Changes and Continuities in Chinese Communism

Volume I: Ideology, Politics, and Foreign Policy

Published in cooperation with the
Institute of International Relations,
Taipei, Taiwan,
Republic of China

Changes and Continuities in Chinese Communism

Volume I: Ideology, Politics, and Foreign Policy

EDITED BY

Yu-ming Shaw

Westview Press
BOULDER & LONDON

Westview Special Studies on China and East Asia

Copyright © 1988 by Westview Press, Inc.

Published in 1988 in the United States of America by Westview Press, Inc., 5500 Central Avenue, Boulder, Colorado 80301

Library of Congress Cataloging-in-Publication Data
Changes and continuities in Chinese communism.
   Contents: v. 1. Ideology, politics, and foreign
policy—v. 2. The economy, society, and technology.
   1. Communism—China—History.   2. China—Politics
and government—1949–   .   3. China—Social
conditions—1976–   .   I. Shaw, Yu-ming.
HX418.5.C473 1988   951.05   87-15928
ISBN 0-8133-7411-1 (v. 1)
ISBN 0-8133-7423-5 (v. 2)

Printed and bound in the United States of America

The paper used in this publication meets the requirements of the American National Standard for Permanence of Paper for Printed Library Materials Z39.48-1984.

6   5   4   3   2   1

Contents

Part One
Methodology

1 How Can We Evaluate Communist China's Political
   System Performance? *Alan P.L. Liu*   3

2 A Normative Approach to China's Modernization
   in Recent Times, *Thomas A. Metzger*   36

3 How Can We Evaluate Communist China's Economic
   Development Performance? *Ramon H. Myers*   86

Part Two
Ideology

4 Giving Marxism a Lease on Life in China,
   James C. Hsiung   117

5 Spiritual Crisis in Contemporary China: Some
   Preliminary Explorations, *Peter R. Moody, Jr.*   127

6 Whither Mainland China: On the Theoretical Study
   Campaign, *An-chia Wu*   153

Part Three
Party and Politics

7 The Reorganization and Streamlining of the Chinese
   People's Liberation Army, *June Teufel Dreyer*   173

8 Chinese Politics: The Bargaining Treadmill,
   David M. Lampton   186

9 Communist China's Civil-Military Relations in
   the Mid-1980s: The Implications of Modernizations,
   Bih-rong Liu   211

10 The Uncertain Future of Hong Kong, *Lowell Dittmer*   230

11 "One Country, Two Systems": Theory and Practice,
    Hsing Kuo-ch'iang   243

12 Another Look at Corruption: Lessons of the Career
of the "God of Fortune," *James T. Myers*   255

Part Four
Foreign Affairs

13 The Impact of the Changing Sino-Soviet Relationship
on Indochina, *King C. Chen*   275

14 China as an Asian-Pacific Power, *Thomas W. Robinson*   289

15 Recent Trends in Sino-Soviet Relations and the
Strategic Triangle, *Donald S. Zagoria*   300

16 Teng Hsiao-ping's Management of the Superpowers,
Harold C. Hinton   306

17 U.S.-PRC Relations: From Hostility to Reconciliation
to Cooperation? *Stanton Jue*   318

18 Relations Between Peking, Washington, and Taipei:
Maintaining the Forbidden Triad or Building Fayol's Bridge?
Peter Kien-hong Yu   337

19 Present and Future Sino-Japanese Relations, 1986–1990,
Donald W. Klein   358

20 Beijing's Relations with Vietnam and Korea: Implications
for Future Change in PRC Foreign Policy, *Robert G. Sutter*   374

21 Beijing's Latin American Policy: An Exercise in
Pragmatism, *Yu San Wang*   393

About the Contributors   413

PART ONE

Methodology

1

How Can We Evaluate Communist China's Political System Performance?

Alan P.L. Liu

For quite some time and, to a certain extent, even at present in American scholarly circles, evaluation of the performance of the Chinese Communist political system has been everybody's utopia. Some U.S. China specialists, before the availability of reliable information, had reached the firm verdict that "the Maoist model" had opened a new path to development and that both developing and developed nations ought to learn from it.[1] Others dispute the exposés and self-criticism of post-Mao leaders, insisting that the Communists on the Chinese mainland have accomplished much more than the post-Mao leaders have acknowledged. For example, just when Teng Hsiao-p'ing and his colleagues stated that the Maoist strategy of development had brought Chinese economy and society to "the brink of collapse," a major textbook in Chinese Communist politics declared, "Yet over the Maoist period as a whole, the Chinese system seemed to be developing stronger capabilities for dealing with its domestic and international problems."[2] Just as the press in the People's Republic of China (PRC) revealed more and more cases of crime, corruption, and rural disorder (e.g., the campaign of establishing "civilized villages"), the same textbook writes: "Social life in the PRC has been relatively orderly and free of crime and corruption"; and, "The PRC has made significant progress toward the development of a social ethic in which compliance with the demands of the political community is recognized as a legitimate obligation of every citizen."[3] Just when the post-Mao regime admitted for the first time that Mao's dictatorship had cost China dearly in terms of human lives, spirit, and welfare, a Pulitzer Prize–winning book on political leadership praised Mao for being the most successful

Revised and reprinted with permission from *Issues and Studies* 23, no. 2 (February 1987): 82–121.

"transformative leader" in the world. According to the author of that book, Mao had succeeded in "raising consciousness and transforming values on a vast scale, mobilizing the higher aspirations of the Chinese people, reconstructing political institutions, producing substantial and real change, the nature of which cannot yet be fully evaluated."[4]

These obviously false and even absurd notions about mainland China call forth a serious evaluation of the performance of the Communist political system since its inception in 1950. A second reason for making such an evaluation is that the present leaders on mainland China themselves have sought to sum up their experience of the first thirty years in order to learn from the past and embark on a new path of national development. Indeed those starry-eyed writers in the West concerning the PRC might well benefit from a reading of the Communist Party's own evaluation of the Mao era.[5] A third reason for a scholarly evaluation of the mainland Chinese political system is to provide a reference framework for an assessment of the reform measures that post-Mao leaders have carried out since 1979.

To evaluate the performance of the Chinese Communist Party (CCP), I shall combine a number of concepts that have been suggested by scholars in comparative politics for evaluating the performance of a government. The main framework that I rely on is the three-dimension scheme on the productivity of political systems developed by Almond and Powell,[6] as presented in Table 1.1. However, I shall not deal with the international aspect of the Chinese Communist system. Though adaptation to the international environment is now a necessity for every nation-state, a political system exists primarily to fulfill domestic needs. (The latter statement, at least, is commonly presumed.) Since Table 1.1 is mainly an outline, in subsequent analysis of the Chinese Communist system I shall make use of other concepts such as legitimacy, penetration, and decisional efficacy that have been suggested by other scholars for evaluation of political performance.[7] Moreover, an evaluation of any political system will not be complete if we do not take into account what the founders or leaders of a particular political system set out to do. To put it bluntly, we must hold leaders accountable to their promises. Subsequent analysis will combine all these references, though the scheme by Almond and Powell serves as the main frame.

System Goods

In evaluating the performance of a political system, Almond and Powell make use of the concept of "political goods" suggested by Pennock. Political goods, according to Pennock, refer to "the consequences of outputs— consequences for the people, for the society as a whole, or for some subset other than the polity, as, for instance, the economy or the family."[8] Political goods are also "goals that satisfy 'needs'—not just needs of the state as such, matters that will enable it to persist, but human needs whose fulfillment makes the polity valuable to man and gives it justification."[9] Whereas Pennock's "political goods" seem to be specifically related to public policy,

TABLE 1.1
The Productivity of Political Systems

Classes of Political Goods		Domestic Goods	International Goods
System goods	System maintenance System adaptation	Regularity and predictability of processes and content Structural and cultural adaptability in response to domestic environmental challenges and opportunities	Regularity and predictability in international interaction Structural and cultural adaptability in response to international environmental challenges and opportunities
Process goods	Participation	Instrumental activity for domestic outputs Activity directly productive of sense of efficacy and dignity	Instrumental activity for foreign outputs Activity directly productive of sense of efficacy and dignity through patriotic or international input
	Compliance and support	Instrumental (sanction-avoiding) compliance with law Fulfillment of duty, opportunities for service, achievement	Instrumental (sanction-avoiding) performance of military and other foreign duties Opportunities for patriotic service and/or international service
	Procedural justice	Equality before the law Equitable procedure	Respect for international law and procedure Encouragement of procedural justice abroad
Policy goods	Welfare	Growth per capita; quantity and composition Distributive equity	Growth; creation of externalities Distributibve equity; facilitation of trade, growth, and welfare abroad
	Security	Safety of person and property Public order	National security Contribution to international conflict resolution˙
	Liberty	Freedom from regulation Protection of privacy	Respect for the autonomy of other nations Encouragement of domestic liberty abroad

Source: Adapted from Almond and Powell, Comparative Politics, 398.

Almond and Powell expand the referent of political goods to system and process. That is, for the production of the three most important political goods—security, welfare, and justice—a political system must first be able to maintain itself through socialization and recruitment and adapt itself to demands and challenges from within and without through structural innovations (special bureaucracies, media of communication, interest groups, etc.). These system goods are equivalent to what is known in industrial economy as capital improvement that will enable a political system to achieve its policy goods with efficiency.[10]

To sum up, the first type of political goods that a political system must produce is system goods, which consist of system maintenance and adaptation. Specifically, we must evaluate a polity in terms of (1) its capacity to change structure and performance in order to cope more effectively with environmental challenges and opportunities, (2) the achievement of the foregoing with efficiency, that is, a favorable relationship between benefits and costs, and (3) a sense of regular order and constructive responses to challenge. Almond and Powell regard the last task—regularity and constructive response to challenge—as the direct consumer goods produced by a political system: "The sense that things are in their proper place on earth and in heaven may be a direct output to consumers. The world acquires a familiar structure and process to which people can adapt—the social orders, ranks, and role incumbents behave appropriately. Interruptions and serious deviations in these routines and behaviors create uneasiness and arouse anxiety; there is a decline in the productivity of orderliness."[11]

As we review the performance of the Chinese Communist political system since 1950, one major conclusion emerges: Except for the initial period of Communist rule, extending from 1950 through 1956, the Communist Party proved to be less than capable of achieving effective or efficient adaptation to environmental challenges. To be more specific, the Communist system was more suited to cope with mobilization for singular tasks such as war or crisis but not so adapted to the complex and integrative task of national development. The key to that observation is that the Communist Party, until after the death of Mao, had not made a serious attempt to transform its psychology and institutions from revolution to national reconstruction. In other words, the Chinese Communist system was initially constructed to cope with revolutionary civil war, and, after 1949, it failed in its first adaptation task—dealing with the needs of ruling and developing a complex society such as that of the Chinese mainland.

The incapabilities of the Chinese Communist system were not immediately evident before 1956, since the environmental challenges then were somewhat similar to that of the revolutionary era before 1949. The postwar situation on the Chinese mainland posed for the CCP almost the same challenge as revolution: the need for mobilizational leadership to bring order to anarchy and uncertainty. The CCP was quite well equipped to meet that challenge before 1956, having a large and relatively disciplined army and party machinery. Because of having these basic political plants (party and army), the CCP was also able to meet the challenge of the initial component of penetration, which is defined as "the capability of the central government to achieve penetration regardless of what may be the views, desires, attitudes, or predispositions of those who are the objects of governmental policy."[12]

Having coped relatively successfully with the challenges of establishing order and effecting penetration, the CCP was confronted with the third challenge in its initial period of rule: that of development. It was in this area that the first signs of the CCP's long-term incapability presented themselves, though it took a while for both CCP leaders (some of them) and the outside world to recognize it. On the surface the Chinese Communist political system had made a major effort to adapt to the requirements of development by establishing functionally specific agencies and implementing its First Five-Year Plan. These seemingly adaptive measures, however, were countered by four fundamental irrationalities in the system. The first one is the personal rule of Mao Tse-tung. In the context of modernization, system adaptation calls for decreasing dependence of the system and its process on individual idiosyncrasies.[13] Personality-dominated systems tend to be erratic rather than flexible or adaptive. The second irrationality in the Chinese Communist political system is its imposition of the Soviet strategy of development without taking into account the lack of comparability of Russian and mainland Chinese social structure and economic conditions.[14] The Soviet preferences for bureaucratic centralism and overcommitment of resources resulted in rigidities, not adaptability, to the challenges of Chinese socioeconomic environment. The third irrationality in the Chinese Communist system is its cadre policy. As the CCP admitted after Mao's death, Mao had never allowed a fundamental change in the standard for the recruitment of cadres from the days of revolution. He had prevented the CCP from turning cadres into knowledgeable professionals of modernization. The fourth irrationality in the CCP system is its erratic policy toward modern professionals, intellectuals, and youth. The policies of the CCP toward these strategic groups in the PRC resulted in their acute role confusion.

These irrationalities inherent in the Chinese Communist political system were submerged for a while before 1957 largely because of the atomistic nature of mainland Chinese social structure (following the devastation of Japan's invasion, the civil war, and Chinese Communist violent mass campaigns), the mobilizational capacity of the Communist civil-military machinery, and the injection into China of massive Soviet aid.[15] However, by the end of 1957, the Communist system was no longer able to hide its weaknesses. The great outpouring of dissent in the Hundred Flowers Campaign in that year showed that the Communist system had not successfully met the twin crises of penetration and legitimacy. As mentioned earlier, the CCP was able to deal with the initial phase of penetration by extending governmental authority to all the regions and groups in society. However, the dissent in 1957 proved that the CCP failed on the second task of penetration, which was defined by LaPalombara as the "ability and predisposition of the objects of policy to receive information regarding policy accurately and to *wish* to conform to such policies voluntarily."[16] This second dimension of penetration shades into the task of legitimacy, which refers "to the extent that a polity is regarded by its members as worthy of support. A polity performs well to the extent that it is so regarded."[17] To gauge the extent of legitimacy, Harry Eckstein suggests that we observe the degree of compliance in society with "value-depriving policies," that is, policies that are clearly disadvantageous to various social segments. "The more 'value-depriving' the policies are for the segments, the more we can be sure that voluntary compliance with them expresses positive political commitments, or at least very closely related 'societal' ones, rather than a mere fortunate coincidence between public and private values."[18] In the 1957 context on mainland China, the "value-depriving" policies and affected social segments were as follows: the collectivization program and the peasantry, the "thought-remolding" policy and Chinese intellectuals and students, the "red experts" policy and Chinese youth, and the "politics taking command" policy and Chinese professionals. The reactions of these segments in the Hundred Flowers Campaign showed beyond any doubt that, on the whole, the CCP did not obtain voluntary compliance from any segment. The agricultural cooperatives were even resisted by a substantial number of regional and local cadres.[19] That these policies were a test of the Communist regime's legitimacy can be testified to by the way the official media propagandized them. In the party-controlled media, all the affected social segments were portrayed as overwhelmingly accepting the policies after overcoming "selfish" attitudes. Another indication of the legitimacy crisis in 1957 is the nature of the Communist regime's response. A large-scale Socialist Education Campaign was carried out in the countryside, and a repressive Anti-Rightist movement sent many intellectuals, students, and professionals to forced labor camps.[20]

The views expressed in the Hundred Flowers Campaign also made it clear that the four irrationalities inherent in the political system of the CCP were the major causes preventing the system from making headway in legitimacy and penetration. Various groups, especially intellectuals and students, expressed disillusionment with Mao's dictatorship, the incompetence of cadres, ideological regimentation, and the various imbalances in the nation's social and economic life caused by the Soviet model of development.[21]

As a result of all these factors, the Chinese Communist political system increasingly, after 1957, failed to perform the function of system maintenance, that is, generating regularity and predictability of processes and content. Conflicts among the topmost leaders of the CCP became more and more serious and destructive of the whole system, culminating in the terror of the Cultural Revolution. The process and content of the CCP system after 1956 reflected Mao's blundering policies, costing tens of millions of human lives in the aftermath of the Great Leap Forward and the Cultural Revolution. Moreover, Mao and his radical followers manipulated at will fundamental symbols of statehood such as the political formula of "proletarian dictatorship" and national constitution. In the process, Mao revised and distorted history in order to accentuate his own status. Those Maoist deeds (misdeeds) belonged to what Almond and Powell refer to as the symbolic output of a political system. To the extent that a system performs its symbolic output well—including political speech, political rite and ritual, political iconography, historical memory, and ideological values—then the other aspects of the system such as legitimacy and penetration will be benefited too.[22] The record of the CCP system under Mao is clear on that count—it failed seriously to generate the three most important values of system maintenance: regularity, predictability, and productivity. It is no wonder, then, that we now see before our eyes the full accompaniments of the CCP's failure in system maintenance. In sociopsychological aspects mainland China is rife with talk of disillusionment with the whole Communist system, for example, "crisis in confidence and faith." In response to lack of faith in the system and extreme sense of uncertainty—that is, anomie—Chinese people on the mainland resort to the ethos of "connection seeking" to protect themselves. Institutionally, the failure of system maintenance on mainland China is reflected in widespread corruption.[23] While scattered cases of malfeasance (existing in all political systems) may be attributed to individuals' greed, rampant and persistent corruption such as that found in mainland China today signifies something deeper. Huntington's comment on corruption and institutional decay is germane here—"Corruption is . . . one measure of the absence of effective political institutionalization, public officials lack autonomy and coherence, and subordinate their institutional roles to exogenous demands."[24]

As an added evidence to the failure of the CCP to establish political legitimacy, the post-Mao regime found it necessary, from 1979 to 1983, to amend criminal laws repeatedly, so that there are now more than forty-seven offenses punishable by death, including bribery, theft, drug trafficking, speculation, and illegal export of valuable cultural relics.[25]

Process Goods

According to Almond and Powell, process goods constitute the second type of political goods whose production forms the basis for evaluating a political system. The three types of process goods are participation, compliance, and procedural justice. Almond and Powell explain the values of these three process goods as follows:

> Process goods are produced at both input and output phases: participation in the formulation of public policy, and compliance and procedural justice in its implementation and enforcement. In their narrower significance, participation and compliance are instrumental; their value as goods depends on their effectiveness in bringing about desired policies. Participation brings important issues to the political process and supports friendly coalitions. Compliance with the law avoids sanctions and penalties and encourages implementation of supported policies. Procedural justice is related to the equitable enforcement of the law.[26]

Since compliance, together with support, overlaps partly with our discussion of legitimacy and penetration and partly with participation (e.g., fulfillment of duty, opportunities for service, achievement), we shall not dwell upon it. On the other hand, in Almond and Powell's scheme there is no accounting for what Eckstein refers to as "decisional efficacy." This term "denotes the extent to which polities make and carry out prompt and relevant decisions in response to political challenges. The greater is efficacy, the higher is performance."[27] Though Almond and Powell regard Harry Eckstein's "decisional efficacy" as a system maintenance attribute, we think that decisional efficacy is also a process variable. The three measures of "decisional efficacy" suggested by Eckstein deal more with process than maintenance: (1) promptness and dispatch in budgeting, (2) the amount of elite dissension in role allocation, and (3) the degree of adherence to normal deliberative process.[28] In subsequent evaluation of the performance of the political process of Communist China, we shall focus on decisional efficacy, participation, and procedural justice.

Decisional Efficacy

Because there are limitations of data, in evaluating the decisional efficacy of the Chinese Communist political system we shall examine economic planning in general, instead of the budgeting process. While Eckstein emphasizes promptness and dispatch in decision making, he recognizes the need of efficiency to balance dispatch. As he notes: "While haste may make waste, reasonable promptness surely always betokens efficiency."[29]

A brief review of Chinese Communist economic planning shows unmistakably (1) that it is neither prompt nor efficient, (2) that elite dissension is very high, and (3) that there is a virtual absence of "normal deliberative process." For example, though the First Five-Year Plan was announced in 1953, long-term planning for it was not initiated until mid-1955. Economic planning subsequent to that was well testified to by the late Alexander Eckstein:

> All available indicators suggest that the Chinese economy was operating on the basis of systematic, more or less comprehensive, and long-term planning for only two and a half to three years, between 1955 and 1957. While a Second Five-Year Plan apparently was formulated and its preliminary targets were announced by Chou En-lai in late 1956, it seems to have been stillborn and swallowed by the Greap Leap Forward.[30]

The Great Leap Forward brought the Chinese economy to the brink of collapse, and years of famine and breakdown followed, so there was no long-term planning from 1963 through 1965. Then, as Alexander Eckstein continued in his last book on the Chinese economy:

> Following a three-year hiatus [1963–1965], the Third Five-Year Plan was promulgated (1966–1970). However, the Cultural Revolution was launched during the first year of its operation and caused considerable disruption in the

urban sector of the economy in 1967 and 1968. It is therefore unlikely that long-term planning was possible during this period. There are occasional references in the Chinese press to a Fourth Five-Year Plan (1971–1975), and it was mentioned in Chou En-lai's Report on the Work of the Government delivered at the Fourth National People's Congress in January 1975.[31]

In 1980, two mainland Chinese economists wrote about the fate of the Fourth Five-Year Plan as follows:

> Due to the chaotic situation in the Cultural Revolution, the Fourth Five-Year Plan was started in 1971 before there was time for economic readjustment. In the 1971–75 period, agricultural and light and heavy industries all suffered from stagnation, decreases and fluctuations. Their imbalances, which had reappeared in the previous five years, became a regular feature of the economy. No readjustment or rehabilitation was possible until after the collapse of the Gang of Four.[32]

In other words, the serious imbalances in Chinese Communist economic planning that were the result of adopting the Soviet strategy from 1953 to 1957 were not corrected until after 1976, the year of Mao's death and the arrest of the Gang of Four.

Meanwhile, just as in our discussion of Chinese Communist performance in system maintenance, the personal rule of Mao and the inefficient results of planning directly contributed to an increase in elite dissension. By 1966 the initial planning elite of Peking, men such as Ch'en Yun, Po I-po, Li Fu-ch'un, Hsueh Mu-ch'iao and Teng Tzu-h'ui, had all been replaced, and most of them were in political disgrace. These must be supplemented by Mao's falling out with one old comrade after another, Kao Kang, Jao Shu-shih, P'eng Te-huai, Teng Hsiao-p'ing, Liu Shao-ch'i, and Lin Piao. In Harry Eckstein's scheme of "decisional efficacy," the Chinese Communist political system displays serious problems of "role allocation." As Eckstein puts it: "Very frequent changes in higher incumbents also imply either the inability of the polity to sustain major decisions, even if particular incumbents can, or else the ability of incumbents to agree only on sharing higher positions, but not on what to do with them."[33]

Through it all, there was virtually no "normal deliberative process" (the third measure of Eckstein's "decisional efficacy") to speak of in the decision-making circle of the CCP. The Eighth Central Committee in 1956 made an attempt to provide for collective decision making by downgrading the role of Mao. However, it was quickly disregarded by Mao in the Great Leap Forward. From then on Mao imposed on the CCP a "patriarchal form of rule."[34] As a general point, decisional efficacy in a personalistic and totalitarian system such as mainland China's is bound to be low because of two factors. The first one is the structure, rather lack of structure, of the elite circle. As Turner and Killian describe the setup of the elite circle in such a system:

There was no defined route nor any set of prescribed qualifications for gaining or losing membership in the inner circle. Members were not assigned to specific offices with defined responsibilities and authority. Instead each member received a vague commission from the [leader] and sought to extend his power at the expense of others among the inner circle. "Purges" resulted when individuals or factions within the inner circle fell from favor.[35]

The second factor that contributes to low decisional efficacy in a system such as mainland China's is that each decision is justified in the name of the leader. Thus failure of a policy implies the leader's loss of his charismatic status. Unless catastrophe occurs, decisions by the leader of such a political system will not be reversed. When a policy is reversed, it is often too late to arrest the consequences. The evidence from mainland China fully bears out this conclusion.

Participation

It should be clear through our discussion of the CCP's "decisional efficacy" that no meaningful participation could have existed in a system such as mainland China's. Almond and Powell were rather specific in the meaning of participation—"participation in the formulation of public policy."[36] Participation not only brings important issues to the political process but also gives the participants a sense of political efficacy, of influence, or of dignity.

The Chinese Communists acquire neither the psychological nor the structural facilities that would allow political participation in mainland China. Psychologically, the CCP as a whole has a strong sense of "ownership" of mainland China (they would like to "own" Taiwan too, if they could) because their power was acquired through long fighting. Among the high elite of the CCP, their sense of ownership of country has been supplemented by ideological-mindedness. The CCP allows followership, not participation. Structurally, the basic requirements for participation—political competition, free choice in election, freedom of association, freedom of speech, equality before law—simply do not exist in the PRC. Instead the CCP has always espoused and practiced the principle of "the unified leadership of the Communist Party" (*tang te i-yuan-hua ling-tao*). A mainland Chinese writer with a reformist bent wrote about the consequence of the principle of "the unified leadership of the Communist Party":

> In farming, not only general planning but also details such as weeding and fertilizing became the central concern of commune, county and even higher Party committees. The day-to-day activity of production has been entirely monopolized by Party branches. The same is true in other enterprises. Everywhere the Party committee "leads all."[37]

This report incidently shows the fallacy of the contention by some U.S. China specialists that though there is little public participation in national policy formulation, there is substantial local participation in matters that affect most people's immediate environment.[38]

On the surface, the Chinese Communist political system has the usual representative institutions such as the National People's Congress, the elitist Chinese People's Political Consultative Conference, and the so-called democratic parties. There are also "people's organizations" (or mass organizations) such as trade unions, women's associations, and peasants' associations. In substance, all these organizations are nothing more than the CCP's "transmission belts"; that is, they transmit CCP directives as tools of the CCP's campaigns of class struggle and thought reform. After the Hundred Flowers Campaign of 1957 in which the "democratic parties" aired their bitterness toward the CCP's total dictatorship, the CCP did not even bother to keep up the pretense of these parties' "joint dictatorship" with the Communist Party. In 1958 the CCP forced the "democratic parties" to terminate their activities in the "heart-surrendering" campaign. From then on none of the parties was allowed to recruit new members until 1979.

The CCP's attitude toward Chinese peasants, supposedly the chief constituents of the Communists, was scarcely any different from its attitude toward intellectuals and non-Communist politicians. The CCP did recruit new cadres from the rank of poor peasantry to staff the party and state bureaucracy in the countryside. These rural cadres were used by the CCP as agents of national authority. From the very beginning, the CCP did not bother to consult local opinions in the selection of these rural cadres.[39] The many campaigns that the CCP had launched, such as the "four cleanups" campaign in the 1960s, ostensibly for the purpose of making rural cadres responsive to "the people," were actually for the sake of making the cadres more responsive to central authority, or practically put, responsive to Mao. These campaigns resulted in cadres' becoming embittered opportunists rather than "servants of the people."[40] The "poor and lower-middle peasant associations" that the CCP organized in the 1960s were just like the peasant associations in the land reform campaign in 1950—temporary expedient means used by the party and dispensed with as soon as the national authorities accomplished their purpose of "class struggle."[41] The specific programs of the CCP's cadre policy, such as selecting cadres from those who were most ready to alienate themselves from their community, granting cadres little or no autonomy, giving cadres the most rudimentary type of education, and open encouragement of cadres' being "rough and ready fellows" (*ta lao ch'u*), were not designed to cultivate in cadres a sense of political efficacy, of influence, or of dignity. Instead the rural cadres have been the objects of public hatred, contempt, and ridicule. They are now regarded as the embodiment of Chinese "feudalism," being one of the most serious obstacles to the Four Modernizations.[42]

Overall, the attitude of the CCP toward participation is best summed up by Mao. In a talk in July 1957, Mao used the metaphor of the digestion process of a cow to describe the genesis and promulgation of the 1952 policy of "general line for socialist transition," which started the process of state confiscation of private enterprises and agricultural collectivization. Mao said: "Every sector of society has studied the General Line but there has been no debate on it, neither within the Party nor in society. It is like a cow eating grass—first you take it down and then you come back to chew it slowly."[43] In other words, except for the top few, the rest of the population on mainland China had to swallow whatever policy had been decided by these few.

To the extent that there were some groups on mainland China that could have "enjoyed" the participation good—that is, acquiring a sense of efficacy, influence, and dignity through their work for the system—they were limited to the ruling elite, a small group consisting of high party, government, economic, and military officials and prominent scientists in defense industry (especially those in space, rocketry, and nuclear weaponry). However, the cases of Marshal P'eng Te-huai, Liu Shao-ch'i, and Lin Piao showed that not even these topmost officials could securely "enjoy" the participation good in mainland China.

Procedural Justice

The last process good that Almond and Powell suggest for us to evaluate a political system is procedural justice, which refers to "the set of conditions, limits, and processes required in the enforcement of the law upon individuals and their property. While it applies in situations in which individuals directly encounter the law, general societal knowledge of the equity and justice of law enforcement is a more general process good contributing to the sense of safety and predictability and the confident exercise of liberties and rights."[44]

Judging by Almond and Powell's definition of procedural justice, there was virtually no procedural justice to speak of in mainland China from 1949 to 1979. For the first few years, the CCP used mass campaigns to dispense "revolutionary justice." These campaigns were designed for the very opposite purpose to procedural justice—creating a sense of insecurity and fear. To the extent that there were some rough equivalents of law before 1979 in mainland China, they were designed to prolong the effects of campaigns. For example, the equivalent to a criminal law before 1979 was the Act for the Punishment of Counterrevolutionaries. Two noteworthy features of the act were first its retroactiveness—acts committed before the establishment of the Communist rule in 1949 were liable to be prosecuted— and its principle of crime by analogy.[45] Laws such as that are intended for the purpose of terrorizing the population. Throughout the first thirty years of Communist rule there was no comprehensive criminal code and no detailed statutes. Party policy was law. When arrested, a Chinese citizen was read not citizen or civil rights, but the state's rights to prosecute, which says: "This is the policy of the government. Leniency to those who confess, severity to those who resist; expiation of crimes through gaining merits; reward to those who have gained great merits."[46]

Before 1979 and to a significant extent even after that there has been no "equality before the law" or "equitable procedure" in mainland China. The enforcement of law depended upon three extralegal factors. First, it depended on whether the accused belonged to the five categories of "class enemies"—former landlords, former rich peasants, counterrevolutionaries, rightists, and "bad elements." A person in one of the five categories, or a descendant of such a person, would receive more severe punishment in a criminal case than would a person outside these categories. Second, law enforcement depended on whether the accused was a member of the CCP. Party members holding higher positions receive greater privileges and immunities. High officials traveling in state-issued black limousines are legally excused from having to stop for unexpected pedestrians or bicyclists. Those who were struck or killed by these cars were not even able to collect civil damages. Third, law enforcement depended on current party policy. For the "need" of party policy at any moment in time the authorities would impose severe punishment, including capital punishment, on certain groups of individuals for the purpose of "educating the public."[47] These methods naturally paved the ground for total lawlessness and extreme violence in the Cultural Revolution period; it is noteworthy that violence then was part of the policy of the government.

Though the regime of Teng Hsiao-p'ing has commenced a reform of the legal system in mainland China—for example, enacting a criminal law and a criminal procedure law and declaring the principle of equality before law—procedural justice in mainland China remains uncertain. First of all, the current regime clearly discriminates against political dissenters. One spokesman of Teng's regime openly declared that "on the question of human rights it is difficult to find a common language between the proletariat and the bourgeoisie."[48] Second, as we have mentioned earlier, the current party leadership has, for political purposes, amended criminal laws repeatedly from 1980 to 1983 to increase the number of capital offenses. That the majority of Chinese people on the mainland feel less fear today than under Mao's rule is not due to any fundamental improvement in procedural justice but to the fact that the present party leaders deem it counterproductive to continue Mao's mobocracy, given the current emphasis on modernization, especially the need to induce foreign investment in China. The CCP is still above the law and uses it for political purposes. As long as this last characteristic remains true in mainland China, Chinese citizens cannot hope to obtain a significant degree of procedural justice.

Policy Goods

To most citizens of the world, of three types of political goods, the most important one is probably the last in Almond and Powell's scheme—policy goods. That is the real payoff of any political system. We can safely make the generalization that most Chinese people would also regard policy goods as the most important one among the three political goods. On the performance of the Chinese Communist political system in producing policy goods, there has been much controversy in U.S. scholarly circles, though less so recently because of the availability of more reliable information on mainland China. We shall examine each policy good in turn: welfare, security, and liberty.

Welfare

Until very recently the predominant view among U.S. China specialists was that the Chinese Communist political system had done a highly commendable job in social welfare on mainland China. Though China remained poor, according to this dominant view among China specialists, the CCP had nevertheless improved significantly the living standard of Chinese people, especially the formerly poor sectors of society. Townsend's 1980 evaluation in this respect is representative of this view: "Despite . . . problems and limitations, per-capita income nearly doubled between 1952 and 1975. Even more significant, however, has been the system's increased distributive capacity which has enabled it to provide a larger share of goods and benefits, in a more secure and orderly way, to less privileged social sectors. Distribution policies have eradicated extreme wealth and alleviated poverty."[49] In the latest edition of the same textbook, Townsend and Womack toned down somewhat the evaluation of the CCP's record in social and economic development: "There were some gains in living standards, primarily in the cities where state subsidies kept housing, food, and transportation costs quite low. Rural areas paid the bill for state extraction, which largely served urbanities and the state itself, with little increase in rural income after the mid-1950s." They acknowledge that "new forms of stratification have emerged, leaving the bulk of the population in a distinctly lower-class status."[50] Nevertheless, Townsend and Womack maintain an overall positive evaluation of the CCP's policy goods, regarding the record as "greatly improved over 1949 and very impressive for a country with limited resources."[51] Readers might want to judge for themselves whether it is meaningful to compare the policy goods of a nation in war and in peace, let alone the fact that the CCP itself was one of the chief causes of the conditions in mainland China in 1949. Later discussion will also shed light on Townsend's contention that the CCP's record in social services is very impressive for a country with limited resources. (Are mainland China's resources limited, for example, as compared with Taiwan and Hong Kong?) But let us first examine the welfare output of the CCP for the first thirty years of its rule.

As Almond and Powell's scheme indicates, data on growth per capita alone do not tell us much about welfare. There must also be information on quantity and composition of growth. Even official Chinese Communist reports show that before 1979 welfare or the standard of living was paid the least attention by the CCP. From 1949 to 1978, the Chinese Communists now claim, heavy industry on mainland China had grown by 90.5 times, light industry by 19.7 times, and agriculture 2.4 times.[52] It is not surprising that economist Nicholas Lardy found that "China is probably the only country in modern times to combine, over twenty years, a doubling of real per capita national income and constant or even slightly declining average food consumption."[53] Moreover, the contention that the CCP had improved significantly the living conditions of the poorer sectors of mainland China is not borne out by facts. The poor sector in mainland China is mostly in rural areas, and we now find that before Teng's reform, over twenty years (beginning in 1957), rural food consumption in mainland China suffered a long-term decline while urban consumption rose. According to Lee Travers, an economist, "Per capita peasant income in China rose only 0.5 per cent per year over the two decades prior to 1978. Rural income growth was not only slow, it also lagged far behind the 1.7 per cent per year rate of the urban sector, which had started from a higher base."[54] In other words, the Communist Chinese regime's policy toward social welfare and services, until 1978, had been regressive, not progressive, quite contrary to the popular view held by many U.S. China specialists.

There is one more myth about Maoist China, the so-called welfare safety net. It is said that Mao's programs of rural development have insured a basic welfare safety net that Chinese peasants had never enjoyed before. Nicholas Lardy looked into the matter of rural relief and reported as follows:

> When the data on rural relief expenditures are expressed in per capita terms, they are modest, well under 1 yuan per capita annually in both 1958–62 and 1976–77, the years of peak rural relief programs. Even if these expenditures were successfully targeted on the poorest peasants, they would be quite small—for example, 6 yuan per capita annually for the most deprived 150 million peasants in 1976–77, an amount sufficient to purchase less than 30 kilograms of grain from the state. Beyond these modest relief expenditures residents of disaster-stricken rural areas are eligible for short-term grain loans to finance consumption. Although these loans are interest-free, they must be repaid within a year, so it is not clear whether state loans generally are available to finance consumption in chronically depressed areas.[55]

In any case, if there had really been a "welfare net" on mainland China, from 16 to 28 million Chinese peasants would not have died of starvation following the failure of the Great Leap Forward.[56]

Next to the myth of a social welfare net that prevailed among many U.S. China specialists is another contention, that of equity or social equality on mainland China. It was said that the Communist regime had created a truly egalitarian society on mainland China. Again facts do not bear out this assertion. According to World Bank data, in 1979 the income of the top 20 percent of the families on mainland China was 2.1 times the income of the lower 40 percent, the same ratio being 1.6 times on Taiwan.[57] Before 1949 the most glaring inequality on mainland China was between the countryside and the cities. Under Communist rule, according to Martin Whyte (not a critic of the Maoist regime), "In spite of the official policy of reducing the urban-rural gap, a large differential remains, and it is not clear that it has been reduced to any extent since 1949."[58] In addition, we now know that the Chinese Communist political system has created a very elaborate system of privileges and perquisites for the elites.[59]

Those who had contended that the Chinese Communists had accomplished impressive deeds in social welfare apparently failed to see the point that given the policy makeup of the CCP before 1978, it was not even possible for the Communist system to achieve the alleged accomplishments. According to the World Bank, based on the experience of successful developing countries (Taiwan being one of the notable examples), there are four policy requirements for equitable economic growth. These are population control; education directed toward enhancing the skills, productivity, and effectiveness of the rural and urban poor; extension of modern health care; and effective delivery of public works and infrastructural elements to the poor. All these were neglected under Mao's rule.

That the Chinese Communists had not instituted a serious population control policy until recent times is obvious. (Mao had even obstructed it.) What needs to be commented on are the three remaining policies, since, just like the myths of social welfare net and egalitarian society, there have been similar allegations by some in the United States about the Chinese Communists' "impressive" record in education, health, and rural infrastructure.

So far as education is concerned, on the surface the Chinese Communists seemed to have had an excellent record. The rate of literacy in mainland China rose from an estimated 10 to 20 percent in 1949 to 75 percent in 1982.[60] Primary school attendance was reported to be 93 percent in 1980.[61] However, just like the crude nature of growth rate, the composition and quality of these educational percentages has to be examined. First of all, from all indications, the 25 percent illiteracy is concentrated in the countryside, especially among rural women. According to the All-China Federation of Women, in 1983 women made up about 70 percent of the country's 200 million illiterates.[62] Undoubtedly these illiterate women are predominantly in the countryside. Second, while the overall school attendance rate is 93 percent, in rural areas only about 30 percent of schoolchildren completed the full six-year course.[63] Universal education remains a goal to be achieved, especially in rural areas. In 1982 only about one-third of China's 2,000 counties reported universal education.[64] In the April 1986 conference of the quasi-parliamentary Chinese People's Political Consultative Conference, a mainland Chinese economist named Ch'ien Chia-chü revealed fully the appalling conditions of rural education. We shall quote Ch'ien's speech at some length:

> Given the state of primary education in our country today, if we do not have resolve, greatly increase funds for education, make major efforts to train teachers, and take a series of effective measures, then the current policy of promoting nine-year compulsory education is a mere scrap of paper. Why? Because up to 1985 many of our primary schools were not equipped with the most basic facilities. Information from certain quarters shows that up to last year there were, over the whole country, 46 million square meters of school houses in disrepair. We frequently hear reports of injuries sustained by teachers and pupils due to collapses of school buildings. The shortage of desks and chairs for school pupils amounts to 37 million sets. One out of every five pupils does not have a desk and chair. We have not achieved the minimal goal set years ago that says "a safe building to every school, a room to every class, and a desk and chair to every pupil." Though the school attendance

rate has reached 96 to 97 percent, the dropout phenomenon is serious. In 1985, the number of students dropping out amounted to 6 million (2 million middle school and 4 million primary school dropouts).

Some try to defend the state of our basic education on the grounds of our country's being poor and economically underdeveloped, and the "debts" incurred in the Cultural Revolution. These arguments are not convincing. Many observant persons (including foreign experts) have pointed out that less than 3 percent of our national income is used for education. (The 1985 national income was 676.5 billion *yuan*, of which less than 20 billion were used for education.) In general, most nations devote 6 to 7 percent of their national income to education. The low proportion of educational funds in our national income can only be explained on the ground that we simply have not given education the importance that it deserves. Take, for example, the excuse of "debts" incurred in the Cultural Revolution. Well, the Cultural Revolution ended ten years ago and we still have 46 million square meters of school buildings in disrepair. In our Sixth Five-Year Plan, the capital investment in state enterprises amounts to 530.2 billion *yuan*. Why can not we use 800 million or a billion *yuan* of that to repair school buildings?

Some have argued that compared with the Sixth Five-Year Plan, funds for education in the Seventh Five-Year Plan have been increased by 72 percent. This amount, so they say, is not insignificant. However, if we analyze the actual purpose of the increased fund, then we discover that most of it is for personnel expenses and next for use in higher education. The amount allocated to basic education is very small. Our educational policy has always emphasized higher education at the expense of basic education . . . . *We are the only country in the world that has free university education but requires payment for attending primary schools.*[65] [emphasis added]

In other words, just like the Communist regime's policy on welfare, its educational policy is also regressive. On Ch'ien's revelation, two points of clarification are in order. First, lacking contextual figures we are not able to say how big a proportion 46 million square meters of school housing is in the PRC. But judging by the way Ch'ien put it, that must be a considerable proportion in the total area of school buildings on the Chinese mainland. Second, in case some U.S. China specialists doubt Ch'ien's account as he is a member of the Chinese People's Political Consultative Conference, not a member of the CCP, Ch'ien has been an ardent supporter of the CCP. In 1951 he enthusiastically supported the CCP's violent land reform and other programs.[66]

The regressive nature of Chinese Communist education is also present in the state of public health in the PRC. Table 1.2 gives the official record of the public health on mainland China up to 1983. Just like the literacy rate, the overall performance of Chinese Communist health service seemed to be impressive. The mortality rate on mainland China had dropped significantly from 1949 to 1982. The average life span of Chinese in 1982 was sixty-eight years as compared with thirty-five years in 1949.[67] It is worthy of note that end of war itself ought to have contributed significantly to the reduction of mortality rate and prolonging of life in mainland China.

TABLE 1.2
Mortality, Hospital-Bed/Population Ratio, and Doctor/Population Ratio in Communist China
(per thousand)

	1949	1957	1965	1975	1980	1982
Mortality	20.0	10.8	9.5	(6.3 in 1978)		6.6
Hospital beds	0.15	0.46	1.06	1.74	2.02	2.03
City	0.63	2.08	3.78	4.61	4.70	4.76
Countryside	0.05	0.14	0.51	1.23	1.48	1.46
Doctors[a]	0.67	0.84	1.05	0.95	1.17	1.29
City	0.70	1.30	2.22	2.66	3.22	3.59
Countryside	0.66	0.76	0.82	0.65	0.76	0.81

Source: "Health Service," *Beijing Review* 26, no. 46 (November 14, 1983): 23.

[a] Includes traditional Chinese medicine.

The internal composition of health service, however, again shows its regressive nature.

While improvement has also been made in the hospital-bed/population and doctor/population ratios in the PRC since 1949, it is moderate compared with world standards, and, moreover, there are sharp contrasts between urban and rural areas. In terms of hospital-bed/population ratio, the world average in 1970 was 1 bed for every 229 persons. In China overall, it was 1 bed for every 500 persons in 1982. But Chinese cities have attained the world average of hospital-bed/population ratio, whereas the countryside is far below the world average. In the availability of doctors, China is ahead of most developing nations but behind the USSR (2.4 doctors per 1,000 in 1970).[68] But again it is the Chinese cities that are impressive by world standards, while the availability of doctors in the countryside is very much in the norm of developing nations. Moreover, one can see from Table 1.2 the deleterious effects of the Cultural Revolution in the availability of doctors; note the decline of the doctor/population ratio from 1965 to 1975, especially in the countryside where the ratio reverted to that of 1949. Yet, one of the rallying symbols of the "radicals" in the Cultural Revolution was to make more physicians available to the peasants.

The development of Chinese medical services is essentially of the "extensive" type at the expense of quality. According to the Ministry of Public Health, one-third of the hospital beds are of the "makeshift" type. The shortage of "specialized beds" is acute. In many cities, two or three women giving birth have to share one bed.[69] In 1983 a high Chinese finance official complained to the Minister of Public Health that even the medical facilities in the *clinics for high cadres* were in poor condition, let alone those in the *hospitals for ordinary people.*[70] The cause of these problems is the same as in other sectors of "nonmaterial production": lack of funds, which were used mostly in heavy industry. The nationally circulated *Chien-k'ang pao* (Health Newspaper) cited the province of Kwangtung as an example: "Public health expenditures in 1979 were 3.94 per cent of the total expenditures of the province, 6.12 per cent less than the 1952 figure. From 1950 to 1981 annual investment in public health capital construction was gradually reduced to only 0.68 per cent of the province's total investment in capital construction."[71]

Though much publicity has been given to Chinese Communist efforts to extend modern medicine to Chinese peasants by such means as "barefoot doctors," the real situation is less rosy than official accounts, which are usually accepted uncritically by the outside world. It is reported that each of China's 2,000-odd counties has a modern hospital and that each commune (50,000 of them) has a clinic. But the problem is that these rural medical facilities are financed locally. As a consequence, the availability of medical care in the countryside depends on the prosperity of an area and the fluctuating condition of harvest. In time of poor crops, commune medical service has to be suspended.[72] Because of the poverty in the countryside, Chinese peasants treat medical service like schools—a luxury that they cannot afford. So, as soon as the new "responsibility system" in farming was established after 1979, peasants refused to contribute to either local schools or clinics. Consequently, the livelihood of the barefoot doctors (paramedics) was immediately threatened. The number of barefoot doctors has been declining steadily since 1977: 1.76 million in 1977, 1.67 million in 1979, 1.46 million in 1981, and 1.39 million in 1982.[73] Part of the reason for the decline of barefoot doctors is the return of one-time urban youth to cities after 1978. Before that time many barefoot doctors were urban youth sent by the government to the countryside to relieve the burden of unemployment in urban areas.

As mentioned earlier, the fourth policy component for an equitable economic growth is infrastructure such as roads, sanitation, and housing. Insofar as Peking's policy of construction of modern transportation is concerned, until recently its main emphasis was for political control and facilitation of heavy industry. Thus the Chinese Communists constructed main trunk rail lines linking major cities and industrial sites but neglected vast rural areas. Highway building, which could have contributed greatly to rural development, was notably neglected in Mao's times. Over the decades, the Communist government steadily reduced its investment in road building. During the First Five-Year Plan, of the total state investment in social overhead, 2.8 percent was allocated to highway construction, and then it declined to 1.6 percent in 1981 and 1.48 percent in 1982.[74] Mainland China now has fewer roads than India, the figure for China being 9 kilometers of highway per hundred square kilometers, and for India, 46 kilometers.[75] Because of lack of roads in the countryside, many rural products could not be transported to other areas and were thus wasted. Every year the government lost about 100 million yuan worth of fruit because of a lack of roads to deliver it to city markets.[76] Moreover, where roads existed, Chinese peasants lacked vehicles to transport goods. In 1984 the national authority announced that for the first time since 1950, it would provide 60,000 vehicles to China's 800 million peasant population.[77]

In sum, none of the policy components—population control, education for skills of rural and urban poor, adequate health care, and public works and infrastructure for the poor—that would have insured an equitable economic growth on mainland China had been emphasized by the CCP for the first thirty years of its rule. Contrary to the contention of Townsend and Womack, for a country with limited resources the record of Communist China in the production of policy goods is not impressive. Other East Asian countries such as the Republic of China on Taiwan, the Republic of Korea, and Singapore, whose resources are much more limited than mainland China's, have done much better than Communist China in the production of welfare goods. Table 1.3 contrasts the living standard in Taiwan and mainland China. These two Chinese societies developed from more or less the same base in terms of per capita income, US$100 in 1952. The data in Table 1.3 show how by 1980 Taiwan had far outperformed mainland China in providing welfare goods to its people. As I argued elsewhere, the usual excuses used by some U.S. China specialists, for example, size, infrastructure, and foreign aid, to downplay Taiwan's success and mainland China's failure in welfare goods are invalid. The real reason for the contrasts in living standards between the Republic of China and mainland China is different policies of development by the two Chinese governments. The positive results concerning welfare goods that Teng Hsiao-p'ing's reforms have brought about on mainland China after 1978 bear out my point.[78]

Security

In Almond and Powell's scheme of policy goods, security as a domestic political good consists of two components: safety of person and property against crime, and public peace and order. As these two scholars point out, just as welfare is a mixed product of the policy and the economy, security is the mixed product of social and political processes. Insecurity of person and of property and public disorder, say Almond and Powell, must be entered into any political ledger in negative terms, regardless of the state of material welfare. Empirically, however, Almond and Powell found that high general welfare, including equality of all population segments, is associated with lower levels of intense domestic political violence.[79]

So far as the PRC is concerned, our previous analysis on procedural justice and welfare under Communist rule has foreshadowed our evaluation of the Chinese Communist system's performance in the security good. Both these previous measures show that security is low in China, and, moreover, insecurity of the people in mainland China has stemmed from two sources: state crime and social crime. The former is commonly known as terror.

Ever since the very first years of the Communist rule of mainland China, Chinese residents there have had to cope with either of the two sources of insecurity, and for most of the time, both of them. U.S. scholars sometimes unwittingly reveal this security dilemma of the people in mainland China. Vogel, for example, saw an enhancement of public security in Kwangtung Province after the terror campaign of suppression of counterrevolutionaries

TABLE 1.3
Standard of Living in Taiwan and Mainland China, 1980

	Taiwan	Mainland China
Disposable income (per capita)	US$1,161.00	US$140.00
Food consumption (kilograms)		
Grain[a]	138.8	218.00
Vegetable oil	7.8	2.30
Pork	26.2	11.20
Sugar	24.0	3.90
Cloth per capita (meters)	53.1	10.00
Sewing machines per thousand	520.2	240.00
		(500 in cities;
		175 in rural areas)
Personal means of transport		
Bicycles per thousand families[b]	908 (1963)	1,200.00 in urban areas;
		333.30 in rural areas
Motorcycles per thousand families	784	—
Automobiles per thousand families	52.2	—
Health facilities		
Hospital beds per thousand people	2.3	2
Physicians per thousand people[c]	0.8	1.2
Culture		
Newspaper circulation per thousand people	120	40
Television sets per thousand families	1,019	44.54
		(147.1 in cities;
		18.9 in villages)
Education		
Percentage of school-age children in school	99.7	93
Number of middle school students per thousand people	91	57.8
Number of college students per thousand people	9	1.2

Sources: Mainland Chinese figures are from *Jen-min jih-pao* (People's Daily), August 14, 1981, 4. Figures on the Republic of China are from *Chung-yang jih-pao* (Central Daily News) (overseas edition), October 12, 1981, 1.

[a]The figures on grain consumption must take into account the fact that on Taiwan, because of improved living standards, consumption of rice and wheat has declined whereas other protein foods such as meat have risen in the components of people's diet. Moreover, the grain consumption in the PRC includes sweet potatoes, which have long disappeared from the diet of the people on Taiwan.

[b]Since bicycles have long ceased to be means of transportation for the people on Taiwan, the government stopped keeping statistical records of them. So the figure of 908 was for 1963 from Neil H. Jacoby, *U.S. Aid to Taiwan: A Study of Foreign Aid, Self-Help, and Development* (New York: Praeger, 1966), 106.

[c]The number of physicians on the mainland includes the "barefoot doctors" whose number has been dwindling since 1980.

TABLE 1.4
Campaigns that Directly Threatened the Security of Persons and Properties of Mainland Chinese

Campaign	Year	Affected Groups
Land reform	1950	Landowners of all sizes
Suppression of counterrevolutionaries	1950	Anyone suspected of disloyalty, mostly former employees of the Nationalist government and American agencies in China
Three Evils (Three-Anti Campaign)	1951	Cadres and businessmen
Five Evils (Five-Anti Campaign)	1951	Businessmen of all types'
Thought reform of intellectuals	1951	Teachers, professors, and members of literary establishment
Suppression of hidden counterrevolutionaries	1955	Members of literary establishment
Agricultural cooperatives	1955	Peasants
Socialist reform of private enterprise	1955	Businessmen
Anti-Rightist	1956	Members of literary establishment, members of "democratic parties," professionals, students, journalists
Party rectification	1957	Cadres critical of the CCP
Great Leap Forward	1958	Peasants
Four cleanups	1964	Rural cadres
Cultural Revolution	1966– 1976	Teachers, literary establishment former landlords and rich peasants, former employees of the Nationalist government, former businessmen, former members of "democratic parties," cadres, professionals of all types, ethnic minorities, and anyone suspected of opposition to Mao

in 1950–1951: "By killing the most serious opposition and intimidating the rest in a well-organized and brutal campaign, the Communists produced more fear than love, but their campaign was the vehicle for establishing a greater sense of public security throughout the Province than the people had ever previously known in their lives."[80] To put it bluntly, the Chinese Communists wish to monopolize all types of social force, including the sources of insecurity and injury to citizens.

It is safe to say that from 1950 to 1978 the chief source of insecurity to most Chinese people on the mainland was state terror. The main vehicle used by the CCP to instill anxiety and fear in the minds of the people on mainland China has been mass campaigns, especially those known as "struggle campaigns." In each of these there were groups designated to be the objects of struggle, which meant one form or another of injury to the bodies or properties of the target groups. Table 1.4 lists all those campaigns that affected the security or properties of the people in mainland China. During the first wave of the Cultural Revolution in 1966, the Communist regime under the leadership of Mao Tse-tung officially advocated lawlessness and induced Red Guards to ransack people's homes and to arrest or even execute anyone suspected of "opposition to Chairman Mao."[81] To the credit of Teng Hsiao-p'ing, one of his first reform measures after 1978 was to compensate some of the victims of the Cultural Revolution and announce state protection of people's "legitimate private property." Nevertheless, the thirty-some years of state crime will not be quickly forgotten by most Chinese. This is reflected in pervasive anxiety and insecurity among current small shop owners who have been allowed to operate after 1978.[82]

In rural areas, Chinese peasants have a source of insecurity in addition to what their urban fellow countrymen have—violent and despotic behavior of rural cadres. In August 1978 the CCP central authorities publicized a case of aggravated cadre despotism in a county in Shensi Province in which cadres' beatings and tortures of peasants resulted in peasant suicides, disablement, and madness. Subsequently the Chinese Communist press launched a campaign to expose cadres' violent behavior in the countryside.[83]

Finally, as we mentioned earlier, the upsurge of crime after 1978 resulted in the CCP's increasing drastically the number of capital offenses. It is highly plausible that the mass violence in the Cultural Revolution and the social crime after 1978 stemmed partly from a common dynamics—the CCP's dismal record of welfare. As Almond and Powell suggested, there is a positive relationship between welfare and security. Before 1978, the Maoist tactic was to divert the incivil mood of the public to political avenues, that is, those used by Mao for his personal power struggle. After 1978, Teng abandoned the use of mass campaigns and lessened state crime against society. The social consequences of low welfare performance in the Chinese mainland then flowed directly to the avenues of social crimes.

Liberty

In Almond and Powell's scheme of policy goods, the last one is liberty, which refers to the exemption and protection of spheres of activity from external interference and the protection of privacy.[84] Given our discussions of the CCP's performance in other types of political goods, the reader is right to anticipate that there is little or no liberty to speak of in the PRC.

To begin with, the Chinese Communist political system is totalitarian in nature. That is, the state seeks to order virtually every aspect of an individual's life. From the very instant of one's birth the state in mainland China intervenes. An identity card is issued on which one's family origin is entered. Under Mao, family origin used to have serious restrictive consequences for the person. For example, before Teng's reform in 1978, if one was born of bourgeois origin, he or she was not likely to be allowed to enter a university. The jobs available to the descendants of bourgeois origin were mostly menial ones. For most people, the residence that is entered on their identification card can be changed only with difficulty; one is likely to be confined to that locality permanently (this is now less strictly enforced), unless, of course, the state chooses to send one elsewhere in the country. The identity card is also necessary for a Chinese citizen to obtain his or her food and cloth ration (rationing has been greatly loosened under Teng).

As one grows to adulthood, the identity card is then supplemented by a confidential dossier which includes information about a person since his school days. The dossier then accompanies a person wherever he or she goes, and no one can obtain employment without it. In daily life an adult on the Chinese mainland is commonly under the surveillance of two organizations: the local police and the work unit, the latter being known in Chinese as the *tanwei* ("unit"). The former keeps an eye on everyone's activity through "street and lane committees" that routinely report to police about the comings and goings of every household. Outside of one's home, a mainland Chinese is then under the comprehensive regulation of his or her employer—mostly state-operated enterprises or cooperatives. The Communist state in mainland China established what Andrew Walder calls "organized dependency" to make employees dependent on the authority:

> Employment in a state-sector enterprise in China is not simply a relationship that confers an income on the employee. China's state enterprises are also institutions that administer the state's provisions regarding labor insurance, welfare, medical care, and social security; they are the points of distribution for housing and ration coupons for consumer goods and some foodstuffs; and they often supply employees with meal services, medical facilities, childcare, and other important items. Those employees who live in enterprise housing also receive their rations of basic foodstuffs and household items from the enterprise. For most of these items, the enterprise is the only possible source for the satisfaction of the needs involved. In the larger enterprises, which are usually able to provide a wider range of benefits for a higher percentage of their employees, this dependence is more complete. In addition, once an employee is assigned a job there is almost no realistic chance of obtaining a transfer to another position that will provide an equally broad range of benefits. There is, in other words, no realistic alternative for state employees, and they usually remain in the same enterprise for most, if not all, of their working lives.[85]

To put Walder's description in perspective, we must note that 76 percent of Chinese workers and staffs are in state enterprises.[86] There are other regulations that a state enterprise imposes on a Chinese citizen, such as marriage and divorce. Without the consent of an enterprise, an employee cannot get married or obtain a divorce.

With collectivization, Chinese peasants (80 percent of Chinese population) lost whatever freedom that they once had in ordering their lives. The cooperatives before 1958 left some "small freedoms" to peasants with regard to their private plots. The people's communes after 1958 took away these "small freedoms," such as planting vegetables or fruits in private plots and selling them in rural markets. Originally, the various components of a commune were given military designations such as "brigade" and "team." In other words, Chinese peasants were treated like soldiers whose duty was to follow orders. One of the first measures of Teng's reform in the countryside was to restore the "small freedoms" to peasants. However, rural cadres readily ignored Teng's policy as the following report (from December 1978) indicates:

> During the years of the "Gang of Four," many communes were made to criticize the so-called capitalist tendency of freedom in labor allocation. The result was that the "small freedoms" that were allowed by the state were canceled. Peasants did not have any free time to themselves. They were not allowed to go up to hills to collect local produce; consequently indigenous products disappeared from markets. After the destruction of the "Gang of Four," down to the present day, some cadres still complain that the peasants have been allowed too many "small freedoms." These cadres watched peasants earning some additional income by collecting local products for markets and they grew jealous. The cadres are fearful lest the peasants become well-to-do.[87]

It is clear from this passage that it is groundless for some China specialists in the United States to contend that Chinese peasants had a great deal of say in the control of their immediate environment.[88] The very opposite was true.

What is noteworthy about the lack of liberty in mainland China is that there is so little trade-off. In some authoritarian countries reduction of liberty is made on the ground of enhancing economic development to improve the welfare conditions of the people, though none of the outstanding cases (e.g., the Republic of China or the Republic of Korea) has restricted liberty to the extent that mainland China has done. In the PRC, liberty is sacrificed pointlessly: Mainland Chinese people obtained neither heightened security nor improved welfare under Mao's rule. It is important to point out that under Teng Hsiao-p'ing, the welfare and security of mainland Chinese have been improved together with some increase in liberty, for example, the freedoms of peasants in the use of lands and disposal of their produce. This experience is contrary to those in the United States who defend Mao's policy on the ground of trade-off between liberty and welfare.

The only reasonable conclusion from the foregoing is that Chinese Communist leaders, Mao Tse-tung especially, suppressed Chinese people's welfare, security, and liberty in order to insure maximum nonaccountability of themselves, or maximum freedom of action to the top few. Liberty and welfare of the few in the Chinese Communist Politburo were obtained at the expense of the overwhelming majority of the people in mainland China.

Elite Goals

Following the suggestion of Almond and Powell, we have evaluated the performance of the Chinese Communist political system according to universalistic standards. However, as is clear from our discussion so far, the concept of political goods inevitably leads to the question of elite goals. The performance of a political system such as mainland China's that has had an inferior record (relative to other countries) in the production of political goods could be due to either one of two major reasons—the elite's incompetence or its lack of interest. So far as normative evaluation of a political system is concerned, it depends on whether an elite is simply incompetent or uninterested in producing goods such as welfare, security, and liberty. One's conclusion about an incompetent though well-meaning elite (or system) certainly differs from that of an elite that shows a fundamental lack of interest in the production of policy goods. Among a considerable number of U.S. China specialists, it is fair to say that the dominant opinion leans toward the stand that the CCP and Mao in particular were a well-meaning but incompetent elite group.[89] In the concluding section of this paper I shall challenge this popular view among U.S. China specialists.

First of all, the performance of a political system depends a great deal on which aspect(s) of the system that a leader (or elite) chooses to pay attention to. We must deal with the question of just what type of life Mao had envisaged for Chinese people—a question to which, interestingly, not many China specialists in the United States have paid attention. Throughout Mao's sayings and writings from 1950 till his death, we find very few occasions when Mao actually touched on the topic of people's living standards. In the few cases where Mao did talk about people's lives, he usually attached careful qualifications, or his remarks were presented in a form of critique. In other words, Mao was either uninterested in the question of people's welfare, security, and liberty, or he was deliberately evasive on that topic. Since Mao's comments on the living standard of the people were sparse, I shall present all that I have been able to locate:

1. It [the CCP] will lead the people of the whole country in surmounting all difficulties and undertaking large-scale construction in the economic and cultural spheres to eliminate the poverty and ignorance inherited from the old China and improve the material and cultural life of the people step by step.[90] [1949]
2. We must lay emphasis on the development of production, but consideration must be given to both the development of production and the improvement of the people's livelihood. Something must be done for their material well-being, but neither too much nor nothing at all.[91] [1953]
3. Liang Shu-ming says that the workers are "up in the ninth heaven" and the peasants are "down in the ninth hell." . . . Your idea is not to have the peasants increase their income through their own efforts in production but to equalize the earnings of the workers and peasants by taking away part of the former's earnings to distribute among the latter. If your ideas were adopted, wouldn't that spell the destruction of China's industry?[92] [1953]
4. Since the beginning of this year there has been one-sided and unrealistic propaganda in the press for improving the people's livelihood, but very little publicity has been given to building the country through diligence and thrift, combating extravagance and waste and encouraging hard work, plain living and sharing weal and woe with the masses, which should from now on be the focus of our propaganda in the press.[93] [1956]

5. Now in many places of this book [Soviet *Political Economy*] the stress is on individual consumption, not on social consumption such as communal culture, welfare and health. That is too partial. The housing in our countryside is not presentable. We must improve peasant housing step by step. In our country housing construction in urban areas is done with public resources, not individual resource. Socialism without socialist enterprises, what kind of socialism is that? Some have said that socialism emphasizes material incentives more than capitalism; this kind of talk is utter nonsense![94] [1961–1962]

Though Mao was vague in all the quoted passages, it is safe to say that he simply was not interested in the question of people's living standards. Now the question is whether Mao was simply being responsible when he downgraded the goal of welfare. When conditions do not permit rapid improvement of people's life, a responsible leader should not make empty promises. Should we then interpret Mao's attitude toward welfare in that perspective? We cannot do so because there was no evidence that Mao was sincerely making an effort to improve the living standard of the Chinese people, in his words, "step by step." As our previous discussions have shown, the welfare standard of the bulk of Chinese declined from the mid-1950s until after Mao's death. Seen in this perspective, Mao's talks about tightening belts for the moment were mainly for manipulative purpose.

In contrast to his vagueness and evasiveness on people's welfare, Mao talked very frequently and specifically on iron and steel production.[95] Mao's evaluation of the performance of any country was in terms of steel production. We shall quote two passages from Mao to illustrate the point:

1. Chiang Kai-shek should be hit because he has not done any good deed. For twenty years he produced a mere fifty thousand tons of steel. Under us in eight years (counting next year) we produced some five million tons of steel.[96] [1956]
2. For long time to come, our country should be known as an industrial-agrarian country. Even after we produce a hundred million tons of steel we should still call ourself that. If we want to overtake England in per capita production of steel, then our steel production must reach 350 million tons.

    Take a country for us to compete with. This is worthwhile to do. We shall use England for our purpose for quite a while. First we shall compete on the basis of gross product, then per capita product. We are still behind them in shipbuilding and automobile production. A small country like Japan has ships of four-million-tonnage. We still do not have this kind of ship.[97] [1961–1962]

Since Mao put so much emphasis on building heavy industry, especially iron and steel, it is legitimate for us to inquire as to what Mao wished to use steel from Chinese factories for. Again we find few clues from Mao's writings. After Mao's death, the CCP under Teng Hsiao-p'ing launched a press campaign on the question of objectives of production. Apparently there was confusion among many CCP leaders and cadres as to the purpose of production. However, Mao was specific on the purpose of his "steel as the key link" strategy in 1958. Mao spoke to the Supreme State Conference in September 1958 on the eve of launching the Great Leap:

> During the start of our liberation, in 1949, there were only eight thousand lathes in the country. They were of inferior type. . . . In the last nine years we produced 180,000 lathes. . . . If we now work hard for another three years, then [so many] lathes would be produced next year, [so many] year after next, plus the 260,000 produced in the past, we will have [that many] lathes. By that time, when we talk with the United States, our position will be strengthened.[98]

There are two noteworthy aspects of the above talk by Mao. First, since his 1958 talk was published in 1969, the editor wished to hide the failure of Mao's goal of lathe production in 1959 and 1960. Hence all the targets that Mao mentioned were deleted and substituted with "xx" (translated here as "so many"). Second, and the more important point, is that for Mao the purpose of production is to gain status for himself internationally. (Of course, Mao regarded himself as the symbol of China, hence his status was also China's.)

From the foregoing there is little wonder why the Chinese Communist political system performed so inadequately in all the aspects of political goods. To put it bluntly, the political system in mainland China exists for the autonomous political goals of the elite, Mao in particular, not for the satisfaction of "human needs whose fulfillment makes the polity valuable to man and gives it justification," as put by Pennock.[99]

How far, then, had Mao accomplished his autonomous goals when he died? Mao had anticipated that, after the Great Leap in 1958 and 1959, production (heavy industry) in China would enter a truly new stage of "great expansion" in 1960.[100] Then, according to Mao, before 1972, most possibly in 1969, China would achieve four modernizations—industry, agriculture, science and culture, and national defense.[101] Socially, by that time, the whole country would have been transformed into "a unitary system of whole people's ownership" (total collectivization of production and social life).[102] Politically, Mao hoped for "a situation . . . in which we have both unity of will and liveliness, that is, both centralism and democracy, both discipline and freedom."[103] Finally, as Mao envisaged, when the diplomatic relationship between mainland China and the United States was reestablished, the Americans would find China totally socialized, so bourgeois ideas could find no room to enter in China. In Mao's words: "When the Americans come to China then and look around, they will find it too late for regrets. For this land of China will have become quite different, with its house swept clean and the 'four pests' eliminated; they won't find many friends here and they can't do much even if they spread a few germs."[104]

When Mao died, neither the autonomous goals of the CCP elite nor the humanistic (or universalistic) goals of mainland Chinese people had been substantially attained by the Chinese Communist political system. While the autonomous goals of the CCP had definitely prevented Chinese people from realizing their humanistic goals, the latter, in the long run, have also defeated the former.

Conclusion

Several conclusions emerge from this evaluation of the political productivity of the Chinese Communist political system:

First of all, we find that when the record of the Chinese Communist political system is subject to the assessment of the universalistic standards of political productivity, it is quite unimpressive as compared with several developing nations in East Asia.

Second, our evaluation brings out the importance of an elite's autonomous goals in the performance of a political system. We have shown that the primary reason for the poor record of the Chinese Communist political system in producing welfare, security, and liberty is that the Chinese Communist system is designed to meet the goals of the Communist elite, especially Mao Tse-tung. Since the political systems of North America and Western Europe have entered into the so-called postindustrial phase and welfare is their foremost goal, there is a natural tendency on the part of Western scholars to assume that welfare is the universal goal of all political systems in the world. We cannot make that assumption. Elsewhere in the world, on mainland China, for example, a political system exists to serve the goal of the elite or even one man. However, there is a limit to a government's using the political system to meet the autonomous goals of an elite. In the long run, as the Chinese Communist experience shows, negligence or betrayal of universal or humanistic goals by an elite boomerangs against the elite's autonomous goals.

Finally, our evaluation of the performance of the Chinese Communist political system also brings out the limit of a political system such as the PRC's that has hitherto neglected in a gross manner the ethical aspect of political systems. Under Mao, the Chinese Communist Party abused, in an extreme manner, the major components of national ethos such as law, credibility of policy, history, and ideology. But in the end the gross neglect of the ethical side of political action by Mao brought the entire system to the brink of total collapse.

Notes

1. Michel Oksenberg, ed., *China's Developmental Experience* (New York: Praeger, 1973).

2. James R. Townsend, *Politics in China*, 2nd ed. (Boston: Little, Brown, 1980), 341.

3. Ibid., 323, 327.

4. James MacGregor Burns, *Leadership* (New York: Harper & Row, 1978), 457.

5. "On Questions of Party History," *Beijing Review* 24, no. 27 (July 6, 1981): 10–39.

6. Gabriel A. Almond and G. Bingham Powell, Jr., *Comparative Politics: System, Process, and Policy* (Boston: Little, Brown, 1978), 391–424.

7. The concept of "decisional efficacy" is from Harry Eckstein, *The Evaluation of Political Performance: Problems and Dimensions* (Beverly Hills, Calif.: Sage Publications, 1971); the concept of penetration is from Joseph LaPalombara, "Penetration: A Crisis of Governmental Capacity," in Leonard Binder et al., *Crises and Sequences in Political Development* (Princeton, N.J.: Princeton University Press, 1971), 205–232.

8. J. Roland Pennock, "Political Development, Political Systems, and Political Goods," *World Politics* 15, no. 3 (April 1966): 420.

9. Ibid.

10. Almond and Powell, *Comparative Politics*, 399.

11. Ibid.

12. LaPalombara, "Penetration," 209.

13. Talcott Parsons, *Societies: Evolutionary and Comparative Perspectives* (Englewood Cliffs, N.J.: Prentice-Hall, 1966), 10.

14. Alexander Eckstein, *Communist China's Economic Growth and Foreign Trade* (New York: McGraw-Hill, 1966), 17–24.

15. Leo A. Orleans, "Soviet Perceptions of China's Economic Development," *Chinese Economy Post-Mao*, a compendium of papers submitted to the Joint Economic Committee, Congress of the United States (Washington, D.C.: U.S. Government Printing Office, 1978), 115–164.

16. LaPalombara, "Penetration," 209.

17. H. Eckstein, *The Evaluation of Political Performance*, 50.

18. Ibid., 60–61.

19. "Editor's Notes from *Socialist Upsurge in China's Countryside*," in *Selected Works of Mao Tse-tung*, vol. 5 (Beijing: Foreign Languages Press, 1977), 242–276.

20. Bao Ruo-Wang (Jean Pasqualini) and Rudolph Chelminski, *Prisoner of Mao* (New York: Penguin, 1973).

21. Roderick MacFarquhar, *The Hundred Flowers Campaign and the Chinese Intellectuals* (New York: Praeger, 1960).

22. Almond and Powell, *Comparative Politics*, 286–287.

23. Alan P.L. Liu, "The Politics of Corruption in the People's Republic of China," *American Political Science Review* 77, no. 3 (September 1983); and Alan P.L. Liu, "Kleptocracy on Mainland China: A Social-Psychological Interpretation," *Issues & Studies* 20, no. 8 (August 1984).

24. Samuel P. Huntington, "Modernization and Corruption," in *Political Order in Changing Societies* (New Haven, Conn.: Yale University Press, 1968), 59.

25. Amnesty International, *China, Violations of Human Rights* (London: Amnesty International Publications, 1984), 53–59.

26. Almond and Powell, *Comparative Politics*, 400.

27. H. Eckstein, *The Evaluation of Political Performance*, 65.

28. Ibid., 76–78.

29. Ibid., 77.

30. A. Eckstein, *Communist China's Economic Growth*, 29.

31. Alexander Eckstein, *China's Economic Revolution* (Cambridge, England: Cambridge University Press, 1977), 111.

32. Yang Jianbai and Li Xuezeng, "The Relations Between Agriculture, Light Industry and Heavy Industry in China," *Social Sciences in China* 1, no. 2 (June 1980): 186.

33. H. Eckstein, *The Evaluation of Political Performance*, 77.

34. Fang Wen and Li Cheng-hsia, "Thoroughly Eliminate the Influence of Worship of Person," *Hung-ch'i*, 1980, no. 24:32.

35. Ralph H. Turner and Lewis M. Killian, *Collective Behavior*, 2nd ed. (Englewood Cliffs, N.J.: Prentice-Hall, 1972), 391.

36. Almond and Powell, *Comparative Politics*, 400.

37. Li Hung-lin, "What Kind of Party Leadership Do We Insist On?" *Jen-min jih-pao* (People's Daily), October 5, 1980, 3.

38. Townsend, *Politics in China*, 236.

39. C. K. Yang, "A Chinese Village in Early Communist Transition," in C. K. Yang, *Chinese Communist Society: The Family and the Village* (Cambridge, Mass.: MIT Press, 1965), 173.

40. Anita Chan, Richard Madsen, and Jonathan Unger, *Chen Village* (Berkeley: University of California Press, 1983), 280–281.

41. See the descriptions of the role or lack of it of the peasant associations in Chan, Madsen, and Unger, *Chen Village*, and William L. Parish and Martin King Whyte, *Village and Family in Contemporary China* (Chicago: University of Chicago Press, 1978).

42. Alan P.L. Liu, "Problems in Communications in China's Modernization," *Asian Survey* 22, no. 5 (May 1982).

43. *Mao Tse-tung ssu-hsiang wan-sui*, no. 2 (reprinted by Center for Chinese Research Materials, Washington, D.C., 1969), 115.

44. Almond and Powell, *Comparative Politics*, 401.

45. Hungdah Chiu, "Socialist Legalism: Reform and Continuity in Post-Mao Communist China," in *Mainland China's Modernization: Its Prospects and Problems* (Berkeley: Institute of International Studies and Institute of East Asian Studies, University of California, 1981).

46. Bao and Chelminski, *Prisoner of Mao*, 33.

47. Chiu, "Socialist Legalism."

48. *Jen-min jih-pao*, October 28, 1979, 2.

49. Townsend, *Politics in China*, 347.

50. James R. Townsend and Brantly Womack, *Politics in China*, 3rd ed. (Boston: Little, Brown, 1986), 407.

51. Ibid.

52. Sung Chi-wen, "On Greatly Increasing the Production of Consumer Goods," *Hung-ch'i*, 1981, no. 6:8–12.

53. Nicholas R. Lardy, *Agriculture in China's Modern Economic Development* (Cambridge, England: Cambridge University Press, 1983), 159.

54. Lee Travers, "Post-1978 Economic Policy and Peasant Income in China," *China Quarterly*, no. 98 (June 1984): 214.

55. Lardy, *Agriculture in China's Development*, 174–175.

56. Ibid., 150–151. Also, John S. Aird, "Recent Demographic Data from China: Problems and Prospects," in *China Under the Four Modernizations*, part 1, a compendium of papers submitted to the Joint Economic Committee, Congress of the United States (Washington, D.C.: Government Printing Office, 1982), 182.

57. Yeh Wan-an, "A Comparison Between the Economic Developments on Both Sides of the Taiwan Strait," *Chung-kung yen-chiu* (Studies on Chinese Communism Monthly) 17, no. 8 (August 15, 1983): 185.

58. Martin King Whyte, "Inequality and Stratification in China," *China Quarterly*, no. 64 (December 1975): 686.

59. Fox Butterfield, *China: Alive in the Bitter Sea* (New York: Bantam Books, 1983), 67.

60. "Facts and Figures: Education," *Beijing Review* 26, no. 40 (October 3, 1983): 26.

61. Li Hai and Hsu Ya-pin, "Educational Growth Must Be Kept Up with Growth in Economic Construction," *Jen-min jih-pao,* April 19, 1980, 3.

62. *Beijing Review* 26, no. 38 (September 19, 1983): 6.

63. Li and Hsu, "Educational Growth."

64. "Facts and Figures."

65. *Hua-yu k'uai-pao* (Sino Daily Express), May 19, 1986, 2. This is an overseas Chinese newspaper published in New York City. The chief editor was formerly a newspaper editor in mainland China.

66. Ch'ien Chia-chü, "Refuting the Nonsense of the Landlord Class," *Hsüeh-hsi* 3, no. 12 (March 16, 1951): 3–5.

67. New China News Agency report as published in *Ming Pao Daily News* (Hong Kong), December 20, 1982, 1.

68. Department of Economic and Social Affairs, *1974 Report on the World Social Situation* (New York: United Nations, 1975), 216.

69. *Jen-min jih-pao,* October 7, 1982, 3.

70. Ibid., March 18, 1983, 3.

71. *Beijing Review* 26, no. 46 (November 14, 1983): 26.

72. David Lampton, "Performance and the Chinese Political System: A Preliminary Assessment of Education and Health Policies," *China Quarterly,* no. 75 (September 1978): 509–539.

73. Pi-chao Chen and Chi-hsien Tuan, "Primary Health Care in Rural China: Post-1978 Development," *Social Sciences and Medicine* 17, no. 19 (1983): 1414; also, Tao Zhenni, "China's Primary Health Care," *Beijing Review* 25, no. 29 (July 19, 1982): 18.

74. Shih Tze-chiang and Ch'en Ta-ch'ing, "Grasp the Key of Accelerating Highway Construction," *Jen-min jih-pao,* August 29, 1984, 5.

75. Hsien Li-chi, "Actively Develop Highway Construction and Motorized Transportation," *Hung-ch'i,* 1983, no. 23:29.

76. Shih and Ch'en, "Grasp the Key."

77. *Jen-min jih-pao,* October 10, 1984, 5.

78. Alan P.L. Liu, *Phoenix and the Lame Lion: Modernization in Taiwan and Mainland China, 1950–80* (Stanford, Calif.: Hoover Institution Press, 1987).

79. Almond and Powell, *Comparative Politics,* 409.

80. Ezra Vogel, *Canton Under Communism* (Cambridge, Mass.: Harvard University Press, 1969), 64.

81. Jerome Alan Cohen, "Will China Have a Formal Legal System?" *American Bar Association Journal* 64 (October 1978): 1511.

82. See most recent report by Merle Goldman and Marshall I. Goldman in "What's New on Peking's Goldfish Lane," *New York Times,* July 22, 1986, 27.

83. *Jen-min jih-pao,* August 3, 1978, 1.

84. Almond and Powell, *Comparative Politics,* 411.

85. Andrew G. Walder, "Organized Dependence and Cultures of Authority in Chinese Industry," *Journal of Asian Studies* 63, no. 1 (November 1983): 53–54.

86. *Jen-min jih-pao,* May 1, 1983, 2.

87. *Jen-min jih-pao,* December 1, 1978, 4.

88. Townsend and Womack, *Politics in China,* 267.

89. Ibid., 399–402.

90. *Selected Works of Mao Tse-tung* 5:20.

91. Ibid., 105.

92. Ibid., 127.
93. Ibid., 336.
94. *Mao Tse-tung ssu-hsiang,* 349.
95. Ibid., 64–65, 72, 84, 99, 126, 142, 147, 149, 154, 205, 225, 230, 235, 240, 264, 267, 277, 303, 304, 320, 368, 390, 498.
96. Ibid., 72.
97. Ibid., 390.
98. Ibid., 244–245.
99. Pennock, "Political Development," 420.
100. *Mao Tse-tung ssu-hsiang,* 321.
101. Ibid., 346.
102. Ibid., 348.
103. *Selected Works of Mao Tse-tung* 5:467.
104. Ibid., 364.

2

A Normative Approach to China's Modernization in Recent Times

Thomas A. Metzger

I. A Methodological Problem

Confusing indeed is the relation today between the study of modernization and the problem of evaluating a modernization pattern as desirable or not. Many social scientists and historians try to minimize such evaluation, concentrating instead on statistical or other factual questions that can be settled rather objectively, such as indices of economic growth or the description of ideologies maximally separated from any attempt to "judge" between them, as Donald J. Munro has put it.[1] This viewpoint has been basic to modernization theory, whether the classical structural-functional form epitomized by Talcott Parsons or more recent, some would say more sophisticated, versions, such as S. N. Eisenstadt's.[2] This standpoint reflects David Hume's widely accepted distinction between "is" and "ought" and Max Weber's linked idea that the social sciences should avoid "value judgments." Robert N. Bellah has pointed out that in thus setting the direction of so much modern social science, Weber won at the expense of Emile Durkheim, who saw a closer relation between empirical investigation and moral judgment.[3] Alasdair MacIntyre has recently shown how prevalent this Humean standpoint has become in Western intellectual circles, where it is widely believed that once one touches on evaluative questions, that is, questions of political or moral judgment, one merely confronts subjective preferences or political interests the contradictions between which cannot be resolved in any objective, impersonal way, not to mention any method based on universal, absolute standards.[4] In the United States, moreover, this viewpoint has been reinforced by two prestigious models of learning, economics and the law. The former supposedly shows how the study of human behavior can be turned into an objective, morally neutral, predictive science, while the latter suggests

Revised and reprinted with permission from *Issues and Studies* 23, no. 2 (February 1987): 19–81.

that moral judgment is just a matter of skillful argument in accord with legal or other conventional rules, something very different from the knowledge pursued by historians or social scientists.

Yet moral evaluation is unavoidable unless one assumes that whatever exists should be accepted, that, in other words, any idea of how a society should develop should accord with the basic interests of the groups currently in power in that society. In fact, however, this conservative view has been applied selectively by American social scientists and historians. We are familiar with the proposition that any reasonable discussion of the development of the People's Republic of China (PRC) must accept as a given the basic interests of the Chinese Communist Party (CCP) and its commitment to Marxism, but many scholars discussing the Republic of China (ROC) do not pay the same compliment to the Kuomintang (KMT).

The discussion of modernization has thus inevitably been infused with counterfactual ideas presupposing that a theory of how societies should develop, a theory of normative development, need not coincide with an empirical account of how societies have actually developed. To be sure, ideas about how societies should develop often just reflect strong convictions developed by people uninterested in if not unaware of any epistemological predicament such as that MacIntyre believed was central to Western culture. What I call "epistemological optimism," the belief that universal moral standards are clearly available and can be easily adduced, seems basic to all Little Traditions and still thrives in the West, as illustrated by the many references to universal "human rights," or by that "promise of freedom and affluence" offered by Milton Friedman.[5]

If, however, we turn to more reflexive or intellectually systematic approaches to the problem of moral judgment, we find three: a tentative if not inconsistent return to the making of value judgments within a Humean or Weberian framework; a pre-, non-, or anti-Humean way of fusing fact and value; and a post-Humean way of respecting the distinction between fact and value while explicitly exploring the possibility of establishing a reasonable method of evaluation. Is any one of these preferable as a way of making normative statements about the development of the ROC and the PRC?

I.1. The Ambivalence of the Humean Approach

The ambivalence of the Humean or Weberian scholars is obvious. Donald J. Munro, for instance, says he does not seek to "judge" between the different "theories of human nature" he discusses. Yet he evaluates the views of Chinese Marxists by inquiring into the "soundness of their reasoning" and the extent to which "empirical evidence" supports what they say. He also implies that "manipulation," "compulsion," and "coercion" are undesirable forms of interaction. Therefore he views central aspects of not only Chinese Marxism but also Chinese culture generally as undesirable. For instance, he states as a fact: "For the Chinese, most mental events are potentially accompanied by promptings to act, and therefore are justifiably subject to manipulation by agents claiming to represent those who might be affected by the acts."[6] Since he at least implies that "manipulation" is undesirable, he depicts this alleged Chinese tendency as undesirable. I am not trying here to debate the validity of either his values or his empirical generalizations, only to show that evaluation plays a basic role in his methodology.

Similarly, while structural-functional modernization theory has eschewed value judgments, this theory, as S. N. Eisenstadt has said, is descended from nineteenth-century optimism and expresses the idea that modernization is good because it promises greater adaptive capacity and the realization of equality, liberty, and rationality. I would also argue that in Eisenstadt's view of modernization, the ability of a civilization to "transform" itself, going "beyond" its inherited "premises," is regarded as a self-evident good. Yet in the eyes of other thinkers, such as modern Chinese humanists, staying true to inherited premises is good: "Chinese must still continuously seek into and open up the sources of their own spirit, renewing their own, already formed system of values."[7] Certainly these two standpoints are not completely opposed to each other, and I am not challenging either here as invalid. Yet they do represent different conceptions of cultural transformation, one valuing ancient premises, the other valuing still more the ability to create premises, the ability creatively to envisage an alternative to inherited premises. Again, my goal is not to criticize either view, just to show how Eisenstadt's view of modernization is linked to a distinctive way of evaluating historical developments.

Karl W. Deutsch's approach to the problem of normative theory is more explicit. In *The Nerves of Government*, he not only analyzes the "essential connection between control and communication" but also treats as a norm the ability "to open" a society's system of communication "to information outside the system": "The task is then, from the point of view of cybernetics, to increase the powers of the human mind, both intellectual and emotional, and the powers of its collaboration with man-made minds or mind-extensions and with the universe around us and within us—that is, with that which Karl Jaspers calls 'the encompassing.'" Thus through Jaspers, Deutsch's positivism is linked to the existentialist quest for transcendence and universal value going back to Kierkegaard, Nietzsche, and Kant. In a partly similar way, behind Wei Yung's behaviorist approach to modernization one can find the humanistic assumption that aspects of China's inherited civilization have lasting value.[8]

The case of Ruth Benedict is still more telling. Famous for emphasizing "cultural relativity," she described cultures in a seemingly neutral way as selecting traits from "the great arc of potential human purposes and motivations." She implied there was no way to evaluate a cultural pattern except by taking for granted the value of another cultural pattern: "No man ever looks at the world with pristine eyes. He sees it as edited by a definite set of customs and institutions and ways of thinking." Yet she also claimed that "we may train ourselves to pass judgment upon the dominant traits of our own civilization," and she went on, indeed, to judge as undesirable various aspects of Western civilization, such as utopian thought and the "obsessive rivalry" associated with capitalism.[9] Indeed her anthropology is a form of social criticism based on an idea that could be developed further: The evaluation of foreign societies should be more closely linked to reexamination of the assumptions we make in defining normal behavior and evaluating our own societies, such as assumptions about the nature of freedom and authority.[10]

Going from Ruth Benedict to the still more venerable Max Weber, one finds that his attempt to separate facts from value judgments also was unsuccessful. This was shown by Leo Strauss, who concluded that the social sciences should return to the question of normative theory, the classical question, as he put it, of what "the good society" is.[11]

I.2. The Non-Humean or Anti-Humean Approach to Evaluation

Though social scientists wary of value judgments have made them nevertheless, there are important schools today holding that universally valid norms can indeed be derived from the nature of things, that "ought" can be derived from "is." After all, Catholic and Aristotelian philosophy is still very much alive, and so are Hegelian outlooks like Marxism. That moral norms are self-evident, implied by the nature of the objective world, or knowable through intuition is also a pervasive assumption in contemporary Chinese intellectual circles. These generally have bypassed what MacIntyre has called "the distinctively modern standpoint," the belief that all moral questions lead only to disagreements for the resolution of which there are no objective standards. As Yü Ying-shih has noted, this kind of "skepticism" has been largely avoided in China. I regard this tendency as a tradition of "epistemological optimism" going back to Confucius and Mo-tzu. Donald J. Munro's discussion of epistemological "clustering" as a continuous, central Chinese trend going back to Chou times partly refers to this same phenomenon. This assumption that "ought" can indeed be derived from "is" is illustrated by all the most prominent modern Chinese philosophies and by the attempts of some political scientists in Taiwan to derive a theory of human rights from David Easton's systems analysis. Yet philosophers like T'ang Chün-i have been so learned and thoughtful in developing an alternative to the Humean position that at the very least the validity of the latter is no longer obvious.[12] At the same time, one has to distinguish between the latter and the views of Hume himself, who took for granted the validity of common-sense moral discourse. Where he differed from T'ang Chün-i was mainly in rejecting the idea that this validity can be rationally demonstrated.[13]

A major point should be noted, however. Whether or not values can be derived from objective, universal standards, the Humean maneuver—suspending judgment by first describing something, then turning to the problem of evaluating it—has obvious value. It helps us reduce bias and examine a cultural pattern in a comprehensive or at least less partial way, instead of prejudging what is worth describing. In Chinese terms, we can separate the task of "analysis" (*fen-hsi*) from that of "affirming" (*k'en-ting*) the "value" (*chia-chih*) of what is described.

I.3. The Post-Humean Approach

This consideration is basic to the post-Humean approach. One version of this approach is the work of Richard W. Wilson, who argues that moral values like "reciprocity," "empathy," and "responsibility" can be used to evaluate the degree of "moral competence" furthered by any cultural pattern.[14] The authors of *Habits of the Heart*, Robert N. Bellah, Richard Madsen, William M. Sullivan, Ann Swidler, and Steven M. Tipton, reject the "quite arbitrary boundary between the social sciences and the humanities," holding that social science, "whether it admits it or not, makes assumptions about good persons and a good society and considers how far these conceptions are embodied in our actual society." Therefore the study of American values "requires not just an evaluation of arguments and evidence but ethical reflection." For these social scientists, the scholarly study of historical or contemporary values is necessarily a "conversation" between the student and the person studied, an argument about which values make the best sense. Living values do not exist except in the form of an argument about options: "Any living tradition is a conversation, an argument in the best sense, about the meaning and value of our common life."[15] This viewpoint partly converges with Benjamin I. Schwartz's view of a historical body of thought as a "problematique" and with S. N. Eisenstadt's view of cultural "premises" as intertwined with arguments about divergent options.[16] I have similarly tried to look at cultural orientations as necessarily mixing shared "perceptions" with "claims."[17] Bellah's emphasis on the need for "ethical reflection" in the study of claims and perceptions, however, brings to the fore the question of normative theory, and his concept of a "conversation" can help us deal with this question (I use "Bellah" to refer to the group of authors who wrote *Habits of the Heart*).

I.4. Developing the Post-Humean Approach

The problem of evaluating modernization patterns is complicated not only by this mixture of Humean, pre-Humean, non-Humean, anti-Humean, and post-Humean methodologies but also by the global interaction between mutually exotic societies and the simultaneous rise of a worldwide debate over the value of a certain non-Humean, revolutionary, utopian ideology, the Marxist one. Certainly when the Ming-Ch'ing rulers were receiving tribute from the King of Korea and the Europeans were fighting with each other while engaged in their Voyages of Discovery, intense diplomatic contact between ideologically competitive, mutually exotic societies was rare. Modernization brought with it a new range of linguistic, methodological, anthropological, and ideological problems for societies having to cope with their international environments.

Today we face a choice. Should we leave well enough alone, suspecting that any further attempt to deal with the methodology of evaluation will only muddy the waters further? Or should we, challenging the positivistic inclination to minimize concern with questions of evaluation, try to develop the post-Humean approach in order to shed light on Chinese modernization?

Taking the latter position, I see Bellah's analysis as implying two points especially. First, one cannot expect a society to realize options not clearly conceptualized by a good number of its more influential members. Moreover, these indigenously conceptualized options must be rooted in the cultural traditions of the society involved. Bellah notes: "Our lives make sense in a thousand ways, most of which we are unaware of, because of traditions that are centuries, if not millennia, old."[18] Indeed his book sees contemporary U.S. culture as rooted in the Biblical and "republican" traditions of Western antiquity. Certainly it would be puzzling should contemporary U.S. culture be rooted in the Western "axial" period of antiquity, while contemporary Chinese culture developed without being significantly influenced by the Confucian and other traditions that arose in China's axial period, the Chou. Thus scholars have increasingly recognized that Chinese modernization patterns have been significantly influenced by the Confucian tradition, both consciously and unconsciously. As Yü Ying-shih notes, the Chinese, Jewish, Japanese, and Indian traditions, among others, have all persisted in important ways amidst the vicissitudes of modernization.[19] This point would not even have to be made were it not for the curious variety of modern viewpoints— May Fourth iconoclasm, modernization theory, and Marxism—claiming that rejection of Confucianism was a necessary part of modernization in China. Yet whether or not indigenously conceptualized options have to be rooted in the inherited cultural tradition in order to be meaningful, they do have to be indigenously conceptualized, that is, they have to be articulated by influential people in ways meaningful to sizable audiences. If such options are envisaged only by foreigners or sophisticated academics whose views remain hidden in learned journals, they cannot serve as goals that a society can be expected to reach.

Second, Bellah suggests that description of such options should be or cannot but be combined with a "conversation" about which options make the most sense. What kind of a "conversation"? Who is entitled to participate in it? No entirely specific answer is possible, but Bellah is referring to some kind of developing consensus that can influence events and to an ongoing effort to be moral and reasonable—to be "intelligent," as John Dewey would have put it.

A fourfold procedure is thus suggested. First, offering to participate in such a conversation, we can adduce widely accepted developmental criteria (e.g., Deutsch's "openness"). Second, we can try to identify the leading developmental options conceptualized in contemporary China. Third, we can logically determine which of these options most accord with these developmental criteria. Fourth, we can specifically study the extent to which economic, political, and other development has realized the indigenous options closest to our developmental criteria.

This fourth step has been attended to by other scholars, such as Ramon H. Myers and Alan P.L. Liu. This paper will deal with only the first three. This procedure might seem either simpleminded or incapable of offering more than a subjective or politically biased way of evaluating Chinese modernization patterns. In fact, though, I do not think this is the case. Developmental criteria cannot be formulated without some controversy, to be sure. Yet the reader will see that all these criteria but one are largely uncontroversial. This simply means that something like Deutsch's goal of opening a social system to information outside it will "strike" many as desirable, even if no proof can be offered that this goal should be pursued. Moreover, the options conceptualized by contemporary Chinese can be described in a reasonably precise and dispassionate way, despite some controversy. One then indeed can logically compare these options to the above developmental criteria, and so broad conclusions can be reached despite remaining areas of controversy. Thus seeing which options most approximate these developmental criteria, we can regard these options as constituting a normative standard by which China's actual development can be judged.

This conclusion can be disputed only by arguing that the criteria or the descriptions of options are inadequate. At the very least, such a systematic approach makes it easier to think dispassionately about matters that easily arouse emotion. Nor is it obvious which options will most accord with widely accepted developmental criteria. The options that seem to, indeed, have not even been discussed in major recent studies of Chinese modernization, democracy, and political thought, noted below. Admittedly, the special nature of "the Taiwan issue" lurks in the background of my discussion, but I think the reader will see that this discussion has an objective foundation and is far from frivolous.

II. Five Developmental Criteria

One largely uncontroversial criterion is economic growth minimizing the ills of growth, such as political instability, inflation, unemployment, increasing crime rates, ecological damage, and any growing gap between rich and poor. Perhaps the only question here is whether unlimited affluence is desirable, as many economists seem to assume. A second virtually uncontroversial criterion is national security. Thus since late Ch'ing, many Chinese have emphasized the goal of "wealth and power" (*fu-ch'iang*), and few will deny a nation the right to protect itself from the aggression of imperialistic powers, totalitarian or not.[20] The third criterion, just and reasonable political development, is the only one entailing major controversy; I discuss it further below. (The controversy revolves around the question of "democracy.") A fourth criterion, overlapping that of just and reasonable political development, is what Karl W. Deutsch describes as the ability of a society to "open" itself to "information outside the system," to establish, in other words, adequate access to traditional and cosmopolitan sources of knowledge and sources of moral and aesthetic value (see I.1 above). This entails what Wm. Theodore de Bary and Charles Frankel describe as "civilizational" and "liberal" values, a formulation overlapping T'ang Chün-i's idea of "civilizational value" (*jen-wen*).[21]

Besides economic growth minimizing the ills of growth, national security, just and reasonable political development, and openness, one other criterion seems important. *Habits of the Heart* argues that a certain kind of moral culture is vital, a concept overlapping the Chinese one of *lun-li* (ethics). In this book, Bellah and his colleagues refer largely to middle-class America, but their position can be generalized. Noting that modernization involves a shift from the more closeknit, face-to-face community (*Gemeinschaft*) to a more impersonal, competitive society built on industrialization, urbanization, and bureaucratization (*Gesellschaft*), they see this shift as impeding the moral integration of society. Such integration, they hold, requires a "moral language" with which to put into a meaningful moral context all the different aspects of life, from the family, education, work, leisure, religion, and the local community to all the broader economic, political, and international patterns. They are looking for concepts that connect these broader economic and political issues to the individual's sense of moral obligation, instead of restricting the latter to the individual's immediate social environment or attenuating it even more. In other words, they worry about how the complex, huge structures of the modern world can appear to the individual as intellectually and morally incomprehensible, and how the individual can thus lose any sense of a larger moral purpose and lapse into a state of loneliness, anxiety, inner emptiness, and anomie. A moral language establishing the ties between an individual and the broader community, they hold, can arise as the people of a society form a "community of memory," becoming conscious of their shared history, suffering, tradition, and hopes. Thus a people can form "those habits of the heart that are the matrix of a moral ecology, the connecting tissue of a body politic." Bellah and his colleagues then offer a complex historical and sociological analysis arguing that this state of moral integration largely existed in the United States during its earlier period and was undermined as the United States modernized.[22]

Thus emphasizing the current U.S. need to repair the breach between the self and the community, however, Bellah and his colleagues also warn against any dominance of group structures, whether in the form of "traditionalism," dogmatism, "conformism," "authoritarian closure," "authoritarian manipulation," or "dependence and tyranny."[23]

In developing this standard of moral integration with which to evaluate American society, Bellah can be seen as harking back to Emile Durkheim's search for a certain ideal balance between self and group. Durkheim advanced this concept in his famous study of suicide. There he saw suicide as stemming from two complementary ways of missing this balance, "excessive individuation" (the problem afflicting the United States, according to Bellah), and "too rudimentary individuation," in terms of which "society holds" the individual "in too strict tutelage."[24] The latter is indeed the shortcoming that some critics claim has been basic to Chinese society, arguing that Chinese culture furthers authoritarianism, collectivism, dependence, and so on.

From this standpoint, therefore, we should look in China for an indigenously conceptualized option that not only promotes the kind of moral integration between self and group that Bellah called for but also emphasizes individual autonomy, "a private realm of beliefs," and "unique and innate inner forces that determine individuality," to use Munro's formulations.[25] This fifth developmental criterion can therefore be added to those of economic growth, national security, just and reasonable political development, and access to traditional and cosmopolitan sources of information and sources of moral and aesthetic value.

II.1. Just and Reasonable Political Development and the Question of Democracy

Our third criterion, just and reasonable political development, is the only really controversial one. First, there is the problem of defining "democracy" or, rather, understanding precisely what different groups have meant by the term. As Andrew J. Nathan says, "We must get behind the international facade of verbal similarity if we wish to understand more fully where we and other cultures fundamentally agree and disagree."[26] The problem here is to describe all the key ideas and assumptions expressed in three main bodies of political discourse, the modern Chinese liberal tradition, epitomized by the writings of Hsü Fu-kuan and Yin Hai-kuang; the literature currently articulating the doctrine of the Three Principles of the People; and what many scholars broadly sum up as the "Western liberal" tradition. To what extent are the ideas and assumptions used in the Western liberal tradition found in the doctrine of the Three Principles as it is currently propounded in Taiwan? Is there a major contrast between the Western and the Chinese versions?

A second area of controversy involves the question of practicability. Are any of these versions impracticable in the Chinese context? Henry Grunwald, Editor-in-Chief of *Time* magazine, holds that "democracy is a complex, subtle system that requires a certain history and certain cultural conditions to function. . . . Today in most parts of the world it does not exist or is not understood."[27] Those disputing this outlook point to Japan and India as cases proving that democracy can be practiced under a wide variety of cultural conditions.

Perhaps the key question here is Manichaeanism, the tendency Chinese themselves criticize as *erh-fen-fa* (seeing every issue in black-and-white terms), as insisting that one always should *fen Ching Wei* (distinguish between the pure waters of the Ching River and the muddy waters of the Wei River, i.e., insist on the distinction between what is absolutely right and what is absolutely wrong). Does not democracy as a system of wide-open political competition that nevertheless is stable require a special degree of tolerance for *i-chi* (the one who disagrees with me)? Doesn't such a special degree of tolerance require a legitimation of the polity as at least partly a system of competing selfish interest groups rather than a system fundamentally based on the dedication of public figures to some objective public good? Still more basically, doesn't such a special degree of tolerance require a cultural definition of the self as a moral mixture of good intentions and frankly selfish interests confronting similarly constituted opponents, as opposed to identifying one's cause with absolute morality and seeing one's opponents as wicked? Classics like Reinhold Niehbur's *The Children of Light and the Children of Darkness* indeed suggest that without this special emphasis on tolerance mitigating the apparently universal tendency to moralistic, Manichaean ways of viewing political conflict, democracy as a system of wide-open political competition for power is not practicable. Yet it would be hard to say that the truth of this thesis has been empirically demonstrated.

Third, assuming that a practicable system of democracy requires that special degree of toleration, does the development of such toleration depend on certain ideological trends missing in China, or can it develop without the latter? Even more to the point, has it already developed in the ROC? Again, to answer this question we only have the differing impressions of various experienced observers, no definitive study.

Fourth, whatever the definition of democracy and the cultural conditions allegedly needed to make democratic procedures practicable, is democracy necessarily the most just and reasonable form of political development? This question was first raised by Plato and Aristotle, who answered in the negative, pointing to the tension between majority will and the goal of wisdom and morality. The modern answer of many Chinese and Americans has been to take for granted the superiority of the American political model. Yet can this be taken for granted? Chang Hao has recently pointed out that with the May Fourth movement, the idea of "democracy" was transformed into *Te-p'u-sa* (Democracy as Bodhisattva),[28] and just about all American scholars similarly regard Thomas Jefferson and the other Founding Fathers as political sages. Yet many today see American democracy as leading to the gravest kinds of problems, whether these are viewed in Bellah's terms as a lack of moral integration between the self and the whole variety of societal groupings or as a failure to put primacy on civilizational values and on the national discipline needed to hold back the threatening power of the USSR. Some Chinese also have been alarmed by aspects of American democracy, pointing to the unequal distribution of wealth, the disproportionate political power of the wealthy, "bad social trends," "moral decline," political "apathy" (illustrated by low voter turnout), and "excessive freedom and democracy."[29] Certainly an annual trade in illegal, escapist drugs now estimated at well above US$100 billion reflects a societal disaster of the gravest proportions, unless a democracy heavily influenced by drug-addicted voters is what Jefferson had in mind. Yet how to stop this illegal trade was not even an issue in the most recent Presidential election (1984)!

Thus American history hardly refutes Plato's and Aristotle's doubts about democracy and suggests that reasonable and just political development depends as much on cultural orientations, the state of public opinion, and leadership as it does on any particular set of formal, legal-political procedures. At the very least, this is a question fully open to scholarly research and reflection.

Bringing up these four questions, we can see something of the scope of the controversy surrounding our third developmental criterion, just and reasonable political development. A lot of this controversy cannot be resolved here, but these unresolved questions need not necessarily preclude our coming to some conclusion about China's normative development. What is necessary, however, is clarifying the distinction between the way democracy has been conceptualized in the leading Chinese trends and in the Western liberal tradition. In this regard, I believe, there is widespread confusion that can be cleared up.

II.2. Defining "Democracy"

Many scholars assume that the nature of democracy is simple and obvious, but at least six aspects of this idea as it has developed in the West can be noted.[30] First, "democracy" refers to the symbolization of the polity using words like "consent of the governed," "rule by the people," "sovereignty of the people," "constitution," "legislature," and "elections."

Second, given the apparent fact that "consent by the governed" or "rule by the people" does not describe the actual operation of any major political system, as Max Weber and Joseph A. Schumpeter noted, "democracy" refers to the institutionalization of the above ideas to the point that there is real competition between the "center" of the polity (to use the terminology of Edward Shils and S. N. Eisenstadt) and groups independent of it. Salient features of such a "pluralist democracy" are a basically open system of electoral competition, usually including two or more major political parties, individual rights, independent judicial review, and a free press.[31]

Third, overlapping the latter is a vigorous flow of formal and informal political communication increasing the center's access to inputs from the rest of society. Admittedly, this flow can also be found in nondemocratic regimes.

The fourth feature is a cultural orientation. To use Andrew J. Nathan's formulation, democracy involves "tolerance for the expression of conflict and antagonism in politics," the "acknowledgment that the political process can legitimately be used by individuals and groups to try to force the state to serve their selfish ends."[32]

The fifth refers to a cultural or intellectual pattern that in much Western thought has been inseparable from the fourth, an emphasis on what Chang Hao calls the "dark" side of human nature (*yu-an i-shih*).[33] As Arthur O. Lovejoy explained, "the American Constitution was framed under the leadership of a group of extraordinarily able men who had few illusions about the rationality of the generality of mankind," believing that "it is entirely possible . . . to frame a rational scheme of government . . . without presupposing that the individuals who exercise ultimate political power will be primarily solicitous about the general good."[34]

The Founding Fathers, in other words, followed the common Western, eighteenth-century view that in political life, selfishness cannot be overcome or minimized, it can only be contained or channeled. Certainly this view was basic to "modern political philosophy" going back to Machiavelli and Hobbes, as Leo Strauss has discussed it.[35] David Hume (1711–1776), for instance, regarded "it as impossible directly to oppose and repress the natural self-interestedness or 'avidity' of men," and so he thought that "entering into society is at most intended to divert or channel that impulse in directions that allow for a higher chance of greater satisfaction."[36]

True, as Bellah says, the Founding Fathers also emphasized that constitutional procedures channeling selfish impulses must be backed by some degree of public morality. They did not, however, expect that such public morality would displace or minimize the competition between selfish interest groups. Therefore they contradicted the Confucian vision of government as based on the determination of at least the ruling group to pursue the public good. Hsü Fu-kuan referred to this Confucian vision as *te-chih* (government based on virtue), and he saw "democracy" as simply a way practically to realize this ancient goal. True, like the Founding Fathers, he looked to the impact of ingeniously designed procedures on human behavior. For Hsü, however, the effect of the mechanism of majority vote was not just to contain selfish impulses but to force leaders to act as "sages" do. In a democracy like Harry Truman's, Hsü held, "Even though a political leader is not a sage, he cannot but act as a sage would."[37] Thus Hsü was confident Chinese could easily erect a system unblemished by either tyranny or license. American pessimism has often led to the idea that because people are bad, one must choose between tyranny and license when designing a political structure, and license is preferable. That is, after all, the rationale for not acting to stop the illegal trade in escapist drugs. Thus Chinese today often feel that the American system suffers from license, from "excessive freedom," and the American answer, that license is the necessary price of freedom, has never been accepted by any Chinese thinker, so far as I know.

This American attitude, apart from the contemporary *reductio ad absurdum*, stems from a most important set of political ideas rooted in the Western philosophical and theological tradition and largely foreign to Chinese philosophy: radical skepticism about the possibility of objectively defining the "public good"; history as made by sinners, an accumulation of corrupt or morally mixed acts (*chi-pi*), a time period lacking any golden age of morally perfect government; politics as necessarily a morally mixed process; the idea of amoral or immoral but still legitimate political authority; the legitimation of prudence in dealing with immoral authority figures, in other words, the legitimation of what the Chinese call "hypocrisy" (*shiang-yüan*); the protection of private property as a central function of the state; and respect for norms based only on custom, convention, or consensus rather than absolute moral principle (*tao*).

Interestingly, the explicit rejection of customary practice (*hsi, su*) as a source of norms can perhaps be found first in *Mo-tzu* (fifth century B.C.). Mo-tzu contrasted custom with "the Way of the sage kings . . . the Way of benevolence and righteousness," but respect for custom, for historically developed practice, became a major principle in the Western tradition of conservative philosophy from Aristotle through Burke. This Western inclination to base political principle on something other than eternal moral truth was connected also to a "moral language" largely differing from the Chinese (see below).[38]

Lin Yü-sheng has similarly noted the Western idea of amoral but legitimate political authority. Seeing this idea as basic to the Western democratic tradition, he pointed out that while the Confucian tradition emphasized the fusion of morality and politics (*cheng-chiao ho-i*), Christianity, beginning in Roman times, recognized that "in the secular realm, the king was the highest authority, and he had a legitimate reason to exist even if he was a tyrant." Yet a recent effort in a Taipei newspaper to note the importance of this concept in the Western intellectual tradition evoked outrage on the part of Chinese liberals. By thus refusing to accept any such separation between absolute morality and political authority, or even to admit that such separation has been accepted by leading Western thinkers, such as Weber, these Chinese liberals showed how strong remains the traditional Chinese view of politics as based directly on morality.[39]

It can also be argued that Western democracy has been intertwined with still another cultural pattern (though one overlapping some of the above ideas): individualism, a culturally distinctive way of thinking about the importance of the individual. It has recently been carefully analyzed by Steven Lukes,[40] and, as Yü Ying-shih and others have noted, differs basically from the Confucian way of emphasizing individual dignity and moral autonomy.[41] Unlike Western individualism, the Confucian concept of individual autonomy and dignity lacks any obvious connection to the demand for individual legal rights, and this focus on legal rights had been interwoven with the typical forms of Western democracy.

II.3. The Relation Between Morality and Politics in the Western and the Confucian Traditions

Of the six concepts above interwoven with mainstream Western thought about "democracy," the fifth involves a basic contrast with the Confucian tradition that is still little understood today, unmentioned in any study of Chinese thought I am aware of. Both the Confucian and the Western tradition have emphasized the highest moral ideals as standards with which to evaluate political life. In the Confucian tradition, however, even though the obstacles preventing realization of the highest ideals were fully recognized, there was a central assumption that overcoming these obstacles through appropriate political action was entirely practicable if not easy. According to the Confucian tradition, therefore, it was entirely reasonable to expect that political action would be directly based on the highest morality.

Confucianism even suggested that any political action not based on absolute morality was not legitimate. I say "suggested" because the Confucian position, as noted below, was not a simple, unqualified one. Nevertheless, its point of emphasis was diametrically opposed to the mainstream Western view.

The latter generated a different sense of what is reasonable. It emphasized that the obstacles preventing political realization of the highest ideals could seldom if ever be fully overcome. From this standpoint, political authority not fully based on morality could be much more easily seen as normal, reasonable, and legitimate. At odds with Confucianism, the idea of politics as "the art of the possible" typifies this Western outlook.

To be sure, the practical implications of this conceptual contrast are open to debate. Many might agree that if the public discussion of policy is to avoid utopianism and respect practicable standards of political life, an intellectual tradition using absolute morality as the standard with which directly to judge governments creates great difficulties: reasonable political discourse is impeded, and therefore using the democratic system of open public debate to determine policy becomes an invitation to disaster. The answer to this point could be that the quality of public discussion is shaped not only by intellectual traditions but also by folk wisdom and other current influences. The behavioral implications of Great Traditions, therefore, raise questions that cannot be settled here. Nevertheless, there should be no misunderstanding about the conceptual contrast we are dealing with here.

It is true that in pursuing the goal of an absolutely moral polity (*jen-cheng, te-chih*), that is, in seeking a king who would not "commit one immoral act, kill one innocent person" (*Mencius,* 2A.2), Confucians still in various ways expressed respect for the authority of morally inadequate political leaders. Confucius himself behaved at the courts of hereditary aristocrats with great respect for them, even though on occasion he expressed contempt for them, and he partly admired the morally inadequate but effective statesman Kuan Chung.[42] In the imperial period, moreover, respect for the emperor's hereditary authority was often combined with awareness of his personal moral inadequacy, and the existence of an immoral polity was seen as due to a kind of fate.[43]

At least by late Chou times (ca. 300 B.C.), however, Confucians and other schools in common assumed that if the leader in the center of the polity acted correctly, he would be enormously if not totally effective in solving all of society's problems. After all, this had been demonstrated by the sage rulers during the golden age of the Three Dynasties. From this standpoint, the center of the polity was like a highly effective lever waiting to be taken hold of by the right hands. Socrates said that an honest man like him could not serve in government without attracting enemies who would eventually bring about his death.[44] Confucius, on the contrary, said he would be very successful if he could serve in government. Confucius similarly said: "If a person's character is good, people will act correctly even without his issuing any orders. . . . If one's character is rectified, what difficulty can there be in governing?" (*Lun-yü,* 13.6, 13.10, 13.13). Mo-tzu, who lived in the fifth century B.C., a little after Confucius, expressed the idea of the political center as a lever still more strongly: "The ruler take delight in [something]. Therefore his subjects carry it out" (*Mo-tzu*, ch. 15). Mo-tzu even took for granted that a ruler could effectively "forbid hatred" (ch. 14). He emphasized that if only a ruler would use his (Mo-tzu's) theories, all people would respond with enthusiasm and act properly, "just as fire rises upwards and water flows downwards" (ch. 16).[45] The idea of a lever is represented as strongly in *Mencius*. Living mostly in the fourth century B.C., Mencius held that "If the ruler is benevolent, no one will not be. . . . No one can oppose someone whose rule as a king is based on benevolence" (*Mencius*, 4A.21, 2A.1). Born a couple of decades or so before Mencius, Shen Pu-hai, possibly the earliest "Legalist" thinker, also expressed this idea of a lever. He is linked to the view that "when the ruler just says one thing correctly, the whole empire is set in order. . . . As for the way an enlightened ruler governs his state, he controls, as it were, a pivot point of three inches: when he turns it, the world is set right."[46] This concept of the political center as a "lever" (our modern term) was still basic in the nineteenth century, as recent research has demonstrated.[47] ("Lever" refers to the efficacy of the king once he acts correctly. Various Chinese thinkers of course differed on the definition of correct action.)

Because the political center was thus perceived as highly efficacious, Confucians regarded the highest moral ideals as politically practicable and tended to hold that political authority is not legitimate unless based on absolute morality. Although neglecting the qualifications noted above, the great expert on Confucian thought Mou Tsung-san is certainly correct: "[A]ccording to all the wise scholars of old, the Son of Heaven was regarded as occupying the highest possible, the most exalted position, the affairs of which were sacred to the utmost extent, and which could not be occupied except by a person who had realized the character of a sage to the utmost extent."[48] In other words, only absolutely moral political authority was really legitimate.

Nothing could be further from Greek thought. To be sure, Plato raised the ideal of the philosopher-king. The Greeks too were interested in defining the highest political ideals. But they absolutely lacked the pervasive Chou idea of the political center as a kind of enormously efficacious lever with which the right ruler could quickly rectify all of society. On the contrary, for the Greeks any kind of practical political progress was enormously difficult, and because of these difficulties, they typically treated as legitimate various forms of political authority which they simultaneously regarded as morally inadequate. The idea of immoral but legitimate forms of political authority was thus utterly central to their thought. Had Confucians been similar, they would have focused their political thought not on the morally perfect "true king" (*wang*) but on the morally imperfect "hegemon" (*pa*), seeing the central political problem as that of "realistically" reaching and maintaining that medium quality of government associated by Hsün-tzu with the idea of the *pa*. In Confucian thought, however, even Hsün-tzu's, this idea of the *pa* is a secondary theme at best. (Mencius in his utopian way completely rejected any respect for the *pa* as realizing such a medium quality of government.[49])

In conceptualizing amoral or immoral but legitimate political authority, the Greeks often viewed political authority in the way that Confucians viewed parental authority, as based on the act of procreation and nurture rather than as contingent on current moral performance. It is paradoxical that while inventing democracy, the Greeks in a sense were more statist than the Confucians. In "Crito," Plato pictures Socrates as demanding respect for the laws of a government that has unjustly condemned him to death. Such immoral state commands are legitimate, says Socrates, because "your country is worthier, more to be revered, more sacred, and held in higher honor both by the gods and by all men of understanding, than your father and your mother and all your other ancestors." This is so, Socrates says, because the state not only "brought" the citizen "into the world" but also "raised and educated" him.[50]

In Aristotle's *Politics*, a document certainly at the heart of the Western tradition of political philosophy, the idea of morally inadequate but legitimate forms of political authority also is central. True, Aristotle's famous typology of the six types of constitutions, along with his many comments about hybrid types, not only is based on factual, amoral description but also puts these six types into "an order of merit—first, second, and so on in turn—according as their quality is a better or a worse quality."[51] Aristotle indeed was concerned with defining the nature of the "ideal" constitution and with helping people aim for that ideal. In that sense, politics for him indeed was closely connected to morality.

According to his typology, therefore, two kinds of constitution, monarchy and aristocracy, were "ideal," since, by his definition, they represented rule by "the best" men; one type, "polity," vested power in "the middle class" and was regarded by him as a "perversion" falling short of "the best form of right constitution"; and three other types, tyranny, oligarchy, and democracy, were still worse "perversions," lying "wholly on the side of error."[52]

This typology, however, not only pointed the way to ideal government, it also legitimated less-than-ideal government. Aristotle emphasized that it "is as difficult a matter to reform an old constitution as it is to construct a new one."[53] Therefore the "ideal" constitutions lay "beyond the reach of most states."[54] He noted: "The attainment of the best constitution is likely to be impossible for the general run of states; and the good law-giver and the true statesman must therefore have their eyes open not only to what is the absolute best, but also to what is best in relation to actual conditions."[55]

Thus concerned with what was "practicable" under "actual conditions," Aristotle endorsed the need to establish and work with "perverted" forms of government. The legitimacy of morally or rationally inadequate forms of political authority could not have been more precisely conceptualized or forcefully emphasized.

First, he held that the "polity," a "perversion" in his eyes, as we have seen, was "the best constitution and the best way of life for the majority of states and men."[56] Second, he saw two still "worse" forms of government as often "necessary": "It is possible, for instance, that democracy rather than oligarchy may be necessary for one sort of civic body, and oligarchy rather than democracy for another."[57] He explained: "The student of politics must also be able to study a given constitution, just as it stands and simply with a view to explaining how it may have arisen and how it may be made to enjoy the longest possible life."[58] Thus he offered many suggestions for stabilizing oligarchies and democracies, in other words, strengthening the authority of political systems that inherently were "perverted" or "erroneous."[59] Again, as with Socrates in the "Crito," political morality lay in the overall nature of the constitution-building enterprise and in the ultimate goal of "ideal" government, not necessarily in current constitutional structures or applications of political authority that still were "necessary." The crucially indirect nature of the relation between actual political forms and absolute morality is clear, in sharp contrast with the Confucian ideal of political authority that still were "necessary." The crucially indirect nature of the relation between actual political forms and absolute morality is clear, in sharp contrast with the Confucian ideal of political authority as a direct "extension" (*t-ui*) of a person's inner, absolute sense of morality.

In the thought of St. Augustine, who as much as anyone defined the direction of Christian political philosophy, the idea is set forth still more strongly that politics only partly reflects the light of morality. For Augustine, "political organized society" was not "natural to man," as R. A. Markus has put it. Even the best polity had nothing to do with ultimate moral questions, which were purely a matter of religion. Government was just "a useful and necessary arrangement for man in his fallen condition," since it could remedy "at least some of the evils attendant upon man's fall state." After all, in any human community or political system, according to Augustine, the lives of those who follow God and those who prefer to sin are "inextricably intertwined."[60]

This "dark" view of man became still more basic with the rise of "modern political philosophy" in the West. According to Leo Strauss's authoritative analysis, "The founder of modern political philosophy is Machiavelli," whose key point was: "Let us then cease to take our bearings by virtue, the highest objective a society might choose; let us begin to take our bearings by the objectives which are actually pursued by all societies. . . . These objectives are: freedom from foreign domination, stability or rule of law, prosperity, glory or empire." Strauss then goes on to show that "Republicanism in the Roman style, as interpreted by Machiavelli, became one of the most powerful trends of modern political thought. We observe its presence in the works of Harrington, Spinoza, Algernon Sydney, Montesquieu, Rousseau, and in *The Federalist*." Strauss also shows how Machiavelli's focus on the actual objectives of political leaders rather than the ideal of virtue was taken over and revised by Hobbes and Locke.[61] Modern positivistic political science itself, eschewing moral judgment, has itself grown out of this tradition of "modern political philosophy" going back to Machiavelli.

To be sure, Bellah correctly points out that the American Founding Fathers, even while influenced by what Strauss calls "Republicanism in the Roman style, as interpreted by Machiavelli," still emphasized the need for "virtue" in public life. They certainly did see democracy as a system not only accepting the "avidity" of people but also seeking to contain and channel that selfish impulse by cultivating the sources of morality, especially religion and the family.[62] But this was a far cry from the traditional Chinese vision of government as action directly motivated by lack of selfishness and dedication to the public good (ta-kung wu-ssu), a concept basic to all the different modern Chinese ideologies, including Chinese liberalism, as represented by thinkers like Hsü Fu-kuan. And this Chinese view is still further away from the mainstream of current American liberalism, which Bellah criticizes precisely for forgetting the American Founding Fathers' emphasis on "virtue" as needed to contain self-interest.

Thus Chang Hao was quite correct in holding that the Western concept of democracy has been closely connected to that "consciousness of the dark side of human life" which is only in the background of Confucian political thought as well as modern Chinese thought about "democracy." This conceptual difference is of the greatest importance, whether or not one also wants to claim that without an intellectual tradition emphasizing this "consciousness of the dark side of human life," a political system cannot institutionalize "tolerance for the expression of conflict and antagonism in politics" and the "acknowledgment that the political process can legitimately be used by individuals and groups to try to force the state to serve their selfish ends," to use Andrew Nathan's formulation. Again, this conceptual difference is crucial whether or not one wants to argue that such special "tolerance" is needed if a political system democratically based on open competition for power is to remain stable.

Many claim that such stability indeed does depend on such tolerance, and that such tolerance does largely depend on establishing a public political philosophy defining politics as "the art of the possible" rather than an extension of the individual's highest sense of moral integrity. This claim is at least plausible. Yet whether or not it proves correct, any Chinese concept of democracy lacking this pervasive Western emphasis on the difficulty of politically realizing the highest moral ideals is very different from the mainstream of Western thought about democracy. Using one word, "democracy," to denote two different concepts is something no serious scholar willingly does.

II.4. Five Models of the Political Center

If, then, we want to equate our third developmental criterion, just and reasonable political development, with "democratization," we find that the definition of "democracy" is a complex problem, and that there is doubt and controversy about the cultural conditions required to set up "democracy" as a practicable system. We may assert that democracy is the most just and reasonable form of government, and that Chinese liberals have called for democracy. Yet what they are calling for, whether it is an absolute ideal, whether it is the same as what Americans call "democracy," and whether it is practicable are all far from obvious. For the sake of clarity, therefore, we can distinguish between five ways of conceptualizing the political center. Once these distinctions are clear, determining which of the five models of the political center should be called "democracy" is a purely terminological matter.

The typical American liberal concept of democracy entails all six of the above ideas: (1) symbolizing the government as based on "consent of the governed"; (2) institutionalizing almost unlimited political competition; (3) effecting a vigorous formal and informal flow of political communication; (4) legitimating politics as conflict between interest groups oriented to selfish ends; (5) combining an emphasis on political morality with a "dark" view of human nature and the nature of political authority; and (6) defining morality in terms of the specifically Western type of individualism with its emphasis on individual legal rights. This model of the political center can be called "American-style democracy."

When, however, we look at the models of the center conceptualized by Chinese liberals and humanists, we find that although they call their model "democracy," they emphasize only the first two of these six ideas, virtually always ignoring or filtering out the last four (see below).

Nathan seems to suggest that "Chinese democrats" on the Chinese mainland have had a vision of democracy coinciding with the Western one in important ways.[63] Yet he presents no evidence that they ever conceptualized any of these six ideas above except for the first two.

The difference between American believers in democracy and Chinese liberals or humanists can be seen in how the latter have sought to put public discussion within certain parameters. True, they have steadily rejected the idea of using a particular "ism" or "ideology" to limit public discussion. Yet they have usually agreed that public discussion must be guided by a certain sense of "reason" or "morality." Said T'ang Chün-i (1909–1978), the eminent humanist philospher:

> We say that the freedom and rights of the individual must be protected by public opinion and the law. People always believe that the legislative and executive organs in a democracy can protect the rights and freedom of the individual so long as public opinion is free. Yet if public opinion is not taken charge of by people who, as I put it, are able to appreciate and fully grasp the true values and ideals of human life and civilization in all its aspects, if the people or officials carrying out legislative and administrative duties are unable to appreciate and fully grasp the true values and ideals of human life and civilization in all its aspects, then correctly orienting public opinion and the law to the public good will be utterly impossible.[64]

It is true that some Chinese liberals have gone further than T'ang Chün-i in calling for a free marketplace of ideas unlimited by any group "taking charge" (*chu-ch'ih*) of the flow of public opinion. A good example is the recent collection of essays *K'ai-fang-te to-yüan she-hui* by the noted social scientist Yang Kuo-shu. I would argue, however, that even Yang keeps public opinion within certain parameters, holding that in a pluralistic society, "law" and "custom," including a "moral consensus," still determine a "certain scope" of thought or behavior that "all must respect," thus avoiding the dangers of "moral relativism."[65] Certainly in this liberal light—and this point applies even more strongly to the two great liberal thinkers of the 1950s and 1960s, Yin Hai-kuang and Hsü Fu-kuan—the consensus on which the polity is based is not left to the open competition of interest groups devoted to their own private ends. This strong Chinese intellectual tendency to intertwine the idea of "freedom" with that of "morality" and "reason" is in turn related to the problem of "moral language" (see below).

If, then, Chinese liberals have still emphasized the idea of a certain moral consensus, the methods available to shape such a consensus are in fact limited: a form of political leadership rising above partisan interests to stand for an overarching principle of morality and reason, such as the political party conceptualized by Sun Yat-sen; the spontaneous wisdom of the masses; and the intellectuals as a somehow united group standing for that same overarching principle of morality and reason.

Chinese liberals and humanists reject the first possibility, occasionally refer to the second, and clearly incline to the third. Therefore, in contrast to the model of "American-style democracy," one can call their model of the political center *hsien-jen cheng-fu* (government by the able and the moral). According to this view, some intellectuals develop an enlightened way of thinking (*k'ai-ming*); gradually the intellectual strata all agree to accept this way of thinking and use it to influence the masses, who, it is often claimed, are still trapped in "feudal" and "unscientific" ways of thought; influenced by these enlightened ideas, the masses will freely elect representatives who are moral and able; and these leaders will then respect the consensus of the intellectuals as they run the government. Thus "democracy" will be realized avoiding not only the problem of tyranny and special interest groups (*chi-te-li-i-che*) but also that of license and moral degeneration.

For many Chinese, however, this vision is not practicable, and so they have inclined toward our third model of the political center, that of Sun Yat-sen, which can be referred to as *wan-neng cheng-fu* (efficacious government). This third model is described below. Among other things, it somehow combines the idea of free elections with that of a political party rising above partisanship; bases itself on overarching principles of morality and reason; and takes considerable responsibility for shaping the nation's moral consensus. Again, in order to understand the plausibility of this model in China, one has to keep in mind the question of a culturally rooted moral language (see below), the fact that the model of American-style democracy has not been clearly conceptualized and propagated in China, and the fact that the model of "government by the able and moral" has often seemed impracticable.

I would suggest, however, that many Chinese sense not only the impracticability of the *hsien-jen cheng-fu* model (rule by the able and moral) but also the danger of dictatorship implied by the *wan-neng cheng-fu* model (efficacious government) and so really incline toward a kind of eclectic mix of the two models. Thus, I argue, the conceptualization of the political process in the ROC today is dominated by a kind of "creative tension" between these two models. Be that as it may, we end up with five models of the political center: American-style democracy, government by the able and moral, efficacious government, an eclectic mix of the latter two, and the model in the PRC, which many would call "totalitarian," though a more precise term may be desirable.

We can now discuss more clearly our third developmental criterion, just and reasonable political development. Which of the five models best accords with that standard? Some hold that the model of American-style democracy does so under all circumstances. Others hold that this model requires cultural or historical conditions. Others hold it is not an ideal solution under any circumstances. Thus unlike the other four criteria, this one is highly controversial. Yet whatever the controversy, many would agree that the totalitarian model least accords with the idea of just and reasonable political development. To that extent, establishing a normative approach to Chinese modernization is feasible.

If, then, we can agree that any society or nation in its development should try to accord with our five developmental criteria, and if we agree that the people in a society can work to meet these standards only to the extent that they have conceptualized these standards, the next question our discussion should deal with is clear. We need to ask: how in fact have major contemporary Chinese intellectual or ideological trends conceptualized the options available to the Chinese people? Which of these indigenously conceptualized otpions comes closest to our five developmental criteria? Curiously enough, however, before we ask these questions we have to deal with still another controversial issue: what in fact are the leading contemporary Chinese intellectual or ideological trends?

III. The Four Leading Options Conceptualized in Contemporary China

III.1. The Three Principles of the People

Trying to describe the currently living Chinese options, I argue that they can be analyzed under four headings. One is the Three Principles of the People as a constantly articulated doctrine in the Republic of China combining ideas from the writings of Sun Yat-sen (1866–1925), provisional president of the Republic of China when it was established in 1911, and Chiang Kai-shek (1887–1975), who led the Republic of China from 1928 until his death, being elected President in 1948. I am here referring to the semi-official version of their ideas propagated in Taiwan in recent years as a unified doctrine and found in well-known studies or textbooks, such as those of Ting Ti, which won three prizes and has been published at least six times, and of Lin Kuei-p'u, also published at least six times.[66] These studies are certainly close to the ideas of Sun and Chiang themselves, but the latter ideas as historical phenomena must be distinguished from secondary attempts to elucidate them and make of them a system of thought that can be conveniently communicated to students and other popular audiences. This paper, however, is interested precisely in the Three Principles as a currently understood way of thinking influencing millions of Chinese, not in the viewpoints of the two authors per se, Sun and Chiang. Therefore such currently used textbooks are a convenient starting point.

At least two groups will not be satisfied with this attempt to describe the Three Principles. First, my outline will seem misleading to scholars like Ting Ti who have put years of intense study into this doctrine and regard it as a living philosophy expounding universal truths, not as a set of arguments intertwined with culturally distinctive premises. Second, a significant group of Chinese and Western intellectuals regard the doctrine as intellectually shallow and refuse to discuss it as a significant current trend.

These intellectuals, in the first place, confuse the question of the doctrine's intellectual value with that of its current influence. Its great influence is obvious to anyone who has lived in Taiwan, read materials associated with it, and talked with a broad range of intellectual and nonintellectual people about it. I recall a discussion I had at the University of California, San Diego, around 1982 with a Chinese student from Taiwan who then was studying as a Ph.D. candidate at this university, working toward a degree in one of the natural sciences. I suggested that Chinese political culture differed from American in emphasizing the need of a nation for some sort of guiding ideology. He was puzzled. "We Chinese don't have such a need," he said. I replied: "What about the Three Principles of the People?" "Oh," he said, "that is not an ideology. That is a kind of science of human behavior." Indeed, this kind of respect for this doctrine as a set of living truths is common among millions of Chinese, especially in the case of the ideas associated with Sun.

Intellectuals brushing aside this doctrine, moreover, overlook the fact that it has been admired by indisputably brilliant Chinese scholars, such as Ho Lin, the astute student of philosophy who was a friend of Fung Yu-lan[67]; Hsiao Kung-ch'üan, perhaps the leading modern authority on the history of Chinese political thought[68]; Ch'ien Mu, regarded by many as modern China's greatest historian; the brilliant philosopher Mou Tsung-san, whose *Cheng-tao yü chih-tao* takes its title from Sun's distinction between the sovereignty of the people (*cheng-ch'üan*) and the derived authority of the state (*chih-ch'üan*)[69]; and the brilliant philosopher-historians Hsü Fu-kuan and T'ang Chün-i, whose political writings frequently include respectful references to the ideas of Sun.[70] In the West, significant new books have argued effectively that Sun's ideas about economic and political development accord with the current views of some prominent economists and political scientists.[71] Trying to adopt a scholarly approach, I am not here trying to evaluate the tendency to glorify Sun's thought, but there is no justification for ignoring his doctrine as a significant contemporary Chinese intellectual or ideological trend.[72]

III.2. Modern Chinese Humanism

A second option has been articulated by a trend that can be called "modern Chinese humanism." This term does not refer directly to the *jen-wen ching-shen* (spirit of civilization) emphasized by many modern Chinese humanists. *Jen-wen ching-shen* denotes a goal or ideal these humanists put forward and also used to describe the historical reality of Confucius and his followers. Rather than the goal of modern China or the historical reality of Confucius, I have in mind an outlook that actually is widespread in China today and takes a variety of forms. These include the historical approach of Ch'ien Mu; the historical-philosophical work of Hsü Fu-kuan; the metaphysical approach of Mou Tsung-san and T'ang Chün-i; Lao Ssu-kuang's less metaphysical if not antimetaphysical approach to Chinese philosophy; a great variety of writings by scholars like Tseng Chao-hsü, editor of *O-hu yüeh-k'an,* a well-known philosophical periodical; and the widely studied historical and interdisciplinary approach of Yü Ying-shih.[73] For the purposes of this paper, Yü's book on Chinese modernization is especially useful. Called *Ts'ung chia-chih hsi-t'ung k'an Chung-kuo wen-hua-te hsien-tai i-i* (Modernization and Chinese culture: a discussion from the standpoint of the traditional value system), this book grew out of a lecture given September 1, 1983, by this Yale University professor at Sun Yat-sen Memorial Hall in Taipei. The event was organized by one of Taipei's two leading newspapers, *Chung-kuo shih-pao,* which has a circulation of about one million. Because this book not only was prominently introduced but also has been widely admired as eruditely summing up things that had needed to be said for a long time, the outlook in this book can be regarded as an important part of at least current intellectual tendencies in Taiwan and indeed in other parts of the Chinese world as well.

Many of the ideas shared by the different versions of modern Chinese humanism have been discussed by Charlotte Furth and others as a form of Chinese "conservatism," but indeed what Furth and her colleagues showed is that the Western concept of "conservatism" cannot easily be used to describe these ideas.[74] What all these writers share is the idea that China should modernize, and that Chinese modernization not only is compatible with the ethical ideals of Confucius but also depends on a reaffirmation, a creative renewal of them (Lao Ssu-kuang, however, would accept this point only with reservations). This viewpoint partly overlaps and partly is in tension with that of the Three Principles, as I will try to show. It goes back to the position taken by Liang Ch'i-ch'ao (1873–1929) in his later years and has some roots in the thought of K'ang Yu-wei (1858–1927). Because K'ang and especially Liang embraced modernization, their emphasis on Confucian values can be distinguished from that of Chang Chih-tung (1837–1909), who with his slogan "Chinese learning as the basis, Western learning as the means" remained committed to the traditional imperial order and so should be placed outside the scope of "modern Chinese humanism."[75]

III.3. Chinese Liberalism

A third option, Chinese liberalism, overlaps that of "modern Chinese humanism," as illustrated by Hsü Fu-kuan's case. "Liberalism," however, has often been based on the iconoclastic, May Fourth claim that modernization cannot be achieved without fundamentally rejecting Confucianism. This approach is illustrated by much of the thought of Hu Shih (1891–1962) and Yin Hai-kuang's (1919–1969) *Chung-kuo wen-hua-te chan-wang* (An appraisal of Chinese culture and its prospects).[76] Liberals have focused on democratization as the prime aspect of modernization, often defining "democracy" as a universally applicable system of majority rule and human rights generally exemplified by the U.S. system. Their viewpoint is important in Taiwan today, being often expressed by political figures, officials, and legislators "outside the Kuomintang" (*Tang-wai*) as well as by the many periodicals in Taiwan critical of the Kuomintang.[77] It is also expressed by those in the PRC called "Chinese democrats" by Nathan.[78]

III.4. Chinese Marxism

The fourth option is Chinese Marxism in its Maoist and post-Maoist forms. It has been much studied.[79] The recent development of Marxist ideology in the PRC has been discussed by Stuart Schram, who sees the PRC leadership as still committed to Marxism: "Despite the emphasis which he places on realistic and successful policies, especially in the economic domain, Deng [Teng Hsiao-p'ing] cannot be properly characterized as a pragmatist because the goals he pursues are defined partly in *a priori* ideological terms." Teng, according to Schram, is trying to reorganize "a socialist system," not replace it "by something else." Moreover, Schram sees an ideological "void left by the mythology of the Cultural Revolution," a void not yet filled by "the emergence of a credible alternative system of beliefs and values."[80]

III.5. Analyzing the Four Options: Modernization, Moral Language, and Seven Points of Controversy

In order to contrast and compare these four options with each other, one can first note their shared commitment to modernization. Some have recently noted that "modernization" cannot be defined in purely abstract terms, since it refers to a series of concrete historical processes, each occurring within a concrete, particular cultural setting. Thus Chinese modernization consists simply of the concrete developments that have occurred in China in modern times. Yet the very scholars who want to equate Chinese modernization with these concrete processes that have already occurred also criticize these concrete processes, saying that China has not yet begun to modernize properly.[81] Thus for them modernization is still at least partly an abstract idea or goal that can be used to evaluate what has concretely occurred, not just a concrete process.

As a goal referred to in many Chinese statements made during this century, modernization can be summed up under these headings: a "secularized" view of the man-cosmos relation influenced by modern science and so either rejecting or revising older ideas about the cosmic or divine basis of morality (as illustrated by Marxist materialism, sociologistical views of human life, or the use of Kant to rephrase the Neo-Confucian view of "heaven"); a multifocal cultural geography replacing the Sinocentric view; nationalism; and an idea of progress emphasizing technology, economic growth, and some form of political participation.[82]

In the modern thought of virtually any society, however, this cosmopolitan goal of modernization is typically intertwined with a moral vision going beyond modernization, as argued especially in Chang Hao's forthcoming book.[83] Thus intertwining the discussion of modernization with a certain "moral language," influential people in any modern society seem usually to hark back to culturally distinctive premises formed centuries or millennia earlier, as Bellah has argued in the case of the United States, and Yü Ying-shih, in the case of China. The nature of these premises in the Chinese case cannot be discussed here, but one point should be noted.

Obviously, modern China's moral language has been unlike the American to the extent that the American has revolved, as Bellah argues, around a certain ideal of "individualism" grounded in the biblical and "republican" traditions of Western antiquity. It has also been unlike the American to the extent that the American has involved what Alasdair MacIntyre called "the distinctively modern standpoint," the idea that there are no objective, impersonal moral standards with which to resolve contradictory views about how people should act. All the four Chinese options listed above include the idea that such objective, impersonal moral standards obviously exist, can be rather easily understood, and should be applied. As noted above, scholars generally agree that there has been no Chinese parallel, in either modern or premodern times, to the prominent Western tendency toward skepticism, which led to what MacIntyre calls "the distinctively modern outlook." Whether Chinese thought has been anti-, pre-, or post-Humean, it has never been Humean to a significant extent. This fact strikes me as a very important one, one indicating a most fundamental aspect of Western modernization that has had little or no influence on China. Moreover this continuing Chinese belief that there are objective moral standards and that these should directly inform the political process is a major reason that Chinese thinkers, in designing the center of the polity, basically avoided the model of American-style democracy and depended on some notion of a political or intellectual force determining the moral parameters of public discussion.

Whatever the nature, however, of the Chinese moral language that has accompanied the Chinese conceptualization of modernity, the four trends above—modern Chinese humanism, the Three Principles, liberalism, and

Marxism—have dealt with at least seven key questions in very different ways.

III.6. Question One: Closure

First, should Chinese development be based on a single, relatively closed philosophical system? Can Chinese depend on one or a few great thinkers who brought forth a virtually perfect system, or should they think of themselves as being in the midst of an ongoing, open quest for the truth?

Chinese liberals and humanists have held to the latter view. Though also tending to identify a particular school or philosopher as having successfully laid down the key principles of learning, such as Bertrand Russell or the *hsien-che* (wise scholars of old) who had formed the Confucian tradition, they have seen themselves as in the process of trying to complete an as yet unfinished intellectual task, not as making clear principles revealed in an already articulated modern doctrine. T'ang Chün-i, for instance, saw himself as trying to show how all the valid points made in all philosophies, old and new, Chinese and Western, formed a single, consistent set of truths (*hui-t'ung*), and he saw his own effort as not yet fully successful.

This relatively open outlook, calling for an unending investigation of all forms of learning in the world, can be distinguished from that of the Three Principles, since according to this doctrine, Sun Yat-sen's thought provides "the highest guiding principles for democratic revolution in the modern world." There is a marked tension between the very concept of such a doctrine and the way liberals and humanists conceive of the quest for knowledge.

Indeed this tension is reflected in the fact noted above, that liberals and humanists so often refuse even to consider the Three Principles as an important aspect of the current ideological situation. Their often contemptuous attitude, in other words, far from demonstrating the insignificance of this doctrine, is itself an important datum regarding the kind of tension between this doctrine and some other trends. In the construction of the modern Chinese polity as a symbolic process, the idea of a perfect doctrine laid down by one or more "great" men has so far proved to be both repugnant to many intellectuals and indispensable for practical leaders grappling with the problem of patriotic mobilization (*t'uan-chieh*). The regimented school activities this mobilization entailed struck a good number of brilliant students as senseless idolatry and left them with a deep and permanent feeling of distaste if not hatred for the group that tried to regiment them, the Kuomintang. Combined with the liberal and humanistic emphasis on the self as the vehicle of morality, the common intellectual inclination toward transformative, socialistic policies, and the spectacle of Kuomintang failure before 1949 (see below), this pattern of distaste has been a major aspect of Chinese ideological life in Taiwan.

Yet the doctrine of the Three Principles is still relatively open. It is significant that Sun's thought is officially represented as derived from not only his own genius but also from a very broad variety of Chinese and

Western writing, ranging from Confucius to Lincoln and Marx: "The father of our country was a magnificent thinker. His thought is a crystallization of the finest ideas produced by all the schools of learning, old and new, Chinese and foreign."[84]

Some dismiss this as shallow eclecticism. This formulation, however, epitomizes the principle of broad access to all forms of learning, a principle Sun managed to combine with the need for conformity and mobilization (*t'uan-chieh*). Moreover, the parameters Sun laid down can be called "fruitfully vague," and his followers have not asked Chinese intellectuals directly to affirm his ideas, only to avoid challenging them publicly. For instance, Yü Ying-shih's book on Chinese modernization nowhere mentions the Three Principles but is still part of the intellectual mainstream in the ROC.

By contrast, Maoists to an extreme extent closed off access to traditional and cosmopolitan sources of learning, though restrictions are easing now. Even in the Soviet Union, no similar steps were ever taken to cut off the Soviet people's access to the riches of their own civilization. This I learned from Count Nikolai Tolstoy, an expert on the Soviet Union and Eastern Europe who, strongly anti-Communist, would not hesitate to see the Soviet leadership as guilty of any barbarous act. Yet however barbarous, this extreme degree of closure in the PRC also reflects the great importance in China of our second question: Should Chinese build up their modern way of thought by basing it on traditional values or on abstractly defined standards seemingly transcending this tradition, such as modern science?

III.7. Question Two: Tradition and the Derivation of Values

In deriving values, all four of our Chinese trends are non-Humean and rely on "reason," observation, and certain assumptions about "morality," but there has been much argument about which kind of learning most accords with "reason" and leads to the most accurate account of "experience" (*ching-yen*). For instance, both the humanist Yü Ying-shih and the liberal Yin Hai-kuang have been much interested in the concept of "culture" developed by social scientists like Clyde Kluckhohn; Kant's way of describing "experience" has impressed humanists like Mou Tsung-san and T'ang Chün-i; "scientific materialism" has attracted the Marxists; and David Easton's system theory has attracted some liberals. Variously using such forms of learning, each of our four Chinese trends has paid an inordinate amount of attention to the question of whether and to what extent modern Chinese should rely on traditional values. It is especially confusion regarding this question that has impeded Chinese modernization, according to many in China, such as Yü Ying-shih.[85]

No Western scholar I know of would put similar emphasis on this issue. Indeed the nature of this issue is at least as significant as is the variety of responses to it. According to this Chinese viewpoint, social-cultural change is the determinative aspect of history. Moreover, it is not an inherently vague process best left to ad hoc, spontaneous cultural activities or the competing insights of different artists, philosophers, and authors all trying creatively to make something meaningful out of the varied symbolic resources provided by their domestic and international environments. It cannot be based just on some fruitfully broad parameters summed up roughly by slogans such as *chi-wang k'ai-lai* (continuing to live by the values of the past while accepting new ideas to open up the future). This well-known slogan actually sums up what is happening in the ROC and strongly resembles Yü's injunction: "Chinese must still continuously seek into and open up the sources of their own spirit" and so establish a proper pattern of modernization. But Yü sees a gulf between his idea and the way Taiwan's society is actually mixing traditional and modern values.

Mixing these values through some loosely structured social process, in other words, is not enough. For many Chinese intellectuals, unlike most Western ones, the interaction between traditional and new values is a process that can be precisely analyzed in normative terms, that has not yet been, that should be guided by intellectuals who have arrived at such an analysis, and that largely determines whether or not China can successfully develop in modern times.

The variety of analyses that have been offered of course ranges from the iconoclastic desire to expunge traditional values to the current debate about the extent to which Chinese should rely on them. Yü Ying-shih's analysis calls for relying on them to a very great extent. They accord, he holds, with the insight of Western thinkers like Robert Nisbet that "science and economic growth" cannot by themselves meet "spiritual" needs.[86] They long ago secured "the dignity of the individual"; indeed, they did so without depending on the idea of an anthropomorphic deity and so enabled Chinese modernizers to bypass that crisis of secularization which in the West has threatened the moral basis of society: "Therefore if we just refer to the idea of human dignity, Chinese culture was modern long ago."[87] Based on a certain concept of "transcendence" (see below), this concept of individual dignity differed from both Western individualism and any "collectivism," Yü suggests, referring to the Confucian view, which he in effect sees as aiming for that very balance between self and group conceptualized by Durkheim. Further elucidating both the inherent appeal of traditional values and the compatibility of these values with modernization, Yü notes that they failed to lead to the discovery of science but did lead the Chinese to welcome the advent of science: Lacking dependence on the idea of God, the Chinese lacked an important religion threatened by the advent of science.[88] Facing death not by emphasizing the immortality of the soul but by recognizing the unending process of cosmic renewal and the eternal value of human achievement, the Chinese traditionally had an approach to the problem of death "very much in accord with what is needed for forming a 'religious faith' in the context of modern life."[89] Moreover, having long emphasized that man has "reason," the Chinese can easily "accept the modern concept of rule by law." In more recent work, Yü has argued that economic values in late imperial China were similar in some important ways to what Weber called "the spirit of capitalism."[90]

This being the nature of their "already formed system of values," which anyway is bound to persist in the future, Chinese can have confidence in these values as helping them reach their modern goals but must make a continuous intellectual and moral effort fully to "seek into and open up the sources of their own spirit."[91] What Yü Ying-shih is calling for is a heightened sense of spiritual alertness based on an intellectual understanding of the very great usefulness and moral worth of the Confucian tradition in modern times.

What I am going to suggest is that while this Chinese discussion is indeed concerned with objective problems of cultural change, it also serves as a form of self-cultivation or *kung-fu* (moral effort) modeled on the Neo-Confucian paradigm: *Chung-kuo wen-hua* (Chinese culture) is a concept that in this modern discussion plays somewhat the role that *pen-hsin* (ultimate mind) played in Neo-Confucian discussions of moral effort. For Neo-Confucians, the key issue was whether the starting point of moral effort was trust in the goodness of one's original nature or "ultimate mind" or a cautious effort to spot and eliminate selfish intentions. Yü's emphasis on a strong spirit of trust in Chinese culture is reminiscent of Wang Yang-ming's emphasis on *tzu-hsin* (self-confidence) in the effort fully to realize one's "ultimate mind."

By contrast, another well-known humanist, Lao Ssu-kuang, emphasizes that although the Confucian tradition has much value, the key to progress is not affirming the value of this tradition but becoming much more precisely aware of this tradition's deficiencies and so becoming able to identify and eliminate them. Lao criticizes T'ang Chün-i for excessively affirming this tradition and so impeding the crucial effort to do away with harmful traditional tendencies. One cannot but see a similarity between his program and Chu Hsi's emphasis on doing away with evil as the first step, rather than beginning by having confidence in the goodness of one's ultimate nature.[92]

To be sure, Lao's point about the need for Chinese to distinguish more effectively between the universally valid aspects of their thought and the culturally particular ones is a thoughtful one. Lao holds that the Confucian concept of the "five relationships" lacks universal validity, while Yü vindicates this concept as envisaging a community based on "natural" relations, such as the "natural relation" between father and son.[93] This argument could be continued by asking whether what Confucians considered to be "natural" is indeed natural universally for the human species or is a form of behavior that, admirable or not, was furthered by a particular culture and so only seemed "natural" to those influenced by this culture.

The issue here, however, does not seem to be one just of biological or anthropological facts. For reasons that require more study, the question of the extent to which Chinese should rely on traditional values became central to the modern Chinese intellectual problematique, and behind the different scholarly answers to this question lie feelings and ideas that have not yet been adequately sorted out.

III.8. Question Three: Transformation Versus Accommodation

Besides facing the question of access to the world's flow of information and that of defining the sources of knowledge and value, modern Chinese thinkers have had to choose between more transformative and more accommodative approaches to change. This distinction is by now well known: Should change be accomplished by transforming the whole society, making it totally moral and rooting out all evils at their source (*pa-pen se-yüan*), or should gradualistic methods be used, trying to reduce rather than eliminate the flow of evil? Both approaches were well established in traditional Chinese thought, and both can be found in the *ching-shih* (statecraft) writings of the Ming-Ch'ing period.[94] K'ang Yu-wei and Liang Ch'i-ch'ao in the 1890s saw modernization in transformative terms, and a transformative, indeed utopian vision was basic to much May Fourth iconoclasm, including Marxism. The Cultural Revolution was an extreme example. An accommodative, gradualistic approach to modernization was increasingly adopted by Liang Ch'i-ch'ao after about 1903, and Sun's thought is accommodative to an important extent, setting the tone for the accommodative policies of the ROC.

Often, however, a belief in eventual transformation has remained part of accommodative thought in China. This is one reason such thought is different from Burkean conservatism. Seeking to revive the Confucian spirit as the basis of modernization and accommodative with regard to practical questions, the philosopher T'ang Chün-i remained nevertheless oriented to the goal of totally transforming China if not the world. In the Three Principles, accommodative views remain linked to the ideal of *ta-t'ung* (great oneness), and even a gradualist like Yü Ying-shih will not give up this hope of transformation: "Perhaps all of mankind one day will truly create a shared value system merging together all the different cultures. That the Chinese dream of a 'great oneness' will never be realized is not necessarily so."[95]

III.9. Question Four: The Scope of Violence

The fourth choice has been between a "conservative" respect for the established structure of power and property (*chi-te-li-i-che*) and a determination to overthrow it using violence if necessary. Violence has been accepted by all four of our Chinese trends (against the Manchus or the Japanese invasion, for instance). Except for the Marxists, however, there has been a strong inclination to deal peacefully with the wealthier Chinese strata possibly opposed to reform. A Burkean respect for them has not been prominent, but the moral transformation envisaged by humanists or liberals has usually been formulated as based on cultural change and education, not violent upheaval of the sort specialized in by Mao with few if any constructive results.

*III.10. Question Five: The State Versus the Individual as
the Vehicle of Morality*

Liberals and humanists have shared a most central belief that morality, the basis of the polity for virtually all Chinese, can come only from the genuine convictions of the individual, and that the state can be moral only to the extent that it acts in accord with the moral understanding thus arrived at by individuals. This widespread emphasis on individual conscience has been somehow overlooked by Western scholars who see the Maoist idea of a state-imposed moral order as similar to some alleged Confucian reliance on hierarchy and authority. It is true that this liberal and humanistic emphasis on individual conscience has often been intertwined with philosophies that have not won mass support, such as Hu Shih's liberalism or T'ang Chün-i's metaphysics. This failure to win mass support, however, does not necessarily mean that such philosophers conceived of the moral self in a way at odds with the Chinese cultural mainstream. This failure can be better explained by looking at the combination of answers offered by such philosophers to all seven of the questions we are dealing with in this paper, the practicability of their approaches overall, and political circumstances. That their emphasis on the moral self was in accord with widespread cultural orientations is suggested by the fact that this emphasis was an idea so broadly shared by so many intellectuals with greatly varying philosophies. Moreover, as noted below, a considerable number of scholars, Chinese and Western, now accept the thesis that the Confucian tradition emphasized the conscience and autonomy of the individual.

Writing as both a humanist thinker and an eminent historian, Yü Ying-shih says: "Chinese believe that moral value has its source within the mind of each self and is something that from the self extends outward to join the self with other people as well as with heaven, earth, and the ten thousand things . . . . To sum up, people have a kind of inner power of spirit, something directing and impelling the self unceasingly to continue its struggle upward." Rooting this concept in the thought of Confucius, Yü describes it as a notion of "inner transcendence" (*nei-tsai ch'ao-yüeh*) different from the Judeo-Christian way of deriving morality from a divine being existing independently of and so ultimately external to human beings: "Chinese infer the concept of a transcendent 'heaven' from the fact that the mind has within itself the ability to become aware of moral value."[96]

As already discussed, Yü puts this concept of the self into historical and cross-cultural perspective, arguing in a striking way that this Confucian concept admirably meets the needs of modernization. This argument is what makes his book distinctive. His view of the Confucian approach to the self, however, is widely shared and cannot be regarded as just the theory of a particular scholar. His idea of "inner transcendence" stems from the formulations of New Confucians like T'ang Chün-i and even resonates with the ideas of Fung Yu-lan, who in *Hsin yüan-tao* (A new study of moral philosophy in China), written around 1944, defined Chinese thought as a quest to merge transcendent moral value with everyday life (*chi kao-ming erh tao chung-yung*).

Another example of this living contemporary faith expressed through devotion to the concept of the self found in Confucian thought is the current writing of Tseng Chao-hsü, editor of a well-known philosophical journal in Taiwan (*O-hu yüeh-k'an*). Tseng focuses on "moral character." Morality is understood in terms of the quality Confucius called *jen*. The idea of *jen* cannot be divorced from that of a certain "transcendent" dimension of the cosmos, a dimension consisting of a "limitless" process of coming into being and renewal (*sheng-sheng pu-i, jih hsin yu hsin*).[97] Yet this transcendence must be realized through concrete human practice (*chi kao-ming erh tao chung-yung*).[98] This effort to subsume under the "limitless" that mundane realm "limited" by obstacles and frustrations can be carried out only by one agent, the individual. Thus it depends on "self-cultivation," which in turn depends on the individual's ability to tap his own inner resources (*yu-chi, ch'iu-chu-chi*). This effort, therefore, necessarily takes the form of a personal, unique experience.

Carrying out this effort, the individual can profit much from the help of a teacher, but what Munro calls "model emulation" or "fosterage" is not what Tseng sees as the heart of the matter. Looking for something within himself, the individual, for one thing, is primarily directing his attention to the words of Confucius contained in ancient writings, not to the words or behavior of his teacher. It is the words of Confucius that he has to memorize, not the words of his teacher, and in trying to figure out the meaning Confucius' words have for his own life, the individual turns just to "reason," carefully avoiding the influence of any "ideology" or state-imposed process of "fosterage" coming between his conscience and the ideals of Confucius himself.[99] If thus studying Confucius is "model emulation," then why isn't that "imitation of Christ" called for by Soren Kierkegaard?

Thus carrying out an "unceasing process of self-strengthening," the individual, refusing to "deceive himself" (*tzu-ch'i*), increasingly frees himself from selfish desires and anxieties, in this way transcending what "limits" his life and so becoming one with the "limitless." Thus he "brings forth that spirit of morality in terms of which each person is his own master," becomes an "integrated" personality, and so attains the "freedom of a spiritual personality."[100] Moreover, this effort to realize fully his own possibilities proceeds hand-in-hand with an effort to do the same for others (*ch'eng-chi, ch'eng-wu*).

Apart from inner and outer moral failure, therefore, the whole social and political order consists only of an accumulation of such moral processes, each carried out by an individual. Therefore, as Yü Ying-shih says, this social-political order is not something "imposed on the individual from the outside."[101] In terms, then, of this relation between group and self, the individual "discovers the direction of his own life" (*fa-hsien tzu-chi sheng-ming-te lu-hsiang*) and realizes the "dignity of the individual" (*ko-jen-te tsun-yen*).

Certainly, like any language claiming to reveal the authentic self, this language putting ancient symbols into a twentieth-century perspective is still a culturally or historically shaped medium not necessarily guaranteeing the absence of what Munro calls social "manipulation." Like Christianity, this Confucian discourse asks us to lift ourselves up by our bootstraps, claiming that certain historically limited texts somehow make clear the nature of the "limitless." Thus caught in all the usual difficulties impeding any such attempt to establish the autonomy of the self, however, this modern Confucian discourse still seems to represent such an attempt as much as does any other such philosophical or theological tradition. One has to keep in mind that the Chinese words making up this language are much more moving in the original than in translation.

Humanists like Tseng Chao-hsü not only reject "ideology" but also eschew any optimism about national or historical development. By contrast, humanists like T'ang Chün-i or Mou Tsung-san, although also rejecting "ideology" and respecting only "reason," do have an optimistic vision of historical development, as illustrated by Mou Tsung-san's Hegelian vision of "Chinese culture" as a moral ideal necessarily unfolding in historical stages and so constituting a cultural "force" or "tide" on which intellectuals can "depend."[102] Yü Ying-shih's humanism also avoids such a concept of "the power of culture." Whether or not perceiving this "power," however, the liberals and the humanists see moral influence as stemming from "the self" or from "intellectuals," not from any political party so far established.

III.11. The Three Principles and the State as a Vehicle of Morality

Their outlook, therefore, is necessarily in tension with not only Marxism but also the doctrine of the Three Principles of the People. To be sure, the Confucian, self-focused logic of the humanists became interwoven with the Three Principles as President Chiang increasingly emphasized Confucian and Neo-Confucian philosophy. Moreover, Sun Yat-sen had emphasized the transition within the self from "understanding" to "faith" to "power," and in dealing with this relation between "knowledge" and "action," he had impressed many intellectuals with his discussion of this central Chinese philosophical problem (*chih nan hsing i*).

According to the current doctrine of the Three Principles, however, the focus is not just on individual moral effort. This is because one political party, the Kuomintang, offers the nation moral leadership based on Sun's and Chiang Kai-shek's teachings, including Sun's Last Testament, and these teachings in turn are represented in the Constitution of the Republic of China, adopted December 25, 1946, through which the Party exercises power.

To some extent, this claim regarding the moral leadership of the Kuomintang is put forward in terms of practicality and political commitment. If Chinese citizens do not commit themselves to a specific political vehicle and submit to its discipline, how can they organize and modernize their society? For many, if the Kuomintang's authority is not accepted, the only alternatives are the totalitarian model of the Communists and the impractical suggestions of the liberals and the humanists, who, I would argue, claim that they are offering the same democratic model realized in the United States but actually have not even conceptualized this model, much less shown that it can be practically implemented in a Chinese setting (see II.1 through II.4 above).

Yet apart from thus referring to practical considerations, the doctrine of the Three Principles bases its claim regarding the moral role of the party on an argument that, like the thinking of the humanists and the liberals, rests on an assumption that most American intellectuals cannot accept: epistemological optimism, the belief that impersonal, objective, universal moral principles can be known and politically applied.

The starting point of the Three Principles is not the philosophy of culture or the moral experience of the individual but the fate of the nation. China is a "society," a "tradition," a "people" of the highest value. But China today exists in a time of peril, like someone struggling in the midst of "deep water or a hot fire" (shui shen huo je). Facing this peril, the textbooks say, is a matter for the group as a whole, for "us," not for the individual alone. Thus the textbooks refer repeatedly to "we." Given this peril, "we" want to "save the nation and save the people."

The individual is thus from the start transposed into a "we-group," into what Bellah calls a "community of memory." The individual is not asked to contemplate fine points about the definition of "modernization" or "culture." His attention is turned not to the original ideals of Chinese culture developed in the Chou period but to what has happened to "us" in the last century. Again and again, the textbooks ask him to remember what is in fact one of the world's great sagas: the 1911 Revolution, the Northern Expedition, the Victory over Japan, the establishment of the Constitution, the loss of the mainland, and the achievements in Taiwan, which "have long since been noted and praised without end by Chinese and foreigners alike."[103]

Yet to bring this saga to a successful conclusion and "save China," a "great doctrine" is needed (ta-tao), one based on universally correct principles (ho-ch'ing ho-li ho-fa-te yüan-tse), and so able to "put an end to all difficulties" (fang-chih i-ch'ieh-te liu-pi). This doctrine already exists; it was established by a "great" man, Sun; and so "we" should accept it, praise it, and act on it.

Today, however, the textbooks continue, it is controversial, unappreciated by many. Therefore "we" need to study it and explain its true meaning to others.

It has an ontological basis in the principle of "the oneness of mind and matter" (hsin wu ho-i). This condition takes the form of a cosmos "unendingly bringing things into being, unendingly progressing" (sheng-sheng pu-i, chin-hua pu-i). Exhibited along with this cosmos are "the principles of mankind" (jen-lei-chih tao-li). Conceptualized by studying all human achievements, these principles accord with the "tide" of history: "The thought of our nation's father accords with the fundamental tendency of the current tide of world events" (*ch'ao-liu-te ch'ü-shih*).[104]

These principles call for the fullest development of all human and cosmic possibilities, especially economic ones (*jen neng chin ch'i ts'ai, ti neng chin ch'i li, wu neng chin ch'i yung, huo neng ch'ang ch'i liu*).[105]

Such development is inherently moral, implying the overarching principle of "devotion to the public good leaving behind all purely private or selfish interest" (*ta-kung wu-ssu*).[106]

Following this principle, the Chinese seek international peace based on "equality" but must also mobilize themselves and, again on the principle of equality, harmoniously cooperate with each other (*t'uan-chieh, hu-chu*). More specifically, to be effective such cooperation requires realizing three principles, the people's livelihood, national development, and democracy. Pursuing these Three Principles in a world still largely not accepting them, even though tending toward them, the Chinese must carry out a "Revolution."

To do this, the Chinese people must (1) respect these principles, (2) retain control as a people over their own destiny, and (3) set up a political party that will on their behalf carry out the "Revolution" by establishing "efficacious government" (*wan-neng cheng-fu*).

Because all three of these actions are necessary in order to carry out the revolution as Sun defined it, there can be no desirable form of freedom that conflicts with them. Thus political freedom in accord with these three actions is necessarily limited from an American standpoint, as Sun and his followers have repeatedly said. "Efficacious government" as a way of designing the political center differs from American-style democracy, just as do the other models of the political center conceptualized in contemporary China (see II.4 above).

According to the Three Principles, political freedom is limited, first of all, because it excludes the freedom to reject "the principles of mankind" and the "Revolution" implied by them: "When Chinese discuss freedom, they cannot do so to the point of departing from the thought of our nation's father."[107] In terms of his thought, moreover, freedom of choice must be balanced if not superseded by other principles, notably equality. At the same time, true equality still calls for a hierarchy based on wisdom and morality.[108]

To be sure, such limits on freedom are not too far from those widely accepted in China, even to some extent by liberals like Yin Hai-kuang. Professor Yin intertwined "freedom" and "democracy" with the principles of "rationality" and "loving compassion" and vigorously distinguished "freedom" from "doing as one pleases" (*kao-hsing tsen yang pien tsen-yang*).[109]

According to the Three Principles, however, the government has rights superseding individual freedom. True, "the people" retain ultimate sovereignty (*cheng-ch'üan*), giving the government only a derived authority to administer their affairs (*chih-ch'üan*), and so they retain their Four Rights (initiative, referendum, election, and recall). Thus the government was seen by Sun as directly controlled by all the people (*ch'üan-min cheng-chih*). This is seen as superior to the Western practice of allowing a single class to control the government, the typical result in a capitalist society.[110]

Thus representing "the people," however, the government does not recognize the rights of the "enemies of the people," those who oppose the "Revolution." This is so because, according to the Three Principles, rights derive from the Revolution, not from nature.[111] The "freedom of the state," moreover, "is more important than the freedom of the individual. . . . When the state has attained complete freedom, it ought to give the people a reasonable degree of freedom." Requiring "efficacious government," the people have to "trust" their government the way a passenger trusts the driver of a car.[112] The need for unity and mobilization thus supersedes the demand for individual freedom especially during the first two political stages envisaged by Sun, the military and the tutelage stages, which lasted until 1947, while the international context of Taiwan in subsequent years has also been seen as justifying restrictions. Thus the followers of Sun saw themselves as conceptualizing "freedom" in a way brilliantly avoiding two Western problems: the excesses of individual freedom and control of the state by special interest groups, as opposed to "the people as a whole."[113]

This conceptualization of political freedom, therefore, differs from the American not only in presupposing that freedom inherently is the structured freedom to carry out a revolution based on certain universal moral principles but also in giving the state a powerful rationale for limiting individual freedom in the name of the Revolution. It differs also in the kinds of devices set up to check or oust the leaders should they violate the wishes of the governed.

According to the Three Principles, the key device consists of the people's sovereign power to exercise their rights of election, initiative, referendum, and recall. Elected by the people, the National Assembly embodies this sovereign power, and the Control Yüan can impeach anyone by addressing its impeachments to the National Assembly. This device is used instead of the two devices basic to American-style democracy: open political competition between two or more major political parties, and the principle of checks and balances between the executive, judicial, and legislative branches. According to the textbooks, the two-party system can "be established only in a country where the political experience of the people is profound and where party policies are managed on a high level of morality; otherwise, it cannot work."[114] So far as checks and balances go, at least some scholars believe this principle applies only to the relation between the National Assembly and the five branches of government, not to interaction between the latter. According to Ting Ti, the five branches—including the executive, the legislative, and the judicial—work together and are coordinated by the President, thus avoiding the danger of one branch's hamstringing another, particularly the legislative's hamstringing the executive.[115]

Thus using the principle of electoral competition and that of checks and balances to only a limited extent, the Three Principles do not give the people any way to check or oust their leaders that is as practical as the methods available to American citizens. One might be tempted to say that in this juxtaposition of "efficacious government" (*wan-neng cheng-fu*) with "government by all the people" (*ch'üan-min cheng-fu*), the power possessed by the Kuomintang is total and fully practical, that possessed by the people, total but somewhat metaphysical. The political reality, however, is different. The system does depend on the continuing commitment of the Party to "the principles of mankind," but electoral pressure does play an important role, as does the powerful flow of public opinion, the quality of the leadership, and the whole institutional, cultural, and international context to the polity, including the commitment to Confucian values, the consequent emphasis on individual moral autonomy, the emphasis on access to the world's sources of information, the free market economy, and the connection to American public opinion. In this system of government, the leadership seeks support and inputs from the rest of society and depends to a large extent on the credibility that results from congruence between its principles and its record.

In thus outlining the nature of the political center as conceptualized in the Three Principles, my purpose has not been to deny that this conceptualization leads to the danger of dictatorship. It certainly does. Nor have I meant to suggest that the ROC's political "center" does a better job meeting the problems of the ROC than the more pluralistic kind of center in America does in meeting American problems. Toting up the disasters and successes on both sides is too complex a task for this writer. My purpose here has rather been to try to explain how the followers of Sun have advanced a claim very different from the liberal and humanistic positions, the claim, namely, that the state as established in the Republic of China is in fact a vehicle of morality.

III.12. Questions Six and Seven: The Design of the Political Center and the Economic Structure

This sixth question, how to design the political center, has thus already been discussed. I argue that the Three Principles, modern Chinese humanism, Chinese liberalism, and Chinese Marxism have respectively conceptualized three models ("efficacious government" [*wan-neng cheng-fu*], "government by the able and moral" [*hsien-jen cheng-fu*], and the totalitarian model), and that an eclectic mix of the first two models is today in fact the mainstream concept in Taiwan. This mix reflects a common kind of ambivalence in facing the shortcomings of these two models: the danger of dictatorship implied by the "efficacious government model" and the impracticality of the "government by the able and moral" model. At the same time, it seems clear that the model of American-style democracy has not been conceptualized by any influential group, though the process of explaining the profound differences between this American model and the Chinese model has now been begun by Chang Hao.

As for the question of how to design the economic structure, many able scholars have discussed this question, such as Ramon H. Myers, H. J. Duller,

Ian M. D. Little, Jan S. Prybyla, and John C. H. Fei, to offer a drastically incomplete list. The basic choice has been between socialism and the ROC mix of a state sector, a private sector, and a kind of "industrial policy" with which to guide the private sector. This choice can also be seen as one between cutting the country off from world capitalism, fully opening the country to the forces of world capitalism (simply stressing the free market, as Milton Friedman suggests), and establishing a kind of modulated relation to world capitalism. As is well-known, the ROC option has led to spectacular record of "growth with equity," including even modern medical care that can be afforded by people with average means.

III.13. An Overview of the Four Indigenously Conceptualized Options

My argument, therefore, is that to understand the developmental options conceptualized in contemporary China, we should take into account four ideological trends, their shared commitment to modernization, their shared effort to establish a moral language with which to envisage the good society, their shared preoccupation with seven key questions, and the distinctive combination of answers to these questions presented by each of these trends. I would argue that unless we look at how Chinese dealt with all these issues, not restricting ourselves to studying just some of their ideas about human nature and the state, and that unless we look at all four of these trends, not looking only at Marxism, we cannot understand the modern Chinese intellectual problematique that developed as Chinese in modern times defined and tried to solve their problems. Table 2.1 sums up each of the four trends, but of course this can be done only in a crude, oversimplified way; the reader should keep in mind the fuller explanations offered in the text above. This table also refers more to Mao's Marxism than to the current revisionism, which tends somewhat toward the other trends.

This overview of contemporary options is of course far from being definitive and instead suggests the need for more study of trends on both Taiwan and the mainland, but perhaps two points are rather clear. First, the Marxist option has become more similar to the others especially in its answer to two questions, the mode of change and the scope of violence. The old Maoist emphasis on violent social transformation or even just on transformation seems at least to have faded into the background. Second, the Marxist option retains certain distinctive features serious alteration of which remains as a great challenge. These can be seen as revolving around the sixth question, that of how to design the center of the polity. Whether or not "totalitarian" is the right adjective for the Marxist design, this design gives centralized, centripetal state structures and the vested interests intertwined with them a dominant position in the society far exceeding that of any similar structures associated with the model of "efficacious government." This seems clear when we look not only at the design of the center but also at the economic structure, the way that the vehicle of morality is

TABLE 2.1
The Four Leading Options Conceptualized in Contemporary China

	Three Principles	Humanism	Liberalism	Marxism
1. *Quest for knowledge:* open/closed	open	open	open	closed
2. *Basis of values:* tradition/science	tradition	tradition	science	science
3. *Mode of change:* accommodative/ transformative	accommodative	accommodative	accommodative	transformative
4. *Scope of violence:* peaceful/violent	peaceful	peaceful	peaceful	violent
5. *Vehicle of morality:* self/state	state	self	self	state
6. *Design of political center:* Efficacious government/ moral rule/ totalitarian	efficacious government	moral rule	moral rule	totalitarianism
7. *Economic structure:* industrial policy/ socialism	industrial	vague	vague	socialism

conceptualized, the way values are derived, and the degree of openness to "information outside the system."

In the case of the economic structure, some loosening of state controls has occurred, but a decisive shift toward the mix of capitalism and industrial policy would require a structural breakthrough that has not yet occurred. It is quite possible that no Chinese state can be legitimated unless it is defined as a vehicle of morality, but in the ROC this definition coexists or is even creatively combined with a strong tendency to view the individual as the prime vehicle of morality. Again, institutionalizing this combination is not a simple matter. I am not aware of any firm tendency in this direction in the PRC, and were such a tendency to materialize, it would very likely be incompatible with the dominant societal role assigned to the ruling party. Similarly, a more open attitude toward traditional values has perhaps begun to arise in the PRC, but were people free fully to explore the intellectual and moral possibilities of the traditional civilization, they would almost certainly become aware of the Confucian definition of the self as a vehicle of morality independent of the state and its ideological apparatus. Thus a really open attitude toward Confucian values would seem to threaten the current design of the political center. This helps explain that continuing reliance on Marxism which Stuart Schram has recently noted, and which some American observers overlook. The need for an ideological wall restricting access to traditional values seems to continue, therefore, and in the same way it will be far from easy to institutionalize openness in the quest for more than technical knowledge. Such openness, it seems to me, requires a reconceptualization of the sources of correct doctrine, a new concept of correct doctrine as eclectically emerging out of a wide survey of all the world's sources of knowledge. This concept is basic to the ideology of the Three Principles of the People, but one cannot easily see how a Marxist ideology can accommodate it.

IV. Conclusion: Developmental Options and Development Criteria

We can ask whether the developmental criteria outlined above are best met by the Marxist option or by that eclectic mix of options which has been institutionalized in the ROC, especially the mix of the humanistic option with that of the Three Principles. Which Chinese option or set of options has promoted or is likely best to promote pursuit of valid developmental goals: economic growth minimizing the ills of growth, national security, reasonable and just political development, openness to information "outside the system," and some kind of balance between group life and the autonomy of the self? Can, in other words, the Marxist emphasis on authoritarian closure and state hegemony be justified in terms of these developmental criteria?

My judgment is that that combination of options developed in the ROC—the mix of the humanistic option with that of the Three Principles—is much easier to justify in terms of these criteria. It logically follows that this mix indicates the normative path appropriate for Chinese society as a whole, it indicates the real "orthodoxy" of modern Chinese history. Conversely, Chinese Marxism appears as an option in conflict with a reasonable view of China's normative course. To put it more abstractly, whether or not the concrete intellectual patterns in the ROC will be copied by the mainland, our analysis here leads to the conclusion that the PRC leaders should adopt answers to our seven questions very different from those answers they now remain wedded to. In other words, to the extent that one accepts the five developmental criteria above, one must hope that the mainland will develop a more open quest for knowledge, a fuller awareness of traditional ideals in its formulation of values, an emphatic recognition of the individual as the prime vehicle of morality, a looser design of the political center, and a shift toward the mix of capitalism and industrial policy. There is no other conclusion possible, unless one rejects these five criteria. If the mainland, however, were thus to turn into China's normative path, an institutional and ideological breakthrough would be needed, although there is controversy about this point.

Many still argue, however, that this normative path is not relevant to the Chinese people outside Taiwan. This standpoint seems to be based on two assumptions. First, going back to our premise that a normative path must be based on indigenously conceptualized options, we can see that it is only in Taiwan that an option approximating this normative path has actually been conceptualized. It follows that this combination in Taiwan of the humanistic option and the Three Principles cannot easily become influential on the mainland. This point, however, presupposes that the people on the mainland will not incline toward the developmental criteria we have outlined. If these criteria are reasonable, and if Chinese on the mainland are reasonable, they may well incline toward options that accord with these criteria. What justification is there for viewing the vast majority of the Chinese as inherently unreasonable?

A second argument, however, is that this Taiwan mixture of the Three Principles and modern Chinese humanism is not a living option for the Chinese, even in Taiwan. This is suggested by the prominent thesis that the Marxist option has become China's "new historical orthodoxy," and that it meshes with the key values of the inherited civilization. That it meshes with them is a point that Donald J. Munro has made in a particularly forceful way. His focus is not on all the issues involved in the formulation of options but on ideas defining the relation between self and group, especially the nature of the group as the vehicle of morality. He holds that the Chinese Marxist emphasis on the group, and on the state as the key group, to a large extent, though not entirely, meshes with the Confucian view, according to which "the social whole always comes first."[116]

Munro certainly knows of the views of modern Chinese humanists, who emphasize the moral autonomy of the individual, who claim that "people have a kind of inner power of spirit, something directing and impelling the self unceasingly to continue its struggle upwards," and who hold that "moral value has its source within the mind of each self." Given his view of the Chinese cultural mainstream, however, this emphasis on the self is a Western idea, or at least a new one. Moreover when Chinese humanists like Yü Ying-shih say that this emphasis on the self was basic to the Confucian tradition, they are, in Munro's eyes, misinterpreting this tradition. Therefore the option they have conceptualized is not likely to make sense to all those Chinese still influenced by the tradition. Not surprisingly then, when Munro wrote a book called *The Concept of Man in Contemporary China*, he equated the contemporary Chinese "concept of man" with Marxist theory and did not even refer to the options conceptualized by modern Chinese humanists and the followers of Sun Yat-sen.

A detailed critique of Munro's carefully crafted book is outside the scope of this paper. I would say that, correctly concluding that Confucianism lacked the particular concept of the self found in Western individualism, he mistakenly concluded that it lacked any strong emphasis at all on individual autonomy and dignity, and he certainly does not cite and discuss much evidence regarding the role of the self in Confucian thought. Recently Benjamin I. Schwartz, in his *The World of Thought in Ancient China*, has taken a more balanced position than Munro's but has still concluded that in Confucian thought, the authority of group structures outweighs the autonomy of the self. In a review of his book, I have tried to argue that he also neglects much evidence regarding the Confucian emphasis on the moral autonomy of the self.[117]

At the very least, scholars who today recognize this Confucian emphasis include not only those fighting philosophical or ideological battles in China but also a good number in the West approaching the question in possibly a more detached way, such as Chang Hao, Yü Ying-shih, Tu Wei-ming, and Wm. Theodore de Bary.[118] Yet I would strongly argue that the interpretation of the Confucian tradition by modern Chinese humanists in China has also been grounded in the evidence, and that they indeed have risen to the challenge of *Verstehen*.

The argument that the Chinese Marxist option best meshes with traditional values is thus fallacious. Contemporary Chinese options should be understood as a "problematique," to use Schwartz's term, to which each of the four leading contemporary Chinese trends has contributed.

The American focus on the Marxist and liberal options, it follows, has been one-sided. It stems in large part, I believe, from a very deep-seated Western view of the Confucian tradition as constricting the individual within a web of particularism, authoritarianism, and ritual, blocking the expression of valuable creative impulses within the individual and so failing to realize that balance between group and self envisaged by Durkheim. Thus regarding Confucianism as unappealing, many American scholars have found it logical to brush aside the views of the many Chinese who found it appealing and to agree with Chinese embracing iconoclastic theories. With this attitude, Americans could hardly develop an adequate normative theory with which to evaluate modernization patterns in the ROC and the PRC.

The relation between normative theory and foreign policy should not be overlooked. Many today accept George F. Kennan's view that foreign policy should be formulated in terms of national interest, not moralistic considerations. Others believe that it is in the U.S. national interest to support governments pursuing appropriate developmental policies, to the extent that such U.S. support can be practically offered.

Such support, however, presupposes an understanding of what appropriate national development is in each case; it presupposes, in other words, an adequate normative theory. If this paper has one point to make, it is that such a theory can be reduced neither to a conservative respect for the ruling group in a particular society nor to ideals cherished by one or another group in our own society. Some effort, I believe, should be made to appreciate the ideals pursued by the members of the society we are trying to evaluate, dissidents as well as conformists, and to grasp the differences between those ideals and our own, avoiding ethnocentrism as much as we can. It is also fruitful, I believe, to engage in a "conversation" about the criteria with which these indigenous ideals can be evaluated. Abstracting such criteria from the heat of particular political controversies, such a conversation can probably lead to a fuller understanding of developmental issues and narrow the areas of disagreement.

Finally, I can try to clear up some remaining questions. Why not deal with the problem of establishing a theory of normative development by just combining some concept of economic growth with the familiar typology of political regimes as either democratic, authoritarian, or totalitarian? Because this typology is just descriptive. Using it is not the same as systematically discussing the question of the standards with which to evaluate one kind of regime as preferable. Moreover, as we saw in the case of "democracy," each of these categories entails problems of definition. "Authoritarian," I would argue, is a particularly unusable term. First, it is so broad that it covers things that are more dissimilar than similar, such as the ROC and the Marcos regime. Second, using it to describe a Chinese political system instead of asking how this system deals with the seven questions above leads to very limited understanding. Third, the word "authoritarian" suggests that the political process in question is fundamentally based on the coercive implementation of decisions made at the top. Therefore the term cannot be properly used to describe systems like the ROC in which other political factors are also most important as ways to secure the power of the regime, especially winning support by following popular policies; emphasizing communication and consultation between leaders and other strata; taking steps to equalize the distribution of wealth, prestige, and, to some extent, power; and respecting widely accepted standards of propriety and morality.

Another question is that of the relation between this paper's perspective and certain very prevalent Chinese ways of thinking about normative development, about *Chung-kuo-chi lu-hsiang* (the direction of China's development). A foreigner, of course, should not deceive himself by thinking that he can discuss this subject effectively by Chinese standards. Nevertheless, it seems to me that two points are worth considering in order to understand some of the most important differences between this paper and much typical Chinese writing on this subject.

First, my view differs from the views of many in Taiwan in that according to it, China's normative path is indicated neither by the Three Principles nor by modern Chinese humanism but by a combination of the two. For many Chinese, such a view makes no sense. Yet if we accept the five developmental criteria above, we can accept the shared ground of the Three Principles and modern Chinese humanism: openness in the search for information and civilizational values; the need to base values on both the tradition and human creativity; and the need for peaceful, accommodative change. With regard to defining the vehicle of morality, however, the humanistic and liberal emphasis on the individual is invaluable, while the definition of the political center and the economic structure offered by the Three Principles is more practical than the conceptualizations found in liberalism and humanism, I would argue.

Second, my view differs from many Chinese views in terms of the reasons I give for favoring one developmental path over another. In other words, in dealing with the second of the seven questions above, the basis of knowledge and moral value, many Westerners would approach the problem of knowledge and norms in a Humean or post-Humean way differing from the pre- or anti-Humean approach common in China. It is claimed in much Chinese writing that the way China should develop can be determined by using "reason" and analyzing some set of facts, whether the moral experience of the individual, the facts of the physical universe, the facts of human behavior, or historical facts. Whether or not laws of history, scientific laws, or cosmic principles can be deduced from these facts, many Chinese hold that scholarly analysis of the "concrete" facts concerning China's traditional "value system" can provide an understanding of how Chinese should deal with their future, since these historical facts include the inherently valuable ideals of the Confucian tradition, and logic can reveal whether or not these ideals fit the needs of the modern age. Valid or not, however, this is a pre- or anti-Humean approach to the problem of normative theory, since it assumes that norms (what should be done) can be determined in an objective way by depending on "reason" logically to examine objective givens, whether the objective, "concrete" facts pertaining to the traditional "value system" or the objective nature of modernization as an inherently valuable goal.

Many Western scholars, however, would question whether the nature of modernization is an objective, fixed given with only one logically possible relation to traditional values, or whether a living moral tradition is an objective "system" of some sort rather than, as Bellah or Schwartz suggests, an ongoing, inherently indeterminate "conversation" or "problematique." In other words, with our Humean background, we Westerners are likely to emphasize the fact that Chinese disagree about all these things, as illustrated by the way Lao Ssu-kuang and Yü Ying-shih disagree about the value of Confucian culture for modernization, and that there seems to be no purely objective or scholarly way to resolve all these disagreements except with regard to purely factual issues. Therefore we Westerners often prefer to try a post-Humean approach, establishing normative goals or developmental criteria not by trying to deduce them logically from objective givens but just by holding a "conversation" among people who want to discuss goals in a reasonable and moral way.

This post-Humean approach is worth considering. First, it has to be considered in order to understand why the Western way of discussing Chinese modernization typically differs from the Chinese. While Chinese scholars invariably adopt a non-Humean way of depending on "reason" and "objective" givens to determine whether Chinese modernization should be based on traditional values and to determine how China's society and culture should develop in the future, the Western trend has been either to try to avoid such "should" questions or to see them as answerable not through direct dependence on "reason" and "objective" considerations but only through use of some post-Humean device such as Bellah's "conversation." I think that by being more aware of the distinctions between Humean, non-Humean, and post-Humean approaches to normative issues, we Western and Chinese scholars will be able to understand each other better. Second, while, as I have tried to argue elsewhere, the non-Humean approach may well be philosophically tenable, the post-Humean approach is much more easily understood in the West. If one uses it to establish a theory of normative development applicable to Chinese modernization, one can more easily engage the international scholarly community in fruitful discussion.

Notes

I am grateful to Professor Robert N. Bellah for criticism that led me to try to discuss more precisely the relation between political authority and morality in Chinese and Western thought. I am also grateful to Professor S. N. Eisenstadt for invaluable critical comments. Obviously in a broad paper of this kind, I cannot cover all the relevant secondary literature, particularly on sociological theory and the theory of democracy, and neither of the above scholars is responsible for any mistakes I may have made in these two areas.

1. D. J. Munro, *The Concept of Man in Contemporary China* (Ann Arbor: The University of Michigan Press, 1977), ix.

2. For an outline of S. N. Eisenstadt's thinking about modernization and bibliographical references, see T. A. Metzger, "Eisenstadt's Analysis of the Relation between Modernization and Tradition in China," and the exchange between Professor Eisenstadt and me. These are respectively in *Bulletin of Historical Research*, Institute of History, National Taiwan Normal University, vol. 12 (June 1984) and ibid., vol. 13 (June 1985). They are also in *The American Asian Review* 2, no. 2 (Summer 1984) and 3, no. 2 (Summer 1985).

3. In a conversation with me, June 1986, Taipei.

4. A. MacIntyre, *After Virtue* (Notre Dame, Ind.: University of Notre Dame Press, 1981), 38.

5. Milton and Rose Friedman, *Free to Choose* (New York: Harcourt Brace Jovanovich, 1980).

6. Munro, *Concept of Man*, 24, ix, 178–184.

7. Yü Ying-shih, *Ts'ung chia-chih hsi-t'ung k'an Chung-kuo wen-hua-te hsien-tai i-i* (Modernization and Chinese Culture: a discussion from the standpoint of the traditional value system) (Taipei: Shih-pao wen-hua ch'u-pan shih-yeh yu-hsien kung-ssu, 1984), 116. See also his "Ju-chia ssu-hsiang yü ching-chi fa-chan: Chung-kuo chin-shih tsung-chiao lun-li yü shang-jen ching-shen" (Economic development and Confucian thought: the religious ethic of late imperial China and its relation to the commercial spirit), *The Chinese Intellectual* 6 (Winter 1985): 3–45. For Eisenstadt's view, see articles listed in note 2.

8. K. W. Deutsch, *The Nerves of Government* (New York: The Free Press, 1966), viii, xiv–xv. Wei Yung, *K'o-hsüeh, jen-ts'ai, yü hsien-tai-hua* (Science, the development and use of human resources, and modernization) (Taipei: T'ai-wan hsüeh-sheng shu-chü, 1985).

9. R. Benedict, *Patterns of Culture* (New York: Mentor Books, 1949), 219, 2, 228–231, 257.

10. For a later effort to develop this view, see my foreword to R. W. Wilson, S. L. Greenblatt, and A. A. Wilson, eds., *Moral Behavior in Chinese Society* (New York: Praeger Publishers, 1981).

11. Leo Strauss, *Natural Right and History* (Chicago: University of Chicago Press, 1953), 35–80, and *What Is Political Philosophy?* (Glencoe, Ill.: The Free Press, 1959), 9–55.

12. T'ang's epistemological thought is in his *Che-hsüeh kai-lun* (An outline of philosophy), 2 vols. (Taipei: T'ai-wan hsüeh-sheng shu-chü, 1974). I have tried to discuss his position in an earlier version of my "Some Ancient Roots of Modern

Chinese Thought: This-worldliness, Epistemological Optimism, Doctrinality, and the Emergence of Reflexivity in Ancient China," *Early China* (in press). The latter version omits this discussion, which will appear elsewhere. Yü Ying-shih's comment about the restricted development of philosophical skepticism in China is in Yü, 85. Also see MacIntyre, *After Virtue*, 38. Munro's discussion of "clustering" is in book mentioned in note 1.

13. For this point I am indebted to Professor Paolo Mario Dau. Hume's position is brilliantly discussed in Barry Stroud, *Hume* (London: Routledge and Keegan Paul, 1977).

14. Wilson, Greenblatt, and Wilson, eds., *Moral Behavior*, 1–20.

15. R. N. Bellah, R. Madsen, W. M. Sullivan, A. Swidler, and S. M. Tipton, *Habits of the Heart* (Berkeley: University of California Press, 198), 27, 301–303.

16. See articles listed in note 2 and Benjamin I. Schwartz, *The World of Thought in Ancient China* (Cambridge, Mass.: The Belknap Press of Harvard University Press, 1985). For my review of this book, "The Definition of the Self, the Group, the Cosmos, and Knowledge in Chou Thought: Some Comments on Professor Schwartz's Study," in *The American Asian Review* 4, no. 2 (Summer 1986): 68–116.

17. T. A. Metzger, *Escape from Predicament* (New York: Columbia University Press, 1977).

18. Bellah et al., *Habits of the Heart*, 282.

19. Yü, *Ts'ung chia-chih*, 114–115.

20. A 1986 M.A. thesis by Hsü Shu-ling, Institute of History, National Taiwan Normal University, shows that the goal of *fu-ch'iang* was important in late Ming *ching-shih* (statecraft) thought already. See Hsü Shu-ling, "Chi-she chi ch'i ching-shih ssu-hsiang" (The incipience society and its thought regarding questions of statecraft).

21. Wm. Theodore de Bary, *The Liberal Tradition in China* (New York: Columbia University Press, 1983), 6–7.

22. Bellah et al., *Habits of the Heart*, 250–251.

23. Ibid., 140, 155, 162.

24. T. Parsons, E. Shils, K. D. Naegele, and J. R. Pitts, eds., *Theories of Society*, 2 vols. (New York: The Free Press of Glencoe, 1961), 1:214, 217.

25. Munro, *Concept of Man*, 25.

26. Andrew J. Nathan, *Chinese Democracy* (New York: Alfred A. Knopf, 1985), ix.

27. *Time*, May 12, 1986, 103–104.

28. *Tang-tai*, issue no. 1 (May 1, 1986): 50.

29. Yu-ming Shaw, ed., *Kuo-shih t'ao-lun-chi* (Collected essays and comments about national affairs; published by the editor, Director of the Institute of International Relations in Taiwan, Republic of China, 1983), 8–9. This essay is by Chiang Ping-lun; its outlook is rather widespread. The great American decline in literacy is discussed in *Time*, May 5, 1986, 68. A full analysis of the whole range of tendencies that can be regarded as dysfunctional in the United States is not attempted in *Habits of the Heart*. While denunciations of American trends are common from both the right and the left, particularly the religious right, scholarly discussion of the root problems of American society is rare. I tried to list some of the problems that are often neglected in my "R.O.C.-U.S. Relations and the Political Development of the U.S.," in John C. Kuan, ed., *Symposium on R.O.C.-U.S. Relations* (Taipei: Asia and the World Institute, 1981).

30. Chinese scholars discussing whether China's traditional values are compatible with the idea of democracy have nearly always focused their scholarly attention

exclusively on the problem of the nature of traditional values, assuming that the nature of democracy is self-evident. This has been a major blind spot in the modern Chinese discussion of this issue. A rare exception is Chang Hao, "Yu-an i-shih yü min-chu ch'uan-t'ung" (The democratic tradition and the consciousness of human nature's dark side), in Shaw, *Kuo-shih t'ao-lun-chi*, 417–436. Chang's article was originally published in *Chung-kuo shih-pao* in 1982.

31. This list is taken from a definition of democracy in Nathan, *Chinese Democracy*, ix. For Schumpeter's view that "rule by the people" does not describe any major political system, see his *Capitalism, Socialism, and Democracy* (New York: Harper & Row, 1962).

32. Nathan, *Chinese Democracy*, ix.

33. Chang Hao's article is referred to in note 30.

34. A. O. Lovejoy, *Reflections on Human Nature* (Baltimore: The Johns Hopkins Press, 1961), 38–39.

35. Strauss points out *The Federalist* too was influenced by Machiavelli's Republicanism. See *What Is Political Philosophy?* 47.

36. Stroud, *Hume*, 202. I am quoting Stroud, not Hume.

37. Hsü Fu-kuan, *Hsüeh-shu yü cheng-chih-chih chien* (Between scholarship and the political realm) (Taipei: T'ai-wan hsüeh-sheng shu-chü, 1980), 125–126.

38. See T. A. Metzger, "Max Weber's Analysis of the Confucian Tradition: A Critique," *The American Asian Review* 2, no. 1 (Spring 1984): 52–53. For the question of "custom" in *Mo-tzu*, see chap. 25, *Chieh-tsang*.

39. Part of this debate, originally in *Chung-kuo shih-pao* in March, April, May, and June, 1983, is in Shaw, *Kuo-shih t'ao-lun-chi*, 592–639. Lin Yü-sheng's view is in ibid., 44–45.

40. S. Lukes, *Individualism* (Oxford: Basil Blackwell, 1973).

41. Yü, 74.

42. For a discussion of the Confucian view of political authority, see my review of Professor Schwartz's book referred to in note 16.

43. Hsü Fu-kuan, "Lun *Shih-chi*" (On Ssu-ma Ch'ien's *Records of the Grand Historian*), *Ta-lu tsa-chih* 55, no 6 (December 1977): 1–48.

44. Plato, "Apology," F. J. Church, trans, xx–xxi. See, e.g., Plato, *Euthyphro, Apology, Crito* (Indianapolis: The Library of Liberal Arts, 1980), 39.

45. This last quote can be found also in Watson's translation. See Burton Watson, trans. *Mo Tzu* (New York: Columbia University Press, 1966), 49.

46. H. G. Creel, *Shen Pu-hai* (Chicago: University of Chicago Press, 1974), 353–354.

47. Huang K'o-wu, "Huang-ch'ao ching-shih wen-pien hsüeh-shu chih-t'i pu-fen ssu-hsiang-chih fen-hsi" (An analysis of the thought of the sections on "learning" and "the basis of government" in "our august dynasty's writings on statecraft") (M.A. thesis, Institute of History, National Taiwan Normal University, 1985).

48. Mou Tsung-san, *Ming-chia yü Hsün-tzu* (Essays on the Logicians and on *Hsün-tzu*) (Taipei: T'ai-wan hsüeh-sheng shu-chü, 1982), 234.

49. The issue of the *pa* is discussed by many scholars. See "hegemonism" and *pa* in the index in Schwartz's study mentioned in note 16.

50. Plato, *Euthyphro, Apology, Crito*, 60–61.

51. Aristotle, *The Politics of Aristotle*, trans. Ernest Barker (London: Oxford University Press, 1950), 218.

52. Ibid., 184–185, 206.

53. Ibid., 182.

54. Ibid., 213.

55. Ibid., 181.
56. Ibid., 213–217.
57. Ibid., 186.
58. Ibid., 181.
59. Ibid., 237, 266–267, 269, 273.
60. The Encyclopedia of Philosophy, 8 vols. (New York: Macmillan Publishing Co., and The Free Press, 1972), 1:205–206.
61. Strauss, What Is Political Philosophy? 40–42, 47, 49. Quotations here are all from Strauss.
62. Bellah et al., Habits of the Heart, 253.
63. Nathan, Chinese Democracy, 226.
64. T'ang Chün-i, Jen-wen ching-shen-chih ch'ung-chien (The reconstruction of the humanistic spirit) (Hong Kong: Hsin-ya yen-chiu-so, 1955), 338.
65. Yang Kuo-shu, K'ai-fang-te to-yüan she-hui (The open, pluralistic society) (Taipei: Tung-ta t'u-shu yu-hsien kung-ssu, 1982), 19.
66. Professor Chu-yüan Cheng has prepared an extensive bibliography, as yet unpublished, pertaining to the study of Sun Yat-sen. Sun's main writings are listed in Lin Kuei-p'u, Kuo-fu ssu-hsiang ching-i (The essence of the thought of our Nation's Father) (Taipei: Cheng-chung shu-chü, 1981), 26–34. A similar study is Ting Ti, Kuo-fu ssu-hsiang yen-chiu (A study of the thought of our Nation's Father) (Taipei: P'a-mi-erh shu-tien, 1978). See also A. James Gregor, Ideology and Development: Sun Yat-sen and the Economic History of Taiwan (Berkeley: Institute of East Asian Studies, 1981). This work effectively argues that Sun's strategy of economic development is close to much current scholarly opinion on that subject. It is also useful bibliographically. The excellent study by Maria Hsia Chang on the Blue Shirts also is bibliographically useful and strongly argues that Sun's view of political development accords with much of the political science literature today. See Maria Hsia Chang, The Chinese Blue Shirts Society (Berkeley: Institute of East Asian Studies, 1985). President Chiang's writings and speeches are collected in Chiang Tsung-t'ung yen-lun hui-pien (President Chiang's collected speeches and writings), 24 vols. (Taipei: Cheng-chung shu-chü, 1956). Some might find it ironical that my copy of these twenty-four volumes is a gift from Professor Yin Hai-kuang. Further bibliographical information is in Lin Yü-hsiang, Chiang Tsung-t'ung che-hsüeh ssu-hsiang t'i-hsi yen-chiu (A study of President Chiang's philosophical system) (Taipei: Chung-yang wen-wu kung-ying-she, 1977). See also Furuya, Keiji, Chiang Kai-shek: His Life and Times, trans. Chang Chun-ming (New York: St. John's University, 1981).
67. Ho Lin, Tang-tai Chung-kuo che-hsüeh (Contemporary Chinese philosophy) (Nanking: Sheng-li ch'u-pan kung-ssu, 1947), 83–142.
68. Hsiao Kung-ch'üan, Chung-kuo cheng-chih ssu-hsiang-shih (A history of Chinese political thought), 6 vols. (Taipei: Chung-hua ta-tien pien-yin-hui, 1966), 1:3.
69. Mou Tsung-san, Cheng-tao yü chih-tao (The philosophy of political authority) (Taipei: T'ai-wan hsüeh-sheng shu-chü, 1980).
70. See note 37 for one collection of Hsü Fu-kuan's politically relevant writings and note 64 for one of T'ang Chün-i's. Another from Hsü is the one edited by Hsiao Hsin-i, Ju-chia cheng-chih ssu-hsiang yü min-chu tzu-yu jen-ch'üan (Confucian political thought and the questions of democracy, freedom, and human rights) (Taipei: Pa-shih nien-tai ch'u-pan-she, 1979). Another from T'ang is his Chung-kuo jen-wen ching-shen-chih fa-chan (The development of the humanistic spirit in China) (Taipei: T'ai-wan hsüeh-sheng shu-chü, 1974). In all these writings, one finds complimentary references to Sun here and there, or, to put it more exactly, references made in passing which take for granted that his ideas are of great value.

71. I am referring to works by A. James Gregor and Maria Hsia Chang. See note 66.

72. I do not want to list the names of scholars who ignore it. Let me say only that this is a problem, discussion of which sometimes leads to passion and irrationality, an historically significant fact in itself (see below).

73. Tseng Chao-hsü, *Lun-yü-te jen-ko shih-chieh* (Confucius' ideal of human character) (Taipei: Shang-yu ch'u-pan-she, 1982). On T'ang Chün-i, see T. A. Metzger, "T'ang Chün-i and the Conditions of Transformative Thinking in Comtemporary China," *The American Asian Review* 3, no. 1 (Spring 1985). For other bibliographical references, see notes 7, 37, 64, 69, 70. Also see Lao Ssu-kuang, *Chung-kuo-chih lu-hsiang* (The direction of China's development) (Hong Kong: Shang-chih ch'u-pan-she, 1981).

74. See C. Furth, ed., *The Limits of Change* (Cambridge, Mass.: Harvard University Press, 1976). I try to discuss the definition of "conservatism" in my review of this book, "The Quest for Traditional Values in Modern Chinese Thought," *The China Quarterly* (March 1978).

75. A recent study based on great mastery of Liang Ch'i-ch'ao's thought is Liu Chi-yao's Ph.D. thesis on Liang, accepted in 1985 by Institute of History, National Taiwan Normal University.

76. Published in Taipei by Wen-hsing shu-tien, 1966, 2 vols.

77. See, e.g., Wang T'o, ed., *Tang-wai-te sheng-yin* (Voices outside the party) (Taipei: Ch'ang-ch'iao ch'u-pan-she, 1978), and Lin Cheng-chieh and Chang Fu-chung, *Hsüan-chü wan-sui* (Long live elections!) (Taipei: Kuei-kuan t'u-shu kung-ssu, 1978). Such works help one understand the viewpoint of liberals highly critical of the Kuomintang, and I believe that in terms of basic political thinking or theory, their ideas remain within the framework laid down by Yin Hai-kuang and Hsü Fu-kuan, but a study of the vast liberal and dissident literature produced in Taiwan in recent years deserves more than one Ph.D. thesis.

78. Nathan, *Chinese Democracy*, 227.

79. See, e.g., Maurice Meisner, *Mao's China* (New York: The Free Press, 1977) or Stuart R. Schram, *The Political Thought of Mao Tse-tung* (New York: Frederick A. Praeger, Publishers, 1969).

80. Stuart R. Schram, *Ideology and Policy in China Since the Third Plenum, 1978–1984* (London: Contemporary China Institute, School of Oriental and African Studies, University of London, Research Notes and Studies No. 6, 1984), 74, 79–80. On still more recent developments, see Tu Wei-ming, "Iconoclasm, Holistic Vision, and Patient Watchfulness—A Personal Reflection on the Modern Chinese Intellectual Quest," in *Daedalus* 116, no. 2 (1987): 75–94.

81. Yü, *Ts'ung chia-chih*, 8, 13, 112.

82. Yü, *Ts'ung chia-chih*, 36, notes that China did not undergo a "secularization" crisis similar to the Western one, but I am using "secularization" in a narrower way. As Professor Yü suggests, secularization in the West was greatly affected by a "skeptical" tradition largely missing in China.

83. This point is made also in Don C. Price, *Russia and the Roots of the Chinese Revolution, 1896–1911* (Cambridge, Mass.: Harvard University Press, 1974). Culturally distinctive premises shaping the modern Chinese concept of the good society are outlined in my "Chung-kuo chin-tai ssu-hsiang-shih yen-chiu fang-fa-shang-te i-hsieh wen-t'i: i-ko Hsiu-mo-hou-te k'an-fa," in Academia Sinica, Institute of Modern History, *Chin-tai Chung-kuo-shih yen-chiu t'ung-hsün* 2 (1986).

84. Lin Kuei-p'u, *Kuo-fu ssu-hsiang ching-i*, 2, 5.

85. Yü, *Ts'ung chia-chih*, 112.

86. Ibid., 49.

87. Ibid., 63, 36, 42, 97–98.

88. Ibid., 38–39, 68–73.

89. Ibid., 106–107.

90. Ibid., 76. See note 7 for Yü's article on economic values in late imperial China.

91. Yü, *Ts'ung chia-chih*, 116.

92. Lao, *Chung-kuo-chih lu-hsiang*, 55–61. Lao's comments about T'ang Chün-i are in Feng Ai-ch'ün, ed., *T'ang Chün-i hsien-sheng chi-nien-chi* (Essays in memory of T'ang Chün-i) (Taipei: T'ai-wan hsüeh-sheng shu-chü, 1979), 266–267.

93. Yü, *Ts'ung chia-chih*, 63, 69.

94. See Huang K'o-wu's thesis mentioned in note 47. For a recent discussion of the distinction between transformative and accommodative thinking in premodern China, see the exchange between Patricia Buckley Ebrey and me in *The American Asian Review* 4, no. 1 (Spring 1986): 1–43.

95. Yü, *Ts'ung chia-chih*, 116. On the strongly transformative orientation of T'ang Chün-i, see my article listed in note 73.

96. Yü, *Ts'ung chia-chih*, 87, 90, 97.

97. Tseng, *Lun-yü-te jen-ko shih-chieh*, 6, 14.

98. Ibid., 18, 23.

99. Ibid., 57–58, 90.

100. Ibid., 31, 6, 90, 37.

101. Yü, *Ts'ung chia-chih*, 72.

102. Mou Tsung-san, *Cheng-tao yü chih-tao, hsin-pan-hsü*, 8–19, 25. For T'ang Chün-i's similar view of Chinese culture as a kind of powerful historical tide, see my article listed in note 73.

103. Lin Kuei-p'u, *Kuo-fu ssu-hsiang ching-i*, 8.

104. Ibid., 154, 158, 27, 8.

105. Ibid., 159.

106. Ibid., 140.

107. Ting, *Kuo-fu ssu-hsiang yen-chiu*, 187.

108. Ibid., 180, 177–178.

109. Yin Hai-kuang, *Yin Hai-kuang hsüan-chi, ti-i-chüan, she-hui cheng-chih yen-lun* (The collected writings of Yin Hai-kuang, Vol. 1, Social and political writings) (Kowloon: Yu-lien ch'u-pan-she yu-hsien kung-ssu, 1971), ii, 205.

110. Lin Kuei-p'u, *Kuo-fu ssu-hsiang ching-i*, 69.

111. Ibid., 69, 120.

112. Ibid., 70. Ting, *Kuo-fu ssu-hsiang yen-chiu*, 187, 189, 192, 261.

113. Ting, *Kuo-fu ssu-hsiang yen-chiu*, 188–189.

114. Lin Kuei-p'u, *Kuo-fu ssu-hsiang ching-i*, 468.

115. Ting, *Kuo-fu ssu-hsiang yen-chiu*, 261–267.

116. Munro, *Concept of Man*, 118.

117. See note 16.

118. See note 21. See also the influential work of Tu Wei-ming, professor at Harvard University. He has wholeheartedly accepted and developed the view of Confucianism set forth by modern Chinese humanists like T'ang Chün-i. Indeed in his latest writings Munro himself may be moving a bit toward this view. See his "Introduction" in Donald Munro, ed., *Individualism and Holism: Studies in Confucian and Taoist Values* (Ann Arbor: Center for Chinese Studies, 1985).

3

How Can We Evaluate Communist China's Economic Development Performance?

Ramon H. Myers

At present we know a great deal about the origins and characteristics of modern economic growth, but few agree on how to evaluate the economic performance of modernizing societies of different cultures, ideologies, and political institutions. The experts use national income accounting measures to evaluate the performance of economic development, but these indicators fail to account for some aspects of modern growth that many regard as important, such as the sources of growth, income distribution, welfare trends, and destruction of physical environment.

If we want to evaluate the economic development performance of the People's Republic of China (PRC) before and after 1978 in comparison with the other Pacific Basin states, what criteria should we use? Can we agree upon some common standards to evaluate the economic performance of societies under different political and economic systems?

This essay tries to answer these questions. The first section introduces some concepts and a framework for evaluating economic modernization. The second section uses these concepts to evaluate the economic growth of several groups of countries. The third section applies these same concepts to Communist China for the periods before and after 1978. A brief conclusion cites some general findings.

Conceptual Framework

Most experts agree on what modern economic growth means. Taking our cue from Simon Kuznets, we can define modern economic growth to be an

Revised and reprinted with permission from *Issues and Studies* 23, no. 2 (February 1987): 122–155.

acceleration of the growth rate of gross domestic product (GDP) per capita on a sustained basis.[1] Most experts also agree on what general developments typically take place after a country has experienced modern economic growth for a half century or more.

Resources have shifted from lower to higher value-added activities; economic activity changes in the three sectors of agriculture (A), manufacturing and construction (M), and services, the public and private ownership of finance, commerce, communications, and transportation (S). The ratio of foreign trade to GDP usually rises; population growth accelerates.

The experts also agree that during the phase of modern economic growth countries experience one or more periods of long swings in economic activity in which economic growth accelerates rapidly and the economy undergoes a dramatic structural change. Conditions are never the same again. These unusual periods have been described in some distinctive terms.

Economic historians have used the term "industrial revolution" to describe developments in England between 1760 and 1860 and on the European continent between 1860 and 1914.[2] Others have used the term "industrialization" to describe developments in the Soviet Union during the 1930s, 1950s, and 1960s.[3] Several economists have described the economic development of Japan in the twentieth century as "trend acceleration" to denote distinctive developments in the 1930s and again from 1952 to 1969.[4] More recently, the term "economic transformation" has been used to describe the unusual economic changes in South Korea and the Republic of China (ROC) on Taiwan during the period 1965–1981.[5]

Whichever term the experts have used, they are obviously trying to understand the unique concatenation of economic changes that fundamentally alters an economy.

We also know that these unique periods described by these terms also revealed great economic variation, and those variations have been the source of considerable confusion and misunderstanding. What confusion and misunderstanding are we talking about?

First, various countries have experienced some very different patterns of early modern economic growth, but these have not been carefully classified to elicit general agreement as to what the distinctive patterns and differences are. We know that the pattern of modern economic growth initiated in Africa, Latin America, the Middle East, and Asia was very different when those regions came under colonial rule from what it was after they gained their political independence.[6]

Second, even among countries that retained their political sovereignty, these early growth patterns differed greatly. For example, imperial Russia and Japan began their modern economic growth much later and at a much lower GDP-per-capita level than the United States, Great Britain, and Western Europe, and their growth was very different from that of the more developed Western countries.[7]

Third, we now know that the early growth patterns in states ruled by Marxist-Leninist parties have been strikingly different from those of Western capitalist societies.[8]

Fourth, more recently, some Pacific Basin states have experienced very unusual economic growth patterns very different from those of the groups of countries just cited.[9]

Finally, we also know that most of the developing countries, like those in Africa, which achieved political independence from Western colonial rule after World War II have experienced very lackluster economic development. Although many countries in Latin America did experience spurts of "industrialization" or "trend acceleration" for a decade or two, they are now experiencing profound difficulties, and their prospects for initiating a trend acceleration are most bleak.

Different patterns of rapid economic growth and structural transformation evolve because of resource endowment, culture, market behavior, state policies, local elite behavior, and the like. State leaders, in particular, have used different strategies and policies to try to initiate modern economic growth. Let us first be very clear as to what kind of pattern of early modern economic growth we want to discuss.

We will only identify those special, distinctive long-swing periods of modern economic growth that occur when unusually rapid economic change takes place. We refer to these distinctive periods as "trend acceleration" or "economic transformation," using the terms interchangeably to denote the presence of several common features. First, the M sector expands more rapidly than before and becomes associated with the application of modern science and technology to the production and exchange of goods for manufacturing and construction. Second, there occurs an accelerated expansion of reproducible capital, which includes inventory, machines, tools, equipment, vehicles, structures, and so on.

All modernizing economies in the last few centuries have experienced these common features, and during certain periods these developments have taken place in very unprecedented ways. But what are the conditions under which new capital has been produced and the economy has been so radically transformed? Some societies have accumulated capital and experienced great improvements in human welfare. Other societies have accumulated capital, but at great social cost. Because the patterns of economic change have varied so greatly during these early phases of development, it is very difficult to judge how well societies perform. If we had some means to classify countries according to their patterns of trend acceleration, we would be in a position to evaluate the economic performance of a country undergoing economic modernization. I propose to classify countries by some normative standards.[10]

But first we must be very clear about how to identify the time period when an economic transformation or trend acceleration is supposed to occur. Some will disagree about periodization and complain that our time period misspecifies the critical economic changes alleged to be taking place. Our key guidelines for periodizing trend acceleration will be to identify when the stock of reproducible capital expands very rapidly as a proportion of GDP and when the value-added output for the M sector accelerates on a sustained basis for a long period before slowing down. Selecting initial and terminal years for trend acceleration will be arbitrary. Such a period should be at least a decade long, and preferably longer, in order to capture the long-swing effect of unusual economic change that historically characterizes trend acceleration. Over time, of course, a society can experience several trend accelerations, each differing significantly from the others.

We now consider five normative economic standards. First, we can measure GDP per capita and examine its characteristics during our trend acceleration to determine whether its rate of growth fluctuates, accelerates and then slows down, or accelerates on a sustained basis. An economy that expands output on a sustained basis and avoids unemployment will utilize resources more effectively than an economy that experiences great output fluctuation and unemployment of labor. Because we have little data about unemployment during early modern growth, we will ignore considerations of unemployment except to assume it must increase when the GDP rate of growth greatly fluctuates or declines.

Second, we can examine the sources of GDP growth by measuring whether labor and capital stock productivity accelerate, fluctuate, or rise and then fall. Another measure of the source of GDP growth is total factor productivity, a more complex estimate that has elicited great controversy but is now widely used to measure both sectoral and total-economy productivity.[11]

Third, we can chart the trend of income distribution to determine whether that pattern becomes more unequal, becomes more equal, or remains unchanged. Measures of income distribution are the Gini coefficient and ranking households by income size and share of total income. By comparing the value of the Gini coefficient (a high value represents very unequal income distribution) and relating the top and bottom shares of income received by the highest and lowest income groups, we also can measure how income distribution changes over time.

Fourth, we can construct a number of welfare measures to show the changes in welfare taking place. First, we can measure real wage trends for all three economic sectors. If the rate of inflation is high, real wage trends will be adversely affected. Second, we can measure the percentage of total household expenditures for food and drink, and compare these percentages (the Engel coefficient) over time, recognizing that any decline in such a percentage reflects expanding consumer utility. Third, we can estimate the principal consumer goods per capita and use these indicators to show whether consumption patterns are improving or declining: the amount of housing space per capita; the quantity of cloth consumed per capita; the number of watches, bicycles, television sets, radios, cars per capita. Fourth, we can measure improvements in diet, longevity, medical care availability, educational opportunity, and the like to determine whether social welfare has improved or declined.

Finally, we can construct measures to monitor the destruction of physical environment, such as the smog content of urban air; amount of pollution of lakes, rivers, and streams; the extent of soil erosion; and the land loss to cultivation.

These five standards permit some common measures of economic performance of a society during one or more phases of trend acceleration. The following findings would reveal a most successful case of economic growth during the "transformative" phase. As a society becomes increasingly efficient and productive, it produces a greater stream of goods and services. Various welfare indicators also increase. If income distribution becomes more equal and the growth rate of GDP per capita accelerates on a sustained basis, more and more people will be benefiting and participating in the modernization process. Minimal destruction to the physical environment would attest to the superior performance of such a modernizing economy. The opposite normative findings would suggest a poor or very inferior economic performance.

As we well know, applying these standards will depend upon the availability of reliable statistics that accurately represent the trends they are supposed to measure. There are numerous measurement problems that cannot be resolved. For example, specialists know that using different temporal price weights will produce a statistical bias in growth rate estimates. They also know that using different money exchange rates will produce different estimates of per capita income change. We must, therefore, interpret the statistical results with caution. But setting aside these caveats, we are still faced with the challenge of how to rank these five normative standards and how to aggregate them into any single standard.

Rather than ranking or standardizing our five standards, we should first strive for a very general level of understanding and agreement. In other words, we will simply try to agree on measures that allow for discussion of our five normative standards. Once we have done that, we can examine specific aspects of economic change according to one or more normative standards to determine whether superiority of one or more standards is really important or not.

Let us begin by asking the following questions: First, can we determine how much GDP might be lost because of acute economic fluctuations, and whether or not GDP per capita accelerates on a sustained basis, or rises and then declines during our period of trend acceleration? Second, can we agree on the importance of productivity as a source of GDP per capita expansion during the period of trend acceleration? This is a very important consideration. If we find that the growth of GDP was achieved primarily through the expansion of resource use and that very little productivity took place during the period in question, we must conclude that resources are being used very inefficiently and that society could produce a much greater output of goods and services if greater productivity had existed.

Third, how can we determine the trend of income distribution during the phase of trend acceleration? Did income distribution become more equal, remain unchanged, or become more equal and then remain unchanged or become unequal? Finally, can we select several important welfare indicators like the percentage of total expenditures that was devoted to food and drink, and various measures showing goods consumed per capita, to demonstrate

TABLE 3.1
Normative Economic Standards and Indicators for a Country Experiencing "Trend Acceleration"

Normative Economic Standard	Change in Value		
	(+)	(−)	(0)
1. GDP per capita:			
Rises (+)			
Declines (−)			
Fluctuates (0)			
2. Sources of GDP growth:			
A. *Partial productivity change:*			
Rises (+)			
Declines (−)			
Remains unchanged (0)			
B. *Total productivity change:*			
Rises (+)			
Declines (−)			
Remains unchanged (0)			
3. Income distribution:			
More equal (+)			
Less equal (−)			
Remains unchanged (0)			
4. Welfare change:			
A. *Engel coefficient:*			
Rises (+)			
Declines (−)			
Remains unchanged (0)			
B. *Goods and services per capita:*			
Rises (+)			
Declines (−)			
Remains unchanged (0)			

whether very little, moderate, or considerable change in consumer welfare took place during the period of trend acceleration? Because developing countries provide little information about the destruction of physical environment, let us disregard any consideration of this normative standard.

By summarizing the available statistical data, we can answer these questions. Table 3.1 presents the framework for organizing these various statistical measures for comparing and evaluating the economic performance of a country during the phase of early modern economic growth.

In the next section, the first and second normative standards can describe the economic performance of Western capitalist and socialist countries during their periods of trend acceleration. We then use the first four normative standards to describe the economic performance of Japan, South Korea, and the Republic of China on Taiwan during the postwar period. We now have enough evidence to compare and evaluate the economic performance of Western capitalist, socialist, and the Pacific Basin states during their relevant periods of economic transformation. These findings then provide the context in which to examine the economic performance of Communist China during 1952–1978, when trend acceleration definitely took place, and during 1978–1983.

Trend Acceleration in Economic History

The most outstanding aspects of Europe's trend acceleration were the rapid growth of capital stock and the rising productivity of capital and labor, which largely accounted for the rapid and sustained growth of GDP per capita. Because of the paucity of reliable data, we still know very little about the trends of income distribution and social welfare.

Great Britain's industrial revolution began around the middle of the eighteenth century, but trend acceleration commenced after 1800. GDP per capita rose at only 0.3 percent per annum from 1761 to 1800, but jumped to 1.3 percent per annum between 1801–1830 and 1831–1860, respectively.[12] The stock of reproducible capital grew at 1.0 percent per year during 1761–1800, 1.4 percent during 1801–1830, and 2.0 percent during 1831–1860.[13] Finally, total factor productivity rose at an annual rate of only 0.3 percent from 1761 to 1800, but then leaped to 1.4 percent during 1801–1830 and continued at a high of 0.8 percent from 1831 to 1860.[14] Associated with this rising productivity was rapid structural change: the A sector's share of GDP fell from 33 percent in 1801 to 18 percent in 1860, whereas the M sector's share rose from 23 percent to 38 percent.[15]

Germany's trend acceleration began after 1860 and continued until World War I. Net product per capita rose 1.7, 1.0, and 1.7 percent during the years 1850–1874, 1875–1891, and 1892–1913, respectively.[16] At the same time, Hoffman's calculations show that productivity rose at an annual rate of 1.7 percent between 1850 and 1913.[17] The A sector's contribution to GDP declined, while the M sector's share rapidly rose. Similar trends occurred in Sweden, France, and Italy, but none was as rapid or as spectacular in terms of sectoral change as Germany's. Productivity became the engine of growth, originating in the expansion of capital stock and improved labor skills.

When we turn to the Soviet Union and socialist-ruled Eastern Europe, however, we note some very major differences in the character of their trend acceleration as compared with Western Europe's. First, the rate of growth of trend acceleration in the USSR and socialist Eastern Europe was much greater than that of the Western European states during their initial periods of modern economic growth and trend acceleration.

Referring to Tables 3.A1–3.A4 in the Appendix at the end of this chapter, we observe that the USSR experienced a 4.5 percent annual growth in gross national product (GNP) and a 3.2 percent annual growth in GNP per capita during 1928–1940 and an even higher growth rate after the 1950s than Great Britain and Western European states had experienced during their industrialization. Using different price weights to make these same estimates might lower the USSR's GNP growth rate, but still not to the same growth rates as those of the West. Sectoral change and the growth of capital stock were particularly rapid. But the USSR's total factor productivity did not rise impressively during the 1930s.[18] It seems to have risen in the 1950s, but then declined in subsequent decades.[19] Trend acceleration in the USSR was achieved by mobilizing more factor inputs. Finally, certain welfare indicators failed to rise significantly. For example, housing improvements have not been conspicuous or outstanding. Calories, proteins, and fats per capita have barely increased since World War II.[20] Similar trends have been observed for other Eastern European countries as well.[21]

The case of the Pacific Basin countries after World War II has been very different from that of Western Europe, the USSR, and the other socialist states of Eastern Europe. First, the GDP growth rates achieved during trend acceleration were even higher. Second, productivity played a much more important role in accounting for that rapid GDP per capita growth. Third, where data exist we can observe that for Japan, South Korea, and the ROC on Taiwan, social welfare rapidly improved, and income distribution became more equal. These developments are briefly described in Tables 3.A5–3.A7 in the Appendix at the end of this chapter.

In the 1950s and 1960s, Japan's annual growth rate of GDP per capita grew at 8.3 and 9.8 percent, respectively. Similarly, for the years 1965–1970, 1970–1975, and 1975–1980, South Korea's GDP per capita grew at 8.7, 7.1, and 5.6 percent, while the ROC's growth rates for the same periods were 6.7, 7.0, and 8.4 percent. These spectacular growth rates for all three countries were associated with a rapid growth of capital stock, so that by 1980 capital formation accounted for around one-third of GDP for all three. Therefore, unlike the countries under socialist rule, high capital formation rates were not achieved at the expense of consumption, but consumer expenditures per capita increased rapidly over these decades for all three countries. Finally, rapid structural change also occurred, with the A sector's contribution to GDP in Japan, Korea, and the ROC declining to 4, 16, and 9 percent, respectively, in 1980. At the same time, the M sector's share of GDP for the same year had risen to 38, 42, and 45 percent, respectively.

High productivity characterized all three countries. In Korea and Taiwan, labor productivity rose at an annual rate of 5.2 and 5.4 percent, respectively, during the years 1965–1981.[22] Ohkawa and Rosovky have estimated that the annual growth rate of the residual for the 1950s and 1960s, which is a crude measure of total factor productivity growth, grew at an average annual rate of 6.75 and 5.61 percent, the highest ever achieved in Japan's periods of trend acceleration.[23]

The Gini coefficient, which measures the degree of income inequality, declined for the ROC during the 1960s and 1970s; it declined and then rose slightly for South Korea and Japan.[24]

Turning to welfare standards, the percentage of Taiwan's household expenditures for fuel, beverages, and tobacco declined from 59.7 percent in 1964 to 39.4 percent in 1981, indicating that more spending went for clothing, education, services, and other consumer goods.[25] Food intake and nutrition on a daily basis also rose dramatically in the ROC over the same period.[26] Real wages in manufacturing rose in both Korea and the ROC over the period 1965–1981, as did consumer spending per capita.[27]

Similar trends occurred in Hong Kong and Singapore, but not in the Philippines, and only in the 1970s for the ASEAN countries. Only in a few Pacific Basin countries, then, was trend acceleration achieved by greater productivity and associated with rapidly improved income distribution and rising consumer welfare. These same countries were not plagued by productive capacity growing more rapidly than market demand for goods and services, a problem that gravely affected countries of Western Europe during their first years of rapid industrialization and trend acceleration. Although the socialist countries of Eastern Europe and the USSR have not been affected by this same difficulty of productive capacity growing more rapidly than market demand, they have experienced widespread inefficiency, poor quality of products and services, and very gradual improvement in consumer welfare. Let us now examine in more detail the economic performance of mainland China before and after 1978 by the normative economic standards that we have developed.

The Case of Communist China

The Pre-1978 Period

Prior to 1978, the PRC's annual growth rate for output per capita first accelerated (1952–1957) and then declined (1957–1965 and 1965–1978). The same trend can be observed for Shanghai except that in the third period (1965–1978) the annual per capita income growth rate rose slightly, but it was still below that of the 1952–1957 period. Declining annual growth rate trends (see Table 3.2) never occurred during the post–World War II trend acceleration of the three other Pacific Basin states.

A second unusual characteristic of the PRC's trend acceleration was that annual output fluctuations were extremely severe. Figure 3.1 compares the changes (not levels) of annual growth of output for the PRC and the ROC for the period 1954–1981. The combined gross values of agriculture, manufacturing, construction, transportation, and commerce for the PRC are compared with the GDP of the ROC. We observe that the annual growth rate fluctuations were much greater for the PRC, and that two exceedingly large dips in the growth rate of output occurred during the Great Leap Forward and the early years of the Cultural Revolution.

A third unusual feature of trend acceleration during this same period was how the three sectors (A, M, and S) contributed to output growth. In the three other Pacific Basin states, the labor force steadily shifted from the A sector to the M and S sectors, and the stock of reproducible capital in the M and S sectors rapidly increased. Not only had the M and S sectors' output rapidly increased, but they had contributed greatly to GDP itself. This process did not take place in Communist China. In Table 3.3 we

TABLE 3.2
Annual Rates of Growth for PRC and Shanghai (percent)

	National Income	Gross Value, Output and Services	Population	Output per Capita
China				
1952–1957	8.9	9.6	2.3	7.3
1957–1965	3.2	6.7	1.4	5.3
1965–1978	6.6	7.3	2.2	5.1
1978–1983	7.1	10.0	1.2	8.8
1952–1983	6.7	8.0	1.9	6.1
Shanghai				
1952–1957	13.8	13.1	3.5	9.6
1957–1965	6.8	8.5	1.0	7.5
1965–1978	9.7	8.3	0.03	8.27
1978–1983	6.6	6.4	1.7	4.7
1952–1983	9.1	8.8	1.1	7.7

Sources: China: *Chung-kuo t'ung-chi nein-chien* (China Economic Yearbook), 1984 (Beijing: Chung-kuo t'ung-chi ch'u-pan-she), data for national income, p. 12; gross value, output and services, p. 20; population, p. 81. Gross value of output expressed in current year prices. National income appears to be valued in 1952 prices.

Shanghai: Shang-hai-shih t'ung-chi-chu, comp., *Shang-hai t'ung-chi nien-chien* (Shanghai Municipality Statistical Yearbook), 1984 (Shanghai: Shang-hai jen-min ta-chang-she), p. 28.

observe that the S sector's contribution to output in 1952 and 1957 was still below its contribution of around 18.0 percent in the early 1930s.[28] Its contribution to output (as well as to employment) declined even further after 1957. Considering the S sector's contribution of around 40 percent for the other Pacific Basin states, that decline was rather extraordinary. In the case of Shanghai, we again observe that the S sector expanded very slightly during the First Five-Year Plan, but declined precipitously thereafter; for a city of such size, in which services had played so important an economic role, this outcome is very strange. Even though Communist national income accounting procedures devalue the contribution of services to output, services still had declined in importance.

Turning to the sources of growth, we have sufficient evidence to show that productivity accounted for very little trend acceleration. This finding is very important, because it signifies that scarce resources were being used very inefficiently and wastefully. Productivity, however, had played a key role in accounting for trend acceleration for our three Pacific Basin countries.[29]

Turning to capital and labor productivity, Shigeru Ishikawa's review of China's economic growth between 1949 and 1976 points out that the productivity of capital declined during certain periods. The state-owned construction industry's utilization of capital is a good barometer of how effectively capital was used. Ishikawa's estimates, based upon Beijing's data, show that less output was being produced from each new unit of capital

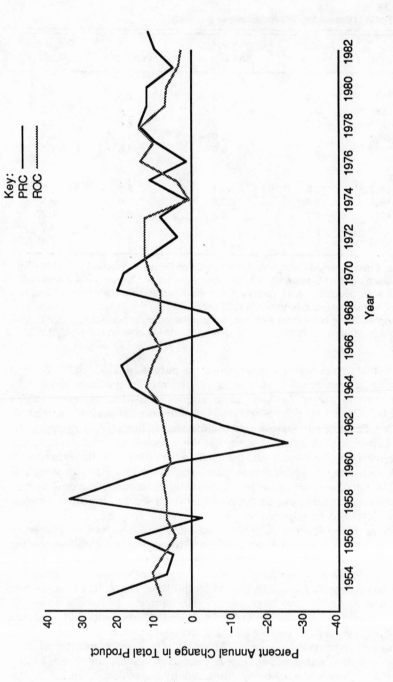

FIGURE 3.1
Annual Growth of GNP

TABLE 3.3
Sectoral Share of National Product and Sectoral Annual Growth Rates

	Sectoral Share of Gross Value Product (percent)			Annual Sectoral Growth Rate (percent)			
	A	M	S		A	M	S
China							
1952	45.4	40.0	14.6	—	—	—	—
1957	33.4	51.2	15.4	1952–1957	4.6	18.0	18.8
1965	30.9	58.6	10.5	1957–1965	1.2	8.9	8.4
1978	22.9	67.7	9.4	1965–1978	4.0	10.1	8.2
1983	28.2	64.5	7.3	1978–1983	7.9	7.9	7.4
Shanghai							
1952	4.0	79.3	16.7				
1957	2.7	78.3	19.0				
1965	2.9	94.1	3.0				
1978	3.6	91.9	4.5				
1983	5.2	86.4	8.4				

Sources: China: *Chung-kuo t'ung-chi nein-chien* (China Economic Yearbook), 1984 (Beijing: Chung-kuo t'ung-chi ch'u-pan-she), data for sectoral share of product, p. 20; annual sectoral growth rate, pp. 12–13.
Shanghai: Shang-hai-shih t'ung-chi-chu, comp., *Shang-hai t'ung-chi nien-chien* (Shanghai Municipality Statistical Yearbook), 1984 (Shanghai: Shang-hai jen-min ta-chang-she), p. 21.

during 1958–1962 than during 1953–1957, and this pattern worsened during 1966–1970 and 1970–1975.[30]

Surveys of labor productivity in the nationally owned industrial enterprises of Shanghai, Nanking, Soochow, Nantung, Wuhsi, and Nanchang also show that labor productivity declined during five years of the period 1971–1978. Productivity had still risen enough in three years to produce an overall average growth of 1.4 percent per annum.[31] But such erratic fluctuations in labor productivity and the very low annual growth rate for labor productivity suggest that low labor productivity was still a serious problem throughout the country.

Turning to factor productivity, Anthony Tang's estimates for total factor productivity in agriculture, and various statements by Chinese economists in the late 1970s indicate that productivity growth in the rural sector (except for land) might very well have been zero during much of the period.[32]

As for income distribution, land reform and the urban campaigns to destroy the capitalist class had greatly reduced income inequality and even reduced the income disparity between the rural and urban sectors. Our evidence of changes in income distribution after 1953 is fragmentary. But Martin King Whyte has reviewed much of the existing information and concluded that after the early 1950s income distribution within the society remained relatively unchanged, with differences between the urban and rural sectors continuing to exist, especially between social strata.[33] Because of limited intersectoral flow of resources, rationing of consumer goods, and slow expansion of real income per capita, income distribution probably remained fairly constant between 1953 and 1978.

But how equal had income distribution become after the transformation of rural and urban property rights? A recent report shows that the Gini coefficient for urban worker income distribution was 0.185 in 1977 and 0.237 for peasant income distribution in 1978.[34] While we cannot be certain that they accurately reflect all segments of the country's huge population, these measures are among the world's lowest Gini coefficients.[35] Even so, low Gini coefficients characterize Marxist-Leninist systems. The Gini coefficients by per capita income for Pacific Basin countries in the late 1970s show that income distribution in the ROC became more equal, while that of Hong Kong, South Korea, and Singapore became equal and then slightly unequal (see Table 3.4).

What about consumer welfare? To be sure, life expectancy increased as public health measures slowly improved, rising from 36 years in 1950 to 64 years in 1979, whereas the average was only 51 years for low-income countries in 1979, and 61 years for middle-income countries. Likewise, the adult literacy rate rose from 20 percent in 1949 to 66 percent in 1979, and primary school enrollment as a percentage of school-age children rose from 25 to 93 percent, although it declined sharply after 1966–1967. Social welfare improvements were even more spectacular in the Pacific Basin states. Yet the PRC's performance was far less satisfactory because the leadership had insisted that the populace postpone consumerism until a modern industrial base had been established.

Before examining the data on household welfare gains, we should mention that an appalling number of people were killed as a result of political repression. Perhaps another 20 million or more died from famine and malnutrition-related disease between 1958 and 1961 when harvests failed because of ill-conceived party-state policies. Therefore, any gains in welfare must be viewed in the context of an immense loss of life caused by deliberate public policies.

Although the data are fragmentary and questionable, recent statistics show only a modest improvement of consumer welfare between 1957 and 1981. To be sure, urban worker household income doubled over this nearly-twenty-year period (see Table 3.5) at roughly a 3.5 percent annual growth rate, but rural household income rose only 82 percent. Meanwhile, the income gap between the two sectors had slightly widened by the late 1970s. Because expenditures also kept pace, the savings ratio, while already high, did not rise over the period.

Readers will observe that the percentage of household spending for food remained about the same for urban and rural worker households, but that that percentage even rose slightly for rural households between 1957 and 1978 (Table 3.5). The regime had initiated consumer rationing around 1954.

TABLE 3.4
Changes in Income Distribution and per Capita Income in Four Pacific Basin Countries

Country	Per Capita Income (US$)	Gini Coefficient
Hong Kong	$5,100 (1981)	0.487 (1966)
		0.439 (1971)
		0.435 (1976)
		0.481 (1981)
South Korea	$1,700 (1981)	0.438 (1961)
		0.344 (1965)
		0.322 (1970)
		0.391 (1976)
		0.389 (1980)
Singapore	$5,240 (1981)	0.498 (1966)
		0.443 (1972)
		0.457 (1973)
		0.434 (1974)
		0.448 (1975)
ROC (Taiwan)	$2,577 (1981)	0.558 (1953)
		0.461 (1961)
		0.321 (1970)
		0.319 (1974)
		0.306 (1978)
		0.303 (1980)

Source: Adapted from Edward K.Y. Chen, "The Newly Industrializing Countries in Asia: Growth Experiences and Prospects," in Robert A. Scalapino, Seizabura Sato, and Jusuf Wanandi, eds., *Asian Development: Present and Future* (Berkeley, Calif.: Institute of East Asian Studies, University of California, 1985), pp. 133 and 151.

Thereafter, the pattern of household expenditures remained roughly the same; for rural and urban families alike, the spending allocations for different groups of goods and services showed little change.

The average consumption per capita of grain and cooking oil greatly declined between 1957 and 1965 (Table 3.6). Average consumption per capita of sugar and cloth virtually remained unchanged between 1952 and 1965, but probably declined from 1957 to 1965. A very modest improvement in consumption per capita occurred between 1965 and 1978.

The picture is little better for the average consumption of luxury commodities per capita: some gradual improvement in the early 1950s, then decline, with modest improvement thereafter (see Table 3.7). To sum up, we observe no substantial improvement in consumer welfare for the Chinese people after 1954–1955 for the period of trend acceleration—a pattern very like that of all socialist economies.

TABLE 3.5
Worker Households and Average Annual per Capita Income and Expenses

Year	Income US$	Growth Rate	Expenses US$	Growth Rate	Food	Clothes	Rent	Fuel	Other
						Expenditure (percent)			
Urban Worker Households									
1957	253	-0.6	222	—	58	12	2	4	24
1964	243	4.5	221	4.5	59	11	3	4	23
1981	500	7.2	457	5.4	57	15	1	2	25
1983	573		506		59	14	1	2	24
Farm Worker Households									
1957	73	—	71	3.7	66	13	2	10	9
1965		2.8	95	1.5	68	10	3	8	11
1978	133	19.4	116	17.4	68	13	3	7	9
1982	270	14.8	220	12.7	60	11	10	6	13
1983	310		248		59	11	11	5	14

Source: *Chung-kuo t'ung-chi nien-chien* (China Economic Yearbook), 1984 (Beijing: Chung-kuo t'ung-chi ch'u-pan-she), data on urban worker households, pp. 463–464; on rural worker households, pp. 463–464, 471, and 473.

TABLE 3.6
Average Consumption per Capita

Year	Grain Catties	Growth Rate	Cooking Oil Catties	Growth Rate	Pork Catties	Growth Rate	Sugar Catties	Growth Rate	Cloth Ch'ih[a]	Growth Rate	Coal Catties	Growth Rate
1952	395	0.6	4	4.6	12	3.7	2	8.4	17	3.4	83	15.4
1957	406	-1.3	5	-6.6	10	2.3	3	—	20	-1.3	170	2.5
1965	366	0.5	3	⸿	12	1.7	3	6.6	18	2.2	208	—
1978	391	3.5	3	22.0	15	18.4	7	5.1	24	5.2	210	7.7
1983	464		8		25		9		31		304	
1952– 1983		0.5		2.3		2.4		5.0		1.9		4.3

Source: Adapted from *Chung-kuo t'ung-chi nien-chien* (China Economic Yearbook), 1984 (Beijing: Chung-kuo t'ung-chi ch'u-pan-she), p. 477.

[a]1 *ch'ih* equals 0.3581 square meter.

The Post-1978 Period

The Communist Party began to initiate important economic reforms after 1978 in order to revitalize the economy. Has a new trend acceleration taken place? To be sure, the new economic indicators for the period 1978–1985 suggest that such might be the case, but the period is still too short to judge.

TABLE 3.7
Average Consumption of Luxury Items per Capita

	Cloth		Watches[a]		Bicycles[a]		Radios[a]		Sewing Machines[a]	
Year	Ch'ih	Growth Rate	No.	Growth Rate	No.	Growth Rate	No.	Growth Rate	No.	Growth Rate
1952	17		0.1		0.1		—		—	
		3.4		14.9		—		—		—
1957	20		0.2		0.1		—		—	
		0.9		9.7		10.4		—		—
1978	24		1.4		0.8		1.4		0.5	
		5.2		22.0		26.2		16.4		14.9
1983	31		3.8		2.6		3.0		1.0	

Source: Adapted from *Chung-kuo t'ung-chi nien-chien* (China Economic Yearbook), 1984 (Beijing: Chung-kuo t'ung-chi ch'u-pan-she), p. 478.

[a]Per 100 people.

We know that considerable resource slack, organizational inefficiency, and structural rigidity had characterized the economy before 1978. As the leadership initiated reforms to encourage resources to move to higher value-added activities, to give collective units greater autonomy to use their resources, and to expand state- and collective-owned units' contacts with foreign investors and traders, an economic spurt took place. How long will this spurt last? When will the growth rate again decline? We cannot answer these questions, but we can refer to our four normative standards to evaluate this brief period's performance for comparison with the period before 1978.

Taking growth rates first, it is clear that the country's output per capita annual growth rate between 1978 and 1983 exceeded that of any previous period since 1952 (see Table 3.2). This was not the case in Shanghai, however, so that regional variation obviously exists. Although some Western studies suggest that factor productivity began to accelerate after 1978,[36] labor productivity in state-owned manufacturing firms in Kiangsu Province declined during 1980–1981.[37] The regime's leaders are clearly worried about low capital and labor productivity and are trying to do something about it. However, as modern enterprises have been urged to employ more workers to alleviate the underemployment problem, labor productivity appears to have declined rather than risen. It is too early to conclude whether productivity is now on the rise and solidly contributing to the growth spurt since 1978.[38] Much of the output growth after 1978 could have been achieved by organizations drawing on resource slack and being allowed to allocate their resources to higher value-added activities.

Even though the regime has allowed small-scale service enterprises (specially licensed) to be active, and has permitted various commodity markets where buyers and sellers can freely exchange goods, the S sector's share of gross value product has still declined (see Table 3.3). Although Shanghai's S sector has definitely expanded, its share of output is still less than in 1952 (see Table 3.3). The expansion of the S sector in various localities represents a shift of some resources from lower to higher value-added economic activity. As this same development has taken place in agriculture, where households allocated more resources to sideline activities, resource redeployment would be a very important reason for the recent spurt in output growth.

As for income distribution, in the countryside a slow tilt toward inequality has been taking place. In 1984 the Gini coefficient for rural households was 0.264, compared to 0.237 in 1978.[39] In the cities, however, the Gini coefficient has declined further, from 0.185 in 1977 to 0.168 in 1984.[40] The egalitarian principles that govern urban enterprises probably account for the high, equal income distribution. The interesting issue, however, is to what extent unemployed households in the urban area are included in the income surveys upon which these Gini coefficients are based. If urban unemployment has been on the rise—and that seems very likely to have been the case—these Gini coefficients are misleading.

Finally, what of consumer welfare? Referring first to Table 3.5, it is clear that urban income has risen, partly because of higher wage bonuses, but rural income has risen even faster. As a result, rural and urban households now spend the same proportion of income for food, despite the income gap between them. That gap has, however, narrowed greatly during the past seven years. We note that a much higher share of expenditures goes for housing in the countryside than in the cities, where housing is greatly subsidized (with the exception of Shanghai; see Table 3.8, Panel A). The enormous boom in rural housing construction indicates that families are finally rebuilding their homes, and many are probably buying additional ones to lease to other families.

Other indicators of consumer welfare show that the consumption per capita of basic commodities has risen more dramatically since 1978 than during any previous time (see Table 3.6). The same trend can be observed for luxury consumer goods per capita (Table 3.7). Although we cannot compare recent consumer welfare improvement with previous years for Shanghai, the percentage change per capita in consumer goods acquired in that city in the early 1980s suggests that more goods and services at last have become available (see Table 3.8).

Suppose, now, that we complete the cells in Table 3.1, using our normative standards to depict the economic performance of mainland China for 1952–1978 and 1978–1983. Table 3.9 presents our results.

Summing up our findings in Table 3.9, the period 1952–1978 reflected a lackluster economic performance for a country beginning early economic modernization. Not only did the long-term GDP per capita growth rate decline, but it violently fluctuated. Productivity accounted for very little growth. After the Communist Party seized power, carried out land reform, and dispossessed the urban capitalist class, income distribution became more equal but remained unchanged thereafter, with poverty shared by everyone except the privileged class in power. Consumer welfare slightly improved between 1950 and 1954, but it is unlikely that welfare in 1978 was significantly better than in the early 1950s. Consumer welfare definitely fell after 1957, probably recovered to the level of the early 1950s by 1965, then stagnated until 1978.

TABLE 3.8
Shanghai: Recent Trends in Consumer Welfare

A. Average Consumer per Capita Annual Income and Spending

Year	Income Yuan	Income Growth Rate	Expenses Yuan	Expenses Growth Rate	Food %	Food Growth Rate	Clothing (%)	Housing (%)	Fuel (%)	Business Spending and Tax %	Business Spending and Tax Growth Rate	Other (%)
1982	594	20	530	31	42	-17	7	22	2	11	91	16
1983	714		694		35		7	23	2	21		15

B. Average Annual Commune Member's Household per Capita Consumption

Year	Grain Catties	Grain Growth Rate	Cooking Oil Catties	Cooking Oil Growth Rate	Meat Catties	Meat Growth Rate	Vegetables Catties	Vegetables Growth Rate	Cotton Synthetic Cloth Ch'ih	Cotton Synthetic Cloth Growth Rate
1980	605	-5.4	7.5	8.9	25.1	12.7	209	5.7	17.9	10.2
1983	507		9.7		35.8		247		24.0	

C. Durable Goods per 100 Households

Year	Bicycles No.	Bicycles Growth Rate	Watches No.	Watches Growth Rate	Television Sets No.	Television Sets Growth Rate	Sewing Machines No.	Sewing Machines Growth Rate	Radios No.	Radios Growth Rate
1980	69	15.7	130	13.2	2	91.3	41	16.0	41	14.2
1983	107		188		15		64		61	

Source: Adapted from Shang-hai-shih t'ung-chi-chu, comp., *Shang-hai t'ung-chi nien-chien* (Shanghai Municipality Statistical Yearbook), 1984 (Shanghai: Shang-hai jen-min ta-chang-she), pp. 342–344.

A major economic spurt has been under way during the past seven years, but it is still too early to determine whether rising productivity has accounted for any of this growth. In the countryside, where about three-quarters of the population still resides and works, income distribution has slightly worsened during this time, but real consumer welfare has begun to improve for the first time since the Communist Party came to power.

Conclusion

When Communist China's economic growth is compared with the experiences of the Pacific Basin countries, it becomes very clear that China's performance has not been as good as it would have been, had the correct policies been initiated. Although China did begin to undergo "trend acceleration" after 1952, the characteristics associated with that performance

TABLE 3.9
An Evaluation of Communist China's Economic Performance: 1952–1978 and 1978–1983

Normative Economic Standard	1952–1978 Value Change	1978–1983 Value Change
1. GDP per capita: Rises (+) Declines (–) Fluctuates (0)	(–) / (0)[a]	(+) / (0)[a]

2. Sources of GDP growth:
 A. Partial productivity change (labor and capital):
   Rises (+)
   Declines (–)
   Remains unchanged (0)
	(–)	(0)?

B. Total productivity change:
   Rises (+)
   Declines (–)
   Remains unchanged (0)
	(–)	(0)?

3. Income distribution: More equal (+) Less equal (–) Remains unchanged (0)	(+) / (0)[b]	(+) urban (–) rural

4. Welfare change:
 A. Engel coefficient:
   Rises (+)
   Declines (–)
   Remains unchanged (0)
	(0) urban
	(+) rural
		(0) urban
		(–) rural

B. Goods and services per capita:
   Rises (+)
   Declines (–)
   Remains unchanged (0)
	(+) / (0)	(+)

[a]First value reflects overall long-term trend; second value indicates serious fluctuations over significant short-term periods.
[b]First value reflects initial change; second value indicates long-term trend.

have been very different from those of Western Europe and the Pacific Basin states during their periods of trend acceleration. There are, however, many similarities between the PRC's economic growth and that of the USSR and the socialist countries of Eastern Europe: a rapid growth of the M sector; a great decline in the importance of the S sector; little or no output growth due to productivity; no significant improvement in consumer welfare; and a very equal distribution of income.

Have we been fair to compare Communist China only with certain Pacific Basin countries, European nations, and socialist-bloc states? Should we not have compared China with India, Brazil, or Indonesia, those developing countries with huge populations and limited land resources? Some will charge that by comparing China as we have done greatly distorts any judgment of its economic performance. But we do not compare the two lackluster racehorses that finish last in a race. We want to compare the loser with the top performers to determine why one wins and the other performs so poorly. China possessed the potential to have performed much better than it did. It shared many of the same characteristics as the labor-surplus, resource-poor countries of the Pacific Basin. Had China's leaders implemented the correct policies to vitalize the private sector instead of destroying and collectivizing it, its economy would not have fallen so far behind those of the Pacific Basin states with which it shares a common culture and a geographical affinity. In 1957 the per capita income of the ROC on Taiwan stood at roughly three times that of Communist China; by 1978 the gap had widened to roughly seven times. Had the PRC at least maintained the same disparity in 1978 as in the late 1950s, how much better its economy would have performed!

The economic reforms launched by the Communist Party after 1978 certainly have initiated a new growth spurt, but has a new trend acceleration taken place? Only the passage of time will reveal whether the new policies will bear fruit.

Notes

I am grateful for critical comments by Thomas A. Metzger, Terry Sicular, Donald Brown, David Granick, George Rosen, and Peter Chow on an earlier draft of this chapter. All errors and omissions are, of course, the responsibility of the author.

1. Simon Kuznets, *Modern Economic Growth: Rate, Structure, and Spread* (New Haven, Conn.: Yale University Press, 1966), p. 1.

2. See David S. Landes, "Technological Change and Development in Western Europe, 1750–1914," in M. M. Postan and H. J. Habakkuk, eds., *The Cambridge Economic History of Europe*, vol. 6: *The Industrial Revolutions and After*, part 1 (Cambridge: University of Cambridge Press, 1965), pp. 274–352; Carlo M. Cipolla, *The Fontana Economic History of Europe: The Industrial Revolution.* (Glasgow: William Collins, 1973), vol. 3.

3. Harry Schwartz, *Russia's Soviet Economy* (New York: Prentice-Hall, 1954), chap. 7, for a discussion of the growth of industrial production; Abram Bergson and Simon Kuznets, eds., *Economic Trends in the Soviet Union* (Cambridge, Mass.: Harvard University Press, 1963), pp. 4–7, for statistical trends of industrialization and capital formation; *Allocation of Resources in the Soviet Union and China, 1977*, Hearings Before the Subcommittee on Priorities and Economy in Government of the Joint Economic Committee, Congress of the United States, Ninety-fifth Congress, First Session, Part 3 (Washington, D.C.: U.S. Government Printing Office, 1977), p. 3, for trends of annual rates of growth of GNP, industry, and net output of agriculture of the postwar period.

4. Kazushi Ohkawa and Henry Rosovsky, *Japanese Economic Growth: Trend Acceleration in the Twentieth Century* (Stanford, Calif.: Stanford University Press, 1973), chap. 2.

5. Lawrence J. Lau, ed., *Models of Development: A Comparative Study of Economic Growth in South Korea and Taiwan* (San Francisco: Institute for Contemporary Studies, 1986). See chapters on Taiwan by Ramon H. Myers, pp. 13–64, and on the Republic of Korea by Sung Yeung Kwack, pp. 65–134.

6. There is an enormous literature on economic development of countries under Western colonization. We will not cite sources here except to say that the debate continues as to what kind of economic development legacy was produced under colonialism for the period of decolonization.

7. See Cyril E. Black et al., *The Modernization of Japan and Russia: A Comparative Study* (New York: Free Press, 1975).

8. See in particular Gilbert Rozman, ed., *The Modernization of China* (New York: Free Press, 1981), chaps. 10 and 14.

9. Lau, *Models of Development*, chaps. 2 and 3.

10. I am indebted to Professor Thomas A. Metzger for suggesting the possibility of normative economic standards, and for identifying them.

11. For a good discussion of the total factor productivity concept, see Robert M. Solow and Peter Temin, "Introduction: The Inputs for Growth," in Peter Mathias and M. M. Postan, eds., *The Cambridge Economic History of Europe*, vol. 7: *The Industrial Economies: Capital, Labour and Enterprise*, part 1: *Britain, France, Germany, and Scandinavia* (Cambridge: Cambridge University Press, 1978), pp. 1–28. For a recent debate over the application of total factor productivity analysis to measure the contribution of productivity to GDP growth in late nineteenth-century England, see Stephen Nicholas, "British Economic Performance and Total Factor Productivity Growth, 1870–1940," *Economic History Review*, ser. 2, vol. 38, no. 4 (November 1985), pp. 576–582.

12. Mathias and Postan, *Cambridge Economic History of Europe*, vol. 7, part 1, p. 84.

13. Ibid.

14. Ibid., p. 87.

15. B. R. Mitchell, *European Historical Statistics, 1750–1970* (New York: Columbia University Press, 1978), p. 408.

16. Mathias and Postan, *Cambridge Economic History of Europe*, vol. 7, part 1, p. 387.

17. Ibid., p. 473.

18. Abram Bergson and Simon Kuznets, eds., *Economic Trends; in the Soviet Union* (Cambridge, Mass.: Harvard University Press, 1963), p. 4, Table I.1. Bergson estimates that net national product per unit of selected inputs (with output in 1937 ruble factor cost and inputs using 1937 weights) declined between 1928 and 1937. On p. 23 the author states, "When we consider the crudity of my calculations for these early years, we must conclude that with the former sort of measure net national product per unit of inputs grew little if at all, and may even have decreased." Again, later, Bergson says, "During 1928–40, the increase in productivity contributes in the former case little or nothing to the growth of output and in the latter case about as much as during the entire period 1928–58. For both calculations, the increase in productivity accounts for about one-half or more of the increase in output during 1940–50 and something more or less than this share during 1950–58." According to research findings presented in 1976, the growth rate for labor productivity in the Soviet Union declined in the 1960s and still further in the 1970s. See Zbigniew B. Fallenbuch, *Economic Development in the Soviet Union and Eastern Europe* (New York: Praeger, 1976), vol. 2, pp. 15 and 33. Aggregate factor productivity in industry stood at an index of 100 in 1960 and climbed to around 110 in 1970, with agriculture performing roughly the same (see p. 108), representing about a 0.9 percent growth per annum for total factor productivity.

19. *Allocation of Resources in the Soviet Union and China, 1977*, p. 5, shows that annual output (GDP) growth rate declined from 5.8 percent to 5.1 percent to 3.7

percent for the years 1951–1960, 1961–1970, and 1971–1975, respectively, and that productivity of capital and labor combined declined for the same period at the rate of 1.2 percent, 0.8 percent, and −0.6 percent per annum.

20. See Paul S. Shoup, *The East European and Soviet Data Handbook: Political, Social, and Developmental Indicators, 1945–1975.* (New York: Columbia University Press, 1981; Stanford, Calif.: Hoover Institution Press, 1981). For calories, proteins, and fats per capita for the USSR during 1961–1974, see p. 417.

21. Ibid., p. 417, for Albania, Bulgaria, Hungary, Poland, Romania, Yugoslavia, East Germany, and Czechoslovakia. For housing in select Eastern European countries, see pp. 408–414.

22. Tibor Scitovsky, "Economic Development in Taiwan and South Korea, 1965–1981," in Lau, *Models of Development,* p. 137.

23. Ohkawa and Rosovsky, *Japanese Economic Growth,* p. 47.

24. Scitovsky, "Economic Development," p. 139.

25. Ramon H. Myers, "The Economic Development of the Republic of China on Taiwan, 1965–1981," in Lau, *Models of Development,* p. 25.

26. Ibid., p. 26.

27. Scitovsky, "Economic Development," p. 137.

28. See the estimate of the service sector's contribution to GDP in the 1930s by K. C. Yeh, "China's National Income, 1931–36," in Chi-ming Hou and Tzong-shian Yu, eds., *Modern Chinese Economic History* (Taipei: Institute of Economics, Academia Sinica, 1979), p. 107.

29. See Edward K.Y. Chen, "Factor Inputs, Total Factor Productivity, and Economic Growth: The Asian Case," *Developing Economies,* vol. 15, no. 2 (June 1977), pp. 121–143.

30. Shigeru Ishikawa, "China's Economic Growth Since 1949—An Assessment," *China Quarterly,* vol. 94 (June 1983), p. 256, Table 5.

31. Feng Lan-rui, Chou Pei-lung, and Lao Ch'ung-te, "Lun lao-tung chiu-yeh ho ching-chi tseng-ch'ang ti kuan-hsi" (An Essay on the Relationship Between Labor Productivity and Economic Growth), *Ching-chi lun-li yu ching-chi kuan-li* (Economic Theory and Management), 1983, no. 2, part 2, p. 59. This informative essay elucidates the serious problem of whether the M sector can generate more employment and still maintain high labor productivity. Survey findings for Kiangsu Province revealed that, as manufacturing firms hired more workers, labor productivity declined.

32. For estimates of total factor productivity in agriculture between 1952 and 1980, see Anthony M. Tang, *An Analytical and Empirical Investigation of Agriculture in Mainland China, 1952–1980* (Taipei: Chung-hua Institution for Economic Research, 1984), pp. 92–93. Tang's corrected estimates show that total factor productivity rose slightly during the First Five-Year Plan, declining thereafter until 1980. For various discussions of low productivity in the economy, see Ma Hung and Sun Shang-ch'ing, eds., *Chung-kuo ching-chi chieh-kou wen-t'i yen-chiu* (Studies of the Problems Concerning China's Economic Structure) (Beijing: Jen-min ta-ch'ang she, 1981), vols. 1 and 2.

33. Martin King Whyte, "Inequality and Stratification in China," *China Quarterly,* no. 64 (December 1979), pp. 684–711.

34. Li Chengrui, "Economic Reform Brings Better Life," *Beijing Review,* vol. 28, no. 29 (July 22, 1985), p. 22.

35. To compare Communist China's Gini coefficient for the late 1970s with those of other countries, see Table 3.10 (following the notes), which presents information published in 1975 by the World Bank. These Gini coefficients were derived from

household income surveys. Note the low coefficients for the socialist countries, which are comparable to those for China, despite China's extremely low per capita income.

36. K. C. Yeh recently made some crude estimates of total factor productivity for the period 1978–1982, but his findings must be viewed with extreme caution. His estimates of factor inputs are based on weights that might be in error. I reproduce his findings for the interested reader in Table 3.11 (following the notes). See K. C. Yeh, "Macroeconomic Changes in the Chinese Economy During the Readjustment," *China Quarterly*, no. 100 (December 1984), p. 711.

37. See note 31. For seven cities in Kiangsu, labor productivity declined in 1980–1981: Shanghai, −1.6 percent; Nanking, −6.6 percent; Soochow, −1.8 percent; Nantung, −0.6 percent; Wuhsi, −1.8 percent; Nanchang, −1.5 percent; and Chungching, −0.8 percent.

38. According to the most recent calculations of factor productivity for state-owned and -operated industries, factor productivity varies enormously among different industries, and such findings must be interpreted with great caution. See Thomas G. Rawski, "Productivity Change in Chinese Industry: Problems of Measurement," a paper presented to the ACLS/SSRC-sponsored conference "Price and Wage Reform in the People's Republic of China," June 17–18, 1986, Washington, D.C.

39. Li, "Economic Reform," p. 22.

40. Ibid.

TABLE 3.10
Gini Coefficients of Pacific Basin and Eastern European Countries

Country	Year	Gini Coefficient
Pacific Basin		
Korea	1966	0.3416
	1970	0.3719
Japan	1965	0.3806
	1971	0.4223
Taiwan	1953	0.5762
	1964	0.3290
	1972	0.2736
Eastern Europe		
Bulgaria	1957	0.2459
	1962	0.2118
Czechoslovakia	1959	0.2060
	1964	0.1938
East Germany	1967	0.1987
	1970	0.2044
Hungary	1967	0.2508
	1969	0.2435
Poland	1956	0.2703
	1964	0.2635
Yugoslavia	1963	0.3451
	1968	0.1791

Source: Adapted from Shail Jain, *Size Distribution: A Compilation of Data* (Washington, D.C.: World Bank, 1975), data for Korea, p. 65; Japan, p. 62; Taiwan, p. 108; Bulgaria, p. 19; Czechoslovakia, p. 30; East Germany, p. 41; Hungary, p. 49; Poland, p. 93; Yugoslavia, p. 120.

TABLE 3.11
Annual Growth Rates in the PRC, 1957–1982 (percent)

	1957–1978	1978–1982	1957–1982
Net domestic product	4.4	5.8	4.6
Employment	2.5	2.9	2.6
Fixed capital	10.0	7.3	9.6
Land	−0.2	−0.9	−0.3
Factor inputs, weighted			
Employment	1.4	1.6	1.4
Fixed capital	3.5	2.6	3.4
Land	—	−0.1	—
Productivity	-0.5	1.7	-0.2

Source: K. C. Yeh, "Macroeconomic Changes in the Chinese Economy During the Readjustment," *China Quarterly*, no. 100 (December 1984), p. 711.

APPENDIX

TABLE 3.A1
USSR: Annual Growth Rates and Other Indicators (percent)

	Annual Growth Rate			Ratio of Gross Capital Investment/ GNP[b]	Sectoral Percent of NNP			Marginal Capital Output Ratio[d]
	GNP[a]	Population[a]	GNP per Capita		A	M	S[c]	
Period 1								
				(1928) 12.5	(1928) 49.2	27.9	22.9	
1928–1940	4.5	1.2	3.2	(1940) 19.1	(1940) 28.9	44.8	26.3	3.5
1940–1950	2.1	–0.8	2.9	(1950) 26.9	(1950) 24.1	49.1	26.8	
Period 2								
1950–								
1958/59	7.2	1.7	5.4	(1955) 28.1	(1959) 22.1	58.0	19.9	3.7
1960–1970	5.1[e]	1.3[f]	3.8	(1970) 29.0[g]	(1970) 22.0	67.0	11.0[h]	
1970–1980	3.2[i]	0.9[f]	2.3	(1980) 24.0[g]	(1980) 15.0	62.0	23.0[j]	

[a]Abram Bergson and Simon Kuznets, *Economic Trends in the Soviet Union* (Cambridge, Mass.: Harvard University Press, 1963), pp. 337 and 352. Annual growth rates from 1928 to 1957 at 1937 factor costs.

[b]Ibid., p. 352.

[c]Ibid., p. 344 for 1928–1959. M includes fishing, forestry, transportation, and communications.

[d]Ibid., p. 356. Incremental capital output ratios based on volumes at 1937 factor costs.

[e]*Allocation of Resources in the Soviet Union and Chnia, 1977*, Hearings Before the Subcommittee on Priorities and Economy in Government of the Joint Economic Committee, Congress of the United States, Ninety-fifth Congress, First Session, Part 3 (Washington, D.C.: U.S. Government Printing Office, 1977), p. 5.

[f]Joint Economic Committee, Congress of the United States, *The Political Economy of the Soviet Union* (Washington, D.C.: Government Printing Office), p. 100 (prepared statement by Murray Feshbach).

[g]United Nations, *National Accounts: Statistical Analysis of Main Aggregates, 1982* (New York: United Nations, 1985), p. 116 for current prices.

[h]B. R. Mitchell, *European Historical Statistics, 1750–1970* (New York: Columbia University Press, 1978), p. 432.

[i]*Allocation of Resources in the Soviet Union and China, 1983*, Hearings Before the Subcommittee on Priorities and Economy in Government of the Joint Economic Committee, Congress of the United States (Washington, D.C.: U.S. Government Printing Office), p. 353 (appendix to CIA briefing paper).

[j]United Nations, *National Accounts*, p. 164.

TABLE 3.A2
Poland: Annual Growth Rates and Other Indicators (percent)

	Annual Growth Rate			Ratio of Capital Formation/NNP[a]		Sectoral Percent of NNP		
	NNP[a]	Population	NNP per Capita			A	M	S[b]
				(1947)	18.8			
1947–1950	20.1	1.0[c]	19.9	(1950)	21.1	41	46	13
1950–1960	7.6	1.7	5.9	(1960)	26.3	26[d]	57[d]	17[d]
1960–1970	7.0	1.0	6.0	(1970)	30.7	17	65	18

Source: B. R. Mitchell, European Historical Statistics, 1750–1970 (New York: Columbia University Press, 1978), pp. 414 and 420.

[a]Calculated from constant prices.
[b]Figures for final year of period.
[c]1946–1950.
[d]Change in definition of national product.

TABLE 3.A3
Yugoslavia: Annual Growth Rates and Other Indicators (percent)

	Annual Growth Rate			Ratio of Capital Formation/ GDP or NNP[b]		Sectoral Percent of GDP or NNP		
	GDP or NNP[a,b]	Population	GDP or NNP per Capita			A	M	S
Period 1				(1921)	19.8			
1921–1931	3.3	1.5	1.8	(1931)	9.8			
1931–1939	2.2			(1939)	16.8[c]			
1939–1948		0.7[d]		(1948)	54.7			
Period 2								
1948–1961	5.4	1.3	4.1	(1961)	61.4	(1960) 26	51	23
1961–1967	6.7	1.0[e]	5.7	(1967)	50.2	(1970) 19	50	51

Source: B. R. Mitchell, European Historical Statistics, 1750–1970 (New York: Columbia University Press, 1978), pp. 416 and 422.

[a]Figures to 1947 are of GDP adjusted for international comparison; subsequent figures are of NNP.
[b]Calculated from constant prices.
[c]Figures are of gross fixed capital formation to 1939. From 1947, stocks are included.
[d]1931–1948.
[e]1961–1971.

TABLE 3.A4
Czechoslovakia: Annual Growth Rates and Other Indicators (percent)

	Annual Growth Rate			Ratio of Capital Formation/ GDP or NNP[b]		Sectoral Percent of GDP or NNP[c]		
	GDP or NNP[a]	Population	GDP or NNP per Capita			A	M	S
				(1921)	8.1	(1921) 24	30	46
1921–1930	4.6	0.9	3.7	(1930)	14.0	(1930) 22	38	40
1930–1937	0.3			(1937)	12.2	(1935) 24	34	42
1937–1950		−0.9[d]		(1950)	5.8	(1950) 17	70	13
1950–1960	7.5[e]	0.9[f]	6.4[g]	(1960)	19.1[h]	(1960) 16	74	10

Source: B. R. Mitchell, European Historical Statistics, 1750–1970 (New York: Columbia University Press, 1978), pp. 410 and 417.

[a]Figures to 1937 are of GDP; from 1948, of NNP.
[b]Gross excluding stocks.
[c]After 1945 percentages are of NNP; prior to 1945, of GDP.
[d]Between 1930 and 1946/47 sub-Carpathian Russia and a few villages in Slovakia were ceded to the USSR.
[e]Calculated from constant prices.
[f]1950–1961.
[g]Estimated using 1960 NNP and 1961 population.
[h]1961–1970.

TABLE 3.A5
Japan: Annual Growth Rates and Other Indicators[a] (percent)

	Annual Growth Rate			Ratio of Capital Formation/GNP[e]		Sectoral Percent of GNP		
	GNP[b]	Population[c]	GNP per Capita[d]			A	M	S[f]
Period 1								
				(1885)	9.0	(1885) 41	9	46
1885–1890	4.4	0.8	3.6	(1890)	9.6	(1890) 39	10	48
1890–1900	2.5	1.0	1.5	(1900)	11.5	(1900) 34	14	49
		(BOP, ¥141 = $70)						
1900–1910	2.2	1.1	1.1	(1910)	15.1	(1910) 30	19	48
		(BOP, ¥156 = $78)						
1910–1920	3.9	1.2	2.7	(1920)	22.1	(1920) 27	21	50
		(BOP, ¥203 = $101)						
1920–1930	2.3	1.6	0.7	(1930)	17.3	(1930) 22	30	45
		(BOP, ¥217 = $109)						
1930–1940	5.8	1.1	4.7	(1940)	28.6	(1940) 14	41	44
		(BOP, ¥343 = $81)						
Period 2								
1940–1953		1.5		(1953)	19.4	(1953) 19	25	56
		(BOP, ¥123,785 = $344)						
1953–1960	9.3	1.0	8.3	(1960)	26.0	(1960) 15	32	53
		(BOP, ¥214,667 = $596)						
1960–1970	10.8	1.0	9.8	(1970)	37.6	(1970) 6	46	48
1970–1980	4.9g	1.1h	3.8	(1980)	33.0i	(1980) 4	38	58g

Source: Kazushi Ohkawa and Miyohei Sninohara, *Patterns of Japanese Economic Development* (New Haven, Conn.: Yale University Press, 1979).

[a]1885–1940 in 1934–1936 prices in millions of yen. 1953–1970 in 1965 prices in billions of yen.
[b]Pp. 278–282.
[c]P. 392.
[d]BOP (beginning of period exchange rate) obtained from R. L. Bidwell, *Currency Conversion Tables: A Hundred Years of Change* (London: Rex Collins, 1970).
[e]Pp. 256–260.
[f]Pp. 278–282. Figures for 1885–1940 do not include depreciation allowances for residential buildings or riparian works, so percentages sum to less than 100 percent.
[g]United Nations, *National Accounts: Main Aggregates and Detailed Tables, 1972* (New York: United Nations, 1985), p. 769.
[h]World Bank, *World Tables*, vol. 2: *Social Data*, 3rd ed. (Baltimore: Johns Hopkins University Press, 1983), p. 122.
[i]United Nations, *National Accounts*, pp. 774–775.

TABLE 3.A6
South Korea: Annual Growth Rates and Other Indicators (percent)

	Annual Growth Rate			Ratio of Gross Capital Invest-ment/GNP[a,b]		Sectoral Percent of GDP		
	GNP[a,b]	Population	GNP per Capita			A	M	S
1950–1956		1.1[c]		(1956)	11.9	(1956)	44	15	41
1956–1960	5.3	3.0	2.3	(1960)	10.6	(1960)	41	18	41
1960–1965	6.5	2.8[d]	3.7	(1965)	14.7	(1965)	39	19	42
1965–1970	10.4	1.7	8.7	(1970)	28.1	(1970)	30	25	45
1970–1975	9.0	1.9	7.1	(1975)	29.4	(1975)	25	33	42
1975–1980	7.1	1.5	5.6	(1980)	33.7	(1980)	16	42	42[e]

Source: Korean Statistical Yearbook, 1968 and 1980, and *Korean Statistical Handbook*, 1982 (Seoul: National Bureau of Statistics and Economic Planning).

[a]GNP and capital formation from 1956–1965 in 1965 constant prices: *Statistical Yearbook*, 1968. From 1968–1980 in 1975 prices.
[b]Calculated from constant prices.
[c]1949–1955.
[d]Using 1965 estimate from 1980 *Korean Statistical Yearbook*, p. 37.
[e]*Korea Annual*, 1983 (Seoul: Yonhap News Agency), p. 111.

TABLE 3.A7
Taiwan: Annual Growth Rates and Other Indicators (percent)

	Annual Growth Rate			Ratio of Capital Formation/GNP[c]		Sectoral Percent of GNP		
	GNP[a]	Population[b]	GNP per Capita			A	M	S[d]
				(1952)	13.9	(1952)	36	18	46
1952–1955	8.9	3.8	5.1	(1955)	11.4	(1955)	33	21	46
1955–1960	6.6	3.5	3.1	(1960)	17.0	(1960)	33	25	42
1960–1965	9.4	3.2	6.2	(1965)	20.0	(1965)	27	29	44
1965–1970	9.7	3.0	6.7	(1970)	26.1	(1970)	18	35	47
1970–1975	8.9	1.9	7.0	(1975)	30.6	(1975)	15	39	46
1975–1980	10.3	1.9	8.4	(1980)	32.4	(1980)	9	45	46

Source: Taiwan Statistical Data Book, 1983 (Taipei: Council for Economic Planning and Development).

[a]P. 21 at 1976 constant prices.
[b]P. 4.
[c]P. 37 for gross capital formation at 1976 constant prices.
[d]P. 34, "Other" included in Services.

PART TWO

Ideology

4

Giving Marxism a Lease on Life in China

James C. Hsiung

For some time, the Marxist ideology was in need of a raison d'être in post-Mao China. That statement may sound incredible, since Marxism had once reigned supreme in the People's Republic of China (PRC) as an unquestioned "absolute truth." The shaken confidence was so serious that Peng Zhen, one of the Chinese Communist Party's "old guards" still around, recently deplored a prevailing notion among Chinese youths that held anyone "conservative" or even "reactionary" who supported the study of Marxism-Leninism.[1]

Of late, the leadership under Deng Xiaoping seemed to be embarking upon a fully coordinated effort to reaffirm the legitimacy of Marxism, to reinterpret and update Marxist tenets, and to rewrite the Marxist textbooks for intensified Marxist studies in colleges. In this chapter, I hope to demonstrate ultimately that there is a logical interrelationship in these endeavors, driven as they are by an inherent political motive. A common view in the West is that Deng was relenting to the pressures of the "old guards" who allegedly wanted to restore the Marxist ideology to its proper preeminence. We shall see if there were other reasons.

To some extent, the confidence crisis among Chinese youths regarding the relevance of Marxism was an outgrowth of the de-Maoization campaign waged by the Dengists. Although tinged with a more immediate power struggle aimed at the "whateverists," the campaign had a higher ideological purpose. The Dengists wanted to make sure that the kind of total insanities and atrocities perpetrated by the followers of Mao Zedong during the Cultural Revolution and, more particularly, the radical ideology spawned during its course would never again appear in China.

To appreciate the extent to which the ideological crisis was directly linked to the aftereffects of the de-Maoization campaign, one has to look beneath the surface of official pronouncements. The most definitive official verdict on Maoism was contained in a resolution adopted by the Chinese Communist Party (CCP), on June 27, 1981, in the course of the Sixth Plenum of the

Eleventh Central Committee. It was a mixed verdict, reflecting a compromise between conflicting opinions within the CCP. The various components of Maoism fared quite differently. For example, Mao's tenets regarding "perpetual revolution," continuing unabated even into the socialist stage, and his developmental strategy, which emphasized "people's interests" at the expense of individual ends, were scrapped. Maoism as a shorthand label for the CCP's official ideology—a symbol of the party's "collective wisdom"—was perfunctorily preserved. The justification was that this "collective wisdom" embodied the best synthesis of Marxist-Leninist strictures and the CCP's revolutionary experience.[2]

The real challenge to the authority of Maosim, however, came from the Dengist thesis of "seeking the truth from reality."[3] The inherent suggestion that "truth" was not something monopolized by any individual, nor derived a priori from any set dogma, obviously, would have wider repercussions. The questions raised over the present relevance of Maoism could be extended to Marxism itself. In reverse, questioning the omniscience of Karl Marx would likewise cast doubt on the claims of Mao's prescience. While acknowledging the positive role played by Marxism-Leninism in the Chinese Communist revolution, Hu Yaobang, on July 1, 1981, declared that "the generalities in Marxism cannot possibly provide a ready-made answer for revolution in any specific country, especially a semicolonial, Oriental country as large as China."[4]

When questions like this were posed, it would only take one step forward to suggest that Marxism was obsolescent for China's current needs. Thus, *Renmin Ribao* (the People's Daily), in a celebrated editorial dated December 7, 1984, declared: "Marx cannot solve all of today's problems."[5] That was the confusing part, because many analysts who were shocked to hear the near-obituary of Marxism cannot now see why the Dengists, after having belittled Marx along with Mao, would once again want to exalt Marxism. We hope we shall be able to find a rationale in this chapter.

Arresting the Decline in Ideological Confidence

If the "seeking truth from reality" thesis were to affect only the fate of Maoism, there probably would not have been too much of a problem within the party, certainly not after the Sixth Plenum in 1981. The Dengist takeover of power was consummated at the Sixth Plenum, as Hua Guofeng, the last of the surviving "Whateverists" in power was replaced as the head of the party by Hu Yaobang, a Deng protégé. But, the ultimate challenge (or its impression) posed by the Dengist thesis to the very sanctity of Marxism could not but have far-reaching effects, some of them probably unforeseen by the Dengists themselves.

There had been, indeed, widespread open disillusionment with the Communist system and its underlying dogma, especially among intellectuals and students.[6] The Dengists' seeming ideological "agnosticism" only served to fan up this fire of discontent. The intellectual unrest obviously soon became alarming to the CCP's remaining "old guards," including Ye Jianying. Equally troubling to them were the growing instances of cadre abuse and corruption in the wake of Deng's economic liberalization, which allowed massive imports of Western ideas as well as technology and goods into China. The party's subsequent campaign against "spiritual pollution" was a natural product of the growing concern of these "old guards." The campaign, nevertheless, was short-lived, as Deng personally intervened to prevent it from being used to hamstring the Dengist reforms. However, the clamor by senior party leaders such as Peng Zhen and Chen Yun for restoring the respectability of Marxism did seem to have an effect.[7] In their view, "spiritual pollution" only in part resulted from imported corrupting influences. The failing grip of the Marxist ideology accounted even more for the loose morals and corruption of cadres and a general slackening of discipline in the country.

After much internal debate, the CCP decided that something had to be done to arrest the decline of ideological confidence. A consensus seems to have emerged regarding three interrelated tasks: reaffirming the legitimacy of Marxism-Leninism; reinterpreting Marxist tenets to fit China's new conditions; and beefing up Marxist education within the party and in schools, especially in colleges.[8] We shall discuss these separately in the following three sections.

Reaffirming the Legitimacy of Marxism-Leninism

Deng Xiaoping made a personal pitch for the importance of the basic Marxist teachings at a congress of CCP delegates in September 1985:

> As we have to acquire more and more new knowledge, to meet the challenge of the new times in our effort to build a socialism fit for China, it is all the more necessary that we grasp the significance of the basic Marxist tenets for our present circumstances. . . . Only in this way . . . will our cadres, especially those who are young and new on the job, be able to find their directions in the increasingly ever more complicated endeavors.[9]

Following Deng's exhortation, echoes of a "Study Marxism" movement were heard from many a proestablishment scholar, writing in the *People's Daily*, among others.[10] In mid-November, a special conference on ideological work was convened in Chengdu by the CCP's Propaganda Department, to discuss how Deng's call for better cadre understanding of Marxist teachings could be translated into reality.[11]

Earlier, on June 7, 1985, Peng Zhen had made a similar plea in a talk to the "responsible cadres" from the various organs of the National People's Congress. "We must persist in the Four Firsts; and must, more particularly, learn from the basic wisdom of Marxism-Leninism," he declared. He pointed out a lack of seriousness among the cadres, including even those at the "leadership" levels, in their attitude toward the strictures of Marxism-

Leninism. However, to learn Marxist theory, he said, was not to learn by rote, but to grasp its true essense, its major standpoints, and methods.[12]

In an article signed by "Commentator," *Hong Qi,* (the Red Flag), official theoretical journal of the CCP, gave renewed emphasis to the "Four Firsts." Formulated at the Third Plenum of the CCP's Eleventh Central Committee, in 1978, the "Four Firsts" refer to the paramountcy of four basics: "the socialist road, the people's democratic dictatorship, the CCP's leadership, and Marxism-Leninism and Mao's thought." Quoting Deng Xioping, the article pointed out the importance of ideological as well as policy "continuity," which could be assured only by adhering to the Four Firsts.[13] The same article noted that "Marxism is the core of Communism," adding: "Our long struggle is to achieve Communism. . . . Without Communist ideals and iron-clad discipline, we would not have been able to achieve our past victory, nor could we achieve socialism in the future."[14] The discourse regarding the legitimacy of Marxism seemed to focus on the following themes:

1. Marxist ideology is necessary to provide a guide for the nation, so that it will not lose its directions in the midst of the "Four Modernizations."
2. One should transcend the written words of Marx and Lenin, and distill the quintessence from them.
3. A yardstick for measuring what is quintessential in the Marxist ideology is whether it transcends the time and imparts purpose into China's current Four Modernizations.
4. Reemphasis on the Four Firsts, which include Marxism-Leninism, is not a return to the "left." It is a prerequisite for building socialism in China.

There seemed to be a conscious effort to appeal to one's reason or sense of duty rather than blind faith. For example, the question of "why China must follow the socialist road," and why not capitalism, was often raised as a starting point. The stock answer was that the peculiar Chinese conditions had proven in the past that neither capitalism nor the Three Principles of the People (*San Min Chu I*) of the Kuomintang could work as well as socialism in China. Furthermore, the revival of Marxism, it was said, must be coordinated with the current economic structural reform launched by the CCP in late 1984.[15] Commenting on the danger of bourgeois contamination, the *Red Flag* discussed why the "commodity exchange" mentality must not be allowed to "pervade the Party's political life." The kind of marketplace commodity exchange that Marx and Engels denounced in *The Communist Manifesto,* it noted, was too money oriented and too materialistic for the members of the Communist Party, who are dedicated to the welfare of the people, and for whom personal utility returns may be moot and immaterial.[16]

Updating Marxism

To reestablish the legitimacy of the Marxist ideology requires reinterpreting its contents to fit the present-day circumstances. The purposeful introduction of the market mechanism by the Dengists, in order to divert the erstwhile disaster caused by the ineptitude of the state planner, has no doubt created wide discrepancies between practice, on the one hand, and what Communist theories require, on the other. If practice is not to be altered to conform to theory, then theory must be made to justify practice. This seems to be exactly what is happening in the People's Republic.

Long before the party had found a comprehensive answer to the problem of squaring practice with theory (or vice versa?), there were discussions, for example, of whether the market mechanism brought into China's socialist economic structure was a capitulation to capitalism or merely a product of China's peculiar brand of socialism. To begin with, the Dengist program had created a "private ownership" problem. As more private entrepreneurship generated more private property and capital, the question became more formidable. Beginning with rural households, private enterprises spread to urban and industrial sectors. By 1985 a number of sizable private corporations owned by individual shareholders had appeared, such as the Minsheng Steamship Company in Wuhan and the Aiguo Construction Company in Shanghai. The total capital in private ownership in the entire country went up from 1 percent in 1979 to 8 percent in 1985.[17]

The earliest discussion of the question whether a sizable private ownership posed a problem for socialism was contained in an article by economist Dong Fureng, in January 1979.[18] A vigorous debate ensued, culminating in a conference held in Peking, on November 21, 1985, to address the very question.[19] There seemed to be an emergent consensus that revisions of classical Marxist theory would be necessary with respect to certain issues: First, appropriate changes should be made to allow more room for private ownership, as the productivity ratios between public and private sectors change. Second, there should be allowance for individual "toiler's ownership" on at least a limited scale. Third, private enterprises may be given utilization rights while ownership may continue to be held by the state or a collectivity.[20]

The most blunt, hence controversial, call for updating Marxist economics came in an article titled "Ten Major Changes in China's Study of Economics" in the *Beijing Review*.[21] In it, Ma Ding (pseudonym for Song Longxiang), a professor of philosophy at Nanjing University, openly deplored the lack of matter-of-fact economic research, as opposed to finding doctrinal justification for the state's economic policies in force. "In the past," he wrote, "Chinese economists only contented themselves with explaining, elaborating and justifying the economic policies in force and seldom thought deeply about them, criticized them, or analyzed them scientifically." Among other things, he noted important shifts, in recent economic research in China, toward (1) an acceptance of the once rejected Western economics, (2) studying the productivity question, and not just relations of production as before,

(3) doing more applied and quantitative research geared to the country's actual conditions, (4) more study of macroeconomic trends and long-range strategy, and (5) greater use of knowledge developed in other disciplines in economic analyses.[22]

The article, which had first been published in the *Worker's Daily*, on November 2, 1985, before it was carried in English translation in the *Beijing Review*, was given wide international circulation by the Japanese press, among others. *Yomiuri Shimbun* even suggested that Ma Ding had sounded the death knell of Marx's *Das Kapital*.[23] That conclusion may have been inaccurate, but there was a clear message in the Ma Ding article and, more important, in the fact that the official Peking press carried the article: that Marxism needed updating and, above all, that China had to borrow from the West. The second part of the message only made the author's true intent more transparent.

Although the Ma Ding article kicked off a controversy in China, it was not totally badly received by the Dengist establishment. Premier Zhao Ziyang reportedly commented at a meeting that any significant reform must first find theoretical breakthroughs and that those who offered pioneering ideas should not be rejected out of hand as either iconoclasts or reactionaries. Zhu Houze, the CCP's propaganda director, also reportedly said that there should be an open and congenial academic atmosphere in which new economic hypotheses could be formulated and tested.[24]

The debate actually had much larger implications. At issue ultimately was academic freedom untainted by Marxist dogma. Liu Zaifu, director of the Institute of Literary Studies, Chinese Academy of Social Studies (CASS), openly espoused literary pursuits outside the straightjacket of class struggle. He was, however, unceremoniously criticized by Chen Yong, of the General Secretariat of the CCP, for having negated the Marxist standpoint and dialectics.[25] Interestingly enough, Chen's views were not widely shared by others in the CCP hierarchy. Hu Qili, a member of the Politburo and also of the General Secretariat, spoke favorably of those who demonstrated courage in endeavoring to break through the existing confines of Marxist achievements and to avoid empirically proven dead ends. Only in this manner, he stressed, could there be the possibility of carrying Marxism and the task of socialism building to new heights.[26]

Hu Sheng, president of CASS, answering Chen Yong in an article in the *Red Flag*, defended the necessity of academic freedom. So long as scholars did not oppose the CCP's leadership and the socialist road, they should be allowed freely to pursue their research and publicize the results. While scholars, like the rest of the country, should follow the guidance of Marxist thought, they likewise enjoyed the freedom of doing scientific research or literary or artistic work, as guaranteed under the Constitution of the People's Republic, Hu pointed out.[27]

Obviously, updating Marxism was a delicate question and had to be handled with extreme finesse. The party could hardly be convincing in demanding respect for Marxism and yet suggesting that Marxism itself had feet of clay. The need for updating Marxist ideology was, therefore, presented in the most positive light possible, so as not to jeopardize its sacrosanct aura, which the party wanted to preserve. A number of arguments were put forth in the CCP's line of defense. In the first place, Marxism was described as a science that "never ceases to develop forward." If Marxism was not a dead science, then it was only logical that it would grow in response to changed circumstances. Second, Marxism was described as the quintessence of the total wealth of knowledge created by humankind. Since it was inseparable from the totality of human activities, the continuing growth of Marxism must not be in isolation from changes in the real world. Third, if Marxism was to continue to be relevant in the midst of external changes, it was important that it impart a correct weltanschauung, or world view, that transcends time and space. As such, Marxist education was inseparable from moral education, which, according to the CCP's view, was indispensable to the Chinese nation. The ultimate defense for updating (i.e., revising) Marxism, therefore, was not that it was obsolete, so much as that its tenets had to respond to the changing times.[28]

At times, the Dengist leadership could be less circumspect than that. Hu Qili, in a May Day address this year, even disclaimed the "universal applicability" or immutability of Marxism and suggested that outdated parts of Marxism must be purged and brought up to date. Without the updating of ideology, he emphasized, China's modernization effort would be indefinitely held back.[29] The last statement was typical of the more recent "establishment" discourse linking success of the Dengist reforms to that of the ideological updating. The *People's Daily*, on March 14, 1986, for example, billed China's current economic reforms as indications of new "breakthroughs" in Marxist ideology.

Augmenting Marxist Education in China

Side by side with reinterpreting Marxism was the effort to strengthen the study of Marxism. In fact, the CCP's call for renewed studies of Marxism went back to the Third Plenum of the Eleventh Central Committee in 1978. What made the new clarion call of 1984–1985 stand out over previous ones was the conscious effort to update Marxism, to bring it more in touch with present-day conditions, as discussed previously. The updating was meant to generate a more convincing justification for the renewed emphasis on the study of Marxism. More specifically, the purposes of studying Marxism were described as follows: (1) to help resolve new problems; (2) to better join theory and practice together, using the former to guide the latter; and (3) to further advance Marxism as a body of living scientific theory.[30]

On October 15, 1984, the CCP issued "Directives Regarding the Strengthening and Reform of the Curriculum in Marxist-Leninist Theories in Institutions of Higher Learning." A specific goal of the new drive, according to the document, was to "resolutely correct any and all erroneous tendencies of belittling the importance of teaching Marxist-Leninist theories."[31]

The CCP Central Commitee, in September 1985, issued another document, "Notice Regarding Reforming the Moral Education and Political Teachings in Schools."[32] Although its specific relationship with the 1984 document ("Directives") is unclear, the "Notice" seems to put greater emphasis on "reform" (as distinct from "strengthening") on a broad scale. Inclusion of Marxist-Leninist studies in the Chinese college curriculum has a long history, going back to 1953. The current mandate for a broad reform of this curriculum seems unparalleled. From the evidence available thus far, "reform" at the operational level entails rewriting the college level textbooks on Marxism-Leninism. This process seems to require an across-the-board review and revision, as is divulged in a series of articles discussing the efforts being made.[33] Most of the points regarding how Marxism should be reinterpreted and updated, as noted in the previous section, were mentioned for consideration in these articles on revisions. The "reform" textbooks, it appears, will most probably give Marxism a very new look.

Under discussion are three basic parts to be included in the final package: the basic theories of Marxism and their social historical origins; the linkages between Marxist theories and the Chinese Communist revolution, and the present tasks of building a Chinese socialism; and the relevance of other philosophies and social sciences.[34] The intended end result of this revision will be that Marxism will be taught as a "living" science (i.e., responding to the demands of changing times). The textbook reform was justified on the ground that students armed with an updated Marxist knowledge would be better able to meet the challenge of building a socialism fit for China and generating an advanced socialist spiritual civilization.[35]

If one pieces together the triple effort of reaffirming the authority of Marxism, updating its contents, and renewing its inculcation through rewritten textbooks, an ultimate political motive seems to become clear. If Marxism is updated to accommodate and sanctify the major Dengist policy reforms, then making students embrace the updated Marxist teachings will have the effect of creating greater acceptance of the reforms. It will ensure their lasting legitimacy.

Conclusion

To recapitulate, there was a logic to the twists and turns over the official status and function of Marxism in post-Mao China. The de-Maoization campaign, as we have seen, had a natural tendency of downgrading the importance of ideology, which affected the sanctity of Marxism itself. Insinuations that Maoism, at least much of it, was out of date somehow cast doubts on the current validity of much of Marxism, too. However, the CCP, under Deng or any other Communist leader, could not for long afford to see the slide of Marxism continue unchecked. There was, therefore, a newly felt need to reestablish the legitimacy of Marxism from late 1984 on. However, it was not any random version of Marxism that would be so honored, but rather one that would best explain and justify current policy.

Hence, Marxism must be reinterpreted and updated, so that it would best lend theoretical support to the building of a Dengist brand of socialism. Of course, inculcating the new Marxist testament in the young would succeed only after two prior steps had been taken, namely, reaffirming Marxism's legitimacy and redefining its textbook meaning.

If this analysis is valid, one has reason to believe that the latest exaltation of the Marxist gospel according to St. Deng is likely to last. For, although its exact shape is yet to be defined, the revised Marxist bible will only lend sanctity to the Dengist reforms. The debate over Marxism in China, from now on, is not whether it should have an exalted place and whether it should be taught and respected. Rather, the right question to ask is, *Which* edition of Marxism, as interpreted and taught by *whom*, is going to perform the guiding and legitimizing function it is supposed to perform?

If the December 7, 1984, editorial in the *People's Daily* lamenting the obsolescence of Marxism was the lowest point in its status in China, that phase is probably over, at least for now. The reason is that the Dengists seem to have discovered the danger of a premature death of Marxism. More important, they now realize that an updated Marxism could be pressed into the service of supporting their own political agenda. The inherent political motive, therefore, holds the key to all the recent shifts regarding the regained primacy of the Marxist ideology and why its redefined content must once again be drilled into the consciousness of the young Chinese. Luckily for Marxism, it has received a new lease on life in Dengist China. Also luckily for the Dengists, they have, after faltering initially, found an ingenious way of enshrining their program in ideological legitimacy.

Notes

1. Hong Qi, no. 6 (1986).

2. I dealt with this point in my paper "Ideology, Maoism, and Developmental Paradigm in Dengist China," delivered at the 14th Sino-American Conference on Mainland China, June 10–13, 1985, Ohio State University, Columbus, Ohio.

3. First exposition of this thesis was in a special unsigned commentary "Practice Is Sole Test of Truth," in *Quangming Ribao*, May 1, 1978. Deng Xiaoping personally elaborated on the thesis in an address to the "People's Liberation Army Political Work Conference." See *Renmin Ribao*, June 3, 1978.

4. Hu's speech on the 60th anniversary of the founding of the CCP, in *Renmin Ribao*, July 1, 1981.

5. *Renmin Ribao*, editorial, December 7, 1984.

6. See, for example, "Why Are Some Reading Materials Not Welcomed," *Dushu Zazhi*, September 1980, p. 2.

7. See, for example, Peng Zhen, "We Must Laboriously Study the Basic Marxist Theories," *Hong Qi*, no. 16 (1985), pp. 3–5.

8. *Renmin Ribao*, October 16, 1984.

9. "Full Text of Deng Xiaoping's Talk at the Conference of Party Delegates," Hong Kong *Da Gong Bao*, September 24, 1985, p. 2.

10. See, for example, writings by Yu Guangyuan, in *Renmin Ribao*, October 18, 1985, p. 5; Su Shaozhi, in *Renmin Ribao*, October 21, 1985, p. 5; also discussion in

Chen Chang-chin, "The Chinese Communist 'Study Marxism' Movement," *China Mainland Studies* (Taipei), vol. 28, no. 7 (January 1986), p. 32.

11. *Renmin Ribao*, November 26, 1985, p. 1.

12. Peng, "We Must Laboriously Study."

13. "The 'Four Firsts' are the Basis for All Policies," *Hong Qi*, no. 22 (1985), pp. 8–12.

14. Ibid.

15. "What We Have Learned from 'Basic Problems of Building Chinese Socialism,'" *Hong Qi*, no. 1 (1986), p. 45.

16. "Why the Commodity Exchange Principle Must Not Pervade the Party's Political Life," *Hong Qi*, no. 16 (1985), pp. 44–45.

17. Figures were provided by the PRC consulate general in New York in response to my inquiry.

18. "The Form That Our Country's Ownership System Should Take," *Jingji Yanjiu*, January 1979.

19. *Renmin Ribao*, November 11, 1985.

20. Ibid.

21. *Beijing Review*, no. 49 (December 9, 1985), pp. 17–20.

22. Ibid.

23. *Beimei Ribao* (New York), May 1, 1986, p. 2.

24. Ibid.

25. Chen Yung, "The Methodology Question in Literature and Arts," *Hong Qi*, no. 8 (1986).

26. Hu Qili's May Day address in Peking, *Beimei Ribao* (New York), May 1, 1986, p. 2.

27. *Hong Qi*, no. 9 (1986), as reported in *Beimei Ribao* (New York), May 2, 1986, p. 2.

28. "Several Questions Regarding Reforming the Curriculum in Basic Marxist Theories," *Hong Qi*, no. 23 (1985), pp. 8–13.

29. *Huaqiao Ribao* (New York), May 6, 1986, p. 2.

30. See discussions cited in note 10.

31. *Renmin Ribao*, October 16, 1984.

32. *Renmin Ribao*, September 13, 1985.

33. See the series of articles in *Hong Qi*, beginning with issue no. 18, in 1985.

34. CCP Committee at Peking University, "The Preliminary Draft Plan for Reforming the Curriculum in Marxist Theories," *Hong Qi*, no. 21 (1985), pp. 42–44.

35. See, for example, Lu Zhichao, "Reform and Strengthen the Marxist Theoretical Education in Institutions of Higher Learning," *Hong Qi*, no. 18 (1985), p. 44.

5

Spiritual Crisis in Contemporary China: Some Preliminary Explorations

Peter R. Moody, Jr.

On September 18, 1985, the anniversary of the Manchurian incident, Peking students held an unauthorized rally directed against Japan. There was another rally in November. These followed a summer of low-key but unrelenting official propaganda against Japan on the occasion of the fortieth year of that country's defeat in war, and the Chinese leadership, like much of the rest of the world, had been vocal in its concern about trade imbalances with Japan. The students denounced Japanese militarism and the possibility of Japanese economic domination. They also demanded freedom and democracy and attacked official corruption, following a well-worn path, leading back at least to the May Fourth movement of 1919 through the Tiao-yü T'ai movement on Taiwan in 1971 and 1972. Baiting the Japanese also serves as a way of expressing demands against the Chinese authorities.

In the context of the conventional wisdom of 1985, however, the rallies were a little anomalous. Concern for freedom and democracy has been a staple of both the democracy movement and the more radical reaches of the reform movement. Vocal concern about corruption, however, in the 1980s was part of the code of those uneasy about reform. The usual assumption has been that young people, especially students, tend to be enthusiastic about the idea of reform, if perhaps skeptical concerning whether reform is really what is going on. Part of the appeal of reform has been the policy of "opening to the outside," allowing into the country foreign goods and foreign ideas. In 1983 the most obvious hostility to this opening came from persons opposed to any kind of liberalization, from cadres worried about spiritual pollution. The college "generation of the '80s" is supposed to be passive and materialistic, not given to making public political appeals in the fashion of their big brothers and sisters at the end of the 1970s or, if it comes to that, in the fashion of the Red Guards. In what is possibly an ominous piece of symbolism, the starting point for one of the 1985 rallies was apparently the large statue of Mao Tse-tung in front of the Peking University library.[1]

The 1985 rallies may be evidence that economic and political liberalization are becoming disassociated from each other and ambiguous in their significance as the unintended moral, social, cultural—"spiritual"—consequences of reform make themselves felt. The main impetus for economic reform has no doubt been a desire for efficiency and efficacy (with greater economic efficiency and efficacy leading to increased stability and legitimacy for the regime). The reformers have believed that greater efficiency requires both some decentralization of the economy and allowance for more spontaneity in economic activity. Some of the more radical among them have argued that it requires political democracy, however ambiguously conceived. In any event, scope for economic spontaneity somehow seems related to the possibility of greater general spontaneity in society. This freedom may for some imply political freedom, or it may merely be the freedom to do what you want to do: to indulge at least your more harmless pleasures; to enjoy what you enjoy even if parents, leaders, or society are unable to understand or appreciate it; to feel what you actually feel and not simply what authority figures tell you you are supposed to feel.

Some students interviewed a party secretary of a textile firm in Wuhsi. The secretary is firm in his "faith" in communism: "If communism is considered as a movement, we are in the process of bringing it about. Considered as a social form, I won't see it and neither will you. But she is an objective truth for whom we all must fight." On modish tastes and fads, however, he has a relaxed attitude. He sees no point in shutting down ballrooms just because bad people sometimes hang out in them.

> 'Evil enters by the mouth.' Does this mean we should stop eating? . . . Young
> people have the right to decide for themselves how they want to live. Everyone
> has his own preferences about what kind of clothes or hat to wear. You can't
> make rules that hair can only be so long, or trousers only so wide, or shoe
> heels only so high. As long as there is no great violence to taste or custom
> (*chih yu pu shang feng pai su*) there should be no arbitrary interference. . . .
> Engels says that man has three demands: existence, pleasure, development.

Life needs to have some beauty. This in no way implies a "bourgeois lifestyle," since that means egotism and worship of money, not the pursuit of beauty.[2]

The point of the interview is not merely to feature the opinions of a particular functionary but to present him as a model; and the issue is not really as simple as he puts it—*ko yu so hao*, to each his own. Hair and clothing styles, in China as in the United States, may be just that, styles; but they may also be ways of making a statement, of identifying for or against a particular mentality (and they may be deliberately offensive to conventional taste, not necessarily all that "beautiful"). Until recently there had been regimentation of personal taste and style in China, partly for what the authorities thought to be economic reasons, but partly also as a way for the authorities to make a political point. An obvious inference from the interview is that there continues to be resistance to individual diversity in taste.

Diversity of style (*to-yang-hua*) is a symbolic manifestation of a more general cultural diversity encouraged by reform. The leadership, whether of the reformist or other persuasion, has detected in elements of this diversity indications of a spiritual malaise, a crisis of faith. Economic, administrative, political, social, and cultural reform is seen to create problems of public morals and public morale.

Anywhere, but especially in a society like China's, a "spiritual crisis" will raise questions of political legitimacy. Traditional Chinese culture was highly moralistic, and in the contemporary period morality in China has been highly politicized. The moralistic orientation of the culture is perhaps still quite strong, but much of the population may no longer be prepared to accept docilely officialdom's definition of the moral. Since 1949, China has been the world of the cadres, those who *kao cheng-chih* (do politics). Part of the logic of reform is to increase the relative status of intellectuals[3] or, among the youngest cohorts, to obliterate the distinction between cadres and intellectuals. The reforms also remove peasants and, to a lesser degree, workers from the direct control of cadres, especially cadres in the party organization. Another reason for the publication of the interview with the factory secretary is to help work out just what, after having lost so many of their old functions, the new role of basic-level party organizations should be. The Wuhsi secretary hopes to exercise his duties with discretion and magnanimity, but a large part of his job seems to be to go around censoring public morals.

In the most narrow sense the spiritual crisis generated by reform becomes a political issue because politicians choose to make an issue of it. The spiritual crisis also serves a political function, if not for the "system" as a whole then for some people in it. It can be made an issue of only because there is objective basis to the uneasiness. But the political use of the spiritual crisis helps perpetuate and intensify it and may serve ultimately to bring into question the legitimacy of reform itself: "The more it reforms, the worse it gets."

Political Functions of the Spiritual Crisis

The Chinese leadership, to counter what it perceives as pernicious side effects of reform, has demanded that people cultivate culture (that is, education), morals, ideals, and discipline. In the spring of 1985, Teng Hsiao-p'ing reiterated this theme, putting special emphasis on ideals and discipline. He demanded faith in Marxism and communism, using language somewhat reminiscent of the Gang of Four and other radical Maoists. We must, he said, have *socialist* modernization, not just any kind of modernization. (The Gang of Four had used this kind of language, and at one time it was held to mean that the Gang wanted no modernization at all.) The "old" reform position was that there is no socialism apart from modernization. Teng also hinted at another Maoist theme: "Some people are now wondering whether China might become capitalist. There is a slight bit of reason for that worry."[4] Much of 1985 was marked by exhortations to develop a "spiritual civilization" to match a modernized material civilization.

The mainstream of traditional Chinese culture made morality the standard for judging political action, and much of traditional morality probably continues to inform the ordinary person's notions of right and wrong, proper and improper. Its rhetoric and even its spirit influenced Chinese communist words and action.[5] Radical Maoism, violently critical of the tradition, remained moralistic in style—even though this style stood in contradiction to its content—and this moralistic style may show the influence of the tradition on Maoism. But any moral system, conventional or otherwise, is not simply a random, arbitrary list of rules, recommendations, and prohibitions. It is grounded in a vision of truth, a vision which, in a stable society, gains plausibility from its function in the social system. The older Chinese system changed, and its vision of truth is alien to Marxism and, if it comes to that, modernism generally. Elements of the traditional morality certainly remain, but those who rule the society no longer officially acknowledge or support the rational basis for those elements.

Confucianism is grounded ultimately in the Way of Heaven. Proximately, morals derive from human nature: Because we are the kind of beings we are, correct, proper, and right behavior is natural to us. Resonances of this traditional notion may explain partly why from pre-Liberation times into the 1980s appeals to humanism have been so popular among modernist critics of certain party practices, and why segments of the party elite have seen these appeals as so threatening.[6]

Marxism itself can be interpreted as a humanistic philosophy, although to do so may do violence to Marx's more mature and considered opinions. This interpretation has not been favored in the official orthodox line of Marxism-Leninism. In this line, strictly speaking, there is no separate, autonomous category of the moral, since morality ultimately reduces to economic interest. Morality is part of the superstructure, contingent upon the stage of historical development and class position. It cannot be based on human nature because there is no unchanging human essence apart from the position of people in the relations of production. Talk of humanity in the abstract or of any absolute and unchanging moral order is a form of false consciousness whose function is to persuade both exploiters and the exploited that the interests of the exploiters do in fact correspond to objective value.

In the Mao period, especially during the Cultural Revolution and afterward, there was a tendency strongly to assert this relativism, coupled with an equally strong tendency to demand conformity to the wishes and ideas of the leadership on moral grounds. Relativism was directed not merely against traditional and liberal ("feudal" and "bouegeois") values, but against classical Marxist-Leninist orthodoxy. Liu Shao-ch'i's exposition of the platitudes of democratic centralism (the minority must obey the majority and so forth) was reviled as "slavishness," a demand for absolute and unprincipled obedience even to erroneous policies and unworthy leaders. Liu was attacked for wanting the country's educated youth to regard themselves as docile tools of the party and people.

Liu was also wrong in his attempt to reconcile duty with desire, for hinting that learning to conform to party discipline could itself be a source of satisfaction. Liu urged that party members train themselves to think as proletarians; the interests of the proletariat correspond to the long-term interests of the human race; and the party as an institution has no interest apart from that of the proletariat, which is the liberation of mankind.[7] Subordination to party discipline becomes a means of both personal and moral fulfillment. For Mao and his spokesmen from about the mid-1960s this party discipline was a way of nullifying the continuing reality of class struggle. For Liu, the party or its members could be corrupted from the outside by influences from the old society. Mao, like some east European dissidents, turned the Marxian critique of ideology against party rule: Liu's theory becomes a moralization, if not of some new class manifested in the party, at least for bad men who occupy positions in the state and party.

Maoist antinomianism was combined with moralistic demands for conformity. Thought and attitudes were supposed to be proletarian, with proletarian defined in terms of thought and attitude rather than by objective social category. If it comes to that, proletarian was attitudinal for Liu Shaoch'i was well; but in radical Maoism there was no thought of universalizing the morality of the proletariat beyond the proletariat, even if the proletariat was defined in terms of this morality.

Radical Maoism urged that human will, spirit, could define and shape social and even physical reality. The mentality had its fullest flowering in the Great Leap Forward (for in this respect the Cultural Revolution was more talk than action), although its roots in Mao's thinking and in Chinese communism generally go farther back.[8] While this might seem an idealism directly contrary to Marxism, as a dialectical system Marxism is probably flexible enough to accommodate it. In the Maoism of the Leap and the Cultural Revolution, most especially in the era of Lin Piao, there was copious talk of spirit—of the spiritual atomic bomb, or of how spirit can transform itself into material force. The Cultural Revolution, as its name implies, was an effort to transform the superstructure by direct action into a proletarian one after a change in the bases of production had failed to do the job. In the post–Cultural Revolution period the bandying about of spiritual this or that is likely to have unhappy connotations.

Confucian moralism is not China's only political tradition. Another is amoral Legalism, which argues that stable and effective rule requires positive law coldly enacted and mechanically enforced. Considerations of justice are at best irrelevant, at worst pernicious, a cover for those who would achieve their own aims in the face of the law and thus throw society into chaos. In the post-Lin period the Maoists, by then mainly the Gang of Four, explicitly grafted Legalism onto their radical moralism, with the effect of dramatically denying the possibility of any moral community between persons on different sides of a power struggle. The radicals continued to arrogate righteousness to themselves, but pictured politics as a raw struggle for power and control.

The criticism of Lin Piao and Confucius may have had no particular social base, but it did have social consequences. For some came a new appreciation of Confucius, particularly among the young, for whom he had been little more than a name. The detailings of his crimes and failings made him look good, especially compared to what the alternatives to him seemed to be. Some who went through the movement in primary school remember it with a perverse nostalgia, since they were then allowed to attack their teachers: By the early 1970s there was still lip service to the antiauthoritarian attitudes of the Cultural Revolution, but overt defiance of authority was not tolerated; nor has it been, except sporadically, since. But to very young children the teachers seemed to be persons with genuine authority, and the organized attacks on the teachers something liberating and daring. A further consequence, this of the entire "ten bad years," was a reinforcement of the earlier sense of demoralization—a feeling that the current constitution of state and society had been drained of moral content. It is interesting that the anti-Confucian slogans repeat those of the May Fourth era. As a *political* order the Confucian system was dead by, say, 1915, and it was certainly no healthier in 1975. But perhaps it had not been replaced by anything more plausible or compelling. Mao's last decade left a generation that *k'an-t'ou-le*, for whom Leninist, radical, and traditional morality were equally empty, who saw through everything and believed in nothing.

The reformers continue self-servingly to blame what they see as persisting demoralization on the Cultural Revolution and the Gang of Four. Public opinion may find these claims plausible on the whole; but the reforms have not yet filled the vacuum in public morals or morale. The anti-Maoist line has its own politicized morality—at first almost an antimorality. It made both intellectual and tactical sense for Hua Kuo-feng and later the more radical reformers under Teng Hsiao-p'ing to return to a more deterministic Marxism opposed to Maoist voluntarism. The famed Maoist revolutionary ideals seemed to be little more than the empty talk of ambitious, hypocritical scoundrels serving to rationalize a political system both ineffective and tyrannical and leading to artificial, unnecessary psychological and social tensions and an artifically low standard of living. "Modernization" became a slogan not only for developing the economy but also for restoring legitimacy to the system. But this tactic raises its own problems of legitimacy.

Hua Kuo-feng deradicalized Maoism but continued to assert that the regime was bound by "whatever" Mao had said or done. Teng Hsiao-p'ing had to discredit this line, if only because one of Mao's decisions was that Hua rather than Teng should be in charge. Teng used the slogan (apparently coined by Stalin, as it happens, although more recently articulated by the Nanking university philosophy professor Hu Fu-ming) that practice is the criterion of truth. The words of Mao (or Marx or Lenin) are, of course, true, but they are not the standard or criterion of truth. They are known to be true only because they have been tested by practice. Strictly speaking there is nothing here that is not in Marx, Lenin, or Mao. In the context of place and time, however, the practice slogan meant a redefinition of ideological orthodoxy and the function of ideology.

The practice mentality superficially fits well into orthodox Marxism. Communism comes from the development of the forces of production. Existence determines consciousness, and morality is ultimately contingent upon the material base. Since communism is the goal of human development, morality is whatever contributes to economic progress, and economic progress contributes to morality.[9] Implicit in the practice slogan is a commitment to some kind of pragmatism, and like all pragmatism it is weak on the ends to be served. Practice may be the criterion of truth, but what is the criterion of practice or, as another version of the slogan helps make more clear, *correct* practice?

Some of the more fashionable schools of Western Marxism have apparently concluded that for human liberation the undiluted development of productive forces is not enough, that there needs to be as well some kind of ethical guidance. In a way, this is something every practical Marxist politician has always known—this is the major function of the party. Some reformers took the pragmatic, "orthodox" line to an extreme: Morality cannot transcend the stage of social development, so in the present era it is fatuous to talk of communist morality; any talk of communist ideals is and can be nothing but Maoist cant.[10] This approach was probably less an appeal for amorality than a demand that the scope of party power be reduced. This kind of talk also allowed those opposed to reform to assert that the new policy meant that people should think of nothing but money.[11]

The Teng tendency in the early period also made use of the concept of democracy, partly because of that concept's intrinsic appeal to twentieth-century Chinese intellectuals, partly to distinguish itself from the Hua tendency's emphasis on order and discipline to counter Maoist antinomianism. In this use the concept was close to that of formal or "bourgeois" democracy rather than to the Leninist usage, although both the reformers and the democracy movement radicals were vague on how democracy should be expressed in institutions. In its handling of the concept of democracy the reform tendency shows some surprising affinities with Maoist radicalism. For Wei Ching-shen, at one extreme of the democracy movement, the value of democracy is that it prevents the moralization of any necessarily transitory order. Wei also articulated a Darwinian-Maoist theory of rights, denying on the one hand any absolute, unchanging standard of human rights but on the other hand asserting that human rights are discovered and unfold through unending (but controlled) political struggle.[12] This thinking captures an interesting antinomianism in the concept of democracy itself, for while we sometimes speak of democratic values, there is a sense in which democracy has no values; rather, it is a set of procedures for assuring that the political regime reflect more or less whatever values may be current in society. Formal democracy has functioned best where there was a strong social order. But in a fragmented society democracy, which reflects rather than creates or asserts values, may only reinforce that fragmentation. Democracy can then serve as a critique of the status quo, but in itself will suggest nothing to replace it with.

Teng at first supported the democracy movement, at least insofar as it involved a certain amount of freedom of speech: "If we let people speak out, the sky won't fall."[13] This sentence has a somewhat Maoist ring to it. During 1979, Teng may also have flirted with the Maoist technique of using democracy as an instrument of class struggle. At any rate, during that year it was his rival, Hua Kuo-feng, who seemed to have had enough of turmoil and struggle. He denounced the democracy movement and also began to talk the way the Maoists had claimed Liu Shao-ch'i did: Class struggle continues, he said, but it is no longer the major problem; and there are no more antagonistic classes in China.[14] On the other hand, Hong Kong writers who in those days seem to have been used to float the more outrageous or advanced opinions of the Peking reformers spoke of the need to use law and democracy to control and eliminate a bureaucratic class, sentiments indirectly echoed in the mainland media.[15]

The Maoists had argued that although China had put the means of production under public ownership, the basic culture of the country had not become socialist or proletarian and the country was, therefore, in danger of capitalist restoration. The early reformist line gave this a different twist. The reformers asserted that China's main trouble was that it had never been properly capitalist and, therefore, had only a weak foundation for socialism. Chinese socialism was distorted by feudal influences from (pick any combination) the strength and longevity of the despotic state, the country's retarded development as a semicolony, or the influence of peasants and persons from peasant backgrounds in the communist movement. By mid-1979 the reformers had two sets of opponents: the "whateverists" still, but increasingly former allies as well, those the Hong Kong commentators sometimes called the restorationists—the old-line economic managers and planners who wanted to "restore" the centralized, Soviet-style economy of the pre–Great Leap 1950s. The reformers held both tendencies to be guilty of leftist errors and found the source of this leftism in the feudal mentality. The whateverists were inclined to fanaticism, the cult of the individual, and to the egalitarian fantasies of traditional peasant rebels; the restorationists were feudal bureaucrats aspiring, like the claws and teeth of the despotic state, to political control of the economy and all facets of life.

If Maoist socialism is really feudalism, the way is open for the introduction of aspects of bourgeois liberalism—for bourgeois institutions, while not reaching the degree of perfection of socialist ones, represent an advance over feudalism and, in some versions of the orthodox line, are historically necessary conditions for socialism. Teng Hsiao-p'ing very early, either reluctantly or with relief, backed away from the democracy movement, but liberalizing reform continued. In September 1979, the party admitted to "serious mistakes in line" in its policies since 1957.[16] This is perhaps the first time a Leninist party has ever admitted that its line itself had been in error (and it is not something the Chinese party has drawn a great deal of attention to since). In 1980[17] there was a flowering of radical reformist opinion in the official press. Direct democracy was no longer in fashion, but a general theme was the need for democratic controls over political power—including, perhaps, some form of checks and balances and separation of powers.[18] Leninism itself was revised: The idea that science, the economy, and culture "can manifest their social existence only by subordination to a certain administrative department" turns out to have nothing to do with Leninist socialism: "This is a post-Lenin mutation."[19]

Whatever the attachment to democracy in the abstract, its advocacy by the leadership was also a political weapon—one given to backfiring and used as long as there was not a safer and more reliable one at hand. The democracy movement had been used against the whateverists, but its immediate consequence was to energize them: They were able convincingly to accuse the reformers of encouraging anarchy, of throwing China into chaos. This claim found resonance not only among cadres but even, despite the general unpopularity of the whateverist position, in society at large, which had grown wary of just what might be behind officially sanctioned questionings of authority. The democracy movement was suppressed and Teng Hsiao-p'ing announced his four principles limiting freedom of speech (discourse must remain within the bounds of the dictatorship of the proletariat, the socialist road, party leadership, and Marxism-Leninism, Mao's thought). Public dissent since that time has been presented by the officialdom as a revival of Cultural Revolution Maoism, of Red Guard anarchy.

The *keng-shen* reforms were directed primarily against the restorationists; and they were moribund before the year *keng-shen* was over. Economic difficulties may have encouraged a change from emphasis on reform to readjustment (a change which, since 1980, has occurred with cyclical regularity). A political effect of the earlier radical reform program would have been to nail home the repudiation of Maoism; but this purpose was perhaps accomplished with less trouble and disruption by the trial of the remnants of the Lin Piao clique and the Gang of Four. The year 1981 saw attacks on unorthodoxy, most prominently on the military writer Pai Hua for his alleged lack of patriotism. In 1982 there was a return to the theme of reform, but with the stress on efficiency rather than democracy. Another major 1982 theme was the elimination of "economic crime," corruption. This had been a 1980 theme as well. Then it referred to the activities of bureaucrats who, by their control of the economy, were able to convert political power to private advantage: one more pathology of an overly bureaucratized, overly politicized system.[20] In 1982 corruption became the vice of those too quick and clever in taking advantage of the liberalizing economic reforms.[21]

Military hostility contributed to the collapse of the drive for reform in 1980. Agricultural reforms may have damaged military morale because the parents of soldiers were no longer being subsidized as much as they once had been, and potential recruits could now, for a change, live as well by staying on the farm as they could by joining the army. The reforms could also be made out to be undermining patriotism. The reform ideology encouraged a jaundiced attitude toward the heritage since 1949 and toward what passed for socialism in that period. All the bad-mouthing of feudalism might leave the impression (so rampant on Taiwan in the late 1960s and early 1970s) that China's history was unrelieved darkness with all progress and light coming from Europe and the United States. Late-era Maoists stressed their radical break with the traditional past; but conservative apologists for Mao in 1981 presented socialist China as the only latest and most glorious unfolding of a long and glorious national history.[22]

Conservatives (or leftists—the terms had become synonymous in official Chinese discourse) could blame the reformers for an alleged crisis of faith in society, and some of the more outspoken reformers were happy to take the blame: The crisis was a healthy reaction to the distortions of Marxism prevalent since the "founding of the state" (a reform code phrase, to be juxtaposed against the restorationist—and still official—notion that the trouble really started in 1957). It proves that the official understanding of Marxism has not kept up with the changes in the world. It shows the liberation of the thought of the Chinese people, their perception of the irrelevance of the old theory to the new realities.[23] The reformers went both too far and not far enough: too far to carry along the timid and conservative, not far enough to satisfy those to whom the reformist critique of the status quo made the most sense. A radical implementation of radical reform might have ameliorated the problem of legitimacy. Instead the reformers, led by Teng Hsiao-p'ing, retreated into lukewarm orthodoxy, mumbling about socialist spiritual civilization and the need for better indoctrination.[24]

The reformers lacked the power to bring about a radical reorientation, but they also lacked the will seriously to try. In the post-Mao period there has been little absolute opposition to change, but equally little inclination to push the reforms to their conclusions, and as reform has progressed and the major reformers have become more secure in their positions, the coalition pushing reform has divided. At the famous Third Plenum, while the democracy movement howled in the streets, the whateverists pronounced a *ch'eng-yü* (set phrase)—*wu hu luan hua*. The literal meaning of the phrase (from the Five Dynasties period) is that five barbarian tribes throw China into chaos. It can also mean that five people named Hu bring chaos to China (or cause trouble for Hua Kuo-feng). The Hus refer to a group of advisers around Teng Hsiao-p'ing. Since the phrase is proverbial the *five* need not be taken too literally. Four of the Hus include: Hu Yao-pang, a long-time client of Teng's, formerly head of the Youth League, in the 1980s secretary general of the party's Central Committee; Hu Ch'iao-mu, an old propagandist, once secretary to Mao Tse-tung; Hu Ch'i-li, a client of Hu Yao-pang's, an apparatchik with something of a liberal reputation; and Hu Chi-wei, in the early 1980s editor of *Jen-min Jih-pao* (the People's Daily), the official party paper. (Beyond these there are at least a half-dozen other Hus to choose from.) By 1986, Hu Yao-pang was, nominally at least, at the top of the heap; a somewhat compromised Hu Ch'i-li was climbing up there; Chi-wei had been purged for being too liberal, too tolerant of spiritual pollution; Ch'iao-mu had turned conservative.

The newly formed Chinese Academy of Social Sciences served in the late 1970s as a kind of reform general staff; but high officials of that organization have a tendency to develop second thoughts about reform. The best known of these are Hu Ch'ao-mu and Teng Li-ch'ün, although it is not obvious how much of a reformer Teng Li-ch'ün ever really was. He had once been Liu Shao-ch'i's secretary and had been purged with Liu. In 1975 he had refused to sell out Teng Hsiao-p'ing when Hsiao-p'ing was under attack from the Gang of Four. After Liu Shao-ch'i's rehabilitation Li-ch'ün wrote an appreciation of him tacitly critical of the democracy movement activists: Liu was selflessly dedicated to the party and people and always submitted to discipline; he never went around bellyaching about his rights.[25] In the late 1970s Hu Ch'iao-mu was in the vanguard of reform, asserting, for example, that even under socialism there are objective economic laws which planners ignore at their peril[26]—which may sound like no big deal, but in the context of the times it was a vigorous challenge to Maoist voluntarist orthodoxy. By 1981 or so reform had outpaced him. That year he argued for ideological orthodoxy and included a small self-criticism of his earlier toleration for the unorthodox.[27]

A more complicated case is that of Ch'en Yun. Unlike most of the other reformers, Ch'en has not been anything like a client of Teng Hsiao-p'ing's. Around the mid-1980s he was sometimes considered part of the restoration group, and has been built up by those uneasy with reform into a kind of anti-Teng. Aside from Teng Hsiao-p'ing he is the only living leader in the post-Mao period to see the publication of his selected works. He is not, however, a standard restorationist, and while he is sometimes in alliance with the restorationists, his economic policy is not quite theirs. He once may have been politically more open than Teng has ever thought of being. According to a Taiwan report he argued that the Communists were in some ways just one more ruling regime like those of the emperor and the Kuomintang and that they have to earn their ruling position. If the party should be overthrown that would not be the end of China.[28] The general direction of economic reform follows proposals Ch'en had unsuccessfully urged in the 1950s.[29] When his proposals, such as giving firms greater autonomy and making greater use of the market to allocate resources, were put into effect, however, Ch'en seems to have developed misgivings about them, worrying particularly about their effect on price stability.[30]

There are many grounds for opposing particular reforms, both technical and ideological. The logic of reform implies a radical transformation of the system, and this implication makes advocates vulnerable to criticism from colleagues and divided in their own hearts and minds. Delayed or halfhearted reform flirts with becoming self-delegitimizing and may spread confusion into society. One reason for proposing reform is to woo segments of society unhappy with the way things are. Dashed expectations of change rarely enhance satisfaction. Democratic agitation comes to be associated with Maoism (one conservative official even announced that from their jail cells the Gang of Four were calling for a two-party system[31]). For some this association may discredit democratic agitation. For others it may enhance the prestige of Maoism. One may wonder whether the 1985 rallies show an undercurrent of nostalgia for the 1960s similar to that which can be faintly detected on U.S. campuses. At the same time, rightly or wrongly, educated young Chinese found the depiction of Maoist socialism as the continuation of feudal despotism enormously persuasive, and the retreat from that line only enhances its plausibility.

In late 1982, Teng purged the propaganda system of the military for its opposition to his policy of favoring intellectuals. At the same time the conservative director of the party's Central Propaganda Department was removed (but only to be replaced by Teng Li-ch'ün). At the Twelfth Party Congress, Hu Yao-pang had talked about socialist spiritual civilization but also deplored the influence of "'leftist' ideas of petty producers" which had led the party to hold intellectuals in contempt.[32] Ch'en Yun, as head of the Central Disciplinary Committee, called for a party rectification (or purge) whose effect would be to eliminate or neutralize those opposed to reform. Ch'en said the party should never promote those who had followed Lin Piao or Chiang Ch'ing, who accepted the ideology of the Gang of Four, who were guilty of acts of violence, who disagree with the resolutions of the Third Plenum, or who have committed "serious" economic crimes. Some press commentary suggests that these "five kinds of people" constituted about a third of the party membership at all levels.[33] By the early 1980s the Maoists were virtually gone from the top of the party but were still numerous at middle and lower levels (say, among the former "worker-peasant-soldier study personnel" from the early 1970s). The purge also hits at the restorationists, however: The reference to acts of violence denies the benefit of doubt to all who were active in the Cultural Revolution, whether rebel or conservative. It contributes to the security of the top reformers, most of whom had been purged at the time, and clears the way for the recruitment of a new generation of technocrats.

Yet after the congress the left somehow resumed the initiative. Writers throughout 1983 were hectored by the Propaganda Department concerning their duty to serve the people, follow the party line, and promote spiritual civilization. The actual onset of rectification was announced at a Central Committee plenum in October 1983, about a year after the Twelfth Congress. The communiqué of that meeting talked about the three kinds of people, although it also complained of comrades who openly reject Marxism and of the malignant spread of bourgeois individualism.[34] A few days after the meeting the head of state, the old-line economic bureaucrat Li Hsien-nien, warned young workers against spiritual pollution; some days after that the head of the Higher Party School announced that at the plenum Teng Hsiao-p'ing had voiced his concern about spiritual pollution,[35] although nothing had been said about it at the time. Hsiao-p'ing had picked up the term (and maybe the concern) from Li-ch'ün, who had been using it for several months.[36] The thrust of rectification shifted from harassing the three kinds of people to chasing down spiritual pollution.

Most crassly, the campaign may have been Li-ch'ün's way of trying to undermine the position of Hu Yao-pang. Beyond that, it was a way for conservative cadres at all levels to show their unease with the way things were going. The concept of spiritual pollution was open-ended. After the fact, party members of a reformist persuasion claimed that it had really been directed only against pornography and that foreigners had made too big a thing of it. But the meaning of pornography was rather broad. It seems to have included rock music. Less defensibly, it included the saccharinely sentimental love songs from Taiwan and Hong Kong that young Chinese girls seem to like so much. New approaches in ideology (the notion of alienation in socialist society and the continuing relevance of humanism) and in literature were also, apparently, obscene. The campaign also impinged on economic reforms—a peasant's concern for feeding his family becoming evidence of spiritual pollution. Chinese intellectuals feared another Cultural Revolution, and foreign businessmen feared for their investments. Just as Li-ch'ün had apparently been able to talk Hsiao-p'ing into the campaign, so Hu Yao-pang and other ranking reformers were later able to persuade him to see its disruptive effects, and after a few weeks the campaign fizzled. Li-ch'ün fell into semidisgrace, but did not then lose his job.[37]

In 1984, the leftist momentum spent, the party moved again toward reform. It reiterated and expanded the liberalizing agricultural reforms[38] and resumed the pursuit of the three kinds of people. In the fall the Central Committee resolved actually to go ahead with the long-discussed urban reforms, an adaptation to industry and commerce of the market reforms used in agriculture.[39] In ideology and culture there was a return to a more relaxed attitude toward "exploration." Socialism was said to be a continuation and perfection of the open society produced by capitalism: it "cannot develop in a germ-free chamber."[40] The *People's Daily* made its famous declaration: "We can't ask that the works of Marx and Lenin written for their time be able to solve the problems we have today" (immediately amended to read: "to solve *all* the problems we have today").[41] In principle there is nothing new about this (the contention is surrounded by Mao's assaults on the notion of Marxism as a dogma), but in the context it indicated a retreat from orthodoxy. At the turn of the year Hu Ch'i-li assured writers of the party's commitment to creative freedom.[42]

Then, in 1985, Teng Hsiao-p'ing voiced his fears of a capitalist restoration. Hu Yao-pang at least amended Ch'i-li's early comments about creative freedom by demanding strict orthodoxy in the party press (which is perhaps reasonable enough) and also complained about literary works showing the dark side of society and about allegedly pornographic "little papers" being published on the free market. He hinted that spiritual pollution may again be becoming a problem—his words accompanied by approving noises from Teng Li-ch'ün.[43] Ch'en Yun had remained largely aloof from the spiritual pollution controversy,[44] but in 1985 he could not say enough about socialist spiritual civilization.[45] The ordinary person thought the dictatorship was being strengthened.

The main reason for the 1985 retrenchment is no doubt the problems encountered by urban reform. But it falls into a long-standing pattern, an alternation of reform with retreat from reform, the retreat based sometimes on practical errors but more often on reform's cultural, moral, or spiritual side effects. This alternation has a basis in objective reality, but is also an artifact of political conflict. Reform and reaction against the side effects of reform even help structure that conflict. There has been some support for a slogan: "In economics oppose the 'left'; in thought oppose the right." The top leadership would no doubt like to have the benefits of economic liberalization without either the questioning or the sleaziness that seems to be built into the reform process. They also know it is hard to have the thing both ways: The slogan is dismissed as something suited only to "brains lacking in independent thought."[46]

Reform and Social Alienation

A symptom of spiritual pollution among the erudite was the notion that there could be alienation in socialist society. This had been a topic of speculation among the early reformers (but not the public at large), and in 1983 it was mentioned by Chou Yang, once the regime's chief literary inquisitor but in the post-Mao period in the forefront of cultural liberalization.[47] In Marxism labor is the source of all value. A laborer can produce more than is needed to sustain him—whence the possibility of human civilization. But in class society this "surplus value" is expropriated by the exploiting class. The value created by a worker becomes something apart from him, no longer his own; his work becomes a commodity like any other, compensated at its factor price (whatever it takes to keep the worker alive and able to reproduce himself). He becomes alienated from his work, and both worker and exploiter become alienated from their human nature. Alienation is usually thought to be a theme of the younger, supposedly more humanistic Marx, and in *The Communist Manifesto* Marx and Engels may sneer at their earlier preoccupations.[48] But as neo-Marxists (and some Chinese writers[49]) point out, the concept remains basic to the Marxian critique of class society.

The attack on Chou Yang, led by Teng Li'ch'ün, was intended, no doubt, to clear the field of fire to get at bigger game. At the same time, Chou's idea of alienation in socialist society is subversive and serves a polemical purpose for the radical reformers. Persisting alienation justifies and even requires basic social change, something unappealing not only to enemies of reform but to reformers coming once again to terms with the way things are. The mainstream of reform had moved away from any notion of transforming the system, relying instead on the tried and true methods of purge and rectification to solve their problems.

In the orthodox line, alienation is a consequence of exploitation; and a socialist system, by definition, contains no exploitation. Socialist society is not yet communist. It is not egalitarian, and surplus value continues to be extracted. But the worker is rewarded according to his labor, and surplus value is extracted by society as a whole for the benefit of society as a whole, not for the good of some lazy capitalist exploiter. Be that as it may, alienation may describe precisely what is behind the spiritual crisis in China, particularly if the term is not restricted to its technical Marxian sense but is used in the broad way once all too fashionable in the postindustrial countries. That sense is broad but still literal: One's life is at the mercy of cold and arbitrary forces outside of and totally apart from oneself, over which one has no control. In China this sense of alienation, especially among some of the young, antedates reform and even the Cultural Revolution. To the extent that the Cultural Revolution was a popular movement it was a manipulation of youthful alienation. One critic notes that if socialist society produces alienation, this fact implies the need for a Maoist unbroken revolution (*pu-tuan ko-ming*). The idea of alienation in socialist society is thus akin to the "theoretical base" of the Cultural Revolution.[50]

The establishment is not totally insensitive to the half-hostile puzzlement of the young, but argues that alienation is no proper response. It points, for example, to Ch'ü Hsiao, "born of an impoverished intellectual family in the old society," the victim of gross injustice both in the Anti-Rightist business of 1957 and the Cultural Revolution. Yet he feels nothing but gratitude to the party for finally, when he was more than fifty years old, acting to correct these injustices and giving him prestige.

Ch'ü in fact has some interesting insights into what may be bothering the young malcontents:

> I often hear people say young people today are hard to manage. Some go so far as to say there is among young people today a crisis of faith. On this problem I don't dare agree. On this, let me make a logical inference. Why did the generations of young university students in the 40s and 50s and others like them ardently love the party and socialism, while the young of the 1980s are not so ardent? Could it be that by the 1980s communism has ceased to be true? Obviously not. I believe that rather than saying the young have a "crisis of faith," it is better to say a crisis of trust. . . . University students of the 80s have a special characteristic: they put special emphasis on reality.

Marxism must be made relevant to reality. Ch'ü lines up on the radical wing of reform: "Since Marx wrote his theories more than 100 years ago, they don't necessarily suffice to explain all the concrete conditions in the world of the 1980s." Still, the young today do have defects. They don't know the bitterness of the old society. They have never lived under capitalism, and, consequently, some of them idealize the West without realizing how decadent the West is. (Ch'ü presumably has acquired firsthand experience of this from his official junkets abroad.) Most importantly, they have never suffered physical abuse; they have never been in the cow pens. They cannot realize what a big thing the Third Plenum was. "Because our young comrades lack that kind of actual experience, on some things their feelings are not all that deep."[51]

Since one mark of maturity is a tendency to make the best of the way of the world, in any society the young (and maybe particularly students, since they have less need than other people to accommodate themselves to reality) may be alienated in greater proportions than other social categories. In China the "generation of the '80s" may be more alienated than their elders simply because they do not realize how much worse things can be. This statement does not mean that older people are necessarily all that content. Many continue bitterly to resent past treatment and are not fully confident that similar things will not happen again, because, though the system has changed, it has not changed all that much. The party asserts that it has seen its errors: but the exhortation to take my word for it is not always the most effective response to a crisis of trust. The younger generation is perhaps inclined to exaggerate the continuity with the past while not fully appreciating the past's evils, and for them talk of the cow pens may be about as relevant as tales of the darkness of the old society under Chiang Kai-shek. Reform, the Four Modernizations, or the Third Plenum become pooh-bahs' bromides, serving the same function as earlier platitudes by earlier authority figures urging earlier generations to exert themselves for the rulers' convenience.[52]

"Some people say: the generation of the '50s loved people; the generation of the '60s rectified people; the generation of the '70s fought people; the generation of the '80s are concerned only with themselves."[53] Recent events have produced differences both within and between generations, and the reform movement may widen the gap. In the old totalitarian system life was politicized: it was through politics that the human race achieved liberation. The generation of the 1980s (along, probably, with many intellectuals of the older generation) sees politics as the main source of oppression and retreats from public concerns, into the self.[54]

The leadership dislikes this hostility to politics because it means that those who share it are difficult to mobilize. The attitude also causes tensions between parents and children, especially, of course, in cadre families: but even in other families parents may see the children's rejection of public concern as indicative of lack of character and harmful to the children's chances in life.[55] It also indicates a gap between the generation of the 1980s and their older brothers and sisters, the generation of the Red Guards and the democracy movement. While most of the former activists now have jobs and families and little inclination to draw attention to themselves as trouble-makers, the older edge of the younger generation can sometimes be impatient with the self-indulgence of the young, particularly if they should happen to reflect that this same generation, then in primary school, served as agents of the Maoist radicals in persecuting their elders.[56] But the main experience of political activism by the generation of the 1980s has been, precisely, as stooges; and they may not be overly impressed with the efficacy of the autonomous political action of their older brothers and sisters. Also, among its demands the democracy movement included privacy and individual integrity, and the younger generation is perhaps simply appropriating without comment what their older siblings thought they had to argue for and justify. The rallies of the fall of 1985, however, may show that there is some volatility under the passivity, and may also be evidence that the withdrawal into the self is a product of alienation more than indifference.

At least until the mid-1980s, though, the general tone of the generation of the decade was passivity, sometimes with the self-pitying world-weariness found mainly among the very young: "There is a little poem: Love is a beautiful flower; the green spring [youth] is the sheen of hoarfrost in the north; the family is a temporary warming; the grave is our everlasting home."[57] The establishment tends to depict this privatism as shallowness and lack of ideals. This depiction is not always fair: Often privatism is simply a different set of ideals.

Chang Chün, a student at the Peking Drama institute and also a soldier in the People's Liberation Army, fell in love with a young Frenchman. Word got out that they planned to marry, and she was arrested and sent to a military prison. There, she says, she was questioned every day from eight in the morning until six at night (on the order of: Did you sleep with that foreigner? How many times?). She was told that he had found a new girlfriend while he, in the course of his frantic inquiries, was informed that Chang Chün was happy and well and no longer wanted anything to do with him.

While she was probably more articulate after the fact than at the time, she says she told her inquisitors:

> There is no standard of right and wrong in the world. . . . Different eras have different standards of morality and so do different societies and different classes. I am absolutely not in error in abandoning feudal morality. . . . You say you represent proletarian thought. I think you are oppressing me with feudal thought. First I am a human being and only then a soldier. . . . You deny my individuality, deny the existence of my personal emotions with your feudal morality. . . . I hate that discipline. I have my own standards of conduct. I respect the lives and rights of others, so why do you stand in the way of my life, tearing away my right to love?[58]

Especially since Chang Chün is so spectacularly pretty it is easy to sympathize with her personally. Her ideas, of course, are banal—to most parents of teenagers in the world today, depressingly banal.[59] It is unfair, though, to treat her mixture of Maoist puerility and puerile self-indulgence as an exercise in moral philosophy. It is the bitter visceral reaction of a vulnerable young girl subjected to intolerable humiliation. Her position would command some sympathy from her educated contemporaries, including the great majority who would not dare do what she did and would not do so if they did dare. It is common enough to hear from students: It is my life, and what I do with it is my business; I have only one life, and they are making me waste it.

Chang Chün is not really making a case for sexual promiscuity but for a highly idealized vision of romantic love, a vision many of her contemporaries share. Others apparently find solace in religion. "Some people," says a commentator, "seek answers from Confucius, Lao-tzu, the Bible, Buddhism, or contemporary Western philosophy" (the last in most cases meaning Sartre). He claims that when they really look into it they discover that Marx is the answer.[60] Actually, it is probably in the area of giving satisfactory answers to ultimate questions that Marxism is pragmatically weakest. If the search for alternatives means too much trouble and bother, too much flack from the leadership, the answer may not be Marxian materialism but plain old material acquisition. "In society today it is popular to find males with the 'five highs': tall body, high cultural level, high degree of talent, a high-prestige job, a high salary. For females it's the 'five professions': the face of an actress, the body of an athlete, the attitude of a waitress, the voice of an announcer, the skills of a chef."[61] It would be otiose to make too much of a joke. Still, not all of the withdrawal into the private self is uniformly high-minded. A general social tone emphasizing material acquision can contribute to alienation, as can failure in such a society to acquire as much as others seem to be able to.

The alleged money madness of Chinese society in the 1980s may be partly a consequence of blocked emotional outlets, but, like this blockage itself, it is also part of the pathology of reform. The conventional reform view of the criticism of everything for money, *hsiang ch'ien k'an*, was that it was the fabrication of obscurantist cadres bitter at their own loss of prestige as poor people came to be able to enjoy a better life.[62] But there also came to be valid grounds for complaints of money fever in society. Among Chinese students of foreign languages the worst job assignment is to teach high school. In 1984 the most desired position was college teaching, and the next was to be a translator in a factory. This was a change from previous years, when to be a college teacher was to be *too much* an intellectual and, therefore, too vulnerable to political bullying. In 1985 the *only* desired position was one in "business," preferably some business engaged in foreign trade.

Apart from its other possible unattractive features, an atmosphere of single-minded pursuit of money disrupts social expectations. The (impression of) 1984 preferences show a return to the traditional Chinese evaluation of intellectual activity, and a major consequence of the reform policies was to raise the status of intellectuals. At one level, both economic and cultural liberalization served the interests of intellectuals to a degree, at the expense of those of cadres. Antipathy between intellectual and cadre has been perennial, but the reforms may foster new social antagonisms.[63] So, one can sometimes detect an undercurrent of hostility between students and young workers.

Unlike the Confucian gentry, Chinese intellectuals today are mainly technical specialists, but a flavor of the old ethos remains. This ethos was aristocratic, not necessarily hostile to wealth or comfort but disdainful of too visible a concern with them. Chinese now as in the past have shown a talent for making money (whence the gibe that the only thing Chinese about Chinese-style socialism is the chase after money), but the ruling intelligentsia which governed the traditional state had interests different from those who lived by the creation and exchange of wealth, and in modern times the more pronounced Chinese economic successes have been outside those areas controlled by the central Chinese government. The reform analysis of the feudal mentality and feudal remnants also focused upon this traditional elite hostility to commerce and industry. The reform policy of encouraging economic enterprise and granting official recognition to the social status of intellectuals made sense in one way, in giving economic influence to the technocracy instead of to supposedly ignorant cadres. But it also helps generate a cultural contradiction. As commerce and speculation boom, intellectuals find their sensibilities offended, their newly restored prestige threatened, and their relative incomes declining. They may come to share the hostility to the pursuit of wealth once articulated by leftist cadres— perhaps just at the time that cadres are discovering that with the economic liberalization, suddenly there is money to be made.

The tensions may become rather complex. In the mass media and in gossip the children of cadres, especially high cadres, are usually presented as degenerates or grafters. In the generation of the 1980s students from low or middle cadre background may be among the most alienated in society. A discussion in *The Nineties*, however, suggests that cadre children from, say, the Cultural Revolution generation, persons now in their thirties or early forties (the lower rungs of the third echelon, as it were), form the social base for the talk of communist ideals. Like the older generation, they genuinely believe in communism, although their ideas of it are different. They are much better educated and more broad-minded than their parents; from rustication or service in the army they learned to appreciate the problems of ordinary people. They were raised from their earliest years, though, in relative luxury and have been shielded from the harshest aspects of reality. Most (except, presumably, those who were most active in Cultural Revolution gang fights and so are part of the three kinds of people) lack struggle experience and may be more softhearted than their fathers. They are said to have a strong sense of collective identity.[64] It is tempting to speculate that people like this are at the core of orthodox reform and may arouse the antipathy of certain older-generation cadres, of the worker-peasant-soldier cadres, and of intellectuals (although their only real difference from intellectuals as a category would be their family background).

More direct pathologies, those attracting the most attention from the media, have to do with inflation and corruption. Long-term inflation tends to demoralize society, and the sudden and high price rises of 1985 were a shock to the Chinese people. The inflation was one result of an extension of the market system, a central part of the program of urban reform. The economist Hsueh Mu-ch'iao constantly and plausibly argues that prices had been artifically low and that while prices are higher than in the past, so, too, is the standard of living.[65] Higher prices should call up greater supply, especially of meat and vegetables. Yet the short-term effect was a decline in the standard of living, at least for some. Food that was plentiful and cheap in 1984 was hard to find at the higher prices of 1985. Those worse off in the short run include cadres and intellectuals who are not well placed for wheeling and dealing on the free market or in other business; students; and peasants who have to supplement their incomes with part-time factory work but who, not being classified as workers, did not qualify for the supplementary bonuses given to full-time workers to offset inflation. Discontent with the price increases led to unrest in Tientsin (and perhaps other places) in the summer of 1985, which was suppressed by the People's Armed Police. It may have been a motive in the football riots of the spring and the anti-Japanese student demonstrations in the fall.

The increases may have been greater than what was necessary to call up higher supply, and the very high prices may be short-term. Vegetable prices were allowed to float during the middle of a cold, wet spring in the north that resulted in a small crop. A major cause of the inflation, however, was the policies entailed by urban reform. In the fall of 1984 enterprises were allowed more freedom to set wage rates and allocate their own profits without administrative orders or guidance from the relevant ministries. Some firms engaged in speculative investment beyond the capacity of the economy's infrastructure, or made investments which would not yield a return for many years (and in fact, there have been complaints since 1980 that the rate of investment is too high). Workers were given wage increases and bonuses in excess of increases in productivity in order to "stimulate their activism." The difference between inputs and lagging productivity was met by issuing new currency, in effect, by printing money.[66]

The use of political power, in China or anywhere else, as a means of personal wealth is not new with the reforms—there is precedent for this even in the Cultural Revolution,[67] although then it took different forms, if only because then there was not as much cash loose in society. Economic liberalization may increase the opportunities for corruption, however, especially since even with liberalization the economic role of the state remains very strong. Many children of high cadres, the story goes, routinely act as middlemen in deals with foreign companies, so reinforcing popular impressions of a privileged stratum, a division in society between those with official power and connections and those without. Other abuses may grow directly from the reform policies themselves without being simply consequences of greater opportunity. In the old fashion firms were run as if they were government offices. Now, the complaint goes, government and party offices operate as if they were businesses.[68] Rural offices charge peasants for services they should be financing from tax revenues. Schools with dormitories and dining halls go into the hotel and banquet business. The most famous confounding of political and business functions is the Hainan Island affair, where state and party units, taking advantage of their special access to foreign currency, imported automobiles for resale into the interior (transporting the cars on naval vessels).[69]

Market socialism must certainly be a possible system, but unless care is taken it may easily institutionalize double standards. At least in the early stages of price reform, the state food stores kept to the old low fixed prices. This policy made it difficult for the managers to run the stores efficiently, as they were supposed to do under the responsibility system. It made it expedient for the managers' relatives to buy up each load of produce as it was delivered to resell on the street. The most pernicious institutionalized double standard must be the system of foreign exchange certificates, a policy so made to be abused that one wonders how anyone could ever have thought it a good idea. The special economic zones are not as indefensible on their face but are still problematical. They seem to have attracted more building speculation from the interior than investment from abroad. They allow conservative cadres to grumble about "special political zones" and foreign concessions, while the ordinary person wonders why, if something is so good for Shenchen (and Hong Kong, and Taiwan) it is not good for the rest of the country. In the meantime, matching the fence between Shenchen and Hong Kong, another fence has been built to separate Shenchen from the rest of China.

Official corruption is always demoralizing (or "alienating"). The reforms blur the distinction between what is corrupt and what is not. After the urban reforms cadres, especially, had unprecedented opportunities to make money, and it is probably not cynical to guess that this helped reconcile many to the idea of reform. But when, say, the wood-purchasing office of a municipality sets up shop in the back room to supply plyboard to private builders, the cadres may well have thought that they were acting in the spirit of the reforms—beginning to pull their own weight, as it were. The Hainan investigation admitted the errant cadres were acting not for personal profit but for the advantage of their particular units (although one effect, presumably, would be higher incomes for those working in the unit). Elsewhere, where the distinction between corrupt and noncorrupt is not all that blurred, the reforms sometimes seem designed to elicit corrupt behavior. The Friendship stores used to have inconspicuous signs outside: "Limited to foreign guests; thanks for not coming in." By 1985 most stores were open to anyone—who had foreign exchange certificates. But for most people there are few legal or completely licit ways of obtaining the certificates.

One way to ameliorate such problems might be a more thoroughgoing reform. The market mechanism has been introduced into an economy which remains highly politicized. If, say, the military can acquire automobiles more easily than other agencies and if, generally, policy continues to reward entrepreneurship, then it may be no surprise if an infantry company sets itself up as a car dealer. A way out might be a more thorough depoliticization— let the army scrabble in the market for cars with everyone else, and if the central leadership thinks it is not getting enough then give it a bigger budget. The 1985 line is that corruption comes from abuses of the policy of liberalization (kao huo). Here, at least, the 1980 line is more persuasive: Corruption is a consequence of a politicized economy; and a consequence of reform has been to increase the opportunities for corruption.

Overall, there may be no stable pattern of support or opposition to reform, but a potential for different combinations and divisions among halfhearted and double-minded people. The democracy movement activists deplored party dictatorship, and they and the party together deplore what they take to be the passivity of the generation of the 1980s. Older intellectuals and younger cadres may be generally liberal in the sentiments but also inclined to see the democracy movement activists as troublemakers, no better than Red Guards—a view encouraged by the party establishment. Conservative cadres and parents are uneasy with youthful impatience with convention, but intellectuals and youth together want greater cultural freedom. Cultural freedom does not always produce culture of the most edifying sort, and an overly vulgar tone to popular culture may encourage second thoughts among intellectuals and notions of general repression from the party. Public opinion desires greater access to foreign ideas—until people come to feel themselves affronted in their national dignity. The ruling establishment wants an opening to the outside without danger to national sovereignty or internal control. Conservative cadres, worried about a cultural liberalism that seems to threaten control, decry the money-mad mentality encouraged by reform— until they discover money, and intellectuals find themselves lost in a sea of vulgar materialism.

Lack of focused opposition may mean that things will work themselves out. But lack of focused support means that society remains in perpetual, unfocused unease. It is tempting to speculate that current problems of morale might be resolved by a radical, rapid, and consistent pushing of reform through to its logical conclusion. This approach would transform the system, and the new system would, of course, have problems of its own. But with the natural uneasiness about reform it is unlikely to be pushed through all the way; and halfhearted reform feeds the spiritual crisis. There are hints of an as-it-were Maoist reaction against reform among at least some students. Such a reaction is less likely to lead to new Cultural Revolution–style radicalism than to authoritarian regression on reform by the authorities in response to a radical critique.[70]

A focus on the spiritual crisis probably exaggerates its depth and extent, as a pathologist might tend to see grim omens in every ache and pain. Because the spiritual crisis serves a political function, the Chinese media probably also exaggerate its significance. Again, it becomes an issue because someone chooses to make an issue of it; and it becomes a way of making points about other things. For example, everyone deplored the 1985 inflation, but economic planners and managers tended to treat it as something perhaps a little more severe than expected but on balance a natural result of prices having been too low too long, while Ch'en Yun's Disciplinary Committee tended to see it as evidence of corruption. This difference shows an organizational division of labor but also political disagreement on economic policy, and this kind of politicization of the spiritual crisis tends to deepen it.[71]

Notes

1. South Bend *Tribune*, September 19, 1985.

2. *Kung-jen Jih-pao*, December 13, 1984; in *Hsin Hua Wen-chai*, March 1985, pp. 7–11.

3. I am using this term in accord with what I understand to be contemporary Chinese usage, to refer to one with an (undefined) degree of education who, as Mencius puts it, labors with his mind.

4. *Jen-min Jih-pao* (People's Daily), March 9, 1985.

5. David Nivison, "Communist Ethics and the Chinese Tradition," *Journal of Asian Studies*, 16 (1956–1957), pp. 51–74.

6. The most famous recent work is Tai Hou-ying, *Jen ah, Jen!* (Canton?, 1980). For a relatively moderate restatement of the official position, see Hu Ch'iao-mu, "Humanism and Alienation," *Jen-min Jih-pao*, January 27, 1984. The humanism both regime and critics have in mind is usually Western rather than Confucian, although from the Cultural Revolution period through the early 1970s Confucian humanism was also heavily criticized. In the view of many modernist critics Confucianism has a "feudal" connotation, and part of their critique is that many current regime practices smack of feudalism. Part of the appeal of humanism is that it provides a way out of Marxist-Maoist relativism without recourse to theism or to traditional systems of values.

7. Liu's most criticized writings include *Lun Kung-ch'an-tang-yuan ti Hsiu-yang* (Chang-chia-k'ou, 1946); *Lun Tang* (n.p., 1945); "On Inner-Party Struggle," *Chieh-fang Jih-pao*, October 9, 1945.

8. Frederick Wakeman, Jr., *History and Will: Philosophical Perspectives on Mao Tse-tung's Thought* (Berkeley: University of California Press, 1973); Maurice Meisner, "Leninism and Maoism: Some Populist Perspectives on Marxism-Leninism in China," *China Quarterly*, 45 (January/March, 1971), pp. 1–36. This mentality in general may be an artifact of conditions in late-modernizing countries. A. James Gregor, *The Fascist Persuasion in Radical Politics* (Princeton, N.J.: Princeton University Press, 1974); compare also Masao Maruyama, *Thought and Behavior in Modern Japanese Politics* (Oxford University Press, 1969), ch. 2.

9. Wang Po-sen, "Preliminary Discourse on the Relationship Between Economic Reform and Moral Progress," *Wen-hui Pao*, July 23, 1984; *Hsin Hua Wen-chai*, September 1984, pp. 21–24.

10. For example, *Kuang-ming Jih-pao*, August 26 and September 18, 1980.

11. *Hsiang ch'ien k'an* (look to money), a pun pronounced exactly the same way as "look to the future." "Look to the future" may originally, however, have been more a "whateverist" slogan than a reformist one; its original implication was that we should move ahead and not dwell on rehearsing the crimes of the Cultural Revolution. *Hung Ch'i*, September 3, 1978, p. 65.

12. Wei Ching-sheng, "On the Fifth Modernization," *Tan-so*, March 1979.

13. *Jen-min Jih-pao*, January 3, 1979.

14. *Jen-min Jih-pao*, June 26, 1979.

15. Chi Hsin, "The Class Situation and Principal Contradictions in Mainland China: An Important Theoretical Issue at the Second Session of the Fifth NPC," *Ch'i-shih Nien-tai*, August 1979, in Foreign Broadcast Information Service/PRC, *Daily Report* (hereafter cited as FBIS/PRC), August 13, 1979, pp. U1–U6; Li Shao-chün, "China's Ancient Feudal Despotism," *Kuang-ming Jih-pao*, August 14, 1979.

16. Speech by Yeh Chien-ying to the Fourth Plenum, Eleventh Central Committee, *Jen-min Jih-pao*, September 30, 1979. Although Yeh delivered the speech, its main author was apparently Hu Yao-pang.

17. That was the year *keng-shen* in the sixty-year Chinese cyclical system, and the proposals of that year have sometimes been called the *keng-shen* reforms. One reason for the term may be that the name of the year sounds a little like *keng-sheng* (rebirth).

18. Feng Wen-lin, "On the Question of Socialist Democracy," *Jen-min Jih-pao*, November 24 and November 25, 1980; see also *Jen-min Jih-pao*, October 7, 1980.

19. Pao T'ung, "A Few Opinions on Opposing Bureaucratism," *Jen-min Jih-pao*, October 30, 1980. This and much of the discussion at the time is a public elaboration of private comments by Teng Hsiao-p'ing in late August. *Chan Wang*, April 16, 1981, in FBIS/China, April 26, 1981, pp. W1–W14. For possible institutional implications of the *keng-shen* reforms, see Liao Kai-lung, "The '1980 Reform' Program in China," *Ch'i-shih Nien-tai*, March, 1981, in FBIS/PRC, March 16, 1981, pp. U1–U19.

20. *Jen-min Jih-pao*, October 17, 1980. This is also the main political point of the attack on the "petroleum gang," whose ultimate backstage boss was probably Li Hsien-nien.

21. See the comments by Li Hsien-nien, *Jen-min Jih-pao*, January 25, 1982.

22. *Jen-min Jih-pao*, March 19, 1981.

23. Li Hung-lin, "What Does the 'Crisis of Faith' Show?" *Jen-min Jih-pao*, November 11, 1980.

24. *Kuang-ming Jih-pao*, February 18 and February 22, 1981.

25. Teng Li-ch'ün, "The Voice of Truth Cannot Be Smothered," *Jen-min Jih-pao*, June 24 and 25, 1980.

26. Hu Ch'iao-mu, "Work According to Economic Laws, Speed up the Realization of the Four Modernizations," *Jen-min Jih-pao*, October 6, 1978.

27. Hu Ch'iao-mu, "Several Questions Concerning the Current Ideological Line," *Hung Ch'i*, December 1, 1982, pp. 2–22.

28. *Chung-yang Jih-pao*, April 26, 1980. The mainland has taken the unusual trouble to deny the authenticity of this report, but many who study the subject accept it. A mainland student in the United States had not heard about the speech, but claimed not to be surprised that Ch'en might have said such things at the time. (Ch'en had not been well-treated during the Maoist period.) The student would, however, be surprised if Ch'en had not since changed his mind.

29. Franz Schurmann, *Ideology and Organization in Communist China* (Berkeley: University of California Press, 1966), p. 86. Dorothy Solinger, *Chinese Business Under Socialism*, (Berkeley: University of California Press, 1984).

30. See, for example, the discussion of his ideas in *Jen-min Jih-pao*, July 16, 1984.

31. Wang Jen-chung, "Unify Thought, Earnestly Rectify Party Style," *Hung Ch'i*, March 1, 1982, pp. 1–13.

32. *Jen-min Jih-pao*, September 8, 1982.

33. *Jen-min Jih-pao*, September 7, 1982, and November 18, 1982. The requirement for adherence to the line of the Third Plenum—in effect, a pledge of allegiance to Teng Hsiao-p'ing—and the business about economic crime were removed in 1983,

reducing the "kinds of people" to three, focusing the attention of the purge on those who profited from the Cultural Revolution.

34. *Jen-min Jih-pao*, October 13, 1983.

35. *Jen-min Jih-pao*, October 19, 1983, and October 25, 1983. For a purported text of Teng's speech (which has not been openly published on the mainland), see *Inside Mainland China*, April 1984, pp. 4–8.

36. *Cheng Ming*, February 1, 1984; in FBIS/China, February 7, 1984, p. W4.

37. Thomas B. Gold, " 'Just in Time!' China Battles Spiritual Pollution on the Eve of 1984," *Asian Survey*, 24:9 (September 1984), pp. 947–974.

38. *Jen-min Jih-pao*, June 12, 1984.

39. *Jen-min Jih-pao*, October 21, 1984.

40. Li Hung-lin, "Some Propositions on Opening to the Outside," *Jen-min Jih-pao*, October 15, 1984. The implication, perhaps, is that exposure to a little pollution is good for you.

41. *Jen-min Jih-pao*, December 7, 1984, and December 8, 1984.

42. *Jen-min Jih-pao*, December 30, 1984.

43. *Jen-min Jih-pao*, April 14, 1984.

44. He deplored what he took to be commercial vulgarizations of the Soochow-Shanghai opera style. *Jen-min Jih-pao*, October 16, 1983, and December 31, 1983.

45. *Jen-min Jih-pao*, July 1, 1984.

46. *Chieh-fang Chun-pao*, January 23, 1985; in *Hsin Hua Wen-chai*, May 1985, p. 5.

47. *Jen-min Jih-pao*, March 16, 1983. On Chou's earlier career, see Merle Goldman, *Literary Dissent in Communist China* (Cambridge, Mass.: Harvard University Press, 1967). For Chou's repentence, see Cho I-hsia, "Remembrance and Concern," *Wen-i Pao*, 3, 1985, in June 1985, pp. 186–187.

48. "German philosophers, would-be philosophers, and *beaux esprits* . . . wrote their philosophical nonsense beneath the French original. For example, beneath the French criticism of the economic functions of money they wrote *Alienation of Humanity.* . . ." *Marx and Engels: Basic Writings on Politics and Philosophy*, edited by Lewis S. Feuer (Garden City, N.Y.: Anchor, 1959), p. 33.

49. Wang Hsueh-chin, "New Explorations of Three Topics on Marx's Theory of Alienation," *Chi-Lu Hsueh-k'an*, 3, 1983, in *Hsin Hua Wen-chai*, September 1983, pp. 38–41.

50. *Jen-min Jih-pao*, February 2, 1984.

51. Ch'ü Hsiao, "Life, Ideals, Pursuit," *Shan-hsi Jih-pao*, April 27, 1985; *Hsin Hua Wen-chai*, July 1985, pp. 3–11, at pp. 8–9.

52. A compelling treatment of the generation gap and, especially, the gap within generations is T'ieh Ning's delightful and powerful story, "The Red Skirt Without Buttons," *Shih-Yueh*, 2, 1983; in *Hsin Hua Wen-chai*, June 1983, pp. 95–120; on this last point, see p. 105.

53. *Kung-jen Jih-pao*, December 13, 1984, in *Hsin Hua Wen-chai*, March 1985, p. 8.

54. This was one of the themes of an extended media discussion on the meaning of life. See "Changing Attitudes Among Chinese Youths," edited and translated by David Owsley, *Chinese Sociology and Anthropology*, summer 1985. For a summary discussion, see *Jen-min Jih-pao*, March 25, 1981. A possible distinction is that the older intellectuals are antipolitical, while the youngest generation is simply apolitical.

55. It is hard to know how to phrase this speculation, since many of the older intellectuals certainly hate and fear politics and hostility to politics has been a major literary theme of the post-"scar" era. But older intellectuals, while perhaps rejecting

the leadership's version of politics, also feel a commitment to public service, something they may not see in the younger generation.

56. See the story by Hsing Cho, "Anniversary of a Death," *Shih-yueh*, 1, 1985; *Hsin Hua Wen-chai*, March 1985, pp. 87–119.

57. *Kung-jen Jih-pao*, December 13, 1984; in *Hsin Hua Wen-chai*, March 1985, p. 8.

58. Chang Chün, "A Prisoner at Changchiak'ou," *Chiu-shih Nien-tai*, July 1984, pp. 70–80.

59. And how many drill sergeants, in any army, can be expected to be patient with recruits who blather about how they are human beings first and only then soldiers?

60. Wang Chih-chang, "Discussing 'Seeing Through,' " *She-hui K'o-hsueh*, 1, 1983; *Hsin Hua Wen-chai*, April 1984, pp. 26–27.

61. *Kung-jen Jih-pao*, December 13, 1984; in *Hsin Hua Wen-chai*, March 1985, p. 10.

62. Chiang Tzu-lung, "Dirge for Yen and Chao," *Jen-min Wen-hsueh*, 7, 1984; *Hsin Hua Wen-chai*, September 1984, pp. 86–123.

63. The manner of the reforms may be reproducing the problems of pre–Cultural Revolution times back into the educational system. In cities the divisions between elite and ordinary educational institutions have become sharper, as has that division between colleges at the national level. As restrictions on earning incomes vanish, peasants have an incentive to keep the kids home, where they can earn some money, instead of sending them to school, especially since graduation from a rural school is likely to be a dead end. The collapse of the commune system means there is no organization prepared to make up for the state's neglect of rural education. For a general discussion, see Stanley Rosen, "Decentralization, Recentralization, and Rationalization: Deng Xiaoping's Bifurcated Educational Policy," *Modern China*, 11:3 (spring 1985), pp. 301–305. It remains to be seen how seriously the educational reforms discussed in early 1985 will address these problems. The Maoist handling of similar problems is not a happy example, but that does not mean that the problems were not real.

64. Chi Chi, "China After Teng Seen in Terms of Political Factions," *Chiu-shih Nien-tai*, February 1986, pp. 54–59.

65. For example, *Jen-min Jih-pao*, December 16, 1985.

66. *Jen-min Jih-pao*, May 17, 1985.

67. Liu Bingyan, *People of Monsters?* (Bloomington: Indiana University Press, 1983), pp. 11–68.

68. *Jen-min Jih-pao*, March 10, 1985; Po I-po, *Jen-min Jih-pao*, March 13, 1985.

69. *Jen-min Jih-pao*, August 1, 1985.

70. This discussion has dealt with only a very limited number of instances of the spiritual crisis. Other causes and symptoms might include juvenile delinquency, the side effects of the birth-control program, increasing polarization in the countryside, and increasing polarization between peasants and workers.

71. For the record, nothing here should be taken to imply that any change of economic, political, or social structures will resolve the question of human alienation; but the forms alienation takes are contingent upon specific social, political, or economic structures.

6

Whither Mainland China: On the Theoretical Study Campaign

An-chia Wu

Let us pull off and shake off from all of us this filthy sweaty shirt of Ideology (Marxism).
—Aleksandr I. Solzhenitsyn

Socialism is to put an end to poverty. Poverty is not socialism, nor is it Communism.
—Teng Hsiao-p'ing

At the National Conference of the Chinese Communist Party (CCP) held in September 1985, such Communist leaders as Teng Hsiao-p'ing, Ch'en Yun, and Li Hsien-nien, all of them standing committee members of the CCP Central Committee's Politburo, asked people to protect themselves from the erosion of capitalism by adhering to the "Four Cardinal Principles."[1] Teng also asked the party's Central Committee to formulate a workable decision so that party cadres at all levels, especially leading cadres, could study and become well-versed in basic Marxist theory.[2] After the conference, a movement for the study of Marxist theory was launched. In this article the writer will attempt to appraise the background and objectives of the campaign and the impact it might have on reforms in the People's Republic of China (PRC).

Challenge from Capitalism

Political movements have always been exploited by the Chinese Communists as a means to attain their goals. After Mao Tse-tung's death in September 1976, although the Chinese Communists had repeatedly proclaimed their intention not to wage any further political campaigns in the course of constructing a socialist society, political movements have never ceased to erupt in mainland China. For example, efforts to eradicate remnants of the Gang of Four led by Mao's widow Chiang Ch'ing, reevaluate Mao Tse-tung and his thought, overcome the tendency toward bourgeois liberalization, promote material and spiritual civilization, consolidate the party,

153

and eliminate spiritual pollution, as well as the current study movement, have all been conducted in essence as political movements and on a nationwide scale, although the measures that have been used are comparatively more moderate than those of earlier times. The current study campaign, which is a continuation of a series of "study movements" initiated since 1978,[3] is aimed at strengthening Communist education, warding off capitalist influence, and eliminating ideological obstacles to reforms.

To revitalize the economy, the Chinese Communists adopted the following measures in the past years: reinstitution of Liu Shao-ch'i's *san tzu i pao* policy (more plots for private use, more free markets, more enterprises with sole responsibility for their own profit or loss, and fixing output quotas on a household basis); enforcement of the production responsibility system in agriculture; extension of the period of farmland contracts to fifteen years or longer; allowing peasants to hire assistants; development of a commodity economy; attaching importance to the regulatory role of the market mechanism; encouraging people to become rich; and opening mainland China to the outside world in order to absorb capital, technology, and management expertise from capitalist countries. In the process of their reforms, the Chinese Communists have taken a critical attitude toward Marxism-Leninism because they want to overcome the ideological obstacles that have emerged. For example, Chou Yang, chairman of the Federation of Literary and Art Circles, said in 1983 that Marxism is a theory in development and that stagnation, retrogression, and even degeneration appeared in its development.[4] In the same year, Su Shao-chih, director of the Marxism-Leninism and Mao Tse-tung Thought Research Institute of the Academy of Social Sciences, declared that Marxism could not solve all the ideological problems that had appeared under new historical conditions because many of the new things and new experiences that had emerged in practical life were beyond imagination in the old days. Taking the system of "contracted responsibilities with payment linked to output" as a case in point, Su said that it was first applied in agricultural sectors and then in other departments. As to this system, no trace can be found in the Marxist classics, the traditional norms, or foreign models. With this understanding, he criticized some theorists on the Chinese mainland for having blindly adhered to outdated and abstract theories.[5] An article in the *People's Daily* on December 7, 1984, reiterated his views and said: "We cannot expect the writings of Marx and Lenin written in their time to solve all our present-day problems."[6] Su Shao-chih reiterated his own views in April 1985[7] and after the September 1985 CCP National Conference.[8]

The imitation of the capitalist way of management of enterprises and market mechanism in the economic reform and the criticism of Marxism inevitably shook the position of Marxism in the eyes of the people. Moreover, the capitalist ideology, system, and way of life that were injected into the PRC along with the influx of foreign capital and technology have also had a great impact on the CCP cadres as well as peasants and students. As a result, the mainland Chinese began to have doubts about the purported superiority of socialism. For example, they raised the following questions: Why should mainland China import capital, technology, and management methods from the capitalist countries after it has practiced socialism for more than three decades? Why is the per capita income in socialist countries lower than that in capitalist countries? Being unable to obtain satisfactory answers to these questions, they lost their faith in communism and began to seek material benefits. As a result, many party cadres speculate on the rise and fall of prices, engage in illegal trade, offer or take bribes, and traffic in smuggled goods. They also have resorted to deception, extortion, evading customs duties, and selling counterfeit and often lethal medicines and liquor just for ill-gotten gains. They also sell obscene videotapes and pictures.[9] Peasants began to engage in industrial and commercial activities instead of growing crops, raising pigs, and planting vegetables. As a result, the call of "no prosperity without engaging in industry" is heard much more loudly than that of "no economic stability without agricultural development."[10] Young students exerted themselves in study with the object of creating an opportunity to go to the United States for advanced studies and then to stay there, get married, and settle down.[11] They were not interested in Communist slogans and treated communism and socialism with bitter contempt.[12]

The Chinese Communist leaders have been cautious about the influx of capitalist influence. At the Third Plenary Session of the CCP's Central Advisory Commission held on October 22, 1984, Teng Hsiao-p'ing confidently assured the top CCP leaders that there was no need to fear "a little capitalist stuff" introduced into mainland China following the open-door policy because it would not be difficult to snuff it out.[13] Not long after that, however, he was forced to back down from his previous assessment of the seriousness of capitalist influence. At the National Work Conference on Science and Technology held in March 1985, he demanded the strengthening of Communist education so as to avoid the risk of making youths captive of capitalist ideology.[14] The capitalist influence was also referred to by Hu Yao-pang in a speech at the commencement of the CCP's Central Party School on October 6, 1985. Hu asserted that the reform policy and the policy of opening the PRC to the outside world had aroused suspicion among people that revisionism, democracy, and capitalism might prevail on the Chinese mainland.[15] Assuring people that mainland China would not take the capitalist road, T'ien Chi-yun, Peking's vice-premier, said at the Conference of Cadres of Central Organs on January 6, 1986, that although individual-owned, joint-ventured, and foreign-owned economies had witnessed a relatively great development in recent years, their industrial output value only constituted a mere 0.6 percent of mainland China's gross industrial output value and that the socialist public ownership system economy still played an absolutely dominant role in the mainland.[16]

The foregoing views bring to light two facts: Teng's reform policy has been criticized by some people as having taken the capitalist road; and mainland China is under the threat of capitalism. As to the question concerning the threat of capitalism, Teng said in his speech at the CCP National Conference that failure to give play to the superiority of socialism, the degeneration of the party's work style, and the corruption of cadres should be attributed to the influence of feudalism and capitalism. Ch'en Yun denounced capitalism as a kind of decadent ideology but attributed the unhealthy tendencies within the party to the policy of opening mainland China to the outside world.[17] In an article by "Commentator" in the People's Daily on January 4, 1986, the degeneration of the party's work style was likewise attributed to the open-door policy and to the commodity economy.[18] If the divergence of opinion on this question is not bridged, Teng will encounter difficulties in carrying out his reform policy. Besides, inflation, income polarization, and the corruption of cadres as a result of the reform policy have forced the reformists headed by Teng Hsiao-p'ing to be on the defensive in ideological matters. In other words, to safeguard their leadership position and to carry forward the reform policy smoothly, the reformists had only to compromise with the conservatives headed by Ch'en Yun and launch the study campaign.

Rationalize the Reform Policy

The study campaign this time is for the following major purposes: to rationalize the current reform policy; to counterattack dogmatism within the party; and to make party cadres understand that the degeneration of the party's work style is not the result of the domestic reform and the open-door policy.

The reformists have found it difficult to work out an ideological guideline for the reform. Although the old policy which was based on Marxist-Leninist theories had proved inapplicable, the Chinese Communists dare not openly abandon Marxism-Leninism because it has been the basis for the establishment and building of the Chinese Communist regime; abandoning it would be tantamount to negating the legality of Communist rule. As a result, the most urgent task now is to find from Marxist classics a basis for the reform. In an article carried in the People's Daily on April 12, 1984, under the title "Theorists Must Enthusiastically Study New Things," theorists are asked to find a basis for the reform measures, including the system of contracted responsibilities with payment linked to output. However, the article disclosed that there were still too few convincing articles to prove in theory that the current reform conformed with Marxism and was by no means equivalent to taking the capitalist road.[19] On June 7, 1985, P'eng Chen, chairman of the National People's Congress (NPC) Standing Committee, called for interpreting major current events on the basis of Marxist-Leninist classics.[20] Of course, this would be a rather arduous task because from Marxism the Communists can find abundant bases for the abolition of the private ownership system and for the equalization of social wealth but cannot find any ready measures to convert a poor agricultural country into a socialist society. As two mainland Chinese scholars, Chang Hsien-yang and Wang

Kuei-hsiu, have observed: "Apart from the arduousness of the construction tasks, it is even more difficult to master basic Marxist theory during the period of construction because the theory regarding construction in Marxist works is not as specific or mature as the theory regarding revolution. . . . We do not have specific theories or completely successful practical experience to draw on in the field of construction."[21]

The following basis has been advanced by some theorists with regard to the reform:

Some theorists defend the reform policy from the historical materialist point of view. For example, Yuan Mu said that a reasonable new economic model should be established because the old system, which is closed and rigid, is incompatible with the demand for the development of social productivity and has made the socialist economy lose its vitality.[22]

Some quarters try to justify the necessity of the open-door policy by saying that Marx, in *The Communist Manifesto,* declared that the development of capitalism had already broken barriers between countries.[23]

Others based their criticism of dogmatism on Stalin's theory that "Marxism is not dogma but a guide to action."[24]

From a series of articles published recently for the study of Marxism, it is clear that a major task in the study is to get rid of dogmatism, which constitutes a formidable obstacle to reform. The most noteworthy Marxist dogma to be abandoned is the one on commodity economy. It is the Marxist theory that commodity production, currency, and profit should no longer be allowed to exist after the enforcement of the socialist public ownership system, for otherwise there would emerge the exploitation of men by men. The current practice in the PRC of developing commodity production and emphasizing the market mechanism, although only to a certain extent, is completely in violation of Marxism. It is in such a situation that the Chinese Communists have to abandon some of the Marxist dogma.[25] Meanwhile, they maintained that the socialist commodity economy is in essence different from the capitalist commodity economy and that to develop the socialist commodity economy is not to develop capitalism and would not turn China to capitalism.[26] Moreover, they argued that to fully develop a commodity economy is a necessary stage for the development of the socialist economy and a revolution in the economic structure.[27] Obviously, the reformists are trying to take the initiative in interpreting ideological matters in the current study movement.

To defend the reform policy is a third objective of that campaign because the conservatives have insisted on saying that evil tendencies such as the corruption of cadres and income polarization are a result of the domestic economic reform and the open-door policy. Maintaining that these malpractices are a result of cadres' being corrupted by feudalism and capitalism, the reformists advanced the following three reasons to defend their policy:

1. The policy currently adopted in the PRC is a unique one that had no precedent or bluepint to follow. As a result, some deviations inevitably

appear in the process of probing forward.[28] In his report to the Fourth Session of the Sixth NPC on the draft of the Seventh Five-Year Plan (1986–1990), Chao Tzu-yang said that the emergence of some problems and contradictions in the process of having the new system replace the old one was inevitable. His reason was that as the reform was probing forward, experience could be accumulated only through experimentation and that, in the process, it was possible that some mistakes would be made.[29]

2. Some of the evil tendencies appeared long before the enforcement of the reform and the open-door policy. The reform itself will not result in those tendencies. Both subjectively and objectively, the root of the evil tendencies should be found from the remnants of the old ideology and social relations and from the old system and the intrusive capitalist influence.[30]

3. Instead of leading the PRC to the capitalist road, the open-door policy would reap many advantages. According to Wei Yü-ming, chairman of the board of directors of the China International Trade Center, the open-door policy plays a constructive role in modernization. For example, it would bring about an increase of foreign exchange earnings and a further advance in industrial and agricultural development, and it would enhance technological and management standards, enrich the market supply, increase government revenue, rapidly accumulate capital, and provide greater opportunities for employment. He maintained that mainland China would be unable to realize its modernization program under the policy of seclusion because no country in the world today can solve its problems in energy supply and technological development by relying merely on itself.[31]

Obviously, the reformists fear that the reform policy and the policy of opening to the outside world may be obstructed or suspended if the voice of the opposition becomes louder. A mainland Chinese economist, T'ao Hai-su, used the "bathtub curve" theory to advise the Chinese Communist leaders not to be misled by the transient phenomenon of a relatively high rate of failure in the early stages of the reform. He said that the problems appearing in the process of reform do not necessarily mean that the policy is irrational but that, because of the obstruction of traditional habits, people have not gained an ample understanding of the policy and that there were still some shortcomings in the policy itself. At this moment efforts should be made to attempt a qualitative analysis of the failure, clear away obstructions, clear up misunderstandings, and improve the measures that have been adopted. Unless the results of the analyses prove that the policy is indeed wrong, the policy should not be rashly changed. Otherwise, there would emerge a situation in which the people always oscillate at the stage of early failures and are unable to switch to the stage of implementing the policy regularly.[32] Chao Tzu-yang urged the Chinese Communist cadres to prepare themselves for handling problems that may have cropped up in the course of the reform and not to be panic-stricken or even abandon the reform of fear of a slight risk.[33] It is generally believed that the Chinese Communists will not abandon the reform, for otherwise they will find no way out. The question now is, Which way will they go for the reform?

The Courses to Follow

Two basic principles have been followed by the Chinese Communists in the past years on ideological matters: abandon outdated theories and restrictions so as to meet the needs of the reform; and find a basis from Marxism so as to rationalize all the reform measures. As we have seen, under the principle of casting away the outdated theories and restrictions, the Chinese Communists have shifted from a blind worship of Mao Tse-tung and his thought to negating part of his deeds and theories; from the past practice of following the Stalinist model to the criticism of that model; from criticism of the revisionist line adopted by Yugoslavia, Romania, and Hungary to an imitation of their methods for economic construction; and from the past practice of regarding Marxism as a universal truth to the current situation of admitting that some Marxist theories were outdated. The change in attitude toward the Marxist classics is for no other purpose but to remedy the continuing poverty in mainland China. Unlike Mao, who extolled poverty,[34] Teng Hsiao-p'ing condemned poverty and said: "Socialism is to put an end to poverty. Poverty is not socialism, nor is it Communism."[35] The methods Teng used to lift the Chinese mainland from the state of "poverty and blankness"[36] are also different from those employed by Mao. In Mao's days, violent political movements were waged to arouse people's enthusiasm for work. However, instead of achieving that goal, the political movements and the theories of "egalitarianism" and "overcoming selfishness and fostering public spirit" further hindered economic development. Teng also initiated a series of political movements in an effort to reform people's thought, but he encouraged people to become rich in the domestic reform and under the policy of opening to the outside world, with a view to enhancing their enthusiasm for work. Nevertheless, the open-door policy brought him troubles as well as benefits, because the influx of capital, technology, and management expertise from the Western countries has been accompanied by the influx of capitalist ideology and way of life. Peking's official attitude is that people should absorb capital, technology, and management methods from the capitalist countries but not their ideology and systems. The *t'i-yung* dichotomy, just as in the reform movement in the late days of the Ch'ing dynasty, would destroy attempts to modernize. This is because the Western *yung* (utility), that is, the capital, technology, and management expertise, is built on the basis of the Western *t'i* (foundation), such as freedom, democracy, experimentation, a critical spirit, and open adversarial disputes.[37] In other words, democracy and the legal system are the key to the success of mainland China's reform. As P'ing Ai-lan, the daughter of a ranking Communist cadre and a Ph.D. candidate at a university in the United States, said: "China should break its existing ideological bondage and gradually cast away the shackles of the 'Four Cardinal Principles' if it wants to make a success of the reform."[38] If the guiding ideology in society is not changed, there will be little prospect of success for the reform. Without casting off the Four Cardinal Principles, it would not be easy for the reform to progress beyond the first two historical efforts of China to modernize—those of the Self-strengtheners from 1840 to 1894 and from 1901 to 1911.[39]

To carry through its reform policy, mainland China will have to walk up and down among the following three ways: the capitalist road, market socialism, and the so-called "Chinese way of socialism," that is, taking one step and looking around before taking another in the reform.

Whether mainland China will take the capitalist road is a matter of much concern to many people. Some observers have maintained that Teng has slowly but skillfully abandoned communism and turned capitalist because he has lost his confidence in the Marxist philosophy which had plunged mainland China into abject poverty in the past three decades.[40] Some observers have adopted the view that Teng's reform was an attempt on a monumental scale to blend seemingly irreconcilable elements: state ownership and private property, central planning and competitive markets, political dictatorship and limited economic and cultural freedom. In other words, they consider Teng's reform an attempt to combine communism and capitalism.[41] Others maintained that if capitalism is defined simply as the use of material incentives, financial levers, managerial prerogatives, and profit criteria familiar in the West, then the PRC is indeed moving in the direction of a revival of capitalism. If, on the other hand, capitalism is taken to mean the value of entrepreneurialism and consumerism, then the PRC is headed that way, too. If capitalism is regarded more strictly and more properly as the private proprietorship of economic activity, then the signs of capitalism in the PRC remain distinctly limited.[42] Still others believe that the reinstitution of the private ownership system would gradually put mainland China on the capitalist road.[43]

Of course, the Western world would be more than pleased to attract the Chinese Communists to the capitalist road. Should the Chinese Communists turn capitalist, it would have two important political implications. One is that the non-Communist world will for the first time be able to attract a "Communist giant" to its own camp, and the other is that the Chinese Communists would finally pull off and shake off the filthy sweaty shirt of the Communist ideology.[44] In other words, the ideal of a Communist society would prove to be both false and unrealistic. Nevertheless, because of the following reasons the Chinese Communists may not and dare not take the capitalist road: First, it would deprive the Chinese Communists of a real basis for legitimate rule over the Chinese mainland. That is why cadres have been asked to persist in the Four Cardinal Principles in the current study campaign. The Chinese Communists have emphasized that "any attempt to find a way out by diverging from Marxism would lead us astray."[45] Second, it would arouse opposition from the conservatives and people with a vested interest. This would occur because the conservatives would lose their vested interest if mainland China takes the capitalist road. Professor Jan Prybyla believes that the market economy threatens the bureaucrats in their capacity as "producers"—planners, supervisors, enforcers, double-checkers, and so on. The market economy also endangers the consumer privileges of the bureaucratic elite. Reform thus threatens the bureaucracy on both counts.[46] Third, the achievements so far attained in the reform have created a sense of euphoria among leading cadres with what they have done and made them believe that socialism is still a superior system and that there is therefore no need to take the capitalist road. According to Chinese Communist reports, reform in agriculture succeeded in increasing the peasants' annual per capita income to 400 yuan in 1985, and the open-door policy enabled the PRC to make use of a total of US$20 billion in foreign investment, to open 1,800 joint ventures, and to absorb advanced technology and thousands of pieces of important factory equipment by September 1985. Contending that these achievements were made by upholding the Four Cardinal Principles and by initiating the domestic reform and open-door policy in relations with foreign countries,[47] the Chinese Communists would think it the best way to make use of the merits of capitalism while opposing the capitalist ideology and system. Hsu Chia-t'un, director of the Hong Kong branch of the New China News Agency, defended Marxism-Leninism in the following statement: "It is not the fault of Marxism-Leninism but the mistakes we have made in our own work that in the past our economy developed at a speed not fast enough and the living standard of our people was not high. Today, we are correcting our past mistakes in accordance with the Marxist-Leninist theories and pushing the socialist cause forward."[48] Hsu obviously overlooked the fact that "egalitarianism" and the one-party dictatorship which stem from the Marxist-Leninist theories are the main causes of the backwardness of the Chinese mainland in the past decades.

In papers presented to the Twelfth Sino-American Conference on Mainland China, Chu-yuan Cheng and Jan Prybyla dealt at length with the question of whether mainland China will take the road of "market socialism."[49] Prior to Mao's death in September 1976, the Chinese Communists did not approve of those Communist nations that practiced their own type of socialism in accordance with the realities in their own countries. For example, they denounced as outright revisionism the kind of socialism practiced in the Soviet Union and Yugoslavia. Today, however, the Chinese Communists themselves are looking for a so-called Chinese way to socialism, and they are trying to learn from Yugoslavia, Romania, and Hungary in economic reform. Among these three East European countries, Yugoslavia abandoned the Stalinist model in adopting its own way of development, while Romania and Hungary revised that model to a certain extent; that is, they try to enhance economic results and productivity by giving material incentives to the people and enterprises while adhering to the principle of centralized planning.[50] In other words, their reforms are made within the framework of the socialist system. It is the Yugoslav model that becomes most attractive to the Communist Chinese reform. The Yugoslav model is characterized by a combination of market socialism with workers' self-management. The principle of this self-management is the core of the Yugoslav model. A mainland Chinese scholar named Kao Fang recommended the practice in Yugoslavia as a "new revelation" to the PRC. He urged the Chinese Communist authorities to grant more authority to workers in the management of enterprises.[51] The Chinese Communists have currently borrowed some of the reform measures from the three East European countries mentioned, such as granting more power to enterprises, developing commodity economy, separating administrative work from business management, and strengthening the role of the market mechanism.[52] However, comparing the reform in mainland China with those in Romania, Yugoslavia, and Hungary, some differences can be discerned in the way to achieve their goals and the degree of decentralization and dependence on the market. As far as the role of the market is concerned, Yugoslavia could be called a market economy, because the prices of industrial and agricultural products are set in accordance with the relative prices in the world markets rather than controlled by the government. In Hungary, the prices of essential consumer goods, basic materials, and fuel are still fixed by the central planners. In the case of the PRC, the market forces are officially identified as only a supplement to the central plan. The role played by the market is very limited. Therefore, the economic system in mainland China is still far away from the market socialism experienced in Eastern Europe. As to the autonomy of enterprises, the Yugoslav workers' council is the most advanced toward workers' self-management. Hungary has delegated considerable micropower to enterprises, but the state control has still not been totally discarded. Management in Hungary is appointed by the higher administration. However, Hungarian directors have far more decision-making power than their counterparts in the PRC. In the allocation of investment funds, income distribution, and agricultural reform, mainland China also differs from the three East European countries.[53] The fact that mainland China's economic reform is different in many ways from that of Yugoslavia, Romania, and Hungary derives from the following causes: First, conditions in China are different from those in the three countries. For example, mainland China has a large population with only limited arable land, and about 80 percent of its population, which totals more than one billion, are peasants. Second, the Chinese Communist leaders have time and again declared that mainland China would not imitate the model of any other country in the course of its own socialist construction. Third, the Chinese Communist Party has exercised a more dictatorial rule than the Communist parties in those three countries and does not want to lose its vested power. In short, mainland China may learn from Yugoslavia, Romania, and Hungary in their spirit and some of their measures for economic reform, but the PRC will not totally pattern itself on the economic construction models of those countries.

The way most likely to be taken by the Chinese Communists is the one suggested by Teng Hsiao-p'ing, that is, taking one step and looking around before taking another so as to find a road suitable to mainland China.[54]

Being extolled as a new model which has dispensed with the outdated, rigid, and dull model used before, the "road with Chinese characteristics" has two distinctive features. One is that it is analogous, to a certain extent, to Lenin's New Economic Policy (NEP), which was aimed at arming the Soviet Union with foreign capital and technology. In the study of the NEP, we should pay attention to the following things: First, that policy was a strategic retreat.[55] Lenin said: "We have to retreat still further, in order, eventually, to go over to the offensive."[56] He also stated: "They [the Russian Communists] are capturing a number of positions by a 'new flanking movement,' so to speak; they are retreating in order to make better preparations for a new offensive against capitalism."[57] Because of that "retreat," Russia's economy was resuscitated. By the same policy, mainland China has absorbed a remarkable amount of technology and capital from Western countries. Meanwhile, however, the Chinese Communists have not stopped their criticism of the so-called bourgeois liberalization (including such systems as parliamentarianism; the two-party system; campaigning for office; freedom of speech, press, assembly, and association; the mentality of "doing things for the sake of money"; and the ideologies of individualism, nihilism, and liberalism). This is a clear indication that mainland China's hostility toward capitalism remains unchanged. Second, the form of economy currently existing on the Chinese mainland is similar to that in the Soviet Union under the NEP. During the period of the NEP, the Soviet economy was composed of five sectors: (1) the patriarchal sector (consisting mainly of individual peasants); (2) the petty commodity sector (including most of the peasants who sold the grain they produced); (3) the private capitalist sector; (4) the state-capitalist sector (consisting primarily of concessions and enterprises leased out by the state); and (5) the socialist sector (consisting of socialist industry as well as Soviet farms, collective farms, and state and cooperative trade).[58] In the PRC today, the economy is also composed of five sectors: (1) the system of ownership by the whole people; (2) the system of collective ownership; (3) the system of individual ownership; (4) the system of ownership of the integrated complexes; and (5) the state capitalism characterized by the joint ventures.[59] The five sectors are in the form of state enterprises run by the state, state enterprises run by collectives, collective enterprises run by the collective, collective enterprises run by individuals, individual enterprises run by individuals, joint ventures run by mainland Chinese themselves or jointly by Chinese and foreigners, cooperative enterprises, and enterprises run by foreigners.[60] Obviously, capitalist elements exist in the economic sector in mainland China today as they did in the Soviet Union during the NEP period. Evidence of the analogy between the PRC's reform and the Soviet NEP is provided by the fact that the former was advanced when a series of leftist policies, such as the Three Red Banners policy and the Cultural Revolution, proved to be ineffective, just as the latter one was advanced in the USSR when "military Communism" proved to be a failure there. In other words, the NEP in the Soviet Union and the economic reform now under way in mainland China were designed to avert an economic crisis in their respective countries. To allay the suspicion of people both in mainland China and abroad about the continuity of its policy, the PRC has time and again announced that its domestic reform and open-door policy will not be changed.

The second characteristic of mainland China's development policy is that it is in line with many of the concepts and measures advanced by Liu Shao-ch'i. For example, Liu proposed that Marxism should not be regarded as dogma but employed as a means to overcome individualism, liberalism, commandism, and bureaucratism.[61] He also proposed the abolishment of the system of lifelong tenure for leadership cadres. All these concepts are now accepted by the Chinese Communist leadership. In the economic sphere, Liu's policy of developing a planned but diversified and flexible system has also attracted renewed consideration. Many of the economic measures currently undertaken are a restoration of those advanced by Liu. These include the production responsibility system in agriculture, the free market and individual economy, greater authority for enterprises, invigoration of commodity circulation by observing the economic law, opening of trusts (integrated complexes), learning from capitalist countries about the management of enterprises, regarding the means of production as commodities, and opposition to egalitarianism.[62]

Mainland China is now still muddling along in its economic development, and it will have to take a long time before it can find the right way to follow. This conclusion can be drawn from the following statement by Chao Tzu-yang at the Fourth Session of the Sixth NPC: "We will strive to lay a foundation for the building of a new socialist economic structure with Chinese characteristics in five years or longer."[63] Whether this prediction will come true will depend upon whether the Chinese Communists will discontinue their hostility toward capitalism. As long as they continue to adhere to this attitude, they will encounter difficulties in developing a "new model" for success. Actually, the most urgent task for mainland China today is to "make up missed lessons on the development of capitalism."[64] Another prerequisite for any meaningful progress in economic development is the discontinuation of the Leninist one-party dictatorship and the Stalinist highly mandatory planned economy.[65]

Conclusion

The reformists have been confronted with two problems in the reform. One is the divorce of theory from practice. In the current reform, many of the measures adopted violate the Marxist principles to which the Chinese Communists adhered in the past. To rationalize the new policy and carry it through, the CCP initiated the study campaign. The other problem confronted in the reform is the emergence of many unhealthy tendencies, such as "worship of money" and corruption, as well as inflation and income polarization. In the current campaign, the reformists defended the reform policy by contending that these unhealthy tendencies are the inevitable "birth pangs" of a new system.[66] Yet no one is sure whether a miscarriage can be avoided and a new baby produced.

In short, ideology will play an important role before a new system is worked out. While it may constitute a hindrance to the formation of a new system, it may also provide the necessary basis for its establishment. Likewise, it may either become an obstacle to the reform policy or serve as a basis to rationalize the policy. Still, under the framework of Marxism-Leninism, the PRC's economic reform is expected to make at best only limited progress. Those who stick to Marxism-Leninism would criticize the policy of pepping up the domestic economy and opening to the outside world as an attempt to develop capitalism, while those interested in "bourgeois liberalization" would be accused of a deviation from communism.[67] What really matters is the official attitude toward Marxism. On the one hand, the Chinese Communist leadership is reluctant to make a break with Marxism-Leninism.[68] On the other hand, however, they intend to enrich the Marxist economics with injections of Western economics.[69] Nevertheless, the problem is how far the PRC can depart from Marxism without causing serious effects ideologically. Meanwhile, the difficulties in making decisions on the attitude to be pursued toward Marxism and capitalism will obstruct economic reform in mainland China.

Notes

1. Teng Hsiao-p'ing, "Uphold the Four Cardinal Principles," in *Selected Works* (Beijing: Foreign Languages Press, 1984), 170. The four principles refer to the socialist road, the dictatorship of the proletariat (or the people's democratic dictatorship), the Communist Party leadership, and Marxism-Leninism and Mao's thought.

2. Teng Hsiao-p'ing's speech at the CCP National Conference, *Beijing Review* 28, no. 39 (September 30, 1985): 18.

3. "Develop a New and Protracted Study Campaign," *People's Daily*, March 28, 1978, 1; and An Zhiguo, "Marxism Endures as Beacon," *Beijing Review* 29, no. 2 (January 13, 1986): 4. The term "study campaign" was used first in these two articles.

4. Chou Yang, "A Preliminary Study of Several Theoretical Issues Concerning Marxism," *People's Daily*, March 16, 1983, 4.

5. Su Shao-chih, "Develop Marxism in the Course of an All-out Reform," *Wen Hui Pao* (Shanghai), March 9, 1983, 3.

6. "Theory and Practice," *People's Daily*, December 7, 1984, 1, and December 8, 1984, 1.

7. Jonathan Kaufman, "Economist Su Looking to Chart New Path for Marxism in China," *Boston Globe*, April 26, 1985.

8. Su Shao-chih, "Study the Marxist Theories with New Demands," *People's Daily*, October 21, 1985, 5.

9. Ch'en Yun's speech at the Sixth Plenum of the CCP's Central Discipline Inspection Commission on September 24, 1985, see *Hsin-hua yüeh-pao* (New China Monthly) (Beijing) 1985, no. 9:43.

10. Ch'en Yun's speech at the CCP National Conference, *Beijing Review* 28, no. 39:19.

11. Li Yü, "On Questions Concerning the Reform of the Marxist Education," *Chung Pao* (Monthly) (Hong Kong), no. 74 (March 1986): 23.

12. Yü Shih-ch'un, "Don't Compose 'Doggerels' Carelessly," *People's Daily*, November 25, 1982, 1.

13. Teng Hsiao-p'ing, *Chien-she yu Chung-kuo t'e-se te she-hui chu-i* (Build Socialism with Chinese Characteristics) (Beijing: People's Publishing House, 1984), 60.

14. *Hsin-hua yüeh-pao*, 1985, no. 3:110. In his speech, Teng said: "Some people are worried that China will turn capitalist. You cannot say that they are worried for nothing. We should use facts, not empty words, to dispel this worry and answer those who really hope us to turn capitalist. Our news media should take heed of this point and imbue the next two generations with lofty Communist ideals. On no account should we allow our youngsters to fall captive to capitalist ideas."

15. *Ming Pao* (Hong Kong), October 6, 1985, 5.

16. T'ien Chi-yun, "Questions Concerning the Current Economic Situation and the Reform of the Economic System," *People's Daily*, January 12, 1986, 2.

17. See note 9.

18. "Reform, Open Door, and the Construction of Socialist Spiritual Civilization," *People's Daily*, January 4, 1986, 1.

19. That article also said: "It is not strange that theory lags behind practice. However, if it is too far behind practice, we cannot regard it as an honor for the theoretical circles. The rapidly developing excellent situation requires that the comrades in theoretical circles rouse themselves to catch up."

20. P'eng Chen, "Strive to Study Basic Marxist Theories," *People's Daily*, August 16, 1985, 1.

21. Chang Hsien-yang and Wang Kuei-hsiu, "Grasp the Marxist Theories in Accordance with the New Realities," *People's Daily*, November 1, 1985, 5.

22. Yuan Mu, "Three Questions Concerning the Understanding About the Reform," *Liao-wang* (Outlook) (Beijing), 1986, no. 6:14.

23. Wei Yü-ming, "On the Open-Door Policy of Our Country and Our Foreign Economic Relations and Trade," *Kung-fei kuang-po chi-yao* (Summary of Broadcasts of Mainland Radio) (Taipei), no. 8325 (February 15, 1986): Economics 5–11.

24. "A Further Study on Theory and Practice," *Hsin-hua yüeh-pao*, 1985, no. 12:31.

25. See note 20. Teng Wei-chih, "A 'Breakthrough' in the Study of Marxism," *People's Daily*, March 14, 1986, 5.

26. Yü Tsu-yao, "The Development of Commodity Economy Is the Only Way to Make People Rich and the Country Prosperous," *Ssu-hsiang chan-hsien* (Ideological Front) (Yunnan), December 1985, 27.

27. Hsu Chia-t'un, "Speech at a Panel Meeting of CPPCC Members from Hong Kong and Macao," *Ta Kung Pao* (Hong Kong), April 1, 1986, 3.

28. Hsu Chia-t'un, "Speech at the Annual Dinner of the Hong Kong Society of Accountants," *Ta Kung Pao* (Hong Kong), November 2, 1985, 5.

29. Chao Tzu-yang, "Report on the Draft of the Seventh Five-Year Plan," *People's Daily*, March 27, 1986, 2.

30. Yuan Mu, "Three Questions," 12; Yuan Mu, "Some Questions Concerning Reform and the Open Door," *Kwangming Daily*, January 25, 1986, 3; and Juan Chiang-ning and Hsu P'ei-chun, "Elimiate Corruption," *Shih-chieh ching-chi tao-pao* (World Economic Herald), no. 276 (February 17, 1986): 16.

31. Yuan Mu, "Three Questions." See also note 23.

32. T'ao Hai-su, "A Theoretical Analysis of the Problems Arising from Reforms," *Ching-chi jih-pao* (Economic Daily) (Peking), October 26, 1985, 1. According to T'ao, the theory applies a "failure rate" in measuring the reliability of a policy, that is, the possibility of achieving the objective of a policy. According to this theory, in the entire process of implementing a policy, failure can generally be divided into three stages: early failure, accidental failure, and failure through wear. In the course of its

implementation, a new policy is often inefficient to varying degrees from the very beginning, and its failure rate is often fairly high. After a certain period, when the new policy has given full scope to its effective function, the situation becomes normal, and its failure rate drops considerably. This is the stage of accidental failure. After the policy has been implemented for a fairly long time, changes in the subjective conditions and the aging of the policy result in a gradual increase of the failure rate. This is the stage of failure through wear. As time goes by, the failure rate forms a "high-low-high" shape in a plane coordinate. It looks like a bathtub, and, therefore, it is called a "bathtub curve."

33. See note 29.

34. Mao Tse-tung, "Notes on the (Part of Socialism) in the 'Textbook on Political Economy'" (1960), in *Mao Tse-tung ssu-hsiang wan-sui* (Long live Mao Tse-tung's thought), vol. 2 (n.p., 1969; reprinted, Taipei: Institute of International Relations, 1974), 181–82. Mao said: "In reality, the more backward the economy becomes, the easier rather than the harder the transition of capitalism to socialism will become; the poorer the people become, the more they are in need of revolution."

35. Teng, *Chien-she yu Chung-kuo t'e-she te she-hui chu-i*, 36. At a meeting with Radovan Vlajkovic, president of Yugoslavia, on April 4, 1986, Teng said: "We cannot say that not wanting capitalist riches is incorrect. But the Marxist viewpoint definitely does not equate communism with poverty." See *Ta Kung Pao*, April 5, 1986, 1.

36. Mao Tse-tung, "On the Ten Major Relationships" (April 25, 1956), in *Mao Tse-tung ssu-hsiang wan-sui*, vol. 1, 59.

37. Chalmers Johnson, "The Failures of Socialism in China," in *Proceedings of the Eighth Sino-American Conference on Mainland China* (Columbia: University of South Carolina, 1979), 36–38.

38. P'ing Ai-lan, "The Possibility of Teng's Success in Reform as Viewed from the Fall of the Ch'ing Dynasty," *Pai-hsing* (The People) (Hong Kong), no. 116 (March 16, 1986): 48.

39. See note 37.

40. *Chung-kuo shih-pao* (The China Times) (Taipei), December 8 and 11, 1984, 1; *New York Times*, December 10, 1984; and *The Economist*, December 15, 1984.

41. *Time*, January 6, 1986, 11.

42. Harry Harding, "Marx, Mao and Markets," *The New Republic*, October 7, 1985, 4.

43. Chang Wu-ch'ang, *Chung-kuo te ch'ien-t'u* (China's Future), 3rd ed. (Hong Kong: Hsin Pao Company, 1985), 158.

44. Aleksandr I. Solzhenitsyn, *Letter to the Soviet Leaders* (New York: Harper & Row, 1974), 48. Solzhenitsyn said: "Let us all pull off and shake off from all of us this filthy sweaty shirt of Ideology (Marxism) which is now so stained with the blood of those 66 million that it prevents the living body of the nation from breathing. This ideology bears the entire responsibility for all the blood that has been shed."

45. "All Party Members Should Pay Attention to the Study of Marxist Theories," *Red Flag*, 1985, no. 24:14.

46. Jan S. Prybyla, "China's Economic Experiment: From Mao to Market," *Problems of Communism* 35, no. 1 (January-February 1986): 38.

47. "What Do the Changes in the Seven Years Account For" and "The Seventy Achievements Obtained Since the Third Plenary Session of the CCP's Eleventh Central Committee," *Pan-yüeh T'an* (Semimonthly Chats) (Beijing), 1986, no. 2:4–13.

48. See note 28.

49. Chu-yuan Cheng, "Economic Reform in Mainland China in Comparison to Yugoslavia and Hungary," in *Perspectives on Development in Mainland China*, ed.

King-yuh Chang (Boulder, Colo.: Westview Press, 1985), 253–280, and Jan S. Prybyla, "Plan and Market: The Bird in the Cage—A Comparative Study of Mainland China and Other State Socialist Economies," ibid., 281–331.

50. For details see Ch'ien Chun-jui, ed., *Tzu-pen chu-i yü she-hui chu-i tsung-heng-t'an* (A Free Discussion on Capitalism and Socialism) (Beijing: World Knowledge Publishing House, 1983), 195–308; Kuan Wei-hung, "A Comparison of the Planned Economy Practiced in the Various Socialist Countries," *Chung-kuo chih ch'en* (The China Spring) (New York), no. 2 (March 1983): 9–16; and Huan Hsiang, "On China's Socialist Modernization," *Cheng-ming* (Contending) (Hong Kong), no. 72 (October 1983): 80.

51. Kao Fang, *She-hui chu-i te kuo-ch'ü hsien-tsai ho wei-lai* (The Past, Present, and Future of Socialism) (Beijing: Beijing Publishing House, 1982), 163–166.

52. "Minutes of the Forum on the Experiment of the Economic Structural Reform in Cities," *Hsin-hua yüeh-pao*, 1984, no. 5:119, and "Decision on Reform of the Economic Structure," *Beijing Review* 27, no. 44 (October 29, 1984): centerfold pages.

53. Cheng, "Economic Reform in Mainland China."

54. See note 20. See also *People's Daily*, June 30, 1985, 1, and *Tung Kung Pao*, April 5, 1986, 1. Teng Hsiao-p'ing said: "Compared with the structural economic reform in rural areas, that in cities is more complicated. What we have been doing now is taking one step and looking around before taking another. We should be fully determined but should walk steadily."

55. V. I. Lenin, "The New Economic Policy and the Tasks of the Political Education Departments" (Report to the Second All-Russia Congress of Political Education Departments, October 17, 1921), in *Collected Works*, vol. 33 (Moscow: Progress Publishers, 1966), 63.

56. V. I. Lenin, "The Seventh Moscow Gubernia Conference of the Russian Communist Party," in *Collected Works*, vol. 33 (Moscow: Progress Publishers, 1966), 96.

57. V. I. Lenin, "The Role and Function of the Trade Unions Under the New Economic Policy," in *Collected Works*, vol. 33 (Moscow: Progress Publishers, 1966, 184.

58. V. I. Lenin, "The Tax in Kind," in *Collected Works*, vol. 32 (Moscow: Progress Publishers, 1965), 331.

59. *Kung-ch'an chu-i li-lun yü shih-chien* (The Theory and Practice of Communism) (Kansu: People's Publishing House, 1984), 163–166.

60. Cheng Hsin-li, "The Second Revolution and the Theoretical Opening Up," *Ching-chi jih-pao*, November 2, 1985.

61. Liu Shao-ch'i, "On the Attitude and Method of Study," in *Liu Shao-ch'i hsüan-chi* (Selected Works of Liu Shao-ch'i), vol. 2 (Beijing: People's Publishing House, 1985), 49–51.

62. Liu Ch'ung-wen, "Exploration and Contribution to the Building of Socialist China," *People's Daily*, December 16, 1985, 5; Ch'en Shao-ch'ou, "Study Comrade Liu Shao-ch'i's Ideology on Socialist Construction," *Ching-chi jih-pao*, December 21, 1985; and Wang Kuang-mei, "A Good Example of Daring to Seek Truth from Facts," *People's Daily*, December 13, 1985, 5.

63. *People's Daily*, March 26, 1986, 1.

64. Ma Hung, "The Importance of Eliminating Spiritual Pollution on the Theoretical Front," *People's Daily*, December 11, 1983, 5. Ma Hung said there were people who had expressed the opinion that as the socialist revolution made mainland China lag behind in productivity, mainland China should go back to the stage of New Democracy and make up lessons for the development of capitalism. He added that there were

people who advocated capitalism and market economy but not socialism and a planned economy.

65. Harry Harding, "Change in Communist Societies: The Transformation of China," *Current*, no. 267 (November 1984): 22–26.

66. Yuan Mu, "Three Questions," *Liao-wang*, 1986, no. 6:12, and Fang Kung-wen, "Have a Correct Understanding of Some of the Phenomena in the Current Economic Structural Reform," *Kwangming Daily*, November 16, 1985, 3.

67. Teng Hsiao-p'ing, "On Opposing Wrong Ideological Tendencies," in *Selected Works* (Beijing: Foreign Languages Press, 1984), 359, and "The Four Cardinal Principles Are the Basis for All Policies," *Red Flag*, 1985, no. 22:12.

68. See note 60. Currently, there is a controversy within theoretical circles as to whether the restrictions of Marxism should be broken through. Some people maintain that as long as there is a need to develop Marxism, there is a need to make a breakthrough to Marxism.

69. Ma Ding, "Ten Major Changes in China's Study of Economics," *Beijing Review* 28, no. 49 (December 9, 1985): 18.

PART THREE

Party and Politics

7

The Reorganization and Streamlining of the Chinese People's Liberation Army

June Teufel Dreyer

Goals

The reorganization and streamlining of the People's Liberation Army (PLA) are the touchstones of Deng Xiaoping's military modernization program. They aim at producing an armed force that is not only leaner, but also younger, better educated, better trained, better equipped, and better liked by the civilian sector of society. Reorganization and streamlining are also intended to produce a force that is more loyal to the central leadership— in this case, to Deng—armed with a better strategy, and amenable to sharing the use of its infrastructure and the capacity of its factories with the civilian economy.

Accomplishments

Some genuine changes have been instituted since Deng began his military reforms; the PLA of the late 1980s is significantly different from that of the early years of the decade. It is clearly fewer in numbers: A 25 percent cut for all services of the PLA except the Second Artillery (the PLA's missile arm) is gradually being implemented. *The Military Balance, 1981–82* (London: International Institute for Strategic Studies) lists the total size of the PLA as 4.75 million; that for 1985–1986, as 3.9 million.

At the same time, the number of military regions in the People's Republic of China (PRC) was reduced from eleven to seven. The new military regions have been given the right to command the different service arms; in the past, these service arms were placed under the armed forces command. Hereafter, again with the exception of the Second Artillery, the service arms were to be under military region command.

There is a new conscription law and a new military service law that establishes a reserve force and allows the reestablishment of a rank system.

The militia has been cut in size as well. In the past few years, the number of grassroots militia members has been reduced by 60 percent, while the numbers of their cadres has fallen by 80 percent. Quality, the central authorities have stated, has been increased even as numbers have fallen.[1] The entities responsible for militia work, the People's Armed Forces Departments, have been removed from joint PLA and city or county control, and placed under local jurisdiction.[2]

Efforts have also been made to give the smaller, more elite military a better appearance: Beginning in May 1985, better tailored new uniforms began to be worn.[3] There has been increasing emphasis on upgrading educational standards. Mass media stress "that the misperception that one can still win battles without knowledge must be rectified."[4] In 1982 units at and above the corps level were ordered to sponsor classes to bring cadres up to the level of senior middle school or technical middle school. Self-study was also to be encouraged: Those willing to enroll in night school, television, or correspondance courses were to be assisted in doing so. Tests of general and special knowledge were to be set up; those who could not or would not meet the required standards would be denied promotion or demoted.[5] At the same time, the Young Communist League was told to mobilize outstanding college graduates to join the PLA.[6]

A three-tiered system was created to train junior, midlevel, and senior officers, with more than a hundred military academies participating. The apex of the system will be the National Defense University, founded in December 1985 by merging the PLA Military Academy, the PLA Political Academy, and the PLA Logistics Academy—the three academies previously operated separately by the individual General Departments of the PLA. The National Defense University will begin classes in the fall of 1986, with the avowed purpose of training officers at and above the military region level, as well as to research strategic issues and serve in an advisory role to the Chinese Communist Party's (CCP's) Military Commission and to the PLA's General Departments. The new academy's leadership would seem to indicate the respect with which high party and government figures would like it to be regarded: Zhang Zhen, a former deputy chief of the General Staff, serves as president, and Li Desheng, a former commander of both the Beijing and Shenyang military regions and Politburo member, was named political commissar.[7]

Training exercises became more sophisticated, involving larger numbers of units. Between 100,000[8] and 200,000[9] men reportedly participated in a mass military exercise northwest of Beijing during the fall of 1981. These and other mass exercises showed a new focus on combined arms operations. Chinese media described a 1984 exercise in the East China Sea as unprecedented in terms of the numbers and kinds of warships taking part; fighter planes and ground forces were involved as well.[10]

Aware of the disadvantages posed by an entire generation of troops never having seen combat, the PLA leadership decided to use hostilities with Vietnam to the army's benefit: Officers are being rotated through four-month tours at the front. New journals such as *Binggi Zhishi* (Ordnance Knowledge) seek to acquaint soldiers with better fighting techniques, and a lengthy *National Defense Modernization Handbook* was published in 1983. There have also been some efforts made in the direction of more efficient recruit training. For example, in the fall of 1985, the Central Military Commission issued a directive providing for separate training of new recruits, rather than taking second- and third-year soldiers through the equivalent of basic training, as had been done in the past.[11]

In terms of weaponry, the argument was made that it would be easier and more efficient to supply the expensive high-technology equipment the PLA needs to upgrade its capabilities to a streamlined and better educated military than to the sprawling and poorly educated mass army of the past. Indigenous research and development efforts were intensified. The PRC built and tested nuclear submarines armed with nuclear missiles and experimented with new airframes and submachine gun designs.[12]

At the same time, extended discussions were held with foreign arms suppliers. Among the notable results of these have been an agreement with Israeli defense contractors for a modern tank firepower system (guns, ammunition, and fire control)[13] and, with the United States, an agreement to construct an artillery munitions factory[14] and, it now seems virtually certain, an avionics upgrade for China's F–8 fighter plane. The last-mentioned agreement, when consummated, will at last give China an all-weather-capable plane.[15]

The United States has also supplied, or agreed to supply, China with Sikorsky helicopters, the Raytheon 12 E 1167 sonar, the Mark 46 Mod 2 torpedo, and five LM 2500 gas turbines for the Chinese navy's destroyers. Shipborne radio systems, degaussing equipment, and the technology to build high-speed catamarans[16] have been obtained from Britain. France has supplied the Crotale surface-to-air missile, artillery-shell-loading equipment, and a coproduction agreement for the Dauphin helicopter. Other contracts have been signed with Austria, West Germany, and Sweden, and the Chinese have also expressed interest in purchasing armored vehicles and military equipment from Brazil.[17]

Some of the results of these activities appeared at an unusually elaborate parade held to celebrate the thirty-fifth anniversary of the founding of the PRC, in October 1984. Observers noted no less than ten new weapon systems of different types, including an updated version of the Type 59 main battle tank, designated the Type 69 and equipped with a 105-mm gun, a new minelaying vehicle, and a surface-to-surface antiship missile whose container/launcher was virtually identical with that of the French Exocet.[18]

In order to encourage better army-civilian ties, the government has tended to place the blame for poor relations between the two on the Cultural Revolution. Lin Biao and the Gang of Four are held responsible for friction in civil-military relations, and lengthy indictments of their specific sins are provided. Although it must be obvious to all those old enough to remember, military perquisites such as better food, housing, and transportation long predated the Cultural Revolution. Deng's government, however, has vowed to make amends. Army personnel have been ordered to vacate premises they have occupied illegally, and in general to live on a more frugal scale. PLA men and civilians have been admonished to work together to create so-called civilized villages. High-ranking officers are described as working shoulder-to-shoulder with ordinary folk in periodic campaigns to clear mud and garbage from city streets, and the army's role in both afforestation drives and disaster relief are well publicized by mass media.

As for producing a force that is more loyal to Deng Xiaoping, the heads of the three General Departments of the PLA have all been replaced since 1980;[19] in the most spectacular of these personnel changes, the head of the General Political Department, who had previously been regarded as supportive of Deng, was removed after blatantly disagreeing with his chief on the matter of spiritual pollution. Similarly, every one of the commanders of the original eleven military regions has been replaced since 1980, and some posts have changed hands more than once.[20] The reduction to seven military regions brought further changes: There are now three new commanders, and all seven political commissars are new. It is highly likely that support for Deng's programs was an important criterion in selection for these positions. In December 1984 an additional forty officers at corps level and above submitted their resignations,[21] followed by several other senior military figures in a major Politburo reorganization in September 1985. The military's representation on the party's Central Committee has fallen to approximately 20 percent, and the army's official newspaper has called for eliminating political work from the command structure.[22]

A new strategic doctrine, to replace People's War, has also been announced for the newly streamlined and reorganized PLA. Known as "People's War under modern conditions," it was described by Chief of the General Staff Yang Dezhi as "a tiger that has grown wings."[23] The details of this strategy have not yet been made explicit. In fact, in consideration of the advantages conferred by secrecy in such matters, they may never be. However, certain features of the new doctrine seem clear. As noted before, there is less emphasis on "luring deep" and on mobile warfare than was characteristic of the original People's War. Positional warfare, though never entirely ignored in the past, is now considered more important. This new emphasis is evident in the way the army has used its tanks on maneuvers. In many cases, and in sharp contrast to past practice, the tanks have been dug in.

As for luring deep, there has been a realization that in present-day China this strategy would involve surrendering a great deal of territory, including valuable assets that would be difficult to recapture. Recent strategy has focused instead on guiding the invaders toward carefully selected battlefields of China's own choosing and counterattacking in these locations. The fall 1981 exercises described previously may be seen as a case in point, the aim being the defense of Beijing.

There has also been a good deal of Chinese interest in developing their forces' ability to engage a front-line military offensive threat. In this regard, Chinese strategists have become very interested in the U.S. Army's concept of the Air-Land Battle. A visiting delegation from the U.S. National Defense University and another from the RAND Corporation were separately asked by their Chinese hosts to prepare lectures on this topic.[24] There is a good deal more interest in the discussion of strategy in general. For example, the Beijing Institute of International Strategic Studies, itself headed by a high-ranking PLA officer, Xu Xiuquan, hosts a "military salon" in which younger and middle-aged officers are encouraged to exchange views.[25]

A streamlined and more efficiently organized PLA would presumably need fewer of the products of defense industry factories and would use the defense infrastructure less, as well. Hence, on the premise that national defense could be modernized only if the agricultural and industrial bases of the country were strengthened first, the PLA was ordered to utilize its factories and infrastructure on behalf of civilian economic development. Arms production facilities typically possessed more sophisticated technology than civilian factories, which could thus benefit from its transfer to them. In addition, even before the PLA's numbers were cut, most defense industry production lines had operated at below capacity and had relied heavily on state subsidies. The new policy might be a way to make them profitable as well.

Accordingly, beginning from 1979, increasing numbers of these factories regeared production lines to turn out goods as diverse as socks, radios, and washing machines. A naval radar plant in Nanjing whose orders were cut by nearly 80 percent in 1980 reportedly saved itself from closure by producing electric fans for civilian use.[26] And a U.S. space team on a 1985 visit to the plant that manufactures China's Titan class booster rocket discovered that the same facility also produced refrigerators.[27]

The military also turned over seventy railroad lines in East China, once used exclusively by the PLA, to local use.[28] Oil and fuel depots and commodity storage warehouses were also converted to civilian purposes.[29] The air force agreed to sell more than 200 transport planes to civil aviation companies at bargain prices, even supplying their crews and assuming responsibility for overhaul and repair work.[30] Some ports and motor vehicles were also transferred to civilian use.

PLA personnel continued to devote approximately 20 million man-days a year to civilian economic purposes and became more heavily involved in nonmilitary construction projects than in previous years. These included such massive undertakings as the Luanhe diversion channel to bring water to Tianjin, and the Beijing subway system. In the words of Chief of the General Staff Yang Dezhi, "It has rarely happened that the PLA devoted so many troops to so many civilian projects."[31] Similarly, a Western defense analyst noted that "there has recently been a considerable increase in the purely civilian tasks troops have undertaken."[32]

Difficulties

Unquestionably the PLA has changed considerably from the force Deng Xiaoping reportedly described in January 1975 as suffering from "bloating, laxity, conceit, extravagance, and inertia."[33] Yet not all change constitutes improvement. While substantial progress has certainly been made, the streamlining and reorganization process has accomplished neither as much nor done so as quickly as some reports might lead one to believe. For example, the recent campaign to lower the ages of officers has indeed succeeded in producing a younger officer corps. However, in the opinions of several U.S. military attachés, many of the individuals may be *too* young: they do not have the experience necessary to cope with the responsibility for units as large as those they now command.

The new educational requirements have produced on the one hand a feverish rush of activity to pass the examinations, and on the other, a thriving industry in cheating to get through or get around them. There have also been instances of newly promoted, better educated officers being ridiculed by their comrades as "university fanatics" or "people who seek fame."[34] The need for "self-study" and "advanced training" have been used as pretexts for many soldiers, especially the sons and daughters of leading cadres, to leave their work posts for extended periods of time. Their numbers were sufficiently large enough for the Jinan Military Region to issue an injunction to return immediately. Those who disobeyed, it stressed, would be punished "regardless of whose sons and daughters they are."[35]

With regard to training, a 1985 all-army forum criticized high-ranking officers who "lack courage and take a passive attitude toward [training] reform" as the number-one problem to be solved.[36] The official *Liberation Army Daily* has also reprimanded units for cheating on training exercises and bribing outside observers to certify the erroneous results.[37]

In terms of equipment upgrades, the PLA has been bedeviled by problems. The submarine development program has had problems of design and testing, and the September 1985 attempt to launch SSBNs from a *Xia* class boat appears to have been unsuccessful.[38] The PRC's efforts to test, proof, and recover torpedoes are advancing very slowly. As for the program to develop advanced fighters, an analyst for the prestigious *Jane's Defence Weekly* noted that "time is not on China's side. It has taken nearly twenty years for the J–8 [F–8] to approach viability, and China cannot afford such tremendously protracted development."[39] The comparably respected *International Defense Review* described the plane as "China's Great Leap Sideways. . . . Far from indicating an encouraging degree of progress in Chinese aerospace technology, as some more sanguine observers have claimed, the design of the J–8 demonstrates that the state of indigenous technology is stagnant and continues to lose ground against the West and the Soviet Union."[40] Further, the new antitank missile displayed at China's 1984 National Day parade was deemed "still very much a developmental weapon and . . . not in production. . . . [I]t has encountered a number of problems, the most serious of which is repeated breakage of the guidance wire at ranges of about 1500 metres."[41]

It is difficult to assess the success of the government's attempts to foster better civil-military relations. Repeated references to attempts to get military families to vacate improperly occupied housing would seem to indicate that their efforts to evade eviction are frequently successful. The recent crackdown on the economic and sexual offenses of leading PLA cadres and their children against civilians may be regarded as either indicative of the problems inherent in the military or as a sign that the system is healthy enough to correct these abuses, depending on one's predisposition.

Certainly service in the military is no longer regarded as desirable, since agricultural reforms have made it more profitable for young men to stay in their native villages. Young people already in the military have been encouraged to write their friends urging them to join, and the punishments for avoiding military service have been made clear.[42] Yet another attempt to solve the PLA's problems in meeting even its reduced quota of conscripts is indicated in a report from Chengdu: New recruits' original work units are to pay them a monthly sum not less than 50 percent of normal wages. As one Western analyst commented, "Just what the industrial enterprises think about being robbed of their best workers while being forced to continue paying their wages is not stated."[43]

As for strategy, a former U.S. assistant secretary of defense who observed PLA maneuvers in the spring of 1985 described them as "Korean War vintage," and expressed doubt that they would have been effective even then.[44] *Jane's Defence Weekly's* analysis of China's positional warfare techniques was far from optimistic. The periodical's commentator noted that even a tank regiment (composed of seventy-eight tanks and two headquarters) would be easily penetrated by a concerted Soviet attack, and concluded that this statement would be true whether the Chinese tanks were the older-style Type 59 or the newer Type 69. Although retrofitted 105-mm guns and lasers will permit improved gun engagement ranges, other support weapons, such as multiple rocket launchers and antitank guided missiles would have to be present to make these effective.[45]

The PLA's adoption of the Air-Land Battle concept is likely to fare no better. While there is an obvious Chinese interest in being able to deal with a front-line military offensive threat, the PRC is very far from having the equipment to make it work. Indeed, there are doubts as to the ability of the much better-equipped U.S. Army to carry out this strategy. The rationale for the Air-Land Battle is the belief that the overwhelming superiority the Warsaw Pact enjoys over the NATO forces in tanks and other fighting vehicles can be compensated for by the extensive use of helicopters to enhance mobility and firepower. Some helicopters would be equipped with antitank guided missiles to shoot enemy tanks, while others would land infantry behind enemy lines.[46]

The Chinese have committed themselves to the Dauphin helicopter and a few years ago signed a contract with France to coproduce the vehicle in a factory in Harbin. However, thus far they have been unable to actually manage the production line. Basically, the French have been supplying kits to the factory, which then assembles them. In addition, even if the PRC could turn out helicopters independently, the Dauphin is unsuited to a role in the Air-Land Battle; it is simply too small. The government has already discovered this fact with regard to other purposes. For example, the size of the helicopter has made it impossible to equip it with both a dipping sonar and a torpedo. Privately, some Chinese officials admit that they made a mistake in choosing to acquire the Dauphin. But it is clear that they intend to continue producing it.

Yet another problem would be maintaining the large number of helicopters needed for the Air-Land Battle. Helicopters require much servicing, and the PRC lacks the necessary number of trained field mechanics to provide it. A China that lacks the capacity to manufacture and maintain adequate numbers of tanks that are a match for the Soviet Union would be ill-advised to adopt a strategy that involves large numbers of vehicles that are still more difficult to manufacture and maintain.

Basically, the obstacle to the Chinese adopting the Air-Land Battle is that it would involve an attempt to compensate for the PRC's technological inferiority against the Soviet Union by employing a strategy that requires a still higher level of technology. The RAND delegation referred to previously interpreted the attention devoted to the Air-Land Battle as evidence of an unrealistic attitude toward strategy in general.[47]

Military reorganization plans have had their problems as well. The proposal to reduce the PLA by a million men was first made in 1982, and it had some effects. The Railway Corps of perhaps 125,000 men, the People's Armed Forces Police, numbering perhaps 300,000, and some units of the PLA's Capital Construction Corps were civilianized, though essentially performing the same duties as before and, in the case of the People's Armed Forces Police, apparently remaining under Military Commission jurisdiction.

Although, as previously noted, enlisted personnel were generally pleased to leave the military, attitudes among the officer corps were quite different. Perhaps the most disquieting development from the government's point of view was the formation of disgruntled groups of men who had been demobilized against their will. Those who were unable to obtain satisfactory alternative employment and found the authorities unsympathetic to their pleas tended to make their protests public. Demonstrations, which included varying degrees of violence, were reported from several different areas of China. Since it was apparently not unusual for demobilized soldiers to retain their weapons, some of the discontented coalesced into bandit groups, staging raids on government offices and preying on local peasants. The best publicized of these, the so-called Disillusioned Army, claimed a membership of 6,000, more than half of whom participated in the temporary takeover of county government offices in western Guangdong province.[48]

In the face of these and other problems, including the unwillingness of many localities to accept demobilized soldiers,[49] the demobilization stopped short of completion. It was revived again in early 1985, with renewed vigor and some changes. One important difference is that the responsibility for resettlement of demobilized veterans has been transferred to the Ministry of Civil Affairs—clearly an effort to remove the stigma of its effects from the military authorities. There has also been much publicity given to the concept of the PLA training "dual competence people"—that is, to advertise that service in the military would teach skills that would be salable on the civilian job market.

This second attempt at demobilization has, however, been accompanied by renewed difficulties, since so many people have a vested interest in avoiding its effects. Chief of the General Staff Yang Dezhi recently complained that there were problems of officers leaving their posts even before their units were disbanded, saying that this and other "unhealthy practices" had caused disorder in the army's work.[50] There have also been reports of rush promotions so as to get higher retirement pay, of improper recruitment of party members within the army, and of soldiers who thought they might be demobilized dividing up military property amongst themselves.

Other soldiers were reportedly denuding their barracks areas of trees and anything else remotely portable. Officers who were forced to retire because of age had used their contacts in the bureaucracy to have their children appointed to the jobs they were vacating. Where units were merged or abolished, one unit would often refuse to accept officers transferred from another. The refusing units were suspicious of both the transferees' loyalties and of their competence. With regard to the former, they expressed un-willingness to work with a complete stranger whom one could not necessarily trust. As to the latter, the units feared that, had the officer to be transferred been a good one, his original unit would not have agreed to part with him, reasoning that "no family would send its beloved child to the temple to serve as a monk."[51]

Clearly, such difficulties in transferring officers among units will severely constrain the development of a modernized, professional army. And if, as seems to be the case, those who survive do so because of their connections rather than their competence, streamlining and reorganization may not noticeably improve the quality of the officer corps.

High-ranking members of the Military Commission have also complained about continued factionalism and the bad effects it is having on the military.[52] They have been critical as well of officers who maintain a passive attitude toward the reforms or choose to wallow in confusion rather than attempt to sort out difficulties.[53] Despite the passage of a law in 1984 reinstituting the rank system, it has so far proved impossible to actually do so. Continued disagreement over who should be assigned which rank appears to be a principal cause. There are also potential problems with reducing the number of military regions and giving them the right to command the different service arms, since larger entities with greater resources at their command have concomitantly greater potential to become foci of resistance to the central government.

Moreover, though Deng has been able to get rid of a number of military commanders and commissars, he has yet to win the military's approval of his choice for head of the Central Military Commission, Hu Yaobang. Since Hu has for the past several years occupied the highest position in the Chinese Communist Party, it is conceivable that he may have trouble keeping the military in line after Deng Xiaoping passes from the scene. Indeed, official sources have sought to quiet speculation on exactly this theme. In a classic example of creative evasion of a question, a spokesperson for the 1985 party conference, when asked by a reporter whether the new younger leaders would be able to handle the military after Deng's departure, replied that the present elections had confirmed the principle of the party commanding the gun, although it was "hard to draw a distinction between who are civilian officials and who are military officials, since eight or nine out of ten of them have experience in leading troops and fighting battles."[54]

The military's greater involvement in the development of the civilian economy has opened newer and more lucrative channels for corruption. Examples abound; one of the more spectacular recent cases resulted in the conviction of several division-level officers in the Guangzhou Military Region, including both the commander and the commissar. The unit had been engaged in a profitable vehicle purchase and resale scheme, which was discovered only when one of their subordinates was robbed and murdered by the owner of a vehicle he was attempting to purchase. The scheme apparently came to light almost accidentally, since the officers were able to conceal information on their comrade's death for several weeks.[55] Military vehicles have frequently been reported as the conduits for smuggling operations, with military personnel of various ranks, as in the example cited, heavily involved as well.

The development of advanced weapons and their acquisition from abroad are being held back by a number of factors. First, there is conflict between the Chinese who would like the PRC to develop its own weapons and those who would prefer to buy from abroad. The National Defense Science, Technology, and Industry Commission, better known as NDSTIC, which would prefer the latter strategy, has resorted to setting up several trading companies to try to get around the resistance from elsewhere in the bureaucracy. It has placed the children of several of China's highest-ranking leaders, including Deng Xiaoping and Nie Rongzhen, in key positions in these companies.[56]

Second, there is conflict over what foreign systems to buy. Differing assessments over the military capabilities of differing weapons are compounded by the international implications of buying from, say, Israel as opposed to France or Great Britain.[57] Third, the PRC has a relatively limited defense budget, and foreign purchases are expensive. Government action to improve a balance of payments position it regards as less than satisfactory, together with China's announcement in January 1986 of a record US$7.61 billion trade deficit, seem to indicate continued constraints on foreign purchases.

Last, and perhaps most important, the PRC lacks an overarching strategy or unifying theme that it could use to judge which weapon systems would be suitable. The aforementioned RAND group felt that the inquiries it received amounted to "an indiscriminate shopping spree for technological targets of opportunity, with detailed discussion of specific menu items, but no overall strategy."[58]

Conclusions

The PRC's efforts to reorganize and streamline its forces have resulted in stripping nearly a million persons from the military's rolls. However, many of these, such as the People's Armed Force Police, the Railway Corps, and some construction units, continue to do the same tasks as before, under different auspices. The raising of educational standards, improvement of training methods, and introduction of more sophisticated weaponry, have all made modest progress, although efforts to improve army-civilian relations are thus far inconclusive. The reduction in the number of military regions and the transfer of additional assets to military region command is efficient at one level, but it may cause inefficiencies at another, since centripetal pressures may be increased thereby. And the PLA still lacks a coherent strategy; continued failure to arrive at one may negate the progress made in other areas. Moreover, personnel and morale problems resulting from merging units and transferring officers remain serious.

In sum, while gains have clearly been made, the rate of military modernization has been slower than hoped for. The lack of consensus on certain crucial matters, combined with continued factionally based frictions and ongoing financial constraints indicates that the outlook for significant near-term improvements in the PLA's fighting capabilities relative to those of the United States or the Soviet Union is not encouraging. Nonetheless, even after major cuts in size, the PLA will remain the world's largest military, and it can draw on the world's largest pool of reservists. Hence its military potential against other Asian states remains substantial and may even increase somewhat.

Notes

1. Beijing Radio, 16 December 1985, in United States Department of Commerce Foreign Broadcast Information, Vol. I, China (hereafter, FBIS-CHI), 18 December 1985, p. K/12.

2. Beijing Radio, 28 August 1985, in United States Department of Commerce, Joint Publications Research Service China: Political and Sociological (hereafter, JPRS-CPS), 25 October 1985, p. 21.

3. Beijing Radio, 11 June 1985, in FBIS-CHI, 11 June 1985, pp. K/2–3.

4. *Xinhua* (Beijing), 18 November 1982, in FBIS-CHI, 24 November 1982, p. O/6; Lanzhou Radio, 18 November 1982, in FBIS-CHI, 3 December 1982, p. T/1.

5. *Yunnan Ribao*, 16 December 1981, in FBIS-CHI, 5 January 1982, p. Q/4.

6. *Xinhua* (Beijing), 29 December 1982, in FBIS-CHI, 30 December 1982, p. K/6.

7. *Xinhua* (Beijing), 18 December 1985, in FBIS-CHI, 18 December 1985, p. K/1; Ibid., in FBIS-CHI, 1 December 1985, pp. K/2–5.

8. *South China Morning Post* (Hong Kong), 23 September 1981, pp. 1, 22.

9. Ibid., 24 September 1981, p. 8.

10. *Banyuetan* (Beijing), 10 April 1984, in JPRS-CPS-84-047 (17 July 1984), pp. 61–63.

11. *Ming Pao* (Hong Kong), 5 November 1985, in FBIS-CHI, 6 November 1985, pp. W/8–9.

12. *Jane's Defence Weekly* (London), 15 December 1984, p. 50.

13. *Die Welt* (Hamburg), 17 October 1984, p. 5; *Jane's Defence Weekly*, 24 November 1984, p. 15.

14. *Washington Post*, 19 September 1985, p. A/33; *New York Times*, 1 October 1985, p. 3.

15. Nayan Chanda, "New Planes for Old" *Far Eastern Economic Review*, 2 January 1986, pp. 11–12; *New York Times*, 25 January 1986, p. 5.

16. *International Defense Review* (Geneva), February 1986, p. 234.

17. *Jane's Defence Weekly*, 21 September 1985, p. 25.

18. *Military Technology*, No. 11, 1984, p. 140; *Flight International*, 27 October 1984, p. 1092.

19. Deng Xiaoping had been named head of the General Staff Department in July 1977; he replaced himself with a protégé, Yang Dezhi.

20. One of these was actually a transfer; You Taizhong, now commander of the Guangzhou Military Region, was previously commander of the Chengdu Military Region, and Qin Jiwei had been first political commissar of the Beijing Military Region before being made its commander in early 1980. You and Qin are also the only remaining military region commanders to have passed their seventieth birthdays.

21. *New York Times*, 31 December 1984, pp. 1, 4.

22. Beijing Radio, 9 November 1984, in FBIS-CHI, 15 November 1984, pp. K/12–13.

23. *Xinhua* (Beijing), 31 July 1983, in FBIS-CHI, 2 August 1984, p. K/1.

24. *Report on a Trip by a RAND Delegation to the PRC* (Santa Monica, Calif.: RAND Corporation, 1985), p. 19.

25. *Liaowang* (Hong Kong), 25 November 1985, in FBIS-CHI, 5 December 1985, pp. K/10–12.

26. *China Daily* (Beijing), 27 February 1985, p. 2.

27. "Chinese Modify CZ-2/3 Rocket Boosters, Focus on Commercial Launch Market," *Aviation Week and Space Technology* (Washington), 22 July 1985, p. 77.

28. Beijing Radio, 6 December 1984, in FBIS-CHI, 7 December 1984, p. O/1.

29. *Xinhua* (Beijing), 28 June 1985, in FBIS-CHI, 28 June 1985, pp. K/14–15.

30. *Xinhua* (Beijing), 3 August 1985, in FBIS-CHI, 7 August 1985, p. K/4.

31. *China Daily*, 4 January 1985, p. 1.

32. Clare Hollingworth, "PRC in Front Rank of Arms Trade," *Pacific Defence Reporter* (Canberra), May 1985, in JPRS-CPS-85-056, 7 June 1985, p. 136.

33. "Army Needs Consolidation," 25 January 1975, in *Selected Works of Deng Xiaoping*, 1 July 1983. Translated in JPRS *China Report* No. 468, pp. 2–3. I have been unable to find a *contemporary* account of this speech.

34. *Renmin Ribao*, 2 November 1982, in FBIS-CHI, 4 November 1982, p. K/8.

35. *Renmin Ribao*, 2 March 1984, in JPRS-CPS-084-032 (2 May 1984), p. 106.

36. *Ming Pao*, 11 January 1985, in FBIS-CHI, 14 January 1985, pp. W/2–3.

37. *Kyodo* (Tokyo), 16 May 1985, in JPRS-CPS-085-057, 12 June 1985, p. 107.

38. Agence France Presse (Hong Kong), 28 September 1985, in JPRS-CPS-085-110, pp. 58–59; *Jane's Defence Weekly*, 12 October 1985, p. 77.

39. Kenneth Munson, "Fishbed, Finback and the Chinese Future," *Jane's Defence Weekly*, 21 December 1985, p. 1369.

40. *International Defense Review*, December 1984, p. 1789.

41. *International Defense Review*, November 1985, p. 18.

42. Beijing Radio, 12 November 1985, in FBIS-CHI, 22 November 1985, p. K/22.

43. David Bonavia, "Half-Pay Soldiers," *Far Eastern Economic Review*, 21 November 1985, p. 18.

44. Author's conversation, 20 November 1985.

45. Carl Jacobs, "China's Type-59 and -69 MBTs," *Jane's Defence Weekly*, 27 July 1985, p. 174.

46. For a generally favorable view of the concept, see Boyd Sutton et al., "New Directions in Conventional Defence?" *Survival* (London), March/April 1984, pp. 50–70.

47. *Report on a Trip*, p. 20.

48. *Cheng Ming* (Hong Kong), 1 December 1981, in FBIS-CHI, 14 December 1982, pp. W/1–2; *Cheng Ming*, 1 January 1982, in FBIS-CHI, 5 January 1982, pp. W/2–4; *Ming Pao*, 26 December 1981, in FBIS-CHI, 6 January 1982, pp. W/2–3.

49. Military resistance to demobilization and civilian unwillingness to accept demobilized soldiers into their midst were characteristic of both imperial and republican China as well. In the latter, civil authorities would sometimes pay to have soldiers loaded on trains and shipped to other provinces for demobilization. See Diana Lary, *Warlord Soldiers; Chinese Common Soldiers, 1911–1937* (Cambridge University Press, 1985), pp. 96–100.

50. *Ming Pao*, 27 August 1985, in FBIS-CHI, 28 August 1985, pp. W/1–2; *Ming Pao*, 9 October 1985, in FBIS-CHI, 11 October 1985, p. W/1.

51. *Ming Pao*, 12 November 1985, in FBIS-CHI, 14 November 1985, p. W/1.

52. See, for example, *Wen Wei Po* (Hong Kong), 10 November 1985, in FBIS-CHI, 12 November 1985, p. W/1.

53. *Ming Pao*, 23 July 1985, in FBIS-CHI, 23 July 1985, pp. W/2–3.

54. *Wen Wei Po*, 25 September 1985, in FBIS-CHI, 26 September 1985, p. W/4.

55. *Ming Pao*, 6 November 1985, in FBIS-CHI, 7 November 1985, pp. W/1–2.

56. See Richard Gillespie, "Marketing to the PLA," *The China Business Review* (Washington, D.C.) July-August 1984, pp. 34–39.

57. For example, Egypt recently canceled an arms contract involving at least US$500 million when it discovered that some items had Israeli-made components. See *Jane's Defence Weekly*, 12 October 1985, p. 763.

58. *Report on a Trip*, p. 20.

8

Chinese Politics: The Bargaining Treadmill

David M. Lampton

Introduction

Since 1979, more than 3,000 American students and scholars have gone to the People's Republic of China (PRC) for study. Of those students and faculty in Chinese studies who went to conduct a month or more of research in China, about 17 percent were in political science and international relations, about 6 percent in economics, and another 13 percent in sociology and anthropology.[1] Accompanying this dramatic increase in direct access to the Chinese polity and society has been a perhaps more startling proliferation of published materials in the PRC. Given all these previously unavailable data and the new perspective from which to view older information, it is fair to ask, What do we know about the Chinese political system? How, if at all, has recent information about the Chinese polity changed our understanding of its operation? What are the implications of such a system for both policymaking and political stability?

What inspires me is not the hubris of grand theory, but the modest hope that we can begin to discern broader patterns of meaning in the many excellent discrete studies that have been undertaken to date.

To state the proposition undergirding this paper in its baldest form, available studies dealing with policy issues in the technical, economic, and social realms reveal a polity best understood as a *bargaining*, not a "command," system. To be sure, there are policy issues (e.g., in the ideological, security, and foreign policy realms) in which bargaining may be quite limited. Equally obviously, when there is a strong elite consensus that an issue brooks no delay (e.g., population policy in 1979–1980), the ability of the regime to enforce its will is impressive. Nonetheless, the bulk of issues that the political system must address, as well as the topics of concern to most Chinese most of the time, are resolved through an intensive process of consensus building in which leadership, at all levels is hesitant to act until there is a clear consensus among subordinates. Consensus often is achieved by implicit and explicit bargaining. This process is evident in both the policy-formulation and implementation phases. The metaphor for the Chinese political system which I have in mind is the rural county fair or market, a setting characterized by protracted haggling, posturing, conditional outcomes, frequent failure to reach agreement, and issues that rise and fall on the agenda, but are rarely fully resolved or discarded.

Among the research questions that arise from this perspective are the following: What basic system characteristics account for the broad range of bargaining activity? In what policy domains is bargaining activity most pronounced; in what areas is it least in evidence; and why? What do political participants bargain over, and who is entitled to enter the process? What tactics do participants employ to enhance their position? What factors account for the behavior of particular bargainers? What consequences does this process have for the behavior and performance of the entire policymaking system?

In the pages which follow I draw from both my own interviews and fieldwork in China and the case studies of other scholars who have examined a broad range of policy issues there. Lest I be misunderstood, a bargaining view of China's polity does *not* imply that all bargainers in the political marketplace are equal (any more than equality is implied in the economic marketplace); it does not diminish the fact that China is exceedingly hierarchical and role conscious (facts which greatly shape who is even consulted as bargains are struck); and it does not diminish the observation that coercive power is important, especially when the individual "crosses the line" (*guo xian*).

The Systematic Causes of Bargaining Activity

The assertion that much of the contemporary Chinese polity is best understood as a "bargaining system" should not be controversial if one considers several structural features of today's Chinese system:

1. Though the scope of state planning has undergone important changes in the last eight years (with guidance planning assuming a more prominent role and mandatory planning playing a declining role), the process of moving resources in society still is a political/bureaucratic decision in considerable measure. Shortages of both needed production inputs and high-quality products, as well as the perennial scarcity of building materials and capital, mean that decision makers at all levels must decide how to allocate exceedingly scarce resources with few, or no, market signals. Unsurprisingly, they respond to political pressure—and frequently pecuniary opportunity. Scarcity that cannot be resolved through a market system becomes the grist for the political bargaining mill.

2. The preceding generic problem with central-planning systems (physical output allocation systems) is further complicated by the fact that China now is in the awkward transition stage of reform. A small but dynamic market sector uneasily coexists with the rigidities of the still dominant administered

economy. The scarcities and rigidities of the dominant system provide opportunities (and problems) for the decontrolled sector—bargaining activity, of all sorts, results. Also, throughout the system, the state is trying to use economic levers (such as tax rates, bonuses, subsidies, tax holidays, preferential investment) to provide incentives for desired behavior. A bargaining process (either implicit or explicit) is essential in order to determine what level and mix of these levers will produce the desired behavior.

3. The technical complexity of many decisions (compounded by the fact that the state is undertaking a directed modernization effort involving thousands of projects simultaneously), in the context of an overloaded political elite with unclear decision rules, means that the elite frequently defers decision until subordinates (experts and various bureaucratic and territorial interests) are able to present them with a consensus decision. The more far-reaching the technical issue and the larger the risk of negative outcomes, the more diligently superiors desire subordinates to strike a consensus bargain that they can then approve. Most technical decisions involve trade-offs. Bargaining and consensus building is endemic to decisions in which trade-offs are involved.

4. It may seem curious to assert that a system that could launch an Anti-Rightist campaign, a Great Leap Forward, a Great Proletarian Cultural Revolution, and a one-child birth control movement is deficient in coercive resources, but it is. The elite has to pick carefully the times it employs coercion, not only because those resources are limited, but also because the widespread use of coercion would diminish the regime's ability to motivate sectors of the populace essential for achievement of its economic goals. The present regime has concluded that technical and economic innovation is generally best achieved in a noncoercive environment.

5. Territorial administrations and functional vertical organizations (the *kuai* and the *tiao* embody a variety of interests, and the minister of a ministry (*buzhang*) has the same rank in the system as a provincial governor (*sheng-zhang*). With respect to any given issue, specific ministries find that their interests and policy preferences correspond with, or diverge from, those of a complex array of other ministries and territorial units. Further, territorial and bureaucratic leaders are judged by subordinates by their capacity to defend their interests against external encroachment. Leaders "brag" (*kuayao*) about their ability to protect "their" domains, whether territorial or bureaucratic. Yu Qiuli's boastful defense of one subordinate who had been criticized in 1964 by the Liaoning Provincial Party Committee is instructive. Yu said, "xx [name unspecified] is an employee of my Petroleum Ministry: Who dares to touch even a hair on his skin?"[2] Finally, each bureaucratic organization develops its own distinctive organizational personality or ideology which frequently sanctifies enduring policy goals and provides the organization with a sense of cohesion.[3] Conflicts among these various territorial and bureaucratic entities arising from these sources result in bargaining.

6. The Chinese system presents us with the seeming contradiction of a massive bureaucracy of about 20 million cadres and 42 million party members,

but a system that is, as yet, weakly institutionalized. By weakly institutionalized, I mean that power and authority still reside substantially in persons rather than offices, stable procedures, and institutions. The individual citizen or subordinate, then, must generally appeal to the interests of the decision maker, and diffuse (but important) concepts of "fairness," rather than to regulations that make decision-making outcomes predictable. Decision making and bargaining tend to shade into one another in a poorly institutionalized system. Of course, attempts to fashion legal and administrative codes are under way in China, and these changes should help diminish the room for bargaining—somewhat. But, the experience of the foreign joint-venture partner who has to bargain with a broad and multilayered Chinese bureaucracy (much of which remains unseen) about wage rates, management authority, water and power supplies, raw materials acquisition, tariffs, access to the domestic Chinese market, technology and copyright protection, and repatriation of profits, confronts a bargaining treadmill only slightly more wearing than the reality which faces any Chinese who wants to initiate an activity.

7. Finally, an important, though less tangible, cause of bargaining behavior is the deeply shared value among both subordinates and superiors at all levels that "fairness" exists when there has been "consultation" and when the outcome of "consultation" is not to leave an individual, family, locality, or organization without adequate wherewithal to subsist and accomplish its assigned duties, unless there is an overwhelming, self-evident, and overriding social interest that can be demonstrated. What constitutes just compensation is the subject of protracted negotiation.

What Do People Bargain About?

The range of issues which is resolved through bargaining is broad. In this section I shall first indicate the breadth of issues over which bargaining occurs and then examine two specific cases in which we can better see the process in operation; the decisions surrounding the construction of the Danjiangkou Dam and the ongoing argument over the Three Gorges Project, a debate that started before the communist era and rages till this day. One point that these cases amply document is that bargaining was an important feature of the system under Mao, even though the range of such activity has expanded as a result of reform policies and the diminished use of coercion in the post-Mao era.

The range of policy issues that generate intense bargaining is broad. In China as everywhere else, one bargains over what is scarce. In the PRC, financial resources, power and position in the hierarchy, access to high-quality goods and services, access to the international system, and access to highly skilled personnel are among those things over which political bargains are most frequently struck.

Predictably, bargaining is intense in the budgetary process. Budgetary resources are allocated among the various functional "systems" (*xitong*).[4]

Each "system's" prior share of the budget is the base from which marginal changes are negotiated for the next year—"the fixed sum system." One recent broadcast explained that this was the "conventional practice" and called for change: "In this way, we will break through the conventional practice of the 'basic sum system,' that is changing the old practice of making the actual level of expenditures in the past the basis for arranging financial expenditure in the new budget."[5] Within "systems" and individual bureaucracies, resources are treated as a "lump" (kuai) to be carved up (qie) among subordinate entities according to the percentages previously applicable.[6]

This incremental approach to budgeting is an almost universal way in which large-scale organizations seek to reduce budgetary complexity, to reduce negotiating time, and to minimize political conflict.[7] Nonetheless, bargaining occurs around the edges of the budget. Which units will suffer marginal cuts and reap modest gains, and which units will have their budgets charged for investments that benefit other systems or organizations, all become important questions.[8] For instance, one of the recurring budgetary issues in building the Gezhouba Dam was how much of the Ministry of Water Conservancy and Electric Power's (shuidianbu) budget should be spent on increasing the lock capacity of the dam to meet the needs and demands of the Ministry of Communications? The Ministry of Communications (jiaotongbu) could make demands for substantial lock capacity, knowing that the cost of meeting its desires would not come from its budget because it was not the lead agency in the project.[9]

In speaking of how investment allocation decisions are made, Barry Naughton explains as follows:

> We can speculate that . . . actual allocation decisions are determined largely by the influence that different Beijing-based bureaucracies can bring to bear, and by various ad hoc sharing arrangements. . . . Ministers struggle to protect their power bases and keep subordinates busy; in order to succeed in this struggle, they must insure that at least their share of the total investment is not too drastically reduced.[10]

In any given year, depending on financial wherewithal and the intersectoral priorities of central planners, investment cuts can be more than incremental. For instance, in discussions at one ministry I was told that in the 1979–1982 period, fixed capital investment (guding touze) declined by about 50 percent, though it rose somewhat in 1982. In reply to my question concerning the process by which this decision was made, I was told, "We talked every day, back and forth [with the State Planning Commission], for two months."[11]

Not only are expenditure-level decisions made in a bargaining framework in which the possible gains and losses are generally limited by budgetary incrementalism, but revenue raising also is a political process characterized by negotiating. In the early 1980s, when Beijing was experimenting with a system in which enterprises were being allowed to keep a portion of profits ("profit retention")—which effectively reduced central revenues in the short run—"enterprises negotiated long and hard for the best possible retention rates."[12]

Given an administered-price system's rigidities and departures from scarcity values and the resulting fact that enterprise profits and losses do not necessarily reflect the enterprise's efficiency, negotiating over profit retention rates was, and is, a critical endeavor for enterprises and industrial bureaus. As explained in a 1982 interview in a Beijing ministry, many factories' retention rates are decided by the local bureau and the province. The State Planning Commission has a "general principle" that the profit retention rate should not be higher than 12–13 percent, though the interviewee noted that it had changed every year and said that the situation had been "chaotic" (*hen luan*). The average is about 10 percent, though in some cases it is as low as 5 or 6 percent, and in some cases it is higher. Critical to determining where in the permitted range the allowed profit retention rate will fall is an assessment of the degree to which the enterprise is disadvantaged by the price system. For example, the price for agricultural machinery is low and in favor of the peasants. So, the enterprises cannot change the sales price, but they can try to retain a higher percentage of the profit.[13] Because the center has created a wide range of possible retention rates, because local enterprises are highly motivated to get the best deal they can, because local officials have considerable discretion in setting these rates, and because the standards for decision are unclear (e.g., disadvantageous prices), one would expect considerable bargaining to characterize the process.

Similarly, with the experimental implementation of a tax system in the 1980s which created the prospect of enterprises keeping more money and then remitting taxes *directly* to the Ministry of Finance (thereby bypassing counties that had previously taken a slice of the financial pie), some counties began to discriminate against enterprises in which the new revenue system was first being implemented, "and may have demanded kickbacks in exchange for supplying the trial enterprises with the desired commodities."[14] In summarizing the politics of the process of moving from a revenue system in which enterprise profit remission would be replaced by taxes, Bachman describes the contours of the budgetary bargain that was struck:

> In an effort to win approval for *ligaishui* [the substitution of taxes for profit remission], central leaders apparently compromised on contentious issues. The Center made two fateful agreements that have checked the more revolutionary implications [of the change]. . . . Beijing stated that enterprises would retain about the same amount of money under [the new system] . . . as they had retained under profit retention. It also announced that there would be no change in the distribution of central-local finances. In other words, to overcome the (potential) resistance of key local interests (factory managers and local officials), the Center agreed that the redistributive dimensions of the *ligaishui* would be minimal.[15]

Localities and bureaucratic organizations bargain not only over expenditures and existent revenue sources, but also over new revenue sources and subsidy levels. For instance, authorities in one county in which I interviewed explained how the center and localities had negotiated an arrangement whereby localities would build small-scale hydroelectric plants (which the center wanted) in exchange for the localities being able to dispose of the resulting revenues as they wished (*yusuanwai*). Moreover, any excess electrical power which these small facilities generated would be purchased by the centrally managed electrical grids, at a high price, even if the grid did *not* need (and could not use) the power at the time the locality wanted to sell the energy.[16] In one Beijing interview, the rationale for subsidies was explained. As recorded in my notes, I asked the interviewee why they subsidize small electric power plants with higher purchase prices and why they sell power in the Gansu highlands at a much lower price than elsewhere? He said in explaining subsidies, "Political factors are key. . . . Sometimes cost benefit analysis counts for nothing." I was also told that "it is the same in the U.S." The case of cheap federal water in California was cited to show how the United States has subsidy problems too. I then raised the case of Gansu with respect to the very low electrical charges there and was told that "economics is not everything." People have to live and you end up having to pay for them one way or another. My interviewee said that provinces are important political powers and they can't be ignored.[17]

In China's half-reformed, highly protectionist, controlled currency system, access to the international market (foreign exchange) and protection from foreign competition are both subjects for bargaining. In a particularly revealing interview in 1986, State Councillor Gu Mu explained why, despite persistent rumors to the contrary, a special currency would not yet be put into circulation in the Shenzhen Special Economic Zone. The idea of a new currency had arisen because Beijing was trying to overcome the problems inherent in having three currencies circulating in Shenzhen (*renminbi*, the Hong Kong dollar, and foreign exchange certificates). This multiplicity of currencies produces considerable black-market foreign-exchange activity. However, the interests of various forces have, thus far, prevented agreement on a new currency. As Gu Mu explained,

> Our original plan was to issue a new currency in Shenzhen, called special zone currency, to bring about a solution, but this problem is too complicated. Some people approved and some opposed it. Moreover, it only provided a solution for the Shenzhen problem; the same problem facing the other special zones and coastal open cities could not be solved by it. Therefore, we must take a prudent attitude and leave this problem alone for another period of time. We will study this problem further with relevant experts at home and abroad to work out a conclusion before we do anything. The problem of issuing a special zone currency can only be temporarily held up as it is.[18]

In the capitalist world, industrial corporations are concerned about maintaining or enhancing their market share. This desire sometimes has produced anticompetitive practices with which antitrust legislation in the United States is designed to deal. In the new more consumer- and profit-oriented environment in the PRC, the desire of firms to enter new, growing, and more lucrative markets, as well as the desire of ministries and enterprises previously in those markets to protect their share, has given rise to some competition and an intense bargaining process.

For instance, washing machines are comparatively simple to manufacture, and previously they were made by the Ministry of Light Industry. Predictably, the Ministry of Light Industry did not want the Ministry of Machine Building to make washing machines. But, the State Planning Commission (SPC) approved the change, and many conferences were held as a result. The Ministry of Light Industry wrote reports to the SPC, and there were intense negotiations to determine how the two ministries would divide the market. Sometimes these negotiations were conducted with each party dealing separately with the SPC, and sometimes all three parties were together.[19]

In 1981 there was a conference on machines for civil use attended by the SPC, the Ministry of Machine Building, and other related ministries. The conference covered bicycles, radios, fans, television sets, watches, clocks, electric meters, refrigerators, and sewing machines. This conference fixed the production levels and determined which factories would make what. The conference lasted ten days, and the meeting was preceded by discussions that occurred over a year. At the conference, every ministry advanced its own proposals. One ministry proposed that a specific number of its factories be allowed to make a specific number of washing machines. Other ministries made their proposals. The SPC decided how many total washing machines the market could absorb. Then all the affected units discussed which factories were suitable for such production. The conferees may decide that, for instance, only one-half of a ministry's proposed factories should be authorized to manufacture the machines. Moreover, the number of machines that a ministry will be authorized to build will likely be below the number that was initially requested by that ministry. There were about 200 persons at this 1981 meeting with most units having about three representatives each. Each province and municipality had representatives as well.[20]

Ministries not only fight and bargain over their markets, they also continually clash over their jurisdictions. Oksenberg recounts the difficulties that Bo Yibo encountered in efforts to reduce the overlapping and duplicative organizational structure of industry, more particularly shipbuilding.

The solution which Bo and other top leaders embraced . . . was to group factories in a single industry into a single, independent corporation operating directly under the Machine Building Commission. A pilot project in the shipbuilding industry was to group the major shipyards in Shanghai into a single corporation. Previously, the shipyards were under several jurisdictions: the Sixth Ministry of Machine Building, the Ministry of Communications, and several municipal departments. However, neither the Sixth Ministry nor Communications wished to lose their shipyards. . . . Bo Yibo, with the staff of the Machine Building Commission behind him, nevertheless had to conduct the extensive negotiations for the formation of the new corporation personally. Several trips to Shanghai were necessary. Even then, with all of his prestige, the result was a hybrid organization. The ministries concurred only when it was decided the head of the new corporation would be one of the vice ministers of the Sixth Ministry and the head of its board of directors would be a vice minister of communications.[21]

Just as enterprises, localities, and ministries negotiate over their respective shares of the domestic market and their organizational domains, it appears that provinces and autonomous regions can, at least under some circumstances, negotiate over the share of foreign trade exports that factories and industries in their locality will be given and over their share of imports. For instance, western China's Xinjiang Autonomous Region has been disadvantaged by the coastal bias of the current "open policy." It appears from the following quotation that perhaps the region's leadership used its disadvantaged status to argue that they should be guaranteed a portion of the newly expanding trade with the Soviet Union: "The Chinese Government has especially provided Xinjiang with a specific share of the total volume of goods turnover envisaged in the trade agreement between the Chinese and Soviet governments."[22]

Water Projects: The Bargaining Environment Up Close

Because water is essential for all persons and all sectors of the economy, because it is a scarce resource that has multiple uses (with one use frequently precluding another), and because water traverses administrative boundaries (with upstream users affecting the interests of those downstream), analyzing how decisions are made in this field reveals the bargaining character of the Chinese political system in its most pristine form. In a 1980 interview, the profusion of bureaucratic "contradictions" in the water planning process was recounted to me. My notes of that meeting record that unified management, and how to get it, is the biggest problem. The Water Conservancy, Communications, Industrial, Agricultural and Forestry, and Railroad Ministries all come into conflict, not to mention the desire of peasants to have full reservoirs and the desire of the Ministry of Water Conservancy to keep reservoirs low so there will be room for flood waters. For instance, the Railroad Ministry wants to put tracks right along the river to minimize grading and construction costs. This shuts off the water's edge to other potential users. The Forestry Ministry wants to use the river to float logs and thus impairs other uses. Shipping users want to use the rivers to the maximum for their purposes.[23]

The controversies swirling around the construction and management of the Danjiangkou and Three Gorges (San Xia) dam projects reveal the broader character of the political system and put flesh on the bones of our view of bargaining in the Chinese polity.

The Danjiangkou Dam. The middle and the lower reaches of the Han River in Hubei Province flood often—it is one of the most troublesome tributaries in the Yangzi River Valley. The Han's discharge capacity progressively diminishes as it moves toward the heavily populated Jiang-Han

Plain.[24] This, combined with the limited discharge capacity of the river at the enormous city of Wuhan, where the Han dumps into the Yangzi, has created a situation in which the Han is a constant menace to one of China's major urban centers. In 1955, China's government began a flood diversion project along the Han (Dujiatai), which was part of the Han River Development Plan. In 1958, the State Council approved construction of the Danjiangkou Dam as the second stage of the development effort.

In building the dam, a number of problems slowed the project, as I have detailed elsewhere.[25] In the context of this paper I want to focus on several issues that became the foci of protracted bargaining during *both* the construction and subsequent management phases: the dam's height; the priorities to be assigned irrigation, flood control, and electrical power generation; the problem of relocating displaced persons; and the issue of local opposition and the preservation of cultural relics. What is theoretically and practically significant in all of this is that *all* of these issues spark intense bargaining today, more than a quarter century later. In China, as elsewhere, issues are just managed, they frequently are never fully resolved. The processes of delay and compromise impose high economic and political costs on leaders at all levels.

When construction started on Danjiangkou, the dam's *initially* planned height was 175 meters, with the water level to be maintained at 170 meters (above sea level).[26] However, throughout the entire construction phase (which ended in 1974), there was intense controversy over what the dam's height should, in fact, be. In the end, work was halted at 162 meters (with the water level normally at 157 meters). This reduced height meant that the structure's flood control, electrical generation, and irrigation capacities were smaller than would have been the case had the dam been built as planned. These diminished capacities, in turn, aggravated the contention among the rival users of the dam. How did it come to pass that the dam they started to build in 1958 was not the dam they finished in 1974 and that more than a decade after construction was halted, the project builders and planners still are pushing to have the height raised to its initially designed level?

During the period of construction, the bargaining process produced agreed-upon dam heights of 140 meters, 152 meters, and 162 meters, as well as the initially planned height of 175 meters. For both engineering and financial reasons, construction on the project was halted for two years (1962–1964), and, even after work resumed, they still had not agreed on the height. In 1965 the planners accepted a dam height of 152 meters, but Hubei and Henan provinces (the two provinces which shared the resulting reservoir) wanted a higher dam (so they would get more electrical power and irrigation water). In 1966 the dam was approved for 162 meters (which Hubei and Henan wanted), *but* the water level was to stay at the 145-meter level (as in the 152-meter dam) until the problem of what to do with displaced persons could be solved. The negotiating process produced a perfectly predictable outcome. The difference between the two sides was split down the middle.[27] As one interviewee explained, "In 1965 . . . the Center approved a revised dam height of 152 meters with a water level of 145 meters. Because Hubei and Henan were unhappy with this . . . the Center agreed in 1966 to a 162 meter dam, with an initial water level of 145 meters to gradually be raised to 157 meters as the relocation problem was solved."[28]

The essence of the problem was that as the dam's height rose, the opposition of counties and special districts that would be inundated became more intense, the number of persons who would be displaced would grow, and all of this would greatly escalate project costs and political conflict. Specifically, if the dam had been built for the initially designed water level, there would have been approximately 100,000 more displaced persons.[29] As it was, between 23.7 and 30 percent of the dam's construction investment was relocation expenses.[30] The kernel of the bargaining outcome was that nobody got all of what they wanted, few persons or organizations lost everything, and the number of dislocated persons and financial expenditures rose more gradually than would have been the case had they proceeded according to the initial plan. Hubei and Henan got more benefits than they would have with the lowest dam alternative; they got less than they had hoped for under the initial 175-meter plan. The surrounding special districts and their counties suffered some inundation, but none were completely wiped out.

Though we cannot see the entire bargaining process, aspects of it are clear. One of the most contentious issues concerned the fact that Hubei Province would get most of the flood control and electric power benefits and Henan Province would get excessive numbers of refugees (in proportion to its benefits). Intense negotiations between the two provinces were initiated in order to resolve this imbalance. The leadership of the two provinces got together, and Hubei agreed to take 80,000 of Henan's displaced persons (*yimin*). According to *central* figures, there were a total of 356,000 refugees, with 130,000 in Henan and 226,000 in Hubei Province. This source said the *local* figures put the total number of displaced persons at 390,000 (obviously higher than the central estimate). When I asked why Hubei agreed to assume this burden, I was told plainly that Henan was poor, its displaced persons' plight was worse, and "Henan's benefits from the reservoir were not as great."[31] These negotiations resulted in a written agreement between Hubei and Henan, an agreement which specified the distribution of electric power, water, and displaced persons.[32]

A second ongoing issue has concerned whether the principal use of Danjiangkou should be electrical power generation, flood control, or irrigation. To manage the dam to maximize one objective is to diminish the extent to which the other purposes can be fully realized. To use water for irrigation means that less water flows through the turbines to generate electrical power. "The contradiction is sharp," I was told in one interview.[33] To maximize power output, the water level needs to be high—to provide insurance against flood, the water level should be kept low. Each of these purposes is organizationally embodied in a different ministry. Agricultural concerns are the responsibility of the Ministry of Agriculture, Forestry, and Animal

Husbandry; electrical power has (at various times) been under the purview of an independent Ministry of Electric Power; and flood control has been a primary interest of the Ministry of Water Conservancy (which at times has been separate from the electrical power ministry). Other interests also intrude into this tangle. Some localities are most concerned with irrigation water (particularly in Henan Province); some areas are most concerned with flood control (particularly areas below the dam in Hubei); and some powerful enterprises (e.g., Wuhan Iron and Steel Company) are desperate for electrical power.

Even before the dam was under construction, complex discussions among ministries and localities occurred over the dam's utilization priorities. Initially, flood prevention was the first priority, followed by electrical power, irrigation, navigation, and aquaculture, in that order.[34] Since then, each ministry keeps raising the issue of the priority of "its" use, continually trying to reopen the case in order to better its position. In the early 1980s, for instance, the Ministry of Water Conservancy and the Ministry of Electric Power came into conflict over the water level at Danjiangkou. The Ministry of Water Conservancy unilaterally imposed its own control level to assure irrigation, over the objections of the electric power interests.[35] Because the dam was not built to its original height, if, in the future, it is raised, the priority of uses would be wide open for discussion again. As my notes taken at the time indicate, if the second stage of Danjiangkou is built, these priorities (flood control, electric power, agriculture) would shift, with flood control first, irrigation second, and electric power third. I asked an interviewee if there wasn't a contradication between irrigation and electric power and he said, "Yes." I asked how they resolve it and he said, "It never is finally resolved, we continually discuss it."[36]

Another contentious issue that resulted in the dam not being built to its designed height, an issue that still weighs against raising the dam today, is the opposition of localities along the reservoir's edge that would be inundated if the water level rises. My notes of one interview recount that another reason the 175 meter dam was not built as planned was because of the displaced persons problem. The fact is, I was told, that Henan Province, even though it had no particular need for the flood control aspects of this dam, would agree to the higher dam, but it was Henan's Nanyang Special District which adamantly opposed it then, and does today, for the obvious reason that it would be one of the areas to be inundated heavily.[37]

In Hubei Province, it is Jun Xian (county), with a long and illustrious history dating from the Tang, and Yun Xian. In Henan Province it is Zhechuan Xian. These three old county towns would go under water and Xiangyang Special District in Henan opposed it. According to my interviewee, the provincial government in Henan would go along with raising the dam because of the benefits to Zhengzhou (the provincial capital) and irrigation, but they can't persuade the affected localities.[38]

Even with the construction of the lower dam, one costly issue involving Jun Xian was what to do with Tang Dynasty cultural relics that would be submerged. Cultural relic costs, alone, ended up at 250,000 yuan.[39]

The Three Gorges Project. The Three Gorges, which sits astride the Hubei and Sichuan border, is a strategic choke point at which the floods that originate in Sichuan Province (and devastate Hubei and Hunan provinces and other areas downstream) could theoretically be stopped. Moreover, the reservoir that would be formed by a dam in the Three Gorges could drive turbines that would supply electrical power to much of central and eastern China's energy-starved industry. Finally, raising the water level in the gorges could improve navigation and increase the size of ships able to reach Chongqing. So strategic is the area, and so attractive has been the idea of a dam there, that leaders from Sun Yatsen, through Mao Zedong, to Deng Xiaoping and Zhao Ziyang, have seriously considered the project.

Indeed, the project has been approved at least twice "in principle" in the post-1949 era (once in 1958 at the Chengdu Meeting and again in April 1984),[40] only to have construction subsequently aborted because approval to commence construction had been made contingent on the resolution of a myriad of technical, financial, and political *"details"* such as the following: How high should the dam be? What is to be done with the displaced persons and inundated factories and administrative centers? Who pays, how much? What would be the effect of such a huge dam on upstream aquatic life? What would be the useful life of the dam due to siltation? Does it make sense to build a dam that may have a short useful life unless one first invests in forestry work upstream? How will shipping across the dam be affected? Is flood control best achieved by one gigantic project or several smaller ones? From where is the enormous investment to come? Who will receive the resulting electrical power, and can it be efficiently transmitted to the distant locations where it is most urgently needed? Is a dam of this scale safe, or would it be, as the Ministry of National Defense and Mao Zedong at times feared, a huge "bowl of water on our heads"?

In this section, I shall not recount the more than three decades of the project's tribulations; these are well-documented elsewhere.[41] Instead, I shall examine the range of interests involved in the Three Gorges decision and then argue that promoters of the project face a bargaining dilemma—in order to weld a coalition big enough to win support for the dam, promoters must provide benefits to a vast constellation of groups. But, this large coalition requires a dam so enormous that the resulting costs and negative outcomes create intense opposition and high financial and other risks that top decision makers are loath to ignore. In this situation, it is unclear that the bargaining process will ever reach closure.

Though there have been hard-core supporters and equally committed opponents of the Three Gorges Project throughout the entire checkered history of the debate, the key to whether an agreement is reached lies in a large number of middle (or contingent) groups. For these middle groups, whether they support a specific plan or not is a function of, to put it crudely, what is in it for them, or what it costs them. The inducements that one group finds attractive may threaten others. In short, the goal of supporters is to win the backing, or at least neutrality, of a large number of groups that could be persuaded, at the "right" price. This process is expensive.

Looking first at the political terrain, the Yangzi River Valley Planning Office (YRVPO), which is the planning arm of the Ministry of Water Conservancy and Electric Power in the Yangzi basin, has been the most ardent supporter of the project, ever since the dawn of the Communist era. The YRVPO has an almost religious commitment to solving the flood problem of the middle and lower reaches of the Yangzi, and this big dam is their solution. Hubei Province, the major flood control and electrical power beneficiary of the project, also has been unwavering in its commitment to this and other dams. A local Hubei radio broadcast put it succinctly in 1985:

> The state has not decided to speed up the construction of water conservation projects on the Chang Jiang [Yangzi River] and to continue to develop and construct such projects. Hubei Province is the greatest beneficiary of this. The provincial CPC Committee and government resolutely support the central policy decision and will provide all-out support for the construction of key water conservation projects on the Chang Jiang.[42]

Hunan Province also has been an "active supporter" of the project.[43]

On the other side, the Ministry of Electric Power (and the electric power interests when they are combined in a joint Ministry of Water Conservancy and Electric Power) has generally preferred smaller hydroelectric (or thermal power) projects that are faster to build (and thereby begin to pay back investment more quickly).[44] The Ministry of Finance continually worries about committing so much money to a single project with such a long gestation time, when other projects could begin generating revenue more quickly. The Finance Ministry also sees that investing so much in a single project is synonymous with deciding not to build many other smaller projects that would satisfy the demands of numerous other localities. The Communications Ministry feels that the needs of inland navigation have been ignored by the dam builders in the past and that this project would represent a genuine threat to shipping on China's main inland navigation artery. And, depending on the dam's height, a variable (but large) number of counties and towns would be inundated by the reservoir that might be as long as 700 km.

In addition to the bureaucracies and localities that tend to be opposed (or whose acquiescence can be purchased at only considerable cost), there are other interests that could be won over. As one interviewee put it, "Their attitude depends on the concrete plan."[45] For instance, Sichuan Province has been worried about what it will do with a million or more possible displaced persons (*yimin*). Plans have proceeded rather far to create a new province (San Xia Sheng) that would relieve Sichuan of most of this burden. Further, the province, *if* it ever is created, would have a vice-governor from Sichuan and one from Hubei. Other inducements can be provided Sichuan such as jobs in the new province for surplus cadres, more electrical power, more investment in improving Chongqing's shipping capabilities, grain to replace crops that would go under water, and industrial investment to more than compensate for the industry that would be submerged.[46] In short, supporters can seek to make it attractive for Sichuan to approve construction. This kind of bargaining, of course, tends to escalate costs which, predictably enough, worries the Ministry of Finance and other interests that need investment capital too. In the inimitable words of one interviewee, "Whoever loses investment is opposed."[47]

Other interests, too, can be persuaded, but only at a cost. Ecological interests in the Ministry of Urban and Rural Construction and Environmental Protection have their worries about the environmental impact of this mammoth project. The Ministry of Agriculture, Animal Husbandry, and Fisheries is concerned about the dam's impact on fisheries, particularly above the dam. Finally, the Travel Service, which sold the natural beauty of the Three Gorges as one of China's premier attractions, is concerned about what filling up the canyon with water will do to tourism. On the other hand, the dam itself would be a potential tourist attraction, *if* they could get more investment in hotels and tourist facilities in the area. Such investment might assuage the concerns of the Travel Service.[48] For those worried about fish, fish ladders will be built. For those who worry about the ecological impact, integrated reservoir management will be better for the environment. For those worried about shipping, the largest vertical ship lifts in the world would be built.[49] All of this costs money, of course. In the effort to buy off the "wavering elements," one ends up with a project that may not be financially feasible. One has the "Christmas tree" phenomenon so familiar in the U.S. Congress. A piece of legislation is so loaded up with benefits for strategic groups that the agreement may collapse under its own weight.

As in the Danjiangkou case, the issue of dam height has been a most contentious and strategic decision. The political system has been unable to reach closure on this issue after almost three decades of wrangling. In May 1983, the SPC, then headed by Yao Yilin, convened a meeting in the national capital to assess the Three Gorges feasibility study that had been submitted to it by the Ministry of Water Conservancy and Electric Power and the YRVPO. This study assumed a water level of 150 meters, which was comparatively low and thereby would reduce both negative outcomes (displaced persons and urban inundation) and benefits (to shipping, flood control, and electrical power generation). Yao declared:

> For more than twenty years the debate over the Three Gorges water resource project has concentrated principally on the problem of the dam's height. That a high dam generates more electricity and that the flood control results are better is easy to see. However, the inundation is too much, the investment is too big, the masses upstream are unable to agree, the burdens on state finance also cannot be borne. However, the relevant ministries and localities have not been reconciled to the low dam and, because of this we have debated for many years and still are unable to decide. If we continue to debate, I think this generation of ours will be unable to accomplish anything on this.[50]

In spring 1984, the State Council approved, in principle, a dam of 175 meters, with a normal water level of 150 meters. Construction was to begin in 1986. The two intervening years were to be used to resolve the remaining technical issues. However, almost immediately, proponents of a higher dam began to push their case. And those opposed began to promote theirs with renewed vigor.[51] It appears that the dispute is still far from resolution, with Li Peng saying, as recently as April 1986,

> The Chinese Government has adopted a "positive and cautious" attitude toward a huge water conservancy project on the gorges of the Yangtze river. . . . The Government has not yet decided whether or not to start construction. Although preparations have been made over the past 30 years, the vice-premier said, there are still a number of problems, such as the control of silt and navigation on the Yangtze, that need further feasibility studies. Li disclosed that the State Council plans to set up a special committee for feasibility studies and invite experts in various fields to join in. Views from foreign experts in hydroelectric power stations would also be heeded, he said.[52]

Only a few days before Li Peng spoke out, Deng Xiaoping indicated that a "final decision had yet to be made, but taken together there were more advantages than disadvantages."[53] It appears that the treadmill of bargaining grinds on. Whether there is any point at which the process can be brought to a conclusion remains to be seen.

Who Bargains, in What Arenas, and What Strategies Are Employed?

Who Bargains?

How are interests articulated in the PRC? To what extent are "interest group," or "interest tendency," models of the Chinese system relevant?[54] Are some interests articulated more effectively in the formulation stage of policymaking while others find greater expression in the implementation phase? What resources are usable for bargaining, in what specific issue areas and political arenas does the bargaining take place, and how are such resources distributed throughout the system? These are questions I shall briefly address below.

One's capacity to affect policy content diminishes greatly as one moves downward from the point of decision. In the *formulation* of policy, bargaining goes on between the principal bureaucracies and territorial administrations. Policy formulation is, in large part, bureaucratic and interregional politics. Who is entitled to remonstrate to whom is tightly structured by the rules of the bureaucratic system. These rules are all carefully specified.

Nonetheless, there is a representative quality to the process inasmuch as each element of the territorial and bureaucratic system sees part of its job as being to reflect the interests of "their" locality or organization. This is done not simply because it is seen as "just" and necessary in order to assure that subsequent policy will be effectively implemented; it also is done because no superior wishes to promote a subordinate who has a demonstrated inability to preserve essential organizational and territorial interests. Each layer of the system endeavors to win the support of subordinates through an elaborate consensus-building process. As I have argued elsewhere, this process of consensus building and negotiation can last, literally, years, indeed decades.

Depending on the policy issue, the *implementation* process involves not only intense bargaining among the territorial and functional bureaucracies, but it also frequently involves officials dealing with a broad range of individuals and small social groups that have no formal political role—nonetheless, they must be reckoned with if policy is to be implemented. Local officials trying to clear land for a public works project must, for instance, bargain with recalcitrant peasants over their relocation compensation. Local officials desirous of building a reservoir find it expedient to promise neighboring villages a share of fish if they will allow some of their land to be inundated. In short, bargaining is endemic to the system at all levels and between all levels. The citizenry is most directly involved in the process during implementation.

To reemphasize, a bargaining view of the Chinese political system does *not* imply that all Chinese citizens and organizations are equally able to bargain effectively, nor does it imply that bargaining necessarily characterizes all policy issues. How much bargaining occurs in each issue area is an empirical question. My evidence suggests that in the process of policy *formulation*, one's capacity to bargain in a way that shapes the ultimate character of policy falls off rapidly as one drops away from the decision-making site in the bureaucratic and territorial hierarchies. Units and localities usually bargain with immediate superiors, immediate subordinates, and horizontal equals. Only under exceptional circumstances does one try to "end-run" the normal chain of authority. However, given the multiple lines of authority in which units are embedded (the plurality of *kuai kuai* ties),[55] the capacity of units to pursue the path of least resistance or to play one superior off against another should not be underestimated.

In the *implementation* phase, bargaining is important and significant at all levels. It is in the negotiations between immediate superiors and subordinates that policy is adapted in ways of most significance to the units and individuals involved. Herein lay the roots of the "implementation bias" which Naughton explains so well.[56] Policy formulation, for the most part, is confined to bargaining among bureaucratic and territorial actors. Policy implementation, on the other hand, involves a much broader range of groups, localities, and individuals, carrying bargaining right down to the grass-roots level.

Where Does Bargaining Occur?

Part of the answer is implied in the previous discussion concerning who bargains. To be more precise, however, there are several arenas (or types of arenas) that play central and recurrent roles: the SPC, other commissions, the Standing Committee of the State Council,[57] state councillors, ad hoc interprovincial committees, ad hoc interministerial committees, and specific policy issue committees. These types of roles and committees are replicated at all system levels. Although we see only the tip of the organizational iceberg, we know enough to outline the process.

The SPC is one of the most important bargaining arenas. As a commission, the SPC stands as a buffer between individual ministries and the State Council. Each ministry must make its plans in accordance with the state plan, and the SPC has sole responsibility for overall economic planning and capital construction, labor allocation, finance, and foreign exchange. Tasks authorized under the plan are thereupon undertaken by the responsible ministry. In an interview I was told that the way in which allocations among ministries are determined is "complicated" and that there is "lots of discussion." The interviewee went on to say that every province and municipality wants allocations that they consider small but that when aggregated become a huge sum. The SPC is the organ charged with rationalizing these conflicting claims and avoiding deficits and materials bottlenecks.[58] Because the SPC is, itself, divided into functional bureaus that reflect the functional divisions among ministries, conflict patterns in the SPC tend to reflect those in the wider bureaucratic system.[59] More research is needed to ascertain whether or not bargaining occurs *within* the SPC and to determine the possible extent to which it does.

From the viewpoint of individual ministries, the role of the SPC is key. My notes of a 1982 interview recount that the ministry opposed this reduction in investment. They made their proposals to the SPC, and, the interviewee said, "We talked every day back and forth, for two months." I asked if they went to the State Council over the head of the SPC, and he said, "Generally this is not good" [*yibande buxing*]. I laughed and said this was not a normal situation, and they laughed and repeated that "generally this is not good."[60]

Another, and indeed higher, arena for bargaining among territorial and functional interests is the State Council, meaning either its Standing Committee or the entire State Council. Conflicts that cannot be resolved by individual commissions or ministries get bumped up to this next higher level. For instance, paraphrasing one interviewee, "Say there is a high value investment to be made . . . and say four provinces or municipalities all want it . . . obviously this is a difficult task. . . . The SPC can reach agreement with mayors, but if that is not possible, it then goes to the Standing Committee of the State Council."[61]

Indeed, it appears from my interviews, as well as the work of Oksenberg, that one of the key systemic problems is that an excessive number of major issues cannot be resolved by the ministries and localities themselves. This difficulty can overwhelm the top echelons of the State Council. In 1982, for instance, the Water Conservancy and Electric Power ministries were merged. One reason for this marriage was to try to reduce the frequency with which disputes between the two ministries were kicked to the next higher level. As one interviewee aptly put it, now discussions are "in the family" rather than "between families."[62]

Not only are conflicts resolved in the SPC and State Council, but there is also a rich repertoire of regularized and ad hoc procedures and committees to resolve disputes in both the *formulation* and *implementation* phases of the policy process. I was in one central China locality and asked how the managers of one water project decide which use of water will have priority over the course of the year. My interview notes recount that I was told that the priorities were (1) power (2) flood control, (3) irrigation, (4) navigation, and (5) water products. They noted that there was a "slight contradiction" during the April-August period, between electric power and irrigation. I asked how this contradiction is resolved, and they said it was discussed at the provincial level and the following departments take part in the discussions: agriculture, planning, electric power, and the Bureau of Water Conservancy. The province then decides and tells the dam what to do.[63]

Similarly, as noted previously, there has been an ongoing battle over the priority among uses to which the Danjiangkou Dam should be put. In times of drought, this dispute can become intense. In one interview concerning the resolution of "use" during droughts, I was told that there is a regular process for solving this, though no specific standing organ. More precisely, if an area has a drought, a special anti-drought headquarters (*zhihuibu*) is set up, and this headquarters always had a vice-minister of electric power, a vice-minister of water conservance, the governors of the affected provinces, and the agriculture ministry, and important related ministries (*youguan bumen*). In the case of Danjiangkou, both the governors of Hubei and Henan would have participated. The interviewee said this body then makes policy and issues the order on how to deal with the problem.[64]

The use of ad hoc interdepartmental committees (which frequently involve *both* territorial *and* functional bureaucratic representatives) is evident not only with respect to recurrent problems, but also with respect to specific projects and one-time issues. For instance, in the course of constructing the Gezhouba Dam, a "technical committee" (*jishu weiyuanhui*) was created at Premier Zhou Enlai's request because disputes and technical problems were hampering the progress of the entire project; indeed, work on the dam stopped from 1972 to 1974. The technical committee's membership gives a clue to the conflicts that arose and the complexity of their resolution: the YRVPO, the Ministry of Machine Building, the Ministry of Communications, the Ministry of Water Conservancy and Electric Power, the SPC, the State Capital Construction Commission, the vice-governor of Hubei Province, and the Gezhouba Construction Bureau.[65]

In short, bargaining is endemic to the system, and there are many arenas in which negotiation occurs. More research is needed concerning both the diversity of arenas and the processes that occur within them.

Strategies for Bargaining

Strategies are contingent on the actor under consideration ("his" skill and resources being particularly salient), the policy issue in question, whether one is trying to promote (or frustrate) a specific initiative, the bundle of interrelated issues, and the wider social-political-economic context. A few examples may serve to illustrate the rich and sophisticated diversity of strategies which are employed.

The Foot in the Door. In the foot-in-the-door gambit, the bargainer tries to secure a commitment that will permit work on a project to start. The idea is to extract an initial commitment that is not threatening to potential or actual opponents, but will not preclude the possibility of enlarging the project at some later date, when the political, economic, and social context is more favorable to the promoters.[66] The object is to create a situation in which each stage's sunk costs (combined with the presumed benefits of the next phase) become justification for the next stage. The Baoshan Iron and Steel Plant may be a classic example of this strategy. The repeated proposals to build the Three Gorges Dam in stages (leaving the subsequent decision on raising the dam till a later date) would seem to reflect this strategy as well. The same process was at work at the Danjiangkou Dam, where the foundation was built to support a much higher dam than actually was constructed. Proponents of raising the dam are still pushing for permission to go ahead, claiming that the present dam is but the first stage of the planned project.

Painting a Black Picture. In the same way that supporters of an initiative try to minimize perceived costs, opponents frequently exaggerate both costs and uncertainties. For instance, in one interview, I asked about the price tag for the Three Gorges Project, noting that I had seen estimates that varied by a factor of five. My respondent, who was an ardent supporter of the project, bluntly replied that those who advance extremely high estimates "oppose the Three Gorges" Project.[67] I noted previously how the localities around the reservoir at Danjiangkou had substantially higher displaced-persons estimates than did central authorities.

A Little Something for Everyone. The something-for-everyone strategy is a coalition-building process in which the scale of a project is enlarged to provide benefits to all of the strategic groups that could obstruct agreement. In cases such as the Three Gorges Dam, there may exist a situation in which enlarging the scale of the project would not only attract some wavering elements, but would also scare away others. The costs of building a big enough coalition may simply be prohibitive.

Cooking the Books. A bargainer who is cooking the books seeks to use facts and figures that support the preferred policy preference. One finds that each ministry is well armed with figures that it uses to bludgeon opponents. For instance, in one interview in the water conservancy "system" (*xitong*) I asked the official why the length of navigable waterways had declined over the previous decades. His immediate reation to my figures was "These are Jiaotongbu [Ministry of Communications] figures."[68] Because the Ministry of Communications is always complaining about how Ministry of Water Conservancy and Electric Power dams obstruct river transport, he assumed that any figures that might sustain the position of the Ministry of Communications naturally came from them.

The Kiss-of-Death Strategy. In his excellent chronology and analysis of the debate over the Three Gorges Project, Lieberthal suggests that because of its historic opposition to the Three Gorges Dam, recent Ministry of Communications support for a dam with a 180-meter water level, rather than 150 meters, may represent a strategy whereby pushing for a higher dam makes it probable that *no* dam will be built.[69] As the dam's height grows, so does potential opposition.

Getting to Key Decision Makers, Old Friends, and Relatives. The utilization of political networks cannot be overlooked.[70] In the bargaining process, one's success may hinge on the "connections" (*guanxi*) that one possesses and the IOUs that can be collected. Personal networks, though not limited to organizations, are built into them. Leaders like Yu Qiuli, for instance, have great power and influence, not only because they directly control powerful organizations directly, but also because they have been able to place loyal friends into a broad range of other organizations.[71] This practice gives rise to what the Chinese refer to as "running organizations by remote control." When asked how political actors promote their interests, one interviewee placed particular emphasis on "face-to-face meetings" with decision makers and contacts with "old friends"; he asserted that close personal ties with key decision makers can be decisive.[72] Herein lies the importance of family ties, both natural and through marriage. Marital ties, along with the conscious fostering of them, are a key aspect of politics in China about which we need to know a great deal more.

The Broader Implications of a Bargaining-System View

If China is profitably understood as a bargaining system, at least with respect to many issues (particularly social, technical, and economic decisions), what are some of the practical consequences of such a system? So what?

1. Decisions in this consensus-building system generally are slow in coming. The negotiation process will be protracted. The more geographic areas and functional bureaucracies that are involved in (or relevant to) the decision, the more laborious will be the negotiation process.

2. It is difficult to definitively say when a decision really has been made. Frequently, decisions are made "in principle," but the most nettlesome "details" are left for future resolution. The requisite resolution of these issues may never come. Decisions concerning building nuclear power plants and the Three Gorges Project are excellent examples of this phenomenon. In short, there is an indeterminacy to outcomes. The same issues seem to rise like Lazarus on the agenda; they never stay buried.

3. Even once a policy is adopted, the implementation process is characterized by negotiation among levels of the hierarchy, sometimes all the way down to the grassroots. This practice gives rise to the situation in which each level slightly deflects policy in a direction favorable to its own interests ("adapting policy in light of concrete local circumstances"). By the

time one has moved through six or seven layers of the system, the cumulative distortion can be great; unanticipated and unwelcome consequences can be the result, from the center's perspective.

4. One of the biggest mistakes that the center can make is to set too many high-priority goals simultaneously. Frequently, the only way a policy can be adopted and subsequently implemented is if the elite is united on the objective and is willing to expend considerable political resources in assuring effective implementation. There is no substitute for elite attention in the protracted negotiation process. However, the ability to focus elite attention often is diluted by the various priorities of elite members themselves, their different support bases, limited resources, and the revolutionary aspirations of an elite whose legitimacy rests on rapid transformation. A developing nation (particularly one with revolutionary pretensions) is almost compelled to bite off more than it can chew.

5. Though bargaining was characteristic of the system under Mao to an extent not generally recognized, three processes have made it an even more conspicuous feature since his death: the importance now accorded professional experts; the involvement of foreigners in domestic change; and what Naughton calls the "internalization" of resources to individual units and localities. Professionals and experts generally inject the element of "trade-offs" into discussions. Once one begins to speak of decisions as trade-offs one can easily slide into bargaining. As the Chinese system deals more with foreigners, who have resources that are desired but beyond the control of Chinese leaders, inducements must be found to elicit the required behavior from afar. Finally, Beijing's decisions to decentralize fiscal resources have provided subordinates resources that they will be reluctant to relinquish to the center. The elite is therefore left trying to find ways to create incentives for local units to use resources in ways consistent with central desires. Implicit and explicit bargaining results.

6. Finally, because bargaining is extensive, it frequently is difficult to separate legitimate activity from corruption. It is essential that the system create a legal framework and a widely shared set of values to govern this activity. It will be a race between the process of establishing these procedures and values and the loss of system legitimacy. This may be the most important race in which Beijing's leaders are running.

Notes

1. David M. Lampton, with Joyce A. Madancy and Kristen M. Williams, *A Relationship Restored: Trends in U.S.-China Educational Exchanges, 1978–1984* (Washington, D.C.: National Academy Press, 1986), p. 56.

2. David M. Lampton, *Paths to Power: Elite Mobility in Contemporary China* (Ann Arbor: University of Michigan, Center for Chinese Studies, 1986), p. 177.

3. Anthony Downs, *Inside Bureaucracy* (Boston: Little, Brown, 1967), pp. 278–279; also, Michel C. Oksenberg, "Economic Policy-Making in China: Summer 1981," *China Quarterly*, No. 90 (1982), pp. 181–184.

4. David M. Lampton, Interview File, No. 25 (1982), China, p. 6.

5. Foreign Broadcast Information Service, *Daily Report: China* (hereafter FBIS), 29 October 1985, p. K3, from *Renmin Ribao* [People's Daily], 11 October 1985, p. 5.

6. Lampton, Interview File, No. 25 (1982), China, pp. 2–3.

7. See Aaron Wildavsky, *The Politics of the Budgetary Process* (Boston: Little, Brown, 1974); also see John Creighton Campbell, *Contemporary Japanese Budget Politics* (Berkeley: University of California Press, 1977).

8. Lampton, Interview File, No. 9 (1982), China, p. 6.

9. Lampton, Interview File, No. 7 (1982), China, pp. 9–10. The same process was evident at Danjiangkou Dam project. I asked my interviewee why it was that at Danjiangkou they had said all investment in Danjiangkou was agriculture and forestry (*nong lin*) investment and some should have been credited against other investment systems. I also asked why I had seen several articles saying that investment ought to be divided into shares for multiuse projects because it was unfair to credit all the investment costs of urban benefits against the rural accounts in multiuse projects. My respondent said that the reason the Ministry of Water Conservancy and rural departments want to divide up investment (*fentan touzi*) is that now *all* project investment is credited against its primary use and so secondary priorities pay *none* of the cost. He felt that this was undesirable in two respects: (1) The Ministry of Water Conservancy has fewer resources this way for doing its job under the existent system. (2) It would help all-around planning because other ministries, and he mentioned the Communications Ministry specifically, would have more control over their investment.

10. Barry Naughton, "The Decline of Central Control over Investment in Post-Mao China," in David M. Lampton, ed., *Policy Implementation in Post-Mao China* (Berkeley: University of California Press, 1987), p. 68.

11. Lampton, Interview File, No. 23 (1982), China, p. 7.

12. David Bachman, "Implementing Chinese Tax Policy," in David M. Lampton, ed., *Policy Implementation in Post-Mao China* (Berkeley: University of California Press, 1987), p. 133.

13. Lampton, Interview File, No. 23 (1982), China, pp. 9–10.

14. Bachman, "Implementing Chinese Tax Policy," p. 138.

15. Ibid., p. 31. See also p. 141.

16. Lampton, Interview File, No. 18 (1982), China, pp. 4–5.

17. Lampton, Interview File, No. 25 (1982), China, pp. 4–5.

18. FBIS, 15 April 1986, p. W5, from *Ta Kung Pao*, in Chinese, 11 April 1986, pp. 2–3.

19. Lampton, Interview File, No. 23 (1982), China, pp. 7–9.

20. Ibid.

21. Oksenberg, "Economic Policy-Making," pp. 176–177.

22. Beijing Radio, in Russian, to the USSR, 15 September 1985, in FBIS, 19 September 1985, p. C3.

23. Lampton, Interview File, No. 1 (1980), China, p. 2.

24. Lampton, Interview File, No. 9 (1982), China, pp. 1–2.

25. David M. Lampton, "Water: Challenge to a Fragmented Political System," in David M. Lampton, ed., *Policy Implementation in Post-Mao China* (Berkeley: University of California Press, 1987), pp. 157–189.

26. Lampton, Interview File, No. 5 (1982), China, p. 7.

27. Lampton, Interview File, No. 9 (1982), China, pp. 3–4.

28. Lampton, Interview File, No. 11 (1982), China, p. 4.

29. Lampton, Interview File, No. 26 (1983), United States, p. 3.

30. Lampton, Interview File, No. 11 (1982), China, p. 2, No. 26 (1983), United States, p. 2.

31. Lampton, Interview File, No. 11 (1982), China, pp. 4–5.

32. Lampton, Interview File, No. 26 (1983), United States, p. 2.

33. Lampton, Interview File, No. 10 (1982), China, p. 3.

34. Lampton, Interview File, No. 9 (1982), China, p. 1.

35. Lampton, Interview File, No. 21 (1982), China, p. 5.

36. Lampton, Interview File, No. 9 (1982), China, p. 1.

37. Ibid., p. 5.

38. Ibid., p. 7.

39. Lampton, Interview File, No. 11 (1982), China, p. 2.

40. Lampton, Interview File, No. 26 (1983), United States, p. 1; also Kenneth Lieberthal, "The Three Gorges Dam Project" (unpublished manuscript), pp. 19 and 49.

41. Lieberthal, "The Three Gorges Dam Project."

42. FBIS, 4 September 1985, p. P3, from Wuhan, Hubei Provincial Service, in Mandarin, 3 September 1985.

43. Lampton, Interview File, No. 4 (1982), China, p. 8.

44. Ibid., p. 9. In another interview, the respondent talked about the thermal versus hydropower debate and said that "it has been this debate which has slowed down construction at San Xia for 25 years." Lampton, Interview File, No. 26 (1983), United States, p. 3.

45. Lampton, Interview File, No. 28 (1986), United States.

46. Lampton, Interview File, No. 26 (1983), United States, pp. 3–4. This interviewee noted that in negotiations between Hubei and Sichuan concerning the Three Gorges Project, many things would have to be worked out. For instance, he said that they would have to agree about how much rice Hubei would provide Sichuan to make up for the farmland in Sichuan that would be inundated. Also, they would have to agree on the distribution of electric power, water, and displaced persons.

47. Lampton, Interview File, No. 2 (1982), China, p. 11.

48. Lampton, Interview File, No. 28 (1986), United States, p. 1.

49. *ENR*, July 26, 1984, p. 27.

50. Li Rui, *Lun San Xia Gongcheng* (Hunan: Hunan kexue jishu chubanshe, 1985), pp. 136–136. This quote is cited in Lieberthal, "The Three Gorges Dam Project," pp. 44–45.

51. Lieberthal, "The Three Gorges Dam Project, pp. 50–56.

52. FBIS, 3 April 1986, pp. K1–2, from Beijing Xinhua, in English, 3 March 1986.

53. FBIS, 1 April 1986, p. B1, from Agence France Presse, Hong Kong, 31 March 1986.

54. Franklyn Griffiths, "A Tendency Analysis of Soviet Policy-Making," in Gordon Skilling and Franklyn Griffiths, eds., *Interest Groups in Soviet Politics* (Princeton, N.Y.: Princeton University Press, 1971), pp. 335–377; also Michel Oksenberg, "Occupational Groups in Chinese Society and the Cultural Revolution," in Michel Oksenberg, Carl Riskin, Robert A. Scalapino, and Ezra Vogel, *The Cultural Revolution 1967 in Review* (Ann Arbor: Michigan Center for Chinese Studies, Michigan Paper No. 2, 1968), pp. 1–44.

55. See the forthcoming dissertation by Paul Schroeder, Department of Political Science, Ohio State University.

56. See Naughton, "The Decline of Central Control."

57. Oksenberg, "Economic Policy-Making," pp. 174–180, provides an excellent description of the roles of commissions, vice-premiers, the SPC, and the Standing Committee of the State Council.

58. Lampton, Interview File, No. 24 (1982), China, p. 7 and p. 4.

59. Lampton, Interview File, No. 27 (1983), United States, p. 1.

60. Lampton, Interview File, No. 23 (1982), China, p. 7.

61. Lampton, Interview File, No. 24 (1982), China, p. 5.

62. Lampton, Interview File, No. 25 (1982), China, p. 1.

63. Lampton, Interview File, No. 15 (1982), China, p. 4.

64. Lampton, Interview File, No. 25 (1982), China, p. 7.

65. Lampton, Interview File, No. 14 (1982), China, p. 5.

66. Lampton, Interview File, No. 7 (1982), China, p. 11.

67. Ibid.

68. Lampton, Interview File, No. 25 (1982), China, p. 9.

69. Lieberthal, "The Three Gorges Dam Project, pp. 50–51.

70. John W. Lewis, "Political Networks and the Chinese Policy Process," an occasional paper of the Northeast Asia–United States Forum on International Policy (Stanford, Calif.: Stanford University, 1986).

71. Lampton, *Paths to Power,* Chapter 5.

72. Lampton, Interview File, No. 27 (1983), United States, p. 2.

9

Communist China's Civil-Military Relations in the Mid-1980s: The Implications of Modernizations

Bih-rong Liu

Introduction

The question of China's civil-military relations has interested many people in the mid-1980s. On the one hand, we witnessed the successful removal by the civilian leaders of eight out of eleven military region (MR) commanders, who were retired or transferred in June 1985, and further, in September, after a special party conference, six out of nine military men on the Politburo resigned. It is noteworthy that even the veteran commander of the Shenyang MR, Li Te-sheng, was dismissed first from the post of commander, then from the Politburo. Li had been stationed in Shenyang for more than ten years and was called the king of Manchuria by some China watchers. Therefore, the 1985 military personnel reshuffle can be regarded as a victory won by civilian leaders to uphold civilian supremacy over the People's Liberation Army (PLA).

However, on the other hand, we also noticed that Teng Hsiao-ping failed to put the former party general secretary, Hu Yao-pang, on the party Military Affairs Commission (MAC). Nor was Teng able to resume the needed military rank system. Although later Chao Tzu-yang was put into the Central Military Commission as the first vice chairman, many analysts doubted that Chao would be able to take over the military power after Teng passed from the political scene. Under these circumstances, whether or not the second- and third-echelon civilian leaders can take over Teng's military power has become a question that merits our attention.

Yet whether or not Chao can chair the MAC is not an isolated question. Other questions should also be addressed: How did the civilian leaders control the military in the past decades? Is Teng able to use these techniques to put Chao at the head of the MAC? And will the current modernization drive complicate or change civil-military relations in the mid-1980s? This paper is therefore a modest attempt to answer these questions.

The Political Control of the PLA:
A Historical Review

Although people tend to label the PLA as a "state within a state,"[1] history shows that China has a good record of civilian control over the military. Despite the fact that the military helped Mao Tse-tung and Chou En-lai to purge Lo Jui-ching and Lin Piao, helped Hua Kuo-feng to arrest the Gang of Four, and helped Teng Hsiao-ping to regain political power, no civilian leader has ever become the military's hostage. To achieve civilian supremacy, the political work system in the PLA is not the only mechanism, and sometimes it is not even a reliable or usable mechanism, particularly when more and more political commissars are now identifying their interests with the military rather than with the civilians[2] and when the functions of political commissars are restricted by the Tengists in order to nurse military professionalism and solve the problem of commissar-commander dual leadership of the Chinese military.[3] As a consequence, many other mechanisms were developed by the civilians during the past decades. The first one is a political campaign launched outside the military to rectify the military's behavior. When the military gradually became an established institution, the political campaign served the function of what Harry Harding calls "internal remedialism," as opposed to the mobilization of the masses to serve as an organizational monitor externally.[4]

Political Campaigns: Manipulation from Above

The purge of Peng Te-huai and Lo Jui-ching, the fall of Lin Piao, the campaign against the ultraleftists, the Anti–Lin Piao Anti–Confucius campaign, and the Anti–Lin Piao Anti–Gang of Four campaign all show that the party can control the gun through a political movement. But who, if not the political commissar, helped the civilians to implement these campaigns in the military?

A close examination of these campaigns would suggest that it was the military itself that helped the civilians to launch political campaigns within the army. We should remember that the PLA is by no means a homogeneous institution. Because the PLA leaders underwent different processes of socialization, their perceptions of the revolution and interpretations of Marxism-Maoism were also different. Furthermore, all the military men have their own functional interests: interests derived from the nature of their primary function to defend the country against aggression by the organized and rational use of means of violence.[5] Although some scholars, given the evidence that the different policy choices, diplomatic or military, presented by different groups are not always based on a bureaucratic position, argue that a bureaucratic model is not applicable to Chinese politics,[6] one can hardly believe that any army officer would fight for the air force budget. The competition for limited resources, together with different perceptions of the "correct" revolution, provide the civilian party with plenty of room to manipulate the various groups within the military and, therefore, to carry out every political campaign.

Much evidence tends to support this argument. In the 1965–1966 strategic debate, Lo Jui-ching asked for more resources, but other military elites opposed them. A coalition of bureaucratic interests finally brought about the purge of Lo.[7]

Lin Piao is another case. A. Doak Barnett relates that it came about not because the civilian party was too strong, but because many important military leaders sided with Mao, making the downfall of Lin possible.[8] Joffe notes that these military leaders belonged to two broad groups: regional commanders and professional commanders. For regional commanders, it was "personal, factional and political rivalries" that made them throw their support behind the civilians. For the professional leaders, it was the hatred of military politicization and the desire for more concentration on military work that made them rise up against Lin.[9]

The Anti–Lin Piao Anti–Confucius campaign of 1973–1974 was a political campaign with its spearhead pointed at military regionalism. If the PLA had been a unified institution, all military leaders should have tried to block this campaign because it was launched concurrently with the 1973 commanders' shift and was itself obviously a threat to the military vested interests. But in practice the reverse was the case. The main forces not only did not block the campaign but were actively involved in it and helped the civilians to propagate their policies.[10]

All of these events suggest that the political campaign is a feasible tactic for the civilian party. However, the political campaign also has a serious drawback: the retardation of the military modernization process. Civilian leaders, of course, foresaw this. But to control the "intensity" of a political campaign is not as easy as to set the "direction" for the policy. When Mao launched the Cultural Revolution, he certainly did not want the revolution to spread to the field of scientific defense research. However, at the climax of the Cultural Revolution, institutions in charge of research and the manufacture of nuclear weapons, such as the Science and Technology Commission for National Defense, the Seventh Ministry of Machine Building, and even China's nuclear arm, the Second Artillery Corps, were swept by the storm of revolution.[11]

Another shortcoming of the political campaign is factionalism. When manipulating one group against another, fueling the existing group rivalry is inevitable. The May 1, 1984, issue of *Red Flag* criticized the factionalism within the party and army and demonstrated the serious side effect caused by previous political campaigns.

All these drawbacks suggest that although the political campaign is the tactic many civilian leaders have successfully used, it is not the best tactic and cannot be used alone. When military autonomy is very strong or existing intramilitary conflict is not intense enough, a conciliatory tactic is particularly needed. And such a tactic will help to reduce the damage done by a political campaign. It is the art of compromise.

Compromise: Manipulation from Below

Many analysts tend to view every compromise the civilians made with the military as an increase of military influence. However, on the contrary, as this research would contend, a compromise is exactly the means civilians used to control the military.

In Lo Jui-ching's case, Mao made a compromise. As Harding and Gurtov observed,

> The compromise involved the rejection of the elements of Lo's program that were especially objectionable to major interest groups within the defense industry, including Lo's proposals to cut back on research and development and the completion of defense preparations on a crash basis. On the other hand, there is evidence that some of Lo's other proposals for the improvement of China's air defense were ultimately accepted. . . . [This acceptance] represented a considerable victory for China's military professionals.[12]

Many scholars also speculate that a compromise had been reached between Mao and regional leaders after the Wuhan incident. The compromise might have included Mao's agreement to proposals that granted commanders at the national and military regional level additional authority in order to save the country from chaos. In return, the commanders might have agreed to give at least nominal assistance to Maoist selectees for revolutionary committees.[13]

The civilians also demonstrated the art of compromise in the Lin Piao case. From the very beginning, the attacks on Lin Piao were by no means aimed at the army as a whole. As Joffe put it, the leadership made a conscious effort to draw a distinction between Lin and the officer corps, and never tried to tamper with the prestige of the army. Most importantly, "The majority of the powerful regional commanders . . . retained their position of power; those who did not seem to have fallen because of their close ties to Lin Piao, and not because they were military men."[14]

Teng Hsiao-ping's agreement to launch the Anti–Spiritual Pollution campaign in late 1983 can also be regarded as a compromise between civilians' more pragmatic policies and the military's more dogmatic ones. But one should note that none of these civilian leaders was defeated or blackmailed by the military after a compromise was made. This evidence suggests that only when a civilian leader enjoys enough political power is he able to withdraw from his policies, or flexibly shift between them, without jeopardizing his political life. And every shift and compromise he makes can only be regarded as a tactic to achieve another political gain rather than as a defeat. Yet compromising with one group and obtaining its support to attack another is only one type of compromise. Two other types of compromise can be further developed.

As has been discussed earlier, every military leader has two major interests: an ideological interest derived from his own interpretation of revolution, his value system, and his self-image; and a functional interest coming from his job. There is always a trade-off between these two interests. A civilian leader can compromise on one of these interests while obtaining a concession on the other. For example, when Teng Hsiao-ping downgraded the priority of China's defense modernization, he certainly affected the military's functional interests. But at the same time, he inspired the military's revolutionary zeal and made the military believe that their temporary sacrifice was good for the revolutionary cause. This action satisfied the military's ideological interests and compensated for their material loss.

On the other hand, Teng could also allocate some resources to a few "target" military leaders and win their support for his pragmatic policy in return. The attitude change of former Shenyang Troop Commander Li Te-sheng is a good example in this regard. Because of his close ties with the radicals, Li rose to power during the Cultural Revolution. In other words, he does not belong to the Teng faction that suffered from the Cultural Revolution. More importantly, Li had held the post of Shenyang troop commander for more than ten years. Analysts have observed that Li's power was strong enough to establish an "independent kingdom." With his radical ideology and power potential, Li constituted a threat to the civilian leaders. Nonetheless, Li survived the 1982 shift of military commanders. But it is worth noting that Li gradually changed his attitude and began to criticize the leftists openly. As he wrote in April 1983:

> Eliminating the "leftist" influence fairly well during a period of time and in doing a certain item of work does not mean that there will be no "leftist" influence during a later period of time and in doing other items of work. . . . In my opinion, only when we have properly solved this problem can we . . . be ideologically and politically at one with the CCP Central Committee, further emancipate our minds, bravely blaze new trails and create a new phase in all fields of work of the Armed Forces.[15]

Obviously, there had to be some compromises between Tengists and Li: Tengists used functional interest to make Li soften his ideological stand and in return won Li's endorsement of the pragmatic policies adopted in the Third Plenary Session of the Eleventh Central Committee of the Chinese Communist Party (CCP). But this compromise by no means implied Teng's weakness. In 1985, when the task of paving the way for the second-echelon civilian leaders to take over political power became imminent, Li was still dismissed, first from the post of military region commander in June, then from the CCP's Central Committee in September. Li's dismissal confirmed our argument about Teng's civilian supremacy.

The third way to compromise is to shift between a hard track and a soft track while dealing with a specific group or service. Beijing's attitude toward the PLA Air Force (PLAAF) perfectly illustrates this tactic.

The PLAAF is a new service to the Chinese. Its development process is, therefore, different from that of other services. Since it needs more modern equipment and professional knowledge than the others, the PLAAF has gradually moved to the model of elitism that is heretical to the old revolutionaries. Bueschel describes the nature of the elite corps of the PLAAF in his book *Communist Chinese Air Power:* "The PLAAF air academy at Xian, along with the many other training schools, produced a substantial number of new pilots, and the PLAAF became widely recognized as the elite corps of the People's Liberation Army. . . . [T]he PLAAF soon found itself in a position where it could pick and choose its candidates for pilot training from the cream of China's youth."[16]

Mogdis also tells of the development of Chinese air forces in his research on the PLAAF. According to Mogdis, because of the progress of the advanced-weapons program, the increased size of the service, and the modernization efforts, the PLAAF has become more specialized and technocratically oriented. This development has put the air force in a position of "having to defend itself against charges of putting elitism and technology ahead of ideology." Furthermore, wrote Mogdis, because it was a new and numerically expanding organization, opportunities for advancement in the air force were much greater than in any of the other services. This situation also raised the question of internal equity within the PLA. "The gap between the levels of possible attainment and the speed with which it could be reached for those in the air force and other services became wider and wider as time passed," observed Mogdis.[17]

All the factors given by Mogdis were enough to fuel the interservice rivalry. As a consequence, the PLA had no choice but to side with the civilians and ask for protection. This request gave the civilians' party an excellent opportunity to control the new service. In 1965, the political commissar of the PLAAF, Wu Fa-hsien, was appointed the new head of the air force following the death of the former commander in chief of the PLAAF, Liu Ya-lou. Scholars believe that it was a political appointment because it sidestepped former deputy commander Wang Ping-cheng and thus put PLAAF under full party power for the first time.[18] In return, the civilian leaders allocated more resources to the air forces. The CIA data on Chinese defense expenditure confirm that the air force budget has been increased since 1965.

On the other hand, a new service such as the air force is so highly professional that the old revolutionaries could hardly take part in its development and strategy. This factor, plus the air force's involvement in the Lin Piao affair, prevents the civilians from trusting the PLAAF whole-heartedly. Beijing's policy toward the PLAAF thus demonstrated the character of shifting back and forth between hard and soft tracks: Sometimes Beijing showed much confidence in its close relations with the air force; sometimes it speculated on the loyalty of the air force.

For example, the PLAAF was praised and cited as a good example in the party rectification campaign by Beijing in June 1978,[19] but in 1983 it was criticized as failing to act "in unison with the party Central Committee politically and ideologically and . . . [as] not conscientious enough in actions."[20] However, in late 1985 the PLAAF was once again given as a good example by the central authority because its cadres were eager to obey orders to reorganize and streamline the military.[21]

Although one might contend that the inconsistency of Peking's attitude toward the air force shows the civilian leaders' discomfort concerning the PLAAF, intentionally or unintentionally, the shift between hard track and soft track has been proven an effective way to control the highly professionalized armed service.

When Lin-Piao was in power, he easily grasped the air force as his power base. The purging of twenty-seven high-ranking PLAAF officers for involvement in Lin's conspiracy is good evidence. The Gang of Four also easily controlled the air force after they came to power. Ma Ning's emergence as commander in chief of the PLAAF shows that while the Gang had problems penetrating the army, they successfully dominated the air force. After the Gang was purged, the PLAAF quickly became a good example of the Anti–Gang of Four campaign. All of these examples show the air force's anxiety to side with the faction in power. Only by doing so could the PLAAF find shelter from intense interservice rivalry. The interservice conflict, therefore, provides the civilians with the best leverage for obtaining party control.

Political campaigns and political compromise, as discussed in previous pages, are two tactics that the civilians employed to uphold civilian supremacy in the past decades. And judging from the fact that in the early 1980s, when the drive of defense modernization caused confusion and misunderstandings in the PLA, such as the 1980–1981 debate over "civilization" and "revolutionary spirit"[22] and the Chao Yi-ya case of 1982,[23] the Tengists still used these two tactics to successfully ferment consensus in the military, we believe that they will continue to employ these techniques to put Chao at the top of the MAC and eventually let Chao take over the military power.

Civil-Military Relations in the Mid-1980s

Through the tactics of "manipulation from above" and "manipulation from below," the Tengists might be able to win the consent of the military and put Chao Tzu-yang at the head of the MAC. However, to have Chao chair the MAC is one thing; to ensure his civilian supremacy is another. In theory, as the party leader Chao can follow Mao's and Teng's examples of using the techniques of "divide and rule" and political compromise to control the military; but in practice, Chao obviously lacks both a strong power base to impose consensus from above and the self-confidence to ferment consensus from below. Under these circumstances, strengthening Chao's power base has become the objective that the Tengists have to achieve in the near future.

Strengthening the Power Base of
New Civilian Leaders

In order to bolster the power base of new civilian leaders, the Tengists are trying to use legal approaches to institutionalize the state and party organs. From history we know that, because of the heterogeneous nature of the PLA and the deep-rooted military ethics of "the party commands the gun,"[24] it would be very difficult for the PLA to overtly launch a military coup and to sell it to the people. Consequently, the only way the military has ever employed to intervene in civilian politics has been through an institutional approach, that is, obtaining political power from "within" the existing political structure in contrast to overthrowing the existing institution from "without."

Lin Piao was an expert in this approach. In 1969, when the Cultural Revolution gradually came to an end, Lin led the military in "reconstructing" the party. As Harry Harding observed, Lin first endeavored to extend close military control over the reconstruction of the party apparatus; then, he sought to increase the number of military representatives appointed to central governmental positions, as well as to the Central Committee and to the provincial party committees; as the third step, he attempted to ensure that government positions would be permanent; and finally, he created conditions under which the military representatives on the party committee could serve as a separate leadership core that could act independently of its civilian party secretaries. It was through this four-step strategy that the military gradually intervened in the civilian sphere and finally dominated Chinese politics without a coup.[25]

To prevent future military leaders from following Lin's strategy, the Tengists take strengthening the party and state structures as their imminent task. The 1982 Party Constitution, for example, devotes seven of its ten long chapters to elaborating in detail the scope and structure of activities for the party organizations. The position of party chairman was also abolished in favor of a collective leadership formula, intended to prevent the radicals from dominating the central authority. As long as the party and state remain stable, the Beijing authority believes, the military will find no opportunity to "reconstruct" the party.

Furthermore, the CCP is in a period of transition to becoming an established party. All the tenures and responsibilities of the party posts will be clearly defined.[26] Although there is still a long way for the party to go, it is foreseeable that the rules of the game are going to be tightened. In other words, it will not be easy for ambitious military leaders to find loopholes.

The Tengists' institutionalization drive was accompanied by the significant promotion of the director of the party's Central Organization Department, Ch'iao Shih, to the post of secretary of the Commission for Politics and Law. This position controls China's legal and security apparatus. Ch'iao was later promoted to the standing committee of the Politburo after the Thirteenth Party Congress in 1987, but he still controls the security and legal organs. China's legal and security apparatus includes the judicial department, the procuracy, the civil administration ministry, and the security bureau. Ch'iao's post therefore provided Hu with an extremely important instrument with which to consolidate his power, particularly at a time when the country is trying to legalize and institutionalize its political machines. In December 1985, for instance, the PLA General Political Department issued a circular to the whole army on its decision to start popularizing common legal knowledge in the army beginning in 1986 and continuing for a period of three years. The circular pointed out that to "earnestly popularize legal knowledge, consciously observe party discipline and state laws, and safeguard and respect state laws under the new historical conditions" is an important political task for the army. Consequently, it called on all PLA units to link this campaign with, among other PLA tasks, "the structural reform and reduction-in-force and reorganization program of the PLA."[27] This circular gives us a good example of how the Tengists are using legal and institutional approaches to pave the road for the second- and third-echelon civilian leaders to take over the political power.

The Increasing Bureaucratic Rivalries

This emphasis on institution building and the popularization of legal knowledge also reveals that the civilian leaders are expecting that civil-military relations in the future will gradually come to be dominated by bureaucratic rivalries. As a result, civil-military relations would be regulated by fixed rules rather than by unpredictable factional conflicts. This expectation is certainly not groundless.

As the first-generation military leaders pass away, all the strong field army affiliations will gradually fade. To the young military leaders, their only power base is their own military region or their own service. Because of the military training they receive, the new military leaders will become more and more professionalized. Inevitably, this professionalization will intensify the interservice rivalries. Most importantly, the post-Teng leaders will not have Mao-style charisma to dominate the central decision-making process. Consequently, they will have to go down to the rank and file to gather enough support. Consequently, professional commanders will have an excellent opportunity to influence the decision-making process in the center. Lieberthal states, in his research on central documents and Politburo politics, that once the person on the Politburo with responsibility for a specific functional area takes over the process of drafting a central document, he typically contacts people in the appropriate executive organs and assigns them the task of pulling together the data necessary for drafting the document. This assignment will usually initiate a process of consultation, research, and investigation that might reach down to the bottom of the functional hierarchy.[28] It is predictable that, in the post-Teng era, consultation of this kind will be more and more frequent. And when military leaders are injecting their opinions, bureaucratic interests are also injected. Bureaucratic interests will gradually outweigh, if not replace, the importance of factional conflict in Chinese politics.

In fact, as defense modernization has continued, we have already witnessed the bureaucratic conflicts, particularly the interservice rivalries, becoming more and more intense.[29] Different methods have been employed by different services to emphasize their importance.

The first method is to emphasize science and technology in future warfare. For example, a theoretical group of the National Defense Industry Office argued in 1977 that the defense industry:

should be developed as fast as possible so that a good foundation may be laid and necessary preparations made before the outbreak of war. At the same time, the defense industry is a sector which makes comprehensive use of the latest scientific and technical achievements. In the course of its development, the defense industry will inevitably continue to make new demands on other industries and on science and technology, thus motivating the development of the entire national economy and helping raise the levels of production, science and technology.[30]

The second method is to use Mao's words to legitimize demands. As the air force lobbyists argued,

> Our People's Air Force has grown, made progress and has even won every victory under the glory of the great banner of Chairman Mao. We can never forget that Chairman Mao formulated the correct line and principles for building our People's Air Force. Chairman Mao and his close comrade-in-arms Premier Chou and Chairman Chu Te time and again reviewed reports on Air Force and requests for instructions.[31]

The third method is to emphasize the external threat (the Soviet Union) or a holy mission (to protect China's territory such as the Hsi Sha Islands, or take back Taiwan). As the navy lobbyists put forward,

> Building a powerful navy is an important problem in bolstering coastal defense, liberating Taiwan and other enemy-occupied islands and defending national security. [The Social Imperialist] expands its Pacific Fleet in a frenzied attempt to surround us from the sea. In recent years, Soviet revisionists have frequently sent aircraft, warships and reconnaissance ships to China's coastal areas to collect military information and even to carry out provocative activities in the Taiwan Straits.[32]

The development of intense interservice rivalries can be attributed to the military modernization effort that made the officers aware of many advanced weapon systems and encouraged them to ask if they could have the same equipment.[33] But, in addition, the change of military strategy also contributed to the intensified interservice rivalries. In the early 1980s, China began to prepare for coordinated warfare. Yang Shang-kun was reported as saying in 1982 that the most important thing in the scientific formation of the armed forces is to strengthen their synthesis. "Without the synthesis of the various branches of the armed forces," said Yang, "there could be no modernization and it would have been impossible to adapt ourselves to modern warfare."[34] A synthesis of various branches therefore broke the long-time emphasis on the infantry and let the voice of other forces be heard.

While the bureaucratic rivalries might be more predictable than the factional conflict and therefore make it easier for Chao Tzu-yang to impose civilian control over the PLA, the vigorous debates among commanders and services might also influence China's current economic priorities and China's perception of the external threat. Determining how to properly lead the bureaucratic rivalries rather than be led by the military officers is a big challenge that faces the civilian leaders.

PLA's Involvement in Civilian Affairs

The military's involvement in civilian affairs is also a noteworthy phenomenon. While the main forces might be eager to modernize and to professionalize themselves, the local forces often harbor a different idea. As Mozingo observed, "Other attitudes aside, their [the provincial military commanders' in charge of regional forces and the militia] career projections turned on making a success out of their imperfectly trained and equipped force in the task of preserving order, security, and the allegiance of the local population."[35]

In fact, some provincial commanders still believe that the military should be a fighting force, a work team, and a production team at the same time. In other words, taking part in civilian work is not only a matter of self-interest but also an ideological commitment. At the same time, it is interesting to find that the civilians have also found that military involvement in civilian affairs has some practical necessities. A *Liberation Army Daily* editorial on December 26, 1979, gave the first reason for military involvement. It said that the army must give aid to the local civilian governments. It must do so because the PLA itself cannot be modernized if the modernization of industry, agriculture, science, and technology does not go ahead. So the military must adapt itself to the conditions of this new historical period and promote the good tradition of "support the government and love the people."[36] In 1980 the National Conference on Urban Social Order and Public Security gave the second reason for military involvement. Some guidelines were laid down by the conference asking the PLA to help various localities reorganize and maintain social order.[37] An all-army conference on supporting the government and cherishing the people held in November 1981 provided the third reason. It called on cadres and fighters of the entire army to "build still closer army-government and army-people relations, to work hard for one year to exalt the prestige of the people's army to an even higher level."[38] All of these are imminent problems and the activities carried out by the PLA indeed served all three of these tasks.

Another aspect of military involvement in civilian affairs is the training of "dual-purpose personnel" for the army and localities. This training is obviously aimed at two problems: the overlapping and overstaffed condition of the military organization and the low military morale. Furthermore, this training program would also help the PLA to improve military training. *People's Daily* reported that in order to manipulate modern weapons and military equipment, cadres and soldiers must command more scientific and general knowledge and master skills in various fields, thus being capable of fulfilling their tasks better. This report also cited several examples to support its argument that the training of dual-purpose talented people would not affect the improvement of the army's military quality; on the contrary, "It will effectively promote the army's military, political and logistics work."[39]

The PLA's production of civilian goods and its transfer of technology to the civilian sector can be also regarded as a means for military involvement in civilian works. To the military, this is a good way to raise funds; to the civilians, it also raised the technological level, quality, and output of civilian products.

Therefore, it is evident that by encouraging the military to take part in civilian affairs, the Tengists skillfully linked the military's functional interests with its ideological commitment to participate in nation building and obtained concrete benefits from the policy at the same time. And we believe that this policy can be expected to continue through the end of the 1980s because it would help Hu and future civilian leaders to pacify the military so that they can continue the current economic reforms. However, some implications of this policy still need to be watched.

First, when ordering the military to actively support civilian works, the Beijing authorities have to be very careful about how far the policy goes. For example, when the military are producing civilian goods, contributing voluntary labor to local construction projects, or training dual-purpose personnel, the civilian leaders have to make sure that the military's regular training will not be hampered by this policy.

In fact, some problems have already appeared. For example, after the ministries of Nuclear Industry, Aviation, Ordnance, and Space had built more than 300 assembly lines producing civilian goods, Peking authorities began to worry that the military industries had overdone the production shifting. According to the civilian leaders, it was technology transfer, not production, that should be the emphasis of the new policy. An article published in the November 1982 issue of *Studies in Economics* therefore warned that "many units have carried out the shifting [of production] because they do not have sufficient tasks or because their funds and income are dropped, and due to the lack of unified leadership, there is serious blindness in their work."[40]

The PLA's contribution of voluntary labor to civilian construction projects also begs the question whether the military can afford to spend that many man-days in civilian works. Hence, Hu Yao-pang was reported as saying in 1982: "It is not really necessary to transfer large numbers of the labor force; for the army itself is quite busy with training. We must study methods. The army can offer technical guidance, give ideological mobilization talks and help local units build important and difficult projects."[41]

The training of dual-purpose personnel brought about some misunderstandings too. The *Liberation Army Daily*, for example, complained on March 30, 1983, that some young cadres put "training for locality use" before "training for military use" and only paid attention to the after-service job hunting.

The previous discussion suggests that controlling the balance between political involvement and military professionalization has become an important task that the civilian leaders have to deal with.

Second, perhaps even more important, when allowing the military to raise funds for themselves, the civilian leaders must prevent the military from becoming corrupted. The September 1985 dispute between Chen Yun and Teng Hsiao-ping on economic reforms is now well known. It is very clear that Chen represents another political force in the government that does not agree to the pace of current economic reforms and wants to shift the priority to rectifying party style and to strengthening discipline. Therefore, if the military became corrupted and lost their discipline, the Chenists' voice would become louder, and the current open-door policy as well as the economic reforms would be inevitably slowed down or reversed. Such a development would signify the failure, at least in part, of Teng's policy, and it would erode the power base of the second- and third-echelon civilian leaders who are expecting their legitimacy to be strengthened by successful economic reforms. Under these circumstances, the post-Teng civilian leaders have to be extremely cautious when they are using the technique of compromise and are trading material benefits for the military's political loyalty.

Third, it is true that the civilian sector has been too weak to take care of its own affairs and has asked the military to help. Vice-Minister of Security Hsi Kuo-kuang's thanks to the military for having given assistance to the police and security organs is a good example.[42] However, as the society becomes more and more developed, the civilian sector will also become stronger and stronger, and more and more civilian professionals will be educated. In comparison with these new civilian professionals, the military transferees' competence will be inadequate to deal with the immediate day-to-day problems, and their rigid value system will also be incompatible with an increasingly complicated world. Friction between civilian intellectuals (for example, a law-school-educated lawyer) and military transferees (for example, a lawyer trained in a six-month short program) is also predictable. It will be very possible for these former military cadres to form an informal coalition to protect their vested interests. If that is the case, then this coalition will have the PLA as its center and gradually develop the role of an interest group lobbying for military resources.

Fourth, how the military adjusts to its position in society also becomes a question. The PLA is in a very difficult position: On the one hand, it is the supplier of technology and professional skills—it uses its technology to help the people, and its personnel are even transferred to the civilian sector to help in nation building; but, on the other hand, it is also the recipient of civilian assistance—it needs civilian intellectuals to help raise its own scientific, cultural level. In other words, the PLA has to play the role of "teacher" and "student" at the same time. Can it play these two roles well? Can it adjust "what it wants to be" and "what it is expected to be"?

Primitive Organization Versus Competitive Organization

The PLA has played a very important role in the past. Its glorious history caused Mao to exclaim, and the PLA itself also deeply believes, that "without the PLA, there would be no new China." But this self-perception and pride gradually became a barrier to defense modernization: The self-pride would prevent the army from seeking advice from the other sectors, particularly from the intellectuals, and also prevent it from correcting its own mistakes.

Maury Feld has introduced two concepts, "primitive military organization" and "competitive military organization," as a framework within which to analyze the performance of the military. Primitive military organizations, according to Feld, "characteristically consider themselves to be the embodiment of rational practices. . . . Insofar as numbers and knowledge are concerned, [such an organization] has nothing to gain from any further dealings with the outside world. Since the organization, moreover, is the embodiment of rationality, there is no higher form of existence than official behavior." The primitive military organizations have few built-in inhibitions about recognizing the existence of rational individuals who do not belong to it. As to the competitive model, Feld put forward the following: "Active collaboration rather than isolated self-sufficiency is, therefore, the guiding objective of a competitively oriented organization. To the extent that they are able to cooperate with other groups of experts, competitively oriented experts achieve an adequate degree of understanding of the outside world."[43]

Using these two concepts as yardsticks, one can find that the PLA is currently in a transitional period. Various evidence shows that the armies realize that they have to seek knowledge from outside the military.

After the September 1981 military exercise, *People's Daily* published an article praising the contribution the intellectuals made to the military: "Without them [the intellectuals], it would be difficult to smoothly realize the strategic and tactical ideas formulated by headquarters, however good they may be, and the combined operations would be in a muddle."[44]

In fact, a large number of intellectuals have been absorbed into the military. In addition, the PLA also began to offer middle-school and college-level education in the military, and most of the instructors were from outside the military. Furthermore, the *Liberation Army Daily* added science columns in July 1978 to "provide an avenue for the exchange of experience in technical innovation and report on trends in science in other countries."[45]

While all these signs appear encouraging, the military continue to demonstrate their tendency toward anti-intellectualism from time to time. They questioned the ideological purity of the intellectuals, and, when they were criticized by the intellectuals for their own mistakes, they furiously struck back. The *Liberation Army Daily*'s attack on Yeh Wen-fu is a typical case. Yeh, a military intellectual, wrote two poems, "General, You Cannot Do So" and "General, Give Yourself a Good Bath," disclosing the dark side of the life of military leaders. Predictably, the military could not tolerate them. They attacked Yeh's poems, saying that he "seriously distorted the history of the Chinese revolution and the reality of our society."[46]

Civilian leaders are worried about the military's anti-intellectualism. A commentator's article entitled "A Strategic Task of Army Building" was published by *People's Daily* on May 5, 1983, saying,

Regarding attitude towards knowledge, we must further eliminate the influence of "leftist" ideas and correct erroneous concepts. We must create an atmosphere of respecting knowledge, welcoming knowledge, being thirsty for knowledge, and making efforts to study science and culture through the army. We also must get rid of various biases against intellectuals, be concerned about them, love them, trust them, depend on them, and create conditions and provide facilities for them to give full play to their wisdom and talents.[47]

All this seemingly contradictory behavior says that the PLA is in its transitional period. When moving from a primitive organization into a competitive organization, the military need to do a lot of adjusting. They have to adjust "what they like to be" and "what they are expected to be." The transition is painful and might also be slow, but it is the key to a successful modernization, and it is also the key to Chao Tzu-yang's successful civilian control.

Conclusion

As far as civil-military relations are concerned, the Tengists are facing three tasks: first, how to put Chao Tzu-yang in charge of the MAC; second, how to help Chao consolidate his power; and third, how to prevent efforts to achieve political control from hampering the defense modernization.

From history, we find that the civilians have developed two techniques, namely, political campaigns and political compromise, to impose their control over the military. And judging from the fact that the Tengists have successfully employed these tactics to ferment consensus of military modernization in the PLA, we believe that they might be able to use these techniques to win the consent of the military and to let Chao chair the MAC.

In contrast, to consolidate Chao's power base would be a more difficult job. To ensure his civilian supremacy, Chao has to build up his legitimacy and self-confidence so that he can also employ the Mao-Teng strategy of campaign and compromise to control the PLA. In order to achieve this objective, and also with the expectation that the party and state systems, particularly civil-military relations, would become more institutionalized and regularized in the future, the Tengists are now attempting to use legal and institutional approaches to strengthen Chao's power base. But legal and institutional approaches alone are not enough; eventually the civilians will still need successful economic reforms to bolster their legitimacy. However, successful economic reforms and military professionalization sometimes might conflict with the Tengist political maneuvers, if the civilians fail to pay due attention to the extent to which the policies go.

For example, in order to win the military's support to the economic reforms, the civilian leaders might decide to give the soldiers some material benefits when allowing the military to take part in civilian projects. This is a technique of compromise, but it also puts military discipline at risk. If military discipline is in question, the economic reforms might be forced to reverse, thereby eroding the power base of Chao and other new civilian leaders who were picked by Teng as political successors and who stand for the Tengist policy of economic reforms. Furthermore, while military involvement in civilian affairs might help to boost the military's morale and prestige, an overinvolvement will certainly jeopardize regular military training and might also make the military's transitional process from a primitive organization to a competitive organization more difficult.

In sum, how to make a balanced choice among these policy alternatives, how to skillfully control the extent to which the policies go after a general direction has been set, and how to conciliate the military without risking military discipline or hampering military professionalization, have become crucial issues that can be expected to determine China's civil-military relations in the mid-1980s.

Notes

1. Mu Fu, "Kuo Chung Chi Kuo: Chieh Fang Chun" (Country within the Country: the People's Liberation Army), *Chiu Shi Nien Tai* (The Nineties) (Hong Kong), July 1984, pp. 53–59.

2. A careful survey of the directory of officials in China and of biographies of Chinese leaders suggests that while political commissars in provincial military districts are staffed by civilians, all political commissars of the main forces and special forces are staffed by career military men. Many military leaders, such as Chin Chi-wei, Wang En-mao, and Li Te-sheng, have been shifted back and forth between the posts of political commissars and military commanders. Other military cadres, while remaining at the post of political officer, transferred from one unit or one service to another for tens of years. As data show, from July 1975 to June 1976, for instance, 85 of the 102 newly appointed political officers were transferred or promoted from another military service or unit. While having spent most of their lifetime in the military, these new political officers certainly identified themselves with the military. See *Chung Kung Nien Pao* (Chinese Communist Year Book), 1976 (Taipei), pp. (8)203–(8)210. In addition to the lifetime career, Whitson and Herspring also pointed out that the new functions of the PLA and the impact of technology might also lead the PLA to identify its interests with those of the civilians. See William Whitson, "Organizational Perspective and Decision-Making in the Chinese Communist High Command," in Robert A. Scalapino, ed., *Elites in the People's Republic of China* (Seattle: University of Washington Press, 1972), pp. 407–408; Dale Herspring, "Technology and the Changing Political Officer in the Armed Forces," *Studies in Comparative Communism*, winter 1977, pp. 390–391.

3. For example, see Sung Shih-lun, "Mao Tse-tung's Military Thinking Is the Guide to Our Army's Victories," originally carried in issue no. 7 (1981) of *Military Science*, reprinted in *Red Flag*, 1981, no. 16, pp. 5–15, trans. in *Foreign Broadcast Information Service, China* (hereafter *FBIS-CHI*), September 17, 1981, p. K23; Ku Kuo-pu, "Ideological Work Must Be Directed Toward Patient Enlightenment and Prevention of Aggravation of Conflict," *People's Daily*, March 29, 1981, p. 1, in *FBIS-CHI*, April 2, 1981, p. K13; and Sun Mao-chin, "On the Trail Blazed by the Older Generation—On Young Deputy Corps Commander Li Lien-hui," *People's Daily*, July 20, 1982, in *FBIS-CHI*, July 22, 1982, pp. K2–K4.

4. Harry Harding, *Organizing China: The Problem of Bureaucracy, 1949–1976* (Stanford, Calif.: Stanford University Press, 1981).

5. Roman Kolkowicz used this concept to analyze the Soviet Red Army. We found it useful also in our analysis of the PLA. See Roman Kolkowicz, "The Military," in H. Gordon Skilling and Franklyn Griffiths, eds., *Interest Groups in Soviet Politics* (Princeton, N.J.: Princeton University Press, 1971), pp. 140–141.

6. See, among others, Byong-Moo Hwang, "Linkage Politics in Chinese Foreign Policy-Making," *Journal of East Asian Affairs* (Seoul), spring-summer 1982, pp. 40–41; and Lucian Pye, *The Dynamics of Chinese Politics* (Cambridge, Mass.: Oelgeschlager, Gunn, and Hain, 1981), p. 86.

7. See Harry Harding and Melvin Gurtov, *The Purge of Lo Jui-Ch'ing: The Politics of Chinese Strategic Planning*, Rand Paper R-548-PR.

8. A. Doak Barnett, *Uncertain Passage* (Washington, D.C.: Brookings Institution, 1974), pp. 86–87.

9. Ellis Joffe, "The Chinese Army After the Cultural Revolution: The Effects of Intervention," *China Quarterly*, July-September 1973, p. 473.

10. *China News Analysis*, no. 1011, p. 3.

11. See, for example, Propaganda Department of the "New 915" Revolutionary Rebel Headquarters of the Seventh Ministry of Machine Building, "Down With Renegade, Special Agent and Capitalist Roader Liu Hsuan," *Flying Whistling Arrow* (Beijing), combined nos. 11 and 12, May 20, 1967. Cited in *Communist China, 1968* (Hong Kong: Union Research Institute, 1969), p. 249.

12. Harding and Gurtov, *The Purge of Lo Jui-Ch'ing*, pp. 59–60.

13. William W. Whitson and Chen-hsia Huang, *The Chinese High Command* (New York: Praeger, 1973), p. 397.

14. Joffe, "The Chinese Army After the Cultural Revolution," pp. 476–477.

15. Li Te-sheng, "Continue to Eliminate 'Leftist' Ideology Influence, Strive to Create a New Phase of Armed Forces Building," trans. in *FBIS-CHI*, April 14, 1983, pp. K1–K5.

16. Richard M. Bueschel, *Communist Chinese Air Power* (New York: Praeger, 1968), pp. 32–33.

17. Franz J. Mogdis, "The Role of the Chinese Communist Air Force in the 1970s," in William Whitson, ed., *The Military and Political Power in China in the 1970s* (New York: Praeger, 1972), p. 257.

18. Ibid., p. 258.

19. Hsin Hua Domestic Service, January 24, 1978, in *FBIS-CHI*, June 29, 1978, p. E1.

20. Kao Hou-liang, "Acting in Concert with the CCP Central Committee is a Concentrated Expression of Party Spirit," *People's Daily*, January 5, 1983, p. 3, in *FBIS-CHI*, January 11, 1983, pp. K15–K19.

21. *People's Daily*, November 18, 1985, p. 4.

22. For this debate, see Chu Liang, "The Armed Forces After the 12th Party Congress—Also Commenting on the Inside Story of the Struggle Revealed by Wei Kuo-ching's Resignation," *Chung Kong Yen Chiu* (Studies in Chinese Communism) (Taipei), October 1982, p. 119; "Guangzhou PLA Cadres Stress Spiritual Civilization," Kuangtung Provincial Service, February 6, 1981, in *FBIS-CHI*, February 9, 1981, p. P1; *People's Daily* editorial, "Clear Up 'Left' Ideas with the Method of Criticism and Self-Criticism," March 10, 1981, p. 1, in *FBIS-CHI*, March 11, 1981, pp. K2–K3; Li Chi-cheng and Li Chu-nan, "Leading Cadres Take Lead in Self-Clearing Up—Xiang Zhonghua Cleans Up 'Leftist' Influence at Guangzhou PLA Political Work Conference," *People's Daily*, April 17, 1981, p. 1, in *FBIS-CHI*, April 21, 1981, p. P1; Contributing Commentator, "Restore the Party Style of Criticism and Self-Criticism,"

1228 Bih-rong Liu

People's Daily, May 11, 1981, p. 2, in *FBIS-CHI,* May 13, 1981, pp. K2–K6; and Hsin Hua Domestic Service, January 20, 1983, in *FBIS-CHI,* January 27, 1983, p. K21.

23. For discussion of Chao's case, see, among others, *China News Analysis,* no. 1245, pp. 3–8.

24. For discussion on the heterogeneous nature of the PLA and the military's self-constraint, see Ellis Joffe, "Party and Military in China: Professionalism in Command?" *Problems of Communism,* September-October 1983, p. 48, and "The Chinese Army After the Cultural Revolution: The Effect of Intervention," *China Quarterly,* July-September 1973, pp. 458–459.

25. Harding, *Organizing China,* pp. 300–302.

26. Frederick C. Teiwes, *Leadership, Legitimacy, and Conflict in China* (Armonk, N.Y.: M. E. Sharpe, 1984), pp. 85–92; also, Teng Hsiao-ping, "The Reform of the Leadership Systems of the Party and the State," *Selected Works of Teng Hsiao-ping* (Hong Kong: Joint Publishing Company, 1983), pp. 280–302.

27. Peking Domestic Service, December 11, 1985, in *Joint Publications Research Service* (thereafter *JPRS*), January 7, 1986, p. 122.

28. Kenneth Lieberthal, *Central Documents and Politburo Politics in China* (Ann Arbor: University of Michigan, 1978), p. 29.

29. Scholars in the last decade refused to recognize the importance of interservice rivalries. Ellis Joffe said, for instance, "On balance, however, there seem to be few grounds for intense interservice rivalries, for in the context of China's . . . military strategy . . . all the services seem to have benefited from the country's limited resources" (Joffe, "The Chinese Army After the Cultural Revolution," pp. 450–477). However, as the defense modernization continued, we did witness the interservice rivalries becoming more and more intense.

30. Theoretical Group of the National Defense Industry Office, "The Strategic Policy on Strengthening Defense Construction—On Studying Chairman Mao's Dissertation on the Relationship Between Economic Construction and Defense Construction," *Kuang Ming Jih Pao,* January 20, 1977, p. 2, in *FBIS-CHI,* January 31, 1977, p. E2.

31. Chang Chih-hui, "Hold High Chairman Mao's Banner and Build a Powerful People's Air Force," Beijing Domestic Service, August 30, 1977, in *FBIS-CHI,* September 1, 1977, p. E2.

32. Theoretical Group of the PLA Navy, "Hold Chairman Mao's Banner High, Build a Powerful Navy—Some Insights Acquired After Reading 'The Chinese People Have Stood Up!' " *People's Daily,* June 24, 1977, p. 3, in *FBIS-CHI,* June 30, 1977, p. E6.

33. In this regard, see, among others, Li Li, "Training Competent Commanders for China—Visiting a PLA Military Academy," *Peking Review,* August 2, 1982, p. 24; and Beijing Domestic Service, April 10, 1977, in *FBIS-CHI,* April 14, 1977, p. H2.

34. Yang Shang-kun, "Build a Strong Modern Revolutionary Army—In Commemoration of the 55th Anniversary of the Founding of the Chinese People's Liberation Army," *Red Flag,* 1982, no. 15, pp. 6–10, in *FBIS-CHI,* August 25, 1982, pp. K20–K27, on p. K25.

35. David Mozingo, "The Chinese Army and the Communist State," in Victor Nee and David Mozingo, eds., *State and Society in Contemporary China* (Ithaca, N.Y.: Cornell University Press, 1983), pp. 98–99.

36. *China News Analysis,* no. 1176, p. 5.

37. "PLA Units Actively Assist Local Authorities in Maintaining Law and Order in Implementing the Spirit of the Urban Public Security Conference," *People's Daily,* January 23, 1980, p. 5, in *FBIS-CHI,* January 24, 1980, p. L1.

38. Peking Domestic Service, November 25, 1981, in *FBIS-CHI*, November 27, 1981, p. K8.

39. Commentator, "An Important Reform in Army Building," *People's Daily*, February 25, 1983, p. 1, in *FBIS-CHI*, March 1, 1983, pp. K6–K8.

40. Yeh Tze-tung, "On Shifting of Science and Technology from Military to Civilian Uses," *Studies in Economics*, November 20, 1982, pp. 44–47, in *JPRS*, no. 82761, pp. 41–48, on p. 45.

41. *Wen Wei Po* (Hong Kong), December 7, 1982, in *FBIS-CHI*, December 8, 1982, p. W9.

42. For details, see *China News Analysis*, no. 1176.

43. Maury Feld, *The Structure of Violence: Armed Forces as Social Systems* (Beverly Hills, Calif.: Sage, 1977), pp. 90–92.

44. Yan Wu et al., "Mighty Troops Shake the Mountains—The People's Liberation Army Marching Toward Modernization," *People's Daily*, October 23, 1981, p. 3, in *FBIS-CHI*, November 2, 1981, p. K5.

45. *FBIS-CHI*, July 24, 1978, p. E2.

46. Gong Yan, "Comments on Yeh Wen-fu's Poems About the General and Others," *Liberation Army Daily*, February 12, 1982, p. 3, in *FBIS-CHI*, February 16, 1982, p. K8.

47. Commentator, "A Strategic Task of Army Building," *People's Daily*, May 5, 1983, in *FBIS-CHI*, May 6, 1983, pp. K3–K4.

10

The Uncertain Future of Hong Kong

Lowell Dittmer

Hong Kong's rise from rags to riches has been one of postwar Asia's most amazing success stories. With very little or no natural resources except its own manpower it has become one of East Asia's four "newly industrialized countries" (NICs) and one of the three largest financial centers in the world; by 1982, Hong Kong had realized Asia's highest GNP per capita after Japan.[1] Yet its political status has remained problematic. Albeit the last of the crown colonies, Hong Kong has assumed a somewhat ironical relationship to its colonizer and its would-be liberator. Whether it is still being "exploited" by British imperialism remains controversial. Although British colonials are accorded discriminatory treatment in the civil service, few of them actually live there, with 98 percent of the population remaining ethnic Chinese. Hong Kong pays only half its own defense costs; British investments in the territory rank well below those of the United States or Japan; and the British Labour Party has long wished to be rid of it, both out of principled aversion to colonialism and the conviction that Chinese sweatshops unfairly compete with British industry.[2] The Chinese, though bereft of their territory for the past 150 years, nevertheless profited handsomely from the arrangement, consistently earning some 30–40 percent of their foreign exchange from the difference in value between exports and imports with the colony.[3]

For some thirty years, this odd reversal of interests has conspired with cold war containment policies to sustain a mutually beneficial status quo. Yet now that the sun begins to set on this lingering imperial outpost, as Hong Kong bids fair to be the first peaceful passenger between communist and capitalist "camps" since the neutralization of Austria in 1955, a host of questions swarms up to bedevil the best efforts of all parties to "ensure a smooth transfer of government." Will the city-state's political autonomy and emphatically capitalist economic arrangements indeed be preserved, not just until the lease on the New Territories expires in 1997, but for fifty years after the red banner displaces the union jack, as promised in the recently concluded Sino-British Joint Declaration? The notion of "one country, two systems," though formally incorporated into Article 31 of the 1982 Chinese Constitution (reportedly at Deng Xiaoping's behest), is even more anomalous than the concept of Eurocommunism—for while capitalism at least claims to be pluralist, communism has hitherto lived under the motto *principiis obsta*—beware the beginnings (of capitalism). That is to say, economic pluralism has been assumed to give rise to political pluralism, which cannot be tolerated without placing the entire system in peril. If this novel experiment misfires, will it be because Hong Kong's economy dovetails with, and further promotes, the ongoing redefinition of Chinese socialism, leading to an eventual market socialist synthesis? Or because the People's Republic of China (PRC) finds it impossible to tolerate Hong Kong's free-wheeling capitalism and takes steps to suffocate it? What will happen to the people of Hong Kong? And who cares?

The purpose of this essay is not to relate the history of the Hong Kong economic miracle or explore the reasons for it, nor is it to recapitulate the chain of events leading to the resolution of Hong Kong's colonial status in the Sino-British Joint Declaration (SBJD) signed in September 1984. These tasks have already been capably performed by others.[4] Our purpose here is rather to examine the progress and prospects of implementation *since* formulation of the "final settlement."

Turning first to the economic consequences of retrocession, it seems at least conceivable at this point, admittedly based on extrapolation from a brief time period, that economic integration may be achieved without prohibitive cost. There has been some capital flight, and for the past two years Hong Kong has suffered from negative fixed capital formation.[5] But there has not yet been any mass exodus, and flight capital may return if financial conditions remain favorable; its loss has for the time being been compensated by an influx of PRC investment.[6] One might have expected Hong Kong's exports to shrink once China itself plunged into the world market beginning in 1978. (Chinese exports and imports essentially doubled in U.S. dollar terms between 1978 and 1981, making China one of the world's biggest developing-country markets and a significant exporter of textiles, petroleum, and a wide range of other goods.) But on the contrary, Hong Kong has benefited more than any other Chinese trade partner (with the possible exception of Japan) from China's "open-door" policy. As Western markets began to erect protectionist barriers, Chinese markets beckoned. Hong Kong's exports and reexports to China have grown more than a hundredfold since 1978; China has risen from being Hong Kong's thirty-seventh-largest market to being its second largest (after the United States) in 1984. (At the same time, imports from China grew nearly sixfold.)[7] Entrepôt trade (involving reexports from China) has emerged as the outstanding feature of the new China–Hong Kong relationship, accounting for 44 percent of Hong Kong imports by 1981; Hong Kong now handles seven times more cargo than all of China's other ports combined. China trade flows through Hong Kong partly because the city boasts the world's second-largest container port, partly because of its excellent infrastructure and disciplined work force, and partly because transshipment facilitates trade with countries without diplomatic ties to the PRC.

Hong Kong has thus been able to prosper while shifting its functions somewhat from manufacturing center to shipping entrepôt. This change represents a return to its prewar function, before the twenty-year American embargo triggered by the Korean War stifled most entrepôt trade and led to the development of textile, consumer-electronic, and other light manufacturing industries. Since China's opening to international trade and investment, significant quantities of Hong Kong capital have begun to migrate into China to take advantage of cheaper labor markets. Thus more than 60 percent of China's joint ventures have been concluded with Hong Kong firms, and 90 percent of the investment in the Special Economic Zones comes from Hong Kong. As industrial capital migrates northward, Hong Kong's economy will shift to trade, communications, finance, and services, assuming a role analogous to that of New York City.

At least three foreseeable difficulties cloud the horizon of Hong Kong's successful economic adaptation to the reversion of sovereignty. First, Hong Kong enjoys a number of special trade quotas and concessions vital to its export-oriented economic development. Taking textile export quotas to the United States as an example, Hong Kong has quotes several times larger than those of the PRC for many items—and these quotas may or may not be honored after retrocession. To be sure, a good-faith effort has been promised; the SBJD in Annex 2 states as follows: "Action is to be taken by the two governments [i.e., Britain and China] to enable the Hong Kong Special Administrative Region to maintain its economic relations in a separate customs territory and in particular to ensure the maintenance of Hong Kong's participation in the General Agreement on Tariffs and Trade [GATT], the Multi-Fibre Arrangement [MFA], and other international agreements." China is not a member of GATT, though it obtained observer status in 1985 and has reportedly applied for full membership; even if it joins after what are likely to be protracted negotiations, however, it is not clear how other members would regard Hong Kong's special status as a Special Administrative Region. The same holds true for the MFA, which is due to expire in 1986. Demands that textile quotas be renegotiated or, worse, that Hong Kong's quotas be subsumed under China's, could devastate Hong Kong.

Second, once sovereignty has reverted to the motherland, it will perhaps become more difficult to turn a blind eye on the sub rosa trade being conducted with Taiwan and South Korea—between 1978 and 1984, China's under-the-counter trade with Taiwan and South Korea rose sixty-three–fold. Hong Kong's top twelve trading partners (in terms of exports, imports, and reexports), in addition to Taiwan and South Korea, include Saudi Arabia, South Africa, Singapore, and Indonesia, none of which has relations with Beijing. Should Hong Kong's official consulates in these countries be downgraded after 1997 to unofficial trade-promotion organizations or altogether canceled, the resulting decline in trade could hurt Hong Kong. The Taiwan–Hong Kong trade relationship deserves special mention: It has been growing rapidly and is imbalanced in Taiwan's favor. The PRC bought only $51,000 in Taiwan goods in 1977, according to Taiwan figures, through middlemen in Hong Kong and Singapore. That figure jumped to $21 million in 1979, to $242 million in 1980, to $390 million in 1981, and to $560 million in 1984, and it was projected to exceed $1 billion in 1985.[8] Although still only about 2 percent of Taiwan's total exports, this trade (which is imported tax-free into the PRC, as Taiwan is regarded as a Chinese province) is of growing importance. Counting simple imports and exports as well as sub rosa reexports, Hong Kong is Taiwan's third-largest trading partner.[9] Taiwan also makes heavy use of Hong Kong for air and shipping links. It seems difficult to believe that China will resist this opportunity to blackmail Taiwan, given its proclaimed intention of incorporating the Republic of China. From Taiwan's perspective, such action would involve sacrificing a market rather than choking off vital supply sources, given the steep trade imbalance; from Hong Kong's perspective, however, the implication is that this trade relationship is subject to sudden cancellation after 1997.

Third, as Hong Kong residents are keenly aware, the Chinese leadership seems to be split between reformers and conservative "leftists," with the latter taking a far more cautious attitude toward the introduction of the market mechanism and the stimulation of commerce. During the 1981 campaign against "bourgeois liberalization" and especially the 1983 campaign against "spiritual pollution," the watchwords warning of "class struggle" and the "capitalist road" were once again occasionally sounded. Should either the closure of Western markets or the rise of Chinese leftists (or some combination of the two) lead to a sudden reversal of China's involvement in the international economy, Hong Kong would obviously find itself in an exposed and vulnerable position. China's admiration of Hong Kong's economic achievements is not without its shadow side.

So far as the political dimension is concerned, Hong Kong's outlook is generally much more sobering. First of all it must however be conceded that Hong Kong has known great liberty but little democracy, having subsisted under crown-appointed rule throughout its colonial history. The British overlords, in a dying gasp of political idealism, first attempted to implant the government they never hitherto deemed the colonials ready to operate during the brief time span before sovereignty reverts in 1997. It is part of the postwar decolonization tradition to decamp in favor of some form of self-determination, and the British also wished to accommodate pressure arising from alarmed Hong Kong colonials in response to the ongoing secret negotiations to decide their future. Yet in Hong Kong's case, the period since the signing of the SBJD has been marked by euphoric expectations of political emancipation plunging quickly in a cold wind from the north. Whereas the British, along with their Hong Kong supporters, thought they had ample legal basis in the agreement documents to continue the movement toward reform that had been initiated just before the agreement was signed, they soon discovered they had not taken due account of their lame duck status.

The would-be reformers certainly started out cautiously enough. In March 1985 the first step toward representative government was taken with the expansion of district-board election suffrage—district boards play an advisory role in such weighty local decisions as street lights, bus stop positions, and garbage collections. Meanwhile, China's National People's Congress (NPC) also met in March to select the membership of Hong Kong's Basic Law Drafting Committee (BLDC), an appointive board consisting of Hong Kong and mainland Chinese delegations—the Basic Law is a mini-constitution for the Hong Kong Special Administrative Region (SAR) that China plans to establish in 1997.

The second significant step toward reform was taken in September, when for the first time 24 (of the 56 total, with the remainder still being appointed) councillors to Hong Kong's advisory law-making body, the Legislative Council (Legco) were selected by indirect elections to an electoral college.[10] Extraordinary pains seem to have been taken to anticipate any accusations of political incivility. In a population of 5.6 million, fewer than 50,000 were entitled to vote, in a number of district councils and functional constituencies defined to give disproportionate weight to business and professional elites (e.g., labor received two of the twelve seats allotted to functional groups). The elections proceeded smoothly if not apathetically, with only 17,000 (less than 34 percent) actually voting.

Yet as events unfolded, the suppressed hunger for democracy seemed to grow with the eating. Many unofficial members of Legco or appointive unofficial members of the smaller and more powerful Executive Committee (Exco), known collectively as UMELCO, began to discuss the prospect of broadening the franchise to facilitate direct elections for at least a portion of the Legco by 1988, with a goal of moving toward a completely elective legislature by 1997. Elections would entail the organization of political parties, for few individual candidates could raise the money to contest territory-wide elections. UMELCO members accordingly began to organize. One emerging group was the Progressive Hongkong Society (PHS), a catchall party headed by Exco and Legco unofficial Maria Tam; another was a grouping modeled after the British Conservative Party led by Legco trio Allen Lee, Selina Chow, and Stephen Cheong.[11] The goal of the parties would be to win a majority in Legco, implying some form of ministerial government, perhaps with unofficials becoming government department heads, taking the reins of power from (appointive) civil servants. It was also suggested that the chief executive of the SAR should be restricted in his appointment of chief advisors to Legco members. All these arrangements, not coincidentally, accorded with the Westminster model.

The hopes of the reform coalition were predicated on a White Paper (policy document) on representative government published by the Hong Kong Government in November 1984, which started the momentum toward electoral government, and on certain glowing but vague passages in the SBJD, such as "Hong Kong for the people of Hong Kong" (*gang ren zhi gang*), "preservation of the existing systems," a "high degree of autonomy" for the SAR, and "one country, two systems" (*yi guo liang zhi*). Annex 1 of the SBJD stipulates that "the legislature of the Hong Kong SAR shall be constituted by elections." The document further states that both government and legislature should be composed of Hong Kong residents; the chief executive, to be selected by election or "democratic consultation," will appoint his principal officials; and the executive authorities are to abide by the law (the existing legal system should be preserved intact) and be accountable to the legislature. Moreover, the government seemed in a strong position to implement these reforms, as Section 4 of the SBJD stated that "during the transition period . . . the Government of the United Kingdom will be responsible for the administration of Hong Kong." In 1987 the government promised to publish a "Green Paper" (consultative document) to review those political reforms already implemented and those recommended for the future.[12]

All indications as of this writing are that the PRC fears that democracy in Hong Kong might set an even more dangerous precedent than the toleration of capitalism. It has, however, attempted to express its aversion rather obliquely in order to avoid possible capital or personnel flight or other adverse developments during the transition period. The Chinese have used "united front tactics" to build a political constituency while forestalling further movement toward formal democracy; those with an historical knowledge of the Chinese Communist Party recall that during the party's long struggle for supremacy, the united front was deemed one of the "three magic forces" that brought eventual victory—along with the People's Liberation Army and the Communist Party itself. These tactics include the following.

1. *The issuance of vague warnings in a context of information deprivation.* Even amid the negotiations the PRC resorted to this tactic, stating that they would impose a unilateral solution if a negotiated settlement were not reached by a stipulated deadline. In response to the prospective development of electoral democracy, on November 21, 1935, Xu Jiatun, director of the local Xinhua news agency (and a BLDC vice-chairman) held his first news conference in the two and a half years since he had assumed his position, in which he declared angrily, "We cannot overlook the trend that some things have deviated from the contract [*bu an benzi ban shi*] . . . such deviations will have damaging effects." He suggested that the Hong Kong government's notion of "returning the government to the people" was inappropriate, observing that since Britain is returning sovereignty to China, it is not up to the British to hand over anything to the people. It would be up to the PRC to decide what role the people of Hong Kong should play. The stock market dropped 50 points amid great (but temporary) consternation. Yet Xu and other local Chinese officials steadfastly refused to identify the "deviations" more precisely, proving equally unresponsive to pleas that they unveil their own position on democracy.

Another example was provided during the visit of Ji Pengfei, director of the state council's Hong Kong and Macao bureau (and the highest Chinese official to visit Hong Kong) in December 1985. More than eighty journalists attended his news conference, but he accepted only written questions submitted four days in advance, spending about fifteen minutes reading prepared answers. In these, he warned that only "small changes" on how the territory is run could be made during the transition period; any proposed big changes must be discussed between China and Britain (implying Chinese veto power). But the best example of all is the Chinese stipulation that all reforms must conform to the Basic Law (a constitutional document to govern political arrangements after 1997) before that law has even been drafted. (The British were sufficiently impressed by this demand that they took considerable pain to avoid preempting the Basic Law in their 1987 Green Paper.) The PRC has also maintained that the Basic Law is Chinese internal politics and that other countries should play no part in it.

2. *Preemption of possibly adverse decisions.* Thus the 180-member Basic Law Consultative Commission (BLCC), intended to advise the BLDC on Hong Kong public opinion, was set up in unseemly haste on the eve of the Legco elections, giving some prospective appointees only a few hours to respond. The Basic Law was originally not due to appear until after 1990, but at one point there was apprehension lest it be published in 1987, to preempt the government's Green Paper (after Hong Kong government agreed to submit the Green Paper to the Chinese side before publishing, this became unnecessary). To be sure, the Chinese are not alone in using preemption; the whole democracy movement was scheduled to preempt retrocession, giving some credence to Xu Jiatun's protests against "huge changes in the coming twelve years and no changes in fifty years" (*shi nian da bian, wushi nian bu bian*).

3. *Cooptation of elites.* The Chinese have made full use of their appointive powers to create a political base, dominating the selection in April 1985 of the 25 Hong Kong members of the BLDC (the other 34 members are from China), as well as the selection of the 180 BLCC members (all from Hong Kong) selected in December 1985. And the Chinese tend to construe their appointive powers broadly: Within days after the BLCC had been constituted, appointment of its standing committee and seven office bearers had been completed; when some raised objections that the whole proceedings had been rushed, contravening BLCC constitutional provisions that meetings require seven days notice and that office bearers be elected by the BLCC standing committee, new elections were held and the same seven names were nominated and elected by show of hands. Those appointed to the BLDC were the 23 topmost elites in Hong Kong, principally affluent business and industrial leaders (many recipients of British orders); the proletarian class had no representation whatever. Composition of the larger BLCC was also skewed in favor of the bourgeois classes (40 percent) and professional elites (30 percent), leaving only 30 percent of the seats for grassroots representation.[13] This kind of representation obviously conforms to the "elite politics" of the British, but shifts from the colonial model of "administrative absorption of politics" toward "political absorption of the economy," aiming to control Hong Kong's political notables through "democratic consultation" in order to maintain the existing market economy.[14]

Among the most noteworthy successes of this tactic has been the gradual muting of Hong Kong's exceedingly lively press. The level of press freedom in Hong Kong is undoubtedly unsurpassed in modern China (broadly defined) and probably in the entire Third World; newspaper consumption in Hong Kong is 350 copies per person per year, second only to Japan (497) and ahead of the United States. Rather than moving to suppress the press, the PRC has pursued a more subtle cooptative strategy, for example by appointing publishers or editors of centrist and rightist papers (*Ming Pao, Sing Pao, Sing Tao,* and *Wah Kiu*) to the BLDC. And these papers, as typified by *Ming Pao,* have accordingly exercised considerable self-censorship in criticizing the PRC.[15] Press organizations have shifted to "normal reporting," establishing beats in Xinhua, printing its handouts, attending its press conferences and briefings. Only those publications directly affiliated with the Kuomintang (such as the *Hong Kong Times*) have stubbornly maintained an anti-Communist stance.

4. *Creation of a "shadow government" in Hong Kong, in the form of the local branch of China's Xinhua news agency.* Xinhua has already played a major role in both BLDC and BLCC, apparently drafting the BLCC constitution, for example. Toward the end of 1985, Xinhua announced that it was not merely a news agency but a department of China's state council. Indeed, the news section even moved out of the Xinhua headquarters in Hong Kong, and ten new departments[16] were created to function under director Xu (a former provincial party secretary) and three new vice-directors, all well-connected with Deng's group in Beijing. One deputy secretary is Qiao Zonghuai, son of a former foreign minister; other senior staff members include Geng Yan, daughter of a former defense minister. There are now no less than 500 people working for Xinhua in Hong Kong, only 30 of whom are in the news department. Xinhua now coordinates and supervises the PRC's interlocking organizations (banks, trading companies, schools, motion picture and publication companies, and labor unions) in Hong Kong and represents the PRC in dealing with the colonial government; it even negotiates with countries (such as South Korea) with which the PRC has no diplomatic ties. What seems to be emerging is a contingency plan (should the British leave prematurely) or prototype for Hong Kong's administrative structure after 1997. Intelligence sources estimate that there are now more than 3,000 CCP functionaries in Hong Kong.

What is perhaps more surprising than skillful Chinese use of such tactics is the capitulation of all resistance to them on the side of would-be reformers. The British position can be appreciated; they have no further economic interest in Hong Kong and are essentially concerned with a face-saving and gracious exit that will not adversely affect Sino-British diplomatic and commercial relations. The business elite seems to have been successfully coopted by the prospect of honorific positions in the transitional organs and profitable contracts to do business with the PRC.[17] Another compelling argument to the business community is that democracy might jeopardize the laissez-faire economic system that has served them so well by encouraging welfare and labor groups to make inconvenient demands on the budgetary process that a more authoritarian order could afford to ignore. This leaves us with the strange prospect from a Marxist point of view of the bourgeoisie opting for communism in order to preserve capitalism. The proletariat, insofar as it is unionized, has already been coopted into the Communist-affiliated Federation of Trade Unions (FTU); nonunionized labor is atomized and politically insignificant. The professional middle classes are regarded as easily intimidated and are being encouraged to put the best face on rule from Beijing by subordinating their desires to the national pride of being ruled by other Chinese, instead of the British. Prospective party leaders have discreetly shelved plans for further political organization until the Hong Kong government's 1987 review of the status of the reforms; "The thing to do now is keep one's head down and make money," commented one.[18]

Thus Hong Kong seems to be moving toward a system that will preserve capitalist economic arrangements under a political regime that is more patriarchal and less democratic than pre-1984 colonial rule, and that seems likely to restrict civil liberty as well.[19] The weakness of the British bargaining position and the early assertion of Chinese preferences for a posttransition regime more similar to Beijing than Westminster[20] seem to have firmly closed the window of opportunity that briefly seemed open to a more democratic future.

But if worse comes to worst, the elite are prepared to leave quickly; and some major trading houses, such as Jardine Matheson Holdings, one of the major British-controlled trading houses, or *hongs*, has set up offices in Bermuda. So, too, has Sir Y. K. Pao.

Conclusions

The implications of these developments—warranting cautious optimism on the economic front, but pessimism with regard to politics—for *Chinese* modernization are on the whole auspicious. China stands to inherit the best deep-water port along the China coast, with its impressive industrial and commercial base virtually intact. The international airport is first rate, and the city's location provides it with communication and transportation throughout the region. Yet the assimilation of capitalism into a communist order may also be expected to present certain difficulties. The device the PRC seems to have opted to use to minimize these problems is a form of tiered federalism, in which different "special" categories of political entity (Special Administrative Regions, Special Economic Zones, and Autonomous Regions) all have different relationships to the center and are all more or less insulated from the rest of the country.

The Hong Kong SAR, like the Autonomous Regions and like China's provinces and municipalities, will be directly under the authority of the central government, but the nature of this subordination will be quite different. In the area of legislative power, the SAR will be required to report locally enacted laws to the NPC Standing Committee "for the record," while the people's congresses of the Autonomous Regions are required to obtain the approval of the Standing Committee before its laws take effect. While laws passed by Autonomous Region legislatures may not contravene the PRC Constitution, the terms of the SBJD seem to indicate that SAR legislation may not be subject to such restrictions. In the Autonomous Regions, courts are under the "supervision" of the Supreme People's Court, and procuratorates under the "leadership" of the Supreme People's Procuratorate; but in the Hong Kong SAR, the judicial system is to remain separate from that on the mainland—no local cases may be appealed above the highest SAR court. The SEZs, unlike either the future SAR or the extant Autonomous Regions, have no separate constitutional status, though SEZ administrative committees do seem to enjoy considerable latitude in practice to introduce economic and managerial innovations. China has also designed the SAR package to appeal to Taiwan, including, however, the additional concessions that both the military and the security forces will remain autonomous and under control of the local authorities.

This sort of tiered federalism, while ideally designed to minimize the glaring inequality involved in the sudden assimilation of 6 million people with an average gross income of $6,000 per year to a population averaging less than $500 annually, may however inhibit the sort of "demonstration effect" deemed useful to motivate Chinese workers. If fences are built around the SEZs and Hong Kong remains insulated from China even after its retrocession, this isolation would seem to hamper the proliferation of innovation. This is a dilemma to which no obvious solution suggests itself.

The implications for Taiwan are of course still very speculative, but because of the perceived interdependency between Hong Kong and Taiwan, the Hong Kong solution may well imply a Chinese drive to recover Taiwan sooner rather than later. If it becomes perceived in Hong Kong that political freedoms are diminishing even as the economic boom continues unabated, Hong Kong will be perceived as a less desirable place to live, even if precipitate flight of capital and personnel can be prevented. Under these circumstances the "Hong Kong option" would soon be discredited for Taiwan, both for its own citizenry and in the eyes of outside observers, and the PRC would have no recourse but a resort to force or threat of force. The lesson for Taiwan would seem to be to accelerate its own progress toward democracy, thereby providing a firm noneconomic basis for legitimacy.

Notes

1. In 1948, the per capita income in Hong Kong was US$180. In 1982, the per capita gross national product of Japan (in U.S. dollars) was $9,684; Hong Kong, $5,390; Singapore, $5,220; Taiwan, $2,587; South Korea, $1,720; and the People's Republic of China (PRC), $300. Japan Institute for Social and Economic Affairs, *Japan 1983: An International Comparison* (Tokyo: Keizai Center, 1983), pp. 1, 9; as cited in Chalmers Johnson, "The Mouse-trapping of Hong Kong: A Game in Which Nobody Wins," in *Issues and Studies*, August 1984. Real gross domestic product grew at about 7 percent per year from 1948 to 1960, accelerating to an annual average of 9 percent between 1961 and 1981. Productivity growth averaged 8 percent per annum during

the 1970s; unemployment remained below 3 percent, absorbing refugee inflows; and capital formation (savings as a proportion of GDP) exceeded 20 percent throughout the 1960s and 1970s. Bruce Bueno de Mesquita, David Newman, and Alvin Rabushka, *Forecasting Political Events: The Future of Hong Kong* (New Haven, Conn.: Yale University Press, 1985), p. 62.

2. The economic benefits Britain derives from Hong Kong seem to consist of the following: (1) profits made by private British firms and by British Airways—Britain grants landing rights at Kai Tak Airport to other countries in exchange for preferential foreign routes for British Airways; (2) funds flow from Hong Kong to Britain in the form of pensions for retired Hong Kong civil servants living in Britain, dividends for British shareholders in Hong Kong firms, and payments for commercial facilities arranged through London (British firms supplied facilities to massive projects in Hong Kong such as the railways and mass transit system); and (3) Britain holds a sizable portion of Hong Kong's sterling balance, accounting for 12 percent of Britain's total foreign liabilities and 27 percent of the total gold and foreign exchange reserves held by the Bank of England in 1973. Norman Miners, *The Government and Politics of Hong Kong* (Oxford: Oxford University Press, 1975).

3. Receipts from Hong Kong are now estimated at US$6 billion per year. In addition, Hong Kong has been the clearinghouse for overseas Chinese remittances to the mainland, amounting to more than US$100 million per year. China's overall trade balance would have had substantial deficits in twenty-four of the past thirty-five years without Hong Kong's contribution. See Y. C. Jao, *China and Hong Kong: The Economic Nexus* (Hong Kong: Oxford University Press, 1983); and Jack F. Williams, "The Economies of Hong Kong and Taiwan and Their Future Relationships with the PRC," *Journal of Northeast Asian Studies*, 4:1 (Spring 1985), pp. 58–80.

4. In addition to works already cited, see G. B. Endacott, *Government and People in Hong Kong, 1841–1962* (Hong Kong: Hong Kong University Press, 1964); David G. Lethbridge, ed., *The Business Environment in Hong Kong* (Hong Kong: Oxford University Press, 1980); Tzong-bian Lin, Rance P. L. Lee, and Udo-Ernst Simonis, eds., *Hong Kong: Economic, Social, and Political Studies in Development* (White Plains, N.Y.: M. E. Sharpe, 1978); Chao-chia Lin, *Society and Politics in Hong Kong* (Hong Kong: Chinese University Press, 1983); David Bonavia, *Hong Kong 1997: The Final Settlement* (Hong Kong: South China Morning Post, 1985); Joseph Y.S. Cheng, *Hong Kong: In Search of a Future* (Hong Kong: Oxford University Press, 1984); *inter alia.*

5. Cheng, *Hong Kong*, p. 241.

6. In early 1984, China made two major investments totaling nearly HK$1.18 billion. Everbright Industrial Corporation, a trading company set up in late 1983 with the help of a loan from the Chinese government, brought several new buildings on Hong Kong Island for HK$4 billion. In addition, Sin King Enterprises, a unit of the state-owned China Resources Company, paid HK$178 million for 34.8 percent of the shares of Conic Investment, Ltd., an electronics manufacturer. China has committed itself to the construction of a seventy-story Bank of China tower that will be the tallest building in Hong Kong and has poured equity into at least two major companies that were facing bankruptcy, one of them a bank. *Oakland Tribune*, January 12, 1986. As of 1984, China held some US$3–4 billion of direct investment in Hong Kong, and it may soon surpass the United States as Hong Kong's largest foreign investor. Bueno de Mesquita, Newman, and Rabushka, *Forecasting Political Events*, p. 108.

7. Total Hong Kong–PRC trade increased by 55 percent in 1984, to reach US$12.2 billion, just slightly less than total U.S. trade with Hong Kong (US$12.5 billion). Williams, "The Economies"; see also "Utilization of Foreign Capital and the Hong

Kong Market," *Ganggao Jingji* [Hong Kong and Macao economic digest], no. 1, 1984, pp. 14–18, as translated in *Foreign Broadcast Information Service—China*, February 28, 1984, pp. k10–15. As PRC–Hong Kong trade has increased, the trade imbalance (in China's favor) has also been closing: In 1984, China bought US$1.4 billion from Hong Kong and sold $7.2 billion, plus $3.6 billion in reexports. There is a great deal of natural economic complementarity between Hong Kong and the PRC—Hong Kong needs raw materials, and Chinese demand for consumer goods is insatiable right now.

8. Williams, "The Economies," pp. 58–80.

9. Bueno de Mesquita, Newman, and Rabushka, *Forecasting Political Events*, pp. 82–87.

10. Before September 1985 the Legco consisted of no elected officials, 29 appointed unofficials (i.e., non–civil servants), and 18 appointed officials, for a total of 47. Previous reform efforts under the MacLehose regime had consisted of increasing the number of appointed unofficial members (in 1973 there were 5 ex officio members in Legco, 10 nominated officials and 15 nominated unofficials; by 1980 the corresponding figures were 5, 18, and 26).

11. See Emily Lau, in *Far Eastern Economic Review*, 128:24 (June 20, 1985), pp. 52–56.

12. This document appeared just before this article went to press in 1987; whereas detailed analysis is not feasible here, the document appears to provide very limited options for wider democratic representation and ignores the questions of changes in the role and power of the Legco vis-à-vis the Exco, in the composition of the Exco, and in the governor's authority.

13. See Chin-chuan Lee and Joseph Man Chan, "Mass Media and Political Transition in Hong Kong," unpublished paper presented to the 36th Annual Conference of the International Communication Association, Chicago, May 22–26, 1986.

14. Ambrose Y.C. King, "Hong Kong's Political Change in Transition," *China Times Weekly* (New York), no. 36 (November 3–19), pp. 16–17.

15. Sir Louis Cha, publisher of *Ming Pao*, is a key member of the BLDC. Responding to criticism of his shifting stand, he said: "*Ming Pao*, which used to launch violent attacks on the CCP, has often praised, and seldom blamed, it in recent years. This is not self-censorship on our part. It is a considered opinion that the CCP's authoritarian policies in the past needed attacks whereas its current open policy deserves encouragement and praise." *Ming Pao*, January 29, 1986, editorial.

16. Administration, research, propaganda, foreign affairs, economics, culture and education, art and sports, coordination, social affairs, and personnel.

17. For example, Sir Y. K. Pao, the sixty-seven-year-old shipping magnate who controls the largest private fleet in the world, since his appointment by Beijing last April as a vice-chairman of the BLDC, has energetically taken on a role as Beijing's "private channel" mediator between Deng Xiaoping and British officials. Indeed, Pao has not been reticent about his role as a power broker and high-level go-between between Deng and Prime Minister Margaret Thatcher, who christened one of the ships he was building in Shanghai during her 1982 visit to China and Hong Kong. Criticism of his role in helping Beijing undermine Hong Kong's belated attempts to install some form of democratic government before 1997 is rejected by Pao, who said recently, "I'm not pro-Beijing. I'm not pro-anybody. I'm a businessman, and I want to make money. I share China's interest in keeping Hong Kong strong."

18. *Far Eastern Economic Review*, 131:3 (January 16, 1986), pp. 37–38.

19. The SBJD guarantees Hong Kong citizens freedom of speech, press, assembly, travel, religion, employment, education and life-style, rule of law, and private ownership

of property. None of these rights and freedoms have been blatantly denied in the brief period since their proclamation, but it is worth noting that most of them are also embodied in the PRC constitution.

20. Ji Pengfei has expressed preference for a tripartite legislature in which one-third of the seats would be allotted to pro-PRC members, another third to pro-British members, and the remaining third to "neutral" personalities. In view of recent public opinion poll findings it seems unlikely that such a legislature could ever be realized through direct elections. See Cheng, *Hong Kong*, p. 242.

11

"One Country, Two Systems": Theory and Practice

Hsing Kuo-ch'iang

On September 26, 1984, the People's Republic of China (PRC) and Great Britain reached an agreement on the "future of Hong Kong." The pact provided that Hong Kong would be allowed to continue its present capitalist system and maintain a high degree of autonomy in legal, financial, and administrative affairs for fifty years after it becomes a "special administrative region" under Peking on July 1, 1997, but that only its defense and foreign affairs would be placed under Peking's direct control. The Chinese Communists said the decision to permit Hong Kong to follow a system different from that in the Chinese mainland after 1997 was based on the concept of "one country, two systems." Maintaining that this concept was applicable not only to Hong Kong but also to Taiwan, the Chinese Communists extolled it as a pioneering undertaking of historical significance. News media in Peking then intensively publicized the concept.

In this article the writer studies the idea in relation to its background, theoretical framework, and feasibility.

Background

Material published by the Chinese Communists indicate that the slogan of "one country, two systems" was advanced by Teng Hsiao-p'ing after repeated deliberations and consultations. Presumably, the slogan was designed as a united front artifice against Taiwan for Peking's practical political purposes.

At the Third Plenum of the Eleventh Central Committee of the Chinese Communist Party (CCP), held two days after Peking announced on December 16, 1978, that formal diplomatic relations with the United States would come into force as of January 1, 1979, the Chinese Communists decided to employ "peaceful united front" tactics toward Taiwan. Consequently, on January 1, 1979, Peking issued a "Message to Compatriots in Taiwan" calling for an exchange of mail, trade, and air and shipping services as well as economic, academic, cultural, sports, and technological exchanges.[1] Peking also made peace overtures to the Republic of China on Taiwan by promising favorable terms. For example, at a reception for Seiki Watanabe, director of Japan's mass-circulation *Asahi Shimbun*, on October 18, 1979, Teng Hsiao-p'ing was quoted as saying that after the unification of China, the people of Taiwan could continue to enjoy their capitalist way of life and that Taiwan could retain its armed forces and enjoy political autonomy.[2] On September 30, 1981, Yeh Chien-ying, chairman of Peking's National People's Congress, advanced a nine-point proposal on the subject of "unification." He maintained that talks should be held between Peking and Taipei on a reciprocal basis; that arrangements should be made to facilitate an agreement for the exchange of mail, trade, air and shipping services, family reunions, and visits by relatives and tourists, as well as academic, cultural, and sports exchanges, under which Taiwan would enjoy a high degree of autonomy as a special administrative region and could retain its armed forces; that Taiwan's current socioeconomic system would remain unchanged, as would its way of life and its economic and cultural relations with foreign countries; and that there would be no encroachment on the proprietary rights and lawful rights of inheritance of private property, houses, land and enterprises, or foreign investments.[3] Article 31 of Peking's Constitution, adopted in December 1982, contained the following stipulation on special administrative regions: "The state may establish special administrative regions when necessary. The systems to be instituted in special administrative regions shall be prescribed by law enacted by the National People's Congress in the light of specific conditions."[4] In Peking on June 26, 1983, at a meeting with Dr. Winston L. Y. Yang, professor at Seton Hall University in New Jersey, Teng Hsiao-p'ing asserted that after China's reunification, Taiwan would maintain certain rights to handle foreign affairs, could handle its foreign economic relations independently, and use a special flag and the title of "China, Taipei." Peking's vice-premier Yao I-lin indirectly admitted that after China's reu-nification, Taiwan would be empowered to purchase defensive weapons from other countries.[5] It is clear from the foregoing that Peking employed the concept of "one country, two systems" in its peace overtures toward Taipei.

The slogan of "one country, two systems" implies Peking's practical needs because the continued prosperity in Hong Kong after the Communist takeover would be of great advantage to the Chinese Communists in the development of the Four Modernizations. The favorable balance of trade and the huge foreign investment in Hong Kong and the income earned in Hong Kong from overseas Chinese remittances and from tourism could be of impressive economic benefit to Peking. On the other hand, an economic recession in Hong Kong would demonstrate serious shortcomings in Peking's overall economic planning.[6] Another relevant point is that most of the more than 5 million Hong Kong residents were Chinese who moved to Hong Kong to escape Chinese Communist rule. Their fears of living under complete Communist rule again are quite understandable. To pacify the people of Hong Kong, the Chinese Communists advanced such slogans as "retrieval of sovereignty, establishment of a special administrative region, Hong Kong people ruling Hong Kong, and maintenance of prosperity." These slogans were consequently developed into the concept of "one country, two systems." Moreover, because of the supposed interrelation between the "Hong Kong issue" and the "Taiwan issue," Peking used the "one country, two systems" formula in its united front machinations aimed at the Republic of China on Taiwan.

From the foregoing analysis, it is clear that the concept of "one country, two systems" began to take shape in 1979 when Peking decided to make peace overtures toward Taiwan. It was not officially employed until September 1982 when Teng Hsiao-p'ing advanced it at a reception in Peking for British Prime Minister Margaret Thatcher.[7] The policy of "one country, two systems" was a product of the objective situation in Hong Kong, Taiwan, and the Chinese mainland, because the current political and economic systems of Taiwan and Hong Kong are diametrically different from that on the Chinese mainland, and the living standards in Hong Kong and Taiwan are much higher than those in mainland China. From the history of the Chinese Communists it is clear that different tactics were used by the Chinese Communists at different stages. During the Communist rebellion against the Chinese National Government in the 1940s, the Chinese Communists resorted to such slogans as "new democracy" and "coalition government" to outflank capitalism.[8] The currently used slogan of "one country, two systems" is also employed to outflank capitalism, because the Chinese Communists have never abandoned their goal of realizing socialism as a steppingstone to communism.[9]

Theoretical Framework

After Teng advanced the concept of "one country, two systems," many scholars and bureaucrats in mainland China wrote articles elaborating on it. The major theoretical framework of the concept can be viewed from the following statements:

Huan Hsiang, an adviser to mainland China's Academy of Social Sciences, said:

> Based on the theory of historical materialism, those superstructures as the political and legal systems are built on an economic base. During the very long historical period before socialism can be realized, a variety of forms of economy will exist: that is to say, there will be a process under which the capitalist system and the socialist system will coexist. Since the economic base in a country will decide its social and political life, the concept of "one country, two systems" should be viewed in the light that while a certain production mode and political and legal systems suited to it are regarded as the main body in a country, other production modes and the political and legal systems suited to it that have been handed down from history in individual areas should be allowed to continue to exist.[10]

Obviously an advocate of historical materialism, Huan Hsiang added:

We should not only allow the state-run, collective and individual economies to exist, but should also allow foreign businessmen to invest in China either jointly with Chinese partners or individually. Besides, they should be allowed not only to exist but also to develop. In such a way, the national economy will have a variety of coexisting forms of economy under the state-run economy as the main body. Three forms of economic system are currently existing in our country: the socialist economy which is now undergoing reforms, the special-zone economy, and the capitalist economy. . . . Therefore, it should be said that the concept of "one country, two systems" has a theoretical basis.[11]

Nevertheless, it is noteworthy that according to the historical materialistic law of development, the socialist state-run economy should be the mainstay of all the economic activities.

Some scholars try to find a theoretical basis from a philosophical viewpoint. Maintaining that all things contain contradictions and are the unity of opposites and that the movement of opposites in all things is a combination of conditional and relative identity with unconditional and absolute struggle, they contended that the Four Modernizations construction in the Chinese mainland would benefit from the capitalist elements introduced from Hong Kong and that the continued progress and prosperity of Hong Kong would need support from the Chinese mainland even though the social systems practiced in these two places are opposite to each other.[12] In other words, Peking's rationale on the slogan of "one country, two systems" is based on the law of the identity of opposites. Of course, the condition for the identity of opposites, that is, for the identity of Hong Kong and the Chinese mainland, is that the two should be unified into one state.

Some scholars interpreted the concept of "one country, two systems," which was originally designed for united-front purposes, from the economic viewpoint, as they noted that the advancement of the concept and Teng's economic policy of "invigorating the domestic economy and opening mainland China to the outside world" might have given people the impression that the capitalist economic system is superior to the socialist system. For example, in Huan Hsiang's article, the concept of "one country, two systems" implies the existence of a capitalist economic system in areas under Chinese Communist rule. Ch'ien Chün-jui, an adviser to Peking's Academy of Social Sciences, says:

It is the policy of the Party Central Committee that after the unification of our motherland, socialism will be enforced in the mainland while Hong Kong, Taiwan and Macao can continue to practice capitalism for a long period. The two systems will be allowed to coexist, to help each other, to reinforce each other and to make peaceful competition. Will this be a good model? It is a question for people throughout the country to study. To meet the new situation, the Party Central Committee has decided to open special economic zones and 14 coastal cities to reform socialism with the merits of capitalism.[13]

Chin Yao-ju, a standing committee member of the Chekiang Provincial Political Consultative Conference, said:

Marx predicted that the dire poverty suffered by the proletariat as a result of the development of capitalism had provoked the crisis of revolution in Europe and put Europe on the eve of victory for a proletarian revolution. Up to Lenin's days, he wrote in his book *Imperialism Is the Highest Stage of Capitalism*, published in 1914, that capitalism had already become decadent and moribund. In his book entitled *On Questions Concerning the Socialist Economy*, published in 1952, Stalin asserted that the capitalist market dwindled markedly and that the high tide of proletarian revolution would soon emerge because the unified capitalist market in the world had already split into the two parallel markets of capitalism and socialism. At the end of the 1940s, Comrade Mao Tse-tung, in an article "On People's Democratic Dictatorship," also predicted that capitalism was "declining rapidly and on the verge of death." All these judgments have been proved outdated and invalid. . . . The theoretical basis of the concept of "one country, two systems" is to abandon the foregoing outdated and invalid Marxist theories on international capitalism from the dialectical materialistic viewpoint and to recognize the fact in a true to fact manner that international capitalism is still in development and will continue to exist in a rather long historical process.[14]

Chin's open criticism of the theories advanced by Marx, Lenin, Stalin, and Mao Tse-tung on international affairs for the purpose of defending the theory of "one country, two systems" implies that the Chinese Communists have made a great sacrifice ideologically.

Teng Hsiao-p'ing interpreted this concept from reality. He said:

China's main body must be socialism, which has produced good results. That one billion people on the mainland implement the socialist system will not change; but certain areas within the country are allowed to implement the capitalist system—for example, Hong Kong and Taiwan. . . . China has adopted the open-door policy and some capitalism is allowed to enter. This is a supplement to the development of socialism and is conducive to the development of socialist productive forces. Importing foreign capital into Shanghai, for example, does not mean that all of Shanghai will implement the capitalist system. Nor is this the case in Shenzhen, where the socialist system is still implemented. Therefore, Shenzhen is different from Hong Kong. Shenzhen will not be moved to Hong Kong, nor will Hong Kong be moved to Shenzhen. The main body of China is socialism.[15]

From this statement, it is obvious that although Teng Hsiao-p'ing advanced the concept of "one country, two systems," he still insisted on taking the socialist road, which is one of the Four Cardinal Principles he proposed.[16]

Some scholars are dissatisfied with the way of interpreting the concept of "one country, two systems" merely from the economic standpoint. For example, Yen Chia-ch'i said in an article published in *Red Flag* that the opening of special economic zones in coastal areas is not an example of "one country, two systems" because these places are different from the hinterland only in the economic sphere. He said, "'One country, two systems' means that the two places are distinctly and greatly different from each other in their political, economic and social systems. If they differ from each other only in individual systems or if they are not distinctly and greatly different from each other in all their systems, they should not be considered in the framework of 'one country, two systems.'"[17] His theory indicates that a consensus has not been reached in theoretical circles in the mainland.

At a reception for three well-known Hong Kong people (Sze-yuen Chung, Lydia Dunn, and Q. W. Lee) in June 1984, Teng Hsiao-p'ing said that if the "one country, two systems" formula could be applied to Hong Kong successfully, there would be an outlet for the settlement of similar international disputes.[18] The October 25 issue of the *Liao-wang* weekly in the same year reported a speech by Teng on the formula in which he is quoted as saying:

> What important significance has the concept "one country, two systems" in settling some major international disputes at present? A series of the world's issues are faced with the question of whether they should be resolved by peaceful means or by nonpeaceful means. International disputes will eventually have to find an outlet—an outlet in a blind alley. In advancing "one country, two systems," we have also considered what methods should be adopted to resolve international disputes. Since there are many knots here and there in the world that are difficult to untie, I think it is possible to use this method to settle disputes between some countries.[19]

Teng's speech was obviously intended for propaganda purposes, and it should be viewed as a reiteration of the slogan of "Five Principles of Peaceful Coexistence."[20]

From the foregoing theories on the concept of "one country, two systems," we can find that the theoretical framework of that concept is built on the following points:

1. From the viewpoint of historical materialism, the coexistence of different forms of economic systems for a long time while taking socialist economy as the main body is a kind of "one country, two systems."
2. From the dialectic viewpoint, the practice of not distinguishing between contradictions within opposites before an opportune movement comes for their unity is the theoretical framework of the concept of "one country, two systems." Of course, the unity of opposites should be made within a main body.
3. The Communist theories that capitalism is decadent and moribund should be abandoned, and there are reasons for "one country, two systems" to exist in the historical process.
4. While a consensus has not been reached on the question whether the implementation of the open-door policy in economic affairs is an example of the "one country, two systems" formula, the Chinese Communists have maintained that it is a formula that could help to settle disputes in countries split apart.

Feasibililty

By the formula of "one country, two systems," the two different systems—socialism and capitalism—are supposedly allowed to coexist within a country. Meanwhile, the Chinese Communists have advanced come concrete conditions for their coexistence. In this manner, the formula should be considered a good way to discontinue confrontation between both sides of the Taiwan Strait and to promote the development of Hong Kong. But whether the Chinese Communists will keep their promise on the conditions for coexistence of these two different systems is something that should be closely watched.

Although it is still too early to predict the feasibility of the formula of "one country, two systems," some conclusions on this question should be reached if it is examined in a cold and detached manner and takes into consideration the opinions of a wide range of people and the political trends on both sides of the Taiwan Strait and in Hong Kong. Based on his research, the author has the following views:

First, although Teng Hsiao-p'ing said that the formula of "one country, two systems" is a pioneering undertaking that has historical significance and although he advanced such theories as "practice is the sole criterion for testing truth" and "be it black or white, as long as it can catch mice, it is a good cat" in formulating political lines, he continues to uphold Marxism-Leninism and Mao Tse-tung's thought. In such a situation, it may be necessary for us to examine the feasibility of the "one country, two systems" formula through a review of the Communist theories. According to Communist theory, the "state" is a "special organization of force; it is an organization of violence for the suppression of some class."[21] After the proletariat organized as the ruling class, the state is under the political rule of the proletariat.[22] On the role of the state, Lenin said:

> That the state is an organ of the rule of a definite class which cannot be reconciled with its antipode (the class opposite to it), is something the petty-bourgeois democrats will never be able to understand. Their attitude towards the state is one of the most striking manifestations of the fact that our Socialist-Revolutionaries and Mensheviks are not Socialists at all (a point that we Bolsheviks have always maintained), but petty-bourgeois democrats with near-Socialist phraseology.[23]

In the light of the foregoing Communist theories, it is clear that Teng's proposal of the "one country, two systems" formula that allows two opposite systems to coexist within a country is diametrically opposed to Communist theory. As Teng continues to uphold Marxism-Leninism and Mao Tse-tung's thought, his advancement of the "one country, two systems" formula should be viewed only as an expedient for united-front purposes.

Second, since the establishment of the Chinese Communist regime in 1949, there have been incessant political movements in the mainland, and the policy of the regime has been capricious. After the ouster of the Gang of Four in October 1976 and the convention of the Third Plenum of the

Eleventh Central Committee of the CCP at the end of 1978, Teng's policy on economic reform has been established. To facilitate the implementation of his policy, Teng used the slogan of "setting things to rights." That actually means a reversal of all past practices. The capriciousness in making policy decisions in mainland China is something incomprehensible to people in the non-Communist world. The only justifiable reason for such capriciousness is that a dictatorial regime enjoys greater power than a democratic government in governing its people. Like an overcoat hanging up on the wall which relies merely on the hook for its uplifting, society on the Chinese mainland is also at the mercy of the hook, that is, the dictator. Once that hook is taken away, that overcoat will fall down.[24] For example, once such policies as "opening mainland China to the outside world and invigorating mainland China's domestic economy," "having Hong Kong people administer Hong Kong," and "one country, two systems" are suspended, the people are powerless against the changes. Therefore, how the continuity of a policy on the Chinese mainland can be maintained should be a matter meriting great international attention. On the other hand, by the slogan of "one country, two systems," Peking aims at placing Hong Kong, Taiwan, and Macao under its control and subjecting them to its rule. In other words, the slogan is advanced for the purpose of achieving the goal of "one country." The people of Hong Kong, however, are attracted to the slogan of "two systems."

Third, as already mentioned, the formula of "one country, two systems" is contradictory in itself. The fact that Hong Kong and Taiwan are separated from mainland China has made it possible for the two diametrically different systems—capitalism and socialism—to coexist in different Chinese communities. If Hong Kong and Taiwan are placed within the main body, that is, under Chinese Communist rule, contradictions will soon appear.

Fourth, the slogan of "one country, two systems" is used to set the minds of the people of Hong Kong at rest so as to maintain its prosperity. But whether this goal can be achieved will depend upon whether Peking can provide the necessary conditions for the maintenance of prosperity in Hong Kong. According to Lydia Dunn, a nonofficial legislator in Hong Kong, the prosperity in Hong Kong depends on the following eight conditions: (1) freedom guaranteed by law; (2) a political system characterized by power equilibrium; (3) a system of consultation with trust; (4) government respect for public opinion; (5) a long-range and stable policy; (6) enforcement of a legal system; (7) the confidence of the people of Hong Kong in their own capability and the existing system; and (8) the manpower resources for the enhancement of Hong Kong's progress.[25] For the present at least, no one is sure that these conditions will exist after the Communist takeover of Hong Kong in 1997. Judging from the situation in Hong Kong in 1985, there have emerged signs that it will be difficult for all these eight conditions to exist after Hong Kong is placed under Peking's rule. At present, a power center headed by the Hong Kong branch of the New China News Agency has gradually replaced the original power center of the Hong Kong government. The representative system currently enforced in Hong Kong has also been stubbornly boycotted by the Chinese Communists.[26] Besides, the slogan of "having Hong Kong people administer Hong Kong" that had been voiced by Teng Hsiao-p'ing, Chi P'eng-fei, and P'eng Chen has now ceased to be used.

Economically, Peking's influence in Hong Kong has also increased enormously. By August 1984, mainland China's investment in Hong Kong was more than US$5 billion.[27] About 300 companies belonging to the Huajun Corporation and the Kwangta Company under Peking's Ministry of Foreign Economic Relations and Trade have been established in Hong Kong. With a total investment of more than US$4 billion, these companies are engaged in almost all the economic activities in Hong Kong, ranging from the stock exchange to real estate and supermarkets. The (Communist) Bank of China and thirteen other related banks in Hong Kong have formed a formidable business network. These banks have loaned out more than US$1 billion.[28] The number of mainland people sent to Hong Kong reached more than 100,000 by 1985.[29] They are satirized as *piao shu* (uncle-in-cousinship), meaning that they are not close relatives but are good at seeking their own profit at the expense of other people. Most of these people are engaged in business, and the others are sent to prepare for participation in cultural, financial, educational, construction, public-security, procuratorial, and legal affairs. With its influence in Hong Kong gradually increased, Peking will find it easy to do whatever it wants; and, when it does, the formula of "one country, two systems" may be changed to "one country, one system."

Fifth, different economic systems have different ideological roots. When places with different economic systems are placed under the rule of one government, the ideological divergence may either give rise to conflict or result in an ideological mixture. No one is sure whether the capitalist system will prevail. Nevertheless, as the capitalist economy is still regarded as a necessary supplement to the development of socialism in the Chinese mainland, the formula of "one country, two systems" is expected to be sustained for some time. With a clear understanding that their fate will be decided by the Chinese Communists, the people of Hong Kong only hope that the Basic Law for Hong Kong will guarantee the perpetual existence of the capitalist system there. At present, some of the people of Hong Kong propose the enforcement of a representative system in the twelve years before 1997; others propose a change of the present system in Hong Kong in the fifty years after 1997. Whatever method they adopt, their struggle for political rights deserves sympathy.

Finally, in the opinion of Professor Weng Sung-jan of the Chinese University of Hong Kong, the "one country, two systems" formula is of a contradictory, overriding, and transitional nature.[30] Its contradictory and transitional nature has been dealt with in this article. By its "overriding" nature, Weng means that the two places under the framework of "one country, two countries" are not symmetrical with each other in size and are not equal in force or position. As a result, one side tends to be overridden or even annihilated by the other side. Because of its overriding nature, the model of "one country, two systems" has been used by the Chinese Communists in their united-front strategy against the Republic of China. As Teng Hsiao-p'ing has said: "Socialism is practiced in China in an area with a population of one billion people. This main body represents a large segment of the total population in China. It is under this premise that we allow capitalism to exist in a small area."[31] If Hong Kong and Taiwan had the capability to override the mainland and play a leading role, no one is sure that Peking would still approve of and have confidence in the "one country, two systems" formula.[32] To the overriding nature of the formula, the reaction of the people of Hong Kong has differed from that of the people of the Republic of China. Under the pressure of events, the people of Hong Kong are helpless. In Taiwan, however, the people are repelled by the idea of any arrangement that would make their government a local one under Chinese Communist rule. Undoubtedly, they would fight to the end to preserve their own identity as the Republic of China.

The concept of "one country, two systems" may serve to pacify the people of Hong Kong at the present stage. For the China issue, however, it is generally agreed that only under a system acceptable to all the Chinese people can the unification of China be achieved. The political development in the Chinese mainland and the economic competition on both sides of the Taiwan Strait will determine the path of China's unification.

The writer will conclude this article with the following quotation from the late Liao Ch'eng-chih, a prominent Chinese Communist leader who used to be in charge of overseas Chinese affairs, which can best describe the real motives behind the "one country, two systems" slogan: "After the peaceful reunification of China, Taiwan will have to walk on the socialist road eventually. It is unreasonable to believe that under the leadership of a proletarian Party, China would implement a socialist system on one side and a capitalist system on the other side."[33]

Notes

1. "Message to Compatriots in Taiwan," *Beijing Review* 22, no. 1 (January 5, 1979): 17.

2. "Teng Hsiao-p'ing on Questions Concerning Taiwan and Others, *Ta Kung Pao* (Hong Kong), October 21, 1979, 2.

3. "Yeh Chien-ying Puts Forth Nine-Point Proposal to the Taiwan Authorities," *Ta Kung Pao*, October 1, 1981, 1.

4. "Constitution of the People's Republic of China," *Beijing Review* 25, no. 52 (December 27, 1982): 16.

5. "Teng Hsiao-p'ing on the Ways for Peaceful Unification," *Ta Kung Pao*, July 30, 1983, 1.

6. Y. C. Jao, "Hong Kong's Role in Financing China's Modernization," in A. J. Youngson, ed., *China and Hong Kong: The Economic Nexus* (Hong Kong: Oxford University Press, 1983), 60.

7. Wei Ta-yeh, "The Formation and Development of the Concept of 'One Country, Two Systems,'" *Wen Wei Po* (Hong Kong), November 12, 1984, 2.

8. Yü Kuan-chih, "One Country, Two Systems and Marxism-Leninism," *Hsin-pao ts'ai-ching yueh-k'an* (Hsin Pao Financial and Economic Monthly) (Hong Kong) 8, no. 7: 64.

9. Ibid.

10. Huan Hsiang, "The Background for the Principle of One Country, Two Systems," *Wen Wei Po*, September 29, 1984, 15.

11. Ibid.

12. Lin Ping-hsi, "The Study of 'One Country, Two Systems' in Mainland China's Academic Circles," *Ta Kung Pao*, January 16, 1986, 5.

13. Ch'ien Chün-jui, "Make Preparations to Welcome 'One Country, Two Systems,'" *Wen Wei Po*, July 18, 1984, 2.

14. Chin Yao-ju, "'One Country, Two Systems' Formula Is a New Movement of Marxism," *Wen Wei Po*, June 25, 1985, 2.

15. "Teng Hsiao-p'ing on the Concept of 'One Country, Two Systems,'" *Wen Wei Po*, October 15, 1984, 2.

16. Teng Hsiao-p'ing, "Uphold the Four Cardinal Principles," in *Selected Works* (Beijing: Foreign Languages Press, 1984), 170.

17. Yen Chia-ch'i, "Scientific Implications and Characteristics of 'One Country, Two Systems,'" *Red Flag*, 1985, no. 6: 18.

18. "A Branch of the New China News Agency Disclosed the Text of the Talks Between Teng and Chung," *Wen Wei Po*, June 28, 1984, 2.

19. See note 15.

20. When Peking and New Delhi signed the "Agreement on Trade and Transportation Between China's Tibet and India" in Peking on April 29, 1954, Chou En-lai advanced the Five Principles of Peaceful Coexistence (mutual respect for territorial integrity and sovereignty, mutual nonaggression, noninterference in each other's internal affairs, equality and mutual benefit, and peaceful coexistence).

21. V. I. Lenin, *The State and Revolution* (Beijing: Foreign Languages Press, 1965), 28.

22. Ibid., 31.

23. Ibid., 8.

24. Lao Ssu-kuang's talks at the five-scholar forum, *Ch'i-shih nien-tai* (The Seventies) (Hong Kong), no. 156 (January 1983): 51.

25. Cited from Hsu Hsing, "On Peking's Blueprint for Hong Kong in 1997," *Cheng-ming* (Contending) (Hong Kong), no. 76 (February 1984): 35.

26. In July 1984, the Hong Kong government published the "Green Paper on the Representative System," saying that the number of legislators in the Administrative and Legislative Councils would be gradually reduced by 1991. In December the same year, the Hong Kong government published a "White Paper on the Representative System," setting forth measures for the election of members to the Legislative Council and regional councils.

27. Ho Hsin-chi, "The Development of Economic Relations Between China and Hong Kong," *Wen Wei Po*, May 19, 1985, 2.

28. Cheng Chu-yuan, "The Basis and the Prospects for the Prosperity of Hong Kong," *Ming Pao Monthly* (Hong Kong), no. 226 (October 1984): 6.

29. Beginning from 1983, the number of people who arrived in Hong Kong with mainland China's passports showed a marked increase. The number reached 49,100 in 1983, 77,800 in 1984, and 104,000 in 1985. *Sing Tao Jih Pao* (Hong Kong), January 20, 1986, 10.

30. Weng Sung-jan, "A Preliminary Study of 'One Country, Two Systems,'" *Chiu-shih nien-tai* (The Nineties), no. 191 (December 1985): 30–40.

31. "Taiwan Should Be Able to Accept One Country, Two Systems," *Wen Wei Po*, January 1, 1985, 2.

32. Weng, "A Preliminary Study," 34.

33. Liao Ch'eng-chih's talks to leading cadres responsible for overseas Chinese affairs on December 28, 1979. Document No. 87 of the Overseas Chinese Affairs Office of Beijing's State Council.

12

Another Look at Corruption: Lessons of the Career of the "God of Fortune"

James T. Myers

The Career of the "God of Fortune"

On December 29 and 30, 1985, the Chinese news media gave front-page prominence to the crimes of one Du Guozhen, a "big swindler" arrested some nine months earlier. The report of Du's misdeeds was transmitted by the Xinhua press agency with a "public notice" requesting all papers to give the item front-page publicity.[1] The following day, *Renmin Ribao* carried a front-page Commentator's article entitled "What Is Shown by the Career Rise of 'Du, the God of Fortune'?"[2] What can "swindler" Du possibly have done to earn himself such notoriety?

Du Guozhen, who because of his spectacular successes became known as the "God of Fortune," had a short but significant career.[3] Du, fifty-three years of age in 1985, was originally a "worker-substitute-cadre" office clerk of a construction team under the Fujian Provincial Highways Bureau. He left that position in 1983 to enter business. By June 1984, Du was engaged in developing one company under contract with Fuzhou city government and comanaging another company together with the (Fuzhou) Jiaoqu District Committee for Foreign Economic Relations. It was in these two positions, between the months of June 1984 and March 1985, that Du Guozhen was said to have colluded with others in committing economic crimes involving a total of some 240 million yuan. In addition to this sum, Du was accused of having purchased illegally from the black market US$108,000 and HK$619,000, which he subsequently transported illegally outside of the country. In the course of committing these economic crimes, Du was said to have passed out more than 200,000 yuan in bribes to the County Party Committee, the county government, the District Court in Fuzhou City, and a number of others. Indeed, a total of twenty-one other individuals accused of accepting bribes or neglecting their duties were arrested with Du Guozhen. Du's accomplices were said to include the deputy commissioner of the

Ningde Prefectural Administrative Office, the former secretary of the Xiapu County CPC Committee, the deputy head of the Jiaoqu District in Fuzhou City, the president of the Lougu District Court, and the director of the Ningde Prefectural Cannery. All in all, these officials constituted a pretty high-level crew of criminals.

Aside from the charge of removing foreign currency from the country illegally, however, the only other specific charge leveled against Du Guozhen was that he was involved in the sale of defective canned mushrooms in Hong Kong, a charge to which we will return in a moment. It seems strange that in a case of this magnitude, involving such large sums of money, that the charges against the culprits were not defined with somewhat more precision. Du, for example, was said to have been guilty of "manipulation," of "cheating and bribing," and of "boasting."[4] It was said that he "swindled and bluffed everywhere," that he was "swollen with conceit," and that the "obtained by cheating" a number of titles, such as chairman of the board and honorary vice-president, which he "unscrupulously" publicized in local newspapers.[5] The authorities charged that Du "bribed some twenty cadres in the financial, economic, communications, customs and judicial departments and signed more than seventy 'contracts' with Fujian and other regions involving more than 240 million yuan."[6] One somehow gets the impression that there was something wrong with the more than seventy "contracts" signed by the God of Fortune, but it is not clear exactly what the problem was or why such activity should be considered criminal or fraudulent.

In another case, Du's "crimes" were described in this way:

> Lured by the promise of dividends, leaders of the Qiaoqu District Committee for Foreign Economic Relations in Fuzhou City approved criminal Du's application to set up a company, as well as the committee's joint management with him in the name of Huafu Company, and notified industry and commerce administrative, tax, banking and other departments concerned to allow him to complete procedures to set up the company. Lacking sufficient funds for his smuggling activities, criminal Du used a fake purchase and sale contract to receive a ten million yuan loan at once from the credit department of the Fuzhou branch of the Bank of China, without going through investigation and review.[7]

Again, other than the charge of using a "fake purchase and sale contract," about which no further information is given, it is difficult to see how Du's activities came to be classified as criminal and fraudulent.

The most detailed information about Du Guozhen and his colleagues is revealed in the charges surrounding the defective mushroom business. In typically unrestrained fashion, *Renmin Ribao* declared: "Committing outrageous crimes, Du Guozhen and his ilk sold a large quantity of defective mushrooms in Hong Kong, seriously damaging the country's foreign trade reputation. Due to the mildew and rot of their smuggled goods and other reasons, the state and collectives suffered over 40 million yuan in immediate economic losses."[8] But what, exactly, was Du's role in this business? The official account suggests some interesting possibilities:

> In purchasing canned mushrooms, he [Du] obtained from the director of the Ningde Prefectural cannery, Chen Liangyuan, at a low price, 986 metric tons of canned mushrooms unqualified or untested for export. In order to receive a several-hundred-thousand-yuan berth fee, former secretary of the Xiapu County party committee, Hu Liangji, and others arranged a berth for loading criminal Du's smuggled goods, and even requested, through the prefectural administrative office, units to dispatch motor vehicles to hurriedly transport the smuggled goods. When the port administration refused to give the exit permit on the grounds that the goods had not gone through joint inspection by the customs, border defense, commerce and quarantine departments, Hu Liangji went so far as to force the county port station, which was only in charge of inland water navigation, to complete the exit procedures.[9]

First, it is clear that mushrooms are a big business in Ningde Prefecture, as the amount in question was given as 986 *metric tons*. This enormous quantity of mushrooms was said to have been purchased by Du Guozhen, not stolen or embezzled. Did he know that they were defective? It is not clear. In fact it is not clear that anyone knew the mushrooms were bad, as they were described as being "unqualified or untested" for export. Were they in fact "unqualified" or simply untested, or both?

Next, it was apparently necessary to grease the palm of the party secretary in order to obtain a loading berth for the mushrooms, which by this point are described as "criminal Du's smuggled goods." At least, such a necessity is implied by the account. It is also entirely possible that the prefecture, and not the party secretary personally, was the beneficiary of the "several-hundred-thousand-yuan berth fee." How the party secretary was able to arrange the berth, even for so sizable a bribe, if the fee was his to keep, is not entirely clear, but his efforts must surely have involved a number of others.

Finally, it seems that the party secretary had to use his influence once again when the port administration refused to grant an exit permit. Was the port administration upholding the law in an honest and exemplary fashion, or did the "customs, border defense, commerce and quarantine departments" want a share of the action? Was their price so high that the secretary was tempted to use his influence elsewhere, for surely he must have had some influence with the port authority as well? Given the scale of the corruption alleged to exist in Ningde Prefecture, the possibility of additional corruption on the part of the port authority does not seem entirely remote.

Nor was this the end of the matter, or of the uncertainties surrounding the mushroom business. The *Renmin Ribao* account asserts that when the mushrooms reached Hong Kong they were unsalable because they did not have a "commodity inspection certificate," and makes no further mention of mildew or rot.[10] A "fake" certificate was subsequently obtained by the deputy commissioner of the Ningde Prefectural Administrative Office. This same official obtained a similar "fake" certificate for a second deal, also arranged by Du Guozhen, which involved a shipment of 2,000 metric tons of canned mushrooms.[11]

That the God of Fortune was well connected there can be no doubt. We are told, for example that the local party secretary went to the provincial capital to "lobby" for Du, and that when Du needed space for his operations, "the leaders of the provincial trade union federation approved the use of an entire floor in the Jinjishan Sanitorium by Du as an 'office,' in addition to four recuperating rooms for senior cadres as a residence for Du and his son."[12] It seems, in fact, that however we view Du's activities—a subject to be addressed subsequently—an extraordinarily wide range of important individuals was involved with him. To recapitulate, according to various accounts, the activities of Du Guozhen are said to have involved the complicity of the deputy commissioner of the Ningde Prefectural Administrative Office, the former secretary of the Xiapu County party committee, the deputy head of Jiaoqu District in Fuzhou City, the president of the Lougu District Court, the director of the Ningde Prefectural Cannery, the Jiaoqu District Committee for Foreign Economic Relations, the Fuzhou Branch of the Bank of China, the Ziapu County Port Station, the provincial trade union federation. Moreover, we are told that when the God of Fortune needed legal advice, he could turn to officials of the "economic court of the Gulou District Court of Fuzhou City," to the advice of the Yufeng Company, and to "his personal legal advisor."[13]

Could the net of corruption really have been so vast? Could so many important officials knowingly have been drawn into a criminal conspiracy devised by the arch criminal and "big swindler" Du Guozhen? How can we understand and explain these events? Are we here, in the case of Du Guozhen, studying corruption, venality, and "unhealthy tendencies" on an unusually large scale? Or is this a case of simpleminded officials being hoodwinked and led astray by a master criminal? Or, could Du have been the victim of a decision to "kill the chicken in order to frighten the monkey" (sha ji xia hou)? And if so, why was Du selected to be the "chicken"?

What the Chinese Learned from the Career of the God of Fortune

In terms of stemming the tide of corruption about which Chinese authorities have expressed such concern over the last year and a half or so,[14] these same authorities seem to have learned little from the rise and fall of the God of Fortune which will help them very much. It seems to me very much the same problem that I have addressed elsewhere,[15] namely: The authorities mistake the symptoms of the disease for its causes. Such explanations usually take the form of blaming corrupt acts by officials on the fact that the officials have forgotten the "lofty ideals" of the party. This explanation amounts to explaining corruption by observing that those committing corrupt acts have deviated from official standards of rectitude. Such an observation may be accurate, but it does little to advance our understanding of the underlying causes of corruption, and without such an understanding, mounting an effective attack on corrupt behavior will be exceedingly difficult, if not impossible.

The Du Guozhen case was analyzed by Xinhua in this way: "What does this case explain? It explains that, in the course of opening to the outside world and invigorating the domestic economy, some of our party-member cadres have completely disarmed themselves ideologically, sold their honor for money, forsaken their communist spirit and the party's goals and programs, and degenerated into sinners, condemned by the people."[16] *Renmin Ribao* condemned the malefactors for lacking "the concept of discipline, a concept of the legal system, and the concept of serving the people wholeheartedly, which all party members and government cadres should have."[17] Another *Renmin Ribao* article, after chastising the officials of Ningde Prefecture for failing to understand the real roots of their problem, offered this assessment: "It seems that we should establish a due concept of discipline, a concept of a legal system, a concept of serving the people heart and soul, and do away with any ideas and conduct of abusing power and bureaucratism on the one hand, and on the other, severely crack down on economic criminals and other criminals."[18]

A circular of the CPC Central Committee Discipline Inspection Commission and the Commission for Political Affairs and Law charged cadres with a "seriously irresponsible bureaucratic attitude," and added that some, "including some leading cadres, have indeed failed to correctly understand the central authorities' policy of firmly combatting economic crimes while opening to the outside world and enlivening the domestic economy, thus ignoring socialist ethics and lowering their guard against the bad capitalist practice of cheating people."[19] The same circular, issued by the highest commission in the PRC charged with dealing with misbehavior by party officials, added this less-than-penetrating analysis:

[Party and government cadres] have forgotten what is right and have disregarded party discipline and state laws upon seeing benefits. Corrupted by capitalist ideas and hit by the "sugar-coated bullet," some cadres, including leading cadres, have been bedazzled by lust for gain, and their eyes widen when they see money. Furthermore, having forgotten the principles, they do everything possible, including abusing their authority, to seek personal gains and begin to solicit and accept bribes disregarding national dignity and their integrity, and eventually they become accomplices of speculators and swindlers.[20]

It is difficult to see how this sort of analysis is going to help the Chinese understand the problem of corruption or venality in their public officials, much less to solve it. Nevertheless, going through the now voluminous reports of corruption, malpractices, and unhealthy tendencies, it is precisely this sort of analysis that prevails. One searches in vain for any meaningful understanding on the part of the Chinese authorities of what seems to be a fairly serious problem.

In the case of Du Guozhen, such analysis of the "lessons" of his career, have, as usual,[21] given rise to prescriptions for solving the problem which strike one as quite feeble, if not actually useless. The Discipline Inspection Commission of the Central Committee of the Chinese Communist Party (CCP) issued the following, presumably hopeful, declaration:

> To promptly reverse this serious situation, we set forth the following require-ments: 1. Party committees and government and judicial departments at all levels must attach great attention to economic speculation and fraud. By dissecting sample cases and analyzing the crimes committed by the speculators and swindlers, they should earnestly sum up the experiences and learn the lessons, study the characteristics and laws of the economic crimes committed under the new situation, especially why such cases of speculation and fraud have occurred repeatedly, and work out counter and preventive measures to firmly deter the recurrence of speculation and fraud. . . .[22]

The message of this crackdown order appears to be that the Discipline Inspection Commission hopes that someone can find out what is causing the problem of "speculation and fraud" and then devise a solution for it. But the Commission does not end its instructions with this one admonition. Three more points follow:

> 2. Party organizations at all levels must intensify educating party members, cadres and other personnel on lofty ideals and a sense of discipline and law. . . . 3. As soon as any speculation and fraud has been discovered, party committees, discipline inspection commissions, and judicial departments at all levels must get hold of them and track them down to the end. . . . 4. The leaders whose units have suffered economic losses due to fraud must have their responsibilities investigated. . . .[23]

Is this really the best advice China's leaders have to offer? An investigation of the literature suggests that it may well be, with, however, one exception. Many of the accounts of wrongdoing stress the importance of swift, sure punishment as a curative or preventative. A typical account states: "It is necessary to resolutely and rapidly crack down on these people, particularly on those who have committed serious crimes. Only by doing so can we frighten bad persons, educate the masses, safeguard the solemn nature of party discipline and state law, fundamentally improve party style and the general mood of society, and guarantee the smooth progress of reform and the consolidation and development of stability and unity."[24] The idea of using punishment to "frighten bad persons," raises the possibility that the wide publicity given to "serious and important" cases such as that of Du Guozhen may indeed be examples of killing the chicken to frighten the monkey. This is especially true when combined with the use of large-scale public executions of the type we have seen in the last several years or so in China.[25] The persistence of corrupt practices, however, as well as the increase in the scale of reported corrupt activities, must give us cause to question the effectiveness of using punishment to "frighten" those who would do wrong.

Nevertheless, official accounts of corruption usually also include a self-congratulatory note to the effect that the apprehension of the latest set of wrongdoers proves that the socialist system of law and justice is, in fact, working just fine. Thus one of the lessons of the Du Guozhen case was that "the speedy arrest of Du Guozhen and his ilk has demonstrated the power of our policy and law."[26] And *Renmin Ribao* trumpeted, "Our socialist China is, after all, not a paradise for adventurers. How can the strong people's democratic dictatorship tolerate a handful of demons who fan the flames of disorder!"[27] These are strong sentiments, to be sure; unfortunately, they are sentiments somewhat at odds with reality. If only a handful of demons were fanning the flames of disorder, we would not be reading about it on page 1 of *Renmin Ribao*.

Lessons the Chinese Might Have Learned from the Case of Du Guozhen

If the Chinese authorities failed to learn important lessons from the career of the God of Fortune, is there anything useful that they might have learned? I believe there are several things to be learned from this case that are both useful and important.

What Did Du Do Wrong?

The first lesson of the Du Guozhen case might be that the values that the Chinese leadership wishes to stabilize and maintain continue to be confused or incoherent.[28] What, exactly, did the God of Fortune do to get himself into so much trouble, trouble that will in the end surely cost him his life?

If we look at the particulars of the canned mushroom business, the case that appears to involve the most serious charges againt Du Guozhen, it is not easy to discern exactly where the aspect of "speculation and fraud" was involved. It certainly does not appear that Du defrauded the authorities of Ningde Prefecture with whom he was involved. On the contrary, it seems just as plausible to suggest that they may have looked to the God of Fortune as someone who could help them with their mushroom business. Considering the quantity of canned mushrooms involved in the two reported deals, the mushroom business must be of some considerable importance to the prefecture. Most of the efforts of Du Guozhen and his coconspirators appear to have been directed toward getting the mushrooms shipped and sold, and though the mushrooms are described as "smuggled goods," Du and the others are nowhere said to have stolen, embezzled, or otherwise illegally obtained them. How the mushrooms were turned into "smuggled" goods is not clear.

And what of the 200,000 yuan in bribes Du Guozhen was said to have passed out to cadres in the "financial, economic, communications, customs, and judicial departments"? Here, two reports come to mind which may be pertinent. First, in a letter to the State Council, a certain Liu Zuolin of a specialized household in Sichuan Province complained that in order to buy some lumber for his township's mechanized brickyard and transport it a total of sixty kilometers, he spent fifty-four days and was required to purchase a total of eleven "permits" at a cost of more than 5,500 yuan in order to buy and transport the lumber that he finally sold for only 3,750 yuan.[29] Second, Alan Liu has cited a 1981 survey made in the city of Changsha in which ninety-nine out of a hundred families responding said that they had paid bribe money (ren qing qian) averaging eight yuan per month.[30] Given the apparent prevalence of this sort of bribery, it would appear to be more than a slim possibility that the 200,000 spent by the God of Fortune was the cost of doing business in Ningde Prefecture.

The suggestion that bribery is extremely widespread, of course, does not make the practice appear any more acceptable in the eyes of the Chinese authorities, but it may help us to see entrepreneurial activities such as Du Guozhen's in a different light. Studies of the Soviet economy suggest that a variety of extralegal practices have become a way of life in the Soviet Union in order to overcome bureaucratic impediments and bottlenecks.[31] Grossman, in fact, describes a range of corrupt activities in the Soviet Union as, "commonplace, everyday phenomena in which virtually the whole population of the USSR is continuously enmeshed, and in which some individuals are involved on a large and at times gigantic scale."[32] In a similar vein, Staats sees corruption in the Soviet system as performing certain necessary functions and describes such corruption as "an important feature of the system rather than an aberration."[33]

In a system where, until recently, virtually all business was the business of the government and where an enormous bureaucracy with the power to delay, impede, and otherwise make trouble is still essentially in place, it is perhaps unreasonable to expect the Chinese bureaucracy to be more upright than it apparently is. But at the same time, if it is the intention of the government to encourage new forms of economic activity, innovation, and entrepreneurship, it makes little sense to kill the entrepreneur because he has had to find ways to contend with the prevailing system. Admittedly, this analysis of the mushroom business may be entirely off base, because so little detailed information about the case is available. Reading the available reports, however, the whole business strikes me as a concerted effort, involving fairly high-level help, to ship and sell the product of a major industry in the prefecture; an effort which, in the end, would probably produce broad economic benefits in the local area.

Is this the sort of economic activity China's leaders wish to encourage, even if it means accepting a certain amount of corruption as the cost of carrying out such activities? It is a question they will have to wrestle with. Though the public statements do not suggest any degree of ambivalence on the part of the leadership toward corruption, such ambivalence may possibly be present, or may evolve. Grossman suggests this to be the case in the USSR, where "economic crimes" have, in his words, "both positive and negative features in terms of the economic performance indicators defined by the authorities themselves."[34] In other words, how does one regard corruption that contributes to the goal of economic growth or development? We will return later to the question of the possible positive benefits of corruption.

If the killing of the bribe-giving entrepreneur has a potentially chilling effect on the conduct of business in China, what of the problem of the bribe taker? How might the Chinese approach the problem of official or bureaucratic corruption?

Force Versus Seduction

Despite the publicity given to "big swindlers" like Du Guozhen, the central point of the persistent campaign against corruption or "unhealthy tendencies," in fact, does appear to be concern over the behavior of party and government officials and cadres. Special and acute concern is expressed about the attitudes of party members who are seen as having forgotten or ignored party ideals, spirit, and discipline. In fact, the problem of official corruption has been seen primarily as a problem to be solved through party reform or rectification.[35] However viewed, the problem, stated in its simplest form, is a problem of behavioral control: How can individuals (the cadres in this case) be made to behave in conformity with certain norms or principles? I suggest here that such behavior may be controlled by using a variety of techniques ranging along a continuum from force to seduction.[36]

At the seduction end of the continuum, the party has relied chiefly on various forms of moral exhortation. If it is accurate to suggest that the ascription of value to the individual, including the self-ascription of value, is an important (perhaps, in fact, the most important) motivating factor in human behavior, the party has relied heavily on rhetoric to achieve this purpose. All of China has been fed a rich diet of "Serving the people," "Learning from Lei Feng," "Upholding the lofty ideals of the party," and so forth, and value was ascribed to those individuals who measured up, who emulated the lives of the heroes, whose lives themselves could serve as an example to others.[37] If the values symbolized by these slogans were believed in, the individual could, by his proper behavior, ascribe value to himself as well. In other words, believing in the values of the model life of Lei Feng, one could be a good Communist and feel good about it.

But what happens when the values of serving the people begin to lose their appeal, when the model life of Lei Feng ceases to be attractive, when it is no longer possible to ascribe value to one's life because one emulates the model life of a good Communist? This is clearly not an either-or proposition but a matter of degree. And much of the loss of appeal of the "Communist" values, as I have argued before,[38] may be a function of lack of clarity about what those values are, or have become. That is, it may no longer be clear exactly what it means to be a good Communist. Whatever the reason, however, whenever, or to what degree, the values cease to be believed in, the rhetoric of seduction based on those values also loses its effectiveness.

Yet, as we have seen, China's leaders persist in serving up a steady diet of such rhetoric. The recent numerous accounts of official misbehavior have been accompanied by seemingly endless admonitions to uphold the "lofty ideals" of communism. But, as we have observed, these admonitions have also been accompanied by recommendations and threats to apply harsh punishments, and, as we noted above, the ultimate sanction of execution has been widely applied. Thus we come to the force end of the continuum. Killing is clearly an excellent method of social control, especially as far as the victim is concerned, but the mere elimination of a single malefactor is not its real purpose. As Peckham has observed of killing: "Its most important task in the redundancy system of force is its effect upon others,"[39] or, to paraphrase the Chinese aphorism, the purpose of killing is not to eliminate the chicken, but to instill fear in the monkeys who witness the execution.

But, what if the killing does not work? What if individuals are not sufficiently frightened to alter their behavior in the desired way? What then? This is a critically important question for, as Peckham also reminds us, if force fails there can be no further recourse.[40] The obvious goal, then, is to avoid the use of force because one who has used force and failed has nowhere left to turn. If, however, the rhetoric of seduction is ineffective, and if threats combined with the application of ultimate sanction also fail to produce the desired results, what modes of behavioral control remain? Here we must return to the seduction end of the continuum, and here, also, the case of Du Guozhen may provide a lesson.

Rhetoric is not the only form of seduction; there are others as well. Other forms of seduction (and the corresponding signs of value) would include the awarding of medals and prizes, various forms of honors or emoluments, and, of course, material rewards. Until very recently, holding political office (in the broadest sense of the term) has provided the principal access to wealth in China. Now, however, that fact is changing because of the new rules of the Four Modernizations campaign. If cadres and officials cannot feel good about "serving the people" because of an erosion of communist values, and if others around them are enjoying financial rewards (signs of value) far greater than those which flow to the power holders, then of what use is political power?

It seems to me that one important lesson of the Du Guozhen case is that as the rules of the game change to allow various groups in the society to grow wealthy, the cadres and officials feel left out. I do not present this as a startling or original discovery, especially given the enormous number of cases of official wrongdoing which have now been reported in the Chinese press. What all these reported cases of venality, corruption, malfeasance, unhealthy tendencies, and the like seem to show is that the self-ascription of value in China is very closely related to the acquisition of wealth, and it strikes me as extremely unrealistic, therefore, for China's higher authorities to expect that those who wield power will not use it in the pursuit of the signs of value associated with the possession of wealth. Yet this appears to be precisely the case, as the authorities continue to rely on the increasingly irrelevant rhetoric of seduction ("Serve the people!") combined with the threat and application of force, a strategy which has thus far failed to yield notable results.

Far from recognizing the difficulties and inadequacies inherent in this approach, the authorities have pressed on, most recently issuing a new set of regulations "prohibiting party and government cadres from engaging in business and running enterprises." On February 4, 1986, the CCP Central Committee and the State Council promulgated a "further" set of regulations updating those issued in December 1984.[41] This was said to be necessary because "some party and government organs and cadres still adopt various tricks to continuously engage in businesses and run enterprises."[42] Under the new regulations not only party and government organs are banned from engaging in business, but also so are "cadres," "workers," and "staff members," including "cadres who have withdrawn to the second line."[43] Children and spouses of leading cadres are prohibited from temporarily leaving their posts to engage in business, and those who do not work for the government or party are prohibited from taking "advantage of the influence and relationships of leading cadres to engage in business, to run an enterprise, or to seek profit illegally."[44] In addition, these prohibitions were intended to be applicable to "mass organizations such as the Communist Youth League, women's federations, federations of literature and art circles, associations for science and technology, and various associations and societies, as well as the cadres, workers, and staff members of these organizations."[45]

If interpreted strictly, these new regulations prohibit large numbers of power holders and their relatives from engaging even in legal business affairs. But if our earlier analysis of the situation is accurate, such prohibitions are unlikely to make more than the slightest dent in the problem of official corruption, and that slight dent will in all likelihood be the result of the authorities having made more precise the boundaries between legal and illegal behavior. But making such a dent (if this analysis has any merit) is not the same as solving the problem, which according to official accounts threatens to become epidemic in its proportions.[46] Another lesson of the career of the "God of Fortune" thus seems to be that checking corruption is going to require that the authorities find some way to allow cadres and officials to participate in the acquisition of the new signs of value, of which material wealth may be the most important.

Changing the rules of the game to allow China's peasants to have increased opportunity to gain access to wealth has no doubt increased the capacity of the governmental institutions to maintain their legitimacy over time. In a certain sense it might be said that Deng has "bought" the loyalty of the peasants through the rural economic reforms. But the same cannot be said of the cadres who now find themselves accused of all sorts of wrongdoing because they have used their political power in order to catch up. Whether the Chinese leadership will attempt to use other forms of seduction in addition to rhetoric, whether, in fact, they will try to buy the loyalty of the cadres as well (perhaps by turning their heads at the less serious forms of corruption), is a question which, for the moment, can be posed but not answered.

Corruption: A Balance Sheet

We have suggested that, based on the Soviet experience, corruption may be said to perform the positive function of allowing those engaged in economic activities to overcome bureaucratic bottlenecks, impediments, and obstacles. And we raised the possibility that this might have been the case with the various "economic crimes" involved in the Du Guozhen affair. Here we want to consider whether there might be other positive benefits which can be ascribed to corruption.

Among those writers addressing the relationship of corruption and economic development, Leff,[47] Nye,[48] and Bayley[49] all argue that, in certain ways, and to a certain extent, corruption may, indeed, be good for the developing economy. Leff, for example, suggests that graft in the form of bribes paid to bureaucrats, "may be the only institution allowing other interests [than those of the ruling group] to achieve articulation and representation in the political process."[50] Leff further observes that bureaucrats may be hostile to entrepreneurial interests, the emergence of which they see as potentially competing centers of power. He suggests, "By enabling enterpreneurs to control and render predictable this important influence [government behavior] on their environment, corruption can increase the rate of investment," and, further, that such graft "may enable an economic innovator to introduce his innovations before he has had time to establish himself politically."[51]

Nye, citing Mandeville's dictum that "Private Vices by the dextrous Management of a skillful Politician may be turned into Publick Benefits," argues that, on balance, corruption has probably been, "a positive factor in both Russian and American economic development."[52] In general, Nye suggests, "If corruption helps promote economic development which is generally necessary to maintain a capacity to preserve legitimacy in the face of social change, then (by definition) it is beneficial for political development."[53] And how might corruption help promote economic development? Nye suggests that where the availability of private capital is scarce and where the government lacks the capacity to tax a surplus out of workers openly, corruption may aid capital formation. Corruption can also assist in cutting red tape and may provide a major means of making use of entrepreneurship and private incentive.[54]

Bayley asserts that "corruption in developing nations is not necessarily antipathetic to the development of modern economic and social systems; that corruption serves in part at least a beneficial function in developing societies."[55] Corruption, Bayley argues, "is not an inherently defective means of arriving at decisions among competing claimants," and, in fact, corruption "may serve as a means for impelling better choices, even in terms of government's expressed goals."[56] And, like Leff and Nye, he asserts that corruption "provides a means of giving those persons or groups potentially disaffected as a result of exclusion from power a stake in the system."[57] Specifically, among the possible benefits that may be ascribed to corruption, Bayley suggests, "The opportunity for corruption may actually serve to increase the quality of public servants."[58] Might the Chinese leadership recognize this possibility and decide to ignore the less serious cases of corruption on the part of cadres and officials in order to increase the material stake of that group in the reform program? It is an interesting thought. As Bayley observes, the corrupt "are not always unable; nor are they always unpatriotic."[59]

Most of the benefits ascribed to corruption by these writers might easily apply to the Du Guozhen case, if the reading I have given that case is at all correct. Likewise, these same benefits would seem to apply to the far more numerous cases of corruption cited in the paper which I delivered to the Fourteenth Sino-American Conference on Mainland China.[60] In other words, there seems to be much good that can be said for the effects of corruption on a developing economy such as China's. Moreover, citing the example of Soviet corruption, Grossman makes the interesting argument that the regime, "by their ability to allot lucrative positions within the hierarchy and to threaten citizens with individual prosecution (since nearly everyone is guilty) may add significantly to their control of subordinate hierarchies and thus strengthen the regime as a whole."[61] But, asks Grossman, "Would Lenin recognize his party and state in these conditions?"[62] Or, we might ask, would Chairman Mao or even Deng Xiaoping?

The negative side of the corruption ledger, I suggest, is to be found chiefly, though not exclusively, in the realm of spirit, values, or ideals. That is, while corruption may have certain positive economic benefits, its effects may be negative in other areas. All of the writers cited above realize this fact, and most of them conclude that, on balance, corruption is probably more toxic than tonic to the developing society.

Even should the Chinese leadership come to recognize the economic benefits that may flow from certain types of corruption, they probably cannot afford to acknowledge such benefits for fear of undercutting the moral basis of party rule and of political legitimacy. Bayley observes that the less a regime depends upon force to maintain itself, the more it must depend upon popular respect: "One element in this process of legitimation is popular faith in government to deal fairly among competing claimants. Corruption weakens this element of support."[63]

Nye draws our attention to the importance of the particular groups in the society with which the regime loses legitimacy. If our analysis of the behavior of cadres is correct and the effectiveness of the rhetoric of seduction decreases because of an erosion of belief in Communist values, such a development may have serious implications. Nye observes: "By destroying the legitimacy of political structures in the eyes of those who have power to do something about the situation, corruption can contribute to instability and possible national disintegration."[64] Already, we have suggested, the basis of legitimacy may be shaky as a result of the erosion of Communist values. In such a situation, where the party has already undertaken large-scale manipulation of material rewards to ensure the maintenance of regime legitimacy over time, the party can scarcely permit the further erosion of the moral basis of its rule by acknowledging the benefits of economic development through corruption. Yet the corruption and the economic benefits of that corruption (both for individuals and for the state) exist in the real world. How should the Chinese attempt to understand and deal with this situation, and what light can the God of Fortune affair shed on the problem?

Conclusion

One lesson of the God of Fortune affair seems to be that the types of "economic crimes" revealed in the case are to a certain extent a function of China's condition of economic and political underdevelopment. At the same time, to the extent that China also resembles a modern Leninist bureaucratic state like the USSR, some elements of corruption may be seen as a response to the bureaucratic inefficiencies, rigidities, and impediments which characterize that system. In other words, corruption in China may be seen to have an important systemic dimension. We have suggested that certain positive benefits may be ascribed to corruption under these circumstances. That is, certain of the economic goals of the Four Modernizations may be said to be advanced by the kinds of activities described as "criminal" in the Du Guozhen affair.

The Du Guozhen affair also reveals that corruption has an important cultural dimension. That is, given the systemic environment, there is a willingness to take advantage of the opportunities for gain in an extralegal manner. In fact, the Du Guozhen case seems to reveal that corruption of the type alleged in that case is widely accepted and that cadres and officials at a fairly high level (or an even higher level in other cases) and on a fairly wide scale, are willing to act in contravention of the formal norms of the system. This second aspect of corruption, we suggested, may be more serious than the first.

In the first instance, China may hope to "outgrow" those systemic features that give rise to corruption as it moves toward the institutionalization of the political system, on the one hand, and developments in the economy, on the other, that reduce or eliminate the functional utility of corruption. It should be emphasized, however, that it is by no means certain that such developments will take place at all, and if they do, they will probably occur only very slowly.

The social or cultural environment in which corruption occurs may prove to be even more difficult to change. Leff observes: "Socially, the elimination of corruption probably requires the emergence of new centers of power outside the bureaucracy, and the development of competitive politics," changes that will come about, if at all, "only as a result of a long period of economic and social development."[65] One must question how likely is the prospect of such change under the Leninist system of party control, which, despite all recent changes, still characterizes the Chinese political system.

In the short run, the Chinese may contain the more gross forms of corruption through vigorous prosecution and punishment. The containment of the more widespread forms of corruption, which, in my opinion, probably characterize the Du Guozhen case, represents a more difficult problem. The regime clearly must find some way to seduce the cadres and officials, but seducing them through material rewards by winking at the less serious (and more economically beneficial) forms of corruption, poses strong negative risks in the realm of values. How the regime might choose to attack this dilemma is anyone's guess, but it is certain that the problem will not be solved by vague moralizing and admonitions to "Serve the people!" As Bayley observes, under such circumstances, "It becomes apparent that considerably more than exhortation may be needed in order to eliminate venality in government."[66]

Finally, we suggested that the case of the God of Fortune demonstrates the incoherence or lack of clarity in the cultural directions for behavior that the regime wishes to maintain and stabilize. I have argued earlier[67] that in the absence of what Apter calls an "articulated moral element"[68] the regime will, in the long run, encounter difficulty in generating support. And this moral element cannot simply be any coherent set of values; it must be able to arouse enthusiasm and, itself, generate support. In short, it must be believed in. Moreover, as Bayley cautions, the mere substitution of one set of values for another will not suffice. "Its defect," he writes, "is that unless buttressed by real social change, it quickly loses force and wastes precipitously."[69]

Before the Chinese can worry about such waste, however, they must first develop the new, coherent, articulated moral element. Is such a development forthcoming? As with so many other questions about China, only time will tell.

Notes

Research for this paper was supported by a research fellowship from the Pacific Cultural Foundation, for which the author wishes to express his appreciation.

1. "CPC Commission Issues Public Notice on Fraud Case," Beijing, Xinhua Domestic Service in Chinese, 29 December 1985, in *Foreign Broadcast Information Service–China (FBIS-CHI)*, 31 December 1985, pp. K1–K3. (Hereafter cited as "Fraud Case.")

2. "Commentator Views Career of Swindler Du Guozhen," Beijing, *Renmin Ribao*, 30 December 1985, p. 1. In FBIS-CHI, 7 January 86, pp. K1–K2. (Hereafter cited as "Swindler.")

3. This summary of Du Guozhen's career is a composite drawn from the following sources: "Fraud Case"; "Swindler"; "Circular Orders Crackdown on Economic Crime," Beijing, Xinhua Domestic Service in Chinese, 14 January 86, in *FBIS-CHI*, 15 January 86, pp. K1–K3 (hereafter cited as "Circular"); "Bureaucratism Blamed For Economic Crimes," Beijing, *Renmin Ribao*, Overseas Edition in Chinese, 26 January 86, p. 2, in *FBIS-CHI*, 28 January 86, pp. K1–K2; "Lessons Learned in Du Guozhen Case Analyzed," Beijing, *Renmin Ribao*, 22 January 86, p. 4, in *FBIS-CHI*, 28 January 86, pp. K2–K3 (hereafter cited as "Lessons").

4. "Fraud Case," p. K2.

5. Ibid.

6. "Circular," p. K1.

7. "Fraud Case," p. K2.

8. Ibid.

9. Ibid., p. K3.

10. Ibid.

11. Ibid.

12. Ibid.

13. Ibid.

14. James T. Myers, "China: Modernization and Unhealthy Tendencies," (hereafter cited as "Unhealthy Tendencies").

15. Ibid.; Also see James T. Myers, "China: The 'Germs' of Modernization," *Asian Survey*, vol. 25, no. 10, October 1985, pp. 981–997 (hereafter cited as "Germs").

16. "Fraud Case," p. K1.

17. "Swindler," p. K1.

18. "Lessons," p. K3.

19. "Circular," p. K1.

20. Ibid., p. K2.

21. See "Unhealthy Tendencies" for a more complete discussion of "solutions" to the problem of corruption.

22. "Circular," p. K2.

23. Ibid., pp. K2–K3.

24. "Xinhua Calls for Crackdown on Economic Crime," Beijing, Xinhua Domestic Service in Chinese, 9 January 1986, in *FBIS-CHI*, 13 January 1986, p. K24.

25. See, for example, David Bonivia, "Repent or Die," *Far Eastern Economic Review*, February 16, 1984. Also cf. *China: Violations of Human Rights* (London: Amnesty International, 1984), especially p. 55.

26. "Fraud Case," p. K1.

27. "Swindler," p. K2.

28. This is a point I have argued in the last two papers I have delivered at the Sino-American Conference on Mainland China and elsewhere; see "Unhealthy Tendencies" and "Germs." Also "Socialist Spiritual Civilization and Cultural Pollution: The Problem of Meaning," in Yu-ming Shaw, ed., *Mainland China: Politics, Economics, and Reform*, (Boulder, Colo.: Westview, 1986), pp. 277–328.

29. "Protection for Specialized Households Urged," Beijing, Xinhua, 17 December 1984, in *FBIS-CHI*, 18 December 1984, pp. K7–K8. For a full account of this episode, see "Unhealthy Tendencies."

30. Alan P.L. Liu, "Kleptocracy on Mainland China: A Social Psychological Interpretation," in Shaw, *Mainland China*, p. 157.

31. See, for example, Gregory Grossman, "The 'Second Economy' of the USSR," *Problems of Communism* (Washington, D.C.: U.S. Information Agency), September-October, 1977; Steven J. Staats, "Corruption in the Soviet System," *Problems of*

Communism, January-February 1972; John M. Kramer, "Political Corruption in the U.S.S.R.," *Western Political Quarterly,* June 1977; Joseph S. Berliner, *Factory and Manager in the USSR* (Cambridge, Mass.: Harvard University Press, 1957).

32. Grossman, "The 'Second Economy' of the USSR," pp. 27–28.

33. Staats, "Corruption in the Soviet System," p. 42.

34. Grossman, "The 'Second Economy' of the USSR," p. 37.

35. See, for example, "Liaowang Urges Higher Standard of Rectification," Beijing, Xinhua Domestic Service in Chinese, 6 August 1984, in *FBIS-CHI,* 6 August 1984, pp. K6–K7; "An Important Step for High-Standard Party Rectification," *Liaowang,* Beijing, No. 32, 6 August 1985; "Wang Heshou Addresses Party Discipline Forum," Beijing, Xinhua Domestic Service in Chinese, 20 August 1984, in *FBIS-CHI,* 22 August 1984, pp. K8–K10; "Xi Zhungxun Speech to Rectification Meeting," Beijing, Xinhua Domestic Service in Chinese, 28 August 1984, in *FBIS-CHI,* 30 August 1984, pp. K1–K5; "Organization Department Discusses Rectification," Beijing, Xinhua Domestic Service in Chinese, 12 September 1984, in *FBIS-CHI,* 19 September 1984, pp. K14–K19; "Bo Yibo Notes Problems in Party Rectification," Beijing, Xinhua, 12 March 1985, in *FBIS-CHI,* 14 March 1985, pp. K1–K8.

36. For an insightful discussion of this concept see Morse Peckham, *Explanation and Power* (New York: Seabury Press, 1979), especially pp. 185–187.

37. For a more complete discussion of the values of such model lives see James T. Myers, "Socialist Spiritual Civilization and Cultural Pollution: The Problem of Meaning," in Shaw, ed., *Mainland China,* especially pp. 302–305.

38. See "Germs," pp. 993–995.

39. Peckham, *Explanation and Power,* p. 187.

40. Ibid., p. xviii.

41. "Cadres, Organs Banned from Engaging in Business," Beijing, Xinhua Hong Kong Service in Chinese, 5 February 1986, in *FBIS-CHI,* 7 February 1986, pp. K1–K3.

42. Ibid., p. K1.

43. Ibid.

44. Ibid., p. K2.

45. Ibid.

46. For examples of predictions of such dire consequences if the tide of "unhealthy tendencies" is not checked, see "Hu Qili Speaks on Combatting Unhealthy Practices," Beijing, Xinhua, 13 March 1985, in *FBIS-CHI,* 14 March 1985, p. K9; "Bo Yibo Notes Problems in Party Rectification," Xinhua, Beijing, 13 March 1985, in *FBIS-CHI,* 14 March 1985, p. K5.

47. Nathaniel H. Leff, "Economic Development Through Bureaucratic Corruption," in Arnold J. Heidenheimer, ed., *Political Corruption: A Reader in Comparative Analysis* (New Brunswick, N.J.: Transaction Books, 1970), pp. 510–520.

48. J. S. Nye, "Corruption and Political Development: A Cost-Benefit Analysis," *American Political Science Review,* vol. 61, no. 2, June 1967, pp. 417–427.

49. David H. Bayley, "The Effects of Corruption in a Developing Nation," *Western Political Quarterly,* vol. 19, no. 4, December 1966, pp. 719–732.

50. Leff, "Economic Development," p. 512.

51. Ibid., p. 515.

52. Nye, "Corruption and Political Development," p. 417.

53. Ibid., p. 419.

54. Ibid., pp. 419–420.

55. Bayley, "The Effects of Corruption," p. 719.

56. Ibid., p. 727.

57. Ibid., p. 729.
58. Ibid., p. 728.
59. Ibid.
60. "Unhealthy Tendencies."
61. Grossman, "The 'Second Economy' of the USSR," p. 37.
62. Ibid.
63. Bayley, "The Effects of Corruption," p. 725.
64. Nye, "Corruption and Political Development," p. 422.
65. Leff, "Economic Development," p. 518.
66. Bayley, "The Effects of Corruption," p. 731.
67. "Germs," pp. 933–997.
68. David E. Apter, *The Politics of Modernization* (Chicago: University of Chicago Press, 1965), p. 271.
69. Bayley, "The Effects of Corruption," p. 732.

PART FOUR

Foreign Affairs

13

The Impact of the Changing
Sino-Soviet Relationship
on Indochina

King C. Chen

Of the several major factors that led to the disputed situation in Indochina today, the Sino-Soviet conflict in the 1960s and 1970s is the most direct and complicated. It is direct because the Sino-Soviet conflict extended its contending model directly to the neighboring countries—China and Vietnam as well as Vietnam and Kampuchea. It is complicated because such a conflict affected not only Indochina, but also the People's Republic of China (PRC), the Soviet Union, Southeast Asian nations, and the United States. From a historical perspective, the Indochina dispute is an offshoot of the Sino-Soviet conflict. Strategically, it is a new arena of the Sino-Soviet rivalry. After the Vietnam War, the "hegemonic" issue was the focus of the conflict between the two Communist giants. In the past few years, they have gradually shifted to work for a rapprochement. What is the significance of the changing Sino-Soviet relationship? And what is the impact of these developments on Indochina?

To probe the problems, we shall deal first with the fundamental positions of three major actors (China, the Soviet Union, and Vietnam) on Indochina; second, with the effect of the "hegemonic" issue on the area; and, finally, with the Sino-Soviet rapprochement and Indochina.

The Fundamental Positions of China,
the USSR, and Vietnam on Indochina

China

China is an Asian power. There are several physical and social elements that serve to fasten its ties with nations in the area, particularly in Indochina. Geographically, the PRC presents a strong potentiality for involvement in Asian affairs. The traditional geopolitical situation virtually dictates China's indispensable role in this area. In history, the rise and fall of Chinese power has significantly affected its neighbors, especially Korea in the north and Indochina in the south. In culture, China spread out its Confucian civilization to neighbors and absorbed outside cultures from them, and Vietnam is the only Southeast Asian nation that received the strongest Chinese cultural influence for a long period of time. Socioeconomically, China and most Asian nations share similar conditions of the family system, rural society, and agricultural economy when compared to those of the West. For these reasons, it is only natural to acknowledge that China has been involved in Asian international politics for centuries, and it will continue being involved for centuries.[1]

Since the establishment of the Beijing government in 1949, Asians have expected the power of the PRC to grow while fearing China's undue interference in their affairs. When former Premier Zhou Enlai attended the Geneva Conference in 1954, Beijing arrogantly stated that Zhou spoke not only for the Chinese people, but also for "the whole of the peace-loving peoples in Asia."[2] North Vietnam echoed enthusiastically. It asserted that "without China, the Asian problem cannot be solved; without China, there can be no solutions to questions of international relations."[3] Obviously, the PRC's assertion of new leadership in Asia was unmistakably accepted by North Vietnam.

For more than three decades, China and Indochina have shared several common interests: Marxist-Leninist ideology, self-preservation and the end of Western intervention, national security, economic development, and social transformation. Their common interests often serve as a guiding principle to promote their relations. However, they are in different stages of national development. Different stages require different policies, which may run against each other's interests. When such a situation is complicated by other factors, such as foreign power's interference, the conflict between China and Indochina arises.

Indochina is an area with which China must secure a friendly relationship. China will not tolerate any foreign power to present a real or potential threat to its security, nor will it allow any nation in Indochina to turn against the PRC. Thus Beijing's Indochina policy since 1949 has been centered on three major items: to exclude both the United States and the Soviet Union from the region, to assist a socialist and friendly Vietnam, and to help establish neutral, independent, and friendly Kampuchea and Laos. Obviously, it can be inferred that the Beijing leadership had never intended to offer assistance to Indochina for Vietnam's occupation of Kampuchea and Laos, much less a Vietnamese-Soviet alliance against China.

Soviet Union

The Soviet Union traditionally has no vital interests in Southeast Asia, although Leonid Brezhnev used to stress that the Soviet Union was not only a European but also an Asian power.[4] Unlike China, the Soviet Union does not border on Indochina. It also shares few common historical, cultural, and socioeconomic conditions with the area. From 1945 to 1947, Stalin actually "abandoned" Indochina.[5] In the early years of the Sino-Soviet dispute (1960–1963), Nikita Khrushchev virtually "gave up" Vietnam.[6] But, the Vietnam War brought about a change in Moscow's policy toward Indochina—renewed interest in the area. The major reasons for such a change are the Soviet competition with the United States in Southeast Asia and its rivalry with China in the Indochina Peninsula.

The Soviet competition with the United States in the international arena led Moscow to pursue a détente with Washington at one time and engage in an arms race at another. To compete against U.S. influence in Asia, the USSR reinforced its relations with several Asian countries by treaty commitments. It concluded friendship treaties with India (1971), Iraq (1972), Afghanistan (1978), Vietnam (1978), South Yemen (1979), and Syria (1980). Vietnam's alignment with the Soviet Union fits well into its global strategy against the United States, much more against China.

The Sino-Soviet conflict in the past had compelled the Soviet leaders to plan for an encirclement of China. To this aim, Moscow offered material aid and ideological ties to its Asian comrades and proposed a "collective security system" for Communist and non-Communist Asian countries. Obviously, such a system was also designed to weaken American influence in the area.

In Indochina, the Soviet objectives can be summarized in the following points: (1) exclusion of Chinese and U.S. influence from the region; (2) usage of Cam-Ranh Bay and other strategic ports; (3) support for and influence on the Indochinese Communist parties and governments; and (4) creation of the dependency of the Indochinese states (particularly Vietnam's) on the USSR by extending generous assistance for their economic and military buildups.[7]

Vietnam

Vietnam is an Indochinese state. It is the most populated, militarily strongest, and most aggressive nation in the peninsula. Acting actually as the leader of the three Indochinese countries, Vietnam has long held a close relationship with Kampuchea and Laos for historical, interest, and geographical reasons.

Beginning with its "annexation" in 1471 of the Kingdom of Champa, which was a "carbon copy of neighboring Cambodia" in ethnicity and culture, Annam (Vietnam) later advanced to control the Mekong Delta area.[8] In the eighteenth and nineteenth centuries, Kampuchea was under the strong influence of Vietnam on the east and Siam (Thailand) on the west. It became a tributary state to Vietnam at one time and to Siam at another. Its dual tributary relationship led to occasional conflicts between the two aggressive neighbors until the French came. But after the French colonialists concluded a protectorate treaty with King Norodom in 1863, Kampuchea continued to lose territory to Vietnam. In fact, the French arbitrarily incorporated large pieces of land, which were inhabited mostly by Khmer people, into today's Vietnam.[9]

Against this background the nascent Vietnamese Communist Party of 1930 was quickly enlarged and renamed to be the Indochinese Communist Party (ICP). In February 1951, when the ICP was reorganized into the Vietnam Lao Dong (Workers') Party, the Vietnamese pledged to establish a "great union of Vietnam, Laos, and Cambodia."[10]

But soon after Indochina gained independence from France in 1954, Prince Norodom Sihanouk argued for Kampuchea's right to sovereignty over the "lost" Mekong Delta area. It yielded no results. During the Vietnam War, the Vietnamese Communists, with or without Kampuchea's and Laos's knowledge, made the Kampuchean-Laotian-Vietnamese border area a sanctuary that was vital to the infiltration of Vietnamese forces to the south. Although both Kampuchea and Laos had repeatedly asked Vietnam to respect their independence and neutrality, Vietnamese troops continuously violated the security of the nations' territories by maintaining the "Ho Chi Minh Trail" throughout the Vietnam War. Small Vietnamese-Kampuchean border conflicts began in 1970 under the Lon Nol regime;[11] frequent clashes occurred thereafter. From 1970 to 1975, the Vietnamese also executed their "international duty" to help train the military personnel of the Khmer Rouge and the Pathet Lao for the liberation of Kampuchea and Laos.

Thus Vietnam, based on historical roots, national-strategic interests, and geographical closeness, has long since planned to establish a "great union" of Indochina under its leadership. The Hanoi government is determined to achieve this goal, allowing no other power to stand in the way.

The Hegemonic Issue and the Struggle for Indochina, 1975–1981

The Sino-Soviet dispute was initiated by the Chinese Communist Party (CCP) under Mao Zedong, although the CCP had its own "justification" for doing so. In the early stage of the dispute, the polemics reached a new high in 1963 and 1964 when the CCP issued its nine "open letters" against the Communist Party of the Soviet Union (CPSU).[12] The March 1969 border conflicts compelled Mao to make a strategic shift to a rapprochement between the PRC and the United States in the 1970s.[13] In 1974, Mao made known his "three-world" theory, launching a campaign against the hegemonism of the superpowers.[14]

The antihegemonic drive practically guided the direction of Chinese foreign policy from 1975 to 1981. Its objective, in a nutshell, was to promote an "international united front" against the two superpowers, especially the Soviet Union. It became a thorny issue complicating the Sino-Soviet relationship, Sino-Japanese peace treaty, and Sino-Vietnamese conflict. Under the influence of the campaign, a three-way struggle for Indochina among China, the Soviet Union, and Vietnam was intensified.

When the Vietnam War concluded in 1975, the Soviet Union had already "won" Vietnam whereas China had "lost" it. The USSR significantly increased its aid to and influence in Indochina. Although it suffered a setback in Kampuchea under the Chinese-supported Khmer Rouge, the Soviet Union rapidly enlarged its advisory group in Laos from 100 in June 1975 to 500 in October of the same year. More significant was the Soviet aid to Vietnam.

With their 1976 annual economic program and a Five-Year Plan (1976–1980) in their package, the Vietnamese went to China and the Soviet Union for aid in September through November 1975. China, displeased with Vietnam's close relations with the Soviets, granted Vietnam only a normal amount of assistance, $200 million for 1976. No aid to the Five-Year Plan was given. Meanwhile, two days before the 1975 aid agreements were signed in Beijing, Chinese Foreign Minister Chiao Guanhua spoke on September 27 at the United Nations. He accused the Soviet Union of filling the "vacuum" in Indochina and warned the Asian countries that they should never "let the tiger in through the back door while repulsing the wolf through the front gate." After the agreements were signed, Le Duan, who led the Vietnamese delegation to China, rushed to Moscow. He showed no need to stay two more days in Beijing for the celebration of the October 1 anniversary of the founding of the PRC.

In Moscow, Le Duan obtained an extremely impressive amount of aid in November 1975. It was reported that the amount reached $500 million for 1976 and as much as $3 billion for Vietnam's Five-Year Plan.[15] This aid encouraged Le Duan, at the CPSU Twenty-fifth Congress in February 1976, to praise the Soviet Union enthusiastically as the "world's mightiest socialist state" and to promise that the Vietnamese people, with "Soviet assistance," would smoothly build up a unified and socialist Vietnam.[16] In return, the Soviet Union also demonstrated clearly its close ties with Vietnam. At the Fourth Congress of the Vietnam Workers' Party in late 1976 in Hanoi, Soviet chief delegate Mikhail A. Suslov relayed Brezhnev's promise that "in the task of rebuilding Vietnam, the Lao Dong Party can always rely on the assistance of the Soviet Union." After the Vietnam party congress, Soviet influence continued to rise. Moscow increased its "experts and advisers" in Vietnam from approximately 2,500 to mid-1977 to 7,500 in mid-1979. And its aid also amounted to $3 million per day.

The Chinese made a substantial gain after the Khmer Rouge took Phnom Penh in April 1975, whereas the Soviets were treated by the Khmer Rouge like hated adversaries. The Soviet embassy in Phnom Penh was attacked by the Khmer Rouge, and Soviet diplomats were forced to go to the French embassy compound with their hands tied.[17] Meanwhile, during 1975–1978, the Khmer Rouge regime repeatedly asked Vietnamese troops to leave Kampuchea. The withdrawal request was made because the Khmers had never trusted the Vietnamese. The Khmer Rouge even regarded Vietnam as their "Enemy Number One" during the days of best cooperation (1970–1972) between Vietnam and Kampuchea.[18]

For a variety of reasons, the Vietnamese resented the Khmer Rouge's withdrawal request. They felt that they had to even the score with the Khmers. First, the Vietnamese asserted that Kampuchea was liberated with their help. They should be treated like a "big brother." Instead, they were asked repeatedly to leave the country. Second, Vietnam was extremely unhappy about the Khmer Rouge's purge of more than 4,000 Vietnamese-trained Khmer forces in 1976. Third, Vietnam was upset by the Khmer Rouge's treatment of Soviet diplomats in Phnom Penh in 1975. Fourth, Vietnam could not make any progress in negotiations with Pol Pot's Kampuchea, as compared to Laos, on a "great union" of Indochina. Fifth, China's strong support for the Khmer Rouge and its gains in Kampuchea annoyed Vietnam. To settle Vietnam's problem with Kampuchea, Le Duan borrowed the wisdom of the formation of the Warsaw Pact and designed a formula of "special relations" for the three Indochina states so that they would be "forever bound together."[19]

This formula was to be carried out either by peaceful negotiations when possible, or by miliary coercion when necessary. In the case of Laos, the "special relationship" was soon established by peaceful negotiations. A treaty of friendship and cooperation was concluded in July 1977, together with an aid pact and a border agreement. In addition, Laotian Defense Minister Khamtai Siphandon led a delegation to Hanoi in September of the same year. He paid a tribute to Vietnamese troops who fought in Laos during the Vietnam War and formally stated that the armies of Laos and Vietnam were strengthening "the alliance of combat, cooperation and mutual help in all fields."[20] Their military ties were officially reinforced.

On the contrary, similar negotiations between Vietnam and Kampuchea went on for three years (1975–1977) with absolutely no result. Worse still, border clashes occurred from time to time, and the Khmer Rouge regime claimed to have foiled a Vietnamese-supported coup attempt in Phnom Penh in June 1977.

Frustrated by the firm resistance of the Khmer Rouge regime, Vietnam planned to exert more military pressure on Kampuchea. Anticipating Vietnam's military attempt, Pol Pot, leader of the Khmer Rouge, visited Beijing in September and October 1977. He requested Chinese military protection. China declined the request but promised to offer more aid. In late November 1977, Le Duan led a party-and-government delegation to Beijing for talks on Kampuchea. Without a positive result, Duan's delegation quietly left Beijing. In late December, Vietnam launched a large-scale attack on Kampuchea.[21] This was the "proxy war," as it was called in the West. In January 1978 the Chinese government issued a statement urging the withdrawal of Vietnamese troops from Kampuchea and a peaceful settlement of the dispute. Meanwhile, China pledged its continuing support and aid to Kampuchea. In February 1978, Hanoi reached a new decision to oust the Pol Pot regime by December 1978.[22] Meanwhile, Vietnam, in addition to its criticism of the Pol Pot regime as "fascist clique" and "murderers," began to shower direct and violent accusations of China for becoming "the main culprit" in genocide in Kampuchea and in Pol Pot's war against Vietnam.[23] China was called by Vietnam "expansionist" and "hegemonist." The tension of conflicts among Vietnam, Kampuchea, and China escalated.

In August 1978 a peace treaty between the PRC and Japan was signed with an "antihegemony" clause. The Soviet Union protested it and perceived that a military alliance of the PRC, the United States, and Japan against the Soviet Union might be in the offing. The Soviet Union responded by tightening its hold on Vietnam. In addition to introducing Vietnam in June 1978 into the Council for Mutual Economic Assistance (CMEA) after China had cut off its aid to Hanoi, the Soviet Union began to build up a military base at Cam Ranh Bay in August of the same year. Then, in November 1978, Moscow concluded a Treaty of Friendship and Cooperation with Hanoi, establishing a Soviet-Vietnamese alliance. One month later, the Vietnamese carried out their February 1978 decision by launching a decisive military attack of 100,000 men to oust the Khmer Rouge regime from Phnom Penh. A Vietnamese-supported regime under Heng Samrin was formed on January 8, 1979. On February 18, one day after China had invaded Vietnam, Vietnamese Premier Pham Van Dong concluded with Heng Samrin in Phnom Penh a Vietnamese-Kampuchean Treaty of Peace, Friendship, and Cooperation. Article 2 of the treaty legitimized the Vietnamese military occupation in Kampuchea. Thus the plan of a "special relationship" between Vietnam, Kampuchea, and Laos was fulfilled by military means.

The causes for China's sixteen-day war against Vietnam in February and March 1979 were generally observed to be Vietnam's "expulsion" of Chinese residents, border clashes, Vietnam's invasion of Kampuchea, and the Soviet-Vietnamese alliance. It should be emphasized that Beijing absolutely could not tolerate a Vietnamese-Soviet alliance against China at its "front gate." To China, it was an alliance between a "small hegemonic" power (Vietnam) and a "super hegemonic" power (the USSR) that Beijing had repeatedly called for an "international united front" to oppose.

However, Chinese restraint, as demonstrated in the sixteen-day war, and the establishment of a diplomatic relationship between the PRC and the United States in January 1979 were probably the two most important reasons that persuaded the USSR to accept the Chinese proposal of April 1979 for negotiations. The talks were held in Moscow in September through November at the deputy-foreign-minister level. Some agreements on trade, scientific, technological, and cultural exchanges were reached. For a time, it appeared that a Sino-Soviet rapprochement was forthcoming, but the initial progress was interrupted by the Soviet invasion of Afghanistan. On the other hand, the Soviets strengthened their 450,000 ground forces on the Chinese border with new weapons, including T-72 tanks and SS-20 missiles.[24]

In Indochina, the Soviet Union reinforced its position. It stepped up its buildup at Cam Ranh Bay and increased its economic aid to Vietnam from $3 million to $5 million a day. Meanwhile, Vietnam's occupation of Kampuchea continued as the Khmer Rouge engaged in guerrilla warfare against the Vietnamese forces. China was able to channel its military and economic assistance to the Khmer rebels through Thailand. Beijing's strategy was to encourage the Khmer guerrillas to keep on fighting in order to drag Vietnam into the Kampuchean quagmire, while arousing the Laotians to be aware of the "colonial rule" imposed upon them by the "Soviet-Vietnamese hegemonists."[25]

Up to this point, China put forward the well-known three "obstacles" to a Sino-Soviet normalization: 450,000 Soviet troops on the Chinese border, Soviet occupation of Afghanistan, and Soviet support for Vietnam's occupation of Kampuchea. As pointed out, the Sino-Soviet conflict had direct effects on the Indochina issue. Ironically, the Indochina issue today has turned out to be an "obstacle" to the normalization of the Sino-Soviet relationship.

The struggle for Indochina was also fought in the United Nations. After two years of effort, the China-ASEAN group (then including Thailand, Malaysia, Singapore, Indonesia, and the Philippines) finally was able to persuade Secretary-General Kurt Waldheim to hold an international conference on Kampuchea. In July 1981, a ninety-two-nation conference was held at the United Nations. But the Soviet Union and Vietnam refused to attend. As the conference concluded, a long-awaited declaration was adopted. It urged (1) a cease-fire by all parties to the conflict in Kampuchea, (2) withdrawal of all foreign forces from Kampuchea, and (3) the holding of free elections.[26] But the declaration was virtually stillborn. First, the Soviet Union and Vietnam, absent from the conference, called it "illegal." Without their participation, the document would be reduced to mere rhetoric. Second, no United Nations peacekeeping force would be introduced into Kampuchea. Third, no date was set for general elections. It was only a moral victory for the China-ASEAN group, offering no immediate help to settle the Indochina issue.

Gradual Sino-Soviet Normalization and Indochina, 1982–1986

As of 1982, Deng Xiaoping's political control, economic reform programs, and conciliatory foreign policy had gained a firm hold in China. Meanwhile, President Ronald Reagan's strong military buildup program and his anti-Soviet stance, including his "evil empire" rhetoric, brought the U.S.-Soviet relationship to a new low. These developments must have convinced the Soviet leadership of the necessity to improve Soviet relations with the PRC.

On March 24, 1982, Leonid I. Brezhnev issued at Tashkent a new appeal to Beijing to improve Soviet-Chinese ties. He said that the Soviet Union was prepared to improve relations with the PRC in economic, scientific, cultural, and political fields "on the basis of mutual respect for each other's interests, noninterference in each other's affairs and mutual benefit." On September 26 of the same year, Brezhnev in Baku once again stressed the importance of reaching a normalization between the USSR and the PRC. On October 28, in his speech to 500 Soviet generals and military officials in Moscow, Brezhnev criticized the United States of preparing for a nuclear conflict and said, for the third time in one year, that Moscow was doing all in its power to normalize relations with Beijing.[27] These repeated appeals certainly signaled a strong Soviet desire to normalize relations with the PRC.

In Beijing, Hu Yaobang, the general secretary of the CCP, issued for the first time China's "independent foreign policy." He also expressed China's willingness to move toward normalization with the Soviet Union if the Soviet authorities took "practical steps" to reduce the Soviet threat to China's security.[28] This response created a favorable atmosphere in which the first round of Sino-Soviet negotiations since 1979 was held in Beijing in October of the same year.

The death of Brezhnev in November 1982 brought China one step closer to the process of normalization. Foreign Minister Huang Hua visited Moscow for Brezhnev's funeral and held an important talk with Andrei Gromyko. On the occasion of the sixtieth anniversary of the founding of the Soviet Union in late December of the same year, the Chinese leadership sent a warm message to Moscow, expressing China's sincere hopes to bring about a gradual "normalization" and urging both sides to make concessions.[29] In the subsequent funerals of Yuri Andropov (February 1984) and Konstantin Chernenko (March 1985), Chinese representatives Wan Li and Li Peng, respectively, held secret talks with the Soviet leaders on normalization. The formal Sino-Soviet negotiations since 1982 have been held systematically and steadily in the following order:

October 1982	Beijing
March 1983	Moscow
October 1983	Beijing
March 1984	Moscow
October 1984	Beijing
April 1985	Moscow
October 1985	Beijing
April 1986	Moscow

The process of Sino-Soviet rapprochement has not been without its setbacks. Criticisms occurred as adverse events developed. In 1984, for instance, Moscow criticized Chinese Premier Zhao Ziyang's visit to the United States and Japanese Prime Minister Yasuhiro Nakasone's and Reagan's visits to China. But, two developments in 1984 and 1985 contributed to the general conciliatory process. The first was Soviet Deputy Premier Ivan Arkhipov's visit to Beijing in December 1984 (postponed from May 1984 to avoid being overshadowed by Reagan's visit in April 1984). During this visit four important agreements were concluded with Beijing to promote trade and to deal with economic matters, science, and technology. The second development was the Reagan-Gorbachev meeting in July 1985 in Geneva. As a result, Deng Xiaoping stated that the "three obstacles" of Sino-Soviet normalization could be removed one by one, and the Soviets expressed the possibility of withdrawing troops from the China border in order to reduce tensions.

In Indochina, nevertheless, the Soviet Union seems to be untiringly increasing its strength. In addition to its military and economic aid to

Vietnam, the USSR has effectively enlarged its submarine depot in Cam Ranh Bay to be an air-naval base, stationing fourteen MiG-23 fighter-interceptors there. In early 1985 when the Vietnamese fought to wipe out the Kampuchean rebels on the Thai-Khmer border, five ASEAN nations (not including Brunei) urged the Soviet Union to stop backing the Vietnamese forces in Kampuchea,[30] but Moscow's policy remained unchanged. It seems that this is an area over which the Soviet Union is not prepared to loosen its control during the process of the current Sino-Soviet rapprochement.

Like the firm Soviet stand on Vietnam, the Chinese continue their unceasing assistance to the Khmer rebels under Sihanouk's coalition, which was organized in 1982 by three factions (the Khmer Rouge, the Khmer People's National Liberation Front, and Sihanouk's faction). The Beijing leadership has rejected Vietnam's proposals for negotiations several times because Vietnam has not agreed to first withdraw its troops from Kampuchea. It has repeatedly pledged its "unconditional support" for the Khmer rebels' struggle "until final victory."[31] China's policy in supporting a neutral and independent Kampuchea under Sihanouk has not been affected by the recent development of the Sino-Soviet contacts.

On the Vietnamese side, a signal of attempting to change has been delivered. The enervated economy, the isolated diplomatic situation, and the quagmire in Kampuchea have caused disagreements in the Hanoi leadership on Vietnam's economic and foreign policies. More significantly, perhaps, the new economic program in China and the process of the Sino-Soviet rapprochement have aroused serious concern and keen interest in Vietnam. As a result, Le Duan, in his February 1985 speech marking the fifty-fifth anniversary of the Vietnam Communist Party, stated Vietnam's desire "to normalize relations with China" and other non-Communist countries in Asia. Also, he preferred a "dynamic and flexible" economic program.[32] Soon after, Vietnam again proposed talks with China. But China demanded that Vietnam withdraw from Kampuchea first.

In August 1985, the Foreign Ministers Conference of the Three Indochinese States in Phnom Penh resolved, in unprecedentedly conciliatory language, to propose the resumption of Sino-Vietnamese talks on normalization. It also decided to withdraw Vietnamese troops from Kampuchea by 1990, talk with ASEAN on Kampuchea, and negotiate with Thailand for a nonaggression treaty.[33] In October 1985, China and Vietnam were reported to have held a secret talk. China made the same demand for Vietnam's troop withdrawal, but the talks had covered three items: reopening Sino-Vietnamese rail transportation, the discovery of oil in the South China sea, and trade and cultural-technological exchanges.[34] In November, China accepted Vietnam as a member of a Beijing trade exhibit in which twenty-six Asian-Pacific nations participated. Phan Hien, who led the Vietnamese exhibition delegation to Beijing, urged the resumption of Sino-Vietnamese trade. He also believed in the possibility of normalizing Sino-Vietnamese political ties.[35] Although Beijing has not yet altered its original political stand, it seems that it has left the door ajar for trade and cultural-technological exchanges with Vietnam. A process of gradual normalization may be forthcoming.

Vietnam, while seeking normalization with China, is firm on its control in Kampuchea. Since 1980, its formula for the "special relationship" of Indochina, a euphemism for the "Indochina Federation," has been further strengthened by the institutionalization of the Foreign Ministers Conference of the Indochinese States (Vietnam, Heng Samrin's Kampuchea, and Laos). The conference has been running systematically in the following order:

January 1980	Phnom Penh
July 1980	Vientiane
January 1981	Ho Chi Minh City
June 1981	Phnom Penh
February 1982	Vientiane
July 1982	Ho Chi Minh City
(February 1983)	(Vientiane, summit meeting)
July 1983	Phnom Penh
January 1984	Vientiane
July 1984	Vientiane
January 1985	Ho Chi Minh City
August 1985	Phnom Penh
January 1986	Vientiane

As Vietnam's occupation of Kampuchea continues, the coalition of the Khmer rebels under Sihanouk is forced to maintain its resistance to the Vietnamese. Up to 1986, the coalition had won the moral or material support of ASEAN and a number of other nations including the United States. Dialogues among Vietnam, ASEAN, Australia, the United Nations secretary-general, China, and even the United States have been held with various proposals and counterproposals. Vietnam's position is that Vietnamese troops will be withdrawn by 1990 but that the Khmer Rouge must be excluded from participation in either military or political affairs and that Thailand and China should stop supplying the rebels. ASEAN holds that all foreign troops should withdraw and a free election must be held with the participation of all the contending factions in accordance with the United Nations declaration of 1981, as previously discussed. China insists that Vietnam should first withdraw its forces before any negotiations could be arranged and Kampuchea should be kept as a neutral and independent country. But nothing concrete has been agreed upon.

In 1985 and 1986 the international conciliatory environment seemed to have rendered some effects on the related parties in regard to Indochina. Hanoi showed its conciliatory attitude toward ASEAN, China, and the United States. The Khmer Rouge also expressed for the first time their willingness to share power with Heng Samrin's regime providing that the Vietnamese leave Kampuchea. In addition, the Khmer Rouge announced in September 1985 the retirement of Pol Pot—a step to improve the Khmer Rouge image.[36] The Sihanouk coalition, too, is moving in a conciliatory direction. After consulting Beijing in early 1986, the coalition announced in March 1986 its eight-point proposal for a political settlement in Kampuchea. In summary, the proposal (1) urged the Vietnamese government to negotiate with the coalition on a Vietnamese troop-withdrawal schedule, which the coalition had suggested to be in two stages; (2) agreed to talk with Heng Samrin's government, after the completion of the first stage of the troop withdrawal, to formulate a four-faction coalition government under Sihanouk's leadership; (3) reasserted that a future Kampuchea should be an independent, unified, democratic, neutral, and nonaligned country free from foreign troops; and (4) expressed a willingness to conclude a peace and nonaggression treaty with Vietnam. Beijing praised it as a "reasonable proposal,"[37] Japan's government endorsed it, and ASEAN supported it.[38] But Vietnam rejected it. ASEAN, nevertheless, urged new dialogues with Vietnam on Kampuchea so as to create a favorable atmosphere for further negotiations.

Conclusion

Several significant points can be drawn from the foregoing discussion.

First, the three major actors have demonstrated that their respective national-strategic interests have largely overshadowed their common bond of Marxism-Leninism in the development of the events under study. But it should be noted that such a common bond is now helping to restore their relations. The role of ideological identity should not be underestimated in analyzing Communist affairs.

Second, the Sino-Soviet relationship in the past decade certainly has strongly influenced the Indochina situation. Currently, the process of gradual normalization has become a trend of the relationship between the two nations. If the development during 1975–1981 can serve as a guide to the future, the conciliatory trend may eventually spread to Indochina.

Third, the development of the "special relationship" of Indochina, which is an oriental copy of the Warsaw Pact, has had several important political and ministry functions: (1) It serves as a forum to coordinate a "united" foreign policy of the three Indochinese states under Vietnam's leadership; (2) it places the Kampuchean and Laotian military forces virtually under Vietnam's control in dealing with both foreign adversaries and domestic revolts; and (3) it provides the power and legitimacy for Vietnam to impose the system of "limited sovereignty" upon Kampuchea and Laos. This development has solidified Indochina into the strongest union the peninsula has ever had.

Fourth, in view of the complicated situation in Indochina today, it appears that three possibilities may provide good opportunities to help settle the issue: a significant Sino-Soviet normalization, a Sino-Vietnamese détente with or without a Sino-Soviet normalization, and a U.S.-Vietnamese rapprochement with or without Sino-Soviet conciliation. How could such possibilities be developed? While the conciliatory trend may eventually arrive in Indochina, the Indochinese states themselves should demonstrate their wisdom and determination for mutual compromise and benefit rather than mutual hostility and rivalry.

The knot of the Indochina issue is Kampuchea. Prince Norodom Sihanouk told this author in 1982 that he sincerely hoped that the Soviet Union and China could one day reach a genuine rapprochement, which would certainly help to settle the Kampuchean problem.[39] However, it is advisable to state that Kampuchea, in ridding itself of Vietnam's occupation, should not submit itself to the control of another power (China) against Vietnam as Sihanouk once inclined to do. Vietnam's model of playing the "Soviet card" against China is too risky for Kampuchea to copy by playing the "Chinese card" against Vietnam.

Notes

1. John King Fairbank, ed., *The Chinese World Order: Traditional China's Foreign Relations* (Cambridge, Mass.: Harvard University Press, 1968); A. Doak Barnett, *China and the Major Powers in East Asia* (Washington, D.C.: Brookings Institution, 1977).

2. "Asian Peoples' Wishes Absolutely Cannot Be Ignored," editorial, *World Culture*, no. 11 (June 5, 1954), p. 3.

3. *Nhan Dan*, "Important Voice of the People's Republic of China at the Geneva Conference," *Vietnam News Agency* (VNA), April 29, 1954.

4. Leonid Brezhnev, "The Decisions of the 24th CPSU Congress Are a Militant Program of Activity for the Trade Union," *Pravda*, March 21, 1972, in *Current Digest of the Soviet Press*, April 19, 1972, pp. 1–9.

5. Donald S. Zagoria, *Vietnam Triangle: Moscow, Peking, Hanoi* (New York: Pegasus, 1967), pp. 37–38.

6. King C. Chen, "North Vietnam in the Sino-Soviet Dispute, 1962–64," *Asian Survey*, September 1964.

7. Consult Donald S. Zagoria and Sheldon W. Simon, "Soviet Policy in Southeast Asia," in Donald S. Zagoria, ed., *Soviet Policy in East Asia* (New Haven, Conn.: Yale University Press, 1982), pp. 153–173. Also Douglas Pike, "The USSR and Vietnam," in Robert H. Donaldson, ed., *The Soviet Union in the Third World: Successes and Failures* (Boulder, Colo.: Westview, 1981), pp. 251–266.

8. John F. Cady, *Southeast Asia: Its Historical Development* (New York: McGraw-Hill, 1964), pp. 105–106; Michael Leifer, *Cambodia: The Search for Security* (New York: Praeger, 1967), pp. 21–23.

9. Stephen P. Heder, "The Kampuchean-Vietnamese Conflict," in David W.P. Elliot, ed., *The Third Indochina Conflict* (Boulder, Colo.: Westview, 1981), p. 23.

10. "The Birth of the Viet Nam Labor Party Is a Great Political Victory," *Voice of South Vietnam* (Ho Chi Minh's), March 13–14, 1951.

11. Norodom Sihanouk, *War and Hope: The Case for Cambodia* (New York: Pantheon, 1980), p. 17.

12. William E. Griffith, *Sino-Soviet Relations, 1964–1965* (Cambridge, Mass.: MIT Press, 1967).

13. For the March 1969 border conflicts, see Thomas W. Robinson, "The Sino-Soviet Border Dispute," *American Political Science Review*, vol. 66 (December 1972).

14. King C. Chen, ed., *China and the Three Worlds* (White Plains, N.Y.: M. E. Sharpe, 1979).

15. *New York Times*, February 1, 1976.

16. The formal name for Vietnam, the Democratic Republic of Vietnam, was changed to the Socialist Republic of Vietnam (SRV) in July 1976.

17. Sydney H. Schanberg, "Evacuation Convoy to Thailand—Arduous Trip Through the Secret Cambodia," *New York Times*, May 9, 1975, p. 14.

18. Sihanouk, *War and Hope*, p. 18.

19. Le Duan, "Outline of the Draft Political Report of the Central Committee of the Viet Nam Workers' Party to the Fourth Party Congress," *Viet Nam Courier*, no. 55 (December 1976), Special Issue, pp. 23–24.

20. *New York Times*, September 30, 1977, p. A5.

21. Heder, "The Kampuchean-Vietnamese Conflict," pp. 21–67.

22. William S. Turley and Jeffrey Race, "The Third Indochina War," *Foreign Policy*, Spring 1980, p. 98.

23. Quyet Tien, "The Chinese Powerholders Are Supporting the Genocidal Fascist Clique in Kampuchea," *Tap Chi Cong San*, no. 8 of 1978, in *Foreign Broadcast Information Service (FBIS)*, September 13, 1978, p. K10. Radio Hanoi, May 25, October 3, 14, 19, November 1, 12, 1978.

24. *New York Times*, May 22, 1980, p. A7.

25. *New York Times*, November 3, 1981, p. A11.

26. *UN Chronicle*, September-October 1981, p. 38.

27. *New York Times*, March 25, September 27, October 29, 1982.

28. Hu Yaobang, "Create a New Situation in All Fields of Socialist Modernization," *Beijing Review*, September 13, 1982, p. 31.

29. *Beijing Review*, January 3, 1983, p. 8.

30. *New York Times*, February 7, 1985, p. A8.

31. *Beijing Review*, December 23, 1985, pp. 7–8.

32. *New York Times*, February 4, 1985, p. A2.

33. "Communique of the 11th Conference of Foreign Ministers of PRK, LPDR, and SRV," in *FBIS*, Asia and Pacific, August 16, 1985, pp. H1–H3.

34. Agence France Presse (AFP), Bangkok, October 1, 1985.

35. AFP, Beijing, November 12, 17, 1985.

36. *Christian Science Monitor*, July 17, 1985; *New York Times*, September 3, 1985.

37. Commentator, "A Reasonable Proposal," *Renmin Ribao* (overseas edition), March 22, 1986, p. 6.

38. "Press Release," Permanent Mission of Democratic Kampuchea to the United Nations, No. 038/86, May 2, 1986, pp. 1–2.

39. This author's interview with Prince Norodom Sihanouk, October 17, 1982, New York City.

14

China as an Asian-Pacific Power

Thomas W. Robinson

As usual, there is a lot of loose talk about China. In contrast with the past, speculation this time is based not so much on a lack of data as on a surfeit, not on uncertainties about China's policies, leadership, and future, but on a solid basis in fact and on clear extrapolation from present trends apparently well established. The evidence, it is said, seems decisively to point to a China finally and firmly embarked on the road to full modernization in almost every area and to a foreign policy of peace, participation, and interdependence, within Asia and in the overall international system. Most look forward to the prospect of the reemergence of the Central Kingdom as the premier Asian nation with hope, anticipation, and support, calculating that it is better to join the race to become a true "friend of China" than to be left behind and risk being left out, particularly as concerns the riches that presumably will flow from that enormous market. If China is on its way to becoming a superpower—Beijing's protestations to the contrary—that trend is apparently all right with most Asians and most of those resident on the eastern coast of the Pacific Ocean. Modernization is assumed to carry with it the means to convert that country into a variant of society (perhaps still socialist, if hardly communist, once the process has been completed) that is relatively open, mostly foreign trade oriented, inclining toward democracy, and dominated by the middle class and that is becoming the pattern in many parts of Asia after having long been firmly established in North America.

A combination of straight-line extrapolation and the infinity curve thus seem to dominate thinking about China's future—no matter that this type of thinking has been seen before, whenever that country seems to have settled in to a predictable path; no matter that, in every single previous instance, dreams or forebodings (depending on which side of the political fence one happens to have been) have quickly and uniformly been shattered or alleviated. The idea is that this time it's different, that China's leaders (to dredge up an old party slogan) really do mean what they say, that the past is no predictor, that modernization will finally work its way on China. No matter that infinity curves always become S-curves, that political change in China has always spelled change in domestic and foreign policies, and that reality is always a low-probability event. The euphoria that has developed since 1979 in China has spread to other nations and has come to dominate thinking about that country's future.

Nonetheless, it is well to replace loose talk with straight talk. Whatever the ultimate level of Chinese economic development and the extent of its modernization (the latter term loosely defined), two things will not change. First, the Chinese drive to modernize will remain a creature of Chinese politics, and hence of the inner maneuvering among individuals and small groups within the Chinese Communist Party. And second, China must obey the dictate of the Iron Law of International Politics, which states that states seek to expand their interests and their influences to the extent that their absolute power increases. The first introduces a major element of uncertainty into any calculation of China's future role as an Asian-Pacific power, while the second, perhaps by way of compensation, clarifies Beijing's coming international proclivities. The role that Beijing may play in the region would thus seem to be indeterminate, were it not for a third verity. That is that all the contributants to a new and dynamic, but reasonably stable, balance of power in Asia are present and ready, if necessary, to contain the Chinese impetus to expand its influence unduly, were it to come. Such containment will take a lot of doing, for a fourth element in the equation must be reckoned with: China's potential possession of all the means of carrying out an expansionist foreign policy that, if left unchecked, could indeed dominate the area. These constitute four themes, each of which deserves inquiry.

It is difficult, these days, to speak of the direction of Chinese politics, despite the relative openness of the system and the comparative accessability of Chinese leaders. A political counterrevolution was carried out in late 1976 against Mao Tse-tung's remnants, and a coalition of the whole, dominated gradually by Deng Xiaoping, took power. Deng firmly put his reformist program into effect in late 1978, and the results were quickly noticeable, in the agricultural sphere from 1979 and in urban areas by 1980. Further reforms were announced, and they were carried out during the early 1980s, in many different areas, ranging from prices to education to law to party structure and membership. The country was progressively opened to the outside world in terms of trade, investment, educational and cultural influences, and tourism. Changes came so fast during the early 1980s that travelers to China often were astonished to find tall buildings or new boulevards where none had stood only a few months before. Deng even persuaded most of his old guard associates to step aside to make room for the new and better educated generation of younger leaders he had readied for power. In particular, the military appeared to step back from center stage for the first time in party history.

But for the discerning eye, some danger signals already were being raised. There had been a "spiritual pollution" campaign in 1983 that, although put down, was notable for having occurred in the midst of the upsurge. More importantly, although Deng had arranged for his own succession in Hu Yaobang, the new party chief, and Zhao Ziyang, the government head, it became clear that the former lacked the requisite support to outlast post-Deng challenges and that the latter might not be able to maneuver so adroitly as to avoid economic pitfalls. Nor did they have the long track record necessary to exert personal authority. Further, Deng himself did not actually retire until 1987, and until he was finally off the political stage, the solidity of his program could not be tested. Finally, and perhaps most importantly, the very nature and the pace of the reforms were engendering their own mounting opposition. Many groups were either being bypassed or damaged by the new system. These included the vast middle rank of the party, of Cultural Revolution vintage, whose ideological skills were no longer needed; the many in the countryside who did not in fact grow rich through reform and who occupied the lowest rung of a new rural class structure; the military, whose budgets were cut, whose prestige was damaged, and who were progressively excluded from the councils of power; those young people, apparently in the millions, who could not find jobs or who were forced into positions and places they heartily disliked; many urban dwellers, who were hurt by inflation; a very large number of women of child-bearing age, who were coerced into forgoing, postponing, aborting, or secretly bearing their children; many youths, who could not obtain the kind or the extent of education that would help them get ahead in the new system; and party ideologues, who questioned on Marxist grounds the efficacy of the new program and who wondered where the Chinese Revolution had gone. The situation was ripe for reaction; the only requirement remaining was a leader who could raise the banner of "true" Maoism to unite all these forces into a single revanchist body.

While there is no way of telling whether such a movement will take place, since in mid-1986 Deng and his entourage were still in place, there is no reason to think that the verities of Chinese politics have suddenly been displaced by the changes of the post-Maoist decade. These verities are at least three. Most importantly, Chinese politics has always centered on the faction and relations between factions. Although the era of Deng Xiaoping has been one of extraordinary movement, in terms of the rise of a whole generation of new political leaders, there is no reason to believe that younger leaders are any less prone to factionalism than their elders. It is merely that the new factions are obscured by the very rapidity of change and by the sheer number of new officials. Second, pendulum-like change has characterized Chinese politics during the rule of the Chinese Communist Party. And although that rule was dominated by Maoist personalism, an element that is now absent, there is no reason to believe that change will not occur again, especially when the enormous reaction to the Cultural Revolution begins to fade. Change is the central rule of politics in any country; why should China be any different? Third, personality, especially that of the top leader, counts for much in China. China during the twentieth century has been ruled by a series of strong personalities—warlords, Chiang

Kai-shek, Mao Tse-tung, and Deng Xiaoping. Emphasis on the personal qualities of one person is inevitable in a country so large and so comparatively lacking in multiplicity and continuity of accepted political and bureaucratic institutions. It is given even more emphasis by the Leninist dictate to concentrate all power within the party and all party power at the center.

Thus, a post-Deng era will bring on a new political situation in China. And if there is to be change, it will have to be away from the extremes of pragmatism, market socialism, international interdependence, and class peace. Such change may be attenuated, it is true, by the momentum and the success of the present program and its enormous popularity among broad reaches of the populace. But even that program is not without its shortcomings, and many of the victories of the last decade may be short-lived if many of the economic experiments prove not to be viable. And it is the party, not the people, that decides the direction and pace of political change in China. The most that can be said, therefore, for China's political future is that it is uncertain. In all probability, after Deng there will be a period at least of taking stock, more probably of political churning, and even (although less probable) of political reversal.

The implication for Chinese foreign policy is twofold. First, to the extent that political uncertainties impede economic progress, the increase in Beijing's power will occur at a slower rate than during the first half of the 1980s. China will thus emerge as an Asian superpower somewhat later than present projections of the turn of the century. Second, a political reaction is likely to have an antiforeign content, as seen already during the "spiritual pollution" campaign. When added to the "normal" assertive nationalism that comes from the pride of expanded national power and the xenophobia of the Central Kingdom complex, a China less liberal than during the Deng era could give its neighbors much more trouble than the putatively peace-loving nation of 1977–1987.

That brings us to the second verity of China's foreign relations, the Iron Law of International Politics. Every student of international relations supposedly is schooled in this simple proposition: Nations expand the range of their interests commensurate with the increase in their national power. They exhibit a propensity to involve themselves in situations and areas farther and farther from their national boundaries. The level of their involvement in places nearer home also tends to expand in the same proportion. All history demonstrates the truth of this assertion, whether it be Greek city-states, Roman empires, Chinese dynasties, industrializing European powers, or contemporary global superpowers. In Asia, it was true of Japan during the first half of this century, and there is no reason to think it will not be true of China during the last third and into the twenty-first century. It is only a question of how much power China has behind its expansionist push (which, we should hasten to add, need not be territorial, since what is most desired is influence over events and trends) and of what sort of power is set up against Beijing. The first concerns the raw elements of power at China's disposal, while the second relates not only to the same elements of power in the hands of other states but also to their capability to organize against expansionism—that is, to the *balance* of power.

Chinese foreign policy under Deng has partially obscured the working of this law. Beijing has found it necessary to seek U.S. support against the Soviet military threat and to seek U.S. assistance in its drive to economic modernization. It has also found it highly desirable to go to other sources of the capital, technology, assembly lines, markets, and educational and cultural institutions necessary to a successful modernization program. These other sources have been Japan, West Europe, and other nations of the Pacific rim, even reaching to South Korea and the province of Taiwan. Soon it will include also the Soviet Union and its East European industrial dependencies. Chinese expansionism has thereby been muted. But it has hardly been absent, even at this early stage. The 1979 lesson-teaching conflict with Vietnam is a good case in point. The "lesson" was that no major change in the international political equation in Southeast Asia could take place without Chinese acquiescence or participation. The attempt to insert China as a middleman in the Iran-Iraq war through sale of arms to both sides is another. The purpose is not merely to help prevent a Soviet invasion of Iran consequent to that country's breakup under the effects of the conflict and Khomeini's rule but as well to introduce Chinese power into Southwest Asia and, eventually, the Middle East. The several pushes against the United States over Taiwan is a third. Each time (1974, 1977, 1982), the intensity rises and with it the threat of untoward consequence for the United States. More can be expected in the late 1980s and into the 1990s, with as yet unforeseeable results. A final example is Hong Kong. China accomplished during 1982–1984 what it was unable to do for a century and a half previous, even though it continues to be in Beijing's interest to extend the life of that city-state, at least partially, into the next century.

The degree to which China elects to push for a greater, even eventually a dominant, role in Asia and beyond depends on two final factors: the assemblage of the requisite means of national power (mostly the product of the modernization drive) and the countervailing power set against Beijing by its Asian-Pacific neighbors. Let us consider the first of these. Any state's national power can be categorized into four elements: military, diplomatic, economic, and cultural. These sum, in some time-differentiated matter, to applicable national power. In China's case, it is not difficult to evaluate the historical and future strengths of each component. In the case of military power, despite a tendency by foreign analysts to disparage the Chinese armed forces in terms of offensive might in a modern conflict and to denigrate both the classical people's war and the Chinese army's level of equipment modernization, Beijing is already the world's third most powerful army and a nuclear power of global consequence. Even at the relatively restrained pace of military modernization characteristic of the Deng period, China has already done much to refurbish its martial base and appears likely to accelerate in years ahead. It is laying the groundwork for a blue-water navy, for a thick air defense, for a logistically dependable projection force, and for an impressive array of up-to-date high technology support systems. It has updated its strategic and tactical doctrine, in both nuclear and conventional arenas. It is going into space in a major way and will soon possess a nuclear strike force capable of reaching, in quantity, all corners of the Soviet Union and most parts of the United States. Within a decade, therefore, China not only will be able to defend itself, in most departments, from Soviet attack (or make Soviet attack exceedingly unwise in terms of the expected level of retaliation), but also will be capable of projecting significant force overland or overseas at distances capable of causing military planners in all Asian states to have to react.

In the diplomatic sphere, Chinese capabilities are well known and highly respected. Diplomacy has two meanings: the degree to which the government succeeds in marshalling national resources to support national goals; and the success the foreign office has in playing the game of international politics. In both areas, China does reasonably well. Its rulers have learned, through their own personal experience and by studying their country's very long tradition of strategy and statecraft, how to use the sometimes slim resources at their disposal. They also have the negative example of Maoist pretentions— when stated goals moved far ahead of national resources—at their disposal. Beijing also has done well not only in negotiations on particular issues and has, from practically the beginning of the party's existence, evolved a particularly accurate understanding of the workings of power politics, especially those in which China (or the party) is the weakest participant. There is nothing unusual about the Chinese negotiating style, and it can be met on equal grounds and even bested, as U.S., Japanese, Soviet, and British (among others) statesmen and businessmen have found out. But the point is that it is of high quality, in contrast to that, occasionally, of the United States and, usually, of the Soviet Union. It serves China in good stead.

In the economic area, where China for more than a century had fallen far behind, the country has become an Asian giant in quantitative measure and, since 1979, has made rapid strides in qualitative and per capita terms. To be sure, it is unlikely that China can maintain the very high pace of the early 1980s all the way down to the turn of the century and beyond. At least one, and perhaps two, economic downturns should be expected, for reasons of domestic politics, weather, and international politics and economics. Nonetheless, even if China continues only moderate progress in agriculture and industry, and presuming it does not again shut itself off from the world commercially, technologically, and intellectually, there seems little doubt that China will become an advanced industrial state in almost every regard, bid fair to dominate Asia's trading system, and even begin to rival Japan for Asian economic leadership. China has always had the domestic base for rapid economic progress, as regards natural resources, a large internal market, a fertile land that still has much potential, and an inventive and entrepreneurial people. Until recently, it lacked the requisite combination of political leadership, motivation, and economic organization. Under Deng, it has gone far to remedy those deficiencies, and if open-minded experimentation continues into the new era, the proper combination of ingredients will be discovered. Beijing is, seemingly, close even now. Economic development not only will provide the wherewithal to enable the country to project its diplomatic and military power abroad. It will also make possible the effective utilization of economic instruments of policy for national-interest purposes. Trade, investment, foreign assistance, and military transfers all are powerful tools of an activist foreign policy. Thus, although today China tends to be a consumer of these commodities, tomorrow it will be a net exporter. With it, Beijing will exert enormous influence in Asia, the Pacific, and throughout the globe.

Finally, with regard to cultural assets, China scores highly. It is often forgotten that cultural instruments of foreign policy are among the most effective in projecting power and influence at a distance. To do so, a nation must possess an attractive and respected culture—art, cuisine, music, literature, philosophy, tradition, and so on—and one that is not merely exotic but practical. China obviously has these qualities, and can, if it so chooses, resume its place as perhaps the most important repository of Asian culture. China was the Central Kingdom for so long not so much because of its location, extent of territory, and power as because it possessed a superior culture freely acknowledged by all of those around it. China thus did not have to conquer Asia militarily; it had already done so culturally. The years since the 1940s have not been kind to China, materially or culturally. It fell behind in the former and lost its preeminence in the latter. Yet, almost forty years after the Communist Party came to power in the country—a party that vowed, among other things, to destroy traditional Chinese culture—enough of that culture remained and was attractive and powerful enough to survive a revolution against it and to reassert itself with enough strength to compete with Leninism for control over the Chinese policy and once again to attract peoples on Chinese borders. There is, of course, a symbiotic relationship between Chinese economic and military power, on the one hand, and Chinese cultural attractiveness, on the other. Since Beijing's material base is once again promising to make the country into the power center of Asia, so Sinic culture may be restored as the cultural standard of the region. That combination could revolutionize Asian international relations. But one final, and critical, element would remain to be put into place: the transformation of the Chinese Communist Party from a Leninist totalitarian organ into a more benign, popular institution with strong elements of democracy. If and when that occurs, Chinese political culture will be added to the other components of Chinese culture to beget a combination difficult to overcome, or to equal.

So China has the policy means to restore its position as the dominant force in Asia and even to expand its influence to other regions. The potential is high and the historical situation without precedent. If such a shift were to come about, it would represent a change in Asian, and probably global, international relations comparable only to the domination of Asia by Japan during World War II. Indeed, if unchecked, China's rise could not only drastically shift the balance of power in Asia but overthrow it. Out of such shifts wars are made, for the balance of power, the only equilibrating mechanism known to the international system, needs both countervailing power properly organized and, equally important, sufficient time to do the job.

Whatever the outcome, it seems reasonably clear that the coming Chinese rise to regional prominence will cause a diplomatic revolution. The only question remaining is, how far beyond that revolution will matters tend? The answer depends on Chinese policy and on that of other relevant states, Asian and beyond. In the case of China, a halt in, or a backtracking of, the present liberal course would not only carry negative implications for eventual economic modernization of the country but would also call into question, once again, the political stability of the country. That could very well take place, as per the previous argument. At the least, such a sequence would delay the benefits to Chinese foreign policy stemming from modernization. At most, it could lock China, once again, into perpetual backwardness. Perhaps, because of the severe domestic and international policy consequences for China, it is unlikely that halts, if they come, will last long, or that reversals will come at all.

What is more likely is a gradual changeover into a Soviet-style economy and polity: reasonably high rates of industrial growth but relative isolation from the global economy, lack of inventiveness, xenophobia, and political stasis. Such a China would gain much of what it wants economically, but at the price of giving up any notion of positive leadership of Asia. China would indeed become a superpower, but more slowly, with less influence, and greater opposition than if it were to persist on the present course. The nature of Leninism argues in favor of a Soviet-like China. No communist party yet extant has liberalized itself to the point of giving up democratic centralism (i.e., its monopoly of power and mode of rule) and of allowing competing world views to vie for the alliegence of the populous. Yet it is precisely such a development, and none other, that will cause other Asian nations to relax about Chinese imperialism and to welcome Beijing as a trusted partner *cum* leader in the region. Until that event takes place, unlikely though it be, China's growth in national power must engender fear and opposition throughout Asia and cause Asian states, as well as both superpowers, to take steps to limit expansion of Chinese power.

We now come to the last of the four elements in our equation: the power and the policies of the other relevant Asian nations, and those of the United States and the Soviet Union. If China were undertaking its current program of rapid modernization and augmentation of national power in the 1930s, with only one other Asian state of consequence, the results in terms of Asian security would have been wildly different from that which eventuated. In a word, war would probably have been avoided, since China would have been too strong for Japan to conquer and since it would have gone on to organize a collective defense system against Tokyo. The 1980s and 1990s are not the 1930s and 1940s, to be sure. But the point is that the national power and the foreign policies of other states must be taken into consideration in any understanding of China's role in Asia during the coming decades.

What will China's international environment be during the last years of the twentieth century? The most important fact is the near certainty that almost all of China's neighbors will be at least as modern domestically, and therefore as activist internationally, as China itself. Wherever one looks in Asia, one is confronted with nations rushing into the modern world, even with nations already there. All Asian states are obeying the two regularities of the modernization process: Every nation eventually modernizes, and according to a reasonably similar path; and once on the path to modernization, there is no going back. In Northeast Asia, Japan is a postindustrial society; South Korea is well into the upper reaches of modernization; and North Korea is behind the south but will accelerate after Kim Il Sung's demise. In East Asia, Taiwan is nearing the end of its drive to industrial strength; Hong Kong has long since modernized and is, consequently, a world capital; and the Philippines, while in great difficulty and facing even more problems, is nonetheless beyond the "takeoff" stage. In Southeast Asia, Singapore is, like Hong Kong, fully modern and an international center; Thailand is moving rapidly, as is Malaysia; Indonesia is at the takeoff point, although it—like the Philippines—faces many problems; Vietnam is a major military power, and if it ever decides to settle back and provide a real industrial basis for popular livelihood and cease its policy of expansion *über alles*, it could become a major regional power in every sense. In South Asia, India is a rival to China in almost every measure imaginable and continues to move steadily into the modern world; Sri Lanka is trying to adopt the Korean-Taiwanese model of growth, with some success despite the Tamil insurgency; and Pakistan stands at the doorstep of rapid growth, ready to pass through if it can solve its domestic shortcomings. Only Bangladesh remains below the threshold, as does Burma in Southeast Asia.

Even this cursory review ought to demonstrate that, given even a few decades, China will be surrounded by very strong, highly nationalist, confident, activist, and, for the most part, Western-oriented states difficult for China to penetrate or, collectively, to overcome. Asia is in fact already divided into two halves: Island Asia, led by Japan, and including the four Newly Industrializing Countries; and Continental Asia, centered in China and including the slower growing, autarchic, inward-looking, and socialist states. Island Asia is the region's leader, and continental Asia must strive to emulate and catch up. That is the most important trend of the late twentieth century in the region, not China's modernization drive. China has little choice but to join the more dynamic portion of its region, lest it fall permanently behind. That is what it is trying to do. If China were to drastically alter its policy, return to a modified version of Maoist isolationism, and use its new power (which would be called into question by such a change in policy), the other states would be in a position to resist Chinese tendencies to expand its influence by force. They would be able—presuming they had their diplomatic thinking caps on—to band together in a regional collective security organization designed to stop Beijing from dominating the region. Thus, on this analysis, China would lose a lot if it chose to "fight" its Asian neighbors and would continue to gain a lot if it elected to "join" them. The exigencies of the modernization process, together with those of the balance of power, more or less lock China into some version of its present policy direction. To be sure, Beijing will always have a policy choice; its very enormity guarantees that. And, as noted previously, a post-Deng leadership will no doubt attempt to reassert a degree of autarchy in its economic policy and will surely try to test the limits of its new power through a more assertive regional policy. But there are severe natural limits to such changes. Both Chinese modernization and Beijing's expansion of influence would suffer, thanks to the equilibrating mechanisms of modernization and power politics.

What shape an anti-Chinese coalition would take, if it were found necessary to form one, is not clear. Much would depend, for instance, on the specific direction of Japanese foreign policy in its new phase of seeking independence from the United States (although still within the framework of the Security Treaty, contradictory though that may sound). There are many other elements that cannot presently be known and that impart a fluidity of unprecedented proportions to coming international relations in Asia. There is, importantly, the continuing participation in Asian international relations of the two superpowers. Their competition throughout the globe will become more severe as the century closes and may even include one or more direct military confrontations. In Asia, it is highly likely that the Soviet Union will attempt to expand its influence—an expansion that will create more direct and more severe military threats—and to incorporate more Asian states into its system of dependencies. Already Afghanistan, Mongolia, and (to some extent) North Korea and Vietnam are in the Soviet system. Moscow will seek to expand its degree of control over these states and add others to it—the Philippines would seem to be the most logical target. The Kremlin will also significantly augment its already very large military presence in Soviet Siberia and the Far East, particularly as concerns air-sea projection forces. These moves will be resisted by the United States, which will have to upgrade its own military capabilities in the region from the much too low levels of the 1970s and early 1980s, maintain its alliances with traditional allies in Asia (especially Japan), seek to knit together the present Washington-based system of bilateral ties into something more formal and multilateral, stress Pacific Basin cooperation and trade expansion, and do its best to retain as much influence as possible in China at a time when Beijing will seek to reassert its regional autonomy and independence. These are tall orders for both superpowers, which will keep them both busy throughout the period and tend to submerge the emerging need to counter Chinese expanionist tendencies into their own global competition. The point is that the very need to do battle with each other will draw Washington and Moscow even further into Asia. Thus both their foreign policy attention and their foreign policy resources will focus on Asia and be available for balance-of-power purposes, in what promises to be a fluid situation.

In sum, Asia as a whole will tend more and more to be composed of strong, modernizing, assertive, and expansionist nations all obeying the Iron Law of International Politics. China will have to fit itself into this new Asia. Although it will have a panoply of policy means at its disposal, so will most of the other Asian states, to say nothing of Washington and Moscow. It follows that China will participate in the new Asian balance of power, no doubt as a principal element, but will hardly be in a position to dominate the region. It will do well, in fact, in the coming years, if it runs fast enough to keep up with the rest. So even though China may tend toward near-superpower status by the year 2000, it will not become the region's new overlord. Too many other factors of limitation are at play.

15

Recent Trends in
Sino-Soviet Relations
and the Strategic Triangle

Donald S. Zagoria

Since the early 1980s, a new stage in Sino-Soviet relations has been developing. By adopting a more "independent" and balanced position in the triangle of the United States, the Soviet Union, and the People's Republic of China (PRC), China has sought to move to the pivotal position in the triangle. Given the nature of the still essentially bipolar world, a more balanced position in the triangle holds out the most promise for China.

In the 1950s, China allied itself with the Soviet Union and became Moscow's "junior partner" in the global rivalry with the United States. This was obviously an uncomfortable position for China, and the strains inherent in this unequal relationship contributed to the Sino-Soviet split in the late 1950s. In the 1960s, China opposed both superpowers, but then it was faced with pressure from both and even with the specter of superpower collusion against it. In the late 1970s, China moved closer to the United States and emphasized opposition to the Soviet Union. But this position encouraged the United States to exploit Beijing's anti-Sovietism for its own purposes and once again threatened to place China in the role of a "junior partner." Moreover, leaning to one side of the triangle deprived China of any maneuverability in its relations with either superpower.

Since 1982 the PRC has been formulating the ground rules for a more balanced foreign policy. It has been improving relations with both superpowers simultaneously and reassuring each of them that it has no intention of aligning with the other. It criticizes both superpowers for "hegemonistic" actions. In some instances, say the Chinese, they will side with one superpower; in other cases, they will take the opposite side.

As a result of its more balanced position in the triangle, China has already gained some advantage. Its relations with each of the superpowers are now better than the two superpowers' relations with each other. This situation gives both the United States and the Soviet Union some incentive to vie for China's favor. In recent years, both superpowers have been increasing economic and technical cooperation with China and aiding China in its new and ambitious drive to modernize. There has been a substantial increase in the volume of trade between China and the Soviet Union. The two erstwhile partners also signed an agreement on scientific and technological cooperation. This followed a substantial reduction of mutual polemics, a resumption of talks about the border dispute, and an increase in cultural exchanges.

At the same time, China's relations with the United States are also improving. In 1985, U.S.-China trade reached some $8 billion, and there was a surge in U.S. technology transfers to the PRC. China and the United States have signed an agreement to cooperate on developing nuclear energy. And both countries are continuing to develop some degree of military cooperation. The Reagan administration has just announced that it plans to sell $550 million worth of aviation electronics to China. This would be the largest sale of military equipment to Peking since diplomatic contacts were established in 1972.

China has managed its superpower relations so well that both the Soviet Union and the United States seem content with, and even optimistic about, their future relations with China. General Secretary Mikhail Gorbachev said in his report to the Twenty-seventh Party Congress in February 1986 that the "reserves" for cooperation between the Soviet Union and China are enormous. And President Ronald Reagan was extremely optimistic about U.S.-China relations during his 1984 visit to the PRC. The United States has now classified China as a "friendly, nonaligned" country and hailed China's reform program as a significant step toward economic and political liberalization.

It is quite likely, however, that each of the superpowers is too optimistic about its relations with China. The Soviet leaders exaggerated the degree to which China would be willing to follow the Soviet foreign policy line in the 1950s, exaggerated the degree of support for Moscow in the disputes among Chinese leaders in the 1960s, and even now seem to exaggerate the possibilities for a deep and substantial rapprochement with China. American leaders, on the other hand, may exaggerate the degree of hostility between China and the Soviet Union, just as they once exaggerated the degree of unity.

Over the longer run, it is certain that China's power and influence will grow and that it will pursue policies in accordance with its own national interests. Those interests will not be the same as those of either superpower. China will not be anyone's "card" or "junior partner."

But China's position in the triangle, while balanced, cannot be described as "equidistant" between the two superpowers. The Chinese themselves are at pains to point out, at least to Americans, that they continue to regard the Soviet Union as the main threat to their own security.

So long as the Soviet Union maintains some fifty divisions of troops on the Chinese border, including several divisions in Outer Mongolia, strengthens its air forces near China, modernizes and expands its Pacific Fleet off China's coast, deploys one-fourth of its nuclear missiles in Siberia, maintains its military alliance with Vietnam, and occupies Afghanistan, the Chinese are likely to adhere to this view. Of course, the Soviet Union has been telling China that its forces in the Far East are intended to balance U.S. forces in the Pacific and are not aimed at China. But it is difficult for Chinese generals to distinguish anti-American from anti-Chinese missiles, airplanes, and ships.

China not only fears the Soviet Union more than it fears the United States, but it also has more to gain from trade and economic cooperation with the West than it has to gain from the Soviet Union. After all, trade with the United States and Japan in 1985 totaled more than $25 billion, while trade with the Soviet Union was less than $2 billion. There are 19,000 Chinese students in the United States and only a handful in the Soviet Union. And the Chinese seem to have a much higher regard for Western than for Soviet technology. In short, for some time to come, it is likely that the Chinese will have much more to fear from the Soviet Union and much more to gain from the West.

There will be other limitations on China's ability to play a truly independent role in the triangle. First and foremost, China will continue to be much weaker than either of the two superpowers. China's official defense budget has accounted for a falling share of total government spending; its military spending remains minuscule by superpower standards; and to meet China's ambitious plans for modernization, China's economic planners depend on switching resources from military to civilian use. Official figures show that the volume of defense plant production of consumer goods almost doubled between 1978 and 1983 and is to continue rising in the future. According to a recent Chinese announcement, output of products for civilian use manufactured by the defense industry quadrupled between 1980 and 1985, and China's defense industry will continue in the next five years to veer toward civilian production.

A second limit on China's ability to play a truly independent role in the triangle is that China will not be able to afford a sharp deterioration in relations with either superpower. A deterioration in Sino-Soviet relations would increase U.S. leverage on China and reduce Chinese leverage on Moscow. By the same token, a deterioration in U.S.-Chinese relations would increase Soviet leverage on China and reduce Chinese leverage on Washington.

It follows from the foregoing that China will have a substantial interest in keeping its differences with both superpowers within limits. Beijing will continue to criticize Moscow for refusing to meet its "three conditions," but this criticism will not interfere with the process of easing Sino-Soviet tensions and developing scientific, technical, economic, and cultural cooperation. By the same token, Beijing will continue to criticize Washington for its policy on arms sales to Taiwan, but this criticism will not interfere with the continuation of economic, cultural, scientific, and even military cooperation with the United States.

At the same time, China will seek to extract from each superpower the maximum possible advantage. China's détente with the United States has gone further than its limited détente with the USSR, and China can threaten the United States with deeper détente with the Soviet Union while threatening the Soviet Union with even deeper détente with the United States.

Meanwhile, while China aspires to a more balanced position between the superpowers on the global strategic level, its policies in Asia are more likely to continue to be parallel to those of the United States.

From a Chinese perspective, Moscow is seeking to encircle China in Asia through its alliance with Vietnam, its invasion of Afghanistan, its pressure on Pakistan, its special relationship with India, and its new strategic presence in North Korea.

The crucial country in this Sino-Soviet geopolitical conflict in Asia is probably Vietnam. China and Vietnam are likely to be long-range adversaries. The Chinese do not accept Vietnamese domination of Indochina, and Vietnam is unlikely to settle for anything short of dominance. Thus there is likely to be continuing tension between Vietnam and China, tension fed by deep-seated suspicions on both sides.

In this conflict between Vietnam and China, the Soviet Union is almost certain to continue supporting Vietnam. Soviet aid to Vietnam has been increasing, and the Soviet Union remains a staunch defender of Vietnam's position against China. As a result, Moscow has gained valuable bases in Cam Ranh Bay from which it can project its power throughout Southeast Asia and into the Indian Ocean. The Soviet Union will not give up these bases in order to improve relations with China, and, in any case, the Vietnamese will not give up their domination of Indochina no matter what Moscow may want.

Under these circumstances, the Sino-Soviet relationship in Asia is likely to continue as adversarial, and China will take a favorable view of U.S. power in Asia as a balance to the more threatening and vastly superior Soviet power. China opposes Soviet policy in Northeast, Southeast, and South Asia. And China's opposition to Soviet policies in these regions is largely shared by the United States. Both China and the United States seek to get Vietnam out of Cambodia and to have genuinely free elections there. Both support Thailand and the rest of ASEAN against Vietnam. Both support the resistance forces inside Cambodia against the Vietnamese-dominated Heng Samrin government. Both support the resistance in Afghanistan and seek to shore up Pakistan against Soviet pressure. Both seek to improve relations with India. And both China and the United States are concerned about the growth of the Soviet military presence in North Korea. Finally, both have a common concern with the growth of Soviet military power throughout the Asia-Pacific region.

In sum, although China pursues a more or less balanced position in the strategic triangle at the global level, in Asia there is a "special relationship" between China and the United States born out of a common fear of Soviet expansion.

What could alter this present pattern of triangular relations? I can imagine several scenarios. First, more aggressive Soviet policies in Asia could drive Beijing and Washington much closer together and even into a military alliance. Second, a substantial deterioration in U.S.-Chinese relations could drive Beijing closer to Moscow. Third, a radical deterioration in U.S.-Soviet relations could stimulate either Moscow or Washington or both to make more substantial concessions to Beijing.

To start with the first scenario, more aggressive Soviet policies in Asia could drive China and the United States closer together. It was the Soviet invasion of Afghanistan in 1979 that led in the early 1980s to the beginning of military cooperation between Washington and Beijing. A Soviet-supported Vietnamese invasion of Thailand or increased Soviet pressure on Pakistan or Korea could have similar effects in the late 1980s or 1990s.

On the other hand, if U.S.-Chinese relations were to deteriorate, Beijing might move closer to Moscow. Such a deterioration might be precipitated by a succession crisis in Taiwan in which a new Taiwanese government declared itself a sovereign state. This would present the United States with an acute dilemma. It might even encourage the Chinese to use or threaten to use force against Taiwan. The ensuing backlash would almost certainly drive a serious wedge in U.S.-Chinese relations.

Finally, a return to a new "cold war" between Moscow and Washington might stimulate either the Soviet Union or the United States to make more substantial concessions to Beijing. The Soviet Union might then begin to think of some "grand compromise" with China involving a substantial troop withdrawal from the Chinese border, a border agreement, and some kind of compromise settlement between Hanoi and Beijing in Cambodia. The United States, on the other hand, might think of trying to increase military cooperation with China.

Apart from the security factors that have been discussed here, there is another important element that will influence China's future position in the great-power triangle. That has to do with the future course of China's "second revolution."

In the past two years, China has begun what Helmut Schmidt has called the greatest single experiment in economic history. China has decollectivized agriculture, adopted wide-reaching measures of decentralization, begun to adopt market reforms, and opened up its economy to the West. As a result, the PRC has taken a significant step away from totalitarianism, revolution, and autarchy and it has acquired a real stake in global peace and stability. It is hard to believe that these far-reaching economic changes will not have profound social and political consequences. Already there has been a significant shift in the relationship between state and society, with society becoming more autonomous. As a result of the opening to the outside world, China is rapidly becoming part of the global culture. It is now exchanging television programs with an American network, CBS. There are 15,000 Chinese students studying in the United States. More than 1,500 Chinese delegations visit the United States annually.

In the meantime, the PRC has joined or is contemplating joining virtually all of the international economic institutions. It has already joined the World Bank, the International Monetary Fund, and the Asian Development Bank, and it is now contemplating joining the GATT. China has repudiated the Stalinist notion of two world markets—one socialist, the other capitalist—and has insisted that all economies are "indivisibly related with the world economy." This statement suggests that China believes that its economic future lies more with the West than with the East.

Moreover, many Chinese leaders and economists recognize the great deficiencies of the Soviet model of central planning. They see a pattern in which autarchic and centrally planned economies of the traditional Soviet variety are technologically backward, unable to keep up with the "information revolution," and unable to produce high-quality goods of a wide variety. Some of these Chinese leaders and economists want to pursue a policy of "radical reform" that could lead China away from the Leninist-Stalinist model of socialism toward a more mixed economy and substantial marketization. Others want to limit the pace and scope of reform in China.

While there is no tight connection between domestic and foreign policy, it seems likely that Chinese cooperation with the West is more likely to flourish if China continues with the policies of reform. On the other hand, a conservative victory in China may give a new impetus to Sino-Soviet relations.

In sum, there are a number of complex factors that have to be weighed in assessing the likely future course of Sino-Soviet relations and the pattern of relations in the strategic triangle.

On balance, it seems likely that in the foreseeable future, the strategic triangle will be fairly stable, and all three parties in the triangle will be relatively satisfied. The PRC will continue to balance between the superpowers at the global level while continuing to tilt to the United States in Asia. China will obtain technology and trade from both the Soviet Union and the United States. China will not soon constitute a serious strategic threat to either superpower. It will continue for many decades to be preoccupied with its own economic and technological development, and it will require a peaceful international climate for this development to succeed.

In the more distant future, however, perhaps even in twenty to twenty-five years, China with its huge population, its diligent people, its new pragmatic development strategy, and its resources will constitute a major new force in the global arena, a force that both superpowers will have to reckon with. The challenge for both Moscow and Washington at that time will be not merely to manage their own rivalry—a challenge they have not so far managed very well—but also to manage the arrival on the scene of a third very powerful player with legitimate interests and ambitions of its own.

16

Teng Hsiao-ping's Management of the Superpowers

Harold C. Hinton

From the perspective of mainland China's leaders, the dominant feature of international politics since World War II has been the "contention" between the superpowers. While denying any aspiration to be a superpower itself, the People's Republic of China (PRC) has tried to play the part of balancing or "swing" power between the two "contenders."

The performance of the current mainland Chinese leadership in this role, which is the subject of this chapter, cannot be fully understood without some reference to that of its predecessors. There are, however, significant differences among periods. The 1950s were essentially the decade of the "tilt" toward the Soviet Union, the 1960s the decade of simultaneous confrontation with both superpowers, the 1970s the decade of the tilt toward the United States, and the 1980s to date the decade of accommodation with both superpowers, as well as priority for modernization.

From Mao Tse-tung to Chou En-lai

According to Henry Kissinger, Mao Tse-tung was a supreme realist in international power politics, even though his values were determined by his "thought."[1] An understanding of Mao's approach to foreign policy, including policy toward the superpowers, must be sought more in his practice than in his writings, which are a most inadequate guide in this case.

Mao evidently perceived the "contention" between the superpowers as a promising opportunity to implement the "united-front" strategy that he had developed in the 1930s. In effect, this strategy was intended to apply to a situation, such as the contention between Japan and the Republic of China under President Chiang Kai-shek, in which the two major adversaries of the Chinese Communist movement were antagonistic toward one another but one (the Japanese) was decidedly more dangerous (to the Chinese Communists) than the other.[2] In that case, a united front, or temporary tactical combination, should be formed with the less dangerous adversary, whose final disposition could be decided after the anticipated joint victory over the more dangerous adversary. In reality, however, the defeat of the Japanese was not achieved primarily by the supposed united front between the Communists and the Nationalists, which deteriorated as the war went on, but by the United States in the Pacific. It is not clear whether Mao ever fully internalized the fact that although his strategy had not necessarily failed, neither had it proved its validity.

Together with other important factors such as shared ideology and history, the united-front strategy played a major role in Mao's celebrated decision, announced in mid-1949, to "lean to one side," that of the Soviet Union.[3] For a number of reasons, including ideological considerations and American support for the Republic of China during the post-1945 civil war, he considered the United States, with much exaggeration, a serious threat to post-1949 mainland China, or in other words, the more dangerous adversary in terms of his united-front strategy. The Soviet Union, although described as a friend, partly because Stalin would have tolerated nothing less, occupied in effect the position of the less dangerous adversary. Among the evidence for this view is the fact that Chinese Communist leaders made it clear, in private conversations with official American visitors to Yenan in 1944, that they expected a Soviet invasion of Manchuria, feared that it might lead to a reimposition of Soviet control, and were determined to avoid any such outcome. It would be a mistake to take at face value the extravagant pro-Soviet statements constantly made in mainland China for a few years after 1949.[4]

Another source of Mao's "tilt" toward the Soviet Union was the fact that the "new" China was too weak to stand alone in a world more or less dominated by the superpowers in "contention." It undoubtedly occurred to Mao, however, that when and if mainland China became a developed country, it would be in a much better position to manipulate the balance between the superpowers.

Mao considered the Soviet Union, as the "head of the socialist camp," uniquely responsible for leading that camp's struggle against the United States, and specifically for supporting mainland China's claim to Taiwan in whatever way seemed most likely to be effective. But this was exactly what Nikita Khrushchev refused to do, beginning in 1954, and two years later he compounded this failure by beginning to commit what Mao regarded as a series of ideological and political blunders.

Infuriated by the Soviet performance, and to some extent under the influence of radical Defense Minister Lin Piao, Mao at the end of the 1950s elevated the Soviet Union to the status of major coadversary together with the United States and adopted what is sometimes called a dual-adversary (or dual-confrontation) strategy.[5] This consisted of a risky and inevitably unsuccessful struggle, mainly ideological and political but with military potentialities, against both the superpowers at the same time. They were held to be "colluding" more than "contending." Inevitably, it was the more accessible of them, the Soviet Union, that felt the main impact of the dual-adversary strategy and that reacted the more vigorously against it. The Soviet response took the form mainly of a major crisis in 1969, which left behind it a greatly strengthened Soviet military presence along the Sino-Soviet border that threatens the PRC to this day.

Beginning about 1969, as Mao told Edgar Snow off the record in December 1970, effective direction of domestic and foreign policymaking passed from Mao and Lin Piao (who was killed in September 1971) to Mao's old colleague Premier Chou En-lai.[6] It could have rested in no more competent hands. The centerpiece of Chou's complex approach to fending off the Soviet threat amounted to a restoration of the Maoist united-front strategy, this time with the Soviet Union as the principal or more dangerous adversary and the United States as the less threatening or secondary adversary and therefore the desired temporary partner. Fortunately for Chou and for the PRC, the United States under Richard Nixon and Henry Kissinger was eager to reciprocate; there is little doubt that during the first few years of the 1970s the new U.S.-Chinese relationship was one of the main reasons why the Soviet Union did not attack mainland China. On the other hand, Nixon and Kissinger were in no mood or position to endorse Chou's private appeals to them for a broad anti-Soviet coalition including the United States and the major nations along the Soviet Union's southern border, from mainland China through Western Europe.[7] Since Chou's radical colleagues, notably Lin Piao, as well as foreign militants such as the North Koreans, opposed his opening to the United States, Chou tried for two years (spring 1970– spring 1972) to deceive and fend them off by claiming that the principal adversary was the hated Japanese, who were then on bad terms with the United States (cast as the secondary adversary) on account of the "Nixon shocks." In reality, of course, Chou was seeking cooperation with the United States in order to manage a threat from the Soviet Union, not Japan.

Teng Hsiao-ping as Chou's Lieutenant

Teng Hsiao-ping, who had been Chou's senior vice-premier down to the Cultural Revolution, was the most important of the victims of that catastrophe whom Chou rehabilitated in the 1970s. Chou intended Teng to succeed him as premier and to be the strong man of the regime after his and Mao's deaths. In the meantime, Chou made Teng his principal lieutenant beginning in the spring of 1973, as his own health started to fail.

In spite of the closeness of their *kuan-hsi*, Teng's personality differs strongly from Chou's. Teng tends to be assertive and even acerbic, where Chou was suave and gracious. Furthermore, Teng is less politically secure than Chou was in his last years and accordingly cannot afford to be as relaxed on the highly charged Taiwan issue. This factor in turn has inevitably complicated Teng's relations with the United States.

These tendencies appeared shortly after Teng's return to office in 1973. At that time he, as well as Mao and Chou in all probability, were disturbed by the current U.S. quest for détente with the Soviet Union—as indicated, for example, at the time of Leonid Brezhnev's visit to the United States in mid-1973—which contrasted sharply with Beijing's preference at that time for superpower confrontation. Teng was also frustrated by the temporary indecisiveness of U.S. behavior in the shadow of Watergate.

Under President Gerald Ford, Kissinger was more than ever the architect of American foreign policy. He clearly had no answer to the upsurge of Soviet activity in the Third World, especially Africa, that followed the fall of Indochina in 1975. This performance did not impress Teng, and his reception of Ford and Kissinger in December 1975 was correspondingly chilly.

The rather poor state of Sino-American relations naturally made caution with respect to the other superpower advisable. For a time after 1974, Sino-Soviet relations were roiled by a seemingly minor but actually explosive issue, the fate of three Soviet army officers captured near the Sinkiang border and accused of espionage. By the end of 1975, it was clear that Chou En-lai would not live much longer, and that after his death Teng might fall victim once more to the hostility of the radicals. If they came to power, they might execute the three Soviet officers, an act that would be extremely provocative in the eyes of the Soviet military. Accordingly, the prisoners were released on December 27, 1975, with an apology. Coming shortly after the summit conference with Ford, this action may have appeared to offer the additional advantage of putting pressure on the United States by suggesting a warming trend in Sino-Soviet relations.

Teng did indeed fall from office in April 1976, three months after the death of his patron Chou En-lai. During the spring and summer of that year, the extreme radicals were more active and influential than they had been since the de facto end of the Cultural Revolution (signaled by the suppression of the Red Guards at the hands of the Army) in late 1968, even though the premiership fell not to one of them but to a compromise choice, Hua Kuo-feng. The radicals, among whom the quartet later branded the Gang of Four were prominent, tried to revive the futile and discredited dual-adversary strategy and did their best to exacerbate relations with both superpowers, although without much effect. Like other problems generated by the extreme radicals, this one was resolved by their arrest a month after Mao's death.

The fall of the Gang of Four inevitably placed the question of Teng Hsiao-ping's return to office on the party's agenda. In spite of Hua's understandable lack of enthusiasm, it occurred in the summer of 1977. There followed a quiet power struggle, whose outcome was a foregone conclusion. Among the efforts that Hua evidently made to dramatize and strengthen his position was a demand, in his report to the National People's Congress in February 1978, for a drastic reduction of Soviet forces near the Chinese border to the level of the early 1960s. The Chinese side had already been making this demand in private at the Sino-Soviet border talks that had been going on since October 1969, but to publicize it was another matter and an unwise provocation. The outcome was a bout of saber rattling on the Soviet side in April and May 1978, probably with some damage to Hua's political position.[8]

This and other mistakes by Hua contributed to a rapid strengthening of Teng Hsiao-ping's position in the second half of 1978. Teng also must have benefited from being the only leader of sufficient stature to cope with the threat posed by the escalating crisis with Vietnam and by Hanoi's increasing closeness to Moscow, which was obviously intended by the Vietnamese to cover an impending invasion of Cambodia, then mainland China's only true client state. As suggested by his trip to Southeast Asia in November 1978, Teng evidently preferred to handle the problem by political and diplomatic means to the extent possible. The military leadership, however, was demanding that Vietnam be given a "lesson" if it invaded Cambodia, and as part of the price of his overall triumph at the celebrated Third Plenary Session of the Eleventh Central Committee (December 1978), Teng had to yield on this point.[9]

War with Vietnam would involve an obvious risk of Soviet retaliation, which Teng proposed to minimize in two principal ways. One was to give Moscow plenty of warning, for example by making no particular effort to conceal the preliminary military buildup near the Vietnamese border. The other was to "normalize" relations with the United States.

Normalization, in the sense of diplomatic relations, had been agreed on in principle in the Shanghai Communiqué of February 1972, but because of various problems including the Taiwan issue little progress was made until 1978. After Zbigniew Brzezinski's visit to mainland China in May of that year, Sino-American negotiations on normalization began, but they were complicated by various problems, including the Chinese side's objections to the U.S. intent to continue selling arms to Taiwan after normalization and to an apparent U.S. desire to normalize relations with Vietnam as well. In early December, however, the United States gave up on Vietnam, and with an invasion of Cambodia obviously imminent Teng intervened in the talks and agreed to normalization in spite of the Taiwan arms issue, on which he had appeared firm up to that point.

Having been named *Time*'s Man of the Year for 1978, as he was to be again for 1985, Teng was presumably in a good mood when he visited the United States at the end of January 1979. Shortly before leaving, he had issued a public call for an anti-Soviet united front to include the United States and of course the PRC.[10] Not only was the Jimmy Carter administration unreceptive to this idea, however, but it made clear its opposition to Teng's evident intent to attack Vietnam. Teng's interest in an anti-Soviet united front therefore faded rapidly. By January 1980, when Secretary of Defense Harold Brown's visit to Beijing suggested an interest on the part of the Carter administration in defense cooperation (the Pentagon's term) with mainland China on account of the Soviet invasion of Afghanistan, it was too late. In effect, modernization, based on the "open" policy toward the outside world, had replaced the idea of an anti-Soviet united front as Beijing's top policy priority. By June 1980, Teng had fallen back on urging, in an interview with a visiting delegation of U.S. strategic specialists, the Carter administration's own line of parallel U.S. and Chinese policies toward the Soviet Union, with the idea that Moscow could not be sure of being able to fight either without also having to fight the other.

Normalization and Teng's trip to the United States served their main immediate purpose, however. The Soviets did not retaliate for mainland China's "lesson" to Vietnam in February-March 1979, although they did further tighten their relationship with Hanoi.

Teng in Charge

Teng's next move was to give notice of termination of the Sino-Soviet treaty of alliance at the earliest time (April 1979) consistent with its terms.[11] There were several reasons for this action. The alliance had been a virtual dead letter since about 1960 and was obviously inconsistent with the state of Sino-Soviet hostility that had existed since about that time, and especially since the border crisis of 1969. Furthermore, the sarcastic joke that the Soviet Union only invades its allies has some obvious historical basis. Finally, the Japanese had always resented being named in the Sino-Soviet treaty as a potential aggressor, and they considered a continuation of this situation incompatible with the Sino-Japanese peace treaty of August 1978.

Moscow does not like to have treaties with it broken off, and in realization of that fact Peking proposed a new series of intergovernmental talks on outstanding issues. It made the mistake, however, of stating as preconditions for such talks Soviet acceptance of the demands Beijing had been making since 1969 for a cease-fire agreement along the border and a "mutual" (actually, Soviet) troop withdrawal from disputed areas.[12] The Soviet side was in no mood for any preconditions. It therefore reintroduced a military component into the 1979 May Day parade, for the first time since 1968. (Military participation had been canceled at the last minute in 1969 as a conciliatory gesture to the Chinese at a time of great Sino-Soviet tension.) On May 5, accordingly, the Chinese side, in an unpublished message, proposed talks without preconditions. When they finally got under way in October, the former preconditions were reintroduced as simple demands, and the talks made little progress.

In January 1980, after only one round of these talks, Peking suspended them on account of the invasion of Afghanistan. It probably felt itself in a strong enough position to do this because the Carter administration, also shocked by the invasion, had just sent Secretary of Defense Harold Brown to Peking to express an interest in U.S.-Chinese defense cooperation. The Chinese side was not really prepared for this proposal, but a highly secret agreement appears to have been concluded at about that time under which the United States has maintained electronic monitoring installations in western Sinkiang, and there were some other visits in both directions by high U.S. and PRC defense officials later in 1980.

One of the main obstacles to an improvement of Sino-Soviet relations had been Mikhail Suslov, the bitterly anti-Chinese senior Soviet ideologue, who had debated Teng Hsiao-ping in Moscow twice, in 1960 and 1963. His death in late January 1982 improved attitudes on both sides. Six weeks later, Brezhnev launched a series of overtures for the resumption of the talks begun in 1979, and they got under way again in October 1982.

At the successive semiannual rounds of these talks, Beijing has demanded the elimination of what it calls the three obstacles, or in other words the Soviet military presence along the Sino-Soviet border (including Mongolia), in Vietnam, and in Afghanistan. This position has subsequently been modified so as to permit the Soviets to begin with the removal of any one of the obstacles, provided all were ultimately eliminated, rather than tackling all of them at the same time. On April 17, 1985, Teng stated that if Moscow would get Vietnam to withdraw its troops from Cambodia, there would be no further Chinese objection to the existence of Soviet bases in Vietnam.[13]

The Soviet response, until Mikhail Gorbachev became general secretary, was essentially to stonewall. Moscow was evidently unwilling to commit itself to ease its pressure on the Chinese border, and it maintained disingenuously that it could not negotiate on the other obstacles because the interests of third countries were involved. Under Gorbachev, however, Moscow has begun to put some pressure on Mongolia and Vietnam to improve their relations with the PRC, although without much visible result. It is not clear whether the purpose is to get the Chinese to waive their objections to the presence of Soviet troops near the border in the interest of an overall improvement of relations with these neighbors and with the Soviet Union itself, or whether it is to persuade Ulan Bator and Hanoi to agree to a Soviet military withdrawal in the interest of better Sino-Soviet, Sino-Mongolian, and Sino-Vietnamese relations; the former seems the more likely possibility.

The coming into office of President Ronald Reagan had a significant impact on Teng Hsiao-ping's superpower policy, in differing ways. On the one hand, the new president was firmly anti-Soviet, and there was therefore no need to exhort him to be firm with Moscow or join an anti-Soviet united front, as had seemed advisable for a time with his predecessors. On the other hand, Reagan was relatively pro-Taiwan, at least to the extent that he was certain not to advocate repeal of the Taiwan Relations Act, which Beijing greatly desired. His belief in capitalism for the Third World also grated on mainland Chinese nerves, as Chao Tzu-yang made clear to him at the Cancún Conference (October 1981). Another irritant was the Reagan administration's reluctance at that time to transfer dual-use (military as well as civilian) technology to mainland China in spite of Beijing's keen desire for it, as contrasted with Secretary of State Alexander Haig's expressed willingness in principle, announced during his visit in June 1981, to sell arms to the PRC, something in which Beijing felt much less interest.

About the time of the Haig visit, accordingly, Beijing began to stress the "independent" character of its foreign policy, thereby abandoning in effect the previous "tilt," more or less openly admitted, toward the United States. The new line was not significantly affected by the Reagan administration's decision, in January 1982, not to sell Taiwan the F-X fighter or by its agreement (in the August 17, 1982, joint communiqué) to keep a qualitative and quantitative ceiling on arms sales to Taiwan.

Sino-American relations in 1983 began rather unpromisingly, with a visit in February by Secretary of State George Shultz. As he made clear in a major speech delivered the following month,[14] Japan, not China, was now to be the cornerstone of the Reagan administration's East Asian policy. It appeared that this might hold true at least until 1989, since Beijing concluded in 1983, after careful analysis, that Reagan would be reelected in 1984.

The second half of 1983 brought a surprising change for the better, from Beijing's point of view. In the fall, the existing U.S. restrictions on the export of dual-use technology to mainland China were drastically liberalized. This major breakthrough, although unwelcome to mainland China's neighbors, rendered acceptable and interesting to Beijing the idea of U.S.-Chinese defense cooperation, including perhaps the purchase of some actual weapons or at least weapons-related technology. The beginning of true U.S.-Chinese defense cooperation appears to date from the visit of Secretary of Defense Caspar Weinberger (September 1983), which also created a better balance in U.S. policy between Japan and mainland China. It is possible that Beijing perceived this improvement, from its point of view, as in part a competitive U.S. response to the "independent" policy and to recent trends in Sino-Soviet relations.

An important characteristic of Teng Hsiao-ping's "independent" policy is that, in considerable contrast to earlier years, Beijing no longer welcomes a confrontation or arms race, let alone actual war, between the United States and the Soviet Union. There appear to be several reasons for this. One is that an arms race between the superpowers inevitably leaves the PRC farther behind than before, and therefore less secure. Another arises from the definite possibility that, in the event of war between the superpowers, the Soviet Union, if unwilling to leave a potentially dangerous neighbor unscathed, might launch a preemptive attack on mainland China. As the best guarantee against such a "hypothetical horrible," Peking in its current mood favors détente and some form of arms control between the superpowers.

A self-imposed compulsion therefore exists on Beijing's part to view the strategic relationship between the superpowers as being in reasonable balance, because if it were not, the weaker party would presumably step up its force improvement programs in a way that would tend to be destabilizing. Having viewed the United States under Carter as lagging behind the Soviets, Beijing considers the United States under Reagan to have caught up[15]—some Chinese sources even claim it is stronger than the Soviet Union—and the superpower balance as reasonably stable, at least for the time being. Whether true or not—and to the writer it seems somewhat optimistic from the U.S. point of view—this belief fits in well with Beijing's present emphasis on stability in the international environment and between the superpowers, as being favorable not only to mainland China's security but to its development.

In view of this underlying attitude, Beijing opposes development by the United States of the Strategic Defense Initiative ("Star Wars"), on the ground that it would be provocative and destabilizing.[16] Furthermore, mainland Chinese strategic analysts sometimes make clear, although indirectly and in private, their concern that a U.S. SDI program would trigger a Soviet counterpart that would nullify Beijing's anti-Soviet nuclear deterrent.

Since the second half of 1985, mainland Chinese leaders have described Beijing's current posture as "equidistant" between the superpowers. These statements have been made in private, and mainland Chinese spokesmen have denied, contrary to the fact, that the term has been used at all. Whether it is an accurate description of mainland China's position will be considered later. Whether accurate or not, it fits well with Beijing's version of its current superpower policy, again as contained in recent unpublished statements: a strategy of maintaining viable relations with both superpowers without getting very close to either, if only because to do so would antagonize the other and would compromise mainland China's proclaimed independence. Furthermore, the notion of equidistance tends to evoke the fewest total objections from the pro-U.S. and pro-Soviet groups within the Beijing elite.

There is no doubt that some plausibility is imparted, at least superficially, to the concept of "equidistance" by the recent trend toward improvement in Sino-Soviet relations. Especially since Deputy Premier Ivan Arkhipov's visit in December 1984, this has taken the form mainly of an increase in Sino-Soviet trade and technology transfer, a mellowing of Beijing's propaganda treatment of the Soviet Union, and a lessening of Chinese pressures on Vietnam.[17] Conversations between the foreign ministers have taken place; on the other hand, Beijing has rejected the idea of a summit conference at least until some progress has been made toward the elimination of the three obstacles.

Some Concluding Reflections

To the writer, the foregoing analysis, as well as his general view of the subject under discussion, supports certain significant interpretations and conclusions.

The foreign policy of the PRC, like that of any other state, is determined, not simply or even necessarily mainly by its domestic politics, but by a fluctuating "mix" of domestic politics and the perceived regional and global environment.

Whether Beijing is sincere or not, it is correct in saying that it will never be a superpower. It has too late a start and too many resource limitations, in relation to its population, to catch up with the United States or the Soviet Union. On the other hand, its geopolitical assets appear sufficient to enable it to become in time a unique great power, with a largely regional reach but on a level above all others except for the superpowers. Even now, mainland China is strong enough to affect the superpower balance; it can, for example, either facilitate or prevent Soviet domination of the East Asian mainland, something that fortunately it opposes.

Beijing still perceives Soviet military capabilities as a serious threat to itself, regardless of Moscow's current intentions, and in fact as the only such threat. Apart from some deployments against Vietnam, Beijing's strategic planning and dispositions are based almost entirely on the assumption of a Soviet threat. The 1982 summer maneuvers in Ningsia, when a tactical nuclear weapon (unreported in the national media) was "used" against hypothetical invading Soviet forces, suggest that Beijing believes it could, and might have to, take such an action in a contingency of that kind, on its own soil, without triggering retaliation by Soviet strategic forces. In addition to the "three obstacles," Beijing is greatly concerned over North Korea's current "tilt" toward the Soviet Union; the aptest comment on Beijing's public statements to the effect that it welcomes this new relationship is one made recently to the writer by a high U.S. official: Anyone who believes that will believe anything.

Regardless of what it may say, publicly or privately, Beijing is not truly equidistant between the superpowers and cannot be equidistant at least as long as only one of them poses a serious threat to its security. (It should be remembered that the United States and mainland China removed each other from their respective "enemies lists" at the end of the 1960s.) Beijing needs a viable relationship with the United States if only to avoid having to accommodate with the Soviet Union more or less on Moscow's terms; the converse proposition is not valid. The United States will continue to be significantly more valuable to China than the Soviet Union is as a source of high technology, capital, and of course access to the non-Communist world. The control rods that Beijing uses to justify its avoidance of a genuine accommodation with the Soviet Union, the "three obstacles," are much more serious than those used against the United States, mainly the Taiwan arms issue, because the former correspond to a genuine threat to mainland China's security whereas the latter do not. A large part of Beijing's current limited tilt toward Moscow appears to derive from what can be called the Chen Yun factor: his political influence as the principal surviving counter-weight in the top leadership to Teng Hsiao-ping, his commitment to principles of Soviet origin in the field of economic planning and administration, and his personal relationship with Arkhipov. Teng has found it advisable to accommodate himself to Chen's views to a degree, but they are not the mainstream of Teng's "thought" and policies.

It has been pointed out,[18] with considerable validity, that mainland China under Teng Hsiao-ping, like the developed non-Communist countries of East Asia, has in effect adopted the so-called Yoshida Doctrine, under which Japan since World War II has deemphasized other means to national power and concentrated on economic development as the safest and ultimately the surest road to it. This course has been followed in more or less conscious reliance on the United States as the guarantor of regional security, as well as regional prosperity through the vastness and relative openness of its domestic market. Beijing is following this path, although less obviously than most. To date, the results have been encouraging on the whole; Beijing's position with respect to the superpowers appears to have improved, an evident testimony to the effectiveness of Teng's management.

As for the long term, Teng pointed out in his report to the important party conference of September 1985 that the PRC expects to become a major industrial power by the middle of the twenty-first century and that it will then be in a position to "make greater contributions to mankind."[19] The attainment of this objective appears a reasonable possibility, although far from a certainty, in the light of current trends. If it materializes, the impact on East Asia is likely to be profound, as mainland China's neighbors already perceive. Beijing of course denies any threatening purposes with respect to Asia,[20] and this restraint is probably genuine at the present time. But a future, stronger, mainland China, which will presumably have both unsatisfied claims (in the South China Sea, in particular) and a military power projection capability, will not necessarily behave in the same way as at present.

In spite of its current declared opposition to any form of "hegemony," a modernized mainland China would probably actualize the ambition that it appears to have already in latent form, a desire for a regional sphere of influence embracing as much of East and Southeast Asia as possible. The superpowers, and others, would be expected to recognize this position, tacitly at least. At the present time, India in effect claims South Asia as its sphere of influence, and the main single source of its continuing good relations with the Soviet Union and its tensions with the United States and China is the fact that the former gives the appearance of recognizing this claim and the latter clearly do not. This situation may turn out to be, if not a model, at least a relevant precedent for the future relationship among the PRC, the East Asian region, and the superpowers.

Notes

1. "Kissinger on Mao: Brilliance and Cold Blood," *Time*, September 20, 1976, p. 49.

2. Cf. Mao Tse-tung, "On Policy" (December 25, 1940), in *Selected Works of Mao Tse-tung* (Beijing: Foreign Languages Press, 1965), vol. 2, pp. 441–449. The concept was significantly reemphasized, although not in a very enlightening way, in "A Strong Weapon to Unite the People and Defeat the Enemy: Study 'On Policy,'" *Red Flag*, 1971, no. 9.

3. Mao Tse-tung, "On the People's Democratic Dictatorship" (June 30, 1949), in *Selected Works*, vol. 4, p. 415.

4. For example, the slogan, "The Soviet Union of today is the China of tomorrow."

5. The classic statement of the dual-adversary strategy is Lin Piao, *Long Live the Victory of People's War!* (September 3, 1965) (Beijing: Foreign Languages Press, 1965).

6. This passage was omitted, presumably at Chou's request, from Snow's published account of the interview.

7. Henry Kissinger, *Years of Upheaval* (Boston: Little, Brown, 1982), p. 55.

8. Cf. Harold C. Hinton, "Moscow and Peking Since Mao," *Current History*, vol. 75, no. 440 (October 1978), p. 122.

9. The communiqué of the Third Plenary Session says, "We must . . . be prepared to repulse at any moment aggressors from any direction" (text released by New

China News Agency, December 23, 1978), a clear departure from Teng's insistence at that time that the threat came from the north (the Soviet Union).

10. "An Interview with Teng Hsiao-ping," *Time*, February 5, 1979, p. 34.

11. New China News Agency dispatch, April 3, 1979.

12. Kyodo dispatch, Beijing, April 25, 1979.

13. Teng Hsiao-ping, interview with a Belgian correspondent (Peking Domestic Television Service, April 17, 1985).

14. On March 5, 1983, in San Francisco.

15. For example, Shi Wuqing, "Superpowers Reach Military Balance," *Beijing Review*, no. 3 (January 21, 1985), pp. 14–15, and no. 4 (January 28, 1985), pp. 25–27.

16. Zhuang Qubing, "United States Prepares for 'Star Wars,'" *Beijing Review*, no. 45 (November 5, 1984), pp. 16–19.

17. Richard Nations, "Peace, Pride and the Rise to World Power," *Far Eastern Economic Review*, March 20, 1986, pp. 64–66, 69.

18. Ibid.

19. Text released by New China News Agency, September 23, 1985.

20. For example, Pei Monong, "China's Future Position in Asia," *Beijing Review*, no. 16 (April 18, 1983), pp. 15–19.

17

U.S.-PRC Relations: From Hostility to Reconciliation to Cooperation?

Stanton Jue

In the twelve years since the long silence between our two nations was broken by the signing of the Shanghai Communiqué, China and America have begun a productive partnership. Our cooperation has helped to provide a counterbalance to aggressive world forces.

—President Ronald Reagan at the Great Wall Hotel,
Beijing, April 28, 1984

Is what President Reagan said in Beijing an expression of euphoria or a notion of realism? There cannot be a simple answer, since U.S.-China relations are inextricably intertwined with a number of complex and even paradoxical factors which, under the best of circumstances, defy ready explanation. To place recent U.S.-Chinese relations in the proper perspective, it is important to look at the major events from Richard Nixon's first term as president, particularly his foreign policy initiatives, and to review the three presidential visits to China in the 1970s and early 1980s. It will also be necessary to examine some of the current issues and misunderstandings besetting the relationship and, finally, to look at the probable course of U.S.-Chinese developments in the 1990s.

From the 1968 election, and perhaps earlier, Nixon and his advisers had the vision and the belief that there could be no durable peace in Asia or in the world without China's participation. Early in his administration President Nixon took steps to correct the anomaly of nonrecognition of China in international relations.

Although Nixon triumphantly characterized his historic visit to China as "the week that changed the world," restoration of relations between the two countries across the Pacific has been arduous and often filled with misunderstanding and distrust, despite good intentions on both sides. After the establishment of formal contacts in 1972, it took the United States nearly seven years to recognize Beijing's claim of sovereignty over the Chinese mainland and adjacent islands in January 1979. Western journalists rightly credit Nixon for his bold initiatives in bringing China out of its self-imposed isolation, dating from 1949 when the Communists came to power on the mainland, but the facts suggest that the emergence of China into the community of nations stemmed as much, and perhaps more, from Chinese perception of the international situation and their desire to develop a new relationship. China had a great deal to say in making the decision for rapprochement with the United States.

China's Move Toward Improving Relations with the United States

During the late 1960s and early 1970s, the United States was deeply involved in Vietnam and eager to extricate itself from the agony of a war that many believed was not in America's priority interests. There was also a perception in China and elsewhere in Asia at the time that the United States, enmeshed in domestic difficulties, was disengaging from the region. The signals were readily apparent, as evidenced in the concept of Vietnam-ization of war efforts and in the various peace overtures advanced in Paris and elsewhere. Yet these efforts achieved few tangible results, as Nixon said in a January 25, 1972, interview: "Our proposal for peace was answered by a step-up in the war on their part. The only reply to our plan has been an increase in troop infiltration from North Vietnam and communist offensives in Laos and Cambodia."[1]

Perhaps more in wishful thinking than in clear reasoning, some leaders argued that normalization of relations with the People's Republic of China (PRC) might increase the prospect for peace in Vietnam, as China could help end the war. Their assumptions were clearly erroneous. If Vietnam's response to the U.S. peace proposal was a step-up in the war, no less unequivocal was China's response, which supported the continuation of the war.

Then there was the Soviet Union, which many believed was the dominant factor in pressuring China into improving relations with the United States. Although the Sino-Soviet Friendship Treaty of the early 1950s provided China some political and economic assistance, China became disillusioned in the ensuing months with Soviet policy on such international and bilateral issues as Soviet curtailment of economic and technical assistance to China; unilateral termination of a science and technology agreement to help China in atomic development; Moscow's questioning of the orthodoxy of Mao's ideology and adherence to the Soviet brand of communism; and Moscow's agreement with the United States on a policy of détente.

In its assessment of the international situation during the late 1960s, China viewed rather grimly the border clashes along the Ussuri River, the Soviet invasion of Czechoslovakia, and the emergent Brezhnev Doctrine, which justified Soviet intervention in socialist countries, and which Beijing saw as an increasing threat to China. These events prompted the Chinese leadership to reexamine the nature of the Sino-Soviet relationship and China's position in the world. In the process, Premier Chou En-lai seemed to have gone to the core of the Chinese character and to have adopted policies designed to give the Chinese a sense of dignity and an independent stature. Of the several policy choices available, Chou selected the one least harmful to China's interests—that is, improving relations with the United States. Chou and his colleagues convinced Chairman Mao that the United States no longer posed a direct threat to China, since the U.S. president was promoting a retrenchment policy in Vietnam and an evolving Nixon Doctrine in Asia.

The abrupt change of Chinese attitude toward the United States, as evidenced by the invitation to the U.S. Ping-Pong team to visit China in April 1971, astounded many people in the world who found it difficult to fully appreciate the communist philosophy and its system of values. To understand China's position, one must consider the degree of dialectic materialism being practiced at the time. From the Chinese perspective it is entirely possible to change tactics abruptly without losing sight of ultimate goals, whether in collaboration with the Nationalists in the war against Japan or in improving relations with the United States to gain technical advantage for economic modernization. China's immediate goals seemed clear: (1) to enter the United Nations, (2) to gain a new status and recognition of China in the world, and (3) to resolve the Taiwan issue. During the early 1970s, China, a close ally of North Vietnam, was in fact in a state of undeclared war with the United States. In the Chinese view, a visit by the U.S. president to China, if he came, would raise China's new status as a world power and ensure its entry into the United Nations. These developments would also accelerate the process of diplomatic recognition of the PRC by a number of countries that hitherto had been reluctant to move toward formal relations. As a consequence, China would gain prestige in Southeast Asia, where overseas Chinese would find a new source of confidence and comfort as the PRC emerged from a weak-power status to one of a great power and potential superpower. Beijing also believed that in the event of war with the USSR, China at least would not have to worry about a military threat from the United States or from Taiwan, as the United States would restrain any open hostility in the Taiwan Strait. In the end, Beijing hoped to achieve greater leverage in dealing with the United States in solving the Taiwan issue.

U.S. Initiatives

U.S. conciliatory moves toward the PRC can be traced to early 1964 when the proposal to place trade of nonstrategic goods with Beijing on the same basis as U.S. trade with the Soviet Union was considered. And there were plans to revise travel regulations for U.S. citizens to visit countries the United States did not recognize, including mainland China, on the understanding that the U.S. government could not provide protection for such travelers. In March 1966, Secretary of State Dean Rusk, testifying before the House Foreign Affairs Subcommittee, underscored the importance of maintaining informal contact and communication with Beijing through the Warsaw channel despite the PRC's continuing hostility toward the United States. In addition, Rusk stated: "We have gradually expanded the categories of American citizens who may travel to Communist China. American libraries may freely purchase Chinese Communist publications. American citizens may send and receive mail from the mainland. We have indicated our willingness to allow Chinese Communist newspapermen to come to the U.S. We are prepared to permit American universities to invite Chinese Communist scientists to visit their institutions."[2] Although the Chinese Communists were not expected to seize upon these opportunities for contact and exchange, it was viewed as important and in the U.S. interest that such channels be opened and kept open.

In 1968, Richard Nixon came to power. From the beginning of his presidency, overcoming China's international isolation was an important part of his foreign policy. Under his direction the National Security Council staff worked closely with the State Department in developing a phased sequence of unilateral measures to be taken by the United States, with or without a Chinese response. Because of existing hostility and suspicion, the United States eschewed dramatic, drastic steps that could rebuke or upset a system that China was not ready to accept. The carefully wrought strategy included the following foreign-policy initiatives:

- July 1969—Noncommercial purchases of Chinese goods by U.S. tourists were permitted. Additional categories of American citizens were permitted to visit China.
- December 1969—Subsidiaries of U.S. firms overseas were allowed to trade with mainland China.
- January and February 1970—Private meetings between Chinese and U.S. ambassadors were held in Warsaw.
- March 1970—U.S. passports would be validated for U.S. citizens for travel to the PRC for any legitimate purpose.
- April 1970—Selective licensing of nonstrategic U.S. goods for export to China was authorized.
- August 1970—Some restrictions on U.S. oil companies operating abroad were lifted so that most foreign ships could use U.S.-owned bunkering facilities on trips to and from Chinese ports.
- October 1970—The president deliberately used the official title "People's Republic of China." A number of public conciliatory statements by the secretary of state made clear the direction of U.S. policy toward the PRC: that the United States sought to promote mutual understanding and mutually beneficial actions. (In the autumn of 1970, Beijing began to respond through private and third-party diplomatic channels.)
- Spring 1971—A series of orchestrated public and private steps were taken in pursuit of a policy of normalization.

- March 1971—U.S. passports no longer needed validation for travel to mainland China.
- April 1971—A U.S. Ping-Pong team visited China and was received by Premier Chou En-lai; several Western newsmen were also granted visas to accompany the U.S. team to Beijing. Nixon announced that the United States would expedite visas for PRC citizens to visit the United States. U.S. currency controls would be relaxed to permit the PRC to use dollars, while eliminating most restrictions on U.S. oil companies providing fuel to ships and aircraft to China. U.S. ships and aircraft would be permitted to carry Chinese cargoes and U.S.-owned foreign flag carriers could call at Chinese ports. Many nonstrategic items could be exported to the PRC direct. (Edgar Snow reported at this time a conversation with Mao to the effect that Nixon would be welcome in China.)
- May 1971—Controls on dollar transactions with China and on certain U.S. bunkering facilities were removed.
- June 1971—The twenty-one-year-old embargo on trade with China was lifted.
- July 1971—Kissinger made a secret visit to Beijing.
- October 1971—Kissinger visited Beijing again to discuss preparations for the Nixon trip.[3]

Chinese Reactions

Chinese initial reactions to U.S. initiatives were neither positive nor negative. Lack of any angry outcry or rejection of U.S. efforts over time was viewed by China specialists as a positive signal, a favorable condition for continuing the process toward normalization. The United States also took meticulous steps to ensure that the Chinese correctly understood U.S. actions and motives. Every policy statement was scrupulously couched to avoid misunderstanding or polemics, particularly in any apparent tilting of position toward the Sino-Soviet dispute. At the time U.S. policy toward the USSR was one of promoting and sustaining détente.

Given these favorable circumstances, with the successful Kissinger secret mission to Beijing and the virtual certainty of PRC admittance into the United Nations in the fall of 1971, China also took some conciliatory steps by releasing two American prisoners and commuting another's life sentence to five years in December 1971, two months before the Nixon visit.

In February 1972, Nixon was accorded a tumultuous welcome in Beijing, instantly transforming the street crowds from old hostility to a new hospitality. The arrival was viewed by large television audiences throughout China and was, without doubt, the most dramatic chapter in the history of recent U.S.-Chinese relations. However, it would be prudent here to point out the problems as well as the successes arising from this historic event, as both sides acted cautiously not to raise the level of expectations. The Shanghai Communiqué of February 28 acknowledged:

There are essential differences between China and the United States in their social systems and foreign policies. However, the two sides agreed that countries, regardless of their social systems, should conduct their relations on the principles of respect for the sovereignty and territorial integrity of all states, non-aggression against other states, non-interference in the internal affairs of other states, equality and mutual benefit, and peaceful coexistence. International disputes should be settled on this basis, without resorting to the use or threat of force. The U.S. and China are prepared to apply these principles to their mutual relations.

Taiwan, clearly too difficult an issue to be resolved quickly, was placed on the back burner by Mao and Chou, who stated that China could wait twenty, fifty, even a hundred years for its resolution. Both sides were nevertheless eager to establish a communications link as an initial step toward normalization of relations. In the Shanghai Communiqué each side stated its assessments and positions independently, without expressing agreement or disagreement with the other's positions. Thus both sides were able to agree to disagree on Taiwan. Procedurally, they agreed that the Chinese position would come first in the Chinese text of the communiqué and the U.S. position first in the English version. Although the phrasing was made deliberately ambiguous to avoid disagreement and contention, Sinologists view and interpret the document variously, especially with respect to the issue of Taiwan.

The 1972 Nixon visit established a new relationship between the world's most populous country and the world's most powerful country, but the lack of mutual recognition presented knotty political, legal, and economic problems, notwithstanding that some progress was made in trade, tourism, and cultural exchange.

In December 1975, President Gerald Ford visited China during the closing months of the Cultural Revolution. China was then in a chaotic state, its political and economic institutions crippled by the Cultural Revolution. Both Mao and Chou were in declining health and Sino-Soviet relations were steadily deteriorating. Deng Xiaoping, twice purged by Mao, reemerged and took over control of the country after Chou was hospitalized in 1975. Not only did Deng perform the functions normally performed by Chou, but he also set about establishing a new program to reconstruct the country, which had been devastated by Mao's policies. It was the beginning of a period of restored domestic tranquillity, economic growth, and diplomatic outreach. With respect to international relations, Deng and his colleagues, perceiving a growing Soviet threat, intensified the rhetorical attack on Soviet hegemonism as Chinese-Soviet relations progressively worsened. And the Soviet border negotiating team headed by Leonid Ilyichev returned to Moscow empty-handed.

When Kissinger visited Beijing in October 1975 to arrange for the visit of President Ford, he was literally lectured by Chinese officials on U.S. naiveté in desiring détente with the Soviets. Hard-line Chinese officials insisted that the only way to deal with hegemonism was to wage a tit-for-tat struggle against it.[4]

In the United States, meantime, some observers questioned the wisdom of sending the president to a country so far away when so many problems beset the administration at home, such as unemployment and other economic woes, as well as the need for negotiating an arms reduction agreement with the Soviets. Was the Ford visit to China really necessary? Was U.S.-China rapprochement in trouble?

Ford administration officials stated that there was good reason for the president to visit China: The leaders of both countries could exchange views and keep the normalization process moving; high-level contacts served to highlight the importance both governments attached to the relationship; and the meetings were part of a continuing process of normalization. The U.S outreach was particularly important, as the Chinese expressed uncertainty as to how strongly the United States was committed to the relationship in the post-Watergate period. Such a visit would also bring about on each side a better comprehension of the major policy directions of the other, while ascertaining the extent to which each agreed or disagreed on certain international issues. Although China sharply attacked détente and the Helsinki Conference, it was nevertheless important for the United States to let the Chinese hear its views on these and other matters, for China's interest in the United States depended on the leaders' perception of how effectively Washington performed internationally and how well the administration was able to carry out its policies or to get domestic support for them. This trip was not so much aimed at negotiating a specific agreement; rather, it was aimed at reaffirming U.S. determination to complete normalization of relations with China on the basis of the Shanghai Communiqué.

The Chinese, on the other hand, wanted an opportunity to tell the U.S. president and his secretary of state directly and in public that Washington's policy toward the USSR was all wrong, and that the United States should adopt a firmer, more aggressive posture toward the Soviet regime.

For some time, as a result of deteriorating relations with the Soviets, the Chinese had viewed the USSR as an expansionist power, aggressive, and hegemonistic, as evidenced in the Soviet military buildup in East Asia and its increased use of seaports and airfields in Vietnam. To the Chinese, Moscow's moves posed a threat to them, potential if not immediate. Clearly, China would like to see Soviet advances halted or retarded by maneuvering the United States into a more active anti-Soviet role. The United States, for reasons of global stability and its own national interests, continued to pursue a policy of détente and was making a serious effort to reduce the level of nuclear arms. Unlike China, which believed in the inevitability of war, the United States considered that any direct confrontation with the Soviets in the nuclear age would be suicidal for both sides. The Chinese criticized this view as one of appeasement to Moscow and one likely to increase rather than decrease tension and the likelihood of war.

A warm welcome was accorded President Ford in Beijing. There was no major diplomatic breakthrough, but the visit did much to nurture a fragile relationship by accelerating the normalization process within the framework established by the Shanghai Communiqué. It also gave the U.S. president a personal view of the changing PRC leadership, while the two sides could pursue parallel policies vis-à-vis certain international issues where Chinese and American interests intersected.

Taiwan remained the most sensitive issue in the discussions. Given the coming elections in 1976 and the strong, residual sentiment in the United States for the people of Taiwan, the U.S. government stood firm on the positions expressed in the Shanghai Communiqué and did not succumb to Beijing's pressure.

Establishing Diplomatic Relations
in January 1979

Watergate was a major factor distracting any concentrated U.S. effort toward China. Thus lack of formal diplomatic relations continued to impede development of bilateral relations. It took another three years following the Ford visit before full official relations were established. The progress was complicated by the fact that the United States recognized the government of the Republic of China (ROC) in Taiwan, while maintaining a mutual defense treaty with that government and stationing U.S. military personnel on the island. In order to move normalization off dead center, the Chinese implicitly set forth three conditions: (1) derecognize the government in Taiwan; (2) terminate the mutual defense treaty; and (3) remove all U.S. military personnel from the island. These requirements surprised some Americans, since Taiwan had been placed in abeyance by Mao and Chou earlier. Negotiations dragged on over many months. Derecognition of the ROC government was most traumatic for that government, as the United States had to remove all its official personnel from the island and close the ROC embassy in Washington and consulates in major U.S. cities.

Equally difficult was termination of the mutual defense treaty. The move engendered adverse reactions overseas as well as in the United States. Within the region the notion that the United States could unilaterally abrogate a mutual defense treaty with a long-time ally raised questions about U.S. reliability and commitment. In the United States, sentiment for Taiwan remained strong, as indicated by public opinion polls and congressional actions to ensure continuation of a viable relationship with Taiwan. The issue of terminating a treaty was particularly troublesome in Congress, though it was recognized that even without a defense treaty the president had the power under the War Powers Act to take any steps deemed necessary to protect U.S. interests in Taiwan or elsewhere. Instead of abrogation, the United States and the PRC finally agreed to the treaty's explicit provision under Article 10, which states that "either party may terminate it one year after notice has been given to the other party."

China took no action to contradict the U.S. position calling for a peaceful settlement of the Taiwan question, while repeatedly stating its own position that Taiwan is a domestic issue and that China alone had the right to settle it in a manner that best suited its national interests. This position was reaffirmed by Deng Xiaoping during his visit to the United States in January 1979, when he refused to rule out the use of force, if necessary, to reunite Taiwan and the mainland.

Establishment of diplomatic relations was announced simultaneously in Washington and Beijing on December 15, 1978, to become effective on January 1, 1979. In the recognition communiqué, aside from reaffirming the principles agreed to in the Shanghai Communiqué, both sides restated their positions to reduce international military conflict, oppose hegemony by any power, and acknowledge that there is one China and Taiwan is part of China. In a sense, for the United States, diplomatic recognition was simply a matter of accepting the realities and formalizing its dealings with Beijing since the Nixon visit.

Many felt, however, that the security and commercial interests of the United States and the needs of the people of Taiwan were not adequately addressed, despite President Jimmy Carter's assurance that the United States was confident that the people of Taiwan faced a peaceful and prosperous future, and that the American people and the people of Taiwan would maintain commercial, cultural, and other relations.[5]

Meanwhile, Senators Alan Cranston and Edward Kennedy, along with twenty-seven other senators, introduced a joint resolution that required the president and Congress to initiate action to protect U.S. interests, peace, and security in the region, as well as the island's people. A similar resolution was introduced by Congressman Lester Wolff in the House. Both resolutions were intended to correct the misperception that U.S. recognition of the PRC meant abandonment of Taiwan.[6]

After several negotiating sessions with the Chinese, the U.S. government was able to keep more than fifty existing treaties and agreements between Washington and Taipei, which later formed the basis for a new unofficial relationship with Taiwan on cultural, social, and commercial activities. Meantime, Congress modified President Carter's draft legislation on Taiwan which, coupled with some of the main points of the Joint Resolutions, became what is known as the Taiwan Relations Act (TRA) of April 1979.

Taiwan Relations Act and Arms Sales

The TRA enables the United States to conduct unofficial relations with Taiwan on a wide range of activities, including sales of defense weapons. The PRC protested most strongly against it as totally unacceptable and harmful to U.S.-PRC relations. After assurances by the Carter administration that the TRA would be interpreted within the context of the U.S.-PRC normalization agreement, Beijing acquiesced to an arrangement that continued to hamper the smooth functioning of bilateral relations in the ensuing months.

At the time of establishing official relations with Beijing in January 1979, Washington acknowledged the Chinese position that there is one China and

Taiwan is part of China, while reiterating that the United States had no intention of infringing on Chinese sovereignty or interfering with China's internal affairs. This principle was mutually recognized and respected. But the question of arms sales to Taiwan, which was not resolved at the time of normalization, remained unsettled.

The TRA, signed into law by President Carter on April 10, 1979, specifically provides Taiwan with arms of a defensive nature under Section 2.5, and under Section 2.6 it asserts the right of the United States to resist force or other coercion that would jeopardize the security or the social or economic system of the people on Taiwan. To this China vigorously objected. In response, the United States assured the Chinese that China's fundamental policy of a peaceful resolution of the Taiwan question would, in due course, permit gradual reduction in U.S. arms sales.

The Chinese demanded a termination date for U.S. arms sales to Taiwan, but the United States refused because the level of arms sales must be determined by the defense needs of Taiwan under the TRA. The guiding principle, according to John Holdridge when he testified before the House Foreign Affairs Committee on August 18, 1982, was that embodied in the TRA: the maintenance of a self-defense capability sufficient to meet the military needs of Taiwan, but with the understanding that China's maintenance of a peaceful approach to the Taiwan question will permit gradual reduction in arms sales.[7]

Given the importance the United States attached to relations with the PRC and the impact those links would have on peace and stability in the region, the United States conceded in the August 17, 1982, communiqué that it did not seek to carry out a long-term policy of arms sales, that arms sales would not exceed qualitatively or quantitatively the levels established since normalization, and that it intended to reduce sales of weapons to Taiwan gradually over a period of time to a final resolution. However, Beijing officials remained dissatisfied particularly over the speed and U.S. intent, and they have raised this issue repeatedly over the past several years as an impediment to the progress of U.S.-PRC relations.

The August 17 communiqué must be read as a whole, since the policies it sets forth are interrelated. Because the communiqué is a vague document, each side interpreted it in its own way. The Chinese claimed a victory in their efforts to limit U.S. arms sales to Taiwan, while the U.S. said it did not give away anything. In a separate statement, President Reagan declared that the United States would continue to sell arms to Taiwan in accordance with the provisions of the TRA, and that if both parties across the Taiwan Strait could agree to become one China in a peaceful manner, then the question of U.S. arms sales to Taiwan would become moot.[8]

In January 1984, Premier Zhao Ziyang visited the United States. In general, the visit was deemed successful, inasmuch as it helped Zhao and his entourage broaden their views and perceptions of U.S. policies and motives, as did the visit of Deng Xiaoping in January 1979. More importantly, the visit exposed Zhao to a wide range of individuals and institutions, enabling him to gain a deep appreciation and understanding of a pluralistic society unlike his own. As a result of this brief exposure Zhao seemed to exude more confidence in himself and more openness in his dealings with foreigners. From this perspective, the Zhao visit was viewed as useful in promoting and expanding U.S.-China relations.

Three months after the Zhao visit, President Reagan paid a "reciprocal" visit to China from April 26 to May 1. In retrospect, the Reagan visit should also be seen as another step in the tedious process of expanding and stabilizing relations between the two countries—not as one keyed to negotiating a treaty or resolving troublesome problems.

The Reagan visit underscored the importance the United States attached to the U.S.-China relationship. The president's personal involvement demonstrated the high-level U.S. commitment to the relationship. It also pointed to the consistency of American policy in the four administrations, from Nixon to Ford to Carter to Reagan, in developing and improving relations with the PRC. The visit provided the president an opportunity to reiterate the durability and reliability of the U.S. commitment and U.S. willingness to help China in its modernization program so that it could play a constructive role in the region. It sent out a message not only to the Chinese but also to U.S. friends and allies in the region.

Reagan met with Deng Xiaoping, General Secretary Hu Yaobang, and Premier Zhao Ziyang. In these meetings and at other forums Reagan took the opportunity to convey U.S. views of the world to the Chinese leadership and people. At an address to a select group of 500 leaders representing various sectors of Chinese society, Reagan criticized Soviet policy while highlighting American freedoms and democratic values. Beijing promptly deleted from a television transmission to the national audience such presidential statements as this: "America's troops are not massed on China's borders; and we occupy no lands. Nor do we commit wanton acts such as shooting 269 innocent people out of the sky for the so-called cause of sacred airspace. . . . We love peace and we cherish freedom because we have learned time and again, in place after place, that economic growth and human progress make their greatest strides when people are secure and free to think, speak, worship, choose their own way."

Reacting to the television omission, White House spokesman Larry Speakes said, "We had made it clear to the Chinese government prior to the trip that we hoped for an opportunity for the President to communicate with the Chinese people on the American approach to world affairs, its basis in our system, and the goals we seek in our relationship with the PRC." Speakes went on to say, "The U.S. Government regrets that statements by the President, which would have given the Chinese people a better understanding of our government and its people, were not included in Chinese media coverage of the speech."[9]

A senior PRC journalist explained to me at the Great Wall Hotel that when Premier Zhao visited New York in January, his speech was neither carried in total by the U.S. press nor broadcast to a nationwide audience in the United States. The Chinese government had the right, the journalist said, to delete portions of the president's speech that might cause further confusion and misunderstanding. He pointed out that most of Reagan's speech had been broadcast by China's national network and there was no reason for complaint. Though the censorship aspect was played up by the Western press and defended by the PRC foreign ministry, the complete and uncensored remarks of the president were later transmitted to radio listeners in China by the Voice of America.

During the visit, several agreements were initialed or signed. These had been in the works for some time and most of them only required an official stamp of approval. The agreement to avoid double taxation, for example, had been completed by Treasury Secretary Donald Regan in his visit to Peking in March 1984. In addition to the tax agreement, an implementing accord to the Cultural Agreement, an expanded agreement on managing industrial science and technology, an agreement on scientific and technical information exchange, and an agreement on peaceful use of nuclear energy were either initialed or signed. Premier Zhao characterized the signing of agreements and protocols as a significant achievement expressing the spirit of "mutual respect and mutual benefit." Several other important agreements, such as those concerned with civil aviation, investment, and maritime matters, were still being negotiated at the time of the visit.

The initialing of the nuclear cooperation agreement was premature, because the Chinese had not agreed in writing to any special safeguards on nuclear energy use, even though China had joined the International Atomic Energy Agency (IAEA) in January 1984. Nor had China signed the nonproliferation treaty, which provides for inspection, guarantees, and other safeguards. Because of congressional criticism, the Department of State delayed for more than a year its submission of the agreement to Congress for review. Beijing accused Washington of insincerity and inconsistency.

Current Issues

Nuclear Cooperation Agreement

One of the more controversial issues is indeed the nuclear cooperation agreement, signed by U.S. Secretary of Energy John Herrington and Chinese Vice Premier Li Peng during President Li Xiannian's visit to Washington on July 23, 1985. President Reagan submitted it to Congress the following day, and despite heated questioning there it became law in December after the administration narrowly defeated several congressional attempts to frustrate it.

The controversy centered on nuclear proliferation. In Congress, Senator John Glenn introduced an amendment to the government spending authorization bill that would require the president to certify that U.S. nuclear materials sold to China are subject to IAEA safeguards against the spread of nuclear weapons. The House also, by a nearly three-to-one vote, passed a resolution that, in essence, expressed concern about the lack of written assurances from the Chinese on their commitment to nonproliferation. They cited the following as evidence: (1) China's refusal to sign the 1968 Nuclear Nonproliferation Treaty (NPT); (2) the fact that Chou En-lai once called the NPT "a great conspiracy" and "the hegemonic practice" of superpowers to deny the small and medium-sized countries the opportunity to develop their nuclear capability; (3) the fact that China undertook no international legal obligations and had no policy to require safeguards and other controls on its nuclear exports; and (4) China's reported assistance in Pakistan's development of a nuclear bomb. With respect to the last point, a series of recent intelligence reports showed China's nuclear scientists spending considerable time at the centrifuge plant in Kahuta where Pakistani scientists were attempting to produce enriched uranium, which can be used to trigger a nuclear explosion.[10]

Reactions from Beijing were swift and loud. The Glenn amendment, said a PRC foreign ministry spokesman, raised "unreasonable demands . . . to unilaterally change some substantive provisions of the pact. . . . And any unilaterally imposed additional provisions beyond the agreement are unacceptable."

What is overlooked by critics, in my view, is the pressure of international competition for the China market. In the last several years European powers and Japan have looked longingly at the huge energy market in China and have been ready to participate in China's ambitious plans for nuclear power generation. The French firm Framatome, for example, using reactor technology originally licensed to it by Westinghouse, already has joined with the General Electric Company of Britain and a Hong Kong firm to open a major nuclear power station at Daya Bay across from the British colony.[11] The Japanese have similarly demonstrated an interest in the nuclear power station near Shanghai.

The United States opened talks on peaceful nuclear cooperation with the PRC in 1981 and intensified them in 1983. During these negotiations, nuclear nonproliferation was, according to Assistant Secretary of State Paul Wolfowitz, the paramount concern of the United States. However, the press tended to highlight the monetary aspect of the deal—that is, enormous economic gains for the United States from large contracts to aid the sagging U.S. nuclear power industry. Although there are profits to be made, the economic element in nuclear cooperation with the PRC has been highly exaggerated.

The agreement is now law, but it should be understood that it simply provides the legal framework within which nuclear cooperation may take place. It is not a U.S. commitment to provide nuclear reactors, components, fuel, or technology to China. The specifics must be negotiated by U.S. suppliers under licenses issued by the Nuclear Regulatory Commission, in accordance with existing U.S. law and regulations.

The question is, how can it be certain that U.S. materials and technology will not be misused? Kenneth L. Adelman, director of the Arms Control and Disarmament Agency, testifying before the House Foreign Affairs Committee on July 31, 1985, made these points:

- First, China pledged that it does not engage in nuclear proliferation, nor does it help other countries develop nuclear weapons. The substance of this pledge has been reaffirmed several times by Chinese officials, both abroad and within China. In fact, China's sixth National People's Congress expressed this policy in a directive to all agencies of that large and complex government.
- Second, in January 1984, China joined the International Atomic Energy Agency, which plays a critical role in international nonproliferation efforts.
- Third, China adopted a policy of requiring IAEA safeguards on its nuclear exports to non-nuclear-weapon states.
- Fourth, during hours of discussions, the Chinese have made it clear to the United States that they will implement their policies in a manner consistent with the basic nonproliferation practices that the United States and others support so vigorously.
- Adelman also attributed China's change of direction from the 1960s and 1970s, when China rejected nonproliferation norms, to its later support of nonproliferation policies and practices as a turnabout of historic significance. He assured the congressmen that the agreement would be an important step in helping China to be part of the nonproliferation solution rather than part of the problem.[12]

Ambassador Richard Kennedy, a key figure in the negotiations with Beijing, also seemed satisfied with the agreement which, he said, met all the requirements in Section 123 of the Atomic Energy Act of 1954, as amended, for nuclear cooperation agreements with nuclear-weapon countries. Section 123 requires that such agreements contain several guarantees by the cooperating partner:

- The first guarantee is that no nuclear materials or equipment subject to the agreement will be used for any nuclear explosive device, for research on or development of any nuclear explosive, or for any other military purpose. This requirement is met by article 5, paragraph 3 of the proposed agreement with the PRC.
- The second guarantee required is that no nuclear material or equipment subject to the agreement will be transferred beyond the jurisdiction or control of the cooperating party without the agreement of the United States. This requirement is met by article 5, paragraph 1 of the agreement.
- The third guarantee required is that adequate physical security will be maintained with respect to any nuclear material subject to the agreement. This requirement is met by article 6 of the agreement.
- The fourth guarantee required is that no nuclear material subject to the agreement will be enriched, reprocessed, altered in form or content, or (in the case of weapons-usable materials) stored without the prior agreement of the United States. This requirement is met by article 5, paragraph 2 of the agreement.[13]

In spite of repeated administration assurances that China's commitments to nuclear nonproliferation are dependable, the issue will remain highly contentious in the months to come. The real test will come at the implementation stage—that is, when U.S. suppliers apply for licenses for exporting specific nuclear equipment and technology to China. Congress will have another opportunity to question and to approve or disapprove.

Arms Sales to the PRC

Since the United States established diplomatic relations with Beijing in 1979, there have been two government-to-government arms transactions. The first was a $98 million Foreign Military Sales (FMS) sale of equipment and a design to build a factory for artillery and other ammunitions in September 1985, although earlier the PRC had purchased twenty-four S70C2 Sikorsky helicopters (a civilian version of the military Black Hawk) and had signed a contract with General Electric for five GE LM2500 gas turbine engines for destroyers.[14]

The second transaction was the advanced avionics package, reportedly worth $500 million, that was agreed to during the unpublicized visit of a PRC delegation headed by Xie Guang, deputy director of China's leading defense procurement and research agency, in November 1985. Under the arrangement, the Chinese would get off-the-shelf electronic equipment, to be integrated by U.S. defense contractors in fifty Chinese-built F-8 interceptors to enable these aircraft to operate in all sorts of weather. Defense contractors such as McDonnell-Douglas, Boeing, Grumman, and Northrop would provide radar, navigational, and fire-control systems for the avionics package.[15]

The package must still go through the COCOM consultation and approval procedures, but such approval is expected, and the deal is considered likely to go forward. Congress will also have an opportunity to scrutinize this transaction. Questions have been raised anew about the implications—whether the transaction will significantly alter the equilibrium of international relations in the region, and whether it will enable Beijing, with advanced military equipment, to use or threaten to use its power beyond its borders. Moreover, what this will mean to the security of Taiwan, in which the United States has a role to play under the 1979 TRA, is a matter of deep concern.[16] Some conservative members of Congress have begun to press the Reagan administration to upgrade Taiwan's F-5E fighters, contending that improved PRC F-8s would erode the island's traditional air superiority and imperil the ROC's defense.

U.S. defense officials downplayed the importance of the avionics package, stressing that it would not pose a threat to Taiwan because the F-8 is designed for the defensive mission of shooting down incoming bombers. Writing for the *Washington Post*, correspondent Michael Weisskopf said: "The proposed sale is seen as an important test of the two-pronged U.S. policy of forging military relations with the communist government in Beijing while guaranteeing the defense capability of the capitalist government on Taiwan."[17]

Several recent exploratory missions indicate that further arms sales to the PRC are likely. Last fall, for example, a group of U.S. defense industry executives visited China to discuss and familiarize themselves with the modalities of U.S.-PRC cooperative ventures. U.S. executives from Boeing, Ford, Honeywell, Hughes Aircraft, Lockheed, Martin Marietta, and Rockwell International visited electronics, armored-vehicle, aircraft, and shipbuilding factories and were well received by the Chinese.[18]

Early in 1986 a large-scale international exhibition of weapons and defense technology was held in Beijing, with more than 160 companies from seventeen countries and regions participating. The largest contingent came from the United States, including eighteen aerospace and defense companies represented in the joint exhibition organized by American Aerospace Industries, Inc. Although the Chinese are noted for "doing much window-shopping but little buying," the fact that defense cooperation is part of the whole process of normalization of U.S.-PRC relations will attract foreign defense industries to the potential Chinese market. The main problem is, of course, the availability of foreign exchange for arms purchases. According to one U.S. defense industry representative in Beijing, China is vigorously pushing an arms sales policy of its own, with more than $1 billion worth of small arms sold overseas in 1984. He expects that China, with increased accrual of foreign exchange from its own overseas arms sales programs, will be able incrementally to buy the more sophisticated equipment it cannot yet produce itself.[19]

Trade and Technology Transfer

Bilateral trade between the PRC and the United States reached $8.1 billion in 1985, a 25 percent increase over 1984. This was about double the U.S. trade with India and almost triple the U.S. trade with the Soviet Union. Despite this dramatic growth, however, there are major commercial frictions, as demonstrated in the joint venture between the American Motors Company and the Beijing Jeep Corporation, which was suspended for a period of time. This and other joint ventures have been confronted with an increasing number of problems, such as shortage of foreign exchange, high cost of doing business in China, lack of skilled workers, uneven application of tax law and regulations, and limited access to local markets and material. On the other hand, it is not unfair to say that unrealistic expectations, emphasis on short-term gains rather than long-term commitment to development, and protectionist legislation on textiles on the part of the United States have also contributed to current misunderstanding and frictions. Moreover, the inability of the two countries to reach an agreement on investment, which would have dealt with arbitration of disputes, problems of expropriation, and contractual arrangements, has likewise hampered development of a more harmonious trade relationship.

In the case of technology transfer, frictions have also increased in frequency, especially over the speed and scope of high technology transferable to China. In many respects, the approval process has been unusually slow and cumbersome because of differing perspectives of U.S. government agencies as well as diverse views among the allies over technology sharing. It is not unusual to see a backlog of export license applications. In February 1985, for example, the United States had 877 applications for export licenses pending at COCOM, the mechanism controlling the flow of strategic products to communist countries, and 807 of these were for products destined for China. For NATO and Japan, about two-thirds of their license applications for export to China were still on hold at COCOM. In recent months, however, the U.S. government has made a determined effort to streamline the procedures for licensing high-technology items in consonance with security considerations. Whether this will lower the level of Chinese discontent remains to be seen. (It is not the intent of this chapter to go into any detailed discussion of trade or technology transfer but merely to refer to them in the context of the overall relationship.)

Looking Ahead

What are the prospects that U.S.-PRC relations will move from hostility to reconciliation to cooperation? The president is certainly optimistic. But political realities tell us otherwise. Of course, no one can predict the future with any degree of certainty, given the fact that so many variables are involved in a given situation—not only the domestic politics and economy of the United States but also the changing political dynamics of China, not to mention the international situation at a given time.

One of the questions one can legitimately raise is this: Can the bilateral relationship be stabilized to the extent that a steady, normal relationship will be the norm? This process calls for a lot of give-and-take by both countries. For example, the United States must give a higher priority to promoting mutual interests rather than national self-interest, on long-term development rather than short-term gains, and on mutual trust rather than distrust. On the other hand, China must continue to develop and maintain enlightened leadership and realistic political and economic reforms while expressing a higher degree of reciprocity in dealing with the United States.

The next several years will be crucial to U.S.-Chinese relations. If both sides can demonstrate maturity and mutual trust in managing the ongoing problems, such as the status of Taiwan and arms sales, there is resaon to expect that a stable relationship can be achieved.

Further amplifications of the preceding scenario are necessary. Given a convergence of interests in the economic area, the United States can more vigorously assist China in its economic modernization with the transfer of appropriate technology and management skills. This effort will also help the United States in economic growth and expansion while offsetting some of the balance-of-payment problems.

Second, it is important that the United States construct a comprehensive, coherent strategy to advance mutual relations over several fronts simultaneously. Any fragmentary approach for short-term gains, as evidenced by some of the recent U.S. initiatives, will not advance but may hinder U.S. goals in the long run. As China vows to pursue a nonaligned, independent foreign policy and not to allow itself to be manipulated in superpower confrontation, it will be more hazardous, not less, for the United States to play the China card vis-à-vis the Soviet Union. Thus, in the area of defense cooperation, there should be a more carefully thought-out plan in consonance with efforts to promote U.S. regional and global objectives.

Third, in dealing with the Chinese leadership, the United States must learn to be more persistent and patient. Vacillation creates distrust, which does not breed a healthy relationship. Similarly, lack of patience is often seen as a sign of weakness and immaturity, and it can hinder development of a mutually beneficial relationship.

Finally, there is a need to fill the sizable communication gap in the cultural dimension. Chinese and American institutions were developed on different bases. The same word in the language is understood differently because of different cultural backgrounds, languages, and expectations. More people-to-people contacts will help, but there is a greater need for mutual recognition of the differences, and more efforts should be made to narrow the gap by increasing the facilities for U.S. and Chinese studies.

From China's perspective, economic modernization is a positive and significant plan. It can transform China into a modern state, but it is no panacea for the country's manifold problems. The scope and nature of the PRC's economic reforms, unless carefully managed and monitored, can also generate potentially disruptive social implications. For example, greater reliance on the market may produce disparities of wealth among groups and among regions in China. One group left behind may be the politically powerful party cadres, who live on fixed and low incomes. Old party members who recall with nostalgia the more puritanical revolutionary days may be unhappy with even limited mixed economic policies.

Thus, in the next several years, potential problems besetting China will still be enormous. Corruption is already emerging in a number of places. There is genuine worry about inflation and the old way of managing the economy. It is true that the PRC has taken a number of steps to correct the social anomalies and has instituted some longer-term structural reforms. The economic experiments and changes are important and necessary, as are the experiments in political leadership in which hundreds of senior party and government officials have been replaced with younger, better trained professionals, who will guide China into the twenty-first century. The Ministry of Education has likewise instituted drastic structural changes to transform a Soviet-style centralized educational system into one more closely resembling Western models. But only time will tell whether these and other measures taken will be sufficient to control the problems associated with China's intense drive toward modernization. Thus it can be said that China's modernization program is not free of risk, nor is it certain of success.

As we look ahead to the 1990s, we should not harbor unrealistic expectations in the bilateral relationship. There are fundamental differences in the political and economic systems between the United States, a capitalist country, and China, a communist one. We should keep our wits about us and not subject ourselves to all sorts of illusions. No less important is our recognition of the limitations on ways the United States can decisively influence the course of Chinese developments. Thus the U.S.-PRC relationship in all probability will continue to go up and down in response to interactive political dynamics at a given time.

Notes

Chinese names in this chapter are rendered in the way they were used at the time. The pinyin system is used in the later period.

1. *Department of State Bulletin*, February 14, 1972, p. 183.
2. *Department of State Bulletin*, May 2, 1966, pp. 694–695.
3. *Department of State Bulletin*, March 13, 1972, pp. 327–329.
4. See Kissinger interview in Tokyo, *Department of State Bulletin*, November 17, 1975, pp. 683–685; Kissinger interview in Peking, *Department of State Bulletin*, December 29, 1975, pp. 926–932.
5. *Department of State Bulletin*, February 1979, pp. 24–25.
6. "Implementation of the TRA: Issues and Concerns," in Hearings of House Subcommittee on Asian and Pacific Affairs, February 14–15, 1979, pp. 2–9.
7. Ibid., June 11, 17, July 30, 1980.
8. *Department of State Bulletin*, October 1982, p. 21.
9. *Washington Post*, April 28, 1984; also text of statement distributed in Peking.
10. *Far Eastern Economic Review*, January 23, 1986, p. 48.
11. *Washington Post*, January 12, 1986.
12. *Department of State Bulletin*, October 1985, pp. 19–20.
13. Ibid., p. 21.
14. *Far Eastern Economic Review*, January 2, 1986, pp. 11–12; *Washington Post*, September 19, 1985.
15. *Washington Post*, March 22, 1986; *Far Eastern Economic Review*, January 2, 1986, pp. 11–12.
16. See Martin L. Lasater's comments in Heritage's Executive Memorandum, January 15, 1986; also "The Taiwan Issue in Sino-American Relations" in Heritage Lectures No. 49; Heritage Lectures No. 53 (delivered by Lasater at the National Security Studies Seminar, Georgetown University, March 8–9, 1986).
17. *Washington Post*, March 22, 1986; also Heritage Lectures Nos. 49 and 53.
18. *Washington Post*, November 5, 1985.
19. *Washington Post*, January 28, 1986.

18

Relations Between Peking, Washington, and Taipei: Maintaining the Forbidden Triad or Building Fayol's Bridge?

Peter Kien-hong Yu

In this chapter, we shall engage in a creative, preliminary exercise on the study of the relations of the People's Republic of China (PRC) with the United States and the Republic of China (ROC). In so doing, we shall first integrate and somewhat modify several interesting concepts as well as models relating to triadic relationships. Second, based on the preceding, we shall study relations between the three actors from Peking's perspective. And in the third section, we shall dwell on Taipei's strategies toward Peking and Washington in the foreseeable future.

Concepts and Models on Triadic Relationships

Relations between three actors are not as simple as they may seem. They range from the simple form of AB, AC, and BC to twenty-seven complex forms. Over the years, close to thirty verbal as well as mathematical models related to triadic relationships have been constructed by scholars.[1] In this study, we shall (1) integrate and somewhat modify those concepts and models as developed by Mark S. Granovetter,[2] Henri Fayol,[3] and Steven J. Brams,[4] (2) arrange them in accordance with the way in which we shall conduct our analysis, and (3) derive appropriate propositions from them. We shall first introduce the concept of the Forbidden Triad.

The Forbidden Triad

Figure 18.1 represents what Granovetter has come up with in his study "The Strength of Weak Ties." A set of appropriate propositions can be drawn from this figure:

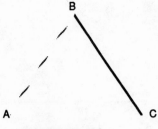

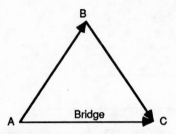

FIGURE 18.1   FIGURE 18.2
The Forbidden Triad   A Triadic Relationship with Fayol's Bridge

1. There are three actors, A, B, and C;
2. A and B maintain ties;
3. B and C are also tied together;
4. There is an absence of ties between A and C;
5. Collapse of the triad is possible—such pressure can come from A because A wants to bring about the demise of C and vice versa; and
6. B plays a unique role in the present form, and it is not likely to disappear from the scene, should the collapse take place, as noted in proposition 5 or as a result of B's destructive action against A and/ or C.

Intuitively, we can speak of three kinds of ties:

1. The strong tie (denoted by solid line), whereby two actors maintain both diplomatic and economic relations;
2. The weak tie (denoted by broken line), whereby two actors have either the diplomatic or the economic relationship; and
3. Absence of ties, whereby two actors lack any relationship and, even if they do, their ties are without substantial significance.

Fayol's Bridge

When there is an absence of ties between A and C, as depicted in Figure 18.1, a message, nonetheless, can still be passed up from A to B and then back down to C. Using Fayol's Bridge, or the path connecting A and C, the message can be sent directly from A to C, as shown in Figure 18.2, and vice versa as the case may be.

Building on Figure 18.1, a set of other propositions can be made from Figure 18.2:

1. The central focus of this figure is on the "linear" bridge-building or the eventual establishment of ties between A and C;
2. Unless the bridge has been completed, the bridge-building process is still considered as part of the era of the Forbidden Triad;

3. The bridge cannot be "built" automatically—that is, efforts must be made by A, if A has a vested interest in such a bridge-building;

4. A can "build" a great portion of the bridge by itself, which means that A has to spend more resources than C and has to make more concessions in return for C's eventual acceptance of A;

5. A can "build" the bridge halfway, waiting for C to complete the other half;

6. Bridge-building can be halted by A for one reason or another;

7. If C finds bridge-building not in its interest, C may find A's bridge-building to be threatening;

8. It takes two to complete the construction of a bridge, that is, to connect from one end to the other end; this statement implies that bridge-building by A could be resisted by C;

9. Without the bridge, A would have to traverse greater distance from A to B and then to C, and the quality of such a relay could be dampened on each wave of retelling; and

10. B can encourage, discourage, or do nothing about the bridge-building.

Twenty-seven Indecomposable Forms

We shall assume that A's desire to build the bridge will be eventually fulfilled, leading to what we shall refer to as the Eternal Triad in the next phase of relationship. Once that process has taken place, relations between A, B, and C will develop into what Brams has called the "twenty-seven indecomposable forms" (see Figure 18.3): "An arrow indicates the direction of asymmetry for each linked dyad (AB, BC, and CA): A⟶B, for example, indicates that the relationship between actors A and B is asymmetrical and, in addition, that the direction of the asymmetry is from actor A to actor B. Two arrows going in opposite directions indicate a symmetrical relationship between two actors."[5] A few more propositions can be made with regard to C. Assuming that C in Figure 18.2 is an underdog, the triads, as developed by Brams, actually help C, whereas the opposite is true of A, which has, in effect, opened a Pandora's box of twenty-seven forms for C to work with. Thus, C can (1) exert "direct" influence on A in nine different circumstances (6, 8, 10, 16, 17, 22, 24, 25, and 26) and (2) "neutralize" A in nine other different circumstances (1, 2, 4, 5, 7, 9, 12, 15, and 18). As to B, we shall assume that it is still the "enjoying third," not to be seriously affected by such structural change.

Having spelled out the basics, we are in a position to conduct our brief analysis of the PRC's relations with the United States and the ROC since 1949.

Peking's Relations with Washington and Taipei

In October 1949, after World War II, the PRC government was proclaimed in Peking after years of civil war. However, its archenemy, the ROC government, managed to relocate its capital from Nanking to Taipei. Given

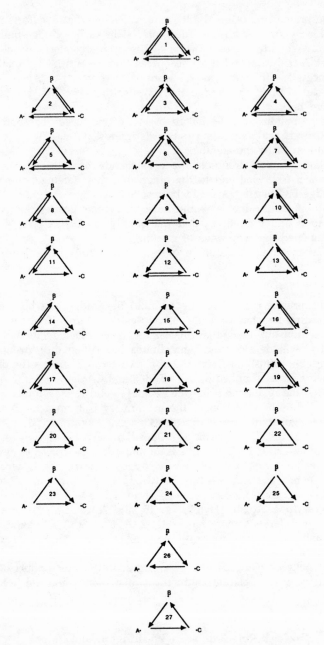

FIGURE 18.3
The Twenty-seven Indecomposable Forms. (Adapted from Steven J. Brams, "The Search for Structural Order in the International System: Some Models and Preliminary Results," *International Studies Quarterly* 13, no. 3 (September 1969), p. 256.)

that it had already been involved in Chinese affairs for a long time, the United States, as the PRC and the ROC would concur, could not avoid being a member of the triad. The stage was thus set for Peking to deal with them.

The Era of the Forbidden Triad, 1949–1979

Relations between the three actors between 1949 and 1979 can be best characterized as the Forbidden Triad, with Peking having weak ties with Washington and an absence of ties or negligible ties with its archenemy, while the ties between Washington and Taipei can be considered as strong from early on. However, toward the end of that era, a fundamental change in the structure of that triad took place, with Peking maintaining strong ties with Washington and negligible ties with Taipei, while those between Washington and Taipei were weakened.

The PRC and the United States. Economically speaking, no visible, direct trade existed between the two powers from the period of 1949–1950 to 1971. However, to curry favor with leaders of Peking, a policy change was made by Washington in April 1971, in which it was stated that the complete, although "informal," embargo on trade with the PRC, implemented since December 1950, would be relaxed. In addition, U.S. vessels would be allowed to ship PRC cargo between non-Communist Chinese ports. Later in June of the same year, a list of goods that could be traded with mainland China and exports shipped from there to the United States could now enjoy the same status as that of the Soviet Union and most East European countries. Although trade between the two sides remained relatively modest until 1978, the PRC bought Boeing jets, fertilizer plants, and substantial amounts of equipment for the exploration and drilling of oil, among other things, from the United States. By 1979, the United States ranked third as a major supplier of goods to the PRC (behind Japan and the Federal Republic of Germany) and third as a major market for PRC exports (behind Hong Kong and Japan).

Diplomatically speaking, the PRC and the United States had no ties to speak of. However, there were various contacts between them from time to time. In June 1949, Huang Hua, then a representative of the Chinese Communists, twice contacted the U.S. ambassador to China, John L. Stuart, in Nanking, discussing future Sino-U.S. relations. In the same month, Mao Tse-tung announced his willingness to discuss the establishment of diplomatic ties with foreign governments. Despite the jailing of the U.S. consul general in Mukden on October 24, 1949, the U.S. diplomatic mission did not completely pull out until January 14, 1950, when the PRC seized the U.S. consulate in Peking.

Then, five months later, the Korean War broke out. This gave the American officials yet another opportunity to meet with the Chinese Communists, which they did at the United Nations (UN) in November 1950. In July 1951, military truce negotiations over the war issue began in Kaesong, Korea, between five-man delegations of the UN, headed by the U.S. Navy commander in the Far East, Charles T. Joy, and North Korean–Chinese Communist commanders.

Dialogue between the PRC and the United States did not end with the signing of an armistice between the parties concerned in July 1953. From 1954 to 1972, despite the obvious hostility between them, they did maintain one tenuous link—a "frail little thread" according to U.S. Ambassador Kenneth T. Young—which allowed officials of the two sides to hold talks first in Geneva and later in Warsaw over matters of mutual concern, including the Taiwan Straits crises.[6] Later, as a result of National Security Adviser Henry A. Kissinger's frequent trips to Peking, those talks were discontinued in 1972, and they were supplanted altogether with the establishment of the liaison offices, a sort of beachhead, in each other's capitals in May 1973. With the issuance of the Shanghai Communiqué at the end of President Richard M. Nixon's historic sojourn in mainland China, it became very clear that diplomatic ties between Washington and Peking would be eventually established.

The PRC and the ROC. There were no ties to speak of between the two Chinese powers. Even if they existed, they could only have been regarded as "negligible." According to Byron S.J. Weng, "During the 1950s agreements were reached on guidelines for civilian air routes and military patrols over the Taiwan Straits airspace, and on the peculiar arrangement of 'alternate-day shelling' to and from Quemoy. . . . In the mid 1970s some [Koumintang] espionage agents released by the [Peking] authorities were received by the Nationalists on board ship at the mid-point in the waters around Quemoy and Matsu. The rendezvous was probably not possible without 'prior and explicit mutual arrangement.' "[7]

Nonetheless, for most of the period under discussion, Peking sought to drive the Chinese Nationalists out to sea. In March 1949 the Chinese Communists for the first time threatened to "liberate" the island of Taiwan because the United States wanted it as "a springboard for future aggression against China proper."[8] Peking was serious and had a very good chance to succeed, as can be seen from the U.S. evaluation of the ROC's prospects for survival in Taiwan, which were increasingly and unrelievedly pessimistic:

> In April, 1950, a reappraisal of the situation by the Central Intelligence Agency merely confirmed an earlier prediction that the [Kuomintang] would be unable to survive a combination of internal and external threats to its existence, and that the [Chinese Communist Party] would be capable of extending its control to the island, probably before the end of 1950. . . . the Secretary of Defense, Louis A. Johnson, reported that during June the People's Liberation Army (PLA) had increased its troop strength opposite Taiwan from "slightly more" than 40,000 to approximately 156,000, backed by a force of some 300,000 additional troops.

This gloomy picture of Taiwan's future continued for a while, even after the outbreak of the Korean War:

In late July [Secretary of State Dean] Acheson was informed that the PLA had the capacity to transport 200,000 troops across the Taiwan Straits; this, combined with the limited American naval forces available for use in the Taiwan Straits due to the hostilities in Korea, made it appear "that Communist craft and military personnel might reach the coast of Formosa in sufficient numbers to jeopardize seriously" the survival of the [Chiang] regime.[9]

Threats continued. Aside from the Taiwan Straits crises of 1954, 1958, and 1962, which were engineered by Mao, the Fukien Military Region commander, Pi Ting-chün, was ordered to prepare for a full-scale attack against Taiwan, immediately after the death of President Chiang Kai-shek and the fall of Phnom Penh, Saigon, and Vientiane in that order in 1975.

Of course, pressures to bring about a collapse of the triad were not one-sided. In a five-year plan mapped by Chiang, the ROC sought to recover the mainland, to deliver the compatriots there from the Communist yoke. However, constrained by the mutual defense treaty and notes of understanding which were signed between Washington and Taipei in December 1954, to the effect that the ROC would not attack the mainland without prior consultation with the United States, Taipei was only able to conduct limited provocations, aerial reconnaissance, and commando raids along the seacoast of mainland China, even though several opportunities emerged for it to conduct successful full-scale counterattacks against the mainland during such times as the Cultural Revolution, as Stanley Karnow of the *Washington Post*, for example, said, reporting from Hong Kong on the eve of the seventeenth anniversary of the Peking government's creation: "For the first time since . . . 1949, even the most sober specialists are speculating on the possibility that . . . Mao . . . could be overthrown by an opposition that has, from all accounts, grown significantly within recent months. Should this come to pass, it might plunge China into a chaos reminiscent of the 1920s, when the country was torn by rival warlords and political factions."[10]

The United States vis-à-vis the PRC and the ROC. There was no question that Washington held an ambiguous China policy during the crucial period of 1949–1950. The collapse of the triad could come at any moment. On the one hand, Washington was hesitant to help Taipei, as can be seen from the controversial white paper *United States Relations with China, 1944–1949.* Various options of handling the Taiwan problem were also considered at the time, among them:

1. establish a U.N. trusteeship over the island under the U.S. administration, until such time as a peace treaty with Japan was signed;
2. support a local, non-Communist administration—or the Taiwanese separatist movement if and when advantageous to U.S. interests—while discouraging the use of Taiwan as a final refuge by the Kuomintang; and
3. call for a U.S.-sponsored plebiscite for the people of Taiwan.[11]

On the other hand, Washington was also not prepared to deal with Peking, as it was committed to revolution and a policy of "leaning to one side," to that of Moscow. On a few occasions during the Korean War, President Dwight D. Eisenhower's administration even contemplated the use of atomic weapons to attack the PRC.

The decision by President Harry S. Truman on June 27, 1950, to dispatch the Seventh Fleet had created a neutralizing effect on the Taiwan Straits. Thereafter, Washington renewed its diplomatic support to Taipei and defended its seat at the United Nations. It also assisted Taiwan in the development and maintenance of a viable, self-supporting economy through the programs of the Economic Cooperation Administration and foreign aid. However, over a period of thirty years, there had been a gradual change in U.S. China policy. If we were to quote some authoritative statements which best reflect such changes, they would have to be Nixon's:

1. Statement made at the time of his vice-presidential candidacy, 1952: "China wouldn't have gone Communist—if the Truman administration had had backbone";
2. Statement made at the time of his presidential candidacy, 1960: "I can think of nothing more detrimental to freedom or peace than the recognition of Communist China";
3. Statement made at the time of his presidential candidacy, 1967: "We simply cannot afford to leave China forever outside the family of nations, there to nurture its fantasies, cherish its hates and threaten its neighbors"; and
4. Statement made at the time of his presidency, 1972: "Let me tell you what the world would be like if I had not taken the trip to Peking. One-fourth of all the people in the world live in the People's Republic of China. . . . They are among the ablest people in the world. Their government is a Communist government. I do not agree with their philosophy. We will continue to have differences with their government. We will have disagreements with their philosophy. But if a billion people in the world, 10, 15, 20 years from now, were lined up in confrontation against the United States of America it would be a dangerous world. I had to take the steps now to reduce that danger. We have done it so we have a better chance for a generation of peace for our young Americans."[12]

As it turned out, a structural change in the triad took place in December 1978 when the PRC and the United States jointly announced that their relationship would be strengthened by the establishment of diplomatic ties on January 1, 1979. It goes without saying that the ROC suffered a severe blow from this change. Ironically, Peking did not follow up with this blow by knocking down Taipei. Instead, it had chosen to build a bridge between Taipei and itself.

The Era of Building Fayol's Bridge, from 1979 to the Present

Since 1979 the PRC has embarked on the construction of Fayol's Bridge, with the ultimate goal of bringing the ROC to the negotiating table.[13] To this end, Peking has periodically come up with policies of one type or another to attract the attention of Taipei and to set limits to constrain Taipei's behavior. Lately it has found a strange bedfellow, the United States, which has indicated an interest in Teng Hsiao-ping's "one country, two systems" and in seeing expanded contacts between the two sides of the Taiwan Straits.

The PRC and the ROC. It takes two to build a bridge, connecting from one end to the other end. Thus far, Peking has been taking the initiative. Since bridges are not built in one day and progress of their construction follows a daily schedule, we shall do the same by highlighting some of the PRC's efforts chronologically. The most important thing to remember, however, is that bridge-building is never smooth.

On January 1, 1979, the Peking government ordered a stop to the bombardment of Quemoy and other offshore islands. On the same day, the PRC issued a statement, adopted by the Standing Committee of the Fifth National People's Congress (NPC), to the "compatriots" in Taiwan. It called upon both sides to engage in "three links," namely, a mail link, a trade link, and air and shipping services, and "four exchanges," namely, visits by relatives and tourists, academic exchange, cultural exchange, and sports exchange. However, it also asked, "Who among the descendants of the Yellow Emperor wishes to go down in history as a traitor?"[14] To signal its sincerity, the PRC announced in January 1979 that it would no longer levy customs duties on certain goods imported from Taiwan, although certain restrictions were reimposed in February 1982.

Three months later, the PRC raised no serious, public objections when the Taiwan Relations Act (TRA) was signed into law by the United States, even though the TRA declared, in part, that it was U.S. policy "to consider any effort to determine the future of Taiwan by other than peaceful means, including by boycotts or embargoes, a threat to the peace and security of the Western Pacific area and of grave concern to the United States" and that the U.S. government "will make available to Taiwan such defense articles and defense services in such quantity as may be necessary to enable Taiwan to maintain a sufficient self-defense capability." To be sure, the Act went much further than the "Japanese solution" in that consular functions would be performed by the American Institute in Taiwan (AIT). That Peking had chosen not to raise objections at this time was mainly due to the fact that President Jimmy Carter had promised Peking a number of things, such as asking the Congress to grant a most-favored-nation trade status to the PRC.

Another action taken by the PRC had to do with the Olympic Games. In October 1979, the Executive Board of the International Olympic Committee

(IOC), meeting in Japan, adopted a resolution calling for the following changes:

  a) to confirm the recognition of the Olympic Committee located in Peking under the name of "Chinese Olympic Committee," and
  b) to maintain the recognition of the Olympic Committee located in Taipei, under the name of "Chinese Taipei Olympic Committee," on the condition that the latter adopts an anthem and a flag which are different from those of the "Republic of China" used until now.[15]

However, to this day, the PRC has not forced the ROC to march with such a flag at the opening and closing ceremonies of the Olympic Games.

Peking's bridge-building came to a halt in 1980 when its attention shifted to the Soviet invasion of Afghanistan. Dramatic renewal of the construction did not come about until the eve of the PRC's thirty-second national day when Yeh Chien-ying, chairman of the Standing Committee of the NPC, offered a nine-point peace proposal for the reunification of China. He urged talks between the two sides for a third time, promised Taiwan the status of autonomy, that is, a special administrative region and the ability to retain its armed forces, and opened the possibility of sharing power with the Kuomintang on the mainland for the first time. On October 10, 1981, the PRC also celebrated the seventieth anniversary of the Hsin Hai Revolution, which founded the ROC. Later in November, the PRC began the construction of its fourth special economic zone at Amoy, Fukien, which is just across the Taiwan Straits, implying that no force will be applied in that area in the foreseeable future.

Then, after months of negotiations between the PRC and the United States, a joint communiqué—referred to by many as the Shanghai Communiqué II—was issued in August 1982, in which the PRC agreed to strive for a peaceful solution to the Taiwan problem. Of course, Peking also asked Washington to eventually cancel its arms sales to Taipei.

Because Taipei was hardly enthusiastic about what Peking had to offer, Peking spoke out again in June 1983. Speaking to Professor Winston L.Y. Yang of Seton Hall University, Teng said:

  a) After reunification Taiwan could retain not only its armed forces, but also purchase arms from foreign countries for its own defense;
  b) Peking would not send military or administrative personnel to the island;
  c) Taiwan could enjoy a high degree of autonomy and keep its present laws as well as an independent legislature;
  d) Judicial organs could be separate and independent from those of the mainland;
  e) Taiwan could have its own flag; and
  f) Taiwan could retain certain diplomatic powers, including the issuance of passports, the handling of foreign economic affairs, and the participation in international bodies such as the Asian Development Bank under the name "China-Taiwan."[16]

Then, in February 1984, Teng, in a conversation with former National Security Advisor Zbigniew K. Brzezinski, revealed Peking's most attractive policy of "one country, two systems," in which Taiwan would be able to retain its present political, economic, and social system but would have to surrender its sovereignty after the reunification. Later, on September 26, 1984, the PRC, in a joint declaration with the United Kingdom, agreed to preserve Hong Kong's system for fifty years after 1997, along the line of "one country, two systems." On the next day, an editorial of *Jen-min Jih-pao* (People's Daily) stated that the declaration will "promote Hong Kong's return to the motherland" and noted how the same formula could be applied to Taiwan.[17] In any case, Peking to this day has not changed a whit from this policy and would very much like to see an early completion of the bridge.

The PRC and the United States. Washington has always had an interest in seeing a peaceful solution to the Taiwan question. Its basic stand is still the following: Taiwan must remain in the hands of non-Communists, no matter who.

Messages sent from the PRC to the United States to be relayed to the ROC were usually not the same when the ROC received them. Thus, prior to the issuance of the August 1982 communiqué, Taipei was told in July 1982 that Washington

a) Has not agreed to set a date for ending arms sales to the Republic of China;
b) Has not agreed to hold prior consultations with the Chinese Communists on arms sale to the Republic of China;
c) Will not play any mediation role between Taipei and Peking;
d) Has not agreed to revise the Taiwan Relations Act;
e) Has not altered its position regarding sovereignty over Taiwan; and
f) Will not exert pressure on the Republic of China to enter into negotiations with the Chinese Communists.[18]

However, a change of attitude has occurred in the United States lately. In October 1985, Defense Secretary Caspar W. Weinberger, probably speaking for President Ronald W. Reagan's administration, stated that he wishes to see increased contact between the PRC and the ROC, provided that Taiwan goes along with that idea and that such contacts would bring benefits to both sides.[19] Later in the same month, a State Department official, Mark S. Pratt, in a paper delivered at the conference "Major Current Issues in East Asia," also encouraged contacts between Peking and Taipei.[20] And a similar statement was delivered by Secretary of State, George P. Shultz, in March 1987 on the mainland.[21] To be sure, these remarks are not made for the sake of making them. Most likely, they are made to suggest that Washington is seeing something "good" about Teng's formula that would benefit not only Washington but Taipei as well in the long run.

Taipei's Strategies Toward
Peking and Washington

Thus far, we have shown that, from 1949 to 1979, the PRC has on numerous occasions sought to bring about a collapse of the Forbidden Triad by attacking the ROC. However, since the establishment of diplomatic ties with the United States, it has attempted to bridge itself with the ROC in 1997, if not earlier. Because of this latter development, Taipei can adopt either a strategy of maintaining the Forbidden Triad, if it can, or a strategy of building a bridge from its end as well, by "meeting" with Peking in 1997 in that part of China which is called neither by the official name of the PRC nor the ROC but simply Hong Kong, China.

The ROC Strategy of Maintaining
the Forbidden Triad

In adopting the strategy of maintaining the Forbidden Triad, what Taipei has in mind is to keep itself as the non-Communist world's "unsinkable aircraft carrier" in the Western Pacific and to render help to its compatriots on the mainland, should they decide to topple the Communist regime. Militarily, the ROC has assigned high priority to establishing a large degree of independence in its domestic weapons production. Politically, it has adopted a policy of the "three nos"—no contacts, no negotiations, and no compromises with the PRC. This means that it would not compromise with the PRC on the issue of its official title, flag, and national anthem. As to Hong Kong, it has made plans to gradually pull out its offices and establishments from there after 1997. Lately, in reference to its troubled membership at the Asian Development Bank (ADB), the ROC has stated that it would not (1) change its official title to "Taipei, China," as demanded by the PRC; (2) withdraw from the ADB, which it had helped to found; or (3) participate in future meetings of the ADB. However, confident that China will be unified under Sun Yat-sen's Three Principles of the People (nationalism, democracy, and the people's livelihood), though not in the distant future, the ROC has called upon the PRC to give up its "four basic principles," to wit, the fourfold persistence in the socialist road, the dictatorship of the proletariat, the Communist Party's leadership, and Marxism–Leninism–Mao Tse-tung thought. Likewise, Peking has been told that "the conditions for peaceful reunification can gradually mature. The obstacles to reunification will be reduced naturally with the passage of time."[22]

Because it has no intention of recovering mainland China by force and yet is feeling military pressures from Peking, Taipei has called the world in general and Washington in particular to the following facts:

> The P.R.C. deploys more aircraft—fighter, bomber and reconnaissance—against the R.O.C. than against the Soviet Union. Today the P.R.C. has close to 5,300 combat aircraft as compared to slightly more than 500 for the R.O.C. Unless the R.O.C.'s requests for more advanced aircraft, submarines and other types

of sophisticated military hardware are fulfilled very soon, the security imbalance will become threatening. Add to this the P.R.C.'s superiority in nuclear weapons, major surface combat ships and submarines, and its massive number of troops, and the R.O.C.'s defense picture becomes even gloomier.[23]

Likewise, the ROC, citing Teng's statements made in October 1984, has reminded the world that the PRC has the capability to "quarantine" the Taiwan Straits. If Peking chooses to do so, it could certainly cripple Taiwan's export-oriented economy in a short time.

In the meantime, with the declining number of countries that are willing to accord diplomatic recognition to the ROC as the sole, legitimate government representing all of China, the ROC is facing the problem of being increasingly perceived by other countries as a "local government" or a "special administrative region (SAR)" of the PRC. To strike back, ROC diplomats, since April 1986, have been pushing for an international acceptance of a two-China policy by referring to the regime in mainland China as the PRC or People's Republic of China; scholars sympathetic to Taipei, notably Hungdah Chiu, have criticized, *inter alia*, the London-Peking accords. They cast serious doubts on the durability and credibility of Hong Kong's "high degree of autonomy," as promised by the PRC.[24] First, Article 67, paragraph 4 of the PRC Constitution provides that the Standing Committee of the NPC shall have the power to interpret statutes. This means that existing Hong Kong laws and, for that matter, the Basic Law of Hong Kong, which will be enacted by the NPC before 1990, can be changed at any time. Second, a contradiction can be noted between Article 2, paragraph 2 of Annex 1 of the Joint Declaration, which provides that the Hong Kong "legislature may on its own authority enact laws in accordance with the provisions of the Basic Law and legal procedure," and Article 67, paragraph 8 of the PRC Constitution, which states that the Standing Committee of the NPC has the power "to annul those local regulations or decisions of the organs of state power of . . . autonomous regions . . . that contravenes the Constitution, the statutes or the administrative rules and regulations." And Third, Article 1, paragraph 3 of Annex 1 of the declaration provides that the "chief executive of the Hong Kong Special Administrative Region shall be selected by election or through consultation held locally and be appointed by the Central People's Government." Since Peking wields the ultimate power of appointing a Hong Kong chief executive, the question that ought to be asked next is, To what extent can the Hong Kong people exercise their free will in choosing their own chief executive? In any case, to protect its own interests, Tibet's bitter experience of the 1950s has always been cited by the Taipei government.

As can be inferred, prospects for a Hong Kong truly administered by its people seem dim, unless Taipei is fully behind it, financially and morally. Likewise, if Taipei chooses to stay in the era of the Forbidden Triad, it may well be stuck with the island province forever. Thus, the question of "Whither the ROC on Taiwan?" has been raised by an ROC scholar in a recent issue of *Foreign Affairs*.[25] Of course, such concern does not mean that the ROC will fade away at the end of the struggle, for the author has also predicted that "after a prolonged period of competition between the R.O.C. and the P.R.C., developments on the mainland will slowly but surely turn in our favor." A reading of the "eternal triad," which comes into play at the moment of the completion of a bridge between A and C, gives a similar rosy picture, because by 1997, Taipei will have more options in dealing with Peking.

The ROC's Strategy of Building a Bridge

There is no question that Taipei will meet Peking head-on in Hong Kong on July 1, 1997. It is a choice forced upon the ROC and a development that can be construed as a golden opportunity for the ROC to project its power—political and economic—into the mainland. A number of reasons can be given to support such a view.

First, the ROC currently maintains several official or semiofficial offices and establishments in the British colony. After 1997, it is expected that most of them will remain open, perhaps under disguise. Thus a newspaper owner who holds an ROC passport has been quoted as saying that his anti-Communist publication, the *Hong Kong Times*, will stay in Hong Kong: "Peking has said Hongkong can exist under a 'one country, two systems' policy. We will stay to test this if they can accept our system. But we won't change to suit their palate, and we won't close down voluntarily."[26] To be sure, it is easier to stay than to retreat and then make a comeback. In addition, by simply staying there, if not taking the opportunity in the meantime to expand as much as possible, the ROC, as a first step in its political and economic counterattack against the PRC, will have to be considered as having "landed" on the mainland. Only by then would other countries be willing to reassess the ROC's new status and to grant diplomatic recognition, if necessary. And domestically, Taipei would be under less pressure from the newly formed Democratic Progressive Party (DPP) members who consciously or blindly opposed the ruling party of Kuomintang to make changes in its electoral representation, such as the Legislative *Yuan* Branch.

Second, indirect and not-so-indirect trade has been going on between the two sides of the Taiwan Straits for some time already, and Taiwan, so far, is getting most of the benefit of that trade. Once Hong Kong becomes part of China, such trade will have to become direct. It is doubtful that Taiwan businessmen will want to stop trading with the people of Hong Kong and that, when reality intrudes, the ROC can stop them. Thus, in order to solve its merchant seamen's unemployment problem, the ROC has reluctantly allowed them to work on foreign-registered, -owned, or -chartered vessels that call at PRC harbors.[27] The explanation offered by Taipei has been that so long as those seamen do not leave those vessels, they are considered on foreign territory.

Third, the fact that Hong Kong will be referred to as Hong Kong, China, and not Hong Kong, People's Republic of China, affords the ROC an opportunity to rule another part of mainland China, besides Quemoy and

Matsu. Such a development is not impossible because an overwhelming number of people in Hong Kong do not trust Chinese Communists. In addition, Hong Kong may elect some forty delegates to the 3,400-member NPC. Although the strength of Hong Kong anti-Communist and non-Communist delegates appears insignificant at first sight, the elected members could be vociferous, just like the DPP in Taiwan, if an analogy can be drawn. Thus, in his directives issued immediately after the signing of the London-Peking declaration, the ROC premier, Yu Kuo-hwa, has encouraged residents of Hong Kong to participate in elections from now on, so as to secure what they have enjoyed thus far. An Ad Hoc Committee on Hong Kong and Macao has also been set up by the ROC Executive *Yuan* (Branch) to assist the people of Hong Kong and Macao in every possible way.

Last, it is also in Peking's interests to maintain Taiwan's presence in Hong Kong after 1997 so as to keep its reunification scheme alive.[28] Thus Hong Kong may sign trade agreements and establish official or semiofficial economic and trade missions in Taiwan. Visitors from Taiwan are welcomed in Hong Kong. Of course, Hong Kong is not the only place. According to an ROC DPP legislator, in the last few years more than 20,000 people from Taiwan have visited the mainland each year.[29] (Starting from November 2, 1987, ROC citizens have been able to visit their relatives in mainland China.) Overseas, mainland Chinese scholars have also publicly and privately met with Taiwan scholars, discussing such sensitive issues as China's reunification.

Speaking overall, the ROC on Taiwan has more assets than liabilities. It has a sound economy, accumulating some US$70 billion in foreign reserve by November 1987. Its brain power is enormous. That it has become more pluralistic and democratic has also enhanced the U.S. interest in continued support. The thing that it seemingly lacks is self-confidence. But with the help of Washington in co-opting mainland China, Taipei would certainly be in a better position to challenge Peking. Whether the United States has such help in mind, we shall now turn to see.

The ROC and the United States

There is a lot in common between Taipei and Washington. But for strategic reasons, Taipei has been left in the cold since the early 1970s. Prior to the PRC's announcement of "one country, two systems," the United States had agreed not to put pressure on the ROC to enter into negotiations with the PRC. For this, Taipei is grateful. But, after that announcement, Washington gradually changed its mind. For this, the ROC should also be grateful because the United States will not only not set it adrift but will eventually ask it to help transform mainland China into a second Japan. When Nixon visited mainland China in 1972, he had such a transformation in mind. Ten years later, he has become more convinced than ever that "a strong, economically healthy China, playing a responsible role, is vital to the future of peace in the world. China today seems to be making some progress in becoming *more* Chinese and *less* Marxist, embracing capitalist-style incentives rather than continuing to wear an ideological strait-jacket. If they continue on this course, they could become the major economic power in the world in the 21st century" (emphases added).[30] Reagan probably shared Nixon's view when he pushed for the congressional approval of the U.S.-China Nuclear Cooperation Agreement in late 1985, allowing sales of U.S. reactors and components to the PRC. With those nuclear plants, mainland China could produce more electricity and, in turn, run its industries and expand its private-sector. There is indeed a great possibility for mainland China to be transformed, to become capitalist-oriented for the next few hundred years, if not forever. Taiwan would be safer if such changes take place and can play a leading, exemplary role in pushing for further changes in mainland China's economy as well as politics, because, in the words of James C. Hsiung, the Taiwan experience can be a catalyst for a future free and democratic China. A number of reasons can be pointed out to support this view.

First, ideologically speaking, China has never gone through the capitalist stage. If the Peking rulers are professed Marxists, then they must accept Marx's interpretation of human history, which comes in terms of several stages, starting from primitive communism to the utopia of communism. Mao attempted to skip the capitalist stage and yet he failed to produce "new socialist men" and made China poorer. Teng, on the other hand, acknowledging certain values of capitalism and thinking that the Chinese Communist Party could retain its control of mainland China, has moved "backward" by encouraging the growth of capitalism. So far, he has abolished the commune system, welcomed foreign investments and technology, and attached greater importance to the idea of incentive. But can communism contain the growth of capitalism, by preventing it from overwhelming the mainland of China someday? The answer has to be no because (1) it has taken some 200 years of practicing capitalism for the United States to become a superpower; it would take an even longer time for mainland China, given its huge population, to become developed; and (2) one does not have to live in a capitalist society in order to understand the dynamics of supply and demand and to appreciate capitalist values. Thus, to avoid political criticisms, many capitalist-oriented programs have been camouflaged under such names as "state-assisted, civilian-operated, and collectively owned programs" and "opening up to the outside world programs." And in a matter of a few years since Teng's consolidation of power, making money and getting rich have become top priorities in the minds of many people. The Hainan Island scandal of 1985, involving high-ranking officials of the PRC, is an excellent case in point. The press in the PRC has also encouraged incentive and attacked Marxism. In an editorial on March 19, 1984, *Jen-min Jih-pao* emphasized the theme of "wealth is a good thing, not a bad thing" and pointed out that Peking's policy is a policy of making the people prosperous. Moreover, on December 7, 1984, the same paper published a commentator's article entitled "Theory and Practice," which stated, "We should never take a dogmatic attitude toward Marxism," because "Marx passed away 101 years ago. His works were written more than 100 years ago. Some were his visions of that time, after which the situation has greatly changed. Some of his ideas are not necessarily appropriate." And therefore, "We cannot depend on works of Marx and Lenin to solve our present-day problems."[31] In any case, China's economic system in the next few hundred years will likely swing between the pendulum of capitalism and the Three Principles of the People, which is a brand of socialism but not the same as the PRC's style of socialism. Should that be the case, the PRC, politically speaking, would certainly be put on the defensive.

Second, in 1980, the PRC adopted a policy, like that of the ROC's export-processing zone, establishing Shenchen, Chuhai, Amoy, and Swatow as "special economic zones." In April 1984, it announced that, in addition to Hainan Island, the following coastal cities—Dairen, Tientsin, Shanghai, Canton, Chinhwangtao, Yentai (Chefoo), Tsingtao, Wenchow, Foochow, Chankiang, and Peihai—were to be opened as "economic development zones" where the basic policies of the "special economic zones," such as greater decision-making power and preferential treatments to investors, would be allowed. (However, because of the Hainan Island scandal, the PRC announced in July 1985 that only the first four cities can continue their operations.) And in January 1985, the PRC declared that three "economically opened regions," namely, the Yangtze River Delta, the Pearl River Delta, and parts of southern Fukien Province, covering the cities of Amoy, Changchow, and Chuanchow, would be opened to the outside world. What these moves meant was that those zones, coastal cities, and regions would become modernized and turn capitalist first. Such a development works only in favor of the ROC, which can move into those pockets, if given the opportunity. By the same token, to test Peking's sincerity in implementing its policy of "one country, two systems," Taipei can ask Washington to help it in making the following demand: to ask it to withdraw from Fukien Province, for example, and to let Taipei transform it into a second Taiwan Province. To be sure, this kind of demand does not go against "one country, two systems," and should the PRC refuse to comply, its intention of ultimately swallowing Taiwan would have been laid bare.

Last, when people are poor, what they think of first is food and shelter; and once they have become rich, they engage in politics. This process is what has taken place in Taiwan. It will also take place in mainland China in the future. Thus, when the PRC proclaimed its program of Four Modernizations, some politically conscious people asked, What about the fifth modernization, namely, democracy? In a Chinese Lunar New Year speech, the PRC president, Lee Hsien-nien, has only to admit that, because of capitalist influence, more and more people are clamoring for democracy in mainland China.[32] If he does, Taipei could singly or in combination with Washington help the people of the mainland to bring about a political change in mainland China like the China spring.

Concluding Remarks

In this chapter we have integrated and somewhat modified several concepts as well as models related to triadic relationships. The first is called the

Forbidden Triad, which means that, in a triad of A, B, and C, ties between A and B and those between B and C are either strong or weak. As to A and C, there is an absence of ties or negligible ties between them. The second is called Fayol's Bridge, which is built on the Forbidden Triad and which stresses that a bridge connecting A and C could be constructed. The Eternal Triad comes in when the construction of the bridge has been completed. It is comprised of twenty-seven indecomposable forms, couched in terms of symmetrical and asymmetrical relationships. Of course, the choice of those concepts and models and the arrangement of them have been deliberate. Had we borrowed, for example, Lowell Dittmer's models of *ménage à trois*, which consists of mutually positive relationships or symmetrical amities among all three members; the romantic triangle, which consists of amity between one "pivot" and two "suitors," with the latter two being in a state of enmity; and the stable marriage, which consists of amity between two members but enmity between each and the remaining third,[33] a different interpretation of the same data could emerge. Thus talks between the officials of China Airlines (CAL) and those of the China Civil Air (CCA) and Civil Aviation Administration of China (CAAC) in May 1986 would not fit into this study; that is to say, they would not constitute the completion of a bridge between Taipei and Peking, for three interrelated reasons: First, none of the actors under study has left the era of the Forbidden Triad. One can remain neutral in that era but not so in the era of the Eternal Triad. That the United States has remained neutral throughout the incident suggests that, at least from the U.S. perspective, the incident cannot be included in my study. Second, the ROC government has reiterated many times that talks between the two sides are nothing but "businesslike" negotiations. And third, even if the PRC government claims that the bridge has been completed by virtue of Wang Hsi-chueh's "inaugural flight" in air transport, it should be remembered that, as I stated at the outset of this chapter, it takes two to bring about the completion of a bridge. So far, Taipei has treated that incident as a "one-shot" affair. In any case, given the complexity of our study, it is fair to say that Dittmer's models are much too simple, whereas ours are closer to reality.

In our study of the PRC, the United States, and the ROC, we have found that there is a change in Peking's strategy toward Taipei. From 1949 to 1979, it sought to bring about a collapse of the Forbidden Triad by eliminating the ROC on Taiwan on several occasions. But since its recognition of the United States, the PRC has attempted to bridge itself with the ROC, by offering numerous overtures along with some concessions, the latest being the formula of "one country, two systems." Nonetheless, such bridge-building does not mean that everything will work in the way that Peking wanted it to—for example, the acceptance of a local government status by Taipei—because by so doing, Peking is actually opening a Pandora's box of twenty-seven forms of relationships for Taipei to work with. With 1997 approaching, it is the PRC that is caught in a dilemma: to continue its bridge-building, thereby allowing the ROC to "land" on that part of China which is called neither by the name of the PRC nor the ROC but Hong Kong, China, or to stop its bridge-building or even return to the era of the Forbidden Triad, thereby further deepening the distrust of the people in Hong Kong as well as Taiwan. In any case, once embarked on the bridge-building, Peking will have to make more concessions in return for Taipei's acceptance of its "new" status.

As to the United States, it has tried to keep the PRC and the ROC apart since 1949. However, not long after the signing of the London-Peking accords, Washington changed its attitude by encouraging contacts between the two sides of the Taiwan Straits, so long as Taipei agrees to it and both Taipei and Peking would benefit from such contacts. In other words, from 1949 to 1985, the United States sided with the ROC, because it was the ROC's desire not to have contacts with the PRC. Now, seeing that many economic programs in mainland China are capitalist oriented, Washington believes that situations there would eventually turn in favor of the ROC. And should Taipei refuse to make a move along the line that Washington has suggested, it would be even more isolated, triadically and extratriadically.

The choice for the ROC, then, is to continue its strategy of maintaining the Forbidden Triad or to change its strategy to that of "building" a bridge from its end, to eventually meet with the PRC. Of course, the ROC should not be in a hurry to build a bridge. It should wait for the day that Hong Kong officially becomes part of *China*. In the meantime, it should try to secure what it has now in that British colony, while at the same time expanding its influence and trying to gain a majority in the Hong Kong Legislative Council and Urban and Regional councils. By controlling the Hong Kong electoral bodies, for example, the ROC, theoretically speaking, would be able to exert direct influence and neutralize the PRC in as many as eighteen different scenarios. Should it be successful, other countries in the world would then be willing to reassess Taipei's new status and to grant diplomatic recognition, if necessary. It is only in this context that the ROC would be able to survive and thrive. In the final analysis, bridge-building from the ROC's side will prove to be a better strategy than the strategy of maintaining the Forbidden Triad, because it will put the PRC on the defensive from 1997 to at least 2047 or 2060, as the case may be.[34]

Notes

I wish to thank Martin L. Lasater, director of the Asian Studies Center at the Heritage Foundation, for his helpful comments on an earlier draft of this chapter. I alone am responsible for the contents of this chapter.

1. See Peter Kien-hong Yu and Phillip M. Chen, eds., *Faces and Phases of Triadic/ Triangular Relationships: Models and Case Studies on Washington-Moscow-Peking* (Taipei: Asia and World Institute, 1987).

2. Mark S. Granovetter, "The Strength of Weak Ties," in Samuel Leinhardt, ed., *Social Networks* (New York: Academic Press, 1977), pp. 348–353.

3. Jerry W. Koehler et al., *Organizational Communication*, 2nd ed. (New York: Holt, Rinehart and Winston, 1981), pp. 19–20 and 104. See also Granovetter, "The Strength of Weak Ties," pp. 351–353.

4. Steven J. Brams, "The Search for Structural Order in the International System: Some Models and Preliminary Results," *International Studies Quarterly*, 13, no. 3 (September 1969), 254–280.

5. Brams, "The Search for Structural Order," pp. 255 and 257.

6. *China: US Policy Since 1945* (Washington, D.C.: Congressional Quarterly, 1980), p. 149.

7. Byron S.J. Weng, "Taiwan's International Status Today," *China Quarterly*, no. 99 (September 1984), p. 6.

8. *China: US Policy Since 1945*, p. 86.

9. Jon W. Huebner, "The Americanization of the Taiwan Straits," *Asian Profile*, 13, no. 3 (June 1985), 197 and 198.

10. *China and U.S. Far East Policy, 1945–1967* (Washington, D.C.: Congressional Quarterly, 1967), p. 199.

11. See Huebner, "The Americanization of the Taiwan Straits."

12. *China: US Policy Since 1945*, p. 54.

13. Guo-cang Huan, "Taiwan: A View from Beijing," *Foreign Affairs*, 63, no. 5 (Summer 1985), 1064.

14. *Beijing Review*, January 5, 1979, pp. 16–17.

15. *Beijing Review*, October 19, 1979, p. 27.

16. Weng, "Taiwan's International Status Today," p. 469.

17. Hungdah Chiu, "The 1984 Sino-British Agreement on Hong Kong and Its Implications on China's Unification," *Issues and Studies*, 21, no. 4 (April 1985), 579.

18. *Free China Weekly* (Taipei), August 22, 1932, p. 1.

19. *United Daily News* (Taipei), December 29, 1985, editorial.

20. See Mark S. Pratt, "The Future of Taiwan," paper delivered at the conference "Major Current Issues in East Asia," Institute of Asian Studies, St. John's University, October 24 and 25, 1985.

21. U.S. Ambassador to Peking, Winston Lord, said in May 1986 that the United States "will seek neither to mediate nor to obstruct reconciliation between China and Taiwan."

22. *Free China Weekly* (Taipei), June 13, 1982, p. 1.

23. Yu-ming Shaw, "Taiwan: A View from Taipei," *Foreign Affairs*, 63, no. 5 (Summer 1985), 1056.

24. See Chiu, "The 1984 Sino-British Agreement," pp. 16–19. See also James C. Hsiung, "The Hong Kong Settlement: Effects on Taiwan and Prospects for Peking's Reunification Bid," *Asian Affairs*, 12, no. 2 (Summer 1985), 47–58.

25. Shaw, "Taiwan: A View from Taipei," p. 1062.

26. *Far Eastern Economic Review*, February 13, 1986, p. 27.

27. *Taiwan Times* (Kaohsiung), May 30, 1986, p. 2, and *United Daily News* (Taipei), May 8, 1986, p. 2.

28. Hsiung, "The Hong Kong Settlement," p. 53.

29. Legislative *Yuan* (Branch) Communiqué (Taipei), March 12, 1986, p. 37. According to the same legislator, some 6,000 to 8,000 residents from Taiwan visited mainland China via Japan last year. See *Taiwan Times* (Kaohsiung), May 30, 1986, p. 2.

30. *New York Times*, February 28, 1982, p. E19. Nixon has called upon the U.S. government to provide a Marshall Plan type of aid to mainland China. Furthermore, he says that the era of containment and détente is over. The world is entering an era of New Realism. International Community Radio Taipei, March 7, 1986.

31. However, a rare retraction was made on December 10, 1984, stating that Marxism-Leninism could not "solve *all* of today's problems" (emphasis added).

32. *United Daily News* (Taipei), February 10, 1986, p. 2.

33. See Lowell Dittmer, "The Strategic Triangle: An Elementary Game-theoretic Analysis," *World Politics*, 33, no. 4 (July 1981), 485–515. However, Peter Burton pointed out that "Dittmer excluded from consideration the fourth pattern of enmity or hostility among all three players" in his study of the Washington-Moscow-Peking triangle. See Peter Burton, "The Asian Strategic Balance and China," in James C. Hsiung, ed., *Beyond China's Independent Foreign Policy* (New York: Praeger, 1985), p. 13.

34. In a 1985 study released by the Japanese government, it has been said that it will take some seventy-five years for the PRC to catch up economically with the ROC.

19

Present and Future Sino-Japanese Relations, 1986–1990

Donald W. Klein

Reduced to its barest essentials, the history of modern East Asian international relations is the history of Sino-Japanese relations. The centrality of these two nations was hidden for a time in the 1950s and 1960s when the two were under the massive shadow of the superpowers. The superpowers still play a crucial role in East Asia, but as we near the 1990s it grows increasingly clear that the ability of the United States or the Soviet Union to alter the Sino-Japanese relationship is diminishing.

Before we assess Sino-Japanese relations today, some preliminary comments are in order. First, a peaceful and stable East Asia requires a stable Sino-Japanese relationship. Second, we will miss important nuances in this relationship unless we recall that the past century of Sino-Japanese relations has been a painful one, and most of that pain has been endured by China. The links are thus colored by a mosaic of ideas and emotions that include admiration, envy, love, hate, guilt, and arrogance. Nor must we forget that the two states are ideological opposites—capitalists and communists. Finally, we should ignore the romantics who in their muddled way insist that both China and Japan are superpowers. Superpowers are capable of projecting all forms of power—military, political, and economic—on a global basis. China and Japan simply do not qualify. Perhaps in the future, but not today.

If we cast about to put Sino-Japanese relations in their proper context, we can ask what is the world's most important bilateral relationship. Soviet-American relations clearly hold that dubious distinction because of the previously mentioned ability to project power globally and because of the nuclear issue. But what is the next most important relationship? West German–Soviet relations? Sino-Soviet relations? Or perhaps U.S.-Japan relations? In any short list of absolutely crucial links, it is evident that we now live in an era in which Sino-Japanese relations rank among the world's most important and seem destined to hold this place into the twenty-first century. It is worth repeating and emphasizing that this is basically a *regional* relationship—but it is the world's most populous region and also one of the most economically vibrant regions.

Current Sino-Japanese Relations

The purpose of this paper is to analyze current Sino-Japanese relations and to explore the factors that might maintain or disrupt these links into the early 1990s. The framework for analysis centers on the positive and negative aspects of three types of relations—military-strategic, political-normative, and economic.

Military Relations

Few would doubt that military power dominated the unhappy Sino-Japanese relationship between the 1870s and the end of World War II. Japan wielded the sword, and China tried none too successfully to defend itself with the shield. It was essentially a direct, one-to-one relationship. There were no superpowers to restrain Japan, and none of the "major powers" (as they were then called) deflected the Japanese sword. Today it may seem superfluous to mention the military component in the Sino-Japanese bilateral linkage. We all "know" that Japan has no intention to attack China. Do the Chinese agree with this view? Not completely, it seems. We must recall that in the famed Shanghai Communiqué of February 1972 the People's Republic of China (PRC) "firmly opposes the revival and outward expansion of Japanese militarism." A decade later we find Beijing accusing "certain circles" in Japan of predatory military designs on China (a point to which we will return).

Despite the seemingly latent Chinese unease about Japan's military power, the military component in Sino-Japanese relations is for the most part not too troubling. For one thing, both the Chinese and Japanese military configurations are far more defensively than offensively oriented. With the possible but probably minor exception of the Senkaku Islands (Diaoyutai), there is no territorial dispute that could trigger military action. The Japanese resolutely shy away from the sale abroad of military items, a fact that should please the Chinese.

It is possible to conceive of situations (such as a second Korean War) that could escalate into Sino-Japanese antagonisms with military overtones, but it seems more probable that some situation (such as aggressive Soviet actions) might in fact lead to limited Sino-Japanese military cooperation. Indeed, there have already been occasional reciprocal visits of Japanese and Chinese military figures,[1] but the idea that these might blossom into some sort of genuine military cooperation is very unlikely. On balance, the military component in Sino-Japanese relations is minor, and we can expect it to stay that way.

Political-Normative Relations

The broad political-normative relations between Beijing and Tokyo are certainly better than at any time in the last century. At elite levels in Japan, there is regular affirmation of good relations. For example, every year the Japanese Foreign Ministry publishes a "diplomatic bluebook" that surveys Japan's relations throughout the world. It is, of course, written in bland diplomatic language, yet the tone is bluntly negative in reference to Soviet-Japanese relations. In striking contrast, Sino-Japanese relations are pictured in exclusively positive terms.[2]

Sino-Japanese political ties are, of course, anchored by the establishment of diplomatic relations in 1972. This was supplemented in the next few years by a host of agreements concerning trade, fisheries, aviation, telecommunications, science, technology, and culture. All these agreements ultimately led to the Sino-Japanese Peace Treaty of 1978.[3] Through most of the 1970s, the Japanese had clung steadfastly to the notion that they might be able to maintain an "equidistant" stance between the squabbling Chinese and Soviets. But by agreeing to a treaty provision renouncing regional "hegemony" (the code word for the Soviet Union), Japan cast its lot with China. Whether or not the Chinese were grateful for this action is a moot point. What is not moot, however, is the fact that Sino-Japanese political relations have blossomed since then. In both quantitative and qualitative terms, there has been an increasingly institutionalized relationship among the highest leaders in both countries. For example, Japan's last three prime ministers (Ohira Masayoshi, Suzuki Zenko, and Nakasone Yasuhiro) have visited China, and China's triumvirate of leaders (Deng Xiaoping, Hu Yaobang, and Zhao Ziyang) have all visited Japan. Deng, in fact, has been there twice.

At a notch below the prime ministerial level, there has been a singularly large number of cabinet-level visits on both sides. For example, since the 1978 peace treaty, all five Japanese foreign ministers (Sonoda Sunao, Okita Saburo, Ito Masayoshi, Sakurauchi Yoshio, and Abe Shintaro) have been to Beijing at least once. A score of other cabinet ministers have also visited China, and equal numbers of Chinese cabinet members have gone to Japan. No "hot line" formally exists, but it seems clear that the top-level contacts are sufficiently elaborate and institutionalized to maintain the momentum of positive relations and to head off any emergency or serious problem that should arise.

Not surprisingly, these executive branch contacts are matched by a steady flow of Japanese parliamentarians. The Japan-China Friendship Parliamentarians' League was established in April 1973,[4] with the ardent blessing of Japan's ruling Liberal Democratic Party. The American predilection to establish one's foreign affairs "credentials" by a visit to China is more than matched by the scores of Japanese Diet members who visit China. Similarly, the powerful and highly influential Japanese business elite is equally well traveled to China. This relationship is also well institutionalized in the sense that by the mid-1980s there were over 100 Japanese business firms with offices in China.[5]

The Japanese media are very well represented in China in terms of numbers, even if the quality of reporting has been questioned at times. At the end of 1982, thirteen Japanese news organizations had a total of twenty-one reporters in China. (Japan has more correspondents only in the United States, Great Britain, and France.) The PRC has a roughly comparable number in Japan—seventeen reporters representing eight news organizations.[6]

A few years ago tourism between the two Asian giants was virtually nonexistent, a situation symbolized by the fact that no direct air route existed between Tokyo and Beijing. Now, however, tourism is booming. Except for Chinese residents of Hong Kong and Macao, the Japanese lead all other countries by a wide margin. From a few thousand Japanese visiting China in the early 1970s, the number increased to about 400,000 in 1985,[7] and all signs point to ever greater numbers as Chinese tourist facilities expand. The word "tourist" does not really describe those Chinese who visit Japan, but by the early 1980s some 20,000 Chinese in one capacity or another were visiting Japan each year.[8]

There are no polls on the Chinese public's view of Japan and the Japanese, but such polls abound in Japan. In the 1960s, and especially during the Cultural Revolution, there was generally a negative attitude toward the PRC.[9] This was complicated by the fact that the Japanese public tended to take a favorable view toward Taiwan (especially regarding Taiwan retaining its seat in the UN). It was also complicated by what might be called a strong measure of realism by the Japanese public: despite its negative views toward China, the public felt that the Japanese government should recognize the PRC diplomatically. Predictably, after diplomatic relations were established in 1972, the Japanese public took an increasingly favorable view of China. This applied both to subjective issues (such as "Do you feel friendly toward China?") and to more rational views (such as "Are relations between Japan and China important?"). For example, a Japanese government poll of mid-1983 found 72 percent of the people "feeling friendly" toward China and 88 percent felt that "relations were important."[10] These figures tell us that Japan's political elite can cultivate close ties with the PRC with the knowledge that it has very strong popular backing.

Economic Relations

It's hard to avoid the point that economic ties are really the ones that bind Sino-Japanese relations. From China's side, Japan has been its chief trade partner since the mid-1960s when Sino-Japanese trade surpassed Sino-Soviet trade. By 1974 this trade constituted no less than a quarter of China's total trade, and it has remained in this percentage range ever since.

On the Japanese side, the trade volume is far less in percentage terms than China's. In 1985, for example, only 7 percent of Japan's exports went to China, and only 5 percent of Japan's imports came from China. Nonetheless, China has steadily moved up on the list of Japan's key trading partners (see Table 19.1), and in 1985 it rose to become Japan's second-largest trade partner, surpassed only by the United States. Unless there is an extraordinary

TABLE 19.1
Japan's Leading Trade Partners

1977	1978	1979	1980	1981	1982	1983	1984	1985
United States	United States	United States	United States	United States	United States	United States	United States	United States
Saudi Arabia	Saudi Arabia	Saudi Arabia	Saudi Arabia	Saudi Arabia	Saudi Arabia	Saudi Arabia	Saudi Arabia	China
Australia	South Korea	Indonesia	Indonesia	Indonesia	Indonesia	Indonesia	Indonesia	
Indonesia	Australia	South Korea	Australia	Australia	Australia	Australia	China	
South Korea	Indo-nesia	Australia	UAE[a]	China	UAE[a]	China		
Iran	Iran	West Germany	China		China			
Canada	West Germany	Taiwan						
West Germany	Taiwan	China						
Taiwan	China							
China								

[a]United Arab Emirates.

rise in oil prices (which would return Saudi Arabia back to the number-two slot), it seems certain that China will remain Japan's second-biggest trade partner for years to come.

Another way to view this great surge in Japan-PRC trade is to examine Japan's trade with the PRC, the Republic of China (ROC), and the Soviet Union. Through most of the 1970s, it appeared that Japan tried to equalize trade among these three nations, but by the 1980s the PRC soared ahead (see Table 19.2). Indeed, by 1984, Japan's trade with China was slightly greater than its combined trade with Taiwan and the USSR, and in 1985 it zoomed to no less than 45 percent larger.[11]

Another very important aspect of Sino-Japanese relations is economic complementarity. Since the mid-1960s, China has relied heavily on Japan for medium- and high-technology goods. Japan, in turn, especially since the mid-1970s, has tapped into China's natural resources, particularly oil and coal. In 1984, for example, 48 percent of China's exports to Japan consisted of oil and petroleum products. However, because Japan buys such vast quantities of resources—especially fuels—its dependence upon China seems relatively slight in percentage terms. For instance, in 1984 only 6.3 percent of Japan's oil imports came from China, and the figure for coal imports for 1983 was a mere 4.4 percent.[12] Yet Japan sees this source of energy as an important part of its quest for diversification, a quest constantly punctuated by the volatile Middle East situation.

TABLE 19.2
Japan's Trade with the USSR, the PRC, and the ROC (in millions of U.S. dollars)

	USSR	PRC	ROC
1970	820	820	950
1971	870	900	1,210
1972	1,100	1,100	1,510
1973	1,560	2,010	2,540
1974	2,510	3,290	2,800
1975	2,790	3,790	2,630
1976	3,420	3,030	3,470
1977	3,360	3,490	3,840
1978	3,940	5,080	5,340
1979	4,370	6,650	6,840
1980	4,640	9,400	7,510
1981	5,280	10,390	7,930
1982	5,580	8,860	6,700
1983	4,280	10,000	7,710
1984	3,910	13,170	9,190
1985	4,200	16,600	7,360

Sino-Japanese trade is not without its troubles. Far from it. In the post-1978 period, much has been made of the erratic nature of China's contractual arrangements with Japanese business firms—especially the huge Baoshan steel complex near Shanghai.[13] The Chinese typically described these as "adjustments" or "readjustments." The Japanese were often stunned, frustrated, and angry, but they persisted. The Japanese government stepped in on a number of occasions to help. The upshot has been that the Japanese government moved steadily from a "fixer" of situations to a giver of foreign aid in its many forms, and this aid is now an accepted part of Sino-Japanese economic relations. This situation, of course, represents a substantial turn-around for China. Deng Xiaoping and Company, in effect, have cast aside Mao's much-touted self-reliance,[14] and Japan is now probably the chief target of China's ever-growing requests for foreign aid.

Japan has responded in many ways. By 1982, China emerged as the chief recipient of Japan's bilateral official development assistance (ODA); Japan's ODA net disbursements of $369 million in 1982, $350 million in 1983, and $389 million in 1984 accounted for 14 to 16 percent of Japan's ODA. To put these figures in another perspective that emphasizes Japan's large role, in 1983 the $350 million that China received from Japan represented no less than 72 percent of all bilateral aid received by China from the seventeen countries that constitute the Development Assistance Committee (DAC) of the Organization for Economic Cooperation and Development (OECD).[15]

The Japanese ritualistically claim that their aid is not "tied." Whatever the Chinese may think of such assertions, they probably prefer Japanese

TABLE 19.3
PRC Technology Imports in 1983 and 1985

Country	Number of Contracts		Value		Percent of Value	
	1983	1985	1983	1985	1983	1985
Japan	44	174	$234,000,000	$550,000,000	41	19
United States	46	137	173,000,000	690,000,000	31	23
West Germany	43	123	54,000,000	790,000,000	10	27
France	3	34	3,000,000	320,000,000	1	11
Great Britain	18	40	15,000,000	79,000,000	3	3
Switzerland	2	36	2,000,000	97,000,000	—	3
Other countries	56	121	85,000,000	434,000,000	15	15
Totals	212	665	$566,000,000	$2,960,000,000	101	101

Source: Beijing Review, no. 10, March 10, 1986, p. 22; and Xue Muqiao, ed., *Almanac of China's Economy in 1984* (Hong Kong, 1985), p. 335.

aid that is tied in an economic fashion to American or Soviet aid that would more probably have strategic or ideological ties.

Still another dimension of the economic links is technology transfer. The record here is very mixed. Middle-echelon Chinese officials will almost invariably complain (sometimes in bitter language) that the Japanese are really not forthcoming in terms of technology transfer. One Beijing official commented that "it's useful to trade with Japan, but don't expect technology." He added that officials in South Korea and Taiwan feel the same way.[16] Such remarks are heard so frequently that one is tempted to think they are planted to force Japan's hand.

Whatever the complaints, it's clear that Japan is one of the key suppliers of technology to China. It is also evident that while China intends to continue to import great amounts of technology, it will diversify the nations from which it gets the technology. To put this statement in a perhaps more revealing fashion, Japan is winning more contracts, but it is losing a large share of the market (see Table 19.3).

Closely related to technology imports (and in fact a source of such imports) are joint ventures. From 1979 to 1983, 188 joint ventures were begun. These are dominated by Overseas Chinese investors from Hong Kong, but the Japanese are playing at least a modest role (see Table 19.4).

The Impact of Sino-Japanese Relations on Other Countries

The analysis so far has been confined largely to bilateral Sino-Japanese relations. We turn now to the impact of these relations on other countries and areas. In doing so, it is important to recognize that the burgeoning Sino-Japanese relations are from the Chinese side a manifestation of an

TABLE 19.4
Joint Ventures in China, 1979–1983

Origin of Foreign Investors	Number of Joint Ventures	Value of Foreign Investment
Hong Kong	128	$110,000,000
United States	21	88,000,000
Philippines	5	42,000,000
Belgium	1	40,000,000
Great Britain	6	38,000,000
Japan	13	19,000,000
Others	14	5,000,000
Totals	188	$342,000,000

Source: Xue Muqiao, ed., *Almanac of China's Economy in 1984* (Hong Kong, 1985), pp. 338–341.

enormous change in China's foreign relations. That is to say, the PRC has virtually abandoned the so-called world communist movement,[17] almost abandoned the Third World (except in normative terms), and moved closer and closer to the trilateral world of North America, the Common Market, and Japan. This statement is particularly true in economic terms, and these economic linkages have tended to nudge all aspects of China's foreign policy toward the West. To put this observation in regional terms, China has moved increasingly away from an Asia mainland orientation and toward the Pacific Region.[18]

By one of those delicious ironies, it is clear that the communist nations involved in Asia are the least happy about improved Sino-Japanese ties. First and foremost is the USSR. Throughout the 1970s the Soviets struggled to prevent improved Sino-Japanese relations. But in typical Soviet style, it was the problem of too many sticks and not enough carrots. In military-strategic terms, the PRC and Japan have clearly not colluded against Moscow, but the Soviets have nonetheless chosen to interpret Sino-Japanese friendship as a hostile act, and, accordingly, have further beefed up their military power vis-à-vis both China and Japan. (In the case of Japan, this increase includes a substantial Soviet military buildup in the so-called Northern Territories that Japan claims as its own.) In political-normative terms, both Sino-Soviet and Japanese-Soviet relations hit a new low following the Sino-Japanese Peace Treaty of 1978. However, after a few years the Soviets learned to live with this fact, and by the mid-1980s—with some give and take on all sides—Moscow's relations improved slightly with both Beijing and Tokyo.

In economic terms the Russians simply can't compete with the Japanese. Soviet trade dipped somewhat with both China and Japan in the late 1970s and early 1980s, reaching a low with China in 1981 and with Japan in 1984. But by the mid-1980s various Russian gestures indicated a renewed interest in greater trade. Among the more important moves were three top-level visits—by Soviet Foreign Minister Eduard A. Shevardnadze to Japan in January 1986 and two by Soviet First Deputy Premier Ivan V. Arkhipov to China in December 1984 and March 1986. In both cases, the Soviet leaders put much emphasis on increasing trade.

On balance, the Sino-Japanese rapprochement is a net loss for Moscow, but it is something the Soviets can live with. The ultimate Soviet nightmare—Japanese industrial might harnessed to Chinese military strength—does not seem likely, even (one hopes) to the more paranoid of the Soviet chieftains.

Vietnam has also been damaged by improved Sino-Japanese ties. The Tokyo-Beijing linkage is no particular military threat to Vietnam, because Japan will certainly not assist China in any attack on Vietnam. But Vietnam is seriously damaged in the world political arena and thus forced to continue its near-exclusive reliance on the USSR, because Japan refuses to have significant dealings with Vietnam as long as Sino-Vietnamese relations are so hostile. So, unless there is a complete Chinese turnabout, there is little chance that Japan will use its "good offices" to mend the Sino-Vietnamese fence, nor will Japan serve as a "bridge" between Vietnam and the West. Vietnam is most damaged in the economic realm. Since the Sino-Vietnamese War of 1979, Japan's trade with Vietnam has been very insignificant. More important, Japan is probably the one and only nation that could help rebuild the shattered Vietnamese economy, but, again, Japan's ties to China preclude such an endeavor.

The impact of improved Sino-Japanese relations on North Korea is rather murky. In military-strategic terms, it is clear that both Japan and China strongly oppose any North Korean military assault on South Korea (a view also shared by Moscow and Washington). In political-normative terms, better Sino-Japanese ties have seemingly coincided with China's slight shift toward somewhat improved relations with South Korea. Chinese officials, for example, are very direct in saying that China will definitely take part in the 1988 Seoul Olympics.[19] A causal relationship may not exist, but in any case since Japan and China established diplomatic relations in 1972, Japan–North Korea trade has increased. Still, it is not a substantial trade—running at slightly less than half a billion dollars during the early 1980s. On balance, better Sino-Japanese relations seem to have weakened North Korea's position by only a small margin.

South Korea has been a net gainer in the wake of better Sino-Japanese relations. Seoul's future rests very heavily on its ties to the United States and Japan—on the former for military, political, and economic reasons, and on the latter for economic ties. To the degree that the PRC can restrain militarily aggressive tendencies of North Korea, then South Korea profits from the Tokyo-Beijing connection. And, as already noted, Beijing has edged a bit toward a more accommodating political position vis-à-vis South Korea. The South Koreans fear that Japan might favor the PRC in terms of economic ties (including aid), but in early 1983 Prime Minister Nakasone went a long way toward reassuring Seoul by agreeing to a huge economic aid commitment.[20] Indeed, the Japanese and Korean economies are so tightly linked in terms of trade, aid, and investments that the Koreans would seem to have little to fear.

The Association of Southeast Asian Nations (ASEAN) has reason to welcome good Sino-Japanese relations. ASEAN has two basic military-strategic worries: China and Vietnam. The bigger of these threats—China (including the internal ASEAN concerns about Overseas Chinese)—is greatly diminished as long as Beijing faces the Pacific Region in a benign and economically oriented fashion. And that is clearly the case today. A current illustration is Beijing's total silence concerning the Communist New People's Army in the Philippines. The ASEAN countries welcome Beijing's abandonment of dissident guerrilla groups in Southeast Asia, not to mention its opposition to Vietnam. So long as Vietnam must deal militarily with China, it is unlikely to move militarily against ASEAN. These military-strategic considerations spill over into the political arena. ASEAN wants to remain neutral, and close Sino-Japanese ties support such a posture. The chief ASEAN concern is economic. It fears that China may absorb increasingly large portions of Japanese aid, and in fact China became Japan's leading aid recipient in 1982. On balance, however, there are many pressures (including some from the United States) on Japan to continue its present levels of trade and aid with ASEAN.

The United States has profited perhaps more than any other nation by the Sino-Japanese rapprochement. For the century prior to this rapprochement, the United States was caught in the perpetual crunch between the two foremost Asian powers. Witness, for example, the last three wars in Asia. In World War II, the United States fought alongside China against Japan. In the Korean War, the United States fought against China, using Japan as a logistics base. In the Vietnam War, the United States battled a close Chinese ally, again using Japan as a logistical base. But now, for the first time in recent history, the United States has good or relatively good ties to both Japan and China. At the military-strategic level, this is an enormous plus for Washington. China and Japan are not militarily allied against Moscow, but close China-Japan links preclude the need for Washington to face, militarily, two giant Communist forces in East Asia as it did from the late 1940s to the early 1970s.

These military-strategic considerations overlap into the political sector. China and Japan share congruent policies in the Pacific Region—both want a peaceful environment and both want to exclude Soviet involvement. These goals, of course, duplicate U.S. goals. In terms of economics, improved and rapidly growing economic ties between Beijing and Tokyo are also a major bonus for Washington. An easily ignored point is that China now helps to absorb the staggering flow of Japanese exports of manufactured goods—such as steel and motor vehicles. In 1984, for instance, China edged out the United States as the number-one customer for Japanese steel products.[21] Given the painful stress of Japan's exports on the U.S. market, such developments are helpful to U.S.-Japan relations.

And finally there is the Republic of China. It is clear that the Japan-PRC rapprochement was psychologically devastating to the ROC. It was a second body blow within a short span of time, coinciding so closely with the Kissinger-Nixon visits to Beijing. The PRC-Japan link represents one more reason why the ROC will not again rule the China mainland, and in political-normative terms it also further isolated the ROC, including the loss of its UN seat.

Still, one must point to the astonishing economic successes of the ROC in the wake of the Sino-Japanese rapprochement. It may not be possible to link these economic triumphs causally to the Japan-PRC rapprochement, but there's no doubt that Taiwan's economic prosperity approximates closely with this period. In any event, Taiwan's economic ties to Japan (not to mention the United States) have never been more elaborate in complexity nor larger in size. In addition, Taiwan has much support in Japan, at both elite and popular levels. It is worth noting that perhaps the most damaging thing that Beijing could do to itself would be to launch an attack on Taiwan. In brief, the fact remains that Taiwan has weathered the storm with stunning success.

The Future

Prediction is exceedingly difficult, especially with respect to the future.

Will the situation that we have analyzed evolve in broadly similar directions into the 1990s? A "straight-line" projection is the most tempting prediction, that is, "more of the same," and the temptation is all the stronger when the present and recent past seem sensible. In this final section, we will raise some points that should support the present trends, and some that suggest difficulties.

Positive Aspects

On the Japanese side, from the most senior officials to the citizenry at large, there is a strong desire to continue and augment the present trends. With almost disarming simplicity, Foreign Minister Abe Shintaro put the case as follows in a mid-1984 interview: "We can hardly find any factors that might alter the present situation in the foreseeable future."[22] In broad outline, the Chinese stress the imperative need for peace as the required framework for accomplishing the Four Modernizations (agriculture, industry, science and technology, and national defense). These are mainly economic goals, and Japan is in many ways the premier modernized economy. In particular, the two economies are complementary. It is commonplace to stress this economic complementarity, but it's equally important to note the steadily emerging military-strategic complementarity. This relationship seems to hold true regarding the two nations' policies toward the key issues and actors in Asia: the United States, the Soviet Union, Korea, and neutrality in Southeast Asia.

In brief, a rational foreign policy for both sides strongly supports a "more-of-the-same" future. Unfortunately, the future is seldom so tidy; so we must turn to the roadblocks.

Negative Aspects

Among the potential trouble spots is the element of change in Chinese foreign policy. No contemporary nation has undergone more decisive and wrenching changes than China. It has been the friend and foe of both superpowers. Indeed, there is no significant country that has not witnessed this volatility—India and Indonesia are two neighboring nations of great importance that have felt both Beijing's warm embrace and its icy scorn. Japan, too, has witnessed these abrupt changes—all of them coming within the adult lives of Japan's current political elite. Most of these abrupt changes occurred during the Maoist era, but note that relations with Vietnam changed from brotherly ally to archenemy during the Deng Xiaoping period.

This potential for abrupt change is of course complicated by the uncertainties that surround the succession after Deng. Deng himself is 82, and his two most senior aides, Hu Yaobang and Zhao Ziyang, are 71 and 67, respectively. The widely shared assumption is that Hu and Zhao will follow Deng's policies. Perhaps. We simply don't know, even if we assume that the scores of newly appointed second-echelon leaders are more pragmatic and technically oriented than the persons they replaced.

On the Japanese side, the succession process is virtually an airtight guarantee of still another Liberal Democratic Party figure who acts like his predecessor. Japanese leaders adjust policies; they don't change them.

This Japanese approach means, of course, that the initiative will be in Chinese hands.[23] China will initiate; Japan will adjust. Japan will attempt to focus relations on economic issues. What China might do is part of the uncertainty.

Some might argue that the most dangerously "negative" action would be a PRC military assault on Taiwan. We should ponder even the most extreme "worst-case" scenario, but a military action of such enormity would go far beyond Sino-Japanese relations. It would, of course, involve the United States. Indeed, it would almost certainly destroy the present fabric of both Sino-Japanese and Sino-American relations, not to mention the still delicate arrangement that provides for the return of Hong Kong to the PRC in 1997. Accordingly, as already suggested, such an attack seems extremely unlikely.

Another problem might be termed the "limits of China's dependence." The PRC was burned once by the Soviet Union in the 1950s when China's economy was massively dependent on the Soviets. In terms of trade alone, China's dependence of about 25 percent on Japan stands in contrast to Japan's dependence on China in the 5 percent range. China, of course, deals with many other nations that can produce the same goods Japan does— virtually any Common Market country, plus the United States, Canada, and Australia, and even a few of the "newly emerging countries" (NICs). This "problem" of dependence on Japan may in fact be less of an abrasive issue and more of a ceiling on Japan's involvement.

One more recurring problem involves the fact that Chinese officials concerned with Japan spend much of their time dealing with *nongovernmental* businessmen. In other words, the China-Japan linkage is in many ways not an *international* relationship, but rather a *transnational* relationship. The problem seems to arise in its starkest form in terms of technology transfer. As Kubota Akira notes, from the Japanese view such transfers carry with them two "unavoidable assumptions."[24] First, the transaction must be profitable and, second, the donor nation is always wary of the "boomerang effect," that is, the very real possibility that the recipient nation will use the technology to outcompete the donor nation. There is a strong tendency within China's huge and generally inefficient bureaucracy[25] to assume that the Japanese government can fix any problem that arises in dealing with Japanese businesses. Sometimes, of course, that's true; often it isn't.

At the military-strategic level, one pitfall may involve atomic weaponry and ballistic missiles. For example, Japan has ratified the nuclear nonproliferation treaty. China has not, even though it has not helped other nations get atomic weaponry. On a related issue, Japan regularly protested China's above-ground nuclear tests, but the PRC announced it was ending such tests in the spring of 1986.[26] Japan also protests China's missile firings. In May 1980, for instance, Tokyo protested Beijing's ICBM tests in the Pacific Ocean on the grounds (always important to Japan) that such tests might damage Japan's fishing industry.[27]

Still another military-strategic issue might arise if China took some precipitous action to "teach Vietnam another lesson." Japan fully supports Beijing's view that Vietnam must pull out of Kampuchea, but fears that another Chinese "defensive invasion" of Vietnam might, unlike the 1979 invasion, provoke the Soviets into some dangerous action possibly harmful to Japan.

A further irritant concerns Japan's alleged militarism. We are four decades removed from World War II, but Chinese sensitivities remain acute on this issue—even granting that Beijing may at times "use" this sensitivity to put Japan on the defensive. The now famous (or infamous) textbook controversy of mid-1982 produced angry reactions from China (and other Asians) who charged that Japan was trying to whitewash Japanese atrocities during World War II. And then in a stunning display of obtuseness, the Japanese allowed the issue to be rekindled in mid-1986 when it was revealed that such ghastly atrocities as the Nanking Massacre of 1937 were being soft-pedaled in a new Japanese history text.[28] Moreover, Prime Minister Nakasone's 1985 visit to Yasukuni Shrine (a symbol of Japanese militarism, especially to those on Japan's political left) was seen by some as proof that the Japanese harbor desires to regain their military prowess. Chinese protests, including student-led rallies in China, forced a fence-mending visit to Beijing by Japanese Foreign Minister Abe Shintaro in October 1985 to tell the Chinese that a second Nakasone visit to the shrine had been canceled.[29] This antimilitarism theme has spilled over into popular protests against Japan's "second invasion," that is, the flood of Japanese consumer goods in China's markets.

Beyond these demonstrations there may well linger a broader concern that could trouble Sino-Japanese relations. Each side seems to hope that the other will get stronger—but not too strong. China looks with favor, for example, at Japan's military establishment and its ties to the United States. But it would plainly take a dim view of Japanese moves toward nuclear weaponry or an emphasis in Japan's military configuration that seemed to have offensive overtones. Japan, in turn, wishes China well in its economic modernization endeavors. Yet it also realizes that China is already the world's largest and most important NIC[30] and thus is capable of challenging Japan's primacy as Asia's greatest economic power.

Conclusion

We can conclude by again reminding ourselves of the temptation to project trends similar to those prevailing today. On balance the present trends in Sino-Japanese relations seem to benefit both sides, and thus a "rational" future would be to continue present policies. We also know, however, that the PRC has often made abrupt changes, and thus at a minimum we should be prepared for changes—however irrational. We must also be prepared for actions by outside forces that might alter Sino-Japanese relations. The two most obvious outside forces would, of course, be the superpowers. The United States basically profits from the current situation; the Soviet Union does not. Accordingly, it would seem more likely that the Soviets might take some actions that could disrupt the current situation.[31]

In brief, we should expect more of the same, but be prepared for the worst.

Notes

I would like to thank Richard K. Winslow, Jr., of the Japanese Consulate-General in Boston for supplying some useful materials. I am also grateful for the helpful comments made at the Fifteenth Sino-American Conference on Mainland China, Taipei, June 1986, especially by the discussant of my paper, David S. Chou, and by Harry Harding.

1. For example, in July 1984, Defense Minister Zhang Aiping visited Japan, and in June 1985, Deputy Director-General Natsume Haruo of Japan's Defense Agency visited China. For a very thorough analysis of Japan-China security links, see William T. Tow, "Sino-Japanese Security Cooperation: Evolution and Prospects," *Pacific Affairs*, vol. 56, no. 1, spring 1983, pp. 51–83.

2. See, for example, Ministry of Foreign Affairs, *Diplomatic Bluebook 1985 Edition* (Tokyo, n.d.), pp. 98–101.

3. For a lengthy treatment of this important treaty, see Robert E. Bedeski, *The Fragile Entente: The 1978 Japan-China Peace Treaty in a Global Context* (Boulder, Colo.: Westview Press, 1983).

4. No less than 374 of the 512 representatives in the lower house of Japan's parliament are members of the Japan-China Friendship Parliamentarians' League. It

is now headed by former Foreign Minister Ito Masayoshi. *Liberal Star,* November 10, 1985, p. 11. The *Star* is the organ of Japan's ruling Liberal Democratic Party.

5. Lin Liande, "Thirty Years of Sino-Japanese Trade," *Chinese Economic Studies,* vol. 16, no. 4, summer 1983, pp. 51–62. This same source has a table showing the large number of Japanese firms and businessmen that take part in the Canton Trade Fair. In the late 1970s and early 1980s, about 5,000 businessmen a year attended the fair.

6. *The Japanese Press* (Tokyo: Japan Newspaper Publishers and Editors Association, 1983), pp. 39, 107, 164.

7. *Beijing Review,* no. 41, October 14, 1985, p. 10.

8. Shinkichi Eto, "Evolving Sino-Japanese Relations," *Journal of International Affairs,* vol. 37, no. 1, summer 1983, p. 62.

9. See Akio Watanabe, "Japanese Public and Foreign Affairs, 1964–1973," in Robert A. Scalapino, ed., *The Foreign Policy of Modern Japan* (Berkeley: University of California Press, 1977), pp. 105–145, especially pp. 124–131.

10. The Japanese government poll, taken by the Prime Minister's Office, was published in mimeograph form by the Foreign Press Center in Tokyo in September 1983 under the title "Public Opinion Survey on Diplomacy." For a useful poll on Japanese perceptions of, interest in, and trust of China, see Masahi Nishihara, *East Asian Security and the Trilateral Countries: A Report to the Trilateral Commission* (New York: New York University Press, 1985), p. 107.

11. The trade statistics for 1985 are preliminary.

12. The oil figure is from Japan Institute for Social and Economic Affairs, *Japan 1985: An International Comparison* (Tokyo, 1985), p. 65; the coal figure is from Japan External Trade Organization, *White Paper on International Trade, Japan 1984: Summary* (Tokyo, 1985), p. 171.

13. For an excellent treatment of this issue, see the second chapter of Chae-Jin Lee, *China and Japan: New Economic Diplomacy* (Stanford, Calif.: Hoover Institution Press, 1984).

14. See, for example, Wang Linsheng, "On the Role of Foreign Trade Under Socialism," *Chinese Economic Studies,* vol. 16, no. 3, spring 1983, pp. 48–65. Wang's article directs several barbs at misguided self-reliance. For instance, "Ideologically, it was the effect of the folly of 'leftist' misconception that lopsidedly emphasized self-reliance" (p. 61), or, "In summing up our historical experience, we can draw the conclusion that the misconception of autarky cost us the golden opportunity of the 1960s" (p. 61).

15. Association for Promotion of International Cooperation, *Japan's Official Development Assistance: 1985 Annual Report* (Tokyo, 1986), pp. 8 and 34. See also a first-rate article that covers all phases of economics by Hong N. Kim and Richard K. Nanto, "Emerging Patterns of Sino-Japanese Economic Cooperation," *Journal of Northeast Asian Studies,* vol. 4, no. 3, Fall 1985, pp. 29–47. Nanto and Kim cover much of the same ground in their "Sino-Japanese Economic Relations," which appears in Joint Economic Committee, Congress of the United States, *China's Economy Looks Toward the Year 2000, Volume 2: Economic Openness in Modernizing China* (Washington, D.C., 1986), pp. 453–471. Further recent and useful coverage is found in Dennis T. Yasutomo, *The Manner of Giving: Strategic Aid and Japanese Foreign Policy* (Lexington, Mass.: Lexington Books, 1986), pp. 96–99.

16. Interview with a Chinese official, conducted in Medford, Mass., March 1986. For an "official" and optimistic view, see *Beijing Review* no. 9, March 3, 1986, pp. 16–17.

17. A typical and recent illustration of Peking's seeming disdain for the world communist movement is found in *Beijing Review*, no. 15, April 14, 1986, p. 9, which blandly reported that "relations between China and the Soviet Union are so far not stable enough for them to resume formal Party relations."

18. This theme is developed in Donald W. Klein, "Mainland China's Role in the [Pacific] Region," in Cecilia S. Chang, ed., *Changing International Relations in Asia* (New York: Institute of Asian Studies, St. John's University, 1985), pp. 37–64.

19. Same interview cited in note 16.

20. This is well covered in Chong-Sik Lee, *Japan and Korea: The Political Dimension* (Stanford, Calif.: Hoover Institution Press, 1985), pp. 129–135.

21. Article by correspondent Tom Ashbrook, *Boston Globe*, December 2, 1985.

22. Interview with Abe in *Journal of Northeast Asian Studies*, vol. 3, no. 2, summer 1984, p. 68.

23. The Japanese scholar Eto Shinkichi stressed this point in an article marking the tenth anniversary of Sino-Japanese relations, published in *Look Japan*, September 10, 1982, pp. 1–3.

24. Kubota Akira, "Transferring Technology to Asia," *Japan Quarterly*, vol. 33, no. 1, January-March 1986, pp. 37–44.

25. Chae-Jin Lee, *China and Japan: New Economic Diplomacy* (Stanford, Calif.: Hoover Institution Press, 1984), pp. 144–145.

26. *Beijing Review*, no. 23, June 9, 1986, p. 18.

27. Tow, "Sino-Japanese Security Cooperation," p. 64.

28. *Japan Times*, June 20, 1986; *Boston Globe*, June 22, 1986; *New York Times*, July 10, 1986.

29. Article by correspondent Tom Ashbrook, *Boston Globe*, December 2, 1985. See also Richard Baum, "China in 1985: The Greening of the Revolution," *Asian Survey*, vol. 26, no. 1, January 1986, especially pp. 51–52.

30. On this point, see Dwight Perkins, "The Economic Background and Implications for China," in Herbert J. Ellison, ed., *The Sino-Soviet Conflict: A Global Perspective* (Seattle: University of Washington Press, 1982), p. 111.

31. For an interesting analysis of the Soviet Union as a "disruptive world power," see Zbigniew Brzezinski, "The Soviet Union: World Power of a New Type," in Erik P. Hoffmann, ed., *The Soviet Union in the 1980s* (New York: Academy of Political Science, 1984), especially pp. 154–158.

20

Beijing's Relations with Vietnam and Korea: Implications for Future Change in PRC Foreign Policy

Robert G. Sutter

One of the critical issues facing analysts of Chinese affairs remains the determination of the likelihood of significant change in the foreign policy of the People's Republic of China (PRC). In particular, analysts and policy-makers in the United States assess repeatedly the possibility that Beijing leaders might shift their general foreign policy orientation of the past fifteen years, which has focused on the Soviet Union as the main strategic danger for China and on the United States as a generally helpful international force, compatible with PRC security and development interests in Asia. They are struck by the repeated tactical shifts that have come to characterize PRC policy—one that seems to stress at times a need for a strong united front with the United States, the West, and Japan against Soviet power, and at other times avers China's lack of interest in such ties with the West in favor of a more independent foreign policy posture that allows the PRC flexibility in encouraging dialogue and possible reconciliation with the USSR.

In determining whether or not Beijing will be inclined to pursue accommodation with the USSR, to a point where it would substantially change the PRC posture between the superpowers prevalent over the last fifteen years, it appears useful to examine closely those factors that serve to restrict or block such change. This chapter follows the analysis of other scholars and the avowed position of the PRC leaders to argue that the impediments to Sino-Soviet reconciliation no longer rest heavily on ideological, historical, cultural, or leadership differences, as they did in the past. Rather, they center on the two powers' continued conflicting interests in Asia.[1] Specifically, the paper views two major points of rivalry—competing Soviet and Chinese policies toward Vietnam and Korea. As is well known, Vietnam's Soviet-backed occupation of Kampuchea (Cambodia) is often explicitly cited by the PRC as the most serious of the so-called three obstacles blocking reconciliation in Sino-Soviet relations. (The other obstacles involve the Soviet military occupation of Afghanistan and the presence of large Soviet forces along the Soviet and Mongolian borders with China.) Recently intensified Sino-Soviet competition for influence in Korea demonstrates that Sino-Soviet relations with Pyongyang have become an important, albeit unspoken, "fourth obstacle" to improved Beijing-Moscow ties.

Change in the overall orientation in PRC foreign policy will not be determined by these two issues alone. Nevertheless, a careful examination of the depth of PRC competition with the Soviet Union in these areas could provide a useful balance to some recent assessments stressing the likelihood of growing independence in Beijing's foreign policy and steady progress toward reconciliation in Sino-Soviet relations.[2]

Determinants of Recent Chinese Foreign Policy and Their Impact on Sino-Soviet Relations

Viewed from Beijing's perspective, the fundamental difficulties in Sino-Soviet relations can be explained by looking at the basic determinants of recent PRC foreign policy.[3] The foreign policy objectives have been determined by a small group of top-level leaders who have reflected the broad interests of the state as well as their own parochial concerns. The primary concerns of these leaders have been to guarantee national security, maintain internal order, and pursue economic development. Especially since the death of Mao in 1976, the top priority has been to promote successful economic development and modernization. This represents the linchpin determining their success or failure. Thus officials have geared foreign policy to help the modernization effort.

But, in order to accomplish economic modernization, as well as to maintain national security and internal order, PRC leaders recognize the fundamental prerequisite of establishing a relatively stable strategic environment, especially around the nation's periphery in Asia. The alternative would be a highly disruptive situation requiring much greater expenditures on national defense and posing greater danger to domestic order and tranquility. The PRC does not control this environment. It has influenced it, but the environment remains controlled more by others, especially the superpowers and their allies and associates. As a result, PRC leaders have been required repeatedly to assess their surroundings for changes that could affect the nation's security and development concerns. And they have been compelled repeatedly to adjust foreign policy to take account of such changes.

At the same time, PRC leaders have nationalistic and ideological objectives regarding irredentist claims (like Taiwan and Hong Kong) and a desire to stand independently in foreign affairs as a leading force among "progressive" nations of the Third World. These goals have struck a responsive chord politically inside the country. Occasional leadership discussion and debate over these and other questions have sometimes had an effect on the course of foreign policy. But, over the past decade, such debates have become progressively less serious, and the foreign policy differences raised in them have become more moderate and less of a challenge to the recent dominant objectives of national development and security.

Thus, Beijing's top foreign policy priority has remained the pragmatic quest for the stable environment needed for effective modernization and development. PRC leaders since 1969 have seen the main danger of negative change in the surrounding environment posed by the Soviet Union. At first, they perceived Soviet power as an immediate threat to national security. Over time, they perceived the USSR more as a long-term threat, determined to use its growing military power and other sources of influence to encircle and pressure the PRC into accepting a balance of influence in Asia dominated by the USSR and contrary to PRC interests.

PRC strategy against the Soviet threat has been both bilateral and global. Bilaterally, it has used a mix of military preparations and tactical, political, economic, and other moves to keep the Soviets from attacking and pressuring it. Globally, PRC strategy has focused on developing—either implicitly or explicitly—an international united front designed to halt Soviet expansion and prevent the consolidation of Soviet dominance abroad.

As the most important international counterweight to Soviet power, the United States has loomed large in PRC calculations. Once the United States, under terms of the Nixon Doctrine announced in 1969, seemed determined to withdraw from its past policy of containing the PRC in Asia, and thereby ended a perceived threat to PRC national security, Beijing was prepared to start the process of U.S.-Chinese normalization. The process has been complemented in recent years by China's enhanced interest in pragmatic economic modernizations, which has emphasized the importance of technical and financial help from the West and access to Western markets.

Closer ties with the United States continue to be complicated by nationalistic and ideological concerns over Taiwan and Third World questions, as well as by fundamental differences between the social, political, and economic systems of the United States and the PRC. Most notably, U.S. support for Taiwan is seen as a continued affront to PRC national sovereignty. But Beijing leaders have differentiated between substantive threats to their security, posed by the USSR, and threats to their sense of national sovereignty, posed by U.S. support for Taiwan.

In short, the PRC has worked hard, and continues to work hard, to ensure that its strategic environment, threatened mainly by Soviet expansion and power, remains stable, so that it can focus on economic modernization. The USSR is seen as having a strategy of expansion that uses military power relentlessly but cautiously in order to achieve political influence and dominance throughout its periphery. Beijing has long held that the focus of Soviet attention is in Europe, but that NATO's strength requires Moscow to work in other areas, notably the Middle East, Africa, Southwest Asia, and East Asia, in order to outflank the Western defenses. The PRC is seen as relatively low on Moscow's list of military priorities, although its leaders clearly appreciate the dire consequences for the PRC should the USSR be able to consolidate its position elsewhere and then focus its strength to intimidate its Chinese neighbor.

PRC strategy of deterrence and defense, therefore, aims basically to exacerbate Soviet defense problems by enhancing the worldwide opposition to Soviet expansion in general, and by raising the possibility of the Soviet Union confronting a multifront conflict in the event it attempted to attack or intimidate the PRC in particular. Beijing leaders see their nation's cooperation with the United States as especially important in strengthening deterrence of the Soviet Union and in aggravating Soviet strategic vulnerabilities. Beijing also encourages anti-Soviet efforts by so-called Second World, developed countries—most of whom are formal allies of the United States—and by developing countries of the Third World.

At the same time, Beijing uses a mix of political talks, bilateral exchanges, and other forms of interchange to help manage the danger posed by the USSR. In fact, circumstantial evidence over the past two years has suggested at times that pragmatism in Beijing and Moscow has prompted leaders in both capitals to attempt to improve the atmosphere in their bilateral relations to a point where questions could be raised as to a possible substantial breakthrough in Sino-Soviet relations. In particular:

- Beijing soft-pedaled anti-Soviet invective in covering the fifth anniversary of the Soviet invasion of Afghanistan, in December 1984, and during the Vietnamese military offensive against PRC-supported insurgents in Kampuchea in 1985.
- The December 1984 visit to China of Soviet Deputy Prime Minister Ivan Arkhipov resulted in agreements on a long-term trade accord, and economic consultations were further developed during the reciprocal visit of Vice-Premier Yao Yilin to the USSR in July 1985. Vice Premier Li Peng traveled to Moscow in December 1985, while Arkhipov returned to Beijing in mid-1986.
- PRC leaders hinted repeatedly in 1985 at an interest in restoring party relations with the Soviet Union, notably by referring to Soviet leaders as "comrade."
- Soviet leader Mikhail Gorbachev repeatedly avowed his strong interest in improving relations with Beijing; and unlike his predecessors, he soft-pedaled anti-China comment in support of allies, like Vietnam, known to be strongly hostile to the PRC. This approach led to signs of Soviet-Vietnamese friction emerging during Vietnamese leader Le Duan's visit to Moscow in June 1985.

But such efforts to improve the atmosphere and increase exchanges in Sino-Soviet relations thus far have not reduced Soviet military pressure around the PRC's periphery in Asia. Indeed, the USSR has used a continued military buildup and support for such allies as Vietnam, Afghanistan, and Mongolia as a key means to help secure its interests in the region. And, beginning in 1984, it used military assistance as a method to strengthen its relations with North Korea, thereby bringing about the most substantial breakthrough in Soviet-Korean relations in twenty years. This military approach was taken in part because Moscow has been unable to build major economic or political influence in the area. As a result, Beijing continues to perceive a growing danger of Soviet military dominance and a strong need to work with the United States, Japan, and other countries to provide a counterweight that would keep Soviet power in check and preserve a balance of influence in Asia favorable to Beijing's security and development.

Beijing, of course, retains the option of attempting to reach, on its own, a serious accommodation with Soviet power in Asia. This course could be seen to help modernization by reducing the need for extensive defense expenditures to deter Soviet power, thereby allowing greater resources to be applied to economic development. But the PRC leadership is doubtless aware that any serious effort to accommodate the USSR in Asia would cause the United States, Japan, and their allies and friends in Asia to reassess their policies toward Beijing, and would run the risk of leaving the PRC isolated as it dealt with the USSR. Under these circumstances, Beijing almost certainly would fear that it would risk mortgaging its longer term development and independence to the dictates of Soviet power and influence.

Beijing, therefore, is unlikely to pursue such a risky course unless it perceives that Soviet leaders are truly no longer interested in using military power to exert dominating influence over the PRC. The proof of such intent would be seen in Soviet efforts to curb their military power in the region. Whether or not the Gorbachev administration will adopt such policies is doubtless a key determinant in the future course of Sino-Soviet relations. While some PRC officials may hope for such a reduction in Soviet power, sober analysis of the obstacles in Sino-Soviet relations, including their competing interests in Vietnam and Korea, would suggest that such prospects are remote. A Soviet military pullback from Asia would seriously jeopardize Moscow's ability to protect Soviet territory and the interests of Soviet allies and friends, not only against possible threat from the PRC, but also against the continuing military buildup of the United States, Japan, and their associates.

Policy Toward Vietnam

Since the late 1970s, Beijing's policy has remained centered on confronting Vietnam's Soviet-supported occupation of Kampuchea and the growing Soviet presence in Indochina.[4] Since the Vietnamese military invasion and the PRC counterstrike of 1978–1979, Beijing has followed a fairly uniform strategy of military, diplomatic, and economic pressure designed to wear down the Vietnamese in a protracted conflict in Kampuchea, and to solidify regional resistance to the Vietnamese and their Soviet supporters.

Beijing's immediate objective, aside from wearing down the Vietnamese in Kampuchea, has been to prevent the Vietnamese from consolidating their position in the country. The PRC also has tried to use its influence with the non-Communist Southeast Asian countries—members of the Association of Southeast Asian Nations (ASEAN)—and more broadly with the United States, Japan, and other countries to establish a balance of power in the region against further Soviet and Vietnamese gains.

In the longer run, the PRC has appeared to hope to force the Vietnamese to withdraw their armed forces from Kampuchea. Beijing almost certainly would prefer to see emerge a new Kampuchean government that would be susceptible to PRC influence, and it has presumably sustained close ties with the Khmer Rouge in part to achieve this end. However, PRC officials also have recognized that such a prospect remains a long way off, at best, and that being seen as favoring a return of the Khmer Rouge would be counterproductive, especially because of strong ASEAN resistance.

Beijing also has ambitions to increase friction between the Vietnamese and the Soviets, hoping to see their alliance come apart over time, thereby leading to the termination of the Soviet military presence in Southeast Asia. As Soviet and Vietnamese influence waned, the PRC no doubt would expect that Southeast Asia would become more open to its influence.

Beijing's strategy to achieve these objectives has involved several elements, including applying military pressure along the Sino-Vietnamese border and in Kampuchea; improving its relations with ASEAN members, especially Thailand, which acts as a conduit of PRC aid to the Khmer resistance forces; promoting international efforts in the United Nations and elsewhere to ensure Vietnam's continued international isolation; and encouraging the United States and other Western countries to become more involved with the anti-Vietnamese resistance as a means to counter Soviet support for Vietnam and to encourage greater ASEAN resolve.

Beijing has directed military pressure against Vietnam on two fronts—northern Vietnam and Kampuchea. Its long experience with the tough, independent-minded Vietnamese almost certainly has caused Beijing to believe that Hanoi would have to feel it was losing on the battlefield before it would negotiate seriously. Beijing's threat to administer a "second lesson"—backed by periodic artillery shelling and shallow incursions into Vietnamese territory—have tied down about half of Vietnam's ground forces. Beijing's pressure prevents Hanoi from diverting these forces—armed with Soviet-supplied weapons—for use against the insurgents in Kampuchea, and it has placed a great burden on Vietnam's already very poor economy. The PRC probably also calculates that its threats deepen Vietnam's dependence on the USSR: Over the short term this policy seems to improve Moscow's position in Indochina, but from one point of view it provides the potential, over the longer period, for tension in Soviet relations with the independent-minded Vietnamese.

Beijing usually reacts to the Vietnamese annual dry-season military action in Kampuchea and incursions into Thailand with military action along Vietnam's northern border. But this reactive approach changed somewhat in 1984, when Beijing was more active in support of the Kampuchean resistance and Thailand, launching attacks on the northern border well before the height of the Vietnamese dry-season offensive in Kampuchea. This new activity led to the longest and most serious period of fighting along the Sino-Vietnamese border since 1979. The height of PRC attacks came during the visit of President Ronald Reagan to China, suggesting that Beijing wished to use its actions both to solidify U.S.-Chinese common interests regarding this issue, and to signal Vietnam and its Soviet backer that the PRC has tacit U.S. support for its tougher stance. The stronger PRC policy in Indochina also came in part as a response to the unprecedented Soviet joint amphibious exercise with Vietnamese forces near Haiphong in March 1984—the first time Soviet naval forces had been reported operating in such a way so close to Chinese territory. The Soviet action posed a clear threat to PRC ability to hold the Paracel Islands, taken by PRC forces in 1974 but still claimed by Hanoi.

In 1985 and 1986, Beijing reverted to a more reactive posture, even though the Vietnamese dry-season offensive in 1984–1985 was successful in wiping out the major Kampuchean resistance strongholds along the Thai border inside Kampuchea. Its position at this time seemed consistent with its effort to avoid undue friction over Vietnam, Indochina issues, and other questions with the newly emerging Gorbachev leadership in the USSR. In late 1985, however, Beijing adopted a somewhat harder stance, calling on Moscow to stop sidestepping the three obstacles and to take concrete actions to do something about the Vietnamese occupation of Kampuchea.

In Kampuchea, Beijing remains the primary supplier of aid to the three Khmer resistance groups—the Communist Democratic Kampuchean (DK) fighters, who have represented by far the most important of the three, and two non-Communist groups, the Khmer People's National Liberation Front (KPNLF), under the leadership of Son Sann, and the National Army under Norodom Sihanouk. The PRC also has provided weapons to all three groups, but most have gone to the Communists. The PRC appears likely to continue to give a much larger share to the Communist insurgents, as Beijing remains wary of moves that could potentially undermine the DK's fighting ability. At least some PRC officials have appeared to judge that a substantial increase in assistance to the non-Communist resistance might hurt DK morale. Beijing also urges that ASEAN and the United States should supply the non-Communist insurgents; presumably it judges that such material support builds stronger ASEAN and U.S. political commitment to the resistance effort.

Beijing also reportedly supplies weapons and training to small, and thus far reportedly ineffective, resistance forces in Laos and Vietnam. PRC involvement with Vietnamese resistance goes back at least to the defection of former Vietnamese Politburo member Hoang Van Hoan to the PRC in 1979. Hoang became the head of the Vietnamese National Salvation Front, a de facto government in exile based in Beijing. The front has been involved mainly with propaganda broadcasts directed against Hanoi, and it has little known armed support inside Vietnam.

Toward the non-Communist countries of Southeast Asia, the members of ASEAN, the PRC attempts to foster better bilateral relations in order to build stronger regional resistance to the Vietnamese in Kampuchea. Good relations with Thailand are vital to Beijing's efforts to provide military assistance and sanctuary for the resistance forces. As the state along the front line facing Vietnamese forces in Indochina, and as the member of ASEAN most threatened by potential Vietnamese expansion, Thailand has found itself closely associating with the PRC as a necessary security guarantor. But Bangkok remains suspicious of the PRC's longer-term intentions— concerns shared to a greater degree elsewhere in ASEAN, especially in Indonesia and Malaysia.

Beijing has attempted to meet these concerns by supporting the ASEAN-fostered, ostensibly neutral coalition government in Kampuchea; by reducing to a bare minimum or ending ties with Communist insurgents in Southeast Asia; and by moderating ties to overseas Chinese communities there. Beijing does not explicitly reject a role for the DK in a future compromise political settlement in Kampuchea, but it clearly has stated its support for a future "neutral and nonaligned" Kampuchea that does not envisage the return of a pro-Chinese regime led by Pol Pot. In this regard, Beijing was probably influential in Pol Pot's 1980 decision to step down as the nominal head of the DK, for the group's decision to abandon communism as its official ideology, and for Pol Pot's reported retirement as military leader of DK forces in 1985.

The PRC reportedly stopped aid to the Communist Party of Thailand in exchange for Bangkok's cooperation in supplying the resistance in Kampuchea. Similarly, aid to the Communist Party of Malaysia ended or was reduced to a bare minimum, and aid to the Philippine insurgents had ended earlier. Beijing also cut off propaganda broadcasts from the PRC in support of Thai and Malaysian insurgents in 1979 and 1981, respectively. Judging from the contents of these broadcasts prior to their going off the air, the PRC was advising local party leaders to put aside past emphasis on armed struggle in favor of political action and united front tactics against the Soviets and the Vietnamese.

Confirming its discreet handling of overseas Chinese, Beijing repeatedly has affirmed its long-standing policy of denying dual nationality. It has emphasized that it expects Chinese residing abroad to integrate themselves into local society and to obey local laws. The PRC rarely has protested unfair treatment of overseas Chinese by ASEAN governments.

Beijing has also used trade, diplomacy, and the development of personal contacts through the frequent exchange of high-level visitors to build its influence. For example, the Malaysian foreign minister held talks with PRC leaders in Beijing in late May 1984. Although differences persisted between Beijing and Kuala Lumpur—especially over China's refusal to sever all ties with the Malaysian Communist Party—the fact that the visit took place at all was a sign of Malaysian as well as Chinese interest in sustaining a working relationship.

To isolate Vietnam diplomatically over Kampuchea, Beijing has insisted that any solution must conform to the general provisions of the resolution adopted by the United Nations in 1980 and the International Conference on Kampuchea in 1981. These require a complete withdrawal of Vietnamese forces from Kampuchea, neutralization of Kampuchea under international guarantees, and free elections under international supervision. Barring Vietnamese approval, Beijing has rebuffed Hanoi's calls for Sino-Vietnamese talks, opposed compromise efforts by third parties that might add legitimacy to Vietnam's hold on Kampuchea, and supported ASEAN-led efforts to preserve the coalition government's seat in the United Nations.

Beijing leaders sometimes have been compelled to adjust their political position to offset Vietnamese efforts to sow dissension in ASEAN's ranks and to portray China as the aggressor. In 1983, for instance, Beijing publicized a five-point peace proposal for the solution of the Kampuchean issue that appeared to be designed to offset Vietnamese charges of Chinese intransigence. However, it deviated from China's standard formula only in stating that if Vietnam agreed to a phased withdrawal of its forces, Beijing would resume the Sino-Vietnamese dialogue after the first installment of troops returned to Vietnam. Beijing had previously insisted on full Vietnamese withdrawal prior to resuming the talks. Similar tactical flexibility appeared in early 1986 when Beijing endorsed the Kampuchean coalition's March 1986 peace proposal that would have allowed the Vietnamese-backed Phnom Penh government to join with the three anti-Vietnamese parties in forming a new Kampuchean government, once Hanoi agreed to withdraw its forces. Vietnam promptly turned aside the proposal.

Beijing has differed publicly with ASEAN on Kampuchea only when it has believed an ASEAN initiative would harm the resistance effort or result in less than complete Vietnamese withdrawal. For example, Beijing at first was reluctant to support ASEAN proposals for the formation of a coalition government and the convening of an international conference on Kampuchea in 1981. And the PRC refused to yield to ASEAN efforts to form a coalition government that would have put the DK in a disadvantageous position.

Beijing has expressed more strenuous opposition to third-party efforts to find a solution to the Kampuchean issue that compromised on the UN formula. PRC Premier Zhao Ziyang warned France and Australia when they put forward their proposals on Kampuchea in 1982 and 1983, respectively.

Regarding the problems posed by ever closer Soviet-Vietnamese relations, Beijing has appeared to believe that its hard policy will eventually exacerbate Soviet-Vietnamese tensions, although in the short run it obviously increases Hanoi's dependence on Soviet support. Beijing's military pressure raises the economic costs of Moscow's special relationship with Hanoi and creates new demands for Soviet military assistance. Moscow's support for Vietnamese expansion also reduces the USSR's opportunities to make inroads in the ASEAN countries. Beijing probably calculates that if it is able to increase these economic and political costs to Moscow, the Soviets will be more likely to increase their demands on the Vietnamese, perhaps to the point of irreparably damaging relations.

Beijing also has tried to use the Sino-Soviet vice-ministerial and other talks to create concern in Hanoi that Moscow might compromise its ties with Vietnam in favor of a deal with China. Hanoi has exhibited some nervousness when Sino-Soviet talks are under way, but the Soviets have been generally successful in reassuring their ally that Vietnamese interests will not be sacrificed.

Beijing also seems to believe that greater U.S. involvement in support of ASEAN and the resistance in Kampuchea will help to counter Soviet support for Vietnam and bolster ASEAN resolve against Vietnam and the USSR. Closer Sino-American cooperation in Southeast Asia also serves to reduce ASEAN suspicions of Chinese intentions by signalling U.S. approval of Beijing's regional posture. As a result, Beijing has publicly supported the U.S. military presence in Southeast Asia, has called for U.S. military support to the Kampuchea resistance, and has emphasized the compatibility of U.S.-PRC interests in the region.

Policy Toward Korea

Beijing's recent policy toward North Korea has been more influenced by tactical shifts in the overall PRC approach to foreign affairs since the late 1970s than has its policy toward Vietnam.[5] The PRC policy toward North Korea has also reflected Pyongyang's increasingly demonstrated proclivity to seek strategic, political, and economic advantage through exploitation of Sino-Soviet rivalry in Northeast Asia—a North Korean effort made more possible after 1984 by the recently unprecedented Soviet willingness to use military and economic assistance to raise substantially Soviet influence with the North Korean government.

During the 1970s, Beijing managed to build and maintain a strong relationship with North Korea while slowly developing improved ties with the United States, Japan, and their friends and associates. And the Soviet Union showed little inclination to attempt to challenge Beijing's position as the most important foreign influence in Pyongyang. Thus, even in times of difficulty in North Korean–PRC relations, Beijing did not seem particularly concerned that North Korea's alienation from the PRC would result in a major gain for Soviet influence on the peninsula.

A distinct coolness in Sino–North Korean relations began to emerge by 1978, coincident with the rapid forward movement in Beijing's relations with the United States and Japan and resulting moderation in the PRC anti-U.S. stance on Korea. The strain began to be seen in public meetings between the two sides and continued until 1981 when the PRC shifted to a more independent posture in foreign policy toward the Third World that gave pride of place to North Korea.

Problems between the Communist neighbors were in evidence in Beijing's subdued treatment of the April 25, 1979, North Korean Army anniversary, with PRC comment cooler and its leadership turnout lower in rank than in the recent past. The visit of North Korean Premier Yi Ching-ok to Beijing in January 1981 underscored the cooling in relations. Yi's arrival on January 10, 1981, failed to trigger the customary welcoming *People's Daily* editorial, and his departure on January 14 was not marked with the usual concluding statement in the press. These omissions served to cloud the assertion by both sides that a unanimity of views was reached during the talks.

As Beijing adjusted its foreign policy approach in 1981 and 1982 toward a posture more independent of the United States and one that emphasized continued differences with the United States and Japan over such questions as Taiwan and Japan's wartime record in China, the PRC was able to solidify relations with Pyongyang more effectively. Downplaying past emphasis on relations with Washington and Tokyo, Beijing was able to reestablish more common ground with Pyongyang through a series of high-level visits in 1981 and 1982. Premier Zhao Ziyang and Defense Minister Geng Biao visited North Korea in December 1981 and June 1982, respectively. Deng Xiaoping and Hu Yaobang secretly traveled there in April 1982—a visit disclosed during Kim Il Sung's trip to the PRC in September 1982.

Zhao Ziyang's visit in December 1981 reflected efforts by Beijing to improve relations after a period of strain following the normalization of U.S.-PRC relations and the signing of the Sino-Japanese peace treaty in 1978. Both sides used the December 20–24 visit, billed as reciprocating North Korean Premier Yi Ching-ok's January 1981 visit to the PRC, to celebrate improving relations. The respective party papers published editorials to mark the occasion; the atmosphere during the visit was portrayed as warm; and the PRC leaders were more effusive than their hosts in describing the visit. Beijing's report of Zhao's meeting with Kim Il Sung seemed designed to put the Korean leader's imprimatur on the relationship, quoting Kim as saying, "We are one and the same family and we don't anticipate any differences among us."

Zhao voiced the routine PRC line calling for withdrawal of U.S. forces from Korea without expressing a sense of urgency. He went beyond the usual formulations in criticizing Washington's Korean policy, however, when he declared at the welcoming banquet on December 20 that the U.S. troop presence was "a major factor in the instability in Northeast Asia." Beijing's standard charge in the past had been that U.S. troops presented the "major obstacle" to Korean reunification. No new ground was broken on the subject of Washington-Pyongyang talks. And the two sides also followed standard lines on reunification, Sino-Soviet rivalry, and succession to Kim Il-Sung.

Geng Biao's visit to North Korea was unusual in that it was the first delegation led by a PRC defense minister in two decades, and because of his more critical tone in characterizing the United States. Geng notably made a gesture to Pyongyang in calling for an immediate U.S. withdrawal from Korea, although PRC media coverage of the visit carefully avoided citing that demand.

Beijing showed unusually lavish hospitality to Kim Il Sung during his September 15–26, 1982, visit to the PRC, thereby dramatizing a special relationship between Beijing and Pyongyang. Each side expressed support for the other's basic policies and took indirect but repeated note of the political succession arrangements under way in both countries by stating that their friendship would last from "generation to generation." Beijing seemed to take care to signal that its close relationship with North Korea would not pose a threat to the stability of East Asia.

The welcome Kim received in Beijing was even more lavish than that given in April 1982 to Romanian Communist party chief Nicolae Ceausescu, another fraternal party and state leader. In addition to attention from Hu Yaobang and Zhao Ziyang, Deng Xiaoping spent an unusual amount of time with Kim, accompanying him on a visit to Deng's home province of Sichuan.

Neither side shed much light on the substantive nature of the "cordial and friendly" talks held during the visit. At the farewell banquet on September 24, Kim and Hu stated that they had reached "identical views" and were "fully unanimous in our views on all the issues discussed." Kim revealed only that they had "wide-ranging" talks on relations between the two countries and "other issues of common interest." Hu said that the talks included "the international situation and major international issues of common interest."

The special Sino-Korean relationship was underlined by Hu's disclosure at the September 16 welcoming banquet that he and Deng Xiaoping had made a previously unpublicized visit to North Korea in April 1982. Statements by both sides during Kim's visit to the PRC generally hewed to standard lines on the Korean question, but the PRC balanced a bow to Pyongyang's position on the U.S. presence there with an apparent concern not to fuel a sense of insecurity on the peninsula. Thus, both the *People's Daily* editorial marking North Korea's September 9 anniversary and the editorial welcoming Kim's arrival supported Pyongyang's demand for an "immediate" withdrawal of U.S. troops. But Hu's speech on September 16 was more typical of past PRC practice when he said that U.S. withdrawal and Korean reunification would be achieved "eventually" in accordance with the "inevitable trend of history."

Increased Sino-Soviet Competition

By mid-1983, Beijing had begun to tack again in foreign affairs. The PRC was particularly concerned over what seemed likely to be a prolonged downturn in Sino-American relations at a time of increasing Soviet pressures on China. Beijing leaders moved to compromise their previous hard line on sensitive bilateral disputes with the United States and Japan in order to solidify relations with the Reagan and Nakasone administrations in anticipation of a period of difficult relations with the USSR. This trend was capped by the exchange of summit visits between Beijing and Washington and Beijing and Tokyo at this time.

As Beijing moved to consolidate relations with both Japan and the United States, it had a difficult time managing relations with North Korea. Its difficulty was compounded by the PRC's evident willingness to exploit more

directly increased exchanges, especially economic exchanges, with the economically dynamic South Koreans—a trend opposed by Pyongyang—and
by the Soviet Union's newly apparent increased interest in cultivating relations
with Kim Il Sung.

PRC leaders continued their effusive public treatment of North Korea in
several exchanges of high-level visits. This amicable approach was seen
notably during the visit of Kim Il Sung's son and heir apparent, Kim Chong
Il to the PRC in mid-1983, and the visit of Chinese Communist Party (CCP)
General Secretary Hu Yaobang to North Korea in May 1984. But differences
between the two sides emerged over North Korea's assassination of South
Korean leaders in a bombing incident at Rangoon, Burma, in October 1983.
Indeed, the bombing brought home to the PRC leaders the unpredictability
of their ally on the peninsula, an ally whose aggressive actions could start
a major conflict involving China and the other major powers in Northeast
Asia that would destroy China's prospects for substantial economic development for the foreseeable future. In response, Beijing made stronger efforts
to move toward a settlement of the Korean conflict under the rubric of
China's formula "one country, two systems," further moderated its stance
toward U.S. policy in the South, and increased efforts to develop contacts
with South Korea.

Although Beijing showed strong support for Pyongyang's peace proposal
announced in January 1984, calling for talks among North Korea, the United
States, and South Korea, and it encouraged North Korea to adopt a more
flexible economic and development approach that would use greater contacts
with the West, the limits of PRC influence were underlined in May 1984
when Kim Il Sung made his first visit to the USSR in two decades. There
was a particular danger to Chinese interests that Kim would attempt to
establish common ground with Soviet officials in opposition to what Moscow
saw as an emerging U.S.–Japanese–South Korean military bloc in Asia; such
a position would have been in stark contrast with Beijing's increased efforts
at this time to improve relations with both Washington and Tokyo, partly
on the basis of common opposition to Soviet expansion in East Asia, and
Beijing's growing economic interchange with South Korea.

A significant decline in Sino-Korean relations was signaled in media
treatment in mid-1984 of the North Korean anniversary of its defense treaties
with both Moscow and Beijing. In contrast with past practice, Pyongyang
sought to strike a semblance of balance in its treatment of the respective
treaty anniversaries. For more than a decade, the North Korean anniversaries
of the treaties with the Soviet Union (July 6) and the PRC (July 11) had
consistently reflected Pyongyang's close ties with the PRC and the relative
coolness of Soviet-Korean relations. This was the case even during 1979–
1981, when Sino-Korean relations were troubled because of Beijing's avowed
interest in fostering a strategic international front with the United States
and Japan against the Soviet Union. Pyongyang saw that PRC effort as
coming at the expense of active support for North Korean ambitions on
the peninsula. Nevertheless, at the same time, Pyongyang still made it clear

that North Korea regarded its relations with the Soviet Union as secondary to its ties to Beijing.

Pyongyang's new, more balanced approach in mid-1984 appeared to be designed in part to capitalize on Kim Il Sung's visit to the USSR and other Eastern European countries from May 17 to July 1, 1984. At the same time, its less effusive treatment of the PRC anniversary underlined the fact that Hu Yaobang's visit to Pyongyang in May 1984—just after President Reagan's trip to the PRC and just before Kim's departure for Moscow—had failed to resolve differences in the policies of the PRC and North Korea.

Moscow's treatment of Kim's visit and the anniversary demonstrated Soviet interest in establishing closer relations after almost two decades of cool relations. For the USSR, the occasions marked its first diplomatic success in Asia since its reputation plummeted after a Soviet fighter shot down a South Korean airliner in September 1983. At first, the Soviets were careful not to commit themselves too closely to the unpredictable Kim Il Sung, and they refrained from endorsing his son as successor. Nonetheless, Soviet comment showed interest in stepped-up economic and technical exchanges; high-level military talks occurred during Kim's Moscow stay; and Moscow highlighted Soviet–North Korean common views on some international issues.

Before Kim's visit, the Soviets had made modest political gestures to convince Pyongyang of Soviet interest in closer relations. These moves included higher than usual representation at North Korean celebrations and unusually warm official greetings on those occasions. The Soviets increased their blandishments to North Korea following the downing of the South Korean airliner; that incident severely curtailed Moscow's heretofore fairly active contacts with South Korea. Moscow also supported North Korea's position on the assassination of South Korean officials in Rangoon in October 1983, and it withdrew from the Interparliamentarian Union meeting held in Seoul that month.

Perhaps Moscow's greatest short-term gain from Kim's visit—and Beijing's greatest concern—was that it demonstrated to the PRC, the United States, and Japan that Soviet interests could not be ignored in talks on the future of the Korean Peninsula, and that Moscow was capable of playing a disruptive role on the peninsula that could severely complicate Beijing's relations with the United States and Japan. It seemed clear that Beijing was anxious to encourage renewed dialogue between North Korea and the United States at this time, in order to reduce the possibility of tension that could disrupt China's plans for economic modernization and provide an opening for the USSR, and in order to reach an understanding among the two Korean parties and three of the four major outside powers that would ensure favorable conditions on the peninsula and keep in check Soviet influence in Northeast Asia.

In any event, the strain in Sino-Korean relations has become all the more apparent in subsequent years, and it has been sharply etched against the backdrop of increasingly active and close Soviet–North Korean ties. The deterioration in Sino–North Korean relations was reflected notably in the North Korean observance of PRC National Day in October 1985. Both Kim Il Sung's annual greetings message and the anniversary editorial in *Nodong Sinmun* noted that the PRC and Korea pursued common goals in the past, but atypically neither went on to suggest that such common purposes continued to bind them. The North Korean leadership turnout for the PRC ambassador's reception was led by only a third-ranked vice-president, whereas an otherwise identical turnout for the East Germany's national day a few days later was led by the first-ranked vice-president.

Earlier evidence of cooling in relations included the following:

- Pyongyang played down changes in the Chinese People's Volunteers contingent to the Korean Military Armistice Commission in late May and early June. Pyongyang media, in an unusual action, ignored an award ceremony for the departing Chinese commander.
- Celebrations of the July 11 anniversary of the North Korean–PRC defense treaty were lower in protocol level and more subdued in media comment than the previous year.
- North Korean observance of the Chinese People's Liberation Army anniversary on August 1 also was less forthcoming than in 1984.

There was mounting evidence of strain in Sino-Korean party relations. Pyongyang in particular began to suggest doubt about the CCP commitment to the goals of world communism. For example, the North no longer credited the PRC with playing a central role in the struggle against "imperialism," which Pyongyang defines as a major task of Communist parties. Moreover, the North implied that China was faltering in its pursuit of the goals of socialism and communism:

- North Korean treatment of the July 1 CCP anniversary was distinctly cooler than in 1985, dropping the previous year's references to the Sino-Korean common goals of "independence, sovereignty, socialism, and communism."
- North Korean media began to slight the CCP leadership on a number of occasions. For example, an August 28 Korean media report on a meeting between CCP General Secretary Hu Yaobang and a North Korean youth delegation—a delegation which Chinese media emphasized was of "great importance" in Sino-Korean relations—repeatedly referred to Hu with neither his party title nor as "comrade," thereby breaking a long-standing North Korean practice. A similarly unusual choice was made in reporting Kim Il Sung's National Day message to the Chinese leaders in 1985, when the Korean message failed to address the Chinese leaders as "comrades."

The downturn in relations also has been reflected in changes in the media's references to the role of Kim Il Sung's son and chosen successor,

Kim Chong Il, in Sino-Korean relations. For example, Pyongyang media accounts of Hu Yaobang's meeting with the Korean youth delegation in August 1985 did not mention that the delegation's head conveyed Kim Chong Il's greetings to the Chinese leadership; such greetings had been a staple in past comment. North Korean media also played down the younger Kim's role in promoting relations with China and the significance of his 1983 visit to the PRC.

Publicly noted differences between Beijing and Pyongyang on foreign policy were underlined at several points in 1985. Thus, for example, Hu Yaobang's May 1985 visit to North Korea saw neither side claim, as was customary in the past, that their standard "unanimity of views" extended to foreign affairs. And there were signs of divergence over domestic economic policy. In a June 9 interview, Kim Il Sung appeared to criticize Chinese policy obliquely in emphasizing that, despite attempts to bolster the North's economy through increased contacts with the outside world, Pyongyang would "never" introduce foreign capital and thus risk becoming a "sub-jugated" economy. Reflecting Chinese sensitivity on the issue, Xinhua's report on the interview in its domestic service omitted Kim's remarks on economic issues. Its English-language account, for foreign consumers, noted Kim's injunction against using foreign capital but deleted his rationale.

In contrast, Moscow and Pyongyang gave unusual public attention to their relationship, including their security relationship, addressing themes that they had previously soft-pedaled out of mutual wariness about directly linking their respective security concerns. The new willingness to acknowledge common security ties accompanied other indications of markedly improved bilateral relations, greater agreement on the North Korean succession and other issues, and stepped up Soviet aid, including provision of MiG-23G fighters to North Korea.

Attention to Soviet–North Korean military ties emerged repeatedly in media comment from both sides marking the August 1985 anniversary of the liberation of Korea from Japanese rule, which was celebrated with an ostentatious display of unity. The focus on bilateral security ties reflected the apparent reassessment by both Moscow and Pyongyang in recent years of each country's strategic importance to the other. Pyongyang gradually revised its long-standing emphasis on the need for independence in relations between communist countries, and underscored the importance of the unity among them to North Korea's security. Soviet media, increasingly ready to identify threats to Pyongyang as threats to the Soviet Union and to view North Korean defense capabilities as serving Soviet security, stressed the strategic importance of the Korean Peninsula to Moscow.

Moscow sent more than twenty delegations to Pyongyang for the liberation anniversary celebrations, including a high-level party and state delegation headed by CPSU Politburo member G. A. Aliyev, only the third Soviet politburo member to visit the North in more than a decade. Also attending was a military delegation led by First Deputy Minister of Defense Vasily I. Petrov and a three-ship flotilla from the Soviet Pacific fleet, which, according to Soviet media, made an "official goodwill visit" to the North Korean port of Wonsan. At the thirtieth-anniversary celebrations in 1975, when Soviet-Korean relations were cool, Moscow was represented in Pyongyang by only two low-level delegations. Representation was higher in 1965, when Moscow sent a "friendship" delegation headed by a Politburo member, but no ranking USSR military officials were seen attending those celebrations, and there was no ceremonial visit by Soviet military units.

Authoritative spokesmen from both sides at anniversary events highlighted the two countries' military cooperation and underlined the significance of their formal security relationship. North Korean speakers repeatedly stressed that the two countries are "allies," a term that began appearing in Pyongyang comment on Soviet-Korean relations after Kim Il Sung's visit to Moscow in 1984. By contrast, the North only rarely implied that its security relationship with the PRC represented an alliance.

Moscow, which for years had been relatively cautious on the question concerning military ties with North Korea, seemed to break new ground. Both Aliyev and Petrov went beyond the routine Soviet claim that the 1961 USSR–North Korean Treaty of Friendship, Cooperation, and Mutual Assistance is important for the peace of the Far East by drawing attention to the military significance of the pact. In his remarks on August 14 at dedication ceremonies for the recently renovated Liberation Obelisk commemorating Red Army soldiers who died in Korea in 1945, Aliyev was unusually outspoken, noting that since the pact was signed, the two sides have pushed ahead with "closer cooperation in strengthening defense capabilities." The same day, in a speech at a Pyongyang rally, Aliyev again drew attention to the security aspects of the treaty, claiming that it has "reliably guaranteed external political conditions conducive to further development of the DPRK and the peaceful national reunification of Korea." In a speech on August 16, Petrov went even further, asserting that the treaty serves as "an important means of guaranteeing the security of the Soviet Union and the DPRK."

Moscow's willingness to publicize the security aspects of Soviet–North Korean relations was accompanied by a parallel readiness to comment on the North's military capabilities. In his speech on August 16, Petrov noted that the "national defense capability of the DPRK has been strengthened and the military capability of the Korean People's Army (KPA) increased." His remarks were in line with a June 25 *Krasnaya Zvezda* article, pegged to the anniversary of the outbreak of the Korean War, that asserted that the North must devote "unremitting attention to ensuring its defense capability" in the face of "militarist U.S. preparations in the Far East." In addition, an August 18 Moscow radio program beamed to Korea praised the qualities of MiG fighter aircraft, noting their use in the Korean War.

The military ties between the two sides were also dramatized by the visit of the small Soviet flotilla to Wonsan, an event clearly intended to symbolize closer defense cooperation. Moscow and Pyongyang had conveyed the same message in marking V-E Day in May 1985 with an exchange of visits by squadrons of fighter aircraft. Meanwhile, Western press reports indicated that around this time the Soviet Union began conducting regularly scheduled reconnaisance flights over North Korea and into the Yellow Sea, presumably to gather intelligence helpful to North Korea's defense against the South, but also useful in Soviet military strategy against its adversaries in the region, including the PRC.

In addition to its focus on military matters, Moscow made a number of gestures that seemed to reflect a willingness to move the improving relations with North Korea forward. In his speeches, Aliyev went out of his way to praise Kim Il Sung, characterizing him as an "outstanding leader" and an "eminent figure" in the world communist movement, language measurably warmer than that which Moscow had used for Kim in the past. Also, Soviet statements pegged to the anniversary appeared to give more credit than usual to the North's own efforts in building its economy after the Korean War, thus diluting Moscow's traditional emphasis on Soviet assistance in the North's postwar reconstruction.

Reinforcing earlier signs that Moscow has accepted succession arrangements in North Korea, Soviet media paid special attention to Kim Chong Il. Soviet media accounts of the liberation anniversary events in Pyongyang noted the presence of Kim Il Sung, Kim Chong Il and "other" North Korean leaders, thus acknowledging the younger Kim's special position in the leadership.

Soviet media claimed that Aliyev's talks with Kim Il Sung on August 14 reaffirmed the two sides' "unity of views" and their readiness to develop cooperation in "bilateral relations and in the international arena." The image of broad agreements between Moscow and Pyongyang had steadily sharpened since Kim's visit to Moscow in 1984, when a more limited expression of agreement was used by both sides to characterize his discussions with the Soviet leadership. USSR Deputy Foreign Minister Mikhail Kapitsa's visit to Pyongyang in November 1984 had evidenced growing signs of agreement between the two sides, and the communiqué capping DPRK Foreign Minister Kim Yong Nam's visit to Moscow in April 1985 registered both sides' "consensus on all problems discussed at the talks."

During later Soviet–North Korean meetings, notably in a visit of several days length by Soviet Foreign Minister Eduard I. Shevardnadze to North Korea in January 1986, Pyongyang deferred to Soviet interest in several ways. It endorsed the newly revived Soviet proposal for Asian collective security and the long-standing Soviet support for the concept of "socialist internationalism"; and it voiced stronger support for the Soviet-backed government in Afghanistan. In each case, Pyongyang's stance implicitly but unmistakably broadened the gap between North Korean and PRC positions on these sensitive international questions.

Notes

The views in this chapter are those of the author and not necessarily those of the Congressional Research Service, Library of Congress.

1. See most recently Harry Gelman, "Continuity Versus Change in Soviet Policy in Asia," *Journal of Northeast Asian Studies*, summer 1985.

2. Such assessments appear periodically in the U.S. media, often coincident with a significant Sino-Soviet leadership meeting.

3. For background and more extensive analysis, see Robert Sutter, *Chinese Foreign Policy: Developments After Mao* (New York: Praeger, 1986), pp. 1–13.

4. For background and more extensive analysis see Evelyn Colbert, "Standing Pat," *Foreign Policy*, vol. 54, spring 1984, pp. 139–155; William Bach, "A Chance in Cambodia," *Foreign Policy* vol. 62, spring 1986, pp. 75–95; "ASEAN's Geostrategic Importance," *Military Technology*, vol. 9, no. 12, 1985. For good weekly coverage of China-Indochina issues, see *Far Eastern Economic Review*. Coverage of Vietnamese media appears in U.S. Foreign Broadcast Information Service, *Daily Report: Asia and the Pacific*. Coverage of Chinese media appears in *Daily Report: China*. See also coverage of Chinese policy toward the countries of the region in *China Quarterly*, "Chronology."

5. For extensive analysis and useful background see Jonathan Pollack, "The Future of Chinese Policy in Northeast Asia," paper prepared for the conference "The Changing Security Environment in Northeast Asia," Seoul, Korea, December 1985. For coverage of North Korean media, see Foreign Broadcast Information Service, *Daily Report: Asia and the Pacific*; for the USSR, see *Daily Report: Soviet Union*. For good weekly coverage of regional developments, see *Far Eastern Economic Review*, especially November 7, 1985, pp. 18–19, and December 5, 1985, pp. 48–49. See also coverage of Chinese policy toward countries involved in Northeast Asia in *China Quarterly*, "Chronology."

21

Beijing's Latin American Policy: An Exercise in Pragmatism

Yu San Wang

A nation's foreign policy generally reflects the sum of its principles, which include its history, belief, power potential, and cultural predilection. The international relations of countries in the nuclear age are, in the main, relations of fear: the fear of fighting a nuclear war between nations that possess nuclear weapons; the fear of mutual problems, which all nations know they cannot solve alone; the fear of declining living standards experienced by developed nations with scarce resources; and the fear of poverty, social instability, and revolution shared by Third World nations. While confronting such profound problems, most nations today, for the sake of survival, take more flexible and less principled approaches in their foreign policies than they did in the past.[1] This approach can be seen in the policies of many Latin American nations toward both the Republic of China (ROC) and the People's Republic of China (PRC).

So far as the principles of Beijing's foreign policy are concerned, five major factors determine its foreign relations, namely, nationalism, the politics of the international Communist movement, domestic affairs, Marxist-Leninist-Maoist ideology, and its strategic-political imagery. Beijing's foreign policy is not flexible concerning its goal but is pragmatic regarding the means of reaching that goal. The "united front" doctrine is a major influence on the formation and conduct of the PRC's foreign policy.

Initially, Beijing had little interest in Latin America. It was convinced that the region was almost impenetrable because of traditional U.S. influence and the existence of a large number of conservative Latin American governments. But the Cuban revolution and increasing Soviet involvement awakened Beijing's interest in this region and led it to reaffirm its theory that revolution in the less developed countries should have its root in the countryside. During most of the 1960s, the PRC provided revolutionary movements with needed financial aid, conducted an active campaign of exporting political indoctrination materials, and supplied guerrilla warfare strategy and tactics. After the violent climax of Cultural Revolution in the late 1960s, Beijing adopted a pragmatic approach in its foreign policy which facilitated its entering into the United Nations, its rapprochement with the United States, and a new strategy for its Latin American policy.

The PRC has long considered itself a developing country belonging to the Third World, for which it tries hard to promote itself as a spokesman. To Beijing, Latin America is an integral part of the Third World. Under its new diplomacy of pragmatism, the PRC, since the early 1970s, has appealed to the Latin American governments to join it to fight a war against superpower domination of Latin American affairs and has tried to promote itself as a major power in the region. In order to achieve this goal, Beijing has to consider the revolutionary movement or the "people's war" to be secondary.

During the past fifteen years, the PRC has conducted an all-out campaign to promote "government-to-government diplomacy" and has been successful in establishing diplomatic relations with more and more Latin American nations, in increasing exchange programs, in expanding economic ties, and in promoting scientific and technological cooperation. By identifying itself as a Third World country, the PRC has shown to Latin American nations its strong sympathy concerning the issues of poverty, international debts, relations with the United States, and superpower domination. Under its Four Modernization programs, the PRC offers Latin America technological exchanges and economic assistance. Many Latin American countries are very interested in Beijing's offering. The PRC's "dollar diplomacy" is instrumental to its political success in Latin America.

Politics, in Harold Lasswell's words, is "a struggle for influence, and there will be less influence if there is less power."[2] More and more nations in the world of the nuclear age take pragmatic approaches toward one another in their foreign policies. This statement is particularly true of many Latin American states. They are now more flexible and less principled in their relations with both the ROC and PRC.

This chapter discusses the dramatic changes in Beijing's foreign policy toward Latin America. It focuses on the PRC's interest, its strategy and tactics, its propaganda and diplomatic activities, and its economic relations. Special attention, however, will be paid to the definition and evaluation of these factors.

The material in this study shows the behavior of nations in the international community to be determined in great part today by the basic structure of the international system in the throes of rapid change.[3] Furthermore, a nation's foreign policy determines its course of action toward other nations.[4] Within these frameworks, Latin American nations have conducted their foreign relations with the PRC.

Beijing's Interest

The overriding intent of the PRC in Latin America during the 1950s was to promote the "people's revolution" against the existing "reactionary regimes" and to achieve communism in the region. It was the deep conviction of the

Chinese Communists that the important contradiction in international politics was a clear-cut division between the oppressed peoples of Asia, Africa, and Latin America and the imperialism of the Western nations. The anti-imperialistic revolutionary war would be won by the "liberation of the peoples of underdeveloped nations."[5] To Beijing the revolutionary war was divided into two stages. The first was a war within, a people's war against the existing governments in Latin America; the people would win by following the Chinese Communist road to power. It was Beijing's belief that the conditions in Latin America were the same as those in China prior to the Communist victory in 1949. The second stage was a war between developing nations of the region and the developed nations of West Europe and the United States.[6]

Initially, the PRC cooperated with the Soviet Union in a joint effort to consolidate the Communist movements throughout the region and to unite the peasants and factory workers in an effort to overthrow local governments. However, the success of the Cuban revolution and the increasing Beijing-Moscow dispute marked a steady increase of the PRC's interest in Latin America. During most of the 1960s, the Chinese Communists took a position of hard-line dogmatic ideology, trying to compete with the Soviet Union for influence in Latin America.

To persuade Cuba to switch to Beijing from Moscow was the PRC's other interest, but it failed. Havana, for the first few years, did facilitate Beijing's influence in Latin America, but their relations became tenuous and unfriendly after the mid-1960s, a shift caused by ever-increasing Cuban influence in the "wars of national liberation" in the region and by closer Soviet-Cuban relations.

The PRC's purpose in Latin America is to establish itself as the spokesman for the Third World opposing superpower domination in world politics. In 1974, Beijing proclaimed an end to the "bloc" system and came to view the international scene in terms of "three worlds." It identified itself as a Third World state. To Beijing, Latin America is an integral part of the Third World. Clearly, the PRC's important interest is to end Soviet-U.S. domination in Latin America.

Last, but not least, to isolate the ROC in Latin America is a major PRC interest. Since 1979, Beijing has conducted a vigorous campaign for China's reunification, a united-front tactic aimed at bringing Taipei to its terms. Because of its economic prosperity, political democratization, and social progress, the ROC does not allow itself to be lured into Beijing's political trap. The PRC therefore has adopted united-front diplomacy to isolate the ROC and has employed "dollar diplomacy" as an effective weapon to pressure those Latin American nations that still maintain official relations with the ROC to switch sides.

Strategy and Tactics

The formation of the PRC's foreign policy is based on the united-front strategy. The term "united front," in J. C. Armstrong's words, denotes "a limited and temporary alignment between a Communist party or state and one or more non-Communist political units with the dual purpose of confronting a common enemy and furthering the revolutionary cause."[7] In a broader sense, the united-front strategy includes four important approaches: aiming at an effort against a single enemy; aligning many diverse forces against that enemy; distinguishing among the "progressive," "middle" and "diehard" components of such a broad united front; and operating a "unity and struggle" strategy within the united front for developing progressive forces and radicalizing other elements in the front.[8]

More than thirty years of the PRC's foreign policy in Latin America clearly demonstrates that the Chinese Communists' behavior is conditioned by the framework of the united-front strategy and tactics, from "the people's revolutionary war" to "government-to-government diplomacy," from "the camp system" to "three worlds," and from "superpower hegemony" to "South-South cooperation." Undoubtedly, the united-front strategy and tactics have secured for Beijing a strong foothold in Latin America.

During the 1950s and 1960s, Beijing tried to impose its ideology on the Latin American Communist movements,[9] which antagonized many local Communist parties. It was Beijing's assumption that the conditions in Latin America were the same as they were in China prior to the Chinese Communist occupation of the mainland in 1949, and, thus, the best way to win the war with imperialism and the reactionary regimes in Latin America was to follow the Chinese Communist experiences.[10]

In pursuing Mao's ideology of inflexibility, Beijing actively supported the "people's war," which, they believed, was the only road to power.[11] The PRC's campaign in Latin America opposed U.S. imperialism, local reactionary regimes, and the Soviet revisionists.[12] Beijing's ideological inflexibility and its pretensions to the leadership of world communism inevitably led to clash with Fidel Castro and other Latin American Communist leaders who did not follow Mao's thinking. The general feeling of the Communist and worker parties in Latin America was that all of them should pursue the common line of the international Communist movement for the purpose of uniting all the revolutionary forces. Beijing's intensified effort to split the Communist movement, however, drew unanimous condemnation from the Havana meeting of twenty-two Latin American Communist parties.[13]

Beijing's effort to dominate the Communist parties in Latin America was obviously a failure, for most of them in that region preferred an approach that would unite the world Communist movement without subordinating it to any particular model. At the end of 1970, there were fifty-nine Communist parties in the region, of which only eight supported Beijing.[14]

In spite of the strong opposition to its policy of Maoist ideology, Beijing decided to split the Latin American Communist parties by setting up the so-called "pocket parties" of pro-Beijing parties or groups.[15] Deeply influenced by the domestic politics of the Cultural Revolution of 1966–1969, the PRC intensified its all-out effort to support pro-Beijing "pocket parties." This hard-line approach, however, did not win any sympathy from the working class in urban areas, nor was it successful in conducting guerrilla warfare in the countryside. The change of strategy toward the end of the 1960s was an important course of action for Beijing, helping to prevent it from being further isolated in Latin America.

The change of the PRC's domestic policy, Sino-American rapprochement, and Beijing's entry into the United Nations brought a decisive shift in Beijing's position in Latin America. As early as 1969, the PRC gradually halted the "people's war" and adopted the strategy of flexibility, that is, "government-to-government" diplomacy. Tactically, Beijing concentrated on such important issues as the 200-mile maritime territorial limit, economic nationalism, a denuclearized zone in Latin America, the North-South conflict, South-South cooperation, and the Latin American nations' position in the United Nations.

The 1952 Santiago Declaration, in which Chile, Ecuador, and several other Latin American states advanced their 200-mile maritime claim, drew sharp disagreement among the major maritime nations—including the United States and Soviet Union.[16] Beijing's active support of this issue won it important friendship in the region. The PRC repeatedly pointed out that Western imperialism had dominated international waters for centuries at the expense of the small nations, and that Latin American states had every right to claim the 200-mile maritime territorial limit.[17]

Immediately after the signing of the Law of the Sea Treaty, which resulted from the third UN Conference on the Law of Sea, in Montego Bay, Jamaica, on December 18, 1982, Beijing's delegation invited Latin American representatives to a victory reception and told them that "it is a great victory for the Third World, especially for the Latin American countries which have successfully defeated atempts of the superpowers to weaken the convention."[18] The Latin American governments were quite impressed by the fact that the PRC was the only great power to actively support their maritime territorial limit claim.

The PRC actively supports the economic nationalism movement in Latin America in its struggle against rich and industrial nations in general and the United States and Soviet Union in particular. The Chinese Communists concentrated their propaganda efforts before 1970 on exploiting the hatred among the Latin American people for their governments and the United States, underscoring Washington as a "protector and defender of corrupt regimes throughout this region and the champion of the large American investors."[19] Beijing, however, has deliberately omitted the "people's war" against the local governments since 1970, devoting all its effort to obtaining a solidarity of agreement in the Latin American regimes concerning achieving economic independence from the First and Second worlds.

To be the part of the Third World that it claimed it was, the PRC called for the revision of the old international economic order in favor of the developing nations. Ever since its entry into the United Nations and its more specialized agencies, Beijing has gained significant influence in its campaigning for economic nationalism in the Third World. At the UN General

Assembly Special Session on Raw Materials in the spring of 1974, Teng Hsiao-ping stated Beijing's position on building a new international economic order.[20] In the same year, Beijing hailed various actions taken by Latin American countries, aimed at gaining economic independence—such actions as nationalization of oil production in Venezuela and new laws limiting foreign investments in several Latin American states.[21] Many Latin American leaders were deeply impressed with Beijing's active support of the Third World's economic independence.[22]

At the Fifth United Nations Conference on Trade and Development (UNCTAD), held in May 1979, in Manila, Beijing's delegation called for destroying the old economic order and establishing a new one. It supported a special resolution, passed by the conference, aimed at reinforcing economic cooperation among the developing countries as a "key element in the strategy of collective self-reliance."[23] In showing its sympathy with Latin American foreign-debt problems, the PRC accused the foreign debtors of being economic imperialists.[24]

The issue of denuclearization in Latin America was an important device utilized effectively by the PRC in opposing the two superpowers. In February 1967, twenty-one Latin American nations signed a treaty prohibiting the testing, using, producing, acquiring, or placing of atomic arms in their countries.[25] The idea of a nuclear-free zone in Latin America was born in the aftermath of the Cuban crisis in October 1962. The countries of Latin America did not want to risk any repetition of the Cuban crisis. Nor did they desire to acquire, manufacture, or permit the deployment of any nuclear weapons in their territories.

The PRC initially refused to support the treaty because it would further assure the Soviet Union and the United States of being the sole nuclear powers to dominate the rest of the world.[26] Beijing, however, through its ambassador in Cairo, informed the Latin Americans one month later that it would not participate in this treaty under UN auspices.[27] When the UN General Assesmbly, on December 5, 1967, adopted the resolution welcoming the Treaty for the Prohibition of Nuclear Weapons in Latin America by an overwhelming majority (82 in favor, none against, 20 abstentions), Beijing immediately issued a statement to the effect that it heartily supported the resolution and appealed to Latin American governments to join together in fighting the revisionist imperialism of the Soviet Union, which abstained from the vote.[28] When it signed the Additional Protocol 2 to the Treaty of Tlatelolco for the Prohibition of Nuclear Weapons in Latin America on August 21, 1973, Beijing capitalized on this occasion by calling for the solidarity of all Latin American nations in opposing the superpowers: "The Latin American countries will strengthen their solidarity and advance together in their struggle against the policy of nuclear threat and blackmail pursued by the superpowers and for the establishment of the Latin American nuclear weapon-free zone."[29] Justifying its own nuclear development, Beijing pointed out that "China is developing nuclear weapons solely because she is compelled to do so, and she is developing them entirely for defensive purpose, as well as for breaking the nuclear monopoly and proceeding from there to the elimination of all nuclear weapons."[30]

The Chinese Communist leaders frequently remind Latin American states that, in order for their region to be truly a nuclear-weapon-free zone, the superpowers, which possess huge numbers of nuclear weapons, must first of all undertake earnestly not to use or threaten to use nuclear weapons against the Latin American countries. To achieve this purpose, Beijing insists that the following steps should be taken: (1) the dismantling of all foreign military bases in Latin America and refraining from establishing any new foreign military base there; (2) the prohibition of delivery by any means of transportation carrying nuclear weapons through the Latin American territorial sea or land and airspace.[31]

The PRC lost no time in using other crucial issues, such as the Panama Canal Zone problem and the antisuperpower contention of hegemony, to wound Washington and Moscow. In January 1971, Beijing issued the following statement supporting Panama's position against the United States: "The struggle now being heroically waged by the people of Panama against U.S. aggression and in defense of their sovereignty is a great and patriotic struggle. The Chinese people stand firmly on the side of the Panamanian people and fully support their just action in opposing the U.S. aggressor and in demanding the recovery of sovereignty over the Panama Zone."[32]

Throughout the negotiations between the United States and Panama for a new treaty, Beijing was constantly critical of Washington. When the final agreement was reached in 1977, the PRC hailed it as an anti-imperialism-colonialism victory.

Ever since its entry into the United Nations, the PRC has most effectively caused the world body to serve its global strategy. In the General Assembly, Security Council, and other important UN organizations, Beijing frequently takes the side of Latin America and other Third World nations. The PRC, for instance, supported unequivocally the proposal of Panama to hold Security Council meetings in Panama City in 1973 to consider "measures for the strengthening of international peace and security and the promotion of international co-operation in Latin America, in accordance with the provisions and principles of the Charter and the resolutions relating to the right of self-determination of peoples and strict respect for the sovereignty and independence of States."[33] In its campaign to elect Javier Pérez de Cuéllar, a Peruvian diplomat, to be UN secretary general on December 15, 1981, Beijing scored another diplomatic victory.

The PRC always considers itself a developing country belonging to the Third World, and Latin America is an integral part of the Third World. It tries to form a united-front strategy among the Third World nations to oppose the First World of the superpowers and the Second World of Japan and West Europe, a strategy to create a North-South conflict. At the sixth special session of the United Nations General Assembly in 1974, Teng Hsiao-ping raised six propositions to support Latin America and other Third World nations:

There should be no hegemony and created spheres of influence by any country in any region; economic and political relations between states should be established on the basis of the principle of peaceful coexistence; the affairs of any country should be governed by its own people; the developing countries must have the right to independently choose social and economic systems; routine international economic matters should be jointly managed by all countries, not just one or two; and international trade should be based on equality, mutual benefit and exchange of needed goods.[34]

In May 1985, Beijing outlined its viewpoints on internationally important issues. In part, the Chinese Communists appealed to the Third World nations to establish various organizations for the united struggle against colonialism, imperialism, and hegemonism.[35]

As a result of several years' serious dialogue and negotiations, the PRC was able to bring the Third World nations together to form the South-South Cooperation Conference in Beijing in 1983. The second and third such conferences were held in Cartagena, Colombia, in 1984, and in Harare, Zimbabwe, in 1985. The primary purpose of the South-South Cooperation Conference is to serve as an important vehicle for "effective negotiations and meaningful relationships with the North."[36] A large portion of the Cartagena Conference was devoted to the issues of Latin America's international debts, superpower domination, regional economic cooperation, Third World solidarity, and the economic "imperialism of the First and Second worlds." Doubtlessly, the South-South Cooperation Conference has become an effective instrument to serve Beijing's global strategic goals.

Beijing strongly sided with Argentina over the Falkland Islands war with Great Britain in 1982. Nevertheless, the PRC remained in a low-key position over the U.S. invasion of Grenada in 1983 against Cuba's presence, for it was the Chinese Communists' long-standing policy to oppose Cuban military influence in Latin America and Africa. Fitting nicely in its antisuperpower line, the PRC endorses the Contadora Group's initiative to settle Central American problems through peaceful negotiations.[37]

The PRC's united-front strategy and tactics in Latin America have seriously jeopardized the ROC's interests in Latin America. One of Beijing's major purposes is to isolate Taipei and eventually to try driving the ROC out of Latin America. Since the Chinese Communists have apparently failed in their united-front campaign to force Taipei to accept their terms for reunification, they intend to disarm the ROC diplomatically.

Propaganda and Diplomatic Activities

Although from 1949 to 1960 not a single country in Latin America had diplomatic relations with the PRC, Beijing's cultural and propaganda activities began with the birth of the Beijing regime. However, an all-out political campaign did not start until 1957, though the PRC already supported the Communist movement and secretly sent propaganda materials to Latin America. It began its Spanish-language broadcasts of about seven hours per week in 1957 and increased them to twenty-eight hours per week in the following year. Broadcasts in Portuguese were initiated in 1960. Programs were transmitted for ten and a half hours per week. Now Beijing spends forty-five hours per week broadcasting in Spanish and thirty hours per week in Portuguese.[38]

From the very beginning, the PRC effectively utilized the New China News Agency (NCNA) correspondents' activities to gain a foothold in the region.[39] It established nine NCNA offices by 1972. The Chinese Communists employed the same pattern in Latin America that they did elsewhere; namely, they promoted the visit of journalists first, then established press offices. As a matter of fact, the NCNA press office played a dominant role that led to the establishment of diplomatic relations between the host nation and the PRC. There are at present NCNA press offices in twenty-one Latin American states, including those which do not have diplomatic relations with Beijing.

The major function of the NCNA office was to provide a news service to local newspapers and propaganda materials to various revolutionary organizations. In addition, the NCNA correspondents also conducted other political activities that frequently violated local laws and regulations.[40] These activities led to accusations by local police that NCNA agents pursued illegal actions such as subversion or espionage. As a result, many NCNA correspondents were arrested and deported, and the press offices were forcibly closed.[41] To further increase its influence in Latin America, Beijing engaged in various activities, both officially and unofficially, including providing films and financial aid to the revolutionary groups.

Diplomatically, the PRC did not have official relations with any of the Latin American countries until 1960. Cuba recognized Beijing in 1960 after Fidel Castro successfully established a Communist regime in Havana. Considering Cuba as a forward base for Chinese Communist activities in Latin America, Beijing initially supported Castro with much enthusiasm.[42] The PRC's attempt to win prestige in Cuba, however, turned out to be a failure, for Beijing could not fulfill promises of trade or economic and military aid to Havana. Castro, therefore, took the side of the Soviet Union in the Sino-Soviet dispute. Obviously, Moscow was in a much better position to supply economic and military aid to Cuba. In addition, Havana found itself competing for leadership with Beijing in the Latin American Communist movement, and this competition led to bitter conflict between Beijing and Havana.[43] Since Beijing adopted a more flexible approach in its foreign policy, relations between them have been improving, for both sides desire to return to normality.

In further improving Beijing-Havana relations, the Cuban minister of external trade paid an official visit to Beijing at the invitation of the Chinese Communist government; the PRC, in turn, upgraded its representation at the Cuban National Day celebrations at the Cuban embassy in Beijing, sending a full minister to lead the Chinese delegation, a sharp contrast with the lower-level Chinese attending in past years; and a conference on bilateral

TABLE 21.1
Nations Having Diplomatic Relations with the PRC

	Year of Recognition
Argentina	1972
Barbados	1977
Bolivia	1985
Brazil	1974
Chile	1971
Colombia	1980
Cuba	1960
Ecuador	1971
Grenada	1985
Guyana	1972
Guadeloupe	1985
Jamaica	1972
Mexico	1972
Nicaragua	1985
Peru	1971
Suriname	1976
Trinidad and Tobago	1974
Venezuela	1974

relations was held in Havana in May 1984 to promote mutual cooperation and friendship.[44] Two months after the conference, Beijing's assistant foreign minister paid a visit to Cuba.[45] Both sides desire to expand their bilaterial relations in the economic field.

Chile recognized the PRC on January 15, 1971, largely because of Salvador Allende's victory in the 1970 presidential election. To Beijing, Allende's Marxist-dominated government was deeply committed to "Chilean people in their fight against U.S. imperialism's ruthless oppression, plunder and exploitation."[46] Beijing tried with some success to use Chile as a forward base on the Latin American continent from which to push for further influence with other Latin American countries. After the military junta overthrew the Allende regime in September 1973, mainland China took a friendly attitude toward the Chilean generals. This policy drew sharp criticism from the Chilean Communist Party.[47]

Because of Beijing's new diplomacy of pragmatism and its entry into the United Nations, the PRC's ability to develop official relations with Latin American states has been greatly enhanced. Not a single Latin American country recognized the PRC from 1961 to 1971. However, during the next fifteen years, fifteen more nations in the region established diplomatic relations with Beijing. At present, eighteen Latin American countries have official relations with the PRC (see Table 21.1).

Three important factors influenced Latin American nations in their shift of attitudes toward the PRC from a nonrecognition policy to the establishment of diplomatic relations. First, Beijing has temporarily abandoned the ideology

TABLE 21.2
Nations Maintaining Diplomatic Relations with the ROC

Costa Rica	Honduras
Dominica	Panama
Dominican Republic	Paraguay
El Salvador	St. Lucia
Guatemala	St. Vincent
Haiti	Uruguay

of the "people's war" against so-called reactionary regimes, replacing it with a "government-to-government" diplomacy. Second, the improvement of Beijing-Washington relations and the PRC's admission to the United Nations have deeply influenced the leaders of the Latin American governments.[48] And third, Latin American countries desire to pursue an independent foreign policy distinct from that of the United States and "to extend their ties with other countries of the world."[49]

In order to establish diplomatic relations with the PRC, Latin American nations usually accept Beijing's condition that the Communist government on the mainland "is the only legal government" of China. Although this condition does not imply suspending all their ties with the ROC, in many cases Taipei voluntarily abrogates its official relations with any government that has decided to recognize Beijing. Currently, twelve Latin American countries still maintain diplomatic relations with the ROC (see Table 21.2).

Cultural, sport, and other exchanges between the PRC and Latin America were limited before 1979. The first exchange program was set up in 1956, during which 200 doctors and specialists were sent to Latin America. In the 1950s, some 300 Chinese students went to this region to study, while more than fifty Latin American experts were invited to mainland China to teach Spanish in schools. The Cultural Revolution literally stopped exchange programs. During the last fifteen years, exchange programs have been expanded, including those related to opera troupes, song and dance groups, delegations of poets, playwrights, editors, essayists, novelists, filmmakers, television and radio personalities, journalists, and others.[50]

To broaden its influence in Latin America, the PRC in recent years has frequently sent top officials to tour the region. Foreign Minister Huang Hua toured Mexico, Colombia, and Venezuela in 1981, and Wu Hsueh-chien was sent to Venezuela, Argentina, and Brazil in 1984. In late 1985, Premier Chao Tzu-yang visited four Latin American countries: Argentina, Brazil, Colombia, and Venezuela. He was the first Chinese Communist premier ever to visit the region. Chao's visit drew considerable international attention, which led to the general belief that Beijing would further its diplomatic offensive in Latin America.[51]

At present, Beijing maintains a dual policy in Latin America. On one hand, it conducts an all-out campaign of government-to-government diplomacy, trying to convince as many governments as possible to establish official relations with it; the PRC's primary reason for this policy is to strengthen its ability to challenge the influence of the United States and Soviet Union in the region. On the other hand, it continues supporting the Communist movement politically and economically; it still believes that Latin America is an ideal place to have its own style of the proletarian revolution.

Many Latin American governments, even though realizing Beijing's continuous support of local guerrilla warfare and other revolutionary movements, do not take issue with Beijing, because the political value of the PRC's friendship outweighs other problems. After all, the guerrilla forces and radical groups in many of the Latin American countries are too small to present a serious threat to the existence of their governments.[52] Nevertheless, the tolerant attitude of the Latin American governments has proven to be important to Beijing, allowing it to continuously support guerrilla warfare and to export Communist movement literature.

Economic Relations

Generally speaking, three important factors have limited the PRC's economic relations with Latin America. First, Beijing's commercial activities in the region have both economic and political objectives; in many instances, the political purpose dominates trade and foreign aid. Second, while Latin America and other Third World nations need technological skills, they also need a lot of capital, especially foreign capital. Attempting to serve as a leader of the Third World, the PRC, as a labor-intensive economy, can provide Latin American nations neither extensive technological skills nor large sums of capital. And finally, Beijing has little to offer in exchange for the commodities; and there is not much demand for Chinese products in Latin America.

The PRC supports a policy of "economic independence" for Latin America. It insisted in the early 1970s that economic independence was a "component part of the national liberation movement in Latin America."[53] The solution to Latin American economic problems, Beijing believes, is the creation of a "new international economic order" through regional economic integration and "South-South cooperation" against superpowers and Second World nations.[54] On the issue of the Latin American foreign debts of more than $360 billion (half the total foreign debts of the entire Third World), the PRC repeatedly calls for the First and Second worlds' creditors to restructure debts due for repayment.[55]

Economic activities of the PRC concentrate mainly in the areas of aid, trade, and technical cooperation. Beijing's aid program, started in 1953, was originally limited to Communist nations and later extended to both Communist and non-Communist countries, from Romania to Zambia and from Mongolia to Peru. From 1953 to 1971, Beijing committed more than $4,600 million in economic aid to foreign nations. The highest level of net disbursements was reached in 1971, representing between 0.3 percent and 0.5

percent of the PRC's estimated gross national product.[56] The financial terms of Beijing's aid to Latin America are far more generous than those granted by other Communist countries. Most loans to these countries have been free of interest with a repayment period of ten to fifteen years and a grace period of around ten years, and carrying a grant element of 75 percent to 80 percent. This policy of favorable loan terms has a great appeal to the nations in the region, for the most serious economic problem that many of these nations have faced has been the rapid accumulation of foreign debts. Naturally, they are willing to accommodate Beijing's political demands in exchange for loans. This policy is termed "dollar diplomacy."

Geographically, Beijing's aid in the past mainly went to Southeast Asia, Africa, and other areas; Latin American states received considerably less. During the period 1953–1971, only $142 million of a total $4,657 million in foreign aid went to Latin America. However, the aid to this region has steadily increased since 1972. Beijing has poured $1.3 billion in aid into Latin America in fourteen years.[57]

Although Beijing's trade relations with Latin America began as early as 1952, the volume of trade grew very slowly. During the Cultural Revolution, the trade with Latin American states was almost completely stopped, but the Chinese delegations have again started to visit Latin America, and Beijing has received visits of trade delegations from many Latin American states since 1970. Today the PRC has trade relations with some twenty Latin American countries.

The PRC's trade with Argentina was impressive from 1959 to 1962, when mainland China badly needed to obtain grains; trading activities between the two countries have declined in recent years because Beijing has little to offer for Argentina's exports. While visiting Argentina in late 1985, Premier Chao promised the host country that Beijing would increase its technological and scientific cooperation with Argentina. In addition, he signed an agreement with Argentina's president for a $20 million loan to the host country.[58] The Chilean government under Allende signed an agreement with Beijing in 1971, a first. Chile agreed to sell mainland China a minimum of 65,000 metric tons of copper annually for four years; trade between the two countries continues in spite of the military coup of 1973.

The prospect for long-term trade between the PRC and Brazil is favorable. Frequent negotiations, conferences, and visits between Beijing and Brasilia have taken place since the late 1950s. The bilateral trade for 1974 was valued at only $17.42 million, but that figure went up to $840 million in the following year, accounting for more than 50 percent of the total PRC–Latin American trade in 1975.[59] Brazil began to import crude oil from the PRC in 1978; it bought 1.3 million tons of crude oil in 1980, 2.5 million tons in 1984, and 2.9 million tons in the following year. The bilateral trade for 1985 was estimated to be near $1 billion.[60] During his official visit in 1985, Premier Chao signed five agreements with Brazil's president on economic cooperation and cultural exchanges.

Mexico was not among the five top Latin American countries trading with mainland China until 1961. The first purchase of 36,000 bales of

Mexican cotton by Beijing was in 1963, and 500,000 tons of wheat were imported to the Chinese mainland under contract in the following year. Beijing–Mexico City trade has been expanded slowly because neither side can offer many commodities and materials needed by the other.

Chinese-Cuban trade reached its high level in 1965, when the two-way trade was valued at $250 million, but trade sharply declined since then because of deteriorating relations. Today their trade is valued at about $165 million annually. The first trade agreement between the PRC and Peru was signed in 1972. Under this agreement, Beijing purchased 40,000 tons of copper, 10,000 tons of fish oil, and 10,000 tons of zinc. Peru, in recent years, has exported Peruvian products to mainland China in repayment for loans granted by Beijing, amounting to some $42 million annually.

In promoting closer economic cooperation, the PRC also has signed trade agreements with many other Latin American countries, including trade and technical agreements with Colombia and Venezuela in 1985.[61]

The PRC, in recent years, has expanded its scientific and technological cooperation with Latin American states. The International Scientific and Technological Cooperation Bureau under the State Science and Technology Commission was created to develop Beijing's scientific and technological cooperation with foreign countries.

The PRC now has scientific and technological agreements with six Latin American countries: Brazil, Mexico, Argentina, Venezuela, Chile, and Colombia. In these countries, Beijing's scientific and technological cooperative ties with Brazil have progressed the furthest.[62] The two countries exchanged seven study groups between 1980 and 1982, involving scientific and technological developments. An agreement was signed in 1982 for cooperation in the fields of agriculture, animal husbandry, fishery, water resources, electric power, and forestry. In December 1984, the PRC and Brazil held their first scientific and technological cooperation meeting in Beijing, to discuss further increases in various cooperative activities.[63]

Mexico was the first Latin American nation to cooperate with the PRC in scientific and technological fields. The two nations signed a scientific and technological cooperation agreement in September 1975; since then, they held seven related meetings, including some 120 programs.[64] Through technological exchanges Mexico sends experts to mainland China to teach coal-mining and orange-growing techniques. In return, Beijing provides Mexico City with Chinese traditional medicine, freshwater fish, silkworm-breeding methods, production and utilization of marsh gas, and irrigation and ceramics processes.

Although cooperation between the PRC and Argentina began as early as 1974, truly meaningful scientific and technical cooperation did not start until 1980, a year in which the two countries signed a scientific and technological agreement in Beijing. And since then, they have frequently held meetings. At the 1983 meeting in Buenos Aires, both sides agreed on a cooperative plan for fiscal year 1984. In that year Beijing sent study groups to Argentina to inspect that country's wool-spinning equipment and techniques, its cattle-raising and -slaughtering methods, its dairy-processing techniques, and its plant-protection methods. During the last two years, Argentina has reciprocated by sending representatives to the PRC to investigate its production and utilization of marsh gas, its railway design and construction methods, its freshwater-fish-breeding techniques, and its methods for treating burns.

The PRC's technical cooperation with Venezuela and Colombia is on a much smaller scale. Beijing has expanded its scientific and technological cooperation with other Latin American nations. During his Latin American visit in 1985, Premier Chao indicated on many occasions that the PRC would increase its scientific and technological cooperation with Latin America in the immediate future.

Conclusion

The formation of the PRC's Latin American policy is mainly based on the united-front strategy and is intended to achieve two purposes: supporting the revolutionary movement designed to overthrow existing governments and, at a later time, aligning the PRC with the so-called reactionary regimes by employing "government-to-government" diplomacy. The support of the people's revolutionary movement, which was Beijing's priority before the 1970s, was intended to promote the PRC as a principal leader in the worldwide Communist movement; the exercise of pragmatism in its government-to-government diplomacy since the 1970s is meant to advance the PRC as a spokesman for the Third World and as a major power in Latin America. Tactically, Beijing has, in effect, created important international issues which it has skillfully utilized for its own diplomatic gain.

In its drive to unite the developing countries of the Third World, Beijing has met with considerable success, mainly by identifying itself as a Third World nation.[65] It has promoted the North-South conflict and engineered the South-South Cooperation Conference, a vital device helping to increase its political influence in Latin America and other regions of the Third World.

In spite of Beijing's relative success, one must recognize the fact that Latin American countries and the rest of the Third World are not monolithic; nor are they always in agreement. How far these countries are willing to follow Beijing's lead remains to be seen. Above all, they will not want to be instruments in the hands of the PRC. However, Latin American states do not have direct conflicts of interest with the PRC on any important issues. Beijing, of course, is quite happy to show its generosity in supporting Latin American positions. This is one of the so-called typical games played by major actors in international politics.

In the area of economic relations, the PRC does not do very well because of its inability to provide substantial amounts of foreign aid to these countries for development. In terms of trade, what the Chinese Communists need is capital goods and technology, now chiefly purchased from Japan, the United States, and West Europe, but at the moment there is little for mainland

China and Latin America to offer to each other. Scientific and technological cooperation has been expanded somewhat in recent years, but the level of cooperation is very limited. Scientific and technological cooperation, more or less, only serves as a symbolic gesture of friendship. After all, the underlying motivation of the PRC in its economic relations with Latin America is more political than economic.

Beijing's "dollar diplomacy" has been relatively successful in further isolating the ROC in Latin America. Nevertheless, in the present world of international politics, with more flexible and less principled approaches, Taipei is there to stay. It is unlikely that most of the ten Latin American states that still maintain diplomatic relations with the ROC will switch sides in the near future. Furthermore, Taipei has been actively campaigning to expand its trade, cultural exchanges, and other unofficial relations with nations that have already established diplomatic relations with Beijing.

In brief, both Latin America and the PRC need each other in order to improve their international positions. As a matter of fact, the foreign policies of most sovereign states are quite effectively designed to serve their national interests in the reality of international relations.

Notes

1. Yu San Wang, ed., *The China Question: Essays on Current Relations between Mainland China and Taiwan* (New York: Praeger, 1985), p. 155.

2. Harold D. Lasswell, *Power and Society: A Framework for Political Inquiry* (New Haven: Yale University Press, 1950), p. 74.

3. M. A. Kaplan, *System and Process in International Politics* (New York: Wiley, 1957), p. 49.

4. Kurt London, *The Making of Foreign Policy* (Philadelphia: J. B. Lippincott, 1965), p. 1.

5. The editorial page of the *People's Daily*, October 1, 1957.

6. In the spring of 1958, the Chinese Communist Party published a pamphlet entitled *The Chinese Communists Look at the World Revolution Movements*, which was distributed to rank-and-file members for study. A portion of this publication dealt with the revolutionary movement in Latin America.

7. J. D. Armstrong, *Revolutionary Diplomacy: Chinese Foreign Policy and the United Front Doctrine* (Berkeley: University of California Press, 1977), p. 13.

8. Ibid., pp. 52–53.

9. James D. Theberge, *The Soviet Presence in Latin America* (New York: Crane, Russak, 1974), pp. 47–79.

10. *People's Daily*, October 1, 1959, p. 3.

11. In its issues of October 6 and November 10, 1967, *People's Daily* thoroughly detailed the concept of Mao's thought on the "people's war."

12. In a broader sense, any Communist parties and left-wing groups not following the Chinese Communist line were accused by mainland China of being revisionists. These included the pro-Soviet and pro-Cuban parties.

13. The meeting was held in Havana in November 1964. In the resolution, leaders of these parties reaffirmed their belief that only a unity of all the Communist movements, based on the principles of Marxism-Leninism, could be successful in the struggle against both reactionary regimes and imperialism. A commission of nine

leaders of Latin American Communist parties was sent to Beijing by the Havana meeting to discuss with Chinese Communist leaders the possibility of uniting the international Communist movements, but the talks produced no result. For details of the Havana meeting, see *Bohemia* (Havana), November 27, 1964, pp. 3–8.

14. Theberge, *The Soviet Presence*, p. 91. Eight Communist parties that supported Beijing were the Communist Party of Bolivia, the Communist Party of Brazil, the Communist Party of Colombia, the Popular Army of Liberation in Colombia, the Communist Party of Ecuador, the Communist Party of Peru (Movement of the Revolutionary Left), the Communist Party of the Dominican Republic, and the Proletarian Voice of the Dominican Republic.

15. Within the two-year period of 1964–1966, the "pocket parties" were set up in Puerto Rico and in the following countries: Argentina, Brazil, Bolivia, Chile, Dominican Republic, Ecuador, Peru, Paraguay, and Uruguay. See *La Nación* (Buenos Aires), January 17, 1967, pp. 2–3.

16. Ken Booth, *Law, Force and Diplomacy at Sea* (London: George Allen & Unwin, 1985), pp. 15–18. The Soviet Union proposed an increase in the territorial-water limit to twelve miles from three, while the United States was opposed to any increase at all. Washington feared that any increase in the territorial-water limit would restrict a huge area of the high seas, hamper coastal navigation, and increase coastal patrolling.

17. New China News Agency (NCNA), September 11, 1952.

18. *New York Times*, December 19, 1982, p. 3.

19. Cecil Johnson, *Communist China and Latin America, 1959–1967* (New York: Columbia University Press, 1970), p. 3.

20. *People's Daily*, April 23, 1974, p. 1.

21. Ibid., September 3, 1974, p. 2.

22. At the Conference of the Nonaligned Movement, which was held in late October 1975 in Lima, Peru's Foreign Minister Miguel A. de la Flor Valle, who presided over the meetings, pointed out that "China is one of the very few major powers that enthusiastically support the cause of the Third World's economic independence." See *La Crónica* (Lima), August 27, 1975, p. 1.

23. *Beijing Review*, June 15, 1979, p. 18.

24. *Beijing Review*, November 18, 1985, pp. 12–13.

25. For the text of the treaty, see *La Prensa* (Buenos Aires), February 10, 1967, p. 1–2. The treaty also provided for an inspection and control system to prevent violations. It is open to participation by all the Latin American countries and all others in the Western hemisphere below the thirty-fifth parallel.

26. *People's Daily*, March 19, 1967, p. 1.

27. The PRC's ambassador told Latin American diplomats that "inasmuch as the United Nations has violated all the rights of the People's Republic of China in the world organization, China cannot participate in its activities and is therefore not in a position to support the treaty for the denuclearization of Latin America."

28. *People's Daily*, December 9, 1967, p. 1.

29. *Peking Review*, September 7, 1973, p. 7.

30. Ibid., p. 8.

31. U.S. Foreign Broadcast Information Service, *Daily Report: China*, January 17, 1974.

32. *Peking Review*, January 22, 1971, p. 13.

33. UN Doc. S/PV. 1684 (16 January 1973), p. 8. The Panama City meeting incurred an estimated cost of $92,000. For detailed analysis of the PRC's behavior

in the United Nations, see Samuel S. Kim, *China, the United Nations, and World Order* (Princeton, N.J.: Princeton University Press, 1979).

34. *People's Daily,* July 24, 1974, p. 1.

35. *Beijing Review,* May 13, 1985, pp. 16–19.

36. *Beijing Review,* April 8, 1983, p. 7.

37. *New York Times,* April 15, 1986, p. 3.

38. U.S. Information Agency, Office of Policy and Research, "Broadcasts from Communist Countries in Latin America," 1984, pp. 34–39.

39. During the summer of 1959, Yao Chen led the first Chinese Communist delegation of four journalists who visited Latin America. This marked the beginning of direct propaganda and political activities.

40. For further information regarding the activities of the NCNA, see "The New China News Agency: Mao's Messengers Around the World," *Current Scene,* April 1, 1966.

41. In Brazil, for instance, two NCNA correspondents were arrested and sent back to mainland China in 1964; three agents were expelled by Mexico authorities in 1966; and Argentine police closed the Chinese Communist press office in 1963. See *Jornal do Brasil* (Rio De Janeiro), September 3, 1964, p. 1; *Esto* (Mexico City), March 1966, p. 1; and *La Prensa* (Buenos Aires), December 19, 1963, p. 3.

42. The PRC hoped that Cuba would serve as an example for other Latin American states to follow, especially as Castro himself and his lieutenant, Che Guevara, were equally interested in promoting armed insurrection in Latin America. During the events of the Bay of Pigs invasion of 1961 and the missile crisis of 1962, Beijing provided Cuba with much verbal support by holding massive rallies and consistent propaganda activities through broadcasting and various official publications.

43. At the meeting of the First Afro–Asian–Latin American Peoples' Solidarity Organization Conference, held in Havana in January 1966, no pro-Beijing parties from Latin America were invited. During the meeting, Castro made his first attack on Beijing by describing Mao Tse-tung as a senile old man, accusing Beijing of carrying out "a criminal sort of economic aggression" against Cuba, and charging the PRC with confusion of Marxism-Leninism with Fascism. Immediately striking back with at least equal harsh words, Beijing accused Castro as being adventurist, a petty-bourgeois romanticist, and a neorevisionist. For Castro's speech, see *Granma* (Havana), February 6, 1966. For materials on Beijing's attack, see *People's Daily,* February 22, *Ta-kung Pao,* February 22, 23, 29, and March 7, 1966; and *Peking Review,* February 25, 1966. At the height of the Cultural Revolution, Beijing called back its ambassador, Wang Yu-ping, and Havana took reciprocal action at once.

44. *Granma,* May 28, 1984, p. 2.

45. *Granma,* July 29, 1984, p. 1.

46. New China News Agency, September 18, 1970.

47. Attacking Beijing's recognition of the Chilean military junta, the Communist Party of Chile openly criticized the Chinese action by saying: "The leaders of the Communist Party of China have once again separated themselves from the world revolutionary and democratic movement, by putting their interests over and above international interests and so helping the imperialists in their moves." See *New York Times,* April 27, 1974, p. 3.

48. In the past, most Latin American states supported the Republic of China's position in the United Nations, but five other Latin republics in addition to Cuba and Chile supported the Albanian resolution to expel Taipei and seat Beijing in 1971. These countries were Ecuador, Guyana, Mexico, Peru, and Trinidad and Tobago.

49. V. Tkachenko, "Peking's Latin American Strategy," *International Affairs*, October 1974, p. 74.

50. *Beijing Review*, October 28, 1985, pp. 11–13. This issue carried a detailed article entitled "China and Latin America Cross-Cultures," which presented a brief history of Beijing's cultural exchanges with Latin America.

51. The press from both the PRC and four Latin American host countries presented extensive coverage of Chao's activities during his visit. In addition, the Beijing government also temporarily increased its Spanish- and Portuguese-language broadcasting hours in order to fully utilize the visit's propaganda value.

52. The Shining Path, a Maoist urban guerrilla group, in recent years conducted a series of terrorist activities in Lima. This group had financial backing from Beijing. The security authorities frequently asked the government to protest to Beijing, but the Peruvian leaders took no action.

53. "Latin American Countries Opposing Hegemonism: Struggle for National Economic Development," *Peking Review*, February 16, 1973, pp. 6–7, 12.

54. "Developing Countries Step Up Co-operation," *Beijing Review*, May 13, 1985, pp. 17–19.

55. "Latin America: Area Economics Get Second Wind," *Beijing Review*, November 18, 1985, pp. 12–13.

56. GNP estimates for 1971 ranged from $75,000 million to $140,000 million, giving a per capita GNP of between $110 and $200. The higher figure was based on Soviet information, using RMB2.45 = US$1, and the lower figure was the estimate provided by the Japanese Economic Planning Agency. The World Bank Atlas, however, gave an estimated $122,000 million.

57. U.S. Department of State, Bureau of Intelligence and Research, *Foreign Economic Aid to the Third World: A Brief Survey* (Washington, D.C.: U.S. Government Printing Office, 1986), pp. 69–70.

58. *La Prensa* (Buenos Aires), November 1, 1985, p. 1.

59. *Jornal do Brazil*, January 26, 1979, p. 4. Beijing's imports were worth $440 million, and Brazil's were worth $400 million.

60. *Beijing Review*, October 28, 1985, pp. 16–17.

61. During his Latin American visit in late 1985, Premier Chao signed trade and technical agreements with Colombian President Belisario Betancur Cuartas on October 28 and with Venezuelan President Jaime Lusinchi on November 9. See *El Tiempo* (Bogotá), October 29, 1985; *Meridiano* (Caracas), November 10, 1985.

62. "China and Latin America Expand Technical Links," *Beijing Review*, October 28, 1985, pp. 17–18.

63. *Jornal do Brazil*, December 17, 1984, pp. 1–2.

64. *People's Daily*, November 21, 1984, p. 3.

65. At a reception given in honor of Alfredo Salazar, president of the Table Tennis Association of Peru and head of the Peruvian table tennis delegation to mainland China in the summer of 1973, Chou En-lai made the remark: "We are of the Third World developing countries which share the same problems and the same wishes, and which must fight for their development and common welfare. . . . Unity brings strength and will make everyone in the world hear our voice, the voice of the Third World." See *Peking Review*, September 14, 1973, p. 16.

About the Contributors

King C. Chen, professor of political science at Rutgers University, New Jersey, is the author of *Vietnam and China* (1969) and the editor of *China and the Three Worlds* (1979).

Lowell Dittmer, professor of political science at the University of California, Berkeley, is the author of *Liu Shao-ch'i and the Chinese Cultural Revolution: The Politics of Mass Criticism* (1974).

June Teufel Dreyer is concurrently professor of politics and director of East Asian Programs at the Graduate School of International Studies, University of Miami.

Harold C. Hinton, professor of political science and international affairs at the Institute for Sino-Soviet Studies, George Washington University, Washington, D.C., has published many books, including *The China Sea: The American Stake in Its Future* (1980).

Kuo-ch'iang Hsing is a research fellow at the Institute of International Relations, Taipei.

James C. Hsiung, professor of politics at New York University, is the author and editor of many books, including *Ideology and Practice: The Evolution of Chinese Communism* (1972).

Stanton Jue, formerly research fellow at the Institute for Sino-Soviet Studies, George Washington University, is a consultant on East Asian and Pacific affairs in Washington, D.C.

Donald W. Klein is a professor of political science at Tufts University.

David M. Lampton is an associate professor of political science at Ohio State University and director of China Policy Studies at the American Enterprise Institute in Washington, D.C. He is the author of numerous articles and books, including *Paths to Power: Elite Mobility in Contemporary China* (1986).

Alan P.L. Liu, professor of political science at the University of California, Santa Barbara, is the author of many books, including *How China Is Ruled* (1986).

Bih-rong Liu is an associate professor of foreign affairs at Soochow University, Taipei.

Thomas A. Metzger, professor of Chinese history at the University of California, San Diego, is the author of *Escape from Predicament: Neo-Confucianism and China's Evolving Political Culture* (1977).

Peter R. Moody, Jr., professor of government and international studies, University of Notre Dame, Indiana, is the author of numerous articles and books, including *Chinese Politics After Mao: Development and Liberalization, 1976–1983* (1983).

James T. Myers, associate professor of government and international studies at the University of South Carolina, Columbia, is the author of many books, including *Cultural Revolution in China: Documents with Analysis* (1974).

Ramon H. Myers, senior fellow and curator-scholar of the East Asian Collection at the Hoover Institution on War, Revolution and Peace, Stanford, California, is the author of many articles and books, including *Understanding Communist China* (1986).

Thomas W. Robinson is a professor at the School of Foreign Service, Georgetown University.

Robert G. Sutter, deputy director of the Foreign Affairs and National Defense Division, Congressional Research Service, Library of Congress, is the author of many articles and books, including *Chinese Foreign Policy: Developments After Mao* (1986).

Yu San Wang, professor and dean of the Division of Social Sciences at Fairmont State College, West Virginia, is the author of *The China Question: Essays on Relations Between Mainland China and Taiwan* (1985).

An-chia Wu, research fellow at the Institute of International Relations, Taipei, is the author of many articles and books, including *Historiographical Studies in Mainland China After 1976* (1983, in Chinese).

Peter Kien-hong Yu is an associate professor at the Sun Yat-sen Institute and an adjunct research associate at the Sun Yat-sen Center for Policy Studies, both of National Sun Yat-sen University, Kaohsiung, Taiwan.

Donald S. Zagoria, a professor at the Research Institute on International Change, Columbia University, is the author of many books, including *Vietnam Triangle: Moscow, Peking, Hanoi* (1967).